Napoleon's Marshals

DAVID G. CHANDLER

EDITOR-IN-CHIEF

Napoleon's Marshals

MACMILLAN PUBLISHING COMPANY
NEW YORK

Macmillan Publishing Company
866 Third Avenue, New York, N.Y. 10022

Collier Macmillan Canada, Inc.

Library of Congress Catalog Card Number: 86-10503

Printed in the United States of America

printing number
1 2 3 4 5 6 7 8 9 10

Library of Congress Cataloging-in-Publication Data

Napoleon's marshals.

    Bibliography: p.
    Includes index.
    1. Marshals—France—Biography. 2. Napoleonic Wars, 1800–1814—Biography. 3. France. Armée—Biography. I. Chandler, David G.
DC198.A1N36 1986   940.2'7   86-10503
ISBN 0-02-905930-5

With gracious permission this book is respectfully
dedicated to
His Majesty King Carl XVI Gustaf of Sweden,
distinguished descendant of Jean Baptiste Bernadotte,
Marshal of the Empire, Prince of Ponte-Corvo, and, from
1818 to 1844, King of Sweden under the name of
Carl XIV Johan

Contents

Acknowledgments

The Editor-in-Chief wishes to express his gratitude to His Majesty King Carl XVI Gustaf of Sweden for graciously permitting this book to be dedicated to Him, the direct descendant of the only Napoleonic marshal to found a lasting royal dynasty; and also to Victor-André Massena, Prince of Essling, direct descendant of the Victor of Rivoli, for consenting to provide a Foreword.

He is grateful to His Excellency Lennart Ahrén, First Marshal of the Court of the Kingdom of Sweden, for advice on matters of protocol in connection with the dedication of this book.

He also wishes to thank his 26 fellow contributors to the volume for their excellent studies of Napoleon's individual marshals, and for observing so scrupulously the various organizational and stylistic guidelines, and above all the necessary deadlines, in the course of their preparation and writing; without such whole-hearted cooperation, and friendly acceptance of the editorial adjustments and occasional excisions, the never-easy task of the Editor-in-Chief would have been rendered far more difficult if not verging on the impossible. He also owes a debt of gratitude to Colonel John Elting, for advice and helpful criticism on several matters. It is with great regret that he has to record the death of General Sir James Marshall-Cornwall (on Christmas Day, 1985), aged 98 years. His chapter on Massena was the first to be received—six months ahead of schedule—which is a tribute to both his efficiency and his scholarship. In his passing we have lost a fine soldier, linguist, and military historian, and the Editor-in-Chief a good friend of some 20 years' standing.

A debt of gratitude is also owed to Stephen Maison for his cartographical services in drawing the 27 excellent maps included in the book.

Finally, the Editor-in-Chief owes a personal debt of gratitude to his patient wife for her help with the preparation of the Index; to Mrs. Anne Nason for undertaking a great deal of the typing of the manuscript; also to Joan Pitsch, Editorial Supervisor, Macmillan; and most of all to Charles Smith, Vice President and Publisher of that company, without whose original inspiration and continuing support and advice, this project—which complements *The Campaigns of Napoleon* (1966), *A Dictionary of the Napoleonic Wars* (1979), and *Waterloo—The Hundred Days* (1980)—would have been unlikely to see the light of day.

David G. Chandler

List of Illustrations

All portraits of the marshals are taken from engravings by Forestier in C. Panckoucke, *Portraits des Généraux Français . . . 1792à1815*, 2 vols. (Paris, 1818).

Explanatory Key to Diagrams

KEY TO MILITARY SYMBOLS USED ON BATTLE AND SIEGE DIAGRAMS

1. SYMBOLS INDICATING PRESENCE BUT NOT THE PHYSICAL LOCATION OF MILITARY UNITS

2. SYMBOLS INDICATING TYPES AND APPROXIMATE PHYSICAL LOCATION OF UNITS ON THE GROUND

NAPOLEON 44,500	KUTUSOV 120,800	— ARMY	INFANTRY	CAVALRY
III DAVOUT 15,000	TUTCHKOV 12,000	— CORPS —	VI NEY 10,000	TOLSTOI 11,500
LEWAL 6,000	PICTON 7,500	— DIVISION —	CONROUX 4,700	HILL 5,200
	(½)		— BRIGADE — (DEMI-BRIGADE)	
		— REGIMENT —		
		— BATTALION —		

NOTE – 1. Name and Roman numeral alongside a symbol reveal the commander and the designation of a unit; arabic numerals denote its numerical strength (when given).

2. Dark symbols represent the French; light or shaded symbols represent their adversaries.

3. MOVEMENT SYMBOLS

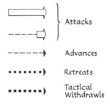

} Attacks

------→ Advances

••••••→ Retreats

•••••••→ Tactical Withdrawls

NOTE – Where necessary, individual diagrams have explanatory keys.

Scales are in miles or yards.

All terrain features are only approximately portrayed.

4. MISCELLANEOUS SYMBOLS

⚑ ⚐ Headquarters

Cavalry Picquets and Patrols

Naval Vessels

∩ Field Fortifications

▲ Camps

Entrenchements and Siege Works

Permanent Defences

Permanent Forts

Cannon

△ Mortars

)(Bridges

SPM '86

Diagrams of Battles and Sieges

Drawn by *Stephen Maison* from designs or references
supplied by the Editor-in-Chief and Contributors

Following the Introduction: The Battles and Sieges of Napoleon's Marshals (with inset of
France, showing the areas of their births).

List of Contributors

JAMES R. ARNOLD is a professional self-employed researcher and writer in the early-nineteenth century and modern periods of military history. His particular interest is in the Napoleonic Campaign of 1809, on which he is preparing a book entitled *Crisis on the Danube*. He lives in Bluemont, Virginia.

IAN F. W. BECKETT took his doctorate at London University, and is a Senior Lecturer in the Department of War Studies at the Royal Military Academy, Sandhurst. His main research interests are English auxiliary military forces and British nineteenth- and twentieth-century civil-military relations and military policy. He has published seven books (three as co-author or co-editor), and *The Army and the Curragh Incident* (the edited papers of Field Marshal Sir Henry Wilson) appeared from the Army Records Society in late 1986. He is a Fellow of the Royal Historical Society, and lives in Yateley, Hampshire, England.

PAUL BRITTEN AUSTIN was educated at Winchester College. He is a professional writer and translator, and has published many books on literary and biographical subjects, including one historical novel. Among other undertakings, he is currently researching an in-depth study of the Napoleonic Campaign in Russia, 1812. He lives alternatively in Sweden and England.

DAVID G. CHANDLER is Head of the Department of War Studies at the Royal Military Academy, Sandhurst, and a Fellow of both the Royal Historical and the Royal Geographical Societies. He is President of the British Commission for Military History and a Vice-President of the *Commission International d'Histoire Militaire*. The author of a dozen works on early eighteenth- and early nineteenth-century military history, he is a recognized authority on the Marlburian and Napoleonic periods, and his books include *The Campaigns of Napoleon* (1966), *A Dictionary of the Napoleonic Wars* (1979), *Waterloo—the Hundred Days* and *An Atlas of Military Strategy* (both 1980). He lives in Yateley, Hampshire, England.

PHILIPP COATES-WRIGHT is a Lecturer at Hounslow College and a military historian with a particular research interest in the Napoleonic period. He is a senior member of the Napoleonic Association, and lives in West London, England.

JOHN R. ELTING is a retired Colonel of the United States Army and a noted American military historian. He was Associate Professor of Military Art and Engineering at the United States Military Academy, West Point. He has published numerous books on military subjects ranging from the late-eighteenth century to the near-present, including being co-author of *A Military History and Atlas of the Napoleonic Wars* and co-editor of *The West Point Atlas of American Wars,* and is currently researching a work on Napoleon's *Grande Armée.* He lives at Cornwall-on-Hudson, New York.

CHARLES ESDAILE is a Doctor of Lancaster University, and currently holds the newly-created post of Wellington Papers Fellow in the Department of Modern History, the University of Southampton. He has a special interest in Spanish early-nineteenth century military history. He lives in Swaythling, England.

MICHAEL GLOVER is a professional writer and author of many works on military history ranging from the early-nineteenth to the late-twentieth centuries. These include *The Peninsular War* (1974), *Wellington's Peninsular Victories* (1965), a life of General Sir Robert Wilson: *A Very Slippery Fellow* (1977), and *Warfare in the Age of Bonaparte.* He lives near Stroud in Gloucestershire, England.

RANDAL GRAY holds an M.A. degree from Oxford University, and is a book and magazine editor and a military historian. He has written many articles on Napoleonic and other military subjects, but his special area is the study of the armies of antiquity. He has been a Casual Senior Lecturer in War Studies at Sandhurst (1986). He lives in Maida Vale, London, England.

PADDY GRIFFITH holds a Doctorate from Oxford University and is a senior lecturer in the Department of War Studies at the Royal Military Academy, Sandhurst. He is the author of a number of books on military history and war gaming, including *Forward into Battle* (1981), *Not Over by Christmas* (co-author, 1983), *A Book of Sandhurst War Games* (1982) and *Wellington, Commander* (editor, 1985). He is presently completing a study of *The American Civil War.* He lives at Owlsmoor in Berkshire, England.

ALAN HANKINSON is a journalist, mountaineer and military historian. He is the author of *Man of Wars,* a biography of the famous Victorian war correspondent, William Howard Russell of *The Times.* He lives in Keswick, Cumbria, England.

T. A. (TONY) HEATHCOTE holds a Doctorate from the School of Oriental and African Studies of London University, and is Curator of the Sandhurst Collection at the Royal Military Academy, Sandhurst. He is the author of *The British Indian Army* (1973) and *The Afghan Wars* (1980). He holds a Major's commission in the Territorial Army, and has been awarded the T.D. (Territorial Distinction). He lives in Camberley, Surrey, England.

PETER HOFSCHRÖER is a specialist book dealer and military historian. He has published two works on the Prussian Army's infantry and light infantry of the period, and most recently, *Prussian Cavalry of the Napoleonic Wars, Vol 1: 1792–1807* (1985). He is a member of the Napoleonic Association, and lives in Gillingham, Kent, England.

DONALD D. HORWARD is Professor in the Department of History at Florida State University. A specialist in the Napoleonic period (particularly the French role in Spain and Portugal) his many publications include *Bussaco, The French Campaign in Portugal, 1810–1811* (the edited journal of General Pelet), *Napoleon in Iberia*, (1984) and *Napoleonic Military History—a Bibliography* (1985). He has been awarded academic distinctions by the French and Spanish governments, and is the organizer of many conferences both in the United States and Europe. He lives in Tallahassee, Florida.

NIGEL de LEE is a senior lecturer in the Department of War Studies, the Royal Military Academy, Sandhurst. He is currently an exchange-lecturer at USNA Annapolis. He has a special interest in Chinese and North European affairs as well as a number of periods of British and French military history. He published *French Lancers* (1976), and was a consultant and contributor to *The Chinese War Machine* (1979), and wrote a section of *World Armies* (1979). He lives in Little Sandhurst, Berkshire, England.

JAMES D. LUNT is a retired Major-General of the British Army, and is a Commander of the British Empire (C.B.E.). He was more recently Bursar of Wadham College, Oxford, and is an author, defense commentator and military historian. He was for many years review editor of the *Army Quarterly*. His published works include *Charge to Glory, Scarlet Lancer*, the *Barren Rock of Aden, John Burgoyne of Saratoga, Imperial Sunset—Frontier Soldering in the 20th Century, Glubb Pasha*, and is at present preparing the official biography of King Hussein of Jordan. He lives in Little Milton, Oxfordshire, England.

STEVEN MAISON, cartographer of the diagrams of battles and sieges, was born in Isleworth, Middlesex, England and educated at the Thames Valley Grammar School in Twickenham, Middlesex. He has worked for the Mapping and Charting Establishment in Feltham as a cartographer, and more recently as an air surveyor, producing maps of many different series. He lives in Hampton, Middlesex.

SIR JAMES MARSHALL-CORNWALL, who died on December 25, 1985, aged 98 years, was a Knight Commander of the Bath (K.C.B.), a Commander of the British Empire (C.B.E.) and held the Distinguished Service Order (D.S.O.) and the Military Cross and many foreign awards. A soldier of great distinction, he was fluent in over 20 languages, and in retirement became a notable military historian. He was President of the Royal Geographical Society (1954–1958). His books included *Massena, Napoleon as a Military Commander*, besides studies of *Grant, Foch* and *Haig*, and in 1984 he published his autobiography, *Wars and Rumours of Wars*. For many years he lived in London, and latterly near Malton in North Yorkshire, England.

JEANNE A. OJALA is a Professor in the Department of History at the University of Utah. Her main research interests centre around French seventeenth-century history, and she is presently preparing a study of *Madame de Sévigny*, but her other publications include a biography on the Napoleonic cavalry commander, *Auguste de Colbert*. She lives between Salt Lake City, Utah, and Tempe, Arizona.

GEORGES OSTERMANN is a French scholar and military historian who holds a Doctorate from the *Université de Paul-Valéry* at Montpellier. He is currently *professeur des lettres* at the Lycée de Serres. He writes on military history and on strategic and tactical war gaming. He lives at Verdeaux, Bedarrides, France.

TIM PICKLES is a historical adviser to film companies, professional costume designer and builder of military model dioramas, and a researcher into military history. He is a member of the Napoleonic Association, and was for many years its chairman. He lives at Knaresborough, North Yorkshire, England.

JOHN L. PIMLOTT holds a Doctorate from Leicester University, and is Acting-Deputy Head of the Department of War Studies at the Royal Military Academy, Sandhurst. He is a prolific author with major interests in post-1945 wars, and above all modern counter-insurgency, and his 10 books include *British Light Cav-*

alry, 1809–1815, War in Peace (editor and contributor, 1981), *Vietnam* (1982), *Middle East Conflicts* (1983) and most recently, with Ian Beckett (noted above), *Armed Forces and Counter-Insurgency* (1985). He lives in Camberley, Surrey, England.

CHARLES RAEUBER is a Swiss banker and military historian. He has a particular research interest in the battle of Bussaco (1810) and has contributed many articles and learned papers to journals and conferences as a member of the Swiss Commission of Military History. He lives in Lugano, Switzerland.

DAVID D. ROONEY holds the degree of Bachelor of Literature (B. Litt.) from Oxford University, and recently retired after a career that included lecturing as a member of the former Department of Modern Subjects at the Royal Military Academy, Sandhurst and two headmasterships—one of a British Army school in West Germany, the other in Cambridgeshire. His main research interests center around West African history, and his publications include *The Building of Modern Africa* (co-author 1966), *Stilwell* (1977), and *Sir Charles Arden-Clarke* (1982). He was recently appointed to hold a Leverhulme Trust Fellowship. He lives in Cambridge, England.

GUNTHER E. ROTHENBERG is Professor of the Department of Military History and Strategic Studies at Purdue University. He is the author of many works, including a study of the *Militargrenze* (or military frontiers of Austria-Hungary in the 18th century), *The Art of War in the Age of Napoleon*, and *Napoleon's Great Adversaries* (a study of Austrian opposition to Napoleon—and in particular of the Archduke Charles). He was recently a visiting professor at the Royal Military College, Duntroon, Australia. He lives in West Lafayette, Indiana.

ALAN SHEPPERD is a retired Lieutenant-Colonel of the British Army, and is a Member of the Order of the British Empire (M.B.E.). He was for many years librarian at the Royal Military Academy, Sandhurst, and is a notable military historian. His books include *The Italian Campaign 1943–1945* (1968), *Arms and Armour, 1660–1918* (1971), *The Connaught Rangers* (1972), *The King's Request* (1973) and *The Royal Military Academy Sandhurst and its Predecessors* (1980). He lives at Camberley, Surrey, England.

ANTHONY G. THOMAS, Lieutenant Commander in the Royal Navy, is a graduate of Oxford University and is a Member of the Order of the British Empire (M.B.E.). He was a Senior Lecturer at the Royal Naval College, Greenwich (1963–1972) before being appointed a senior lecturer in the Department of War Studies at the Royal Military Academy, Sandhurst—a position he still holds. He is a researcher in naval and military history and a regular reviewer of books. He lives between Camberley and Worcester, England.

PETER YOUNG is a retired Brigadier of the British Army, who was awarded the decorations of the Distinguished Service Order (D.S.O.) and the Military Cross (M.C.)—with two bars. A graduate of Oxford University, he became a famous Commando leader in the Second World War. After a period in the Arab Legion, he was appointed Reader in Military History at the Royal Military Academy, Sandhurst (1959–69). He is a prolific military historian with over two dozen published works, many being devoted to the English Civil Wars, and including *The British Army 1642–1972, World War Two, 1939–1945, Edgehill 1642, Naseby 1645* (1985) and *The Marshals of Napoleon* (1973). He lives at Twyning-in-Tewkesbury, Gloucestershire, England.

Foreword

Victor-André Massena, Fifth Duke of Rivoli, Seventh Prince of Essling

France has dignified her most distinguished soldiers with the proud title of marshal since the reign of King Henri I^{ier}. The first known to have been so honored was Marshal Gui in the eleventh century; the latest, posthumously, was General Koenig in 1984. Many famous names appear on the intervening list (and, it must be admitted, one or two disastrous ones), but no period of French history has seen a more prolific display of martial talent rewarded with the baton than the 11 years between 1804 and 1815.

History sadly shows that every nation undergoes times of dire military crisis; the "call to arms" can bring out the best in a people (and sometimes the worst), but invariably a number of soldiers respond to the challenge with valor, vigor, great professional skill, and, above all, outstanding leadership. The 25 Frenchmen and one Pole whom Napoleon appointed Marshals of the Empire owed their preferment to political as well as to military considerations, as David Chandler makes clear in his General Introduction, but military history has seldom—if ever—seen a more colorful, varied, and distinguished body of soldiers called to assume the highest responsibility. The Emperor's original motives have been variously interpreted. On the one hand, he wished to unite around his person a group of influential generals—some already devoted to him, others not—to ensure the French Army's acceptance of the Empire. On the other, he wished to integrate the leadership of that same army into the new civilian aristocratic hierarchy. As is discussed elsewhere by the Editor-in-Chief, it is important to appreciate that the marshalate was essentially a civil institution rather than a military one per se. Although the desire to recognize proven military talent was in most cases an equally important factor, particularly in appointments to the baton made after the initial, 18-strong creation of 1804, the dignity of Marshal of the Empire was essentially a conferred title rather than a military rank. The favored men were to become *grands seigneurs* in the imperial hierarchy, placed fifth in terms of court rank, subordinate only to the Emperor and Empress, the imperial family, the grand dignitaries of the Empire, and the ministers. "Marshals of the Empire, chosen from among the most distinguished generals," ran part of the *Senatus Consultum** dated *"28 floréal an XII"* (or May 18, 1804), were, among

*Decree of the Senate

other privileges, entitled to receive a cannon salute of 11 discharges on certain official occasions (a minister was entitled to 15).

These 26 men were essentially tough fighting men rather than respectful courtiers—few of them being temperamentally suited to the latter role in any case, a few of them being very "rough diamonds" indeed, my great-great-grandfather included. As soldiers their services would be repeatedly and pitilessly called upon in return for the generous honors, titles, estates, and monetary grants lavished upon them. Nor would their exalted positions remove them from the threat of shot and shell on the battlefield. Napoleon himself was wounded at Ratisbon, albeit lightly, and no less than half the marshalate became battle casualties—some several times—between 1804 and 1815. Three—Lannes, Bessières, and Poniatowski—died of wounds, were killed outright, or drowned (in the last case) as a result of injuries received in action. The position of Marshal of the Empire was far from being a safe sinecure.

My own ancestor was among the 13 more fortunate marshals not to have been wounded by enemy fire. Nevertheless he by no means escaped scot-free, losing an eye in 1808 to "friendly fire" from a very exalted sportsman and suffering an exceedingly painful fall from his horse just a few days before Wagram in 1809, seriously injuring his thigh, an injury that he refused to take to the hospital. Instead, after the fashion of Marshal Saxe at Fontenoy, he insisted on exercising command from an open carriage. There is no denying that our forebears were tough, and that all officers, no matter how senior, exposed themselves unflinchingly at what today would be called "the forward edge of the battle area," as did my forebear at both Rivoli and Essling and on many another occasion. But, then, so did Napoleon himself, both as General of the Republic (as at Arcola) and as Emperor (as at Ratisbon).

This book sets out to describe the careers and characters of Napoleon's 26 marshals. The 11 years of the First Empire saw France continually at war, and this must constitute the most dramatic and action-filled period in European history. David Chandler and his team of scholarly authors have produced a noteworthy work that will interest, inform, and instruct a new generation of readers attracted to the study of Napoleon and his key subordinates, and I deem it a pleasure to have been invited to provide this brief Foreword.

Massena

December 2, 1985

(181st Anniversary of Napoleon's Coronation and
180th of the Battle of Austerlitz)

Editor-in-Chief's Note

At the outset I wish to make one or two points concerning the planning and execution of this book for the assistance and guidance of the reader. The challenge of producing a reasonably comprehensive treatment of 26 of the most colorful and dramatic military careers in modern military history within the compass of a reasonably sized volume posed considerable problems. Rather than accord each subject an equal amount of space, I felt it necessary to establish an order of priority. Thus, seven subjects were selected to receive some 8,000 words apiece, nine more were allotted 6,000 words, and the remaining 10 were given either 4,000 or 5,000 words apiece. The allocations will doubtless appear arbitrary and possibly ill-conceived to some readers. Is it justifiable to relegate Berthier to the third category and yet award greater spatial preference to Jourdan or Lefebvre? The selection of the top seven was somewhat easier, but the overall problem was insoluble. All I can say is that I took decisions in the light of my own estimation of the relative importance of each marshal, and that I am solely responsible for any injustices or maladroit allocations that may have resulted, however unintentionally.

As it had been decided to approach each marshal as a separate individual (rather than seek to achieve an overall mélange or incorporated treatment of the marshalate as a whole of the kind undertaken by Macdonell or Delderfield in earlier years—see Select General Bibliography p. 547) and to invite 26 authors to contribute a chapter apiece, it was necessary to lay down certain guidelines to achieve a broadly similar approach and to avoid too much repetition. Thus, each contributor was asked to divide his or her chapter into four sections, the last to be a discussion of an engagement or operation of war of particular importance—whether for better or for worse—in the career of the particular man. The majority understandably opted for subjects that earned their marshals their batons or ducal titles or contained some special passage of arms. A number selected engagements that were personal disasters for their subjects (for example, Eylau for Augereau in 1807, Albuera for Soult in 1811, Salamanca for Marmont in 1812, and Vitoria for Jourdan in 1813), and one—the writer on Bernadotte—opted for a battle (Dennewitz in 1813, again) in which his subject fought *against* his former colleagues! A fair spread of battles and sieges in terms of both date and geographical location has resulted with no duplications, although it will be noted that Waterloo is conspicuous by its absence from the list. However, aspects of this subject appear under Ney and Grouchy.

The team of contributors were left to tackle their subjects within these broad limits according to their own inclinations, and a fascinating variety of treatments has been the result. All have laid stress on the personalities of their subjects, but obviously in the space available have needed to be selective rather than comprehensive in their approach.

Finally, I would wish to point out that the main purpose of this book is not to break new ground or to make stunning revelations based on newly-discovered primary evidence. Although many novel points of detail and interpretation will in fact be found in the pages that follow, one main purpose has been to reassess the marshals in the light of modern scholarship. Another main purpose, above all, is to make available to new generations of readers details of the lives, careers, strengths and foibles, achievements and failures, and above all their personalities as human beings and capabilities as leaders in time of war, of "the Twenty-Six", who, after the Emperor himself, are among the most interesting and dynamic figures of those eventful years that have gone down into history as "the Wars of the French Revolution, Consulate and First Empire"—assuredly one of the most dramatic and action-packed periods of European-New World history, which still has no inconsiderable impact on the lives we lead today, nearly two centuries later.

—David G. Chandler

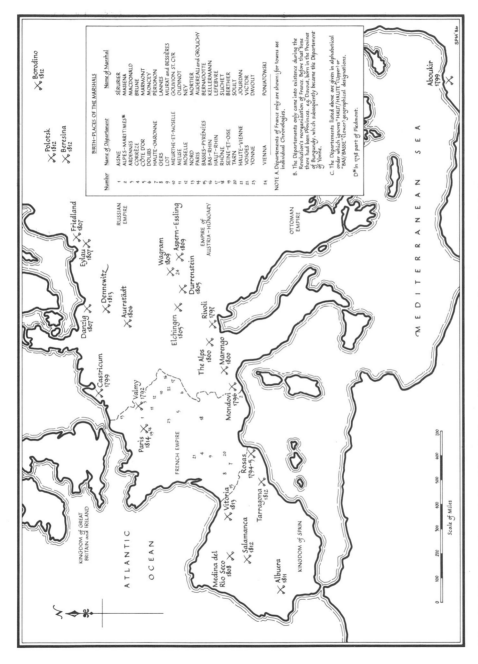

Map B. The Battles of the Marshalate, 1792–1815, and their areas of birth.

General Introduction

NAPOLEON AND HIS MARSHALS

David G. Chandler

On May 18, 1804, Napoleon Bonaparte was proclaimed Emperor of the French people by formal decree of the Senate. The establishment of a hereditary Empire was subsequently endorsed by a plebiscite, which voted 1,390 to one in favor of this significant constitutional development; and on December 2, Napoleon, in the presence of the Pope and the assembled notables of the land— including his family and the marshalate—crowned himself in the cathedral of Notre Dâme. The change from the Consulate to the Empire was embodied in the "Constitution of the Year XII,"[1] which in Article 48 announced the creation in principle of 16 active "Marshals of the Empire" and a further unspecified number of honorific appointments to the same dignity, whose main purpose was to represent the army's interests in the Senate. On May 19, the day after the issue of the *Senatus Consultum* of *28 floréal an XII*, the names of the first promotion (14 active and four honorary marshals) were made public.* The list was headed by Alexandre Berthier, Napoleon's indispensable chief of staff, followed by Joachim Murat, imperial brother-in-law and *beau sabreur*† of the French Army. In eighteenth place came the name of Jean Sérurier, 62-year-old veteran, one of the honorific appointees. The oldest on the list was François Kellermann the Elder, nine days short of entering his seventieth year. The youngest—not half the age of the hero of Valmy—was Louis Davout, who had celebrated his thirty-fourth birthday just nine days earlier. His nomination attracted some surprise and criticism, as alone of the favored few he, unlike a good many passed-over more senior generals, had no experience of a major command in time of active war. His relationship by marriage to the late General Leclerc, husband of Pauline Bonaparte, was widely and uncharitably canvassed as the main reason for his selection.

---

*The order of appearance (or at least of publication) of the first promotion was as follows: (1) Berthier, (2) Murat, (3) Moncey, (4) Jourdan, (5) Massena, (6) Augereau, (7) Bernadotte, (8) Soult, (9) Brune, (10) Lannes, (11) Mortier, (12) Ney, (13) Davout, (14) Bessières, (15) Kellermann, (16) Lefebvre, (17) Pérignon, (18) Sérurier. (The honorary marshals were Moncey, Kellermann, Pérignon, and Sérurier.) The order did *not* represent a statement of true seniority—and certainly no marshal on the list conceded seniority to any other. However, there were two exceptions: all other marshals obeyed Berthier because he spoke or wrote "in the name of the Emperor" as chief of staff, while Murat was designated as "the Emperor's Lieutenant," and thus had some claim to seniority.

†Dashing blade, or swordsman

Over the next 11 years, a further eight distinguished soldiers—seven Frenchmen and one Pole—would also receive their batons from Napoleon: Victor in 1807; Macdonald, Marmont, and Oudinot, all three at or after Wagram in 1809; Suchet in 1811; and Gouvion St.-Cyr, Poniatowski, and Grouchy (the twenty-sixth and last) in 1812, 1813, and 1815, respectively. The average age of the 18 marshals of 1804 was 44 years (the inclusion of the four veterans of the revolutionary wars having an effect), and that of the later eight was coincidentally also 44. At the time of his coronation, Napoleon was 35. Only two of the marshalate were younger—namely, Davout and Marmont; eight were 10 or more years older; a further seven were his senior by between four and nine years; the remaining nine were under two years older—three of these (Ney, Soult, and Lannes) sharing Napoleon's birth year of 1769.

Les Gros Bonnets ("the Big Hats"), as the subalterns of the army nicknamed them, had in many cases already enjoyed dazzling and meteoric careers in the service of the Republic and the Consulate—and for some the future would hold still further unimagined advancement. Conversely, all would, in the fullness of time, taste either directly or indirectly the bitter fruits of defeat, disappointment, and (in some cases) disgrace. Almost all would suffer the stresses and strains of over a decade of practically continuous warfare, a full half would sustain one or more wounds in action between 1805 and Waterloo, and another three would be killed or die as a result of wounds. A fair number would suffer varying periods of disgrace and disfavor, two (Murat and Ney) would end their eventful lives in front of firing squads and one (Brune) would be messily murdered by a mob. The brighter side of the medal would, however, see many of them accumulate by fair means or foul substantial personal fortunes, while titles, honors, orders, and estates would be showered on the deserving. Six would become princes; two would progress to become monarchs, and one of these—Bernadotte, Prince of Ponte-Corvo—would found a royal dynasty destined to prosper down to the present day. It all amounts to a very dramatic and dynamic, if stormy, story, and the purpose of this Introduction is to pull together certain threads and present an overview and summation of what is to follow in the course of the book.

Inevitably, the uncertainties and balancing opportunities of the Revolutionary Wars launched the careers of the future marshalate just as they did that of their chief. Many enjoyed spectacular promotion. Bernadotte, for instance, was first commissioned a lieutenant in the 36th Regiment on November 6, 1791, and just under three years later was promoted general of division in the Army of the *Sambre-et-Meuse* on October 22, 1794. Gouvion St.-Cyr's early rise was even more meteoric. Enlisted as a volunteer on September

1, 1792, two years and one day later he received confirmation of his promotion to general of division in the Army of the Rhine from the Committee of Public Safety. But at a troubled time when ideological probity was as important as military valor or skill, there were many pitfalls awaiting the incompetent, unwary or plain unlucky. Between August 1792 and November 1799, no less than 994 general officers of 1,378 holding commands during that 7-year period were disciplined in some degree for one reason or another—all of 75%. A total of 81 were condemned to death (41 for alleged political crimes) and 55 were actually executed by firing squad or guillotine.[2] However, if a thrusting general officer was fortunate enough to avoid enemy shot and shell, to keep his head upon his shoulders through the Revolutionary period *and* to earn the ultimate accolade of selection for the award of the baton from Napoleon for reasons to be discussed later in this Introduction, there were indeed many glittering prizes awaiting the faithful, the relations, the favorites (very few), and the deserving. In the days of the Republic, decorations as such had been scorned as inegalitarian, but awards of weapons of honor, letters of commendation, and the occasional grant of money for deeds of notable valor or other distinction were from time to time authorized. Among the future marshals, such awards had been received by Macdonald and Gouvion St.-Cyr before 1800, and rather later, in some cases retrospectively, by Lannes, Murat, and Massena. Such marks of distinction continued to be issued until late 1803, but became increasingly superseded by the Legion of Honor from its first inception on May 19, 1802. This celebrated honors system, with its four classes ranging from *Légionnaires* (simple members) through officers, commanders, to grand officers headed by holders of the Grand Eagle, was organized into 15 (later 16) cohorts with a nominal establishment of 408 award holders apiece. Inevitably, the highest awards went to the marshals. Each received the Grand Eagle, some—Gouvion St.-Cyr, Marmont, and Victor (all 1805), Suchet (1806), Grouchy (1807), and Poniatowski (1809)—before gaining their batons. Fourteen of the cohorts were headed by marshals of the first promotion (the remaining two by admirals), the exceptions being Brune, Kellermann, Pérignon, and Sérurier. At various later dates, most marshals also received one or more orders from foreign or allied countries. Georges Six's researches reveal that the 2,248 generals who held that rank between 1792 and 1814 divided between them—excluding various awards of the Legion of Honor—a total of at least 188 Grand Crosses, 186 commanderships, and 445 Knights Crosses, 95 of them belonging to six French orders and the rest to 44 foreign orders from 23 countries.[3] Naturally, the marshalate came in for the lion's share. The most decorated of the marshals was probably

Berthier who accumulated no less than 13 orders (to include his Grand Eagle) in just over three years.

If decorations and orders were one form of recompense, titles of nobility were another as Napoleon set out to re-create a social hierarchy around his throne. In 1805 Murat—his brother-in-law—was made a prince. Next year Berthier was created prince of Neuchâtel, and Bernadotte prince of Ponte-Corvo, both endowed with principalities. Then, in 1807–1808, Napoleon began to create a complete nobility, endowing each title with monetary grants drawn on French sources or (increasingly) on those extorted from conquered or assimilated territories. In all, between 1807 and 1815, Napoleon ennobled 897 generals (including 19 foreigners), issuing a total of 985 patents. Some officers received more than one: Thus, Oudinot, a count in 1807, was made duke of Reggio in 1810, to cite a single example. Sixteen of the Marshalate became dukes, and six became princes [Berthier twice, in 1806 and 1809; Murat was Grand Duke of Berg and a Prince of the Blood by marriage; the others—as we shall read below—were Bernadotte, Davout, Massena, and Ney (we exclude Poniatowski who was a Polish prince in his own right)]. Only Brune and Jourdan held out against this flood of honors because of republican principles, but both ultimately succumbed to become peers of France in 1815 during the Hundred Days, and the latter was made a count by Louis XVIII in 1816.

To support their new dignities, Napoleon distributed very substantial sums of money among the "military" princes, the 23 dukes, 193 counts, 648 barons, and 117 knights who made up his martial aristocracy. In all, he disbursed over 16 million francs in 1,261 awards in favor of 824 generals. The actual sums varied enormously, but once again a majority of the marshals did very well for themselves. Berthier—besides his principality—received eight *dotations* (endowments) to a total value of over 1.254 million francs. Ney—close on his heels—benefited from five awards to a total value of 1,028,973 francs (receiving 800,000 in a single gift in late 1812). Davout received six awards totaling 910,840 francs and Massena some 638,375 francs in five (besides his notorious "little savings," which were another matter entirely). Lannes received almost 328,000 francs—and doubtless would have had more but for his premature death in 1809. Others of the marshalate did not do so well. Gouvion St.-Cyr reputedly was awarded only 30,000 francs, and Brune and Jourdan received nothing at all. As we shall see, many another marshal besides Massena looked after his own interests in foreign parts—causing many a problem thereby—not least Brune, who earned the nickname (as Alan Shepperd recalls) of "the intrepid looter" from the Emperor himself, although Soult was apparently the worst depredator.

But if wealth, honors, and rewards were one part of the story of being a Marshal of the Empire, there was (as already mentioned) another, darker side to the coin. Apart from the honorary senatorial appointees, few marshals were allowed much time to enjoy their privileges—unless, like Brune, Gouvion St.-Cyr, Macdonald, and (ultimately) Massena, they fell out of favor with the Emperor and were consequently not employed in the Grand Army for long periods. As the table of Major Campaigns shows (see p. lxii), he was a relentless master, and when not engaged on active service most marshals were required to undertake time-consuming administrative tasks or tedious court functions. And, of course, the marshals were by no means immune from shot and shell, as will become quite clear in the chapters that follow. All of half would receive wounds as marshals, and three would succumb—Bessières killed outright at Rippach on May 1, 1813; Lannes as a result of wounds sustained at Essling on May 22, 1809; and Prince Poniatowski, drowned while trying to swim the Elster with severe wounds at Leipsig on October 19, 1813. Lannes had also been hit at Pultusk in 1807. The invincible Oudinot—as Paul Britten-Austin recalls—received at least eight wounds as a marshal, three of them in Russia in 1812, to add to his incredible total of battle injuries, which did not prevent his living to the age of 80. Davout, Bernadotte, Marmont, and Ney were all wounded on two occasions (the first-named, in fact, sustained two injuries at Borodino and so really counts as three times stricken), while Murat, Augereau, Suchet, Gouvion St.-Cyr, and Victor were individually laid temporarily *hors de combat* on one occasion in a whole range of battles from Eylau on February 8, 1807, to Craonne on March 7, seven years later.[4]

It would be quite wrong to assert that the "untouched" marshals tended to hang back or avoid the firing line. Many had been wounded in their service before 1804. Only Massena, Kellermann, Moncey, and Brune enjoyed charmed lives, surviving their entire active careers without sustaining a single wound in battle—but the first-named had performed legendary feats in full view of his men and the enemy on numerous occasions, as at Rivoli where he rode alone toward the Austrians at a critical moment while reinforcements were being rushed to an unguarded sector, to distract attention, and was almost taken prisoner; or again at Essling on the morning of May 23, 1809, where he was the last man to cross onto Lobau Island after skillfully extricating the French rear guard from the north bank of the Danube. As for Brune, his luck on the battlefield did not extend to the events of August 2, 1815, when he was attacked and murdered by royalist terrorists in a particularly brutal manner. Such exceptions, however, only serve to prove the rule. Officers of all ranks were closely involved in physical terms in the battles of the early nineteenth century. Interestingly, Georges Six has calculated that 1,013 of the 2,248 general officers of the 1792–1815 period escaped being wounded in action—almost 50%. The same authority has also calculated that the 1,235 who were less fortunate (230 being killed) accounted among them for a daunting total of 4,055 wounds.[5] Death and injury on the battlefield were clearly no respecters of persons. Napoleon himself was twice wounded—at Toulon (1793) and Ratisbon (1809)—and had a number of other near escapes.

Clearly, high command brought commensurate physical risks as well as considerable recompenses and privileges. The tough old Duke of Danzig, Lefebvre, twice wounded himself (the first time while protecting the royal family from the attentions of the Paris mob outside the Tuileries in 1791), assuredly said it all when an old friend was enviously admiring his fine Paris mansion. "So you're jealous of me," exclaimed the veteran. "Very well; come out into the courtyard and I'll have twenty shots at you at thirty paces. If I don't hit you, the whole house and everything in it is yours." The friend hastily declined to take the chance, whereupon Lefebvre remarked drily, "I had a thousand bullets fired at me from much closer range before I got all this."[6]

What kind of men, therefore, were these Napoleonic paladins, who provided "the brawn, muscle and courage" to complement the Emperor's "inspiration, brains and willpower"?[7] What were their origins and backgrounds that suited them for the undoubtedly grave challenges posed by grasping the gold-embroidered marshal's baton?

The future Marshals of the Empire—as the chapters of this book will confirm—came from widely differing social and family backgrounds. It is interesting to note that seven of the marshalate (or 27%) came from aristocratic families, although most of these belonged to the *petite noblesse*. Poniatowski was, of course, a Polish prince, and Grouchy (as James Lunt points out) a French marquis, in their own rights, but Berthier, Davout, Macdonald, Marmont, and Pérignon were also men of good family, the descendants of officers in the Royal Army or of important officials. Some would also place Sérurier in this category. Not only was he a major and a Chevalier of St. Louis before the Revolution, but his father certainly regarded himself as a landowner and royal office holder under the Bourbon monarchy. However (as David Rooney informs us below), Sérurier-senior was the royal mole catcher at Laon, so his marshal son should probably be classified alongside Augereau, Lefebvre, Murat,

Mortier, and Ney—sons of a fruit dealer, a miller, an innkeeper, a wealthy peasant farmer, and a barrel cooper, respectively—as a man of relatively humble origin although the "royal" appointment might signify. The remaining 13 (half the total) came from professional, commercial, or lower-middle-class backgrounds. Four had fathers who were lawyers, two were medical men, and the remainder were a bailiff, a tailor-cum-tax collector, a silk manufacturer, a brewer, a tanner, a shopkeeper, and a well-to-do farmer. In all, at least six fathers (those of Berthier, Davout, Victor, Marmont, Sérurier, and Marmont) could claim some form of army service.

In terms of geographical location, their birthplaces (we exclude Poniatowski as foreign born) were divided between Paris and 22 of the 90 *Départements* of metropolitan France. Only the capital and Lot could boast of two apiece, namely, Augereau and Grouchy, and Murat and Bessières, respectively. The northern and eastern frontier regions could claim a dozen, and a further eight were born in a straggle of Departments between Haute-Vienne and Basses-Pyrenees; the rest in eastern–central France. Few came from the Midi or the southeast, and only a couple from the western or northern coastal regions. None at all were born in Normandy, Brittany, or the Bordeaux or Toulon areas. But nothing of great consequence emerges from a survey of geographical origins.

More significant and revelatory is the study of the marshals' educations and of their previous military experience. Napoleon laid some stress on the importance of the former. "There are scant resources to be found in men who have not received a primary education," he once reflected. "They can feel keenly, they can sense, but they cannot analyse anything; and when they come up against novel circumstances they only perpetrate stupid mistakes."[8] According to Guy Godlewski, eight of the marshals—like Napoleon himself—had received some formal military education, namely, Davout, Grouchy, Kellermann, and Marmont at royal military schools of one sort or another, and Macdonald (as Alan Hankison discusses), Pérignon, Poniatowski (in Vienna), and Sérurier should also be regarded as educated men.[9] Bernadotte, Bessières, Brune, Moncey, Oudinot, and Murat were all students (in the last instance, a seminarist, as Tim Pickles reminds us) in early life, but all abandoned the pen (or the soutane) for the sword, and the book for the barrack room, at an early stage; Ney was training to be a notary, Mortier (Randal Gray reveals) to be a merchant's clerk, Gouvion St.-Cyr to be an artist. All the remainder were literate in varying degrees, although Augereau, Lannes, and Lefebvre owed more to their native wits than to any formal education. But in terms of innate intelligence, all rated quite highly, especially Berthier, Davout and Soult, Massena and Suchet. Napoleon did not surround himself with fools—far from it.

There was also a great reservoir of variegated experience— both military and civil—among this band of 26 men. When Louis XVI was arrested at Varennes in June 1791, nine future marshals were serving as officers in the Royal Army. True, Pérignon, Davout, and Marmont were only junior subalterns, Macdonald a lieutenant, and Moncey a captain; but Kellermann was the equivalent of a general of brigade, Berthier was a staff colonel, Grouchy a lieutenant-colonel, and Sérurier a major. At that moment in time, a further 10 future marshals were either serving as non-commissioned officers or other ranks, or had recently done so. Ney, Murat, Soult, Bernadotte, and Lefebvre came into the first category (although the last-named, after 16 years in the *Gardes Françaises* (French Guards), had, in fact, become a lieutenant in the paid National Guard in 1789); while Jourdan, Augereau, Massena, Victor, and Oudinot (as James R. Arnold and Paul Britten-Austin discuss in due course) belong to the second, not on that date being members of the regular army, although all five were already serving in the National Guard or volunteer formations in various capacities (Oudinot was, indeed, a paid captain-instructor). Massena, of course, had been a regimental sergeant major when he quit the army in 1789. At the same date in 1791, the remaining six (discounting Poniatowski who was in Poland) were all still civilians following various employments, although once again several were already part-time members of the National Guard. Bessières was working as a hairdresser (but would join the Royal Constitutional Guard in April 1792). Brune was a printer with literary leanings in Paris— and already an elected captain in the National Guard (since 1789). Lannes was a painter, but may have had some military experience as he was elected a *sous-lieutenant* (subaltern officer or second lieutenant) the same day he joined the Volunteers of Gers (June 20, 1792). Suchet was busy learning the family profession of silk merchant (he would enter the cavalry of the Lyons National Guard at an unspecified date later in 1791). Gouvion St.-Cyr was an artist in Paris—and would join the Volunteers in September 1792. And last, Mortier, training to be a merchant's clerk, was already a member of the Dunkirk National Guard. All six were members of the bourgeoisie, and clearly every man was patriotically inclined and probably politically aware as their association with National Guard or Volunteer formations might indicate. In troubled times it was prudent to be seen as actively committed to the defense of the Revolution.

The true political attitudes of the serving or former soldiers at this, the constitutional crisis of the Revolution, are less easy to categorize. A study of their known declarations, and above all their actions at the time and in later years, gives certain indications, but they need to be treated with care. Clearly none were out-and-out Bourbon royalists or they would have joined the emigration of officers that rapidly boosted many of their careers by facilitating rapid promotion to vacancies so caused. However, it seems that Sérurier, Macdonald, and Moncey all considered leaving the country. Marmont considered himself a constitutional royalist, and in general terms this description might well, with varying shades of graduation, have also been applied to Berthier, Bessières, Moncey, Mortier, Pérignon, and Sérurier. Berthier (as Charles Raeuber recalls) actually commanded troops protecting part of the royal family from the mob in early 1791, and Bessières—once he had joined the Royal Constitutional Guard—was similarly involved in what could certainly be deemed anti-revolutionary activities during and after the mob's storming of the Tuileries Palace on August 10, 1792, as Charles Esdaile's account reveals. Moncey's leanings are probably revealed by the identity of his main friends, who included Moreau and Pichegru and the notorious plotter Georges Cadoudal, all royalists of varying complexion. Mortier kept his opinions to himself and remained enigmatic, but Pérignon accepted the Bourbon Restoration in 1814 with less qualms than most. At the other political extremity were the outspoken Augereau, the equally violently-expressed Suchet, and the rather sinister Brune, friend of Danton, who became involved in denunciations and purges. Bernadotte was a Jacobin (or extreme left-winger) in his earlier years—or such was his reputation—although he would mellow with the passage of time. Murat was a blazing patriot during the early revolutionary period, but soon cooled. Jourdan was a simple-hearted man who, with Brune (for other reasons), clung to revolutionary principles for much of their lives, refusing preferments until later years, as we have already noted and as Michael Glover mentions in his chapter on the former. Of the rest, Davout, Grouchy, and Kellermann were certainly patriots, the first two genuinely enthused by the new ideas at the expense of the Old Regime and their own class in society, but the first- and last-named ultimately placed discipline as the highest virtue, and determined to protect the army from the worst forms of extremism, whether from right or left. The remainder—including Ney, Lannes, Massena, Oudinot, and Gouvion St.-Cyr, together with Lefebvre and Victor—were middle-of-the-road republicans without unduly strong personal convictions, although Gouvion St.-Cyr was probably more committed than the rest (as Philipp Coates-Wright reveals below).

Politically, therefore, the future marshalate represented a wide spectrum. All, however, save possibly Jourdan, were opportunists to a marked degree, as indeed was Napoleon Bonaparte himself. A high degree of flexibility was a desirable characteristic in a revolutionary period with its abrupt swings and about-faces; and the relative ease with which many of the surviving marshals were re-assimilated after the First and Second Bourbon Restorations of 1814 and 1815 would also seem to reinforce this impression.

Rarely has any group of men called to high military rank at a single period been more varied in terms of temperament and character. The flamboyance and quarrelsomeness of the touchy Murat contrasts with the icy-coolness of Davout or the reserved, stalwart fidelity of Bessières; or with the sensitivity of Moncey that Ian Beckett illustrates below. The red-headed Ney had a flaring temper to match, not least in battle, the coarseness of Augereau or the drive of Lannes. Soult was both able and vain. None seems to have been highly religious, although Bernadotte made much of being a Protestant in later years, and Lefebvre made no secret of his Catholicism. Gouvion St.-Cyr was a confirmed agnostic. A few had a feeling for music and the arts. Ney played the clarinet, and Victor, Marmont, and Gouvion St.-Cyr (possibly) the violin. Their ages, as we have seen, varied as markedly as their degrees of military seniority. In their private lives, the great majority were unremarkable—they were good, if unspectacular, husbands and fathers in the main. The exceptions only proved the general rule. Marmont had a miserable marriage, Bessières was notorious for squandering his money on a mistress, and Massena's taste for women was apparently insatiable. As Sir James Marshall-Cornwall reminds us on a later page, Massena's mistress, Silvia Cepolini, accompanied him for most of the first Italian campaign: also, in 1810 the Prince of Essling took another, Henriette Leberton, fetchingly (if wholly unconvincingly) disguised as an officer of cavalry, to Portugal—although this caused much trouble with his corps commanders, who refused to talk to her at mealtimes (for whatever reason—*Madame Junot* kept her unfortunate husband on a very short lead); and Baron Marbot blamed the slow pursuit of Wellington's army from Viseu on his chief's solicitude for the lady in question. Berthier accepted an arranged marriage but pined for his beloved Madame Visconti and eventually set up a *ménage à trois*. Four were divorced but remarried—Lannes, Macdonald, Victor, and Davout, whose second marriage proved very close. Other examples of marital tenderness and total fidelity included Lefebvre and his devoted Catherine Hubscher, the sometime washerwoman nicknamed *Madame Sans-Gêne* for her lack of tact and sometimes devastating bluntness; and Gouvion St.-Cyr and his wife were equally devoted through a marriage that lasted 36 years. Macdonald married three times in all, and Augereau, Davout, Grouchy, Lannes, Oudinot, and Victor twice. As a group the marshalate proved prolific. Although four were childless (Brune, Marmont, Sérurier, and Poniatowski—the only marshal who never married), the remaining 22 produced 104 descendants. The Lefebvres had 14 children, but tragically all but two died as infants. Pérignon and Oudinot produced 11 apiece, Davout eight (of whom four survived infancy). Guy Godlewski has calculated that today only nine family titles survive in direct male lines,[10] but in 1956 Murat was calculated to have 300 descendants, and in 1962 Grouchy had all of 474.

If the marshalate shared one vice other than quarrelsomeness, it was venality. Their appetite for riches seemed insatiable, and represents the more sordid side of the ambition that drove them forward without exception. The names of Augereau, Brune, and Massena are often associated with tales of peculation and looting on an impressive scale, with Victor only a shade behind them. Their bare-faced depredations became legendary. Soult also looted in the grand manner—holding large towns and whole provinces to ransom, gathering the finest collection of paintings in Europe in the process. One notorious case occurred in 1807, at Erfurt, where Imperial Intendant-General Count Daru uncovered one marshal (commanding the local occupation forces) who had levied 300,000 francs in taxes and split them two to one with his senior paymaster. The latter was made to disgorge his gains, but the marshal—probably Victor—stood his ground and bluffed his way out of the impasse without repaying a single sous.[11] Napoleon, of course, knew every detail of what was going on from his spies, and occasionally used his knowledge ruthlessly to control—even blackmail—his subordinates. Sometimes he insisted on ill-gotten gains being returned: both Brune and Massena were on occasion made to disgorge. More often he turned a blind eye on such irregularities. "Don't talk to me about generals who love money," he enjoined Gourgaud on St. Helena. "It was only that which enabled me to win the battle of Eylau. Ney wanted to reach Elbing to procure more funds."[12] It seems the Emperor had hoped to check the cupidity of his senior generals by awarding them proud titles, with appanages and monetary grants to match—but if anything it proved the opposite. The newly ennobled needed fine houses, hunting lodges, and all that went with them, and above all to outshine their rivals. Even on campaign a number of them kept almost regal state. The day after the Battle of Valutino, an officer reported to Ney's headquarters to find to his astonishment a feast comprising all of 25

covers being served in splendor on the grass. To maintain this
kind of standard cost money, and many senior commanders did
not hesitate to milk the conquered provinces through which they
passed—some (as noted above) with flamboyant gusto, others
more discreetly. But not all were tarred with the same brush, or
to the same degree. Some—including Davout (save when the
French interest was involved), Bessières, Mortier or Suchet (as
Jeanne A. Ojala tells us), and certainly Bernadotte (as Tony
Heathcote discusses)*—were men of probity who set an example
to their men and enforced similar standards, protecting civilian
populations from the depredations of their troops to the best of
their ability and, in the case of Suchet, winning substantial local
Catalan support, or at least a measure of acceptance, in supposedly implacable northeastern Spain, as a result. It must be
admitted, however, that these fine examples were exceptional.
Some marshals were mean as well as grasping—not least Massena as the incident of the reward for his coachman and postil-
lion at Wagram reveals all too convincingly. These were for the
most part tough men set in rough times, and they acted accordingly. Napoleon had few illusions on this score. He once on St.
Helena reproved General Gourgaud who was reminiscing in
glowing terms about Lannes and Ney. "You are fooling yourself
if you regard Lannes thus. He, and Ney, were both men who
would slit your belly if they thought it to their advantage. But on
the field of battle they were beyond price."[13]

That was indeed the point: military valor and performance
rated higher than the moral virtues, at least in the Emperor's
book. The basic requirements Napoleon sought in a senior
commander were as follows: "A general's principal talent con-
sists in knowing the mentality of the soldier and in gaining his
confidence," he once asserted. Or again, "A military leader must
possess as much character as intellect—the base must equal the
height." Before appointing a general he would inquire, *"Est-il
heureux?"* ("Is he lucky?"—and by "luck" the Emperor really
meant a flair for taking properly calculated risks). In 1804 he
advised Lauriston that a successful general must achieve concentration of force, display activity of body and mind, and firmly
resolve "to perish gloriously. These are the three principles of
the military art that have disposed luck in my favour in all my
operations. Death is nothing, but to live defeated is to die every
day." And brave men the marshals certainly were—and for the
most part very able, a number definitely gifted. One has only to

---

*The Prince of Ponte-Corvo was considered parsimonious. On one occasion, when
his personal wagon had been captured by the enemy, he remarked—to the pointed
amusement of his men—that this unfortunate event would make it impossible for him to
distribute his habitual rewards to deserving soldiers.

think of Lannes (as Don Horward describes it) wrestling with his aides to take up a scaling ladder outside Ratisbon when the spirit of the storming party faltered. Or Ney, commanding the rear guard, musket over arm, during the retreat from Russia, arriving at last in safety totally unrecognizable even to close associates (as Peter Young recounts). Or again, Marshal Soult, responding stoutly to an untypical remark from Napoleon after Eylau concerning the harm the Russians had wrought: "And we them, our bullets were not made of cotton."[14] Old Lefebvre, charging at the head of a battalion at a critical moment in the Siege of Danzig in 1807, Murat bluffing his way over the bridge at Vienna two years earlier, and Massena fighting intrepidly among his men in a desperate situation two years later at Essling are further well-known examples of the personal valor of these famous figures, and many another example might be cited. Inspirational leadership of this type was much appreciated by both Napoleon and the ordinary soldiers—but there was sometimes a price to be paid. The instincts of the warrior sometimes overwhelmed the cool calculations of the strategist. Murat's cool demonstration of sangfroid at Vienna does not conceal the fact that he was not supposed to be anywhere near the Austrian capital—and his presence there was, in fact, allowing the Russian army to escape. Ney's impetuous attack at Jena in the wrong place caused his exasperated master to remark that the Duke of Elchingen knew as much about soldiering "as the last-joined drummer-boy," and the performance of "the bravest of the brave" at both Quatre Bras and Waterloo in 1815 would attract more well-founded imperial criticism.

All the marshals were brave men without doubt, but only a few were "great captains" in their own right. Davout and Massena—and probably Suchet—merit such a description, being men capable of independent command, strategic insights, and intuitive flashes of inspiration. Soult, as Paddy Griffith makes clear, was a superb tactician on the battlefield—"the first manoeuverer in Europe"—but a lamentable strategist who compromised French strategic operations in the Peninsula on three occasions—in 1809, 1810, and 1811—although we must admire his stalwart "last-ditch," defensive campaign conducted amid the Pyrenees and in southern France against Wellington in 1813–1814. Lannes was another fine but impetuous fighting soldier whom the Emperor allowed a comparatively free rein in Spain, and as advance guard commander, probably wisely. As for the rest, most were, if the truth be told, pretty mediocre commanders. Marmont was something of a paradox (as John Pimlott reveals), but Berthier—the chief-of-staff *sans pareil*—was hopelessly at sea in temporary command of the army in Austria during Napoleon's absence at the outset of the Campaign of 1809, although nine years earlier, as Charles Raeuber reveals, he organized and in fact commanded the dangerous crossing of the Alps by the Army of the Reserve with great skill (albeit with the First Consul nearby to tender advice). Some generals of division—including Lasalle, Lecourbe, and Vandamme—were probably capable of more initiative than Soult, Marmont, Macdonald, or Oudinot. But, then, Napoleon as we shall see, did not always encourage independence of mind in the men he chose for the highest honors, and took scant pains to inculcate in them an appreciation of the finer points of the art and science of war (pace certain historians).[15] This is not to discount the great administrative and training achievements in earlier years of such commanders as Kellermann the Elder or his valorous command successes during the Valmy Campaign of 1792 (as Peter Hofschröer so vividly describes), or those of the practically unknown Pérignon in northern Spain (as Georges Ostermann reveals).

That many of the chosen 26 were awkward subordinates to control, with their fits of feuding, quarreling, and plain insubordination, there can be no denying. Napoleon was not above playing the game of Caesar Caligula, *divide et impera* ("divide and rule"), to keep the hounds at bay by encouraging them to savage one another, but at times his patience must have been sorely tried. Murat became ever more difficult to handle, partly because of his sense of being a ruling monarch and needing to act out the role accordingly, as Tim Pickles discusses. Soult's aspirations to an Iberian crown reached near-treasonable proportions. Gouvion St.-Cyr—after clashing with Murat and Massena—had to be ordered back to Naples on pain of death after abandoning his duty station in 1806 for a visit to Paris in order to protest his treatment. Bernadotte allowed his rivalry for Davout in October 1806 to overbear his military responsibility and his flagrant disobedience of orders almost earned himself a court-martial thereby—and his conduct at Wagram finally cost him (rather unfairly) his place in Napoleon's favored circle (although this did not preclude a brilliant future as crown prince and then monarch of a Baltic kingdom). But the marshals rowed, snarled, and snapped at each other in campaign and out, and were repeatedly complaining to the Emperor about one another's behavior. Thus, Davout—whom Berthier alternatively liked or disliked—loathed Bernadotte and despised Murat, who in turn was barely on speaking terms with Ney from 1805 onward. Brune gave as much criticism as he attracted. Ney rowed with his superior Massena in 1810 and was, as a result, removed from his command, but so a little later was the Prince of Essling himself. Murat and Lannes prosecuted a lively fued from 1799; and Oudinot had scant time for Ney, and achieved possibly the perfect revenge at Dennewitz in 1813 when, smarting from being superseded in command by his rival, he *obeyed* an order knowing it to be wrong. The list could go on almost indefinitely, but many of these clashes of personality and temperament will be found in the chapters that follow. Nevertheless, it should be appreciated that, however problematical were these evidences of rivalry, the great majority of the marshalate cooperated to considerable effect on campaigns and in battle. The "feuding" and "non-cooperation" that occasionally broke out (especially in Spain in Napoleon's absence) was the exception rather than the rule.

Why, then, it may be wondered, given all these problems and uneven levels of ability, did Napoleon create the marshalate in the first place, and then appoint to it the men he did? His reasons were many and complex, and only the more important can be indicated here. The dignity of Marshal of France had been abolished by the Convention in 1793, but the re-establishment of the position in May 1804 was no passing whim on the part of the Consul for Life, soon to become Emperor. At one level, it was a coldly calculated political act designed to rally a number of highly influential but critical senior army commanders to his support. Ever since the coup d'état of Brumaire in 1799, there had been some generals who showed open hostility toward the institution of the consulate for reasons of ideology or of jealousy plain and simple. Hard-bitten military critics—particularly those of the extremist Jacobin persuasion—regretted the passing of the austere, idealistic days of the Republic from the establishment of the Directory onwards, and distrusted the regime headed by the jumped-up Corsican (as some regarded Bonaparte) who was in most cases so very much younger than they. These initial reactions hardened when the Concordat with the Papacy—"restoring the ancient altars" to a France that had formally abolished religion—was pushed through. This did not prevent, be it noted, die-hard Republicans such as Brune from being among the greatest depredators. But as Napoleon steadily increased his hold over state and people, many generals positively disliked the deliberately fostered cult of personality surrounding the new ruler and the pomp and ceremony of the quasi-regal style he came to adopt. Not all the conspiracies—both royalist and diehard republican—of the years between 1800 and 1804 were figments of Minister of Police Fouché's imagination. Bernadotte, the sometime strong Jacobin, set up a large-scale plot against Napoleon: it is remarkable that (despite some of the watchful Davout's "telltale relevations") he was not called to account. But then, as Napoleon once remarked, "war [and one's attitude to subordinates?] is a matter of tact". It is equally remarkable that the crisis did not occur until 1809—and that even then, Bernadotte got away with it—and even transformed the situation to his own advantage from 1810. The Prince of Ponte-Corvo was probably the most politically-conscious and adept of the marshalate.

Napoleon in his earlier years was a supreme realist as well as an egotistical opportunist. Aware that his rise owed everything to (after his own abilities) the French Army, he knew his power must be firmly based on its unquestioning support, and that meant the whole-hearted cooperation of its commanders. Otherwise it would require only a determined group of dissident generals and a few regiments and cannons placed in strategic positions around Paris on an awkward date to bring off yet another coup and institute another regime. One answer to this problem was clearly to buy the support of the influential soldiers—pandering to the human frailties of ambition, lust for position, and appetite for gain of whose existence in almost every man, Napoleon Bonaparte, close student of human nature, was very well aware. "It is with baubles that men are led," he once cynically remarked. Accordingly, he decided, at one level, to re-create the marshalate as a means to win over, and if necessary compromise and even corrupt, the soldiers he had to rely upon. He would pay the necessary price to purchase their consciences, and then leave it to the lure of the trappings of apparent power and social pre-eminence—the fine city mansions and country estates, the gifts, honors and decorations, cannon salutes and guards of honor (and above all, perhaps, the newly-awakened aspirations of the newly elevated's womenfolk and families), together with the power of his own magnetic personality, to consolidate his power over them. "If I wanted a man enough I would kiss his arse," the Emperor once crudely remarked. Once caught in the spider's web of privilege, few men, Napoleon calculated, would be strong-willed enough to break free.

As he moved nearer to the restoration of, if not a monarchy on the ancient type then at least an empire modeled on that of Charlemagne in the ninth century, Napoleon was also aware that the re-creation of the marshalate—with origins going back to the eleventh century and its close associations with the royal dynasties of France—would be an important institutional step in restoring the links with the past that would ease his own progress toward the throne. Furthermore, it was important in his eyes to restore an equivalent dignity for France's senior military men to that of field-marshal, which existed in the Austrian and Russian empires and the Prussian and British monarchies. The marshalate would, he calculated, help earn acceptance on an equal footing for the new French Empire, and add dignity and luster to occasions of international negotiation and summitry. Napoleon often made use of his marshals as ambassadors-extraordinary for special diplomatic missions (and sometimes as a punishment to be sure), as will emerge from reading this book.

Furthermore, Napoleon appreciated the need to create an imperial court and to associate the army as well as the civilian notables with it. The marshals and their wives would have an important part to play in support of the imperial family on grand occasions associated with the Tuileries, Rambouillet, Fontaine-bleau, and Malmaison. This particular aspiration was never, in fact, brought to full realization. Ney, Davout, and several others loathed attendance at court with its deadening formalities and protocol; and the former rarely, if ever, appeared there. Berthier and Bessières took to its pomp and ceremony rather more easily, and at times gave sumptuous balls and other festivities. On other occasions there were events bordering on the farcical, including the celebrated rabbit shoot arranged by Berthier, (and spite-fully described by Madame Junot and the later occasion when Napoleon managed to shoot Massena in the eye—an event the present Prince of Essling alludes to in his Foreword—but induced poor Berthier—in fact a keen and capable hunter and horseman—to shoulder the blame. The association of the marshalate with the court was also important for another fundamental reason. It is important to appreciate that the title of marshal was a civil dignity and *not* a military rank. It is true that only the most senior military men could qualify for the award of the baton, but Napoleon was adamant that a marshal per se was only a ceremonial appointment. On several occasions he was quick to emphasize the point when he deemed it necessary to check the arrogance of his commanders. "Know, then, that you are only a military figure when with the Army," he pronounced on one occasion. "The title of Marshal is a purely civil dignity . . . which carries with it no authority whatsoever. You may be generals on the field of battle, but you are only *grands seigneurs* when you are about me at court."[16] Thus, he also used the marshalate as a means to distance himself from his comrades of equivalent rank in earlier years, and even, when necessary, to put them firmly in their places.

When it came to selecting the men to carry the baton, Napoleon was again the subject of conflicting pressures and priorities, in which politics within the army had an important part to play. Prominence in the army and personal valor were certainly basic criteria, but military distinction per se was not the sole, or even the most important consideration. Relationship by marriage with the Bonaparte clan was most certainly one factor in the appointment of both Murat and Davout to the dignity, and the inclusion of a number of staunch heroes of the early republican period such as Kellermann, the other honorific marshals, and Lefebvre, was clearly a sound decision. This at once helped quell any charges of anti-republican bias in the selection process and stressed the continuity of the institution. But it was even more important to strike a balance between significant power groupings within the army itself and to keep them under control, allowing no single cabal to exert a decisive influence. There were two main groups, and one minor, to be placated, controlled, and integrated. These were in the first place the generals who had served under General Bonaparte in the famous Army of Italy, many of whom had followed him on to Egypt and Syria; second, there were those soldiers who had made their reputations serving on the northern and eastern frontiers of France under such notable commanders as Dumouriez, Kellermann, Moreau, Pichegru, and Kléber, without any recourse to Napoleon or experience of serving under him; and in third place, there were commanders who had served mainly on the southern frontiers in the Armies of the Pyrenees, of whom the same might be said. There was considerable mutual suspicion, even a degree of antagonism, between the groups, particularly the first two. The "Italians" considered themselves as the elite owing to their long-established proximity to Napoleon's person—and some were inclined to take liberties on this basis—another tendency the Emperor was determined to check. The "men of the Rhine," on the other hand, believed that they had carried the brunt of the revolutionary wars and achieved just as much, if not considerably more, than the Corsican's "mafioso" who had fought on what could be deemed the secondary front against, in the main, second-class opponents in Italy. By 1804 Dumouriez had defected, Moreau had been disgraced, and Pichegru and Kléber were dead, but Napoleon realized the need to rally the remaining veterans of the Rhine armies in order to avoid any danger of schism and conspiracy, and to achieve his determination to create a single, united French army without strong regional loyalties and attitudes that might cause problems. Accordingly, the first list of 18 names was a carefully conceived balancing act designed to unite the factions, giving each a fair share of representation. Seven of the "active" marshals were drawn from the generals of the Army of Italy, namely, Berthier, Murat, Massena, Augereau, Brune, Lannes, Bessières. Seven were selected from the Armies of the Rhine, namely, Jourdan, Bernadotte, Soult, Mortier, Ney, Davout, and Lefebvre. The Armies of the Pyrenees (which had been largely quiescent since 1795) were represented by two of the honorific appointments, namely, those of Moncey and Pérignon. The remaining two batons were awarded to an old soldier from each of the two main factions: Sérurier representing the veterans of "Italy," Kellermann those of "the Rhine." All four incarnated the achievements of the first armies of the Republic—and also represented a salute to the old Bourbon Royal Army that preceded these, and in whose ranks at least three had earned considerable distinction. So much for the "Promotion of 1804." It is interesting to note that roughly the same balance was preserved in the later appointments, although the distinction between "soldiers of Italy" and "men of the Rhine" had become less critical with the passage of time. Thus, Victor, Marmont, and Suchet had originally served under Bonaparte in 1796–1797, while four more—Macdonald, Oudinot, Gouvion St.-Cyr, and Grouchy—had first earned their reputations on the eastern frontiers. Poniatowski, of course, as a foreigner, belonged to no faction.

Thus, the two formative "schools" or cliques that had produced victory for France between 1792 and 1800 against the First and Second Coalitions were fairly and evenly represented in those selected for inclusion in the marshalate. Personal sentiment would seem to have played only a muted role in the selection process. Berthier, Murat, Marmont, and Bessières, together with Lannes, were those regarded by Napoleon with something approaching personal affection—but this was of a very special nature, compounded of "brutality, generosity, inaccessibility, and even rancour."[17] It is notable that Junot, something of a favorite, and d'Albe, after Berthier probably Napoleon's key confidant and—as controller of his Map Office—strategic planner, never received their batons, and it would be possible to mention another half-dozen names of experienced soldiers whose individual records were more brilliant and comprehensive in terms of demonstrable military skills than those of an equivalent number of the less-gifted among the marshals.* But, as always in military matters, "luck" enters into the equation—being at the right place at the right time to earn the necessary personal approval of Napoleon. He would live to regret some of the appointments he made, and even to question the wisdom of restricting the award of key commands to marshals alone, above all in the later years. "He found fault with himself for having made so much use of the marshals in these latter days," recorded Caulaincourt in 1814, "since they had become too rich, too much the *grands seigneurs* and had grown war-weary. Things, according to him, would have been in a much better state if he had placed

---

*It is interesting to note (see Appendix A on pp. 536–7) that a further 17 soldiers of the Grand Army, many of whom had served as generals and one (Bugeaud) as colonel, would receive batons from the Bourbons between 1815 and 1851.

good generals of division, with their batons yet to win, in command."[18] But in the great years, before disillusion set in, he owed much to the men he had selected to wear *les gros bonnets*, as the chapters that follow will reveal.

In conclusion, it remains to reach some sort of an estimate of Napoleon's opinion of his 26 marshals, and also some of their feelings toward him. He was always aware of his debt to them individually—for good or ill. Anyone criticizing, for example, Augereau would be reminded (as John Elting recalls), "Ah, but remember what he did for us at Castiglione!"[19] Ney's conduct during the retreat from Moscow was frequently recalled in the last years of the Empire as at least partial absolution for his errors in judgment. The Emperor could equally be devastatingly scathing to those he regarded as having let him down. He rarely minced words, either face to face or on paper. "I cannot approve your manner of march," he wrote to Murat in 1805. "You go on like a stunned fool taking not the least notice of my orders."[20] On another occasion he compared the Prince's latest splendid uniforms to those of "Franconi the circus rider." Again, after Bernadotte's major *faux pas* in mid-October 1806, Napoleon declared, "This matter is so hateful that if I send him before a court martial it will be the equivalent of ordering him to be shot. . . . [However] I shall take care he shall know what I think of his behaviour."[21] When Marmont was responsible for a near-disaster in the Festieux Defile (March 1814), the Emperor fulminated at "the crass stupidity of the Duke of Ragusa, who behaved himself like a second-lieutenant,"[22] which at least gave him some seniority over Ney at Jena, compared scathingly to "the last-joined drummer-boy." "Write him a truly dry letter," directed the master, sacking Victor for idleness in 1814; and no man was better at phrasing a telling expression of imperial displeasure than Berthier, of whom Napoleon once admitted, "No-one else could replace him."[23]

There is no question but that the Emperor drove his key subordinates hard. Berthier was once found in tears. "A mere soldier is happier than I. I am being killed by hard work."[24] Marshals and staff were bullied mercilessly—and Napoleon's rages were widely feared (and not without reason: the Prince of Neuchâtel was once seized by the throat and his head hammered against a stone wall). The Emperor's demands were incessant, allowing for no argument, and immediate compliance was expected. As already noted, Napoleon sometimes deliberately played his marshals off against one another, encouraging rifts and jealousies, in order to ensure their complete reliance upon him. As we have also seen, he could be generous—but few were given much chance to enjoy their privileges. The system worked well enough in the great days of the Empire, but several grave penalties had to be paid in later years. First, because Napoleon demanded absolute obedience, few of the marshals were happy when situations arose that demanded genuine initiative in their master's absence. This became particularly evident in Spain from 1809, when successive teams of marshals—deprived of the Emperor's dominating presence—proved incapable of fully effective action, and furthermore wasted much time and energy prosecuting their personal feuds against one another. Even the great Massena fell prey to this tendency in 1810–1811 with dire results. Moreover, if even Napoleon was incapable of controlling events on the Tagus or Ebro from Paris in mid-1809, what hope had he of doing so from Moscow in 1812 or central Germany in 1813? Thus, the strictly centralized direction of campaigns upon which he insisted—and which was operable enough in the campaigns he personally commanded with armies of up to 250,000 men—eventually broke down when the size of armies burgeoned to a half-million and more, as war zones extended ever more widely, and as a second front—and a Russian one at that—was finally added to compound the problem. As disasters began to mount, so the morale of his key subordinates began to sink. "It would be difficult for me to describe the gloomy inquietude which I saw on the face of the gold-spangled courtiers and generals assembled in the Emperor's apartments," claimed the wily and unscrupulous Austrian statesman Metternich of peace negotiations in early 1814. "The Prince of Neuchâtel said to me in a whisper—'Do not forget that Europe needs peace—France above all wants nothing but peace'."[25] And in the end, the system let him down, when a group of marshals, led by Ney, totally demoralized and wearied beyond bearing by the incessant demands of Napoleonic warfare, mutinied at Fontainebleau on April 4, 1814, and refused to obey orders to march on Paris. "The Army will obey me!" proclaimed the Emperor. "The Army will obey its Chiefs," riposted the prince of the Mosckova. The nadir of the French Empire, of its directing genius and of the marshalate, had been reached at that moment. The outcome was the first abdication and Napoleon's exile to the island of Elba. On his return next year for the final gamble of the "Hundred Days," he exacted a revenge. No less than five marshals were proclaimed to have forfeited their batons: Augereau and Marmont for their misconduct in 1814; Pérignon for having supported the Bourbon prince, the Duke of Angoulême, in the Midi; Victor and then even Berthier for having followed Louis XVIII over the frontier into Belgium in 1815. Furthermore, he totally disowned his brother-in-law, Murat, refusing his proffered saber and insisting that he return to Naples. Conversely, when Oudinot refused the summons to serve, he was formally exiled to his estates although he retained his baton. After Waterloo the Bourbons exacted their vengeance by shooting Ney and by depriving several more marshals—including Davout—of their batons and other privileges at least temporarily. Brune and Murat also paid with their lives.

How, then, did Napoleon see his marshals? The long years of exile on St. Helena gave him plenty of leisure to consider their strengths and abilities, their failings and foibles, and the services of Count Las Cases and General Gourgauld to record his verdicts for the benefit of posterity. Here it will be possible to cite only a single recorded opinion (or at the most two) on each of the marshals. Of course, some allowance has to be made for the circumstances of disillusion and bitterness that surrounded the exile of St. Helena, which inevitably colored Napoleon's verdicts to at least some degree, but they do provide a guide to Napoleon's innermost feelings at that time.[26]

The justice or otherwise of the Emperor's sometimes somewhat inconsistent views will have to be judged by the reader. Comment would be superfluous and indeed out of place in an Introduction. The marshals are placed in alphabetical order—as indeed are the ensuing chapters forming the main body of the volume for the reader's greater convenience:

Augereau: "It is a long time since the Marshal was truly a soldier; his courage, his outstanding virtues certainly elevated him far above the crowd; but honours, titles, and money plunged him back into it. The conqueror of Castilgione could have left a cherised name to France; but she will recall the memory of the deserter of Lyons."

Bernadotte: "I can only say that Bernadotte let me down. He had become a sort of Swede, but never promised or declared an intention to stay true. I can therefore accuse him of ingratitude, but not of treason."

Berthier: "I have been betrayed by Berthier, a true gosling whom I had made into a kind of eagle" (1814). "There was not in the world a better Chief-of-Staff; that is where his true talent lay, for he was not capable of commanding 500 men" (St. Helena).

Bessières: "If I had had Bessières at Waterloo, my Guard would have brought me Victory."

Brune: "[He] was justly proclaimed the saviour of the Batavian Republic. The Romans would have awarded him the honour of a Triumph. By saving Holland he also saved France from invasion."

Davout: "[He] will have his place in History because of Auerstädt. He also performed well at Eylau, but, although urged on at Wagram, . . . [his slowness] was the cause of the failure to conclude the battle on the first day. . . . He also made mistakes at the Moskowa [Borodino]."

Gouvion St.-Cyr: "My mistake was to have employed St. Cyr; he never exposed himself to fire, made no visits, left his comrades to be beaten, and should have been able to save Vandamme [at Kulm, 1813]."

Grouchy: "Marshal Grouchy, with 34,000 men and 108 cannon, solved the apparently undiscoverable secret by being, on the morning of the 18th [June 1815], neither on the battlefield of Mont St. Jean nor on that at Wavre. . . . His conduct was as unforeseeable as if his army, on the march, had undergone an earthquake and been swallowed up."

Jourdan: "I certainly used that man very ill; nothing would be more natural than that he should think that he owed me little. Ah well! I have learned with great pleasure that since my fall he invariably acted very well. He has thus afforded an example of that praiseworthy elevation of mind which distinguishes men one from another. Jourdan is a true patriot, and that is the answer to many things that have been said of him."

Kellermann: "I think that I was probably the boldest general who ever lived, but I wouldn't have dared to take post there [the ridge topped by a windmill at Valmy, 1792]."

Lannes: "In the case of Lannes, his courage in the first place carried him further than his spirit; but each day his spirit rose to the occasion, and restored the balance. He had truly become a superior being by the time he perished; I found him a pygmy, but I lost a giant."

Lefebvre: "A truly brave man . . . whose only thought was to fight better . . . He had no fear of death. . . . He possessed the sacred fire."

Macdonald: "He was a reliable man, good to command between 15,000 and 20,000 men. Brave, but slow and lazy." "Macdonald and others like him were good when they knew where they were and under my orders; further away, it was a different matter." He was ". . . good and brave, but unlucky."

Marmont: "The ungrateful fellow—he will be much unhappier than I" (1814). "Many others were worse than he, who did not have the sense of shame that he felt. . . . Vanity was his undoing . . . an excess of folly."

Massena: "[He] was once a very superior man who, by a very special dispensation, possessed that greatly desired coolness in the heat of an action; he came alive when surrounded by danger. Massena, who was endowed with rare courage and such remarkable tenacity, also had a talent that increased the greater the danger; when defeated, he was always ready to begin again as if he was in fact the victor."

Moncey: "[He] was an honest man."

Mortier: "The three best of my generals were Davout, Soult and Bessières. Mortier was the most feeble."

Murat: "I cannot conceive how so brave a man could be so unreliable. He was only brave when confronted by the enemy, and then he was perhaps the bravest man in the world . . . but if he was placed in council he was a poltroon with no judgment and was quite incapable of making a decision. Murat's character, however, was nobler than Ney's, for he was generous and frank."

Ney: "Ney only got what he deserved. I regret him as a man very precious on the battlefield, but he was too immoral, too stupid to be able to succeed." "He was good for a command of 10,000 men, but beyond that he was out of his depth."

Oudinot: "He was a brave man, but none too bright. He let himself be dominated by his young wife of good family." "I should not have made either Marmont or Oudinot marshals. We needed to win a war."

Pérignon: Napoleon is not known to have ever commented upon this deserving officer. See Georges Ostermann's evaluation.

Poniatowski: "He was a man of noble character, brimming-over with honour and bravery. I intended to make him King of Poland had I succeeded in Russia."

Sérurier: "[He] retained all the characteristics and the severity of an infantry major—an honest man, with integrity and reliability; but unfortunate as a general."

Soult: "I should have made a great example and had Soult shot; he was the greatest pillager of them all." "Both [Soult and Talleyrand] put money before everything else; they wanted a royal suite and money, always money."

Suchet: Asked by Dr. O'Meara to say who was the ablest of his generals, Napoleon replied; "That is difficult to say, but it seems to me it may have been Suchet; once it was Massena, but eventually one had to consider him as virtually dead; Suchet, Clausel and Gérard were the best French generals in my opinion."

Victor: "[He] was better than you might think. At the passage of the Beresina he commanded his corps very well indeed."

So much for the master's views on his key military subordinates (save the shadowy Pérignon). They, of course, also had some very decided views about him. In 1796 Massena recalled how the newly arrived General Bonaparte, "suddenly put on his hat, and seemed to have grown two feet."[27] Augereau commented, "This little bastard of a general actually scared me." Even the hardened and totally intractable republican general Vandamme later admitted, "So it is that I, who fear neither God nor Devil, trembled like a child when I approached him."[28] All respected, most admired, but by no means all liked Napoleon. Massena was for many years not wholly his man, and during the consulate pointedly asked an officer of the Consular Guard when he had joined "the janissaries" and how the "Sultan Bonaparte" was getting on. On another occasion he pointed out to a friend that the stream that watered Malmaison had its source on Massena's property, and that accordingly, "I piss on him when I want to."[29] Augereau could be even blunter. In 1814, as the Empire collapsed, the Duke of Castiglione issued a proclamation at Valence releasing his soldiers from their oath to Napoleon, "a man who, having sacrificed millions of victims to his cruel ambition, has not known how to die like a soldier."[30] Little wonder he found himself struck off the list of marshals on the Emperor's return to France next year. Ney's 1815 comment about bringing Napoleon back to Paris "in an iron cage" is well known, but Bernadotte—when changing sides to the Allies in 1812—referred to Napoleon as "that rogue, that scourge of the world who must be killed."[31] Again, given his pusillanimous behavior the previous year, we are not surprised that Napoleon rejected Murat's proffered services in 1815. Even Lannes, loyal though he basically was to Napoleon and something of a favorite, never accepted all his pretensions; nor did Gouvion St.-Cyr—perhaps the least favored of the marshalate. But Napoleon had their measure. As he once confided in a realistic if disillusioned moment to Minister Molé in 1813, "I have nobody I can put in my place, neither here [in Paris] nor in the Army. Without a doubt I would be very happy if I could make war through my generals. But I have accustomed them too much to knowing only how to obey; amongst them all there is not one who can command the others, for all they know is to obey me alone."[32]

How did the marshalate appear to outsiders? Many admired them—but inevitably others did not. Among the latter we must place the egotistical Stendhal. "Posterity will never know the grossness and beastliness of those people once off the field of battle. . . . No, posterity will never appreciate what dull Jesuits those heroes of Napoleon's bulletins really were."[33] He did, how-ever, express admiration for Moncey, a man "incapable of cer-tain types of ill-conduct." Madame de Rémusat found them maladroit, "too puffed up by their still too recently acquired glory."[34] Wellington could also be scathing, although one must allow for a degree of understandable scorn (probably based upon the previous year's mutiny at Fontainebleau), when, shortly before the French attack toward Brussels from Charleroi in 1815, he was asked by a friend whether he counted upon any desertions from the Army of the North. "Not upon a man," he said, "from the colonel to the private in a regiment—both inclu-sive. We may pick up a marshal or two, perhaps; but not worth a damn."[35] On other occasions the Duke was more flattering. "When Massena was opposed to me, and in the field, I never slept comfortably," he once admitted. The two men met in Paris in 1814. "You turned every hair on my head white," stated the Prince of Essling. "We were pretty even!" gallantly responded the Duke.[36] British posterity has been equally chivalrous. It is not always recalled that the Royal Navy named two monitors*— H.M.S. Marshal Ney and H.M.S. Marshal Soult—both brought into service in 1914 and continuing in commission until 1957 and 1946, respectively. Great Britain thus has proved a generous enemy; although, to French distaste, London has its Waterloo Station. Paris, after all, has the Gare d'Austerlitz and Pont de Iena. Many other comments could be cited, but these few must suffice.

The marshals, like so many others, succumbed to the tre-mendous personal appeal that Napoleon could exert. I conclude with the celebrated passage from Hendrik van Loon (written in 1921) which goes some little way to explaining this phenomenal appeal and personal magnetism:

> Here I am sitting at a comfortable table loaded heavily with books, with one eye on the typewriter and the other on Licorice the cat, who has a great fondness for carbon paper, and I am telling you that the Emperor Napoleon was a most contemptible person. But should I happen to look out of the window, down upon Seventh Avenue, and should the endless procession of trucks and carts come to a sudden halt, and should I hear the sound of the heavy drums and see the little man on his white horse in his old and much-worn green uniform, then I don't know, but I am afraid that I would leave my books and the kitten and my home and every-thing else to follow him wherever he cared to lead. My own grand-father did this and Heaven knows he was not born to be a

---

*A *monitor* is a shallow-draught, heavily-gunned (two 15-inch gun) warship, used for inshore attack.

hero. . . . If you ask me for an explanation, I must answer that I have none. I can only guess at one of the reasons. Napoleon was the greatest of actors and the whole European continent was his stage. At all times and under all circumstances he knew the precise attitude that would impress the spectators most and he understood what words would make the deepest impression. . . . At all times he was master of the situation. . . . Even today he is as much of a force in the life of France as a hundred years ago.[37]

How much he owed to the 26 marshals he created, individually and collectively—for better or for worse—and what they owed to him, the reader must now estimate for him–or her–self in the chapters that follow.

David G. Chandler
Sandhurst and Yateley,
December, 1985

TEXTUAL REFERENCES

1. See Appx C p. 000 for the revolutionary calendar that remained in use until 1805.
2. G. Six, *Les Généraux de la Revolution et de l'Empire* (Paris, 1947), p.236, fn. 1.
3. *Ibid.*, pp.326–29 (Table L).
4. A. Martinien, *Tableaux par corps et par batailles des Officiers tués et blessees pendant des Guerres de l'Empire 1805–1815* (Paris, n.d.), Pt.2, Sec.1, p.11.
5. Six, *op.cit.*, pp.301–2.
6. Cited from A.G. Macdonell, *Napoleon and His Marshals* (London, 1934), by Max Hastings, *The Oxford Book of Military Anecdotes* (Oxford, 1985), p.200.
7. D.G. Chandler, *The Campaigns of Napoleon* (New York, 1966), p.161.
8. G. de l'Ain, *Dix Ans de mes Souvenirs miiltaires de 1805 à 1815* (Paris, 1873), p.109.
9. G. Godlewski, "Les Maréchaux de Napoléon," an article in *Souvenir Napoléonien No. 326* (Paris, November 1982), p.2.
10. *Ibid.*, p.5; namely, the descendants of Bernadotte, Massena, Murat, Pérignon, Lannes, Suchet, Gouvion St.-Cyr, and Grouchy. See also *Souvenir Napoléonien No. 329* (May 1983), p.17, for details of *Mesdames les Maréchales*.
11. Baron C.F. Méneval, *Mémoires* (Paris, 1894), p.266.
12. Gen. G. Gourgaud, *Journal de Ste Hélène* (Paris, n.d.), Vol. 2, p.449.
13. *Ibid.*, p.48.
14. Chandler, *op.cit.*, p.549.
15. See R.M. Epstein, *Prince Eugène at War* (Arlington, 1984), p.10, who challenges my view. However, as an imperial stepson, Eugène Beauharnais was probably a special case; in any case, the gulf between theory and practice was immense.
16. Madame de Rémusat, *Mémoires* (Paris, 1880), Vol.2, p.281.
17. Godlewski, *op.cit.*, p.4.
18. A. de Caulaincourt, *Memoirs* (London, 1950), Vol.3, p.371.
19. Cited by Macdonell, *op.cit.*, p.15.

20. *La Correspondance de Napoléon 1er* (Paris, 1858–70), Vol. 11, No.9470, p.392.
21. Speaking to General Savary, as cited in M. de Bourienne, *Memoirs* (London 1844), Vol.2, p.374.
22. *Correspondance, op.cit.*, Vol. 27, No. 21461, p.301.
23. Cited by Godlewski, *op.cit.*, p. 6.
24. E. Las Cases, *Memoirs of the Emperor Napoleon* (London, 1836), p. 231.
25. A.F.L.V. Marmont, *Mémoires* (Paris, 1857 et. seq.), Vol.5, p.140.
26. Rather than cite 26 or more separate references, please refer passim to the works of Gourgaud and Las Cases, and to Godlewski's articles in *Souvenir Napoléonien*, Nos. 326–329.
27. Chandler, *op.cit.*, p.56.
28. Cited by W.H. Hudson, *The Man Napoleon* (London, 1915), p.213.
29. A. Bigarre, *Mémoires du Général Bigarre: aide-de-camp du Roi Joseph* (Paris, n.d.), p.130.
30. Cited by J. Lucas-Dubreton, *Soldats de Napoléon* (Paris, 1948), p.96.
31. M. Rochechouart, *Souvenirs* (Paris, 1933), p.293.
32. M. Molé, *Mémoires* (Paris, 1922), Vol.1, p.154.
33. Stendhal, *La Vie de Henry Brulard*, ed. by M. Arbelet (Paris n.d.), Vol.1, p.244.
34. Rémusat, *op.cit.*, Vol. 2, p.281.
35. T. Creevey, *Papers* (London, n.d.), p.228.
36. Cited by P. Young, *Napoleon and His Marshals* (London, 1973), p.65.
37. H. van Loon, *The Story of Mankind* (New York, 1921), reprinted at least 30 times. The quotation is taken from the British edition of 1972, pp.352–53.

THE MAJOR CAMPAIGNS OF THE MARSHALS 1792–1815

Campaign	Augereau	Bernadotte	Berthier	Bessières	Brune	Davout	Gouvion St. Cyr	Grouchy	Jourdan	Kellermann (hon)	Lannes
Later active service		═	∕∕∕	∕∕∕	∕∕∕						∕∕∕
The Hundred Days, 1815		═	∕∕∕	∕∕∕	X			X			∕∕∕
France, 1814		═※═	X	∕∕∕		X		⊠			∕∕∕
Germany, 1813	X	═※═	X	⊠		X	X				∕∕∕
Russia, 1812		═	X	⊠		⊠		⊠			∕∕∕
Austria, 1809		X	X	⊠		X		X			⊠
Spain, 1808–1813	X		X	X			X	X	X		X
Portugal, 1808–1811											
East Prussia, 1807		⊠	X	X		X		X			⊠
Poland, 1807	⊠	⊠	X	X		⊠		⊠			X
Prussia, 1806	X	X	X	X		X		X			X
Austria, 1805	X	X	X	⊠		X		X			X
Italy, 1800			X	X	X						X
Egypt, 1798–1799			X	X		X					⊠
Italy, 1796–1797	X	X	⊠	X	X						⊠
Pyrenees, 1792–1795	X			X							X
Campaigns on Eastern frontiers, 1792–1800	⊠	X	X		X	X	X	⊠	⊠	X	
Year of appointment	1804	1804	1804	1804	1804	1804	1812	1815	1804	1804	1804

Marshals (in alphabetical order)

	Year													
Lefebvre	1804	⊠				X	X	X	X	X			X	X
Macdonald	1809	⊠					⊠	X	X	X	⊠	X	X	X
Marmont	1809	X	X	X	X	X	X	⊠	X	X	X			⊠	X
Massena	1804	X	X	X	X	X	X	X	X	X	X				
Moncey (hon.)	1804		X	X				X							'23
Mortier	1804	⊠		X	X	X	⊠	⊠	X	X	X	X	X		
Murat	1804	X	⊠	X	X	X	X	X	X	⊠	X	⊠	X		/////
Ney	1804	⊠			X	X	X	X	X	X	⊠	X	⊠	X	/////
Oudinot	1809	⊠			⊠	X	X	X	⊠	⊠	X	⊠			'23
Pérignon (hon.)	1804	⊠	X												
Poniatowski	1813									X	⊠	⊠			/////////
Sérurier (hon.)	1804	⊠													
Soult	1804	X		⊠	X	X	X	X	X	X	X	X	X	X	X
Suchet	1811	X		X	X	⊠	X	X	X	⊠					
Victor	1807	X	X	X	X	X	X	X	X	X	X	⊠	X	⊠	

Notes: Service on all the Eastern Frontiers during the revolutionary wars, 1792–1800, has been concentrated into a single column. "X" denotes a marshal's active participation in the campaign in question. "⊠" denotes a marshal having been wounded in the campaign in question. No account is taken of the receipt of more than one wound. "'23" indicates the year a marshal saw active service after 1815 under the Bourbons. "X̄" indicates service in a campaign against France. Hatchmarks indicate years following the death of a marshal. Minor campaigns are not shown; thus, Perignon was wounded at Novi in Italy in 1799 and taken prisoner. Other marshals campaigned in Naples, etc.

CHRONOLOGY

1757, October 21	—Born in Faubourg Saint-Marceau, Paris
1774–1791	—Soldier, deserter, adventurer in various nations
1792, September 7	—Adjutant major in the German Legion
1793, September 27	—Adjutant General in *l'Armée*
December 23	—Promoted *général de division*
1794, August 13	—Defeats Spaniards at San-Lorenzo-de-la-Muga
November 17–20	—Leads main attack in breaking the Lines of Figueras
1795, September	—Transferred to *l'Armée d'Italie*
1796, August 3	—Defeats Austrian column at Castiglione
1797, May 1–16	—Commands *l'Armée d'Italie* rear areas during the "Veronese Vespers"
August 8	—Appointed commander of troops in the Paris area
September 4	—Commands troops during the coup d'état of 18 *Fructidor*
September 23	—Appointed commander of the armies on the Rhine frontier
1798, January 29	—Transferred to Perpignan on Spanish frontier
1799, December 28	—Appointed commander of French forces in Holland
1804, May 19	—Named *Maréchal d'Empire* (sixth as published)
1805, November	—Commands VII Corps at Feldkirch; forces Austrian surrender
1806, October 14	—Commands VII Corps on the left wing at Jena
December 24	—Commands successful river crossing at Kolozomb, Poland
1807, February 8	—Commands VII Corps at Eylau; wounded
1808, March 19	—Created *duc de Castiglione*
1809, March 30,	—Appointed commander of VIII Corps in *l'Armée*
June 1	—Appointed commander of *l'Armée de Catalogne*
1810, April 24	—Replaced by Macdonald
1812	—Commands VIII Corps on occupation duties in Prussia
1813, October 9	—Commands XVI Corps at Naumberg; wins battle
1814, January 5	—Appointed commander of *l'Armée du Rhône*
April	—Denounces Napoleon
1815, April 10	—Struck from the list of marshals
1816, June 12	—Dies at La Houssaye

CHAPTER ONE

"THE PROUD BANDIT"

Augereau

by
Colonel John R. Elting

Soldier of Misfortune (1757–1791)

He comes swaggering into known history in 1792, already 34 years old and more than a little scarred by Fortune's teeth.

Pierre François Charles Augereau had been born in Paris, on Rue Mouffetard in the unstylish Faubourg Saint-Marceau. His father is generally described as a domestic servant, sometimes as a fruit dealer or grocer. (Later, Augereau would tell his admiring young aide-de-camp, Lieutenant Marcellin Marbot, that he had been a fruit merchant, successful enough to give his children good educations.) Also, he apparently had once been a soldier. Augereau's mother was from Munich; she habitually spoke German at home and so taught Augereau that language. By some accounts she ran a fruit stall, which—one might guess—developed into a reasonably profitable family business. Certainly Augereau must have received some sound schooling; if his handwriting was "a little pretentious, that of a noncommissioned officer who has applied himself [to mastering] calligraphy,"[1] yet his letters show good style and grammar, as well as considerable common sense. Moreover, he once was moved to comment on Victor's lack of education!

Young Augereau, however, was not meant to be a domestic or a fruit store clerk. A tall, lean youngster, handsome and strong, he was fond of physical exercises, which probably included fencing and possibly a fondness for public brawling. In 1774, when he was 17, he joined the French Army.

His first enlistment apparently was in the Infantry Regiment Clare, in theory an Irish unit, in fact full of Bretons, Belgians, and anyone else its recruiters could catch. Young Augereau,. however, did not find a home in Regiment Clare. According to one story, he was allowed to purchase his discharge in 1775; according to another, he was discharged for having falsely claimed to be Irish. Neither version seems particularly credible, unless we assume that he had proved too much of a handful for Clare's sergeants.

Augereau promptly enlisted in a dragoon regiment, and may have become a noncommissioned officer, but in 1777—possibly after more or less accidentally killing a young officer who had struck him—went over the hill. For the next 13 years or so, he would be one of those thousands of wandering soldiers of misfortune who drifted across Europe, following the wars and the seasons. Originally (so he told it later) he took refuge in Switzerland, where he made the acquaintance of a family of watchmakers who traded extensively in the Middle East. Traveling with, or as one of, their salesmen, he passed through the Balkans into southern Russia, and there enlisted in the Russian army and served under the celebrated General Suvorov against the Turks. (Unfortunately, the actions in which he claimed to have taken part actually occurred some 10 years later.)

Deserting from the Russian army (if he actually ever did serve in it), Augereau moved on into Prussia, enlisting in Prince Henry's well-reputed infantry regiment. Later (he claimed) he served in one of the starkly disciplined units of Frederick the Great's Royal Guard. It is certain that the Prussian Army—still esteemed as the world's finest for drill, discipline, and appearance—definitely established Augereau's concept of military efficiency. Eventually, it also bored him, and he left it without the formality of a discharge. (His excuse would be that he personally overheard Frederick decree that no Frenchmen were to be promoted.) Desertion in Prussia, however, was extremely difficult, the peasantry around each garrison being rewarded if they captured a deserter and fined if he got away; consequently, an average of 98 of every 100 deserters were apprehended. Punishment was drastic. Augereau's solution was to organize and lead a mass breakout by 60-odd fellow foreigners, who fought their way into nearby Saxon territory. He thereafter went to Dresden, where he supported himself as a fencing and dancing master.

In 1781 the celebration of the birth of France's new dauphin, Louis XVI's short-lived first son, included an amnesty for all French deserters. Augereau came back to Paris and enlisted in the cavalry Regiment *Royal Bourgogne* in 1784. The next year he transferred to the *Carabiniers de Monsieur*, an elite cavalry unit that ranked next to the king's household troops, where he further polished his reputation as a duelist. In 1786 the king of the Two Sicilies (Naples), having decided to modernize his ornamental army, asked for the assistance of a French military mission. Augereau may have been one of the sergeant instructors detailed to it, or he may simply have deserted again—but he was in Naples during 1786–1787, scratching out a living as a fencing master.

In Naples he somehow met and fell in love with Gabrielle Grach. Whether or not she was, as Augereau maintained, the daughter of a rich Greek merchant, she obviously was a girl of courage and character. When her father, undoubtedly a sensible man, refused Augereau's request for her hand, she eloped with him. The lovers fled to Lisbon (more vulgar versions say that the Neapolitan government expelled Augereau as a suspicious character). According to Augereau, they lived pleasantly enough in Lisbon until 1790 when the flare-up of the French Revolution put the Portuguese government on guard against all stray Frenchmen. Augereau was thrust into the "dungeons of the Inquisition"[2] where he was held for several months until a

French merchant ship put into Lisbon harbor, and Gabrielle persuaded its captain to intercede for him. Back in Paris Augereau joined the National Guard, later shifting to a battalion of volunteers.

Altogether, it is a strange tale of adventure and mishap, based on little more than Augereau's own word and various yarns told by other men who claimed to have "known him when." Asked to produce records of his prior service on his promotion to general in 1793, Augereau responded that he had none—the Portuguese Inquisition had confiscated all his personal papers. A War Ministry check failed to find any trace of him in the muster rolls of the French regiments in which he claimed to have served. (There is the possibility that, having deserted once, he may have enlisted again under an assumed *nom de guerre*.)

Sifting through the various tales, we can be certain that he had some years of service in the Prussian Army, and quite possibly with others; vague stories have him in the troops of one of the Swiss cantons and the "Royal Carabiniers" of Naples. Part of this service must have been as a cavalryman—in 1797 he would ask General-in-Chief Napoleon Bonaparte of the Army of Italy to put his pet half-brother, Jean Pierre Augereau, into a cavalry unit to "give him the proper bearing and appearance."[3]

Despite the wolf-eat-wolf life he had led, and whatever the whole story of their courtship, there is no doubt that he was devoted to his Gabrielle.

The Big Prussian (1792-1804)

Augereau welcomed the French Revolution. By birth he was genuinely a man of the people; his military service would have given him a bellyful of a society in which aristocratic ancestry counted far more than valor and competence, and a pretentious sprig of a lieutenant could casually strike a veteran sergeant. The Revolution was changing all that—in the old American phrase, "The bottom rail's on top now"—and a determined, shifty soldier could rise as high as his sword, wits, and luck could take him.

In September 1792 Augereau finally becomes historically established as the adjutant of the "light cuirassiers" of the "German Legion"—certainly the most exotic of volunteer organizations hastily raised around Paris during 1792–1793. Except for the cuirassiers (mostly ex-troopers of now-unpopular national police), enlisted men were Germans, Swiss, and everything else. There was a surplus of officers, mostly of dubious repute, given to denouncing one another as traitors and to confusing the

Legion's funds with their own pay. Yet the Legion made a brave display of gaudy uniforms, and its initial service earned it a reputation for "elegance." In April 1793 it was sent to the bloody civil war flaring across the Vendée district of western France.

There, the Legion lasted barely one inglorious month. The cuirassiers served valiantly, but many of the Swiss and Germans promptly deserted to the Vendeans, giving their peasant levies a tough professional core. Those who did not desert looted with notable enthusiasm. Before May was out, Augereau and 30-odd other Legion officers were in prison for alleged royalist sympathies or various misconducts. Among them was Lieutenant François S. Marceau of the cuirassiers, whose brother-in-law, a "Citizen" Serjent, came to visit. Artillery fire was rumbling in the distance; Augereau, Sergent remembered, was banging his head against the wall in frustration over being kept out of the fight. They were released in June, to find that the Legion—after a futile reorganization—had been disbanded. Its surviving cavalrymen went into the new 11th Hussar Regiment, Augereau being promoted to captain. (Marceau would be a general in 1794 at 24, to take his death wound in a rearguard battle three years later, mourned by comrades and enemies together.)

Augereau soon left the 11th Hussars, serving first as army "wagonmaster general" (supply trains required hard-handed supervision), then as aide-de-camp to General Jean Rossignol, a thieving, usually cowardly incompetent, who marched with a headquarters detachment of whores. The assignment made Augereau a lieutenant colonel, but a week or so of it was too much. Somehow, he wangled a transfer to the hard-luck Army of the Eastern Pyrenees, with promotion to *adjutant general, chef de brigade* (colonel on staff duty).

His first assignment was training recruits for a division General Charles Marbot was forming near Toulouse; young Marcellin Marbot, then visiting his father, remembered Augereau's martial appearance, "always immaculate, hair curled and powdered white, long queue, gleaming tall boots,"[4] which made him conspicuous among his carelessly dressed comrades. These, however, refrained from invidious comment, having proper respect for Augereau's red-hot patriotism—and swordsmanship. To his men, Augereau was the "Big Prussian" who drilled and disciplined them as if they were Frederick's foot guards, yet gave them pride in their new skills. General Marbot praised his work; pleased by such appreciation (probably something he seldom had experienced), Augereau thereafter was a conscientious friend to the Marbot family.

In December 1793 Augereau was promoted to general—yet, even here, there remains confusion as to whether he was jumped directly to major general or was simply a brigadier general during 1794. That year he was placed in command of one wing of the army—some 6,000-odd men, including crack light infantry battalions he had trained himself. He quickly proved a first-rate tactician with a good eye for the terrain, deciding quickly and hitting hard. Independent, sometimes almost insubordinate, he tended to slip off to make war on his own, yet was always ready to answer a call for assistance. His men liked him; if strict in training and discipline, he looked after them and set an example of courage and endurance. His great day was May 19 at San-Lorenzo-de-la-Muga when 12,000 Spaniards, advancing in five columns, attempted to trap him. Holding his troops concentrated, choosing his ground expertly, he struck and routed each column in turn. That November he led the main attack that shattered the massively fortified Spanish "Lines of Figuerias."

Spain having sued for peace in 1795, four divisions from Eastern Pyrenees were dispatched to reinforce the Army of Italy. They shed deserters whosesale, yet "took with them . . . the spirit; the confidence given by victory; the somewhat noisy swagger of Augereau, their principal chief, as well as the practice in enduring all sorts of privations without complaint."[5] That last quality was essential in the Army of Italy. Augereau and his subordinates, Victor and Lannes, had a creditable part in the French victory at Loano (November 24, 1795), making a successful secondary attack while Massena led the main drive through the Austrian position, and Sérurier covered the French left. Through the bitter winter that followed, Augereau showed firmness and understanding in keeping his hungry, tattered soldiers together. He did write a cheerful letter asking the government for a new coat; the one he was wearing had been through three campaigns and was all he had.

General Bonaparte took command of the Army of Italy on March 26, 1796. Older and more experienced though he was, Augereau joined the other division commanders in welcoming him. (There seems considerable backing for the story of Augereau telling Massena afterward, "That little bastard of a general actually frightened me!") Augereau's drive and courage were invaluable as the French offensive swept across northern Italy. Bonaparte's first reports praised him: "His attacks are on time and carried out carefully; he spaces his columns expertly, locates his reserves wisely; fights with intrepidity" and "strong character, firmness, energy, has the habit of war, liked by his men and is lucky."[6] General Desaix, on his visit to Bonaparte's army, penned a famous description: "Fine, big man; handsome face, big nose, has served in many countries, a soldier with few equals, always bragging."[7]

The first battle at Castiglione (just south of Lake Garda) was probably Augereau's masterwork. An Austrian counteroffensive under Marshal Würmser had struck southward from the Tyrol, one strong column advancing on either side of the lake. Considerably outnumbered, Bonaparte concentrated against the western column, which threatened his communications; he gave Augereau the mission of delaying the eastern column. Augereau caught its advance guard near Castiglione and defeated it in a hot, scrambling fight. Bonaparte crushed the western column, then countermarched to pick up Augereau and complete Würmser's defeat.

Castiglione begot a myth—that Bonaparte had been rattled by the swift Austrian advance, that other French generals had urged him to retreat, that only Augereau had voted to fight and thereby saved the army. The single source of this legend is Augereau himself.

Though Napoleon never forgot what Augereau "did for us at Castiglione," it was increasingly obvious that he considered Massena the better general. (A somewhat poisonous staff officer, Paul Thiébault, wrote that, alongside Massena, Augereau looked like a drum major, a fencing master, or a recruiting sergeant.) Massena was always dogged and resourceful; Augereau was fatigued and usually despondent after a battle, even a battle won. Increasingly, to Augereau's discontent, Massena got the bigger commands and the crucial missions.

There was more friction over Augereau's looting, which did not spare French sympathizers. Desaix told how Augereau went into a Romagna municipal pawnshop, filled his pockets with diamonds and precious objects, posted a sentry over it—and later had the soldier shot for taking some trifle. He broke up a famous collection of religious medallions, taking gold and silver and leaving copper, on the excuse that he was a "sworn enemy of superstition."[8] Withal, he was reputed an unenlightened looter, more concerned with quantity than quality, who grabbed for the sparkling and gaudy. His baggage wagon soon was famous as a mobile treasury.

Augereau's health also was weakening. Between campaigns in September, he requested sick leave. His piles kept him from riding, rheumatism racked him, his chest hurt. (Malicious individuals suggested his conscience also was aching—Bonaparte had learned that he had sold captured horses for his own profit.) Nevertheless, Augereau fought gallantly through the desperate Battle of Arcola in November, but—left again to cover Bonaparte's flank and rear during the Rivoli campaign—let himself be badly outmaneuvered. After the capitulation of the fortress of Mantua, Bonaparte honored Augereau by sending him to Paris with 60 captured flags. There Augereau swaggered joyfully. His public utterances were moderate, but in private conversations he exalted himself as the Army of Italy's actual guiding genius. Nobody took him seriously; one of the Directors (the five-man executive committee that more or less ruled France) labeled him "a proud bandit."

On his return to Italy, Bonaparte, then moving northward into Austria, ordered him to take over the army's rear area where a pro-Austrian revolt had erupted around Verona. The situation was well in hand when he arrived, but he promptly began a civil war with his new subordinates, over both punishment of captured rebels and the loot squeezed out of the area under the guise of indemnities for French losses. It was an ugly affair; he was accused of selling justice, and got into a grabbing contest with General Charles Kilmaine, a failed cavalryman but a talented thief with excellent political connections.

Meanwhile, France sagged into political crisis. Weary of wars and misgovernment, public opinion turned conservative and even royalist. Fearful of their fate if they lost power, the three most "revolutionary" Directors decided to purge the government by military force, and called on Bonaparte for a general to handle that task. Bonaparte sent Augereau, as possessing the appropriate combination of revolutionary zeal and political ineptitude. Augereau entered Paris trumpeting dire threats against enemies of the Revolution, yet initially flinched at using force. Finally—reportedly well primed with champagne—he blustered through the bloodless "coup of 18 *Fructidor.*" That done, he felt himself a mighty power in the new French government; Antoine Lavalette, an aide-de-camp whom Bonaparte had sent to Paris as an observer, thought Augereau "a man beside himself." As a start, Augereau got the minister of war to authorize him to draw 600,000 francs from the Army of Italy, and sent an aide off to collect. (The aide returned chewed out and empty-handed.)

The victorious politicians, however, had no further use for this military bull in their rickety shop. Deftly, they eased him off to the Rhine frontier to command their new Army of Germany, formed by linking the existing Armies of *Sambre-et-Meuse* and *Rhin-et-Moselle.* Augereau's arrival was a major spectacle. General Macdonald described his as covered with gold lace, even to his boots. A glittering staff, including many revolutionary riff-raff that had adhered to him in Paris, clattered behind him. Gabrielle followed, in a white-satin–lined state carriage picked up in Italy, escorted by Augereau's new guides, flaming in hussar uniforms of yellow, green, and red. There soon would be three squadrons of these, recruited out of the Black Legion and similar roughnecks, and commanded by wild Colonel Fournier-Sarlovese, later the "Demon of the Grand Army."

As army commander, Augereau frightened the French more than the enemy. His new command had endured in poverty in the ravaged Rhineland, and developed a creed of simplicity and discipline. Augereau tried to reassure and accommodate its generals, but—except Lefebvre—few accepted him. (He did denounce Davout and St.-Cyr.) His entourage spread disorder; Augereau seemed less concerned with military operations than seizing and selling church property. Macdonald claimed that Augereau tried to break down the army's discipline, but this may be another of Macdonald's yarns.

Augereau's appointment did convince Bonaparte that it was high time to make peace with Austria: "[Augereau] is incapable of conceiving an extensive plan. He will get beaten, or will not advance at all; all the Austrian forces will then fall on me."[9] The subsequent peace negotiations produced a wry incident. En route to them, Bonaparte passed through Offenbach where Augereau had his headquarters. Halting his carriage outside, Bonaparte sent in word that he was rushed but would like to see Augereau for a minute. Augereau sent back word that he was "engaged at his toilette." Bonaparte drove on; two days later Augereau rethought the situation and wrote a humble-pie letter. Bonaparte apparently ignored it. Augereau boiled up and decreed that no military honors be shown Bonaparte when passing through the Army of Germany's area.

The politicians still were trimming Augereau's plumes. His army was steadily reduced; in February 1798 it was abolished and he was reduced to a territorial command at Perpignan on the Spanish frontier. His guides were scattered through various hussar regiments. As a partial compensation, he was elected to the Council of the Five Hundred (the French legislature's lower house), where he spoke loudly, but not always to the point.

He was in Paris during Bonaparte's *Brumaire* (November 1799) coup d'état. Along with Bernadotte he is described as fluttering about in civilian clothing, unable to decide which side would be the most profitable. The coup accomplished, Augereau made his submission, and was placed in command of the French forces in Holland. During the 1800 campaign, he commanded a small French–Dutch corps, which remained largely inactive until after Bonaparte's victory at Marengo. His opponents were miscellaneous German levies, largely second rate and unenthusiastic. Augereau took Würzburg and won one minor victory, then was almost trapped by Austrian reinforcements. Probably only the Armistice of Steyer (December 25) saved him.

In 1802 the Treaty of Amiens brought a pause in Europe's wars. Augereau purchased a fine estate at Houssaye-en-Brie, improving it to include separate apartments for each of his aides-de-camp. He was a lavish host, but did rule Gabrielle's portion of the chateau "off limits" because of her failing health. When Lannes, his comrade and friend in Spain and Italy, got into financial difficulty while uniforming the Consular Guard infantry, Augereau voluntarily loaned him the 300,000 francs needed to clear his accounts.

England declared war in 1803. Bonaparte sent Augereau south to Bayonne to organize troops for a Franco–Spanish invasion of Portugal, England's ally. Young Marcellin Marbot, who joined him there as his junior aide-de-camp, made the interesting observation that Augereau was training his troops for irregular warfare. Portugal, however, made peace; Augereau was transferred to command of the new VII Corps organizing at Brest for a projected "descent" on Ireland.

Common tradition has it that Augereau opposed Bonaparte's elevation to Napoleon, Emperor of the French, that he tried to slip away from the coronation procession and talked loudly during the ceremony. This may be so, in whole or part, but Marbot, who accompanied him, mentions nothing of the sort; and Augereau readily accepted his appointment as a Marshal of the Empire. Also, he joined the 17 other new-minted marshals and Grand Marshal of the Palace Duroc in contributing 25,000 francs apiece for a ball for their new Emperor and Empress. All Paris wanted to attend; the marshals' aides distributed the invitations, and Marbot humorously noted that he "never had so many friends."

Augereau did most of his commanding from the comfort of Houssaye, while his aides rode back and forth with reports and orders. Napoleon did not object; he still was housebreaking some of his senior officers, and Augereau could hardly create any disturbance at Houssaye. There *was* trouble in VII Corps: Brigadier-General Jean Sarrazin—able, but overambitious and erratic—quarreled with everyone, and then wrote Napoleon that Augereau and his generals were traitors. Napoleon sent his letter to Augereau, who settled the affair to the emperor's satisfaction without leaving Houssaye. (Sarrazin later deserted to the English.)

The Good Marshal (1805–1816)

Augereau's lines had fallen in pleasant places. He was wealthy, comfortably established, happily married, honored among men. Napoleon had made him a Grand Officer of the

Legion of Honor, and would ennoble him in 1808 as Duke of Castiglione. The only shadow was Gabrielle's worsening health.

Good fortune noticeably mellowed Augereau. He loaned Marshal Bernadotte 200,000 francs without interest as casually as Sergeant Augereau might have stood Sergeant "Pretty-Legs" Bernadotte a drink before the Revolution—"When a Marshal is fortunate enough to oblige a comrade, the pleasure of doing him a service is enough."[10] There was no more looting. Marbot, Augereau's aide-de-camp during 1803–1807, wrote with obvious sincerity, "Of the five marshals under whom I served, [Augereau] was without a doubt the one who most alleviated the evils of war, who was the most considerate of civilians and treated his officers the best, living among them like a father in the midst of his children."[11] To him, Augereau was the "good marshal."

During the Ulm-Austerlitz campaign, Augereau's VII Corps had a mop-up mission in the rear of the Grand Army. A German clergyman praised its discipline as "exemplary," noting that Augereau was taking milk baths for his rheumatism. Except for gathering in fragments of a fleeing Austrian column at Feldkirk, there was little excitement. Afterward, Augereau was dispatched to occupy Hesse-Darmstädt and discipline the anti-French free city of Frankfurt-am-Main, carrying through both missions efficiently and humanely.

Gabrielle died while he was away at the wars. His aides shared his grief; she had been kind and thoughtful of them.

The 1806 campaign against Prussia was rougher. Forcing his march northward (83 miles in 50 hours) to support Lannes, Augereau bagged Prussian fugitives, including Infantry Regiment Prince Henry. His old company still had the same captain and first sergeant. Augereau had the captain to dinner (both men acting as if they had met for the first time), loaned him money, and gave him letters of introduction. But he called his former sergeant by name, shook hands with him, and gave him 500 francs for himself and 40 for each of his former comrades still with the company.

At Jena the next morning, VII Corps formed Napoleon's left flank, attacking against Prussia's unenthusiastic Saxon allies. Augereau made rather a hash of it. During the subsequent advance into Poland, however, he showed considerable drive, especially at Kolozomb where he forced a crossing of the Ukra River.

The campaign paused with VII Corps around Plonsk, "an accumulation of filthy huts," but a Russian winter offensive brought it out into the field again. At Eylau (see below p. 13), sick and feverish, Augereau strapped himself to his saddle and went forward with his men. One aide remembered "always the stern face . . . that tall figure, that incisive glance, and that nose [like the beak of] a great bird of prey."[12] Overwhelmed by snow squalls, artillery crossfires, and surges of Russian cavalry, VII Corps was driven in. A grapeshot struck Augereau's arm; losing its footing his horse fell with him, crushing his sword hilt against his left hip.

Napoleon sent him home to recover. He was still unfit for the 1808 Spanish campaign, but did become infatuated with a 19-year-old impoverished aristocrat, Adelaide-Josephine de Chavange. Recalled to service in 1809, he guarded Napoleon's communications with the small VIII Corps. Then he married Adelaide, which required settling pensions on her father and brother. And Adelaide had Gabrielle's tomb moved deep into the woods behind Houssaye. Three months later Napoleon put Augereau in command of the Army of Catalonia. He began well, but soon showed a lack of energy and lost several detachments. Napoleon transferred him to Germany.

During the 1812 Russian campaign, he commanded in northern Germany, working shrewdly to train his polyglot recruits. When Napoleon's campaign began to recoil, Augereau stayed calm, reminding his generals that they had the "essentials"—muskets, bayonets, and cartridges. When cossacks scouted Berlin in late February 1813, he rode out with 300 dubious Westphalian troopers to clear the area. But he was aging—an observer noted his scanty white hair, wry lips, and gloomy stare. As Prussia turned openly restive, something cracked in him; he reported sick, and the Viceroy Eugene ordered him home.

A month later, however, Augereau was organizing a new corps and guarding Napoleon's communications from the Rhine eastward toward Dresden. In early October, Napoleon summoned him to the main army at Leipzig. En route a slightly smaller Austrian force intercepted him near Naumburg; Augereau's rookies squashed it. At Leipzig he was once again the "Augereau of Castiglione." He may have said, as Macdonald later claimed, that he was not fool enough to be killed for a Leipzig suburb, but he held the French right flank against all odds, and brought off his survivors in good order.

This conduct led Napoleon to entrust him in 1814 with an "Army of the Rhone," to be formed around Lyons. Once the enemy had advanced deep enough into France to expose their communications, Augereau was to strike northeastward to cut them. Instead he complained and dithered, failed to exploit subordinates' successes, finally abandoned Lyons, and fled south to Valance. There, learning of the emperor's abdication, he issued a proclamation abusing Napoleon and urging allegiance to Louis XVIII.

Louis confirmed his title as marshal and made him a peer. He was in Caen, denouncing Napoleon, when news of the

Emperor's return reached him. Calling on his soldiers to "revive the colors of the nation," he attempted to switch sides again. Napoleon struck him from the list of marshals, and thereafter ignored him. After Waterloo Louis XVIII dismissed him, cancelling all his emoluments. He died the next year, reportedly of dropsy. He left no children.

Augereau's character naturally made him subject to caricature by later writers. He *was* a bundle of contradictions: brave to heroism, but often a moral coward; an ingrate to Napoleon, yet kind and merciful; greedy, but generous. Failing health undoubtedly weakened his resolution. But there was always something of the ancient Gaul about him—more than a man at the battle's onset, less than a woman at its ending.

The Battle of Eylau (February 8, 1807)

It was January 1807 across the freezing dreariness of East Prussia and Poland. The wearied Grand Army was settling into winter quarters north and west of Warsaw.

General Levin Bennigsen, the Hanovarian mercenary commanding the Russian army, chose then to launch an offensive. Knowing little of Napoleon's dispositions, he blundered into the two northernmost French corps—first Ney, then Bernadotte—and pushed them back, then came to a bloody-nosed halt, wondering what Napoleon was doing.

Napoleon was mounting a counteroffensive northward to cut Bennigsen off from his base at Konigsberg. The countryside being wormy with cossack patrols, the first seven of the eight officer couriers—most of them new lieutenants—Berthier sent to Bernadotte were intercepted. One youngster failed to destroy his dispatches. Thus warned, Bennigsen began pulling back.

Impatient, Napoleon moved out before his troops were fully concentrated. Nevertheless, his drive sent Bennigsen stumbling back until February 7, when—realizing he was in danger of being cut off from Konigsberg if he retreated further—Bennigsen (60,000) decided to halt and fight on high ground east of Eylau. To cover his deployment, he left a strong rear guard on a ridge west of the town. Toward dark the French drove it back into Eylau. Napoleon chose to halt on the captured ridge: He had only Soult's and Augereau's corps, Murat's cavalry, and the Imperial Guard (44,500 in all) in hand. Ney (10,000) was off to his left, seeking to intercept Lestocq's Prussian corps (9,000); Davout (15,000) was to his right rear; Bernadotte far behind. However, soldiers of both armies wanted Eylau for shelter; their im-

13

promptu squabblings swelled into a night battle in which Soult cleared the town.

Outnumbered and heavily outgunned, Napoleon decided to stand on the defensive initially the next morning. He deployed Soult's strong corps, covered on its left by light cavalry, as his front line; Augereau, Murat, and the Guard were massed in reserve behind his right wing. Once Davout arrived, Napoleon would commit him, supported by this reserve, to envelop Bennigsen's left flank. Ney was called in to attack Bennigsen's right, but his orders were delayed.

If Bennigsen had a plan, he never explained it. Most of his army stood massed on a forward slope, a perfect target for French artillery. Over 200 Russian guns replied. Though partially sheltered by buildings and rough ground, Soult's men suffered considerable loss. Around 9 A.M. Soult beat off a Russian attack on his left. Shortly thereafter, Davout's leading division came into action, clearing Serpallen and driving on Klein-Sausgarten. Napoleon ordered Augereau forward through Soult's right–center. Soult's right-flank division, under General St. Hilaire, also advanced, linking Augereau and Davout.

Augereau moved up under heavy artillery fire, deploying his two divisions after clearing Soult's line. Almost at once a dense snowstorm drove into the faces of Augereau's men. Losing direction and formation, they strayed to their left, drifting into a blind crossfire of French and Russian artillery. Bennigsen loosed his cavalry, with strong infantry supports, against this struggling mass. Having the storm at their backs, the Russian horsemen rode through it, except where several hard-bitten regiments formed square to cover the retreat. St. Hilaire also was hustled back, uncovering Davout's left flank. Russian cavalry drove into the gap.

Then the snowstorm passed, and Napoleon could see his battle. Augerau's corps was streaming to the rear; Augereau and both division commanders were among its 5,100 casualties. Soult was battered, Davout stalled. Napoleon calmly ordered Murat to charge. Grouchy's and Klein's dragoons routed the Russian cavalry, Grouchy continuing to break the first line of Russian infantry. D'Hautpoul's cuirassiers smashed completely through Bennigsen's center. Bennigsen committed his reserves; some of the Russian infantry lines re-formed, trapping part of Murat's cavalry. Napoleon launched his Guard cavalry, which chopped their comrades loose. Amid this melée a Russian infantry column blundered up to the edge of Eylau. The Guard destroyed it. Murat's troopers took heavy casualties, but left Bennigsen's center in complete disorder.

Meanwhile, Davout got his entire corps into action, hammering Bennigsen's left flank and left–center back through Ank-lappen and Kutschitten. From ridges west of Klein-Sausgarten his artillery raked the whole Russian front. Part of Augereau's corps rallied on Soult's line; a Russian cavalry charge against the French left failed expensively. Bennigsen's army was crumbling when Lestocq—having sacrificed two flank guards to elude Ney—came panting onto the field. His attack, reinforced by rallied Russians, enveloped Davout's right flank, forcing Davout back to the hills north of Klein-Sausgarten. There, Davout beat off all attacks, then again drove forward until darkness and exhaustion halted him.

About 7 P.M. Ney's leading brigade appeared, chased Lestocq's rear guard out of Althof, and pushed on to Schloditten, where it wrecked a counterattack by Bennigsen's last reserve. Ney, however, pulled back to Althof for the night.

Napoleon readied his army for a renewed battle. (The story that he contemplated retreating is another of Jomini's inventions.) Around 3 A.M. Soult reported the enemy moving off. Bennigsen—his army crumpled and almost out of ammunition—had reported another great victory over Napoleon, and hastily departed.

Napoleon held the field, but it had been costly, with no worthwhile result. He had lost perhaps 20,000 men and five eagles. Bennigsen left some 11,000 dead, 2,300 prisoners, 21 guns, and 16 flags on the field.

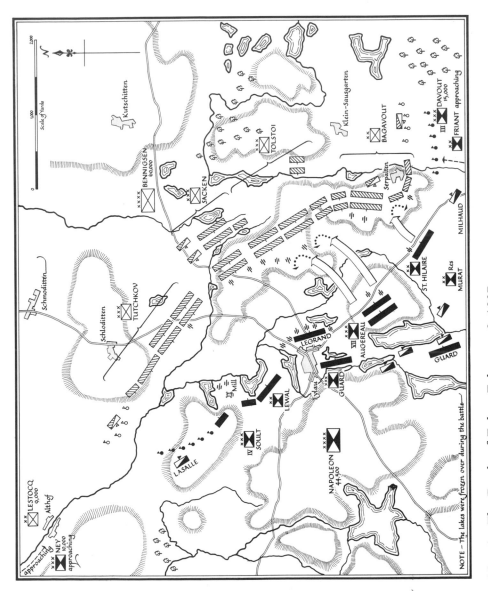

Map 1. The Battle of Eylau, February 8, 1807

TEXTUAL REFERENCES

1. F. Bouvier, *Bonaparte en Italie, 1796* (Paris, 1899), p.74, fn.
2. M. de Marbot, *Mèmoires du général Baron de Marbot* (Paris, 1892), Vol. 1, p. 187.
3. R.W. Phipps, *The Armies of the First French Republic and the Rise of the Marshals of Napoleon I* (Oxford, 1935), Vol. 4. p.156.
4. Marbot, *op.cit.*, p. 19.
5. J.D., *Le General Beyrand (1768–1796)*, in *Carnet de la Sabretache*, 1913), Third Series, Vol. 1, p.562.
6. Phipps, *op.cit.*, p.85.
7. Desaix—Note de Voyage du Général Desaix: Suisse et Italie—1797 in *La Sabretache*, 1898, p.703.
8. Phipps, *op.cit.*, p.206.
9. A.M. de Lavalette, *Memoirs of Count Lavalette* (Philadelphia, 1894), p.145.
10. R.P. Dunn-Pattison, *Napoleon's Marshals* (Boston, 1909), p.259.
11. Marbot, *op.cit.*, p.180.
12. *La Sabretache*, 1895, p. 5. Reprinted part of *Les Souvenirs du Général baron Paulin . . . le 7ᵉ Corps à Eylau*

BIBLIOGRAPHICAL NOTE

Augereau never has had a biographer of any note. Usual descriptions of him—as in A.G. Macdonnell's specious *Napoleon and His Marshals* (New York: Macmillan, 1934) and R.F. Delderfield's unoriginal *March of the Twenty-Six* (Philadelphia: Chilton Books, 1966)—are quick caricatures. This chapter therefore is something of a mosaic, made up of bits of information from many sources. Outstanding among these has been Col. Ramsay W. Phipps, *The Armies of the First French Republic and the Rise of the Marshals of Napoleon I* (Oxford, 1935–39), Vols. 1,3–5, which shows Augereau's service through 1799, the period in which his characteristics as a commander became fully developed. Marcellin de Marbot's *Mémoires du général Baron de Marbot*, 3 vols. (Paris, 1892) is a respectful account of a mature Augereau's good years, while Napoleon's empire still was glorious and strong. More information came from a screening of the 32 volumes of *Correspondance de Napoléon 1er* (Paris, 1858–70); the four volumes of Arthur Chuquet's *Ordres et Apostilles de Napoleon* (Paris, 1911–13); and the five volumes of Gabriel J. Fabry's *Campagne de Russe (1812)* (Paris, n.d.). Also useful were Lefebvre de Behaine's *La Campagne de France: Napoleon et Les Alliés sur le Rhin* (Paris, 1913) and Henry Houssaye's *1814* (Paris, 1899). Finally, numerous useful items were picked out of issues of the *Carnet de la Sabretache* (Paris, 1894–1984).

CHRONOLOGY

1763, January 26	—Born at Pau (Gascony)
1780, September 3	—Enlisted in the Royal Maritime Regiment
1782, May 20	—Joined grenadier company
1790, February 7	—Promoted to regimental sergeant major
1791, November 6	—Commissioned as lieutenant.
1792, November 30	—Appointed regimental adjutant
1794, February 13	—Promoted to major
April 4	—Appointed to command 71st Demi-Brigade, *l'Armée du Nord*
June 26	—Serves at Fleurus; promoted *général de brigade*
October 22	—Promoted *général de division*
1797, January 4	—Joins *l'Armée d'Italie*
1798, February	—Ambassador at Vienna (until April)
August 17	—Marries Désirée Clary
1799, July 3	—Appointed minister of war (until September 14)
1800, April	—Appointed commander in chief, *l'Armée de l'Ouest* (until September 1802)
1804, May	—Appointed governor of Hanover (until August 1805)
May 19	—Appointed *Maréchal d'Empire* (seventh in seniority)
1805, December 2	—Commands I Corps at Austerlitz
1806, June 5	—Created *Prince de Porte-Corvo*
October	—Commands I Corps during the Campaign of Prussia (to November)
1807, January	—Commands I Corps in East Prussia (to June); wounded at Spanden
July	—Appointed governor of the Hanseatic towns (until March 1809)
1809, March	—Commands I Corps in the war against Austria
July 5 and 8	—Commands I Corps at Wagram; resigns command and returns to Paris
August 12	—Appointed commander in chief, *l'Armée d'Antwerp* (until September 24)
1810, August 21	—Elected crown prince of Sweden
1813, June	—Commands allied *l'Armée du Nord* against France (until July 1814)
August 23	—Defeats Oudinot at Gross Beeren
September 6	—Defeats Ney at Dennewitz
October 16–18	—Participates in the Battle of the Nations (Leipsig)
1814, May–June	—Commands Swedish army in occupation of Norway
1818, February 5	—Succeeds to the thrones of Sweden and Norway as King Carl XIV
1844, March 8	—Dies at Stockholm

CHAPTER TWO

"SERJENT BELLE-JAMBE"

Bernadotte

by

T.A. Heathcote

Soldier of the King and General of the Republic (1763–1804)

Jean Baptiste Bernadotte was born, prematurely, on January 26, 1763, in the town of Pau, once the capital of the kingdom of Béarn, in the furthermost southwest corner of France. The earliest recorded inhabitants of this region are the Basques, that strange mountain people from whom is derived the name by which it is better known, Wasconia, or Gascony. The most famous fictional son of Béarn is D'Artagnan, of the King's Musketeers, whom some say was modeled by Dumas upon none other than Bernadotte himself.[1]

Jean Baptiste was the last of five children born to Henri Bernadotte and his wife, Jeanne. Of these, only two others were still living when he was born, his brother, Jean, then aged nine, and Marie who was not yet four. Henri was the son of a prosperous master tailor who had used his wealth to provide a decent education for his two boys, both of whom went into the legal profession and became *procureurs* or official attorneys at the Royal Court of Justice in Pau.

After the death of Henri Bernadotte in March 1780, his student son decided to abandon the pen for the sword. A recruiting sergeant of the Royal Maritime Regiment, a native of Pau, was then on furlough in his hometown, while the regiment's colonel, the Count de Lons, also came from Pau, and knew Bernadotte's father. The sergeant let the young man try on his uniform coat to see how well it looked, and, as is the way of recruiters, declared that he was sending him forth to become a marshal of France.[2]

A keen and intelligent young soldier, Bernadotte soon began to do well. He was promoted to corporal of the grenadiers on July 10, 1785 and to sergeant of the *chasseurs*, or light company, at the end of the following month. Three years later he became company sergeant major. To achieve this rank at the age of 25, within eight years of joining the Colors, and at a time when the French Army was being cut by half as part of a desperate attempt to restore a bankrupt national economy, was a signal achievement. Bernadotte was always noted for his tall and well-turned-out appearance, and gained the nickname of *Sergent Belle-Jambe*.[3]

In May 1789 Bernadotte's regiment went to Marseilles, where civil disturbances had grown alarmingly and where the garrison badly needed reinforcements. For want of sufficient barrack accommodation, the regiment was billeted among the local population. Bernadotte was sent to the house of François Clary, a wealthy silk merchant of Irish descent, but promptly sent away again with a request that the billet be filled by an officer instead of a soldier. Clary's youngest daughter, Désirée, a girl of 12, noticed the incident but thought little enough about it.

In February 1790 Bernadotte became regimental sergeant major, the senior other rank of his unit. He maintained his reputation for efficiency, and soon had the opportunity to display it. The Bastille had fallen the previous July, and all France was in a ferment. New ideas and plans for reform poured out of Paris. Military reform included the abolition of the old regulations that prevented anyone who was not a member of the nobility from becoming an army officer. In November 1791, after 11 years in the ranks, Bernadotte was appointed lieutenant. In the following May he was confirmed in the rank and transferred to the 36th Infantry Regiment.

At the end of May 1793, Bernadotte (now adjutant) took part in his first major engagement at Ruzlheim, near Mainz. A panic occurred in the French advanced guard, and men began to run. Bernadotte's account of what followed is the epitome of his Gascon style:

> I shouted, sometimes cursed, and I begged and commanded but my voice went unheard. Bullets flew all round, and I escaped many by striking the muskets aside with the point of my sword. I rushed to the head of the battalion, where conditions had become critical, and my horse fell, but I did not lose my head. "Soldiers" I shouted "assemble here. There must be no more retreating. You can make a stand here, I know it. Your bayonets and your courage are your defence: those who flee are unworthy of freedom. We will stand fast at our posts, and die, too, if need be with the cry: 'Long live the Republic! Long live the Nation! Form up!' and advance against these paid slaves with the fixed determination to conquer." Speechmaking, convincing, decision and regained obedience to orders were the work of a minute. The soldiers shouted "Let us march against the enemy with our regimental adjutant." In reforming our battalion I succeeded in preventing the confusion infecting six other battalions which were marching in the rear. . . . All the officers congratulated me on my zeal and success, and the soldiers were full of enthusiasm for me.[4]

The following year, 1794, was to prove one of the most dramatic in Bernadotte's career. He began it as a captain. On February 13 he was promoted to field rank as battalion commander. On April 4 he became colonel in command of the 71st Demi-Brigade, a formation whose mercurial spirit was typical of revolutionary armies. Bernadotte repeatedly had to rally his men when their patriotic ardor was suddenly cooled by the realities of the battlefield. In one incident near Landrecies, he tore his epaulettes from his shoulders and threw them down before his retreating men, shouting that if they so dishonored themselves he would refuse to remain their colonel.[5]

Twice he met the sinister St. Just, Representative of the People, sent by Robespierre to visit the army and ensure the ideological reliability of its leaders. Emboldened by the presence of this democrat, a delegation of 12 sergeants appeared before Generals Kléber and Marceau demanding better quarters. Kléber called for Bernadotte, by now a noted queller of indiscipline, and asked him to draw to the attention of these noncommissioned officers the difference between a camp and a club. Bernadotte did so by drawing his sword and belaboring the sergeants with the flat of his blade until they fled back to their unit, to the amusement of their own men and the astonishment of St. Just. He seems, however, to have by this act established his credentials as one zealous in the defense of the Republic.

On June 26, 1794, came the decisive battle of Fleurus. Bernadotte led a brilliant assault against a wood occupied by Austrian infantry and was promoted to brigadier general on the field. On October 22, 1794, he was promoted general of division, at the age of 31, two and a half years after having been commissioned and 14 years after enlisting as a soldier.

After a year in which he had risen from captain to major general, there came a year of consolidation. In November 1794 Bernadotte was appointed military governor of Maastricht, which had been occupied by the French, and gained his first experience of civil administration. Brought up in the traditions of the old regular army, he gave, and enforced, strict orders against looting or unlawful interference with private property. This principle he was to maintain throughout his career, in marked contrast to the revolutionary principle of making war pay for itself. He and his men were to become noted for the correctness of their behavior, and although incidents of indiscipline occurred, as they do in any army, they were never condoned.

During the Campaign of 1795, Bernadotte commanded a division of the Army of the Sambre and Meuse in the Rhine theater of operations. The final battle was on December 12, 1795, at Kreusnach, which was taken by Bernadotte's division after fierce street fighting.

In June 1796 Bernadotte for the second time led his division across the Rhine. Once more the French were driven back. On July 2, they renewed their offensive and for the third time Bernadotte and his men reached the far bank of the Rhine. On August 10, they marched into Nuremburg, and a few days later Bernadotte occupied the ancient university town of Altdorf.

The academics, fearing for the virtue of their maidservants, the modesty of their wives and daughters, the safety of their wine, and the good atmosphere essential for their writing, waited in a body upon Bernadotte with a claim for exemption from billeting. He, who on the march through Hesse and the Rhineland, had maintained good discipline and respected the rights of private property, was in no mood to indulge those who wished to avoid the unavoidable consequences of war. Rounding upon them with his Gascon temper, he threatened to burn their university to the ground if they failed to comply with his orders.[6]

A few days later, leaving the professors to resume their interrupted studies, the Army of the Sambre and Meuse marched on, deeper into Germany. On August 22, 1796, separated from the main force, Bernadotte was at Teining, near the city of Ratisbon. Here was fought a brisk action against superior numbers of Austrians under the Archduke Charles. Outflanked, and with his only means of retreat under threat, he placed himself at the head of his reserves, reminded them of how well he had always looked after their interests, and bade them seize this chance of showing their gratitude, deserving well of their country, and covering themselves with glory.[7] Once more his oratory and leadership saved the day, and the counterattack drove back the Austrians from the vital road. When the whole French army fell back to the Rhine, Bernadotte commanded the rear guard, and went into winter quarters at Coblenz having been hailed as a modern Xenophon.

A Paris newspaper then inflated the incident of the Altdorf professors into a story that Bernadotte had sacked and burned the city of Nuremburg. Bernadotte, the man who prided himself on the correctness of his actions, the man who had fought a duel with his own chief of staff whom he felt had taken a bribe, the man who had astonished the burghers of Nuremburg by refusing the money customarily accepted by Prussian and Austrian generals, asking only that his wounded and sick be cared for, was not prepared to accept such a slur. He called upon the Directors to demand justice. They assured him that his services and character were too well known for the story to be believed. Bernadotte was not satisfied, and failing to obtain further action determined to leave the army. He was only dissuaded by his friend and comrade, the gallant General Kléber.

Reinforcements were needed by General Napoleon Bonaparte's Army of Italy. Bernadotte led his division across the Alps at the beginning of February 1797, maintaining his usual iron discipline, both on this difficult march and after his arrival. This led to friction with the veterans of the Army of Italy, who dubbed the newcomers *Les Messieurs* from their regular army ways, for which they themselves, as true citizens of a democratic republic, had little time. Duels and free fights between the "gentlemen" and the "citizens" became common. One officer of the Army of Italy, Colonel Dupuy, military governor at Milan, declared that he was not obliged to comply with the orders of a general of the Army of the Rhine, at which Bernadotte promptly placed him under arrest for insubordination.[8] Dupuy was a friend of General Berthier, Bonaparte's chief of staff, and the episode led to ill feeling between the two generals, which remained strong throughout their subsequent careers.

At the beginning of March, Bernadotte reported to Bonaparte at the castle of La Favorita on the outskirts of Milan. The two men were prepared to meet on cordial terms, each hoping to gain by supporting the other. Bernadotte and the Rhine troops wanted a chance to prove themselves, and Bonaparte needed a dashing subordinate to carry out his plans. Their interests lay in working together, and they concealed any reservations they may have had about each other.

The offensive began on March 10, 1797. Bernadotte led the vanguard of the right wing, which was under Bonaparte's direct command. On the sixteenth they crossed the swollen Tagliamento River, Bernadotte plunging in on foot to show that it could be forded, and going back to rescue two men who had been swept away. On the nineteenth they crossed the Isonzo, and Bernadotte was ordered to take or blockade Gradisca where the Austrians held a strong and well-fortified position. "I see it all," he cried to his staff. "He is jealous of me and wants to disgrace me. I have no resource left but to blow my brains out. If I blockade Gradisca I shall be blamed for not having stormed it. If I storm it I shall be told I ought to have blockaded it." And so it turned out, for he took Gradisca by a brilliant *coup de main*, and was coldly told by Bonaparte he had behaved recklessly and need not have lost a single man had he waited for support.[9]

On April 17, with the Army of Italy only 80 miles away from Vienna, an armistice was signed and the lightning Campaign of 1797 came to an end. In August Bernadotte was sent by Bonaparte to Paris to lay before the Directors the captured Austrian standards and the dispatches of the campaign. This was both a mark of honor for his services in the field and a way of removing a potentially too popular general from his own command. He was still in Paris at the beginning of September, when the coup d'état of 18 *Fructidor* took place, in which he played no part other than to declare his inflexible loyalty to the Republic.

Early in 1798 Bernadotte was nominated as the new French ambassador at Vienna. The appointment of a Gascon soldier of the Revolution to one of the most protocol-ridden courts in Europe was unlikely to be a success. Bernadotte did not want the job, but went under orders. Arriving at the border ahead of his credentials, he threatened to regard any attempt to turn him back as an act of war. In Vienna he had a mixed reception, some commenting on his Gallic charm, others on his lack of social graces, and most seeing him as the bloodstained representative of a regime that had murdered an Austrian archduchess. He himself, either through conviction or expediency, paraded his republican principles and emblems, culminating in an incident in which the Viennese mob tore down the tricolor that he flew from his embassy and sacked the building while the police looked on. Bernadotte harangued the mob and complained to the Austrian foreign minister, but failing to obtain redress from either, demanded his passports and left the capital on April 15, 1798.

Bonaparte, in Paris, argued that Bernadotte had behaved without proper regard for Austrian sensitivities, but the Directors, remembering that it was Bonaparte who had persuaded them to appoint him in the first place, would have none of this. They encouraged Bonaparte to depart on his Egyptian adventure, patched up relations with Austria, and invited Bernadotte to be ambassador at the Hague, a post that he declined.

While waiting for a more acceptable posting, Bernadotte met and married a pretty girl of 23, Désirée Clary, whose father had refused him the billet in Marseilles. Her family had run into difficulty during the Revolution, but had been befriended by a rising politician, Joseph Bonaparte, to whom Désirée became betrothed. Joseph was then persuaded by his brother, Napoleon, to marry, not Désirée, but her sister, Julie, who, though plainer, was older and already of marriageable age, so that Joseph could obtain her handsome dowry without further delay. Napoleon offered to marry Désirée himself, and the two exchanged passionate letters until he broke off the engagement in order to marry Josephine de Beauharnais. At first completely distraught, Désirée was made much of by the rest of the Bonaparte family, and entered society under the protection of her new brother-in-law. Nor did she lack for more suitors, including Generals Duphot, Junot, and Marmont. Her preference for Bernadotte was clinched when she was told he was a man who could stand up to Napoleon Bonaparte. Her marriage, in August 1798, made the two brothers-in-law.

The following year, when on leave in Paris, Bernadotte was invited by Barras and Siéyès to play a part in the coup of 30 *Prairial.* As on 18 *Fructidor*, he declined to act against established authority, but made no move without orders to defend it, on the grounds that he had received no orders to do so. His reward was to be appointed, in July 1799, Minister of War, with the support of Joseph and Lucien Bonaparte, now leading men in the government.

Bernadotte brought to the Ministry of War the same zeal and energy that he had displayed on the battlefield. On being informed by the finance minister that there was no money to fund the troops and stores he demanded, he drew his sword and threatened to use it, though eventually having to accept that the Republic really was, for the moment, bankrupt. A stream of exhortations and orders of the day, couched in heroic terms, was sent to the commanders in the field, to newly joined conscripts, to the veterans of Italy. Supplies were found and hurried to the theaters of war. Siéyès, a member of the Directory, grew alarmed at Bernadotte's growing popularity and influence. Taking advantage of one of Bernadotte's gasconades in which he declared that he would, as a soldier, rather be in the field than at a desk, he removed him from office in September 1799.

The following month, when Napoleon Bonaparte returned from Egypt, Bernadotte, ever a stickler for the regulations and suspicious of the underlying political motives, tried unsuccessfully to have him arrested on a charge of desertion and evading quarantine. Despite attempts made to keep their differences, quite literally, "in the family," relations between the two continued to be strained. On November 7, the eve of the coup of 19 *Brumaire*, Bernadotte was asked plainly by Bonaparte to support him in overthrowing the Directory. He refused but promised to take no other action without orders from the government. The orders never came, and when the coup succeeded, he had no alternative but to lie low until tempers cooled.

By the end of the year, with Napoleon Bonaparte firmly installed as first consul and head of state, both sides judged it safe to attempt a reconciliation. Bernadotte was appointed a member of the Council of State in January 1800, and then given command of the Army of the West, in anticipation of the British fleet landing an allied army on the shores of France. The threat materialized in the form of a landing by French royalists at Quiberon Bay in June 1800. The affair proved an utter fiasco, and Bernadotte found himself engaged in suppressing an insurrection in Vendée.

His hopes of leading an invasion of England were dashed by the Peace of Amiens (March 1802). This led to the disbandment of the Army of the West and a farewell order to his troops by Bernadotte. This included a number of references to Liberty, which Bonaparte took as a reflection upon his own regime. More seriously, a number of Bernadotte's subordinates became involved in secret meetings and plots against the growing absolut-

ism of the first consul. Although no real proof was ever forthcoming against Bernadotte himself, his name was linked with
them, so that Bonaparte threatened to have "this stupid South-
erner"[10] shot if he did not mend his ways.

Again Bernadotte had to lie low, and after a few weeks
Napoleon relented, gave in to the tears of Désirée and Julie, and
offered him the post of governor general of Louisiana probably
with a view to getting him out of the way. Bernadotte declined to
go but eventually accepted the post of ambassador to the United
States of America. He was still awaiting passage in May 1804
when news came that Louisiana had been sold to the United
States and war had been renewed against England. Abandoning
his embassy which with the sale of Louisiana had lost much of
its importance, Bernadotte returned to Paris without orders,
declaring that his first duty was to place his sword at the disposal
of the state. For a year he remained without a post of any kind.
Then, early in May 1804, Bonaparte had need of him again. The
plan was for the Republic to give place to the Empire. Bernadotte, seeing that the Republic was finished, and with no other
chance of employment, bowed to the inevitable. He promised his
loyalty and cooperation. Ten days later, when the first 18 marshals of the new order were created, Bernadotte's name was
seventh on the list.

Marshal of the Empire (1804–1810)

Bernadotte received, along with his marshal's baton, the
appointment of governor and commander in chief in Hanover.
His arrival there, at the end of June, brought an end to a period
of looting and free quartering. As in Italy and the Rhineland, Bernadotte's men were to behave according to the regulations, and
every effort was made to protect the inhabitants and their property. He did his best to reduce the economic hardships suffered
by an occupied country, and took advantage of his return to
Paris for Napoleon's coronation in December 1804 to obtain a
reduction in the size of the army of occupation it had to support.

In August 1805 Bernadotte's army of occupation became I
Corps of the Grand Army, and in November he held the left flank
as the French drove south eastward to Austerlitz. The Emperor
found fault with the speed of Bernadotte's advance, and accused
him of crossing the Danube a day late. On the morning of the
great battle, as Napoleon gave orders to each of his five marshals, it was noticed that he addressed Bernadotte in a particularly imperious tone. The battle was decided by the final attack
upon the allied center by Soult and Bernadotte's corps together

though Davout subsequently complained that Bernadotte lacked energy in the pursuit.

Peace with Austria brought Bernadotte a new post, governor of Ansbach, ceded to the French by Prussia in January 1806. In June 1806 he was created Prince of Ponte-Corvo, a former papal state that was then made a direct fief of the Empire. After Berthier, he was the first of the marshals to be made a prince, somewhat to the chagrin of Davout, who was himself equally connected by marriage to the imperial house.

On the advance to Jena, Bernadotte was ordered to cross the Saale at Dornburg, and Davout to cross at Kosen, 10 miles distant, to fall upon the Prussian flank. Neither of them reached Jena (October 14, 1806) in time, though Davout met and defeated the retreating Prussians at Auerstädt. Bernadotte himself was rebuked by Berthier, the chief of staff, for having disregarded Napoleon's instructions and taken part in neither action, and he narrowly avoided total ruin. Stung to action, he hurled his men in pursuit of the Prussians. On October 17 he stormed the town of Halle, advancing against superior numbers along a narrow causeway. "Bernadotte hesitates at nothing," said Napoleon. "One day the Gascon will get caught."[11] The chase continued until at last the Prussians were trapped at Lubeck. There, he received the surrender of a Swedish division—and unknowingly (through his courtesy to its officers) began a connection that would prove significant a few years later.

Bernadotte's corps was in action against the Russian offensive in East Prussia during January 1807, but missed the Battle of Eylau, Berthier's couriers having been intercepted by cossacks. Napoleon's comment that had Bernadotte been there the victory would have been less costly and more decisive was countered by a reply that had Berthier not entrusted his letters to subalterns fresh from military college the enemy would not have been better informed than their intended recipient.

Hostilities resumed at the beginning of June. Bernadotte, plunging into the fighting at Spanden, was wounded in the neck by a musket ball. Désirée forsook the life of an imperial princess in Paris and traveled to East Prussia to nurse her wounded hero back to health. In July he was appointed governor of Hamburg, Bremen, and Lubeck—a post he held for 21 months. In the spring of 1809, war again broke out with Austria, and Bernadotte took the field at the head of the IX corps of Napoleon's Saxon allies.

On July 5, 1809, the Grand Army met the Austrians at Wagram. The Saxons were driven back with heavy losses, and Bernadotte complained bitterly that Berthier deliberately diverted his supports. The battle was renewed the following day, and again the Saxons failed to hold their ground. Napoleon arrived to chide the marshal for failing to carry out his orders, and angry words were exchanged. Bernadotte saw only a plot to discredit him, and offered to resign rather than have his men sacrificed for such a reason.

The ill effect of this open quarrel was made worse by a grandiose order of the day in which Bernadotte praised his men for their share in the victorious battle. Their columns, he told them, had stood like bronze, and more to the same effect. Then on July 8 he handed over his command and left for Paris. Napoleon was furious and published an official rebuke, stating that the prince of Ponte Corvo's order had been contrary to truth, policy, and national honor.[12]

Bernadotte was rescued from disgrace by the British landing in Walcheren at the end of July 1809. On Napoleon's orders the marshal was sent to form the Army of Antwerp. He waited for an attack that never came, as the unfortunate redcoats dropped like flies before the onslaught of bad weather, malaria, and dysentery, and the survivors reembarked for home in early December.

Bernadotte himself derived little benefit from this, as Napoleon suspected that he was using the opportunity to renew contacts with those who secretly wished to restore the Republic. A bombastic order of the day in which Bernadotte told the Army of Antwerp that, though only 15,000 strong, it would within 10 days have repulsed any attack that the English might have launched made matters worse. In September 1809 Bernadotte's army was combined with the army in Flanders, to form a new force under Bessières. Napoleon renewed his complaints against Bernadotte. He had been late at Jena, so allowing the Prussians to escape. He had been missing at Eylau. He had failed at Wagram. "I intend no longer to leave the command in the hands of the Prince of Ponte Corvo, who now as before is in league with the Paris intriguers, and who is in every respect a man in whom I can no longer place confidence." There had been 60,000 men on the Scheldt, wrote Napoleon, and even if there had been only 15,000, Bernadotte had no business to disclose his order of battle to the enemy. "This is the first occasion on which a General has been known to betray his position by an excess of vanity."[13]

In 1809 a coup d'état in Sweden had driven King Gustavus IV into exile, and replaced him by his childless and elderly uncle, who was crowned Charles XIII. In June 1810 Charles's adopted heir died suddenly and a new successor had to be found for the Swedish throne. Charles himself wished to nominate a Danish prince. This was opposed by a group of Swedish patriots who feared that their country would fall under the domination of

Denmark, an ancient enemy and rival. Charles appealed for support to Napoleon, an ally of the king of Denmark, and secured a half-promise of agreement. The patriots then took the idea of French involvement one stage further. They proposed that the new heir should be one of Napoleon's own family, or one of his marshals.

Bernadotte fulfilled both conditions. He had a good record as an administrator, and a good reputation among the Swedes with whom he had dealt when in north Germany, where Sweden had territorial and commercial interests. Napoleon—after some initial hesitation—raised no objection, since the idea enabled him simultaneously to be rid of a Gascon intriguer and obtain for a relative an exalted position among the crowned heads of Europe. Moreover, he judged that a French marshal on the throne of Sweden, irrespective of his politics or competence, would mean the final closure of the rich Baltic trade in naval stores above all to his arch-enemy England.

Though Bernadotte was not the Swedish emissaries' first choice at the imperial court, he was the only one who, like his fellow townsman Henry IV, was prepared to change his religion for a throne. On August 21, 1810, the Swedish Parliament, with royal assent, unanimously elected Bernadotte as their crown prince. Napoleon released him from his oath of allegiance and French nationality, though failing to extract from him a promise never to bear arms against France, and the two parted on terms of mutually insincere flattery. They would never meet again.

Crown Prince and King of Sweden (1810–1844)

The new crown prince landed in his adopted country on October 20, 1810, taking the names Charles John. To the ordinary people he let himself be seen as a conquering hero, to the apprehensive king and queen as a grateful son, to the military as a confident leader, and to the nobles as a grave and reserved statesman. He soon became a popular figure in the country, avoiding undue involvement in internal politics and advocating a peaceful foreign policy to restore the national economy.

He soon decided that he would have to disappoint the general hope that he would reconquer Finland, lost to the Tsar by Gustavus IV. There were neither the men nor the finances available to hold the province against an expanding Russia. Instead, he determined to reconcile his new countrymen to its loss by obtaining the kingdom of Norway, which seemed to him, from a geographical standpoint, a more natural arrangement. Napoleon refused to hear of such a thing. Norway belonged to the king of Denmark, whose friendship he needed to secure the Baltic.

The Emperor had other plans for Sweden. She was required to join the Continental System, by which none should trade with Britain, and, under French pressure, actually declared war in November 1810. The British response, that those who did not trade with Britain should not trade at all, at least by sea, would have damaged Swedish interests so seriously that both sides soon agreed to behave as though they were still at peace. Napoleon responded by occupying Swedish Pomerania in January 1811. He added insult to injury by placing it under Marshal Davout, with whom Charles John had long been on bad terms. In Germany in 1808 he had discovered Davout intercepting and reading his letters, and had threatened to horsewhip him.[14]

Crown Princess Désirée, who had needed to look up Sweden in an atlas, joined her husband there in 1811. She stood the climate for a year before plucking up the courage to risk another bout of seasickness and then fled back to Paris, where she remained until 1823. Her 12-year-old son, Oscar, remained with his father. One other close companion remained, Bernadotte's foster brother from his childhood at Pau, whom he created a baron and a general.

As Napoleon grew more hostile, Tsar Alexander became more friendly. In April 1812 Sweden and Russia agreed to guarantee each other's territories. In case of hostilities, both sides would send troops to the German coasts, though Sweden was not bound to do so before Russian troops had helped her conquer Norway. This was followed by the Treaty of Vilna (June 15, 1812), which declared Swedish ports open to the ships of all nations, the first open breach in the Continental System.

A week later Napoleon invaded Russia. As the Grand Army marched steadily eastward, Tsar Alexander looked for allies. In July 1812 he met Charles John at Abo in Finland. They exchanged flattering addresses, and gave each other extravagant promises of support that neither was in a position to fulfill. The Tsar, with the Grand Army halfway to Moscow, offered 35,000 men for the conquest of Norway. Charles John, never to be outdone, said that if St. Petersburg were in danger, he would land in person on the coast of Brittany.

In December 1812 General York declared the neutrality of the contingent that Prussia had been forced to contribute to the Grand Army. In mid-March French and Prussian forces came into open conflict. In the same month Sweden signed a treaty with Great Britain and agreed to send 30,000 men, paid for by the British, to North Germany. In return the British withdrew any objections to Bernadotte's designs on Norway. Charles John wrote to Napoleon that he was acting not against France, but for Sweden, and that the rupture between them was caused by Napoleon's invasion of Swedish Pomerania and seizure of Swedish ships. Bidding a soldier's farewell to his old commander, he added that he would nevertheless always preserve for the Emperor the sentiments of an old comrade in arms.

Scarcely had the Swedish army landed in Germany, in May 1813, when news came that the allies had been defeated at Gross-Gorschen. The Tsar sent a message urging Charles John to forget Norway, as the allies hoped the King of Denmark might join them, and instead to think of becoming king of France. About the same time Désirée wrote to him not to fight against the French, as Napoleon must soon fall, in which case her lord might have a great role to play in the affairs of France.

Charles John reacted angrily to the vagaries of his allies. He spoke of having been betrayed by the Tsar and by the King of Prussia who had not yet sent him a single battalion. Only England had kept her promise, and as long as England remained in the field so would he. He declared that rather than suffer further indignities, he would take his army home, retire from politics, and go to live in Lapland. Denmark's subsequent decision to enter the war on Napoleon's side solved the Norway question for the allies, and in July 1813 Charles John met the Tsar and the King of Prussia at Trachenberg. He told them what he knew of Napoleon's methods in warfare, and expounded on the weaknesses of, and rivalry between, his marshals. He advised the use of delaying tactics to wear down Napoleon in the field and on the home front, and proposed that if any one of the three allied armies (the Army of the North, under himself; the Army of Silesia, under Blücher; and if the Army of Bohemia under Schwartzenberg) were attacked, it should fall back and win time for the others to come up.

The fighting during the autumn of 1813 vindicated this plan, though Charles John's delays in following up his victory at Dennewitz (see p. 35) led to further difficulties with his allies. Allied generals at his headquarters protested at his slow progress, only to be treated to a series of gasconades. The Prussians were reminded of who beat them at Lubeck. The English were asked if this was the way to repay Sweden's loyalty. It took a broad hint from the Russians that there were other pretenders to the Swedish succession to induce him to sacrifice his lines of communications and to follow Blücher across the Elbe at the end of September.

There is no doubt that Charles John felt he had everything to lose, and little to gain, by incurring the risk of another battle. Before he left Pomerania he had declared he would not allow himself to be argued into accepting battle on unequal terms, a condition that by this time, it had become clear, meant on any terms other than those in which victory was certain. Every drop of French blood shed by the Army of the North would make it more difficult for its commander to aspire to the throne of France. A single defeat, he felt, might cost him his reputation as a general and with it his position as crown prince of Sweden itself.

It was not until October 18, 48 hours after Blücher had joined the battle, that Charles John finally arrived on the field of Leipzig, and even then only after Blücher had agreed to placing half the Army of Silesia under his command. Though cautious with his army, Charles John behaved with his customary personal courage, and the Russian attaché reported him as being mounted on a great gray charger and wearing a gold braided pelisse of violet velvet. "He held in his hand a baton draped in violet velvet ornamented with gold. He looked superb, in the middle of the firing, surrounded by dead and wounded, and encouraging by his presence a brigade of English artillery,"[15] the Royal Horse Artillery's rocket troop, which Wellington declined to employ in the Peninsula.

After their victory at Leipzig, while Blucher and Schwartzenberg followed Napoleon to the Rhine, Charles John marched north to deal with Davout and the Danes. He liberated Lubeck on December 5, drove back the Danes, and at the Treaty of Kiel (January 14, 1814) secured their cession of Norway in exchange for Swedish Pomerania. Rather reluctantly, he crossed the Rhine at Cologne on February 10, 1814, and issued a proclamation to the people of France, informing them that the sight of the great river, on whose banks he had so often fought victoriously on their behalf, impelled him to express to them his innermost thoughts: "All enlightened men cherish the wish to see France preserved. Their only object is to prevent her from continuing to be the scourge of the world."[16]

This did him little good. His former comrades resented their achievements being represented as the scourge of the earth. His allies were by no means sure they wished to see France preserved, at least as far as the "natural boundaries" for which Charles John had fought. To everyone he was a former French general who had entered his native land as a foreign prince at the head of an invading army. At the critical time, as so often in his career, Charles John was absent. He was at Liège when the news of Napoleon's fall reached him, and by the time he reached Paris, any chance he had of obtaining the French throne with Russian aid had been lost.

He stayed two weeks in Paris, reunited with Désirée, who was concerned to do something for her sister, Julie, once Queen of Spain, now facing exile. He met Ney, Augereau, Marmont, and Lefebvre, the cordiality of their exchanges being somewhat marred by Lefebvre's lady, *Madame Sans-Gêne*, who loudly said she was not at home to a traitor. After a fortnight he rejoined the Army of the North at Liège and prepared to take his Swedes home.

Charles John started for Lubeck on May 4, 1814, and none too soon, as on May 17 the Norwegians declared their independence. His last campaign was a brief and bloodless affair, which ended with Norway remaining a separate kingdom under the Swedish crown. During the Hundred Days, Charles John made no move, asserting that he had already fulfilled his obligations to his allies. This did not endear him to the Bourbons, who saw in him the last of the crowned Jacobins. A final touch of irony came in 1830 when the Bourbons were again dethroned and Louis-Phillipe came to the throne of France. His representative, the son of Marshal Ney, arrived in Stockholm, only to be ordered to take down the tricolor which he hoisted over the French Embassy, while Sweden, largely out of deference to her powerful Russian neighbors, still recognized the Bourbon lilies.

Désirée remained in France until 1823, acting as Charles John's eyes and ears at the Bourbon court. She caused a great deal of gossip by throwing herself at Richelieu, the French foreign minister, who thought she was simply some kind of spy. Nevertheless, it was only after his death that she joined her husband in Sweden. She assumed the Latin version of her name, Desideria, and spent the rest of her life in Sweden, dying in 1860 at the age of 84.

Charles John succeeded to the thrones of Sweden and Norway by the death of Charles XIII on February 7, 1818, taking the title Charles XIV John. He proved a capable though cautious monarch, and Sweden prospered under his rule. He remained fond of making emotional speeches, though he was never able to master Swedish or Norwegian, and the hard-headed Scandinavians were never as easily swayed as had been his Frenchmen. Opposition in both parliaments of both his kingdoms constantly caused him to inveigh bitterly against the ingratitude of his subjects. Nor were his famous gasconades as successful as they had once been. When he threatened to deal with student unrest by making the gutters run with blood, Desideria told him plainly that everyone knew he couldn't even kill a kitten.

His determination to stand by the established constitution led him to be attacked, in his latter years, as an arch-conservative. During the 1830s he was constantly criticized in the liberal press, and in 1840 the Swedish Parliament called on him to abdicate in favor of his son; but, by judicious concessions to public opinion, he managed to ride out the storm.

During the four years that followed, he rarely appeared in public life, but regained something of his early popularity. His silver jubilee in 1843 was the occasion for general celebration, and his death, on March 8, 1844, in the eightieth year of his age and the twenty-sixth of his reign was greeted with a sense of national loss. His own words, delivered when he heard that Napoleon had been brought home from St. Helena and carried by his veterans under the Arc de Triomphe, provide a fitting conclusion: "You may say of me, that I, who was once a Marshal of France, am now only King of Sweden."[17]

The Battle of Dennewitz (September 6, 1813)

It was not until he fought against Napoleon that Bernadotte first served as an independent commander in chief in the field. He commanded the Army of the North, one of the three allied armies in the 1813 War of Liberation. All told, his troops amounted to some 119,000 men, including 38,000 Prussians (a large number of whom were militia) under von Bülow, 30,000 Swedes, 9,000 Hanoverians and others in English pay, 6,000 Mecklenburgers, some American volunteers, a British rocket troop, and a large force of Russians. In support 30,000 strong was the Count of Tauenzien's 4th Prussian Corps. Against him the French forces in northern Germany, including Saxons, Wurttembergers, and Bavarians, totaled approximately 111,500.[18]

In August 1813 the Army of Berlin, led by Marshal Oudinot, began its advance upon that city. Bernadotte, anxious to avoid a battle, planned to retire to the north, but was persuaded by his Prussian allies to meet the French before they reached Berlin. Oudinot, advancing with his three corps widely dispersed, ran into the Army of the North at Gross Beeren on August 23, and was defeated by von Bülow. The Prussians complained that they had been left to do all the fighting, but were met with assurances by Bernadotte that they were, in his entire army, the men whom he considered most fit to conduct the defense of their capital. Napoleon, furious at Oudinot's mishandling of his army, sent Ney to take command, with orders to renew the march on Berlin.

When he assumed command on September 3, Ney had at his disposal 58,000 men, consisting of IV Corps under Bertrand, VII Corps under Reynier, and XII Corps under Oudinot. Bernadotte's main army lay to his north, and Berlin to the northeast, with the route to Berlin via Dennewitz and Jüterbog held by von Tauenzien. When the French advance began on September 5, Bernadotte ordered von Tauenzien to fall back to Dennewitz and win time for the Army of the North to attack Ney's left flank and rear. Von Bülow, forming Bernadotte's eastern flank, marched through the night to make contact with von Tauenzien and by dawn on September 6 was encamped within two miles of him.

As at Gross-Beeren, the Army of Berlin was not expecting a

major battle, and its three corps were widely separated. The first to reach Dennewitz was Bertrand's IV Corps. At about 11 A.M. he launched an attack against von Tauenzien who had taken up a position with 19 guns and 10,000 men on an area of high ground north of the village. The Prussians were forced back, and saved from defeat only by the arrival of their compatriots under von Bülow. These reached the neighboring village of Neider Gorsdorf at about 12:30 P.M., and forced the French to withdraw their left flank. By 2:30 P.M. the French had been driven back south of Dennewitz. The arrival of Reynier's VII Corps enabled Ney to launch a counteroffensive that succeeded in crossing the Agerbach, a deep but marshy stream that flows southeast from Nieder Gorsdorf through Dennewitz to the next village, Rohrbeck. Von Bülow, with the last of his corps reaching the field, counterattacked in his turn, drove the French back across the Agerbach, and advanced on the village of Gorsdorf a mile to the south. The arrival of Oudinot's XII Corps enabled the French to retake Gorsdorf without difficulty; and von Bülow then stood in danger of being attacked on his right flank, or at best of being driven westward, away from the struggle still raging at Dennewitz.

There Marshal Ney himself had joined the battle, fighting sword in hand with his customary bravery, but allowing his impetuosity to cloud his judgment. The whole battlefield was by this time engulfed in a sandstorm, the light soil of Prussia having been kicked up by the feet of thousands of men and horses and whirled along by a strong wind from the northwest. Oudinot's delay in reaching the field was due in part to this. He had been ready to march at 10 A.M., but stayed where he was as Ney's last orders had been to allow Reynier's corps to pass him first. In fact, Reynier, having taken a completely different road, never did pass him, and it was not until 2 P.M. that, in response to further orders from Ney, Oudinot actually started out for a battle he could not see was in progress. Ney himself could not see what was going on around Gorsdorf, and ordered Oudinot to join his right flank and support Bertrand in an attack at Rohrbeck. Oudinot disregarded the pleas of Reynier that Ney could not know that the decisive point of the battle had been reached around Gorsdorf. Still in a bad temper because Ney had superceded him, he said he was under orders and would do exactly what he was told.

Ney's mistake and Oudinot's wounded pride thus threw away an almost certain victory. Von Bülow committed in the last of his reserves and drove Reynier, now unsupported, out of Gorsdorf. At 5 P.M., before Oudinot could reach Rohrbeck, Bertrand was repulsed by a furious Prussian attack. As Ney's right flank fell back from Rohrbeck, his left began to come under fire from Russian and Swedish artillery.

Bernadotte reached the field of battle at 5:30 P.M., having marched 15 miles in 6½ hours. The fire of the 36 cannons that announced his arrival turned the French retreat into a rout. At 6 P.M. Ney ordered a general retreat, and his men streamed away from the field in various directions, infected by the very kind of panic that Bernadotte, as a young officer, had seen so often. His plan had worked very well. The Prussians had held the Army of Berlin long enough for Bernadotte to take it in the flank, and, as a bonus, they had done most of the fighting before the Swedes arrived.

The Prussians did not quite see things in this light, as the following memoir by an officer of von Bülow's staff makes clear:

> The Crown Prince of Sweden arrived and drew up his troops in battle array. But as he did not come any closer and remained where he was, General Bülow became extremely angry and ordered me to ride immediately to the Crown Prince to inform him that the battle was not yet over and to beg him therefore to advance immediately.
>
> "The battle is won," replied the Crown Prince to me "I have arrived with forty battalions. Tell General Bülow he is to pull back his troops into the second line."
>
> I could hardly believe my ears when I heard this order. We, who had already suffered over 5000 killed and wounded were to give up the fruits of our almost superhuman efforts and surrender the honour of the day to those who had hitherto been mere onlookers.[19]

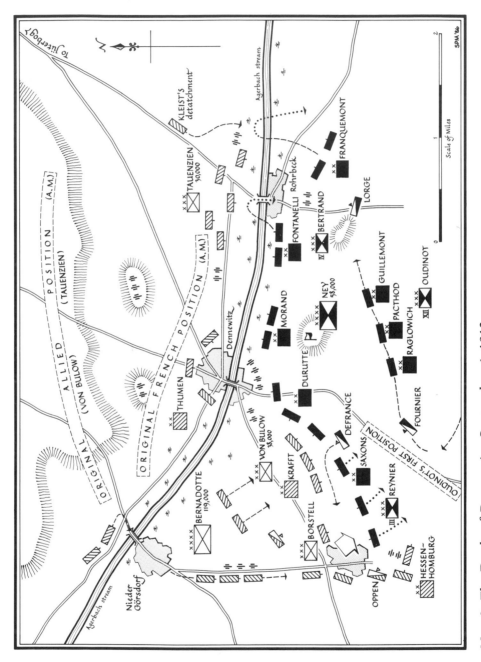

Map 2. The Battle of Dennewitz, September 6, 1813

TEXTUAL REFERENCES

1. P. Barton, *The Amazing Career of Bernadotte 1763–1844* (London, 1929), pp. 2, 5.
2. Wencker-Wildberg, *Bernadotte. A Biography*, trans. by K. Kirkness (London, 1936), p. 17.
3. Barton, op. cit. p. 11.
4. Author's translation of Bernadotte to his brother, May 26, 1793, quoted in slightly differing translations by Wencker-Wildberg, *op. cit.*, pp. 47–84, and Lord Russell, *Bernadotte, Marshal of France and King of Sweden* (London, 1981), p. 16.
5. Wencker-Wildberg, *op. cit.*, p. 48; Barton, *op. cit.*, p. 18.
6. Wencker-Wildberg, *op. cit.*, pp. 56–58; Russell, *op. cit.*, pp. 27–28.
7. Russell, *op. cit.*, p. 30; Barton, *op. cit.*, p. 32.
8. Barton, *op. cit.*, p. 43.
9. *Ibid.*, p. 47.
10. Translated by Wencker-Wildberg as "this damned southern blockhead," *op. cit.*, p. 151.
11. Barton, *op. cit.*, p. 193.
12. Wencker-Wildberg, *op. cit.*, pp. 207–10; Barton, *op. cit.*, pp. 220–23.
13. Napoleon to Clarke (minister of war) September 11 and 12, 1809, cited in Wencker-Wildberg, *op. cit.*, pp. 220–21; Barton, *op. cit.*, p. 226; and Russell, *op. cit.*, p. 127.
14. Barton, *op. cit.*, pp. 144–45, 183, 213.
15. *Ibid.*, p. 301.
16. Bernadotte's Proclamation "to the French People" dated February 12, 1814 cited in full in M. Philippant, *Memoirs and Campaigns of Charles John, Prince of Sweden* (London, n.d.), p. 488.
17. Barton, p. 343.
18. F. L. Petre, *Napoleon's Last Campaign in Germany 1813* (London, 1912), Chs. 3, 26.
19. Memoirs of Ludwig von Reiche, *cited* in A. Brett-James, *Europe Against Napoleon. The Leipzig Campaign 1813 from Eye-Witness Accounts* (London, 1970), p. 35.

BIBLIOGRAPHICAL NOTE

Three volumes by Sir D. P. Barton—*Bernadotte, The First Phase 1763–99* (London, 1914), *Bernadotte and Napoleon 1799–1810* (London, 1921), and *Bernadotte, Prince and King 1810–44* (London, 1925)—form the earliest, and still the most exhaustive, complete biography. With numerous appendixes and letters, this work remains the definitive source. An abridged version of the above, but still with a wealth of detail well supported by references, is Sir D. P. Barton, *The Amazing Career of Bernadotte 1763–1844* (London, 1929). Though obviously an admirer, the author presents an objective portrait aimed at achieving a balance between the extreme adulation or hostility with which Bernadotte has been treated by most previous writers. Catherine Bearne's *A Queen of Napoleon's Court. The Life-Story of Désirée Bernadotte* (London, 1905) is based on various published memoirs of the imperial family and their society. She avoids political and military events to concentrate on social details of the woman, but for whom Napoleon said he would on three occasions have had Bernadotte shot.

Probably the most readable of the Bernadotte biographies is Simon Dewes, *Sergent Belle-Jambe—The Life of Marshal Bernadotte* (London, 1943). This book gives a lively but still detailed account of his life until 1818. The final chapters are overgenerous both to the importance of Bernadotte's part in the War of Liberation and to the extent by which dynastic ambitions influenced his actions in 1814–15. An uncritical contemporary account of Bernadotte's public life is John Phillipart, *The Memoirs and Campaigns of Charles John, Prince Royal of Sweden* (London, 1814). It contains many letters and dispatches that exemplify the Gascon extravagance of Bernadotte's prose style. The only biography in English currently in print is Lord Russell of Liverpool, *Bernadotte, Marshal of France and King of Sweden* (London, 1981). It is a straightforward narrative with some analysis of its subject's career, but lacks many of the anecdotes that enliven other works. Friedrich Wencker-Wildberg's *Bernadotte. A Biography*, trans. by K. Kirkness (London, 1936), is a reliable and competent work in the meticulous German style, faithfully captured by its translator. Not recommended as light reading, but well worth consulting as a cross-reference.

Another German work, useful for the War of Liberation though strongly anti-French in approach, is H. Klober, *Marschall Bernadotte, Kronprinz von Schweden* (Gotha, 1919). Of titles in French, P. de Pressac's *Bernadotte* (Paris, 1932) displays, like so many French works, hostility toward Bernadotte for his part in the War of Liberation; while L. Pignaud's *Bernadotte, Napoléon et les Bourbons* (Paris, 1901) recognizes Bernadotte's personal qualities and is considered scholarly and interesting, though its objectivity when dealing with Bernadotte's conduct toward Napoleon is open to question. The two volumes by B. Sarrans, *Histoire de Bernadotte, Charles XIV Jean* (Paris, 1845), constitutes a reputable work that deals objectively with its subject except when in opposition to Napoleon. Two works strongly pro-Bernadotte are C. Schefer, *Bernadotte Roi, 1810–1818–1844* (Paris, 1899), and G. Touchard-Lafosse, *Histoire de Charles XIV*, 3 vols. (Paris, 1838), a lengthy work based primarily on sources close to Bernadotte.

CHRONOLOGY

1753, November 20	—Born at Versailles
1766, January 1	—Topographical engineer
1770, March 11	—Lieutenant of infantry
1776, August 18	—Lieutenant of dragoons
1777, June 2	—Captain of dragoons
1780, April 26	—Captain, Soissonnais infantry regiment
1787, December 2	—Assistant, General Staff Corps (*aide maréchal-général des logis*)
1788, July 1	—Major
1789, July 11	—Lieutenant colonel
1791, April 1	—Colonel adjutant general
1792, May 22	—*Maréchal de camp* (brigadier general)
September 20	—Suspended
1795, March 2	—Reinstituted as *général de Brigade*, chief of staff, *l'Armée d'Italie*
June 13	—*Général de division*
1797, December 9	—Commander in chief, *l'Armée d'Italie*
1798, March 8	—Chief of staff, *l'Armée de l'Orient*
1799, November 10	—Minister of war
1800, April 2	—Commander in chief, *l'Armée de Réserve*
August 11	—Ambassador extraordinary to Spain
October 8	—Minister of war (until September 1, 1807)
1804, May 19	—Appointed *Maréchal d'Empire* (first in seniority)
July 11	—Senator, Grand Officer of the Palace, Grand Master of the Hunt
1805, August 29	—*Major-général*, chief-of-staff of *La Grande Armée* (until 1814)
1806, March 30	—Sovereign Prince of Neuchâtel and Valangin
1807, August 9	—Vice-constable of the Empire
1809, August 15	—Prince of Wagram
1810, February 27	—Ambassador-extraordinary to Vienna
June 13	—Colonel general of the Swiss
1814, June 1	—Captain, 5th Company of the king's *Gardes du Corps*
June 4	—Peer of France
1815, June 1	—Died at Bamberg, Bavaria

CHAPTER THREE

DUTY AND DISCIPLINE

Berthier

by

Charles Raeuber

The Development of a Staff Officer (1753–1796)

Louis Alexandre Berthier was born on November 20, 1753, the first of four sons,[1] to Jean Baptiste Berthier (lieutenant colonel of Topographical Engineers) and Marie Françoise l'Huillier de la Serre, and it was early decided that he was to follow in his father's steps.

In 1766, at 13 years of age, Alexandre Berthier joined the Topographical Engineers. In 1770 he got his lieutenancy and served with the Legion of Flanders, and in 1777 he was commissioned captain in the Royal Lorraine Dragoons. In 1779 he transferred to the *2nd Chasseurs-à-cheval,* acting as aide-de-camp on the staff of the Army of Normandy. It has often been said that he had served with the Military Engineers. This was not the case, although during the last years of the Old Regime he had been in daily contact with them.[2]

On April 26, 1780, Berthier joined the Soissonnais infantry regiment, so he could participate in the American expedition, serving as a supernumerary assistant on Marshal Rochambeau's staff. Though an interesting experience, he saw, besides an insignificant skirmish near Philipsburg[3] and the Siege of Yorktown, little actual fighting in America. Rochambeau's expeditionary corps left Baltimore in October 1782 and, after some cruising in the Caribbean, returned to Brest in June 1783.

The following years were rather uneventful. Berthier participated in General Custine's mission to study the Prussian army, but mainly he dedicated himself to tactical studies.

Then, in 1789, things began to happen. On July 11 Berthier was promoted to lieutenant colonel and appointed chief of staff to General Besenval, commanding the troops stationed around Paris. However, this troop concentration was to prove only an abortive attempt at intimidating the revolutionary movement in Paris.

Next we find Berthier as commander ad interim of the National Guard at Versailles, playing a secondary role in the escape of the sisters of the late King Louis XV. Now a full colonel, he was to serve as instructor to some 30 volunteer infantry battalions until, on May 22, 1792, he was promoted to brigadier-general and chief of staff to Rochambeau's Army of the North. In the same capacity, he was also to serve Generals Luckner and Kellermann.

Then, on August 21, 1792, the revolution caught up with Berthier. The Assembly ordered his destitution, confirming the decision on September 20 in the milder form of a suspension from all duties. However, he was permitted to serve as a volunteer private, and as such he signed up in the Army of the

West. On May 11, 1793, the People's Representative requested him to act as chief of staff to General Biron. This, to say the least, was a rather dubious arrangement, and Berthier did not like it. Neither did the Committee of Public Safety. When he had to make a short trip to Paris, he was not allowed to return to the army, and so went into what must have appeared to him as permanent retirement.

When, in early 1795 the armies of the Republic were to be reorganized, Lazare Carnot, minister of war, remembered Berthier and, on March 2, reinstated him as brigadier general and chief of staff to the Armies of the Alps and Italy. Carnot was fully aware of Berthier's value. He, like Berthier, was a honest man. However, for him conviction had precedence over duty and discipline, and this difference of character became most evident when both of them came into the orbit of Bonaparte, for whom, of course, expediency came a long way first.

As chief of staff to Kellermann, then to Schérer, Berthier was able to set up his own staff organization. When Bonaparte took over the Army of Italy, he found Berthier already well established. If—and the accent is on "if"—there existed any equivocal situation, Bonaparte very soon made it clear who was giving orders, and who was to execute them. This was how matters would stand as long as they remained together. A short abstract of Berthier's staff organization might here be appropriate. The staff was subdivided into several "divisions," the first division comprising Berthier's personal offices, that is, the services working on matters demanding his immediate decisional attention. The second division provided the material needs: armament, equipment, clothing, food, forage, remounts, etc. Inspection, particularly of food and forage, was the domain of the third division, which was also responsible for intelligence and reconnaissance. The fourth division was in charge of army quarters and police matters, besides keeping the roster of liaison posts and guides.[4]

This organization does not look very logical, but Berthier had fashioned it according to his own needs, and in its empirical way it ran with the precision of a Neuchâtel pendulum clock. In addition, Bonaparte had his own "household staff" or *maison*. Both organizations having overlapping duties, it is not always clear whether Bonaparte's staff was complementing Berthier's, or vice versa.

The "historical bulletins" to be sent to the Directory were elaborated by Bonaparte and Berthier under the strictest exclusion of any third party, very often days after the events, and always with "posterity" in mind.[5]

The Italian Campaign of 1796–1797 offered ample opportunity to show Berthier's efficiency, and at Lodi (May 5) he proved that he knew how to wield not only the pen but also the sword; he gave further proof of personal courage by leading a cavalry charge at Rivoli on January 14, 1797.

After the 1797 campaign, Berthier met Giuseppina Visconti,[6] having shown earlier some interest in Bonaparte's sister, Elisa. At first, Bonaparte favored the liaison with Madame Visconti, mainly in order to get that somewhat overbearing woman off his own back. The 44-year-old Berthier promptly fell in love. He adored and adulated Madame Visconti, and was to remain loyal and faithful to her to the end. So would she, at least when he was present.

The Indispensable Chief of Staff (1797–1815)

When Bonaparte left Italy, Berthier was appointed to the command of the Army of Italy (December 9, 1797). He occupied Rome, proclaiming the Republic, but on February 2, 1798, handed over the command to Massena. On March 8 he was nominated chief of staff of the Army of the Orient (formerly Army of England). The expedition to Egypt was getting under way.

This expedition was certainly a grandiose undertaking. Although a failure in the end, Bonaparte reaped no end of glory and praise. Behind the scene, however, there was Berthier, the ever-hard-working organizer, managing the less glorious task of keeping the army fit for the fight under heavily unfavorable conditions. Add the heat, the Middle-Eastern dirt and stench, and dear Giuseppina so far away, and it becomes understandable that he was not unhappy when Bonaparte decided that he could accompany him on the return voyage to Paris.

Berthier had no active part in the coup d'état of 18 *Brumaire* (November 9, 1799), but immediately after, on November 11, he was appointed minister of war, facing the huge task of reorganizing the Republic's armies. He gave up this post again on April 2 of the next year, when he was assigned to command the new Army of the Reserve. As First Consul, Napoleon was technically debarred from command of the army, but of course commanded it in fact.

The crossing of the Alps in 1800 will be treated below (see p. 52). Berthier again proved to be the perfect organizer and a good fighter. Montebello (June 9, 1800) was his battle as much as Lannes's, and from the battlefield of Marengo he emerged with a wounded arm.

Two months later we find Berthier at Madrid as ambassador-extraordinary. Well instructed by the First Consul and Talleyrand,

Berthier concluded the secret treaty of San Ildefonso to the satisfaction of everybody. On his return he was renominated minister of war, and as such he would serve until September 1, 1807.

Although there was now a short period of peace, there remained enough work for Berthier. The Grand Army that, by and by, would be assembled near Boulogne needed all his attention.

On May 19, 1804, the day after Napoleon had been proclaimed emperor, Berthier was named as the senior of the 18 marshals of the Empire. This was followed by a seemingly endless stream of honors and dignities for everybody. On August 29, 1805, Berthier in addition was made *Major Général*[7] (or chief of staff) of the Grand Army, two charges he would retain until the Emperor's abdication.

The Grand Army was now ready, with a general staff that essentially retained its former structure. The army and its staff grew in size as the circumstances demanded, with the staff adding here and there some new offices and departments, something like building new wings to an old country house, so as to accommodate an ever-growing family.

Berthier's personal cabinet was now the most important part of his staff organization. It was to this cabinet that the Emperor came when he wanted to see the maps covered with varicolored pins indicating the army's and its adversary's positions.[8] The system had been invented by Desaix and was later perfected by Berthier.[9]

It would be anachronistic to compare the Grand Army's staff with a modern organization; but a short look at contemporary Prussia, Austria, and Russia may here be given. In 1806 Prussia had nothing resembling a general staff. It was only after the collapse that Scharnhorst started methodical work. In 1810 the Allgemeine Kriegsschule* was opened, and by 1813 we find that famous and efficient Scharnhorst–Gneisenau–Blücher team, which in its time would develop into the renowned grand general staff.[10] Austria started in 1801 by creating a quartermaster general. After the defeat of 1809, the energetic and efficient Radetzki took over, and during the 1813–1814 campaigns the Austrian army was relatively well served by its staff. However, it should not be forgotten that for many years the "Aulic Council" residing at Vienna had a negative impact on all operations.[11] Russia suffered from a chronic lack of competent officers. There were a few exceptions, like Muraview, but it was not until 1813

*The Prussian War College.

47

that Jomini was allowed to talk about staff duties, and only after 1815 that the building up of a staff organization was started.[12]

The great Campaigns of 1805–1807, filled to the brim with hard work for Berthier, would bring him also new honors. On March 30, 1806, he was made prince of Neuchâtel and Valangin. The first result was that henceforth he would sign with a lapidary "Alexandre," thus demonstrating his "sovereign" status. To a deputation of his new subjects, he appeared a quite understanding and affable ruler, who declared that he regarded them as members of his family and was against introducing any unnecessary changes.[13] Berthier never managed, or cared, to visit his principality, although several attempts were undertaken to get him there. His prime concerns were the supervision of the execution of imperial decrees—so much for "sovereignty"—and matters financial.[14] Over the seven years of his reign, 610,000 livres,[15] or almost half the gross revenue of the principality, was directed to Berthier's personal account—so much for any "family" preoccupation. The Neuchâtel battalion, raised by imperial decree on May 11, 1807, saw service in Spain, Russia, and the 1813–1814 campaigns. During its existence a total of 1,983 men served in its ranks. The last 64 were disbanded on June 1, 1814.[16]

On March 9, 1808, Berthier married Princess Maria Elizabeth of Pfalz-Zweibrücken-Birkenfeld, who, apparently, was of a trusting and conciliatory character, to the point of even finding a kind of modus vivendi with Madame Visconti. Berthier would have preferred to regularize his relation with the latter, but Napoleon almost literally pushed him to the altar. It is not without irony that old Visconti died two weeks after Berthier's wedding, but it may be presumed that Napoleon would have forced through the Bavarian marriage anyway.

The 1809 campaign against Austria, with Berthier serving as the nominal commander in chief, got off on the wrong foot. Berthier, trying to follow the Emperor's somewhat confused directions (of which the Austrians probably had some knowledge), got things so messed up that he did not know what to do next. Then the Emperor made his appearance, and lo, everything was soon proceeding as planned. There is no doubt that Berthier had blundered, but the timing of Napoleon's intervention was so perfect that it may well have been one of his greatest propaganda stunts—an aspect that might be worthy of further examination.

It was after the Battle of Wagram (July 5–6, 1809) that Berthier received yet another title: Prince of Wagram. This added an annual income of 250,000 francs to his already considerable endowments, bringing the total up to over 1.3 million francs per annum.[17]

The next year, 1810, was a year of relative peace. On March 3 Berthier was at Vienna where, for and on behalf of His Majesty the Emperor of the French, he was to formally request the hand of the Archduchess Marie Louise. Another honor came his way when on June 13, 1810, he was nominated colonel-general of the Swiss.[18]

Now came the time of organizing and putting into the field the Grand Army that was to invade Russia. The results of that campaign are well known. As to whether Berthier can be held responsible for the logistical breakdown is an idle question. No doubt, the transport system was inadequate for such a huge undertaking, the more so because it seems that horses were regarded as something expendable, all the way down the line from King Murat to the last wagon driver.

Berthier's moral stamina reached its nadir at Smorgoni, when Napoleon refused to take him onto his sled when he left for Paris. With tears in the eyes, Berthier continued to do his duty, first with Murat and then with Prince Eugène, but his enthusiasm was gone. Even so, Berthier stolidly kept up his working standard during 1813 and the Campaign of 1814, coming out from the Battle of Brienne (January 29) with yet another wound.

In the end, Berthier, like everybody else, had to face the facts. After the Emperor's abdication on April 11, 1814, he adhered to the provisional government. King Louis XVIII, if not actually showering him with favors, at least made Berthier a peer of France and commander of the Order of St. Louis. How he was induced to accept the ridiculous command of the 5th Company of the King's Gardes du Corps is a question that only some of his old comrades could have answered, Marmont, for example.

When Napoleon returned from Elba, Berthier had some difficulty making up his mind. He could not entirely repudiate his former master; on the other hand, he had sworn allegiance to the king. The result was that, in the end, he was acceptable to neither side. When finally he followed the king to Ghent, he found himself confronted with the distrust of the king and his "court camarilla," and then packed off to his in-laws at Bamberg, whence his family had already preceded him. There, on June 1, 1815, from a window on the third floor of the Bamberg castle, Berthier observed the Russian cavalry as it sauntered by on its way to France—and fell. Bouncing off several sills and balustrades on the way down, Berthier was probably dead before he hit the flagstones of the castle square.[19]

Some Considerations on Berthier's Personality

It is said that for the basic formation of a person's character, the first three years of life are the most important. Whatever happens later is then a development or logical extrapolation of the formation acquired during that time. There are, of course, no records preserved that would give a hint as to the first three years of Berthier's existence. However, his later actions and reactions to outward influences will allow some sort of appraisal of his personality, which, anyway, must have been deeply marked by his being an engineer by profession.

Berthier's early life seems to have been uneventful, comfortably sheltered in the fold of a well-to-do family. His father knew how to encourage and develop his mathematical talents, his neatness and orderliness; and, having access to the court of Versailles, he was also able to further his early career to a certain extent.

Coming to America (1780–1783) with such a background, the colonials and their army must have appeared to Berthier as utterly backward and undisciplined rabble. The experience was obviously of no help, either in giving him a wider horizon or in enhancing his power of imagination.

This lack of imagination must also have helped Berthier to survive the revolutionary period by always keeping a low profile. Never in the forefront, never active in matters politic, he just adhered to "duty and discipline." It was then that he must have realized that he was not the man to seize and exploit opportunities. With a truly admirable self-discipline, he was to keep this insight to the end of his days.

This attitude was to serve him well in the years with Napoleon Bonaparte. Berthier never pretended to be anything else but Napoleon's servant. Meanwhile, their relationship had its ups and downs. This went from "Berthier: talents, energy, courage, character. Has everything"[20] to "I have been betrayed by Berthier, just a gosling transmuted by me into some kind of eagle,"[21] with in between a series of sarcastic, ironic, and often downright offensive observations that, however, reflect more on Napoleon's character than on Berthier's.

Berthier never seems to have criticized his superior, but he often pitied himself. On several occasions he was on the verge of throwing in the sponge, clamoring to be left in peace, that he wanted to retire to his estates, and that any private soldier was better off than himself.

Considering the preceding, a slightly masochistic trend in Berthier's character is not to be excluded. Indeed, an appraisal of his infatuation and excessive adoration, love, and loyalty for Madame Visconti seems to bear out this suspicion.

Berthier is described as small and stout, with a disproportionately big head and unsightly hands.[22] However, this disproportional head also contained an disproportionate amount of knowledge and information, and, small as he was, his work capacity was extraordinary. When scolded or humiliated by Napoleon, Berthier took refuge in his work, redoubling his activity—the workaholic *ante littera!*

Although good natured, if somewhat uncouth, Berthier knew how to drive his subordinates. There was no love lost. He demanded, and obtained, that everybody work according to the rules he had set himself. It is said that he never conceded anything with grace, but that what he refused was refused with harshness.[23]

But there is also another side to Berthier: the good-humored man, more often than not laughing off any adversity. He just loved to give sumptuous receptions and fancy dress balls and to organize hunting parties. (Let us forget that famous shot at Massena and the ridiculous rabbit hunt. Both events must be attributed to Bonaparte's desire to imitate royalty.)

Berthier's death in 1815 is a mystery that, it may safely be said, will never be solved. Did he fall? Did he jump? Was he pushed? Assassination is the least probable and, incidentally, never seriously advanced theory. Most historians believe in suicide, but, despite appearances, Berthier was not the suicide-prone type. He was too self-disciplined, too single minded, and too obstinate for that. So there remains death by accident. He had been standing at the window, perched high on a chair, leaning outward to have a better view. It needed but an awkward movement or a slipping chair or both. It could have been as simple as that.

There exists a so-called eyewitness account by Anselm von Feuerbach, which, after all, was not truly such. Feuerbach was 15 minutes late for the fall, but several hours later was permitted to examine the body; and he gives, not without some relish, a description of all the gory details.[24]

Berthier left no memoirs. Short of being able to conduct a full-scale research project, one is entirely dependent on hearsay, often to be taken with more than a grain of salt. But when all is said and done, Berthier remains the outstanding chief of staff of modern and contemporary times, a professional of the very first order, a highly talented executive, and a powerful worker, endowed with an exceptional sense for grasping the essentials in any given situation.

The Crossing of the Alps (April 20–May 27, 1800)

After the coup d'état of 18 *Brumaire* (November 9, 1799), there was no doubt left in Bonaparte's mind that he would have to settle accounts with Austria. A first indication of his intentions was revealed when, on January 24, 1800, he ordered that no further conscripts were to be sent to the armies in the field.

The First Consul, in close collaboration with Berthier, his minister of war, began planning the coming campaign. The organization of units of volunteers, veterans, and invalids for the Army of the Reserve began in late March. This army was to be stationed in and around Dijon. No effort was made at keeping it a secret. On the contrary, particularly the units of invalids were meant to deceive the Austrians, who thought the whole operation to be just a bluff, and continued to do so until a highly efficient French army poured out of the Alps and into the plains of Lombardy.

Since the First Consul as head of state could not take the command of just one of the armies of the Republic, Berthier was appointed commander-in-chief of the Army of the Reserve on April 2, 1800. His chief of staff was to be General Dupont de l'Etang.

On April 20 Berthier arrived at Dijon, his first order being that all divisions were to present muster rolls every day without fail.

On April 27 the troops set out to march to Geneva and along the northern shore of Lake Geneva. This movement mystified not only the Austrians but practically everybody, including the French. The Army of Reserve still had three options open: It could march to the Rhine River above Basel and join Moreau's army; it could go through Switzerland for an attack on Vorarlberg and Tyrol; or it could cross the Alps to Italy, there to disengage Massena under close siege in Genoa since April 20.

The First Consul decided for the third option, and on April 26 sent his detailed orders to Berthier. It is most interesting to see how Berthier transferred these rather lengthy orders to his chief of staff in a most clear and concise manner.[25] On April 28 General Marescot was sent to reconnoiter the pass of Grand-Saint-Bernard. Berthier brought his headquarters forward to Geneva on May 5, and the day after the First Consul left Paris for Geneva.

The Army of the Reserve was now strung out from Ville-neuve, at the upper end of Lake Geneva, back to Dijon, where the last elements were being assembled. Orders were issued to send 400,000 to 500,000 rations by lake barges and land trans-port to Villeneuve, to arrive there on May 9, and the same quan-tity again for the next day. This gives only a small idea of the logistical problems. Add to this ordnance, clothing, shoes, forage, etc., for 40,000 men, and only then do the real dimensions of this undertaking become apparent. Of course, grand strategy was the exclusive domain of the First Consul, but the nitty-gritty was all Berthier's. Berthier, in reality a kind of "grand chief of staff," was indispensable; what is more, he was in his element.

This army of 40,000 men with 44 pieces of artillery was com-posed of the divisions of Loison (7,312), Chambarlhac (8,123), Boudet (6,911), Watrin (5,165), Monnier (4,830), Mainoni's bri-gade (2,800), Lecchi's Italian Legion (1,200), Rivauds' cavalry (1,124), and Murat's cavalry corps (2,372). Chabran's division (6,400) would cross the Alps by way of Little-Saint-Bernard to join the main army at Aosta. The right flank would be covered by Thurreau (10,000) advancing over Mont Cenis, while on the left flank Moncey's division (11,000), released by Moreau, would come across the Saint-Gotthard pass.

Watrin's division and Rivaud's cavalry, later to be joined by Mainoni's brigade, formed the vanguard commanded by Lannes. On May 6 Marescot informed Watrin that the Aosta valley was occupied by the Austrian regiment of Kinsky and some Croats, a total of about 2,000 men. Fort Bard, a very important place, seemed to have a garrison of 150, and was apparently being restored.

On May 9 the First Consul arrived at Geneva. Watrin's divi-sion was now between Villeneuve and St. Maurice, the rest of the army being strung out behind for almost 60 miles along the northern shore of Lake Geneva. Berthier arrived at Lausanne on May 11. Orders were given that all troops passing Villeneuve (the main depot) were to be furnished with five days' rations and cavalry forage for two to three days, and that muskets were to be issued to all officers and noncommissioned officers.

On May 14, the day before the first Austrian resistance was met, the situation was the following: Lannes with the vanguard (Watrin plus Rivaud) had reached the hospice of Grand-Saint-Bernard, rear elements at St. Pierre. Boudet was at St. Maurice, Loison at Aigle, Chambarlhac at Villeneuve, and Murat's cavalry with a detachment of the Consular Guard bringing up the rear between Lausanne and Vevey. The artillery had not yet closed up.

On May 15 Lannes started the descent from the pass. A picket of 50–60 Austrians was brushed out of the village of St. Rhémy. Berthier was now up at St. Pierre, urging the preparation of tree trunks for the transport of gun barrels and hunting up mules and peasants, in short, getting things on the move. This continued also on May 16, while Lannes skirmished down the valley through Etroubles and La Clusa, taking Aosta in the evening, where some looting occurred.

Latest information gave the strength of the Austrians as 2,200 men and 16 guns. Fort Bard was said to have 26 pieces. Berthier ordered Lannes to circulate proclamations announcing the arrival of an army of 100,000 men.

The Army of the Reserve was extremely fortunate as far as the weather went. Cloudless days alternating with clear, cold nights held the snow in place during the mornings when the army marched from earliest light to noon, thus avoiding the afternoon avalanches. Reaching the summit of the pass, the men found the monks and their dogs, the former distributing astonishing quantities of food and wine,[26] the latter without brandy barrels, alas.[27]

By the evening of May 16, Lannes, now joined by Mainoni, was holding Aosta. Boudet was between St. Pierre and the hospice; Loison just behind; Chambarlhac at Martigny; Murat, Lecchi, and the Guard still near Villeneuve. The Austrians had retired to Châtillon, apparently with the intention of making a stand there.

On May 17 Berthier carried his headquarters from St. Pierre forward to Etroubles, making only a short stop at the hospice.[28] Lannes was ordered to clear the Aosta valley as far as Bard, and to attack the fort without delay. The First Consul arrived at Martigny, preparing the ascent to the pass, which he was to cross almost incognito on muleback and in civilian garb.[29] Lannes was now on the way to Châtillon, Boudet was at the pass with Loison, and Chambarlhac was close behind. Monnier, Lecchi, and the Guard had reached Martigny, Murat and his cavalry, St. Maurice.

On May 18 Lannes attacked the Austrian position in front of Châtillon, clearing the place with a bayonet charge, taking 300 prisoners and two guns. Meanwhile, the bulk of the artillery was still stuck at St. Pierre. What with mules disappearing, (Lannes's vanguard did not like to give them up) and slow pay for services rendered, the local people were less and less enthusiastic about giving help. Marmont, in command of the artillery, depended now almost entirely on the French troopers who were not so enthusiastic either. But orders were orders, and, by and by, the guns were dragged over the pass.

On May 19 the vanguard arrived at Fort Bard, and Watrin's division started the siege. Fort Bard is situated on a high rock in the middle of what is more a river gorge than a valley. On the right flows the River Dora Bàltea, from which an inaccessible mountain wall rises straight up. To the left of the fort, in a smaller gorge of its own, lies the small town of Bard. On that side the mountain has easier access, and a track called the Albard trail leads up the mountainside and around the town and fort.[30]

On May 20 Berthier transferred his headquarters to Verrès, to remain there until May 26. Lannes invested the fort and, using the Albard trail, pushed pickets down the valley to Carema. The fort was held by Captain Bernkopf—no fool, that one—with two companies of grenadiers of the von Kinsky regiment. When summoned to surrender by Dupont, Bernkopf answered with a salvo from the fort's batteries and the declaration that he was as fully aware of the means he had to maintain himself as of the importance of the place.

May 21 saw some skirmishing farther down the valley (50 prisoners taken), and on May 22 the French occupied the town of Bard and installed a battery of nine guns directed against the fort. On the same day, Lannes, with Watrin's division in the vanguard, took the town of Ivrea, defended by 6,000 Austrians, who lost 300 prisoners and as many killed and wounded, besides 14 guns. Since no artillery was able to pass by Fort Bard as yet, these 14 guns represented a real boon to Lannes.

In the evening of May 22, Lannes occupied Ivrea with Watrin and Mainoni. Boudet's division had passed Bard, while the fort remained surrounded by Loison's division. Near Verrès Lecchi's Italian Legion was preparing to march up the Sesia Valley so as to protect the immediate left flank of the army. Murat's cavalry was now at Aosta, having overtaken Monnier at St. Rhémy and Chambarlhac at Etroubles. One of Monnier's demi-brigades was still at Martigny, bringing up the rear. Chabran's division, coming down from Little-Saint-Bernard, also had reached Aosta.

Time was now pressing: the fort had to be bypassed at all costs if the surprise effect was to be maintained. During the night of May 23–24, a first attempt was made to pass artillery along the main road through the town. It failed because Bernkopf had "fire pots" thrown from the fort, thus providing enough light for his artillery to take aim. A new attempt was made the following night. In the hope of reducing the traffic noise, the road was covered with manure and the gunwheels were wound with hay and straw. Two four-pounders got through, but two eight-pounders were dismounted by the fire of the ever-alert Austrians. However, from then on some artillery was passed every night, until only the siege guns remained in place.

In the early morning of May 26, a half-hearted attack on the fort was launched, only to be easily repulsed by the Austrians. The siege operations were then taken over by Chabran's division, while the rest of the army passed down the valley to Ivrea. On June 1 Chabran could open fire with two 12-pounders. In the evening Bernkopf asked for terms, surrendering 400 prisoners and 18 guns on the morning of June 2.

Meanwhile, on May 27 Berthier advanced his headquarters to Ivrea, where he was then joined by the First Consul. The army was disposed as follows: Lannes with the vanguard (Watrin, Mainoni, Rivaud) advanced to Chivasso, on the road to Turin. Murat's cavalry and Monnier's division were at Vercelli, on the road to Milan, followed by Boudet's division. Loison had passed Ivrea, with Chambarlhac close behind and Chabran still covering the siege of Fort Bard. Thurreau, coming down in leisurely fashion from Mont-Cenis, had finally reached Susa, while Moncey was still far up in the Leventina valley, having only just passed Saint-Gotthard.

The crossing of the Alps from Martigny to Ivrea was accomplished by Lannes's vanguard in eight days, and in 13 days by the main body of the army, artillery included. The distance covered was almost 100 miles, with an ascent of 7,455 feet up to Grand-Saint-Bernard and a descent of 8,125 feet from there to Ivrea.

The feat had been accomplished. Now thanks to "a little help" from Berthier and his staff, the plains of Lombardy lay at the feet of Bonaparte, the First Consul. Accounts with Austria could therefore at last be settled.

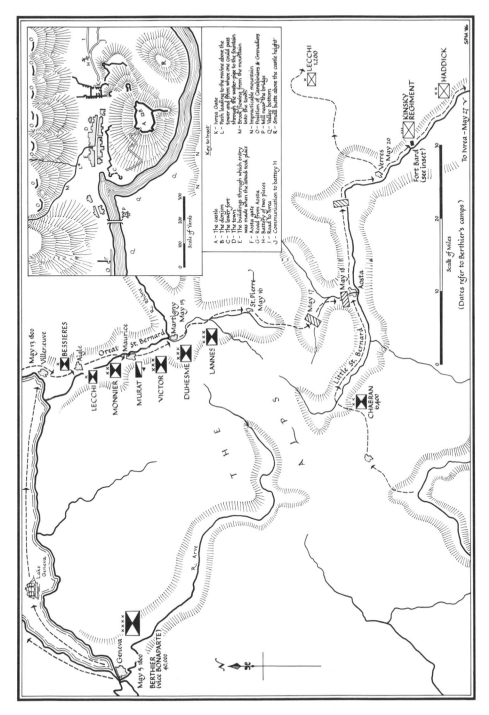

Map 3. The Crossing of the Alps, April 20–May 27, 1800

Key to inset:

K – Ivrea Gate
L – Path leading to the ravine above the tower and from where one could pass through the water-pipe to the fountain
M – Brook flowing from the mountain into the town
N – Impracticable mountain
O – Position of Carabiniers & Grenadiers
P – Mill near the bridge
Q – Valley bottom
R – Small butte above the castle height

A – The castle
B – The donjon
C – The lower fort
D – The town
E – The buildings through which entry was made when the attack took place
F – Aosta gate
G – Road from Aosta
H – Battery of two pieces
J – Communication to battery H

TEXTUAL REFERENCES

1. The other three sons were Charles (1760), César (1765), and Léopold (1770).
2. A. Blanchard, *Les ingénieurs du "Roy" de Louis XIV à Louis XVI* (Montpellier, 1979).
3. Philipse Manor near Yonkers, New York.
4. M. Reinhard, *Avec Bonaparte en Italie d'après les lettres inédits de son Aide de Camp Joseph Sulkowski* (Paris, 1946), pp. 63–66; and H. Giehrl, *Der Feldherr Napoleon als Organisator* (Berlin, 1911), pp. 20–25.
5. Reinhard, *op. cit.,* p. 77.
6. Giuseppina, born Carcano, widowed Sopranzi, remarried Visconti.
7. The term "major general" is to be taken literally, meaning the major—or senior—of generals.
8. Giehrl, *op. cit.,* p. 21.
9. D. Reichel, *Davout et l'art de la guerre* (Neuchâtel, 1975), p. 270. A box containing one of these sets is conserved at the Musée de l'Armée, Paris.
10. G. Rapp, *Les états-majors des principales armées pendant la Ire moitié du XIXe siècle*, in *L'Etat-major général suisse* (Basel, 1983), Vol. 1, p. 53.
11. *Ibid.,* p. 56.
12. *Ibid.,* p. 58.
13. J. Courvoisier, *Le maréchal Berthier et sa principauté de Neuchâtel (1806–1814),* (Neuchâtel, 1959), p. 61.
14. *Ibid.,* p. 167.
15. One livre was equal to 1.41 gold francs or 0.01 ounce of gold.
16. A. Guye, *Le bataillon de Neuchâtel au service de Napoléon 1807–1814* (Neuchâtel, 1964), p. 223.
17. Général Derrécagaix, *Le maréchal Berthier, Prince de Wagram et de Neuchâtel* (Paris, 1905), Vol. 2, pp. 615–16.
18. Nominal commander-in-chief of the Swiss regiments in French service.
19. A. von Feuerbach, *La mort du maréchal Berthier, Prince de Wagram, raconté par un illustre témoin,* in *Revue des Etudes Napoléoniennes* (Paris, 1936), pp. 340–43.
20. *Correspondance de Napoléon Ier* (Paris, 1858), Vol. 1, No. 890.
21. Comte de Las Cases, *Mémorial de St. Hélène,* Ch. 4, see entry for March 27, 1816.
22. Duchesse d'Abrantès, *Mémoires* (Paris, 1831–33), Vol. 2, p. 383.
23. L. A. Bourrienne, *Mémoires* (Paris, 1829–30), Vol. 1, p. 190.
24. Feuerbach, *op. cit.,* p. 342.
25. Capitaine de Cugnac, *Campagne de l'armée de réserve en 1800* (Paris, 1900), Vol. 1, pp. 201–8.
26. According to the archives of Grand-St.-Bernard, a total of 27,703 bottles of wine, 1,758 pounds of meat, and 495 pounds of bread were distributed between May 13 and July 9, 1800. See Cugnac, *op. cit.,* p. 483.
27. The monks and the dogs are still there. For the motor tourist, it might be worthwhile to drive over the pass, open from June 15 to September 25, instead of using the tunnel.
28. Berthier would have liked to buy one of the dogs, but apparently none was readily available. See Cugnac, *op. cit.,* p. 404.
29. L. Lathion, *Bonaparte et ses soldats au Grand-Saint-Bernard* (Neuchâtel, 1978), p. 67.
30. The fort was considerably enlarged during the last century, but is not in use anymore. Anyone wanting to visit the town and the fort should leave the autostrada at Verrès, rejoining it farther down the valley at Pont St. Martin.

BIBLIOGRAPHICAL NOTE

General works on the subject include the following: Jean Cour-voisier, *Le maréchal Berthier et sa principauté de Neuchâtel (1806–1814)* (Neuchâtel, 1959), an exhaustive account of Berthier's relations with his principality; Général Derrécagaix, *Le maréchal Berthier, Prince de Wagram et de Neuchâtel,* 2 vols. (Paris, 1905), the basic, thoroughly researched, but not unbiased biography of the Marshal; Hermann Giehrl, *Der Feldherr Napoleon als Organisator* (Berlin, 1911), which covers in a concise manner the organization of the grand headquarters, Napoleon's command technique, intelligence and signal services, cartography, etc.; and S. J. Watson, *By Command of the Emperor, a Life of Marshal Berthier* (London, 1957), a somewhat apologetic work, depending heavily on Derrécagaix.

A work dealing with Berthier's personality is Louis Chardigny, *Les Maréchaux de Napoléon* (Paris, 1977, reprint), which depicts the marshals under various aspects: origin, education, character, physical appearance, wives, etc.

The crossing of the Alps is usefully dealt with in the following: J. Campana, *Marengo, étude raisonnée des opérations militaires qui ont eu pour théâtre l'Italie & l'Allemagne au printemps 1800* (Paris, 1900), an indifferent text, but containing a valuable set of 19 sketch maps; G. J. M. R. Cugnac, *Campagne de l'armée de réserve en 1800,* 2 vols. (Paris, 1900), on which the foregoing section on the crossing of the Alps was essentially based—a hitherto unsurpassed work, giving a day-to-day account of the Italian campaign in 1800; and Lucien of Lathion, *Bonaparte et ses soldats au Grand-Saint Bernard* (Neuchâtel, 1978), in the main based on Cugnac, doing away with many local legends.

CHRONOLOGY

1768, August 6	—Born at Prayssac (Lot)
1792, April 5	—Enters Constitutional Guard
August 10	—Participates in defense of the Tuileries Palace
November 1	—Enlists in *Légion des Pyrennées* in *l'Armée des Pyrennées*
1794, April 31–May 1	—Distinguishes himself at Battle of Boulou
1795, August	—Transferred with his regiment to *l'Armée d'Italie*
1796, May 30	—Captures gun single handedly at Borghetto
June 5	—Appointed to command Bonaparte's bodyguard—the *Guides*
November 15–17	—Carries out successful diversion in enemy rear at Arcola
1797, January 14–15	—Leads successful cavalry charge at Rivoli
January 27	—Sent back to Paris with dispatches and captured standards
1798, May 19	—Sails for Egypt with Bonaparte
1799, July 25	—Fights at Aboukir; promoted *général de brigade*
August 22	—Returns to France with Bonaparte
November 9–10	—Supports Bonaparte in coup of 18 *Brumaire*
November 11	—Appointed second in command of newly created Consular Guard
1800, June 14	—Fights with distinction at Marengo
1801, October 26	—Marries Adèle Marie Jeanne Lapeyrière
1804, May 19	—Appointed *Maréchal d'Empire* (fourteenth in seniority)
1805, December 2	—Commands Guard cavalry at Austerlitz; repels last Russian counterattack
1807, February 8	—Supports Murat's great cavalry charge at Eylau
June 25–July 9	—Participates in Conference of Tilsit
1808, March 9	—Appointed to command the *corps d'observation* of the Western Pyrenees
July 14	—Defeats Cuesta and Blake at Medina de Río Seco
1809, May 21–22	—Holds French center at Aspern–Essling
May 28	—Created *duc d'Istrie*
July 6	—Slightly wounded at Wagram
1811, January 8	—Appointed to command *l'Armée du Nord* in Spain
May 3–5	—Accompanies Massena at Fuentes de Oñoro
September 20	—Returns to Paris
1812, September 7	—Present at Borodino; persuades Napoleon not to use Imperial Guard
1813, May 1	—Killed by cannon ball on eve of Lutzen

CHAPTER FOUR

THE MISNAMED BAYARD

Bessières

by
Dr. Charles Esdaile

The Making of a Marshal (1768–1801)

Jean Baptiste Bessières was born on August 6, 1768, in the village of Prayssac (Lot) to a prosperous barber surgeon and the daughter of a local notary. His family being comfortably off, at the age of 14 he was dispatched to the Royal College of Cahors to receive a secondary education. He proved an excellent student; more importantly, in a development of great significance for his future, he became friendly with a certain Joachim Murat. Originally, Bessières was to have studied surgery, but in 1787 economic difficulties forced him to return home. His entire region was suffering severe hardship, so it is hardly surprising that Bessières rallied to the French Revolution. He enlisted in the local National Guard and, along with Murat, in 1792 was chosen to represent his department in the new Constitutional Guard.

By 1792 the Revolution was becoming steadily more radical. It was not a development that Bessières, the son of the quintessential local notable, found to his taste. As a devout Catholic, his personal opinions were strongly conservative. It is perhaps significant in this respect that he continued to powder his hair in the old style throughout his life.[1] When the Constitutional Guard was disbanded in June 1792, Bessières remained with the royal family and participated in the defense of the Tuileries on August 10. Afterward he fled south and, on November 1, 1792, enlisted as a trooper in the Legion of the Pyrenees (later 22nd *Chasseurs à Cheval*), a regiment attached to the Army of the Eastern Pyrenees. He served with this unit throughout the war with Spain, distinguishing himself at the Battle of Boulou in 1794, and ended the campaign as a captain.

In August 1795 Bessières's regiment was transferred to the Army of Italy. This proved to be a phenomenal stroke of luck: He soon found himself under the command of Napoleon Bonaparte, among whose aides-de-camp was his old friend, Joachim Murat. Bessières soon won a considerable reputation for courage, so that when Napoleon decided to form a personal bodyguard in June 1796, it was not surprising that he appointed him as commander. At the head of this unit—the *Guides de l'Armée d'Italie*—he won much glory in the subsequent campaign, particularly at the Battle of Arcola where he reputedly led a raid on the Austrian rear that precipitated the collapse of their left wing. This story is denied by Lacroix, who claims that the officer responsible was not Bessières but a young lieutenant named Hercule. Nevertheless, Bessières's feats in the Italian campaign were such that in March 1797 he was rewarded with the prestigious task of escorting the captured enemy standards back to Paris.[2]

Bessières then rejoined Napoleon in Italy and soon became

one of his few real friends.[3] Promoted to colonel, he was included in Napoleon's retinue for the invasion of Egypt and during the campaign helped to quash opposition to his patron's leadership. His devotion was rewarded by a place among the chosen few who slipped back to France with Napoleon in August 1799. By now a brigadier general, he supported the general in the coup of 18 *Brumaire* and in return was appointed second in command of the Consular Guard and tutor to Napoleon's stepson, Eugène de Beauharnais.

In the Campaign of 1800, Bessières took the field at the head of the Guard cavalry, playing an important role in the Battle of Marengo (June 14, 1800), where he first helped to cover the retreat of the French right wing under General Lannes, and then participated in the last-minute counterattack that ultimately won the day for Napoleon. Marengo set the seal on Bessières's success, bringing him promotion to general of division. His influence was reinforced by his association with the Guard, of which his control was now considerably enhanced, thanks to one of the sordid intrigues typical of the future marshalate. The original commander of the Guard was General Lannes. This officer was engaged in a bitter feud with Bessières's friend, Murat: the two were bitterly jealous of each other's glory and by 1800 were also rivals for the hand of Napoleon's sister, Caroline. Bessières not unnaturally attempted to use his influence to advance Murat's case: apart from the ties of friendship, he had the further reason that Lannes had been publicly accusing Bessières of failing to give him adequate support at Marengo.[4]

Bessières not only supported Murat but also set out to ruin Lannes. As Lannes's deputy, Bessières knew that he had overspent the Guard's budget for 1801 by 30,000 francs. So far Lannes had managed to hide the deficit, but Bessières now betrayed him, passing the information to Murat, who immediately told Napoleon. The First Consul was furious and dismissed Lannes, who was packed off to a diplomatic exile in Portugal as ambassador. He escaped imprisonment only because General Augereau lent him the money to pay off his debts. Meanwhile, Murat married Caroline Bonaparte and Bessières was appointed colonel general of the Guard calvary.[5]

Bessières was now a central figure in Napoleon's entourage, and it came as no surprise when he was among the 18 leading generals promoted to the rank of marshal on May 19, 1804. Though he had demonstrated considerable courage on the battlefield, his elevation was not a tribute to his skill as a commander—he had still not led more than 500 men in the field. Far more important was his absolute loyalty to Napoleon. His wife may also have played an important role in his success: in 1801 he had married the young and beautiful Adèle Lapeyrière, whose modesty, simplicity, and charm soon made her a particular favorite with both Napoleon and Josephine, a situation from which her husband was obviously likely to benefit.[6]

Fluctuating Fortunes (1804–1810)

Bessières's first command as marshal was of the Imperial Guard in the Campaigns of 1805 and 1806. However, as Napoleon consistently refused to make use of this force except in moments of extreme crisis, the marshal soon discovered that his opportunities for winning glory were severely circumscribed. At Austerlitz, for example, the Guard was sent forward only toward the end of the battle, though Bessières did play an important part in beating off the efforts of the allies to recapture the vital Pratzen heights; in particular, he led a brilliant cavalry charge that shattered the Russian Imperial Guard and thus sealed the allied defeat. In the Campaign of Jena and Auerstädt, the Guard saw no action at all, being kept firmly in reserve. Bessières did not get another chance to prove himself until the "winter war" of 1806–1807. On December 13, 1806, he was appointed to command the newly formed Second Corps of Reserve Cavalry, which constituted part of the left-hand pincer of an offensive designed to trap the Russian army north of Pultusk. Though Bessières won a minor victory at Biezun on December 21, the Russians made good their escape. The failure was not entirely his fault—the roads were bad, the weather terrible, the supply situation difficult, and his fellow commanders uncooperative— but the Marshal's performance still did not auger well for his future as an independent commander.

Napoleon showed his displeasure by dissolving Bessières's new command and returning him to the Guard. The desperate nature of the subsequent Battle of Eylau (February 8, 1807) gave him a chance to redeem himself, for Napoleon was forced to make use of this force: following Murat's great cavalry charge against the Russian center, Bessières covered his withdrawal by a series of successful charges of his own.

Eylau proved to be only a brief moment of glory, however: At Friedland, the Guard again did nothing. On the whole, Bessières's contribution to the Campaigns of 1806–1807 had hardly been outstanding. As he was already disliked in the army because of his association with the much envied Imperial Guard, Napoleon's decision to include him on the famous raft at Tilsit on June 25, 1807, caused considerable resentment. Marshal Lannes—who was not included in the party—was particularly displeased: he already believed that Murat had cheated him of his rightful share of the glory at Eylau; to see a mere 'courtier' like Bessières preferred over "fighting generals" like himself was to add insult to injury.[7]

Lannes's jealousy was irrelevant, however: Napoleon continued to shower Bessières with favors, increasing his income and sending him to Wurtemberg to arrange the marriage of Jérôme Bonaparte with Princess Catherine. More importantly, the Marshal was again given a field command. The Emperor was becoming increasingly embroiled in Spain and Portugal and his decision to overthrow the Spanish Bourbons required the dispatch of more troops. In March 1808 Bessières was therefore entrusted with the 19,000-strong Corps of Observation of the Western Pyrenees and given the task of protecting the main road between Madrid and the French frontier.

The great Spanish uprising of May 1808 placed Bessières in a very difficult position. His men were dispersed along the main road, the population was violently hostile, and insurrectionary armies were gathering on all sides. However, for once he acted with decision and promptitude. Punitive columns were dispatched in all directions, Santander occupied, the Castillians beaten at Cabezzón and Torquemada, and the Aragonese bottled up in their capital of Zaragoza.

These early successes were crowned by the major victory of Medina de Río Seco on July 14, 1808 (see below, p. 70), but five days later an entire French corps was forced to surrender at Bailén. Panic stricken, the French hastily evacuated Madrid and the whole of Old Castile and withdrew behind the Ebro. Furious at this humiliation, Napoleon now came to Spain himself at the head of a new army in which Bessières was appointed to command the reserve cavalry, in which capacity he participated in the Campaign of November 1808–January 1809. Once again, he saw little action, however. After a brief period as governor of northern Spain, in March 1809 he returned to France to take part in the new war against Austria.

As commander of the reserve cavalry, Bessières was present at Eckmühl (April 20–22, 1809) where he was entrusted with the pursuit of the Austrian left wing, but it was only at Aspern–Essling (May 21–22, 1809) that he was offered a real chance to distinguish himself. Together with IV Corps, his cavalry was sent to establish a bridgehead on the north bank of the Danube. While the infantry of IV Corps garrisoned the villages of Aspern and Essling under the command of Marshals Massena and the long-since-reinstated Lannes, now Duke of Montebello, Bessières occupied the open space between them with 7,000 cavalry.

The three marshals and their 24,000 men now settled down

to await the rest of the army and were taken completely by surprise when the Archduke Charles suddenly attacked them with an army of 111,000 men. Napoleon frantically attempted to rush reinforcements across the Danube, but the bridge kept breaking and the French position quickly became desperate. Bessières's troops were driven back, but, fortunately for him, the main brunt of the attack was borne by Lannes and Massena. Prior to the battle, Napoleon had temporarily placed Bessières under the command of the former. Seeing Bessières's cavalry unengaged, the Duke of Montebello now convinced himself that his old enemy was deliberately leaving him to be slaughtered and therefore sent Bessières an order to charge home against the enemy without delay; contained in the message was a clear implication that Bessières was not doing his duty.

Though he complied with Lannes's orders, throwing back the Austrian center by a brilliant cavalry charge, Bessières was furious. Encountering Lannes that night, he demanded an apology, but his old enemy accused him of being a cowardly incompetent who had secured promotion only by spying on his colleagues. Only the timely intervention of Massena prevented the two Marshals from coming to blows. In the event, the quarrel was settled by fate: on the following day, Lannes was mortally wounded, leaving Bessières to vindicate himself by several more highly successful cavalry charges.[8]

Napoleon rewarded his efforts by making him Duke of Istria. The marshal went on to win fresh laurels at Wagram (July 5–6, 1809), covering Napoleon's transfer of Massena's corps to meet the threat to his left flank by a massive charge against the Austrian center. In the process, his horse was shot from under him and a rumor spread that he had been killed; the news made the Guard weep.[9] Though only slightly wounded, Bessières was still forced to return home to convalesce. Nevertheless, by September 1809 he was well enough to succeed Bernadotte in command of the forces deployed against the British expedition to Walcheren, not that this could be considered an onerous appointment.

It was to prove his last command for some time. In November 1809 Napoleon decided to divorce the Empress Josephine, an action denounced by a Catholic Bessières, who ostentatiously maintained his contacts with Josephine. Napoleon was furious and proceeded to rub the marshal's nose in the affair by appointing him governor of Strasbourg, thus forcing him to welcome Marie-Louise when she crossed the French frontier on her way to Paris.[10]

The Last Campaigns (1811–1813)

Bessières remained out of favor until 1811. The news from Spain was not good: the six different generals governing the northern provinces were proving completely incapable of defeating the Spanish guerrillas. A single commander was the obvious answer and Bessières's past experience made him the natural choice for such a post. On January 8, 1811, he was duly appointed commander of a new Army of the North, consisting of four infantry divisions, two cavalry brigades, and the regular garrisons of San Sebastián and Pamplona.

With these troops Bessières was supposed to keep open communications with the Portuguese frontier and Madrid, contain the regular Spanish army based in Galicia, and defeat the guerrillas. Given the size of his territory, which stretched all the way from the French frontier to Portugal, Bessières soon realized the impossibility of his task. He simply did not have enough men both to hold down this military government and to form field armies to fight the Spaniards. Unless an offensive strategy were adopted, the Spaniards would clearly never be beaten, yet the adoption of an offensive strategy would simply give the French still more territory to defend. It was an impossible dilemma and the marshal had the courage to tell Napoleon so, arguing that Portugal, Extremadura, and Andalucía should all be evacuated and the French armies concentrated in the north.[11]

Napoleon obviously could not accept these proposals and instead poured yet more troops into Spain. This was of little immediate help to Bessières, and he was forced to lessen the burden on his resources by evacuating Asturias. The respite proved short lived: in March 1811 Massena's battered Army of Portugal retreated over the border into his territory; its commander demanded that Bessières supply all its numerous wants on the grounds that, as the main French *masse de manoeuvre* in the Peninsula, the Army of Portugal should have first claim on the available resources.[12] In itself this argument was not unreasonable, but Massena would do nothing for Bessières in return, refusing, for example, to accept responsibility for the defense of the frontier districts that he occupied. Bessières sent forward some supplies and money but Massena remained dissatisfied.[13]

It is probable that Bessières could have done more to supply Massena's material needs, but the latter was also soon demanding extra troops so that he could launch a counterattack against Wellington's army.[14] There was simply no way in which Bessières could meet these demands for, as was graphically shown in July

1811, when he concentrated a small army to beat off a sudden offensive by the Army of Galicia, he could concentrate a field force only at the cost of letting the guerrillas run riot in his rear.[15]

After much prevarication, Bessières appeared with 1,500 cavalry, six guns, and enough horses for 36 more. Massena was furious: not only were the reinforcements inadequate, but his colleague's personal arrival made it only too obvious that he was determined to seize a share in Massena's glory.[16] There was little glory to be had: the French were defeated at Fuentes de Oñoro (May 3–5, 1811), a failure that Massena and many others sought to pin on Bessières.[17] The Duke of Istria was certainly less than cooperative during the battle, but the chief allegation against him—that he frustrated a massive cavalry charge against the British right wing at the climax of the great flank march of May 5—is supremely irrelevant: the largest force of cavalry could not have hoped to defeat formed infantry and the participation of Bessières's cavalry in such an attack would not have made the slightest difference to its outcome. As for the claim that he should have come with more troops, had he done so there would have been no battle to fight, for Wellington would simply have withdrawn into Portugal.

After Fuentes de Oñoro, Bessières returned to his own territory and in July 1811 successfully drove off the Spanish Army of Galicia when it invaded León. However, he was soon recalled to Paris in some disgrace. Already annoyed by the marshal's pessimistic view of the Spanish war, Napoleon chose to make him a scapegoat for Fuentes de Oñoro.[18] The Emperor's displeasure was also made manifest in the arrangements for the Campaign of 1812: instead of being given a corps, Bessières commanded no more than the 6,000 cavalry of the Imperial Guard.

Bessières's influence on the Russian campaign lies chiefly in the realm of strategy. With typical caution, he opposed the march on Moscow and, according to Marbot, was instrumental in persuading Napoleon not to throw in the Imperial Guard at Borodino in a last attempt to win a total victory, the only hope the French had of winning the war.[19] Though the story is not repeated anywhere else, it certainly accords with the caution he displayed later in the campaign: he was strongly in favor of the evacuation of Moscow, and at Maloyaroslavets (October 24–25, 1812) he helped dissuade Napoleon from risking another battle with Kutusov in order to gain the vital Kaluga road on the grounds that a French defeat would mean complete catastrophe.[20]

After the horrors of the retreat from Moscow, Bessières, still convinced that France's interests were synonymous with those of the Emperor, was plunged into the deepest gloom. His pessimism was increased by a strong premonition of death, a premonition that was fulfilled on May 1, 1813: riding forward to reconnoiter allied positions near Lutzen, to Napoleon's deepest sorrow, he was struck by a cannon ball and killed instantly.[21]

Bessières is in many ways one of the more attractive figures among the marshalate. Contemporary accounts are united in praise of his nobility, generosity, kindness, piety, and courage. Unlike many of his fellows, he was no brutal, avaricious *condottière*, but a man of culture who shunned all forms of venality.[22] Handsome and affable, he was also described as "the most amiable and polite of men."[23] Perhaps his greatest quality was his honesty. Though certainly devoted to Napoleon, he was no court sycophant. If his candor frequently brought Napoleon's wrath upon his head, the Emperor seems to have respected his honesty and always numbered him among his closest friends.[24]

Bessières's many good qualities led to him being known as "the Bayard of the Grand Army," an image that has been exploited to the full by his later hagiographers.[25] Yet, in reality, he was very far from being a saint. His conduct with regard to Lannes in 1801 and Massena in 1811 is definitely open to challenge. In Spain, too, he showed that he could be just as brutal toward the civilian population as any of his fellows.[26] His wife also suffered cruelly at his hands. Unbeknown to her, Bessières had a mistress named Virginie, a young opera singer in Paris. When the grief-stricken *Madame la Maréchale Bessières* received his effects after his death, her distress was greatly augmented by the discovery of his adultery.[27]

Bessières is far easier to assess as a general. His skill as an administrator is shown by the high quality of the Guard Cavalry, of which he was colonel general, and there is no doubting his excellence as a battlefield subordinate. Yet presented with even the slightest room for personal initiative, he began to waver and hesitate: Lannes's allegations concerning his "fiddling about" at Marengo and Aspern were certainly not without a grain of truth. Even at Medina de Río Seco he is reported initially to have doubted the wisdom of attacking the Spaniards.

As a strategist, his faults came even more to the fore. He could react sensibly in the face of a crisis—as in Spain in June 1808—but on the offensive he often seemed to be at a loss as to what to do, as witness the maneuver on the Narew in December 1806 and the aftermath of Río Seco. These hesitations were born of an excessive caution that was to have disastrous consequences in 1812. But for the chariness he exhibited at Borodino and Maloyaroslavets, the horrors of the retreat from Moscow might have been avoided.

Thus, in spite of his undeniable talents and good qualities, Bessières was no paragon of military virtue. As fallible as most of his fellows, his reputation as a latter-day Bayard is therefore sadly undeserved.

The Battle of Medina de Río Seco (July 14, 1808)

Bessières's victories against the Spanish insurgents in June 1808, (see p. 65) had not improved his strategic situation. In addition to his original commitments, he now had to hold down the provinces of Valladolid and Santander and find troops for the siege of Zaragoza. His forces also had to face the threat represented by the Spanish Army of Castile under General Gregorio Garcia de la Cuesta, which was reforming behind the River Esla. There were also rumors that General Joaquin Blake's Army of Galicia, together with a (fictitious) British expeditionary force, were moving to its support with the aim of launching an offensive in Old Castile.

The marshal's only advantage was that he was well-informed: one of his aides-de-camp had been captured by insurgents but had managed to escape by pretending to be a British officer; en route to safety he had gleaned much useful information which Bessières was able to put to good use.[28] Hastily recalling the garrison of Santander, the marshal concentrated all the troops he could muster at Palencia. He still had only 10,700 men but Napoleon, realising the danger, sent him an extra division under General Mouton (though by the time this force reached Bessières, it had been so depleted by detachments dropped off en route that it only numbered 3,000 men). Napoleon also ordered more troops to be sent from Madrid but they did not arrive in time.[29]

With only 13,700 men and 32 guns, Bessières was still hopelessly outnumbered: even without British aid, the Spaniards could still theoretically call upon 45,000 men. To make matters worse, his army contained a large number of raw conscripts formed into ill-organized and poorly-officered provisional regiments.[30] However, on July 9, 1808, the new King Joseph had entered his domain; before he could proceed to his capital, it was politically essential that the Spaniards be dealt a heavy blow. In any case, Joseph could hardly be allowed to march straight into the path of a Spanish army. Bessières thus had no option but to attack at once: at 1 a.m. on July 13, 1808, he duly marched out of Palencia to find the Spaniards at the head of 11,800 infantry, 1,150 cavalry and 32 guns. These troops were organized into the infantry divisions of Merle and Mouton, a composite division under Lasalle consisting of that general's own cavalry brigade and the infantry brigade of General Sabathier, and finally a Guard Reserve under Dorsenne.

Had the insurgents immediately launched a concerted assault upon the French, then Bessières would indeed have been in trouble, but fortunately for him the Spaniards were hopelessly disunited. The juntas of Asturias and Galicia were deeply suspicious of General Cuesta, rightly believing that he desired to establish himself as a military dictator. Consequently, Cuesta's demands for help in launching an offensive in Old Castile met with a hostile reception, particularly as the juntas wished to retain their armies within their own borders so as to bolster up their authority. Only their fear of the job persuaded them to send any troops at all. Even then the junta of Asturias would send only two battalions of levies. The junta of Galicia, on the other hand, did send its whole army, but it gave Blake strict instructions to ensure the safety of Galicia and not to trust Cuesta. Naturally cautious, and unhappy at the prospect of fighting in the Castillian plains, where the French could make use of their superior cavalry, Blake therefore left behind one of his five divisions in Galicia and would only advance at a snail's pace.

The two Spanish generals met at Benavente for a council of war and immediately fell to quarreling. Cuesta was furious at Blake's tardiness and insisted that, as the senior of the two, he should have command of both armies. Under protest, Blake agreed to this arrangement, but it was only with the greatest difficulty that Cuesta was able to persuade him to advance any further. Even then, Blake's movements were as slow as ever and he insisted on leaving another division at Benavente. Out of a potential of around 45,000 men*, the Spaniards were thus left with less than 22,000 (that is, Army of Galicia—15,204 infantry, 150 cavalry, 20 guns; Army of Castile—6,000 infantry, 560 cavalry).[31]

The dissension in the insurgent ranks played straight into Bessières's hands. In terms of quality, their armies were hopelessly outclassed by the French. The Army of Castile was composed entirely of raw recruits; there was too little cavalry and what there was was extremely badly mounted (centuries of mule breeding had ruined Spain's horses); finally, the artillery was also inadequate, though more in quantity than in quality. The vast open plains of Old Castile could not have been more disadvantageous to such an army.

---

*Spanish forces present: Army of Galicia—Vanguard, 1,962 infantry, 150 cavalry, 6 guns; first division, 6,470 infantry, 5 guns; fourth division, 5,818 infantry, 5 guns; attached troops, 804 infantry, 4 guns. Army of Castile—first division, 3,100 infantry, 260 cavalry; second division, 2,900 infantry, 300 cavalry.

In these conditions, the Spaniards' only real hope was to strike hard and fast with all their forces, but between them Cuesta, Blake, and the juntas had ended all hope of such action. The French were allowed to concentrate and the result of the campaign became a foregone conclusion.

By July 13 Cuesta had reached the town of Medina de Río Seco when he received news that Bessières was marching toward him from the direction of Palencia. Blake's troops were spread out on the roads to the south and southeast, and Cuesta hastily sent out messages recalling them to Río Seco. Leaving his troops to cover the distance in their own time, Blake rode ahead to meet Cuesta. The accounts of what happened next are confused and contradictory, but it appears that Blake convinced himself that the attack would come from the direction of Valladolid and drew up his troops as they arrived in a position covering the southern approaches to Río Seco. Both generals were in a state of the most complete ignorance as to the strength of their enemy, which Cuesta reckoned at 7,000 men. Only at 2 A.M. on July 14 did news reach Blake that the French were not approaching from Valladolid but from Palencia. In total darkness he had to move his men to occupy a flat-topped ridge dominating Río Seco from the east, known as the Paramo de Valdecuevas. This position was as good as any available to meet a French assault as its eastern slopes are extremely steep. Nevertheless, it was not without its defects. It is dominated from the north by a high mound known as the Tesón de Monclín, near which a large spur juts out to the east, terminating in another prominent knoll on which Bessières was later to establish his headquarters. Behind the spur lies a reentrant whose slopes form the only point at which cavalry can ascend the Paramo.

None of this need have mattered had the ridge to the north of the Paramo, crowned by the Tesón de Monclín, been occupied by Cuesta's forces. It is apparent from the account of Blake's aide-de-camp, Joaquín Moscoso, that this was what Blake expected to happen. Instead, however, Cuesta halted the Army of Castile just outside the town of Río Seco, while the Fourth Galician Division, which had been placed under his orders to bolster up his raw recruits, occupied a ridge 1,000 yards to the west of the Tesón de Monclín. The reason for these dispositions remains a mystery. It is conceivable that Cuesta's advance was delayed and that he was deterred from occupying the ridge by the appearance of French troops on its summit. Equally, since his line was deployed in echelon to the left, he may have been seeking to take the French in the flank as they came over the ridge; such a plan would also have the political advantage of enabling him to rescue Blake from certain defeat.

Whatever Cuesta's reasons, the effect of his actions was disastrous: The Spanish forces were divided into two halves, which could not even see each other, and Blake's left flank was left entirely exposed to the French cavalry at the only point where it could ascend the Paramo. It is even conceivable that Blake did not know of the absence of his rival. Meanwhile, Bessières's troops were approaching from the east. Advised of the faulty Spanish dispositions, the marshal was quick to take advantage of the situation. While the infantry of Merle and Sabathier attacked Blake from the front, Lasalle's cavalry would attack his vulnerable left flank. In the meantime, Mouton's division would occupy the northern slopes of the ridge and contain Cuesta's forces.

From his position, Blake could only see the French troops marching across his front. Convinced that Bessières intended to turn his right flank, Blake sent a message to Cuesta asking for some cavalry to be sent to strengthen the right wing. Surprisingly, Cuesta complied but to little purpose: supported by a powerful battery established on the spur below Blake's position, Merle and Sabathier suddenly turned to their right and advanced toward the Paramo. At first their assault, disordered by the steep slope, was checked; but then Lasalle's cavalry suddenly burst over the lip of the reentrant and crashed into Blake's flank. The unfortunate Spaniards could have had no idea of their approach. Taken in both front and flank, they immediately turned and fled despite Blake's desperate attempts to rally them. The Spanish cavalry was ordered to charge the French, but it, too, retreated in disorder. Only the artillery and Blake's personal guard, the *Voluntarios de Navarra*, held firm, and they were soon overwhelmed.

At this point, Cuesta's forces at last entered the battle. Provoked beyond endurance by the French artillery fire, Cuesta's two squadrons of Guard cavalry and the Fourth Galician Division advanced toward the Tesón de Monclín. The attack was pressed home with great courage, and the Spaniards even succeeded in capturing four guns. Their success was short lived, however. They were immediately counterattacked by Mouton's division and the Guard from the front, while Merle and Sabathier assailed them from the flank. Hopelessly outnumbered, the Spaniards collapsed. Seeing the fugitives pouring back toward him, Cuesta, who had played no part in these events, now led the Army of Castile off the field.

The Spaniards were not pursued. Exhausted by the heat, the French halted to sack the unfortunate town of Río Seco. It is claimed that the troops had been fired on from the town and were enraged by the discovery of the horribly mutilated corpses of some French prisoners. Nevertheless, the sack was not justified under the laws of war, and the affair remains a considerable stain on Bessières's reputation.

In other respects, Río Seco had been a splendid victory. For the loss of 500 men, the French had inflicted 3,300 casualties and taken 15 guns. Moreover, Joseph was now able to proceed to Madrid. Yet Bessières did not make proper use of his victory. The Spaniards were in complete chaos and had to cross many miles of empty plain before they could reach safety. A vigorous pursuit might have wrecked Blake's army for good and done much to counter the unfortunate effects of Bailén. Instead, Bessières became siezed by a fit of timidity: advancing with the utmost slowness, he let the Spaniards escape and contented himself with a vain attempt to subvert Blake by letter. The result was that, within days, the catastrophe of Bailén wiped out the effects of his victory at a stroke.[32]

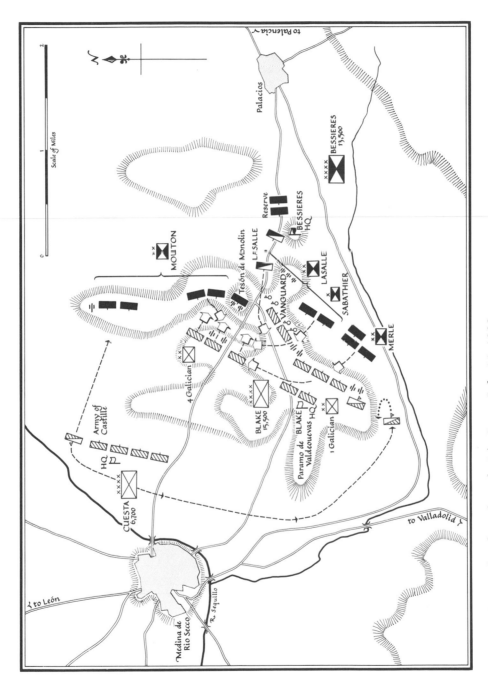

Map 4. The Battle of Medina de Río Seco, July 14, 1808

75

TEXTUAL REFERENCES

1. L. Junot, *Mémoires de Madame la duchesse d'Abrantes* (Paris, 1831–35), Vol. 3, p. 31.
2. *See D. LaCroix, Mémoires pur servir a l'histoire de France sous la regne de Napoléon, éscrits á Sainte Hélène sous sa dictée par les généraux qui ont partagé* (Paris, n.d.), Vol. 1, pp. 95–256, 328–81; and A. Ravel, *Le Maréchal Bessières* (Paris, 1903), pp. 14–22.
3. M. de Baudus, *Etudes sur Napoléon* (Paris, 1841), Vol. 1, p. 41.
4. E. de Beauharnais, *Mémoires et correspondance politique et militaire du Prince Eugene.* (Paris, 1858–60), Vol. 1, p. 83.
5. J. Marbot, *Mémoires du Général Baron de Marbot* (Paris, 1891), Vol. 1, pp. 189–90; and Junot, *op. cit.,* Vol. 5, p. 307.
6. Junot, *op. cit.,* Vol. 16, p. 164.
7. see Junot, *op. cit.,* Vol. 9, pp. 367–71; Baudus, *op. cit.,* Vol. 2, pp. 229–30; Marbot, *op. cit.,* Vol. 1, p. 373.
8. Marbot, *op. cit.,* Vol. 2, pp. 186–92, 228.
9. Baudus, *op. cit.,* Vol. 1, p. 122.
10. *Ibid.,* pp. 132–44.
11. Bessières to Berthier, June 6, 1812, cited by J. Delmas, *Journaux des sièges faits ou Soutenus par les français dans le peninsule de 1807 à 1814,* Vol. 1, pp. 560–62.
12. Massena to Bessières, April 29, 1811, cited in *ibid.,* pp. 530–31.
13. A. C. Thiébault, *Mémoires du Baron Thiébault* (Paris, 1895), Vol. 4, pp. 473–76; Massena to Berthier, April 17, 1811, cited by Delmas, *op. cit.,* pp. 513–17.
14. For example, Massena to Bessières, April 22, 1811, in Delmas, *op. cit.,* pp. 528–29.
15. A. von Schepeler, *Histoire de la revolution, d'Espagne et de Portugal, ainsique de la guerre qui en resulta* (Liege, 1829–31), Vol. I, pp. 336–37.
16. Thiébault, *op. cit.,* pp. 478–79.
17. For example Massena to Berthier, May 7, 1811, in Delmas, *op. cit.,* pp. 531–33.
18. Berthier to Bessières, May 19, 1811, in *ibid.,* pp. 531–33; and Baudus, *op. cit.,* Vol. 2, pp. 315–22.
19. Baudus, *op. cit.,* Vol. 2, pp. 35–36; Marbot, *op. cit.,* Vol. 3, pp. 135–36.
20. Baudus, *op. cit.,* Vol. 2, pp. 124–26; Marbot, *op. cit.,* Vol. 3, pp. 135–36; General Gourgaud, *Napoléon et la Grande Armée en Russie* (Paris, 1825), pp. 329–30.
21. Baudus, *op. cit.,* Vol. 1, pp. 159–61; Marbot, *op. cit.,* Vol. 3, p. 250.
22. Baudus, *op. cit.,* Vol. 1, pp. 186–87.
23. Junot, *op. cit.,* Vol. 10, p. 273.
24. *Ibid.,* Vol. 5, p. 294.
25. E. las Cases, *Le Mémorial de Sainte Hélène* (London, 1823), Vol. 1, Pt. 2, p. 160.
26. For example, decrees of Bessières, June 5 and 6, 1811, in Delmas, *op. cit.,* Vol. I, pp. 563–67.
27. Mlle. de Avrillon, *Mémoires de Madamoiselle Avrillon, premiér femme de chambre de l'imperatice, sur la vie privéade de Josephine, sa famille et sa cour* (Paris, 1833), Vol. 2, pp. 120–22.
28. Baudus, *op. cit.,* Vol. 1, pp. 110–11.
29. Schepeler, *op. cit.,* Vol. 1, p. 429.
30. A. Foy, *History of the War in the Peninsula Under Napoleon* (London, 1827), Vol. 2, pp. 123–25.
31. G. Garcia de la Cuesta, *Manifestio de presenta a la Europa el Capitán General de los Reales Ejércitos Don Gregorio de la Cuesta sobre sus operaciones militares y politicas desdè el mes de junio de 1808 hasta el dia 12 de agosto de 1809 en que dejó el mando del Ejército de Extremandura.* (Palma de Mallorca, 1811), pp. 6–7; Conde de Toreno, *Historia del leva-*

namiento guerra y revolución de España (Liege, 1829–31), Vol. 3, pp. 336–37.

32. For the battle of Rio Seco, see Schepeler, *op. cit.,* Vol. 1, pp. 431–34; Toreno, *op. cit.,* Vol. 1, pp. 314–39; Foy, *op. cit.,* Vol. 2, pp. 171–82; Baudus, *op. cit.,* Vol. 1, p. 107; Cuesta, *op. cit.,* pp. 7–8; J. Moscoso, *Memorias para las campaña . . . desde 1808 hasta 1812* (Mss.) and *Relación de la batalla . . .* (Mss.), both in the Archive of the War of Independence at the Servicio Histórico Militar Madrid, Caja 3, Leg. 4, Carp. 23 (Doc. No. 1) and Carp. 25, respectively.

BIBLIOGRAPHICAL NOTE

The standard biographies of Marshal Bessières are A. de Bessières, *Le Maréchal Bessières, Duc d'Istrie* (Paris, 1941), and A. Rabel, *Le Marechal Bessières* (Paris, 1903). A bibliographical essay also appears in J. Ambert, *Cinq Epées* (Tours, 1884). Though useful for reference, all are highly laudatory in tone.

For contemporary anecdotal material, see M. de Baudus, *Etudes sur Napoléon,* 2 vols. (Paris, 1841); L. Junot, *Mémoires de Madame la Duchesse de Abrantes,* 18 vols. (Paris, 1831–35); E. las Cases, *Le Mémorial de Sainte Hélène,* 5 vols. (London, 1823); and J. Marbot, *Mémoires du Général Baron de Marbot,* 3 vols. (Paris, 1891). Baudus was Bessières's chief aide-de-camp and Madame Junot a close friend: Their work provides a useful contrast to that of Marbot, who is bitterly hostile toward Bessières.

All these works contain information on Bessières's campaigns, but for a detailed account of the Austrian Campaign of 1809 by an officer who served under Bessières, see D. Chlapowski, *Mémoires sur les guerres de Napoléon 1806–1813* (Paris, 1908).

For the Fuentes de Oñoro affair, see A. C. Thiébault, *Mémoires du Baron Thiébault,* 5 vols. (Paris, 1895). Finally, for 1812, P. de Ségur, *History of Napoleon and the Grand Army in Russia,* 2 vols. (London, 1825), is unreliable. General Gourgaud's *Napoléon et la Grande Armée en Russie* (Paris, 1825) is much more useful.

A vital source of information for this chapter has been the battlefield of Medina de Río Seco itself, visited by the author in April 1985. It is almost entirely unchanged.

I would like to thank Monsieur R. Kann of the French Senate for help in researching the Bibliographical Note and the Trustees of the De La Salle College, Middleton, Manchester, England, for financial assistance permitting research to be undertaken in Spain.

CHRONOLOGY

1763, May 13	—Born at Brive-la-Gaillarde (Corrèze)
1789,	—*Capitaine, Garde Nationale de Paris*
1791, July 17	—Took part in Champ-de-Mars demonstrations
August 10–31	—Arrested and imprisoned; released through intervention of Danton
October 18	—*Adjutant-major,* 2nd Battalion *Volontaires de Seine-et-Oise*
1792, September 5	—Deputy to *adjutants-généraux* at the camp at Meaux
September 7	—Appointed *commissaire général* for movements
October 12	—*Adjutant général chef de brigade* supernumerary
1793, July 10	—Chief of staff to Sepher in Normandy; commanded advance guard at Pacy-sur-Eure
August 18	—*Général de brigade* while serving in *l'Armée du Nord*
September 10	—Envoy in the Gironde; commandant at Bordeaux
December 25– **April 2, 1795**	—Employed with the Military Committee of the Convention in Paris
1794	—Married Angélique Pierre
1795, April 13– **October 13**	—Posted to 17th Military District; under Barras and Bonaparte during rising of October 5
1796, September 28	—Joined *l'Armée d'Italie;* given a command under Massena; Battles of Arcola, San Michele, and Rivoli
1797, April 17	—Temporary rank of *général de division;* rank confirmed November 7
April 24	—Commanded Massena's, and later 2nd Division
1798, February and **March**	—Crushes Swiss resistance and plunders their national treasure; sent to take over *l'Armée d'Italie*
1799, January 9	—Commands all French troops in Holland and later Batavian army
October 6	—Battle of Castricum; forces allies to evacuate
1800, August 22	—Succeeds Massena as commander in chief in Italy
1801, June 1	—President of War Department, Council of State
1802, September 11	—Ambassador to Turkey
1804, May 19	—Created *Maréchal d'Empire* (ninth in seniority)
1805– **1807**	—Commanded army forming at Boulogne; governor general of Hanseatic towns; commander of *Corps d'Observation* of *La Grande Armée*
1807, October 27	—Recalled in disgrace by Napoleon over treaty with Sweden; unemployed for 7 years
1814, June 1	—Rallies to the Bourbons; made Chevalier de St. Louis
1815, March	—Transfers his allegiance to Napoleon
April 16	—Appointed governor of Provence and commander 8th Military District
July 31	—Hands over Toulon to Marquis de Rivière
August 2	—En route to Paris, is assassinated in Avignon and his body thrown into the Rhône

CHAPTER FIVE

THE PATAGONIAN

Brune

by

Lt. Col. (ret'd.) Alan Shepperd

Poet into Revolutionary (1763–1796)

Like a fair number of Napoleon's marshals, Guillaume Brune came from a middle-class background that was associated with the law. His father was a judge, and among his uncles were a canon, a doctor, and a cavalry officer who had received the Cross of St. Louis. Brune's early years were spent at Brive la Galliarde; and after a schooling in the humanities by the Benedictines, he was sent to Paris to study law. Preferring to spend his time drinking and gambling, however, he was soon in debt. Forced to earn his living, he became a reader and typesetter for a printing firm. Pretensions to authorship led to his writing a volume of prose and verse, based on a holiday spent with two school friends, which he published anonymously. Fancying himself as a poet, and that his future lay in the realms of literature, Brune acquired a small printing press and helped to launch the satirical *Journal de la Cour et de la Ville*, a daily news sheet with "patriot" undertones.[1] Soon, however, the opening events of the Revolution, which Brune enthusiastically supported, warned of the storm that was about to break, and he abandoned his journalistic efforts.

Brune was already a member of the newly raised National Guard, and his rank of captain owed much to his impressive height and martial bearing, backed by a fine display of patriotism. Indeed, of all the future marshals, Brune was one of the six who came neither from the officer class nor from the ranks, but were civilians owing all to their earlier participation in the revolutionary movement. As for Brune, he was one of the founders, alongside Danton, Marat, Camille Desmoulins, and Hébert, of the *Club des Cordeliers*,[2] which met in an old convent and thus named after the knotted girdles of the Franciscans. Here Brune was privy to all the intrigues and seditious plots that led to the fall of the monarchy. Following the "Champ-de-Mars Massacre," Brune was arrested and thrown into prison and his printing press was seized. Through Danton's intervention he was soon released. To his friend and mentor, Brune was "my Patagonian,"[3] so called for his tall stature and ardor; and he now became Danton's man, body and soul. With the latter's rise to power in September 1792, Brune's promotion from adjutant of a volunteer battalion to the rank of colonel followed in a matter of days.

The spring of the following year found Brune on the staff of General Dumouriez with the Army of the North campaigning in Belgium, where he earned praise for rallying the troops after the defeat at Neerwinden. That same summer, rebel federalists under the Girondin General Wimphen concentrated around Caen, threatening to march on Paris. An improvised "army of pacification" was quickly assembled, and the threat was easily suppressed. Brune, appointed chief of staff and put in command of the advance guard, claimed the sole credit as the victor at Pacy-sur-Eure. His suggestion that he should now be made minister of war was laughingly rejected by Danton, but his promotion to brigadier general came within a month. His return to the Army of the North, ostensibly "to take knowledge of everything concerning the state and supply of the armies and the fortresses and to report on them," coincided with a witch-hunt of a number of generals, many of whom being falsely accused went to the scaffold. In this calumny, aimed at the "nobles and foreigners," there is no doubt that Brune played a major role.[4] Meanwhile, an insurrection by the Girondists in the southwest had flared up to alarming proportions. Alongside Ysabeau and Tallien from the Committee of Public Safety, Brune was sent into the Gironde to subdue the royalists. As commandant in Bordeaux, he carried out this task with all the brutal cruelty of the Terror.

Returning to Paris, Brune was employed on the Military Committee of the Convention, an appointment that lasted through 1793 and into the spring of the following year. Brune now decided to marry and set up an established home. His bride was a young woman of humble birth, Angélique Pierre, who was employed as a metal burnisher. Their liaison was of long standing, but resisted by her family. Brune's rank and position were now overriding arguments in his favor. Of a modest and retiring nature, Angélique was well content to live in the shadow of one whose pretensions and ambitions meant little to her. Later, as *La Maréchale*, her attendance at the Emperor's court was strictly confined to the obligatory state occasions. She died childless in 1829.

A struggle for power within the Convention in the spring of 1794 could well have ended Brune's career and even cost him his life. First Danton and then Hébert fell to Robespierre's venomous attacks, and both were executed. Brune, a fellow traveler of Danton and Hébert and a prominent Cordelier, survived the Robespierre purge through the support of Barras and his own ability to adapt to the changing scene. The events of 9 *Thermidor* and the execution of Robespierre, however, brought the "Dantonists" such as Tallien and Barras into power. Brune's instincts had paid off.[5]

In the spring of 1795, food shortages brought the mobs on to the streets of Paris. Brune was posted to the 17th Military District. Under martial law, 16,000 militants were crushed into the city's jails and the rising was easily suppressed. The autumn, however, saw the more serious threat of a royalist insurrection. Barras, however, had made plans to bring together a number of generals known for their heavy-handed methods. These included Carteaux, Brune, and Bonaparte who was to command the artillery and act as chief of staff. Standing by were 4,000–5,000 regular troops and three battalions of volunteers. "On 13 *Vendémiaire* Paris was under arms for the very last time. The Insurgents numbered twenty to twenty-five thousand men, but they had no cannons to set up against those brought by Murat during the night from the camp at Sablons."[6] A day later the rising had been crushed. The decisive part played by Bonaparte's handling of the artillery did not go unrecognized. Thanks to Barras, and indeed to Fréron, the lover of his sister, Pauline, Bonaparte's promotion to divisional commander and appointment as commander in chief of the Army of the Interior followed within days. Nor did the future Emperor forget the tall brigadier general who had briefly come under his command alongside a howitzer detachment at the bottom of the Rue Vivienne, and who had driven out the royalists holding the French theater. When the threat of risings spread to the south, Fréron was dispatched on a mission of "pacification." As his deputy in Marseilles and Avignon he took Brune, confident in his ruthless and uncomprising methods in dealing with troublemakers. Again, Brune briefly came under Bonaparte's command, and, as it later transpired, the citizens of Avignon also retained memories of another tall man who came among them with the power of life and death. Within the year, in October 1796, Brune joined Masséna's division with the Army of Italy.

Revolutionary into Soldier (1796–1799)

When Brune joined the Army of Italy, it was as an outsider, without battle experience and unknown to the troops. So it came as a surprise to many that he was given a command by Bonaparte. But in the next five months of campaigning, he proved that this patronage was not misplaced, and his personal bravery won praise from both Massena and the army commander. Bonaparte, indeed, seemed particularly impressed by his conduct in defense of San Michele in January 1797, when Brune with a regiment and some cavalry beat off strong attacks in which the Austrians lost over 500 prisoners and two guns. In his report to the Directory, Bonaparte wrote, "The grenadiers of the 75th took the guns with the bayonet: they had at their head General of Brigade Brune, who had his clothes pierced by seven balls."[7] After the armistice Brune commanded a division with acting rank, and by the end of the year was promoted to general.

With the proposal to mount an expedition in Egypt, the

Directory was faced with an urgent need for money. Over and above what could be seized by plundering Piedmont and Naples, their covetous eyes fixed on the millions that lay in the treasury in Berne. Early in January 1798 Brune had been nominated as head of a mission to Naples, but was recalled to Paris by Barras for secret instructions. Strategically the occupation of Switzerland was necessary to ensure the conquest of Germany and Italy; officially republican France was seeking to "liberate" the Swiss from their autocratic rulers; privately the seizure of the country's considerable treasure was an urgent priority. To achieve this needed audacity and cunning, an ability to mix threats and tough action with deceit and false promises. Brune was the man to send. His old division under General Menard had already been ordered to assemble near Geneva, while a further 15,000 men from Augereau's Army of the Rhine were marching down from the north. Meanwhile the plans to occupy Switzerland were kept a closely guarded secret.

Brune based himself at Paverne near the lake of Neuchâtel. The canton of Vaud had already fallen to revolutionary propaganda and become a separate republic, and Brune opened his campaign of deceit by trying to persuade Berne and the other states to follow suit. He soon realized, however, that until his troops arrived he must temporize and appear to negotiate. In a series of conferences at Basel and elsewhere, he declared that France wished only for the happiness and liberty of its neighbors, and that as soon as a more democratic constitution had been achieved their independence would be respected. This web of deception was cemented by Commissioner Mengand, whose sordid intrigues succeeded in sowing confusion and dissension in both the Bernese senate and their army.

Early in February Menard's division was halted at Lausanne and the stronger force under Schauenbourg had reached the frontier near Basel. On February 5, 1798, the Army of Switzerland officially came into being, and under Brune's command both columns were directed on Berne. The main action of the month-long campaign was the crossing of the River Saane at Fribourg that was bravely contested by Swiss Commander Erlach. Brune described the fight as like that at Lodi (which he had not been at), while Pelleport with long experience in Italy, and later to become a general, said the affair did honor to the Berne militia.[8] In the north Schauenbourg in a more rapid advance took Soleure on March 2 and entered Berne two days later, a few hours before Brune's advance guard. The timing of these events should all be seen in relation to Bonaparte's secret preparations for the expedition to Egypt, which were well advanced; and on March 8 Brune was appointed commander of the Army of Italy to relieve Berthier who was to join the expedition. But Brune had much to do before leaving for Italy; in fact, one suspects he underestimated the time it would take to crush the Swiss and occupy their country. It took Brune and his agents only three weeks to collect 14 million francs, seized in cash and ingots and by the sale of title deeds (this apart from considerable sums raised by requisition), together with quantities of war-like stores, which included over 350 pieces of artillery.

His prime task completed and with part of the treasure en route for Toulon, Brune, seeking to emulate Bonaparte in the role of conqueror and legislator, attempted to impose a revolutionary system of government on the Swiss, dividing the country into three republics. It did not suit the Directory, however, to allow one of its generals to hold so much power, and an excuse was made to hasten Brune back to Italy. He did not go empty handed, for he levied the sum of 200,000 francs on the Swiss for his "expenses" in plundering their national treasure. "Only part of this was handed over, the rest was to be sent after him to Milan. As it was, his carriage was so heavily laden—with gold, said his enemies—that it broke down a short time after quitting Berne."[9] No wonder Napoleon later spoke contemptuously of this *déprédateur intrepide.*

Reaching Italy, Brune found many of his troops were embarking for Egypt. With little to do, he started meddling with the management and constitution of the nominally independent Cispadine Republic in north and central Italy. This brought him into conflict with the Directory, where one member found him mediocre, pleasure loving, vain, and a swindler, and Suchet, his chief of staff, "one of the most shameless plunderers." It seems that Brune, regarding the Italians as having been conquered, turned to his usual methods of extortion; by the time he was recalled in October 1798, his personal fortune was greatly increased. It was about this time that he bought the Château of St.-Just in Marne for 160,000 francs; and later from "feudal rents in conquered regions [he purchased] in turn, the two halves of a farm near Choisy."[10]

After a two-month leave, Brune was sent by Barras to take command of 15,000 French troops stationed in Holland. The arrival of this important revolutionary, notorious for his conduct in Switzerland and Italy, alarmed the Batavian government. Were the United Provinces about to be absorbed like Belgium, and if the Allies invaded would their army be committed in the name of France on Dutch soil? For five months all Brune's efforts to persuade the Batavian Directorate to raise more troops, provision their fortresses, and even agree to a united command were countered or ignored. Only after Fouché had been sent to intervene on his behalf was Brune given overall command of both armies. But there was a bare month left for him to organize the country's defenses before the British under Abercromby landed at the Helder. Much credit is due to Brune for his initial dispositions of the three French and two Batavian divisions, and the energy he showed in getting forward reinforcements, including those brought in from France, to hold the front in the north against the final buildup of some 30,000 British and Russian troops commanded by the Duke of York.

Before the arrival of the Russians, the British beat back the combined French and Batavian attack on the Zijpe Canal line, but Brune, bringing up his army reserve, halted a concerted attempt by the Allies to break out at Bergen. Two weeks later, however, in the Battle of the Dunes, close by Alkmaar, he failed to stop the British from reaching Egmont aan Zee. The final battle of the seven-weeks campaign was fought at Castricum. In this defensive battle (see p. 88), Brune was at his best as a field commander. The Duke of York, his troops ravaged by sickness and virtually starving, was forced to withdraw and negotiate their evacuation, for in George Canning's words, "Better have our army without Holland than Holland without our army."

Ambassador to the Porte—And the Gathering Shadows (1800–1815)

Brune's recall from Holland coincided with the coup d'état of *Brumaire;* He was made a state councillor and given appointments in Vendée and with the reserve army. Then, in August 1800, Massena was removed from the Army of Italy for barefaced plundering, and Brune took his place as commander in chief. In the subsequent winter campaign, Brune's handling of the passage of the River Mincio nearly brought disaster, and he was replaced as soon as the armistice was signed. Bonaparte later remarked that Brune's conduct on this occasion demonstrated that he was not fit for high command. Back in Paris, Brune was appointed president of the War Department of the Council of State, but within months he was sent as ambassador to Turkey. The circumstances were not auspicious. Bonaparte's venture into Egypt and Syria was not to be easily forgotten or forgiven, and Turkey's prestige had suffered from the prolonged occupation of Egyptian soil by French troops. Indeed, the peace treaty between France and Turkey had been ratified by the latter only after Bonaparte had secretly guaranteed the sultan's territories against retaliatory moves by both Russia and Britain. In return the sultan reluctantly agreed to open the Dardanelles to

French merchantmen seeking access to the trade of the Black Sea ports.[11]

While Bonaparte sought to save face and regain an important part of France's overseas trade, Russia, ever sensitive to any threat to the Dardanelles, turned from her policy of aggression against Turkey to one of support. These undercurrents in a pool of intrigue were perhaps only fully understood by Pierre Ruffin, France's chargé d'affaires in Constantinople. Unfortunately he and Brune never got on and his advice was invariably ignored. The task Brune had been given, to reestablish France's position in the Near East, called for patience and well-mannered diplomacy. The first consul evidently considered that the appointment of a general who had "driven" the British and Russians out of Holland would be more likely to impress the sultan and his ministers. A numerous staff, together with Madame Brune and several other wives, now assembled at Marseilles ready to be transported by a naval squadron. Here Brune was being wined and dined by the merchants who hoped to gain from his negotiations. His secret instructions included orders that he should seek the personal friendship of the Ottoman foreign minister and "consort with the Ambassador of Russia, but be more friendly with the Ambassador of Prussia [and] always be in the limelight and see that the Turks focussed attention on him."[12]

The mission finally reached Constantinople in December, upstaged perhaps by the arrival of the Russian minister, Italinski, who landed from an English frigate a few days earlier. Nevertheless, Ruffin was favorably impressed by the show and pomp of Brune's arrival. Ruffin, now downgraded and often snubbed by his new master, soon became disillusioned and applied to return to Paris, but was refused. At first Brune was able to make progress. French consular services were reestablished and extended to cover many outlying parts of the Ottoman Empire, and he reported that the Turkish ministers seemed tacitly disposed toward his plans for trading. The Dardanelles had now been opened to France albeit the same right had been given to Britain, Austria, and Prussia. Italinski, however, was being very stubborn, insisting that Russia had the right to hold all foreign ships passing into the Black Sea for quarantine and inspection, and that this was with Turkey's agreement, although outside any treaty. Moreover, he kept a frigate on station off Constantinople to enforce his rules, and to Brune's fury and despair would make only rare exceptions in allowing the passage of French merchantmen. In desperation Brune requested that a French frigate and two brigs be dispatched urgently, under the pretext of mapping the coast of the Black Sea, but in reality to force the issue. The warships were never sent, for within days Britain and

France were again at war. While peace lasted, "considerable commercial activity began in the Black Sea. Approximately 815 foreign ships called at Russia's southern ports in 1803. Twenty-five per cent of the grain from southern Russia went to Marseille. . . . Only fifteen ships under France's own flag loaded at Odessa, however the Anglo-French war forced this commerce to go into new channels or to cease altogether."[13]

In a move to circumscribe Napoleon's European conquests, Russia had for some time been sending troops through the Dardanelles to the Ionian Islands. Convoys destined for Corfu, carrying some 16,000 troops, had been reported by Brune, who was now told by Talleyrand to persuade Turkey to close the Straits. But the sultan and his advisors preferred to listen to the representatives of Britain and Russia rather than to the threats and cajoling of this arrogant revolutionary, who recently had announced that he should be addressed as "Marshal of the Empire." Indeed, it was the refusal of Turkey to recognize the newly proclaimed Napoleon as "Emperor of the French" that led to Brune's recall 7 months later. To the Ottomans, titles had much importance and precise usage. Seeking to establish the equivalent for "Emperor," which they hesitated to accept, Brune claimed that Napoleon was "Padishar," meaning "Great King" and probably suggested by Ruffin.[14] But all Brune's arguments were countered and his requests blocked, as neither the sultan nor the czar was prepared to acknowledge a "commoner's" right to either title. Frustrated by Turkish prevarication, and cold shouldered by Italinski who was talking openly of Napoleon's "perfidious designs" on the Ottoman Empire, Brune could see only one way out. Claiming that Napoleon had been insulted, which he as a Marshal of the Empire could not countenance, Brune threatened to leave for Paris immediately. Twice he called for his passports; twice he hung on for several days, hoping for a change of mind by the Porte. Then, as a last act, he again tried to halt the Russian troop ships. But the sultan was only waiting for Brune's departure before renewing the alliance with Russia. Among a people who delighted in outward show, Brune's natural flamboyance could have been his greatest asset, but by now the Turks were thoroughly scandalized by his arrogance and surly behavior; nor were they impressed by his sternness and threats that came to nothing. Turkish neutrality had been maintained, but little else was left to show for his efforts over two long and frustrating years in Constantinople, and Brune's departure went almost unremarked.[15]

His mission to Turkey undoubtedly damaged Brune's career, showing him to be unsure of himself with a predilection for half-measures, and to some a soldier in rank alone. Reaching Paris he received his baton and the Grand Eagle of the Legion of Honor, but now he was excluded from any top appointment. In the autumn of 1807, when serving as governor general of the Hanseatic towns, having seized the town of Stralsund, he signed a treaty with Sweden giving France possession of the adjacent Island of Rugen. When Napoleon saw the wording "the French Army," instead of "the Army of His Imperial and Royal Majesty," he was furious and immediately dismissed Brune from his command.

For the next seven years, Brune never left St.-Just. During the Hundred Days, the Emperor and the Marshal were reconciled, and Brune was sent to Toulon as governor. Here, long after Napoleon's defeat and abdication, Brune defiantly continued to fly the tricolor. Finally, threatened with imprisonment, he handed over his command and set out for Paris. Leaving his cavalry escort and baggage to take the direct route through Orange, he diverted to Avignon to change horses. But his uniform was spotted and an excited crowd quickly collected. Mistaken for a tall revolutionary who had carried the head of the princess of Lamballe on his pike during the massacres over 20 years before, Brune's attempt to escape in his carriage was halted by a mob screaming for revenge. Forced back into the Royal Palace Hotel, he was discovered while writing a last letter to his wife, shot down, and his body thrown into the Rhône. Brune, the revolutionary turned soldier, met his death with characteristic courage.

The Battle of Castricum (October 6, 1799)

After the allies broke through to Egmont aan Zee, they still faced Brune's main defensive positions covering the narrow neck of land 5 kilometers wide between Beverwyk and the sea at Wyk aan Zee. To the east the Lang Meer and the Alkmaar canal, with beyond the polder deep in flood water, effectively blocked any major enveloping move round the right flank. Tied to the coastal strip, the allies had only three roads southward, along the edge of the dunes, from Heiloo through Castricum, and through Akersloot and Uitgeest. Beside the coast itself, the sand dunes and scattered copses made controlled deployment impossible and provided the defense with endless concealed positions. Inland the criss-cross patterns of canals and ditches, and especially the broad-flowing Schilp-water, where every bridge had been destroyed, would confuse and slow down any attack, allowing the defense to concentrate at key crossing points. Here Brune had taken great care to fortify the villages astride the river line and right back to Beverwyk, giving a defense in depth of over nine kilometers.[16]

The Duke of York, desperately short of supplies, unaware of the full extent of the French reinforcements, and overestimating their losses, decided he must renew the attack as soon as possible. His plan was for a phased advance; first to drive in the enemy's outpost line, then to mount a coordinated attack on the rear positions, in front of which the ground gave better scope for maneuver. With hindsight it could be said that the balance of forces, combined with the difficulties of the terrain, were overriding factors in favor of the defense, but it is certainly true that Brune's foresight, sound dispositions, and aggressive policy in defense, together with energetic leadership and control on the battlefield, clinched the matter.

When the allied divisions advanced on October 6, Abercromby moved into the dunes in the face of the French skirmishers, while the Russians quickly overran Bakkum, and Limmen and Akersloot fell to Dundas's brigades. "There the advance should have ended; but at Bakkum the Russian commander Sedmoradsky pushed forward in pursuit, entered Castricum, and forced the French defenders into the dunes, where he attacked them again. . . . Brune had already alerted Boudet to concentrate his division near Castricum, and soon a heavy counter-attack developed. More Russian battalions were called into the battle; Abercromby's reserve brigade was drawn into the fight from the west; and soon a disorderly general action flared up along the whole front, with attack and counter-attack swaying to and fro for many hours in ferocious Combat."[17]

News of these events reached the Duke of York while at dinner in Alkmaar. Completely out of touch and apparently unconcerned, his reaction was too slow to influence the last stages of the battle. Brune, however, had already sent Boudet's French battalions into action at Castricum and gone himself to the left flank. Here he quickly organized a second counterattack, gathering up the whole of Gouvion's division and all the available cavalry. Marching directly on Castricum, the French columns drove the Russians back beyond the Schilpwater, being checked only by Abercromby's reserve battalions sent to stem the rout. As darkness fell, the fighting ended around the villages of Bakkum and Limmen where it had started 10 hours before, and with both sides falling back to their previous positions. That night the Duke assembled his field commanders. "They pointed out the shrinking strength in relation to the enemy's, the supply problem, the condition of the troops, the unwillingness of the Russians, and the failure of the Dutch people to provide help or even information . . . and [the army] was not now able to conquer the country or maintain its present position." Twenty-four hours later, "in pitch darkness and torrents of gale driven rain,"[18] and with great secrecy, the exhausted men who had come as liberators were in full retreat to the line of the Zijpe and eventual evacuation. Napoleon later wrote, "Brune was justly named the saviour of the Batavian Republic. The Romans would have awarded him the honours of a Triumph. By saving Holland he saved France from invasion."

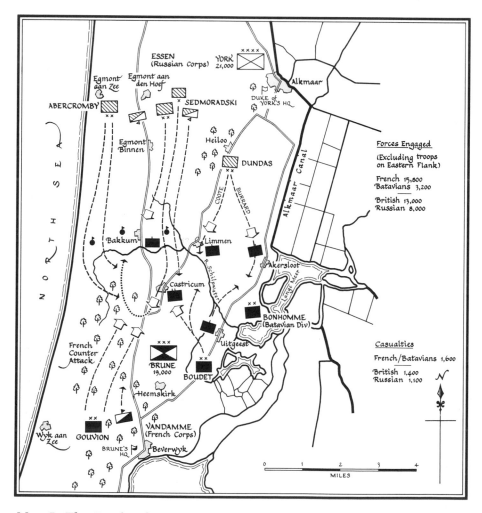

Map 5. The Battle of Castricum, October 6, 1799

TEXTUAL REFERENCES

1. *Revue des questions historiques,* July 1, 1912, pp. 223–24.
2. J. M. Thompson, *The French Revolution* (Oxford, 1944), p. 109.
3. P. Barras, *Mémoires de . . .* (Paris, 1825), Vol. 4, p. 36.
4. R. W. Phipps, *The Armies of the First French Republic and the Rise of the Marshals of Napoleon I* (Oxford, 1926–39), Vol. 1, pp. 200–2.
5. F. Furet and D. Richet, *The French Revolution,* English ed. (London, 1970), p. 227.
6. *Ibid.,* p. 263.
7. Phipps, *op. cit.,* p. 140.
8. *Ibid.,* Vol. V, p. 69.
9. For plundering, see Sciout, *Le Directoire* (Paris, 1895–97), Vol. 3, p. 388ff.
10. L. Bergeron, *France Under Napoleon,* English ed. (Princeton, 1981), p. 124.
11. V. Puryear, *Napoleon and the Dardanelles* (Berkeley, 1951), pp. 2–3.
12. *Ibid.,* p. 6.
13. *Ibid.,* p. 9.
14. *Ibid.,* pp. 27–28.
15. *Ibid.,* p. 39.
16. E. Gachot, *Les campaignes de 1799: Jourdan en Allemagne et Brune en Hollande* (Paris, 1906), pp. 286–87.
17. P. Mackesy, *The Strategy of Overthrow, 1798–1799* (London, 1974), pp. 295–96.
18. *Ibid.,* pp. 298–99.

BIBLIOGRAPHICAL NOTE

For background to the marshal's revolutionary activities, *The French Revolution* (London, 1970), in the English edition by François Furet and Denis Richet, is a useful, if discursive, guide. Brune's military career, except as commander in chief in Holland in 1799, was unexceptional and has attracted scant attention. Colonel R. W. Phipps in his *Armies of the First French Republic and the Rise of the Marshals of Napoleon I* (Oxford, 1926–39), however, painstakingly follows Brune's progress and gives a brief account of the campaign to despoil the Swiss in 1798. For an account of the campaign in North Holland, Edouard Gachot's *Les Campaignes de 1799: Jourdan en Allemagne et Brune en Hollande* (Paris, 1906) overstresses the achievements of the French and takes little note of the logistical problems. Sir John Fortescue in his *History of the British Army* (London), Vol. 4, Pt. 2, also published in 1906, devotes two chapters to the campaign and deals in particular with the difficulties in supply and transport that faced the allies. Fortescue and to a lesser extent Gachot rely extensively, in their account of the Battle of Castricum, on Baron Jomini's *Histoire critique et militaire des guerres de la Révolution, 1820–24* in Vol. 12. The strategy of the campaign is briefly covered by A. B. Rodger in *The War of the Second Coalition, 1798–1801* (Oxford, 1964). The most recent and objective study, however, is contained in Piers Mackesy's *The Strategy of Overthrow 1798–1799* (London, 1974), which includes details of orders of battle and of the buildup of opposing forces. Brune's two years in Constantinople, a turning point in his career and largely ignored by French writers, is admirably covered in the opening chapters of Vernon Puryear's *Napoleon and the Dardanelles* (Berkeley, 1951).

CHRONOLOGY

1770, May 10	—Born at Annoux (Burgundy)
1788, February 2	—Commissioned into the Royal Champagne Cavalry
1791, November 8	—Marries Marie-Nicolle Adelaide (née de Seuguenot) (divorces her January 4, 1794)
1793, July 25	—Promoted *général de brigade*
1795, September 18	—Taken prisoner at Mannheim (later exchanged)
1799, February 12	—Defeats Hassan Bey at Redecieh in Upper Egypt
July 25	—Present at Aboukir (and captures castle August 2)
1800, March	—Captured by Royal Navy en route for France (subsequently freed)
July 3	—Promoted *général de division*
1801, November 9	—Marries Aimée Leclerc
1804, May 19	—Appointed *Maréchal d'Empire* (13th in seniority)
1805, December 2	—Commands III Corps at Austerlitz
1806, October 14	—Commands III Corps at Auerstädt
1807, February 8	—Commands III Corps at Eylau; slightly wounded
July 15	—Appointed governor general of the Grand Duchy of Warsaw
1808, March 28	—Created Duke of Auerstädt (confirmed by letters patent, July 2)
1809, April 22	—Commands III Corps at Eckmühl
July 5 and 6	—Commands III Corps at Wagram with distinction
August 15	—Created prince of Eckmühl (confirmed by letters patent, November 28)
1810, January 1	—Appointed to command *l'Armée d'Allemagne*
1812, June 24	—Enters Russia in command of I Corps
September 7	—Commands I Corps at Borodino; wounded
October 26	—Placed in command of rear guard of retreating
November 17	—Fights at Krasnöe
1813, March 9–19	—Defends Dresden at head of I Corps
May 30	—Assumes command of Hamburg and area
1814, May 27	—Evacuates Hamburg on orders of Louis XVIII; exiled to his estates
1815, March 20	—Appointed minister of war by Napoleon (holds post until July 8)
June 2	—Created a peer of France
June 24	—Appointed military governor of Paris
July 3	—Evacuates Paris (takes command of *l'Armée de la Loire*, July 5)
July 14	—Resubmits to Louis XVIII; exiled to his estates
1817, August 27	—Restored to the dignity of *maréchal de France*
1819, March 5	—Readmitted to the French peerage
1823, June 1	—Dies of consumption at Paris

CHAPTER SIX

THE IRON MARSHAL

Davout

by

David G. Chandler

Emergence of the Soldier (1770–1804)

Of all the 26 members of the Napoleonic marshalate, Davout was one of the least liked as a man, the ablest as a commander, and the most feared—and respected—as an adversary. He was also, from 1798, one of the loyalest of Napoleon's key subordinates, but paradoxically never enjoyed his master's unquestioning trust.

Louis-Nicolas Davout was born on May 10, 1770, at Annoux (Yonne) into a noble Burgundian family with martial ancestry stretching back to the Crusades. An ancient local saying ran: "When a d'Avot is born, a sword leaps from its scabbard."[1] Not surprisingly, he opted for a military career, and after studying at the military school of Auxerre, on September 27, 1785, at age 15, he entered the Royal Military School in Paris just after a certain Napoleon Bonaparte had left on first commissioning. His course completed, in February 1788 the young Davout joined the Royal Champagne Cavalry Regiment in garrison at Hesdin. He was soon known for strong political views—openly supporting the dangerous new ideas sweeping through France—and these were not long in landing him in trouble. On August 18, 1790, he was arrested for championing a regimental delegation that had visited Paris without orders,[2] imprisoned at Arras for six weeks, and required to resign his commission. Upon release, he returned home to Ravières, after successfully claiming that his resignation was invalid, having been obtained under duress, and he was granted extended leave. Over a year of relative inactivity followed, at the end of which he married his first wife, and soon regretted it. Marie-Nicolle Adelaide (née de Seguenot) proved an unfaithful hussy of the first order.

On September 22, 1791, the Volunteers of the Yonne met to elect their senior officers; they chose Davout to serve as *lieutenant-colonel en second* of their 3rd Battalion. After months of equipping and training, with some local duties at Auxerre, in July 1792 the battalion was posted to the Army of the North on the frontiers. The young colonel rapidly gained a reputation for dash, boldness, and revolutionary single-mindedness in a series of surprise attacks against Austrian outposts around Condé. Early 1793 was spent near Liège, and Davout fought at the Battle of Neerwinden on March 18. He abruptly rose to public notice two weeks later when, on April 4, he led his men in a vain but determined attempt to arrest their own commander-in-chief as Dumouriez defected to the allies. The general made good his escape, but not without Davout's bullets whistling after him. This incident doubtless hastened Davout's appointment as brigade major and, in July, his promotion to general of brigade after his transfer to disaffected Vendée where he undertook counterinsurgency operations.

All seemed set fair, and still further promotion was in the offing, when disaster struck in late August. By order of the Convention, all *ci-devant* aristocrats were to be debarred from the army and required to reside beyond a stipulated distance from Paris. Davout—staunch republican that he was—at once sent in his papers, although not without bitterness.[3] Once again at Ravières, his troubles were not over. For a short while his mother was jailed as a suspect, but her son managed to destroy dangerous correspondence and she was freed. A little later both were briefly re-arrested as suspects. But at least he was away from Paris during the height of the Terror, where the "swings and roundabouts" of revolutionary politics continued to operate unpredictably. In July 1794 came the coup d'état of *Thermidor*, and the fall of Robespierre and the Jacobins. Under the milder regime that followed, it became possible for Davout to resume his military career, and on September 21 he was re-appointed general of brigade. He managed to have his initial appointment changed to a cavalry command in the Army of the Moselle; Davout had certain friends in high places. So it was that November found him reporting to General Debrun, his new divisional commander, as the Army of the Moselle prosecuted the siege of Luxembourg.

He was soon to display his talents as a daring cavalry commander. At the head of some 4,000 men, he harassed the Austrians mercilessly, scoring success after success. When the full siege of Field-Marshal Bender and his 15,000-strong garrison was under way, Davout was instrumental in repelling a large enemy sortie, following this up on another occasion by capturing several guns and burning three grain stores within musket range of the main defenses. He transcended all by leading two companies of grenadiers through a foggy night to infiltrate deep within the Austrian positions on March 4, 1795, to destroy the Mill of Eich—a feat he brought off for the loss of one man wounded and one missing.[4] Thenceforward he was a noted commander— and when the Austrians attempted a retaliatory sortie they were repulsed with 1,200 casualties.

When Luxembourg fell on June 7, Davout was not present, having been transferred to the Army of the Rhine and Moselle. Taking part in operations near Mannheim, he came in contact with General Louis Desaix, who became one of his staunchest friends. He also came to know Oudinot over this period. Mannheim had been captured by the French on September 20, but Austrian Commanders Würmser and Clerfayt counterattacked with skill, and by October 29 the fortress was reinvested and

Davout within it. The French garrison commander, Montaigu, decided to surrender on November 21, and Davout became a prisoner of war. To make amends for some insults paid him by a young Austrian officer, Würmser (who had known his uncle in earlier times) freed the general of brigade on parole.[5] Returned again to his home, awaiting an exchange, he used his time to good effect by studying military history and theory, particularly the works of Chevalier Folard, which impressed him a great deal and helped form his concept of war. This interlude ended in October 1796, when he found himself posted back to the Rhine; although not at first holding an active command, he continued to add to his military experience under Moreau, the army commander, and Desaix, in charge of a force at Kehl. In April 1797 he was given a command in General Duhesme's division, and on April 20 played a prominent part in the major crossing of the Rhine at Diersheim. He captured the town at the third attempt after Duhesme was wounded. He proceeded to hold the town against determined Austrian counter-attacks. Next evening, at the head of cavalry, he pursued the Austrians for 25 miles to Biberach and Zell; en route he captured a wagon belonging to General Klinglin, which proved to contain incriminating letters between Pichegru and the Austrians. Pressing on up the Kinzig valley on the twenty-second, news arrived of the signature of the armistice of Leoben. Operations thereupon came to a halt. To his great chagrin, he was not mentioned in the Directory's first letter of congratulations to Moreau's army, but the oversight was remedied in a subsequent missive on May 24. It would seem that Moreau—closely associated with Pichegru—was not particularly pleased about the revelation of the latter's intrigues, thanks to the zeal of Davout, although he appreciated his fighting qualities. Davout also came under a cloud when General Augereau took over command in the area; some sarcastic remarks were reported by an innkeeper—and this led to Davout and a staff officer being posted away from their units as a disciplinary measure.

But help was at hand. His friend and patron, Desaix (already highly thought of by the hero of the hour, General Bonaparte), arranged for Davout to be posted to the Army of England on January 12, 1798. Two months later he introduced Davout to his new commander-in-chief in Paris.[6] No details of the interview have survived, but Bonaparte clearly accepted Desaix's recommendation, and on April 14 Louis Davout found himself awarded an appointment in the Army of the Orient, which was about to set out for Egypt. Thus was first forged a professional relationship that was to last until 1815.

If his experience up to 1798 had firmly founded his grasp of interarm combat, the next years would broaden his military horizons considerably. For Davout, Egypt was a hard experience, but like many another who came through the fire, it tempered his character and abilities. Initially attached to Dumas's division, he was transferred to command the cavalry under his friend Desaix from July 11, and thereafter remained closely associated with him until both men left the country in 1800. Short of horses, the French cavalry were little more than spectators, placed within the infantry squares, at the Battles of Shubrakhit and the Pyramids, but Davout apparently earned a commendation from General Bonaparte.[7] Arrived in Cairo, he survived a serious attack of dysentery, and was then charged with finding mounts for the cavalry. The Army of the Orient had brought only one-third of its requirement from France, and hopes that horses captured from the ferocious Mamelukes might make up the numbers proved illusory. Davout issued draconian edicts and requisitioned many horses from French officers and civilians, which earned him scant popularity, but his commander approved his ruthless resolve, on December 2 Bonaparte was able to review Davout's fully mounted brigade.

Desaix was now detached to conquer Upper Egypt and hunt down the Mameluke leader, Murad Bey. As a result, Davout never went to Syria, but instead shared in Desaix's brilliant campaign at the head of just 4,000 men. Somehow a huge area was little by little subjugated, the cavalry playing a critical role throughout. In the process, by May 1799 six combats had been won. These were small but dangerous affairs, and Davout won special distinction at Sonagui (January 3, 1799), Samhoud (January 22), and Redecieh (February 12), where he eliminated the Mameluke force of Hassan (or Osman) Bey by adroit maneuver, and yet again at hard-fought Bir-el-Bar on March 31. By May 1 he could write, "The country has entirely submitted to us."[8] His greatest moment in Egypt came, however, in late July. After rejoining the main Army of the Orient (following its return from Syria), he marched with it despite a serious fever to meet the Turkish invaders at Aboukir. Although Murat gained most of the glory at the ensuing battle on July 25 (Davout's cavalry being used in only a covering role), he volunteered to serve under General Menou for the subsequent siege of the Aboukir town and castle. On July 30 he managed to capture every building in the former at great risk. "Good news," wrote Menou to Bonaparte on July 30. "General Davout has conducted himself with the greatest distinction. . . . He has taken the entire village as far as the fort. A large number of Turks have been killed in the houses."[9] This vigorous blow was decisive, and 3 days later the Turks in the castle surrendered.

Neither Desaix nor Davout was selected to accompany the

commander back to France a few weeks later, but stayed on in Egypt under Kléber, with whom they were soon at odds. When Kléber proposed to accept the terms of the Convention of El Arish (which ultimately proved abortive), Davout was the only general at the council of war to oppose him. On March 3, 1800, Desaix and Davout were given leave to return to France, but en route, despite their passports, they were detailed by a royal naval vessel and forced to linger in quarantine at Livorno for a month. At last, on May 6, they disembarked at Toulon. Their return was welcomed by Bonaparte, now First Consul. Desaix was at once summoned to take part in the North Italian campaign, where he was killed at the critical moment of the Battle of Marengo, thus depriving Davout of possibly his most appreciative and influential friend. However, after a period of sick leave at Ravières, he found himself promoted to general of division (July 3), and by August he was commanding the light cavalry in the Army of Italy. In this capacity he fought in several actions, most notably at the passage of the River Mincio at Valeggio on December 26, where he effectively took over from Brune, the overall commander, at the critical moment. His subsequent denunciation of Brune to the First Consul for incapacity earned him a future fellow marshal's lasting hostility. The Peace of Luneville brought hostilities to an end early in 1801.

After his return to France in July, Davout was made inspector general of the cavalry, and in late November was appointed commander of the grenadiers of the Consular Guard. The first consul's wish to associate with Davout more closely had already shown itself when he and Josephine strongly encouraged him to marry Aimée Leclerc earlier the same month. The bride's elder brother was married to Pauline Bonaparte, so a distant family connection with the Bonaparte family was the result. As will be seen below, the match would prove very happy—despite the death in infancy of several children—and lasting. In 1802 they purchased an estate at Savigny-sur-Orge.

The sunshine day now shown on Louis-Nicolas. He used the period of peace to develop his administrative and training skills. As a new war with England developed, from August 1803 he commanded the Camp of Bruges, and aided by Generals Oudinot, Durutte, and Friant, he set about creating what would become III Corps. He paid attention to the career prospects of noncommissioned officers, insisted upon varied and carefully structured training (including amphibious drills and invasion practices), and published a training manual on interarm tactics. He had his men trained to march hard and long and to row to encourage physical fitness, frowned on smoking, encouraged gardening in the camps, and imposed the most exacting discipline (setting an example by sharing in the life of his troops, unwillingly depriving himself on his beloved wife's company at Bruges). He trusted his subordinates and interfered little, but sacked ruthlessly—including Rear-Admiral Magon—when they fell below his standards. Above all, he paid great attention to the health and well-being of the ordinary soldiers, and was at pains to keep them informed of and up to date on developments.

These measures were beginning to take effect when, on May 19, 1804, his name was included as thirteenth on the list of Marshals of the Empire. This surprised many and horrified a few, particularly those senior generals not so honored. Not only was he, at just 34, the youngest on the list, but Davout had never conducted truly independent operations, and was still regarded as an "unknown quantity." His strict attitude toward his profession had not earned him many friends, and indeed had provided him with a fair number of highly placed enemies, including Bernadotte and Brune. His outspokenness had alienated many more, and he was difficult to please, earning respect rather than affection from his subordinates. But Napoleon was aware of his proven and potential qualities. The period of military apprenticeship was over. The greatest days lay close ahead.

Davout the Terrible (1805–1814)

To serve under Marshal Davout's orders was no sinecure. He was in every sense a hard taskmaster, a man endowed with phenomenal powers of concentration and application second only to those of the Emperor, his master. If he expected much of his troops, he demanded far more of his officers and most of all from members of his staff. "I can assure you," his future chief of staff in 1814 once declared, "that to serve under him is a truly serious matter."[10] The sole consolation was that he drove no one harder than himself. Increasingly laden with honors though he was from 1804, he had little time for social occasions or court festivities: The saddle, the campfire, and, in rare time of peace, his home at Savigny or the office table—although he detested "desk work"[11]—were his preferred locations. The justification for this almost inhuman single-mindedness was the proven battle worthiness of his creation, III Corps of the Grand Army (to which he was formally appointed as commander on September 23, 1805), over the next four years of campaigns and battles.

The Napoleonic wars have received much attention and here it is only feasible to mention certain highlights of Davout's contribution. As Napoleon conducted his famous sweep from the Rhine to the Danube in late 1805, the 26,000 men in Friant,

Gudin, and Bissot's divisions made good time on the march, often to their disadvantage. "The speed of our march made it impossible for supplies to keep pace with us," noted Corporal Blaise of the 108th, "and so we were often short of bread in spite of all the efforts of our commanding general, Marshal Davout. . . . Fortunately it was the height of the potato season, and they were plentiful in our area. How many times did we ruin the hopes of the villagers!"[12]

After Mack's surrender at Ulm, the French set about catching his elusive ally, Kutusov. On November 8 Davout drubbed Merveldt's Austrians at Maria Zell, but still the Russians retreated, and the capture of Vienna by Murat on November 12 was no substitute for a decisive action. Leaving Davout around the capital, Napoleon plunged north into Moravia—to the extreme limit of a possible advance—and at last found his adversaries near Olmütz. Feigning weakness, he lured them forward to Austerlitz and the Pratzen Heights. To redress the numerical balance, he summoned Bernadotte from Iglau and Davout from Vienna by forced marches to strengthen the northern and southern extremities of his battle position, respectively. The performance of III Corps in responding to this challenge was superb. Friant's division covered 70 miles of road in 46 hours to reach Raigern late on December 1. Ahead of the infantry moved Davout and the corps cavalry. Next day, Davout's cavalry helped sustain Legrand's outnumbered division of IV Corps around Telnitz during the early morning phase, but Friant's intervention proved decisive. Just as Legrand was giving ground before the vast Russian envelopment, the arrival of the weary and foot-sore men of Heudelet's brigade at the critical moment, followed by a determined drive toward Sokolnitz by Friant's remaining two brigades, blunted Doctorov's ardor, and by 10 A.M. the Russians had been halted. This permitted Napoleon to launch Soult's corps against the Pratzen Heights in the center an hour later. Meanwhile, at the tactical level, Davout had drawn up his scanty resources in three echelons, and despite daunting odds preserved the ability to outmaneuver the enemy. At 2 P.M. III Corps shared in the advance to rout the Russian left wing once and for all. There was inevitably a grim price to be paid: III Corps lost 1,494 casualties, including 224 killed. Proportionately, only Gudin's division (too far distant to fight at Austerlitz) would suffer heavier losses at Auerstädt next year.

The "right of the line" has long been the place of honor in the armies of many countries when engaged in battle. Davout had occupied it in his first great battle under Napoleon's command in 1805, and was to do so again on at least three more occasions before 1810. At Auerstädt in 1806 (probably Davout's masterpiece—see p. 110), III Corps was very much on the extreme right wing—and on its own—during the double battle of October 14. Next year on February 8, at the height of the desperate winter Battle of Eylau in Poland, it was Davout's arrival in the early afternoon that permitted Napoleon to turn an almost-lost battle into at least a draw. Again, Davout came up on the right to launch his three divisions under Friant, Morand, and Gudin (the trio who had fought so doggedly at Auerstädt) against Bennigsen's exposed left flank.[13] But it can be argued that he reached peak form in 1809, back in Austria. Before Napoleon's arrival in the theater, Davout loyally if critically obeyed Berthier's confused orders to hold Ratisbon in an attempt to delay the Archduke Charles's sudden offensive south of the Danube, and then played a vital role in the 3-day battle of Abensburg–Eckmühl (April 20–22) that regained Napoleon the initiative. In recognition of his achievements, above all on April 22, and at the subsequent recapture of Ratisbon, on August 15, 1809, Napoleon could create Davout prince of Eckmühl. But before that distinction was conferred, the Marshal would have served once again on the right wing at the great Battle of Wagram on July 5–6. On this occasion III Corps comprised all of 45,000 men—Friant, Gudin, and Morand being joined by Demont and another German division. Napoleon was somewhat critical of the time it took Davout to capture the village of Markgrafneusiedl on the morning of the second day, but by 1 P.M. the Austrian left flank was being rolled back as intended, and the Archduke Charles eventually conceded the day. In the day's fighting, Davout had a horse killed under him, while at his side the trusted Gudin received four wounds. The local action had been almost lost at one moment before midday when the archduke launched his reserve cavalry against III Corps and broke through its first line of units. But Davout rallied his men and his second line stood firm, and the Austrians recoiled, permitting the marshal to resume his advance yard by hard-won yard.[14]

Between the major campaigns, Napoleon was not slow to use Davout's great administrative skills to the full, and this was possibly one reason why he never shared in the bitter campaigns in Spain—a country that dimmed the reputations of so many of his fellow commanders. After Tilsit he had been appointed governor general of the Grand Duchy of Warsaw, and eventually came to trust the patriot Poniatowski. In late 1808 he was put in charge of the Army of the Rhine to watch the Emperor's back as he led the Grand Army into Spain. After Wagram he was placed over no less than three army corps, the reserve cavalry, and the allied contingents in central Europe, and from January 1810 was commander-in-chief of the Army of Germany. Eventually he established his headquarters in Hamburg, where he became noted for his severity and probity, and soon added the name of Bourienne—the Emperor's former secretary and later governor of the city—to his burgeoning list of enemies by revealing his illegal trading activities with Great Britain. As always, he was implacable in cases of corruption brought to his attention, and his strict enforcement of the Continental System in north Germany did not add to his local popularity. Napoleon's reward, in due course, was to make him governor general of the newly annexed Hanseatic towns and the Duchy of Oldenburg.

As tension rose with Russia during 1811, Napoleon soon gave further proof of his esteem for Davout. On November 24 he warned the Marshal to prepare to move to the Vistula at the head of "an advance guard of 150,000 infantrymen, over 30,000 cavalry and between 4 and 500 pieces of artillery, which will give you an army of almost 200,000 men. I will be in your support with 200,000 more."[15] Although this command was designed to cover only the preliminary preparations for the attack on Russia, it was nevertheless a sizable responsibility. As "saber rattling" continued, this force was fined down to become the First Observation Corps of the Elbe and then, from April 1, I Corps of the Grand Army. Two months later, as the advance into Poland began, this formation comprised five infantry divisions, one of cavalry, and 150 guns—a total of possibly 72,000 men. This was far and away the largest single operational command. Furthermore, I Corps was a model of preparedness. It had rations for 24 days—only to be used after crossing the Niemen. Every soldier's knapsack held the same clothing and equipment. Each regiment was made as self-sufficient as possible, containing "masons, bakers, tailors, shoemakers, gunsmiths; in short, workmen of every class. They carried everything they required with them; his army was like a colony; handmills followed. He [Davout] had anticipated every want; all means of supplying them were ready."[16] Less fortunate was a blazing altercation with Berthier at Marienwerder, which exacerbated an older feud and induced Napoleon to hearken to the Prince of Eckmühl's growing band of foes and critics.

Russia held mixed fortunes for Davout. When Jérôme Bonaparte threw up his command on July 14, Davout temporarily assumed overall charge. Although he had occupied Minsk a week before, even his drive failed to trap the elusive Bagration. Davout mauled the Russians at Mohilev on July 23, but the foe again slipped away eastward. At Smolensk the Marshal led his corps with skill in the battle, but Bagration—now united with Barclay de Tolly—eluded the net. The death of the trusted Gudin on August 19 was a bitter blow. The pursuit toward Borodino saw a major row on July 28 with Murat, whom Davout accused of mishandling the cavalry and exhausting the infantry: the two men almost came to blows. Then Kutusov took command of the Russian armies, and the result was the gory Battle of Borodino. On September 6 the Marshal begged Napoleon to send him on an enveloping move to turn Kutusov's southern flank, but the Emperor would have none of it. "Ah, you are always for turning the enemy. It is too dangerous a manoeuvre."[17] In the struggle of attrition that ensued next day, Davout was bruised in the belly and wounded in the thigh, but captured a key earth work in the Russian center and insisted on remaining in command.

Borodino, although indecisive, gave the French Moscow, and there Davout found time to convalesce. On October 19 the French left the city. The Marshal took no large part at Malojaroslavetz on October 24, but the next day was appointed to command the Grand Army's rear guard as the retreat proper began. This did not prove his most successful responsibility. On November 3, I Corps was cut off near Fiodoroivskoy, and had to be rescued by IV Corps. Napoleon then ordered Ney to take over the rear guard with III Corps. The retreat continued; but by the time Smolensk was reached, I Corps was down to 10,000 effectives. Nevertheless, it fought well at Krasnoe on November 17, but shortly thereafter Davout was accused of abandoning Ney when III Corps in its turn was cut off by the Russians west of Smolensk and came near to total disaster. In fact, the relics of III Corps survived by a near-miracle and rejoined the army, but much criticism was aimed at Davout—the scapegoat—and Napoleon noticeably cooled toward him. By the time the army reached the crisis of the Berezina (November 25–29), Davout's fighting strength was down to an estimated 4,000 men. The river was crossed, and the survivors limped on through terrible weather conditions to Smorgoni. There, on December 5, Napoleon held his last conference in Russia, which Davout attended, to announce his decision to leave the army and head for Paris. The retreat continued under Murat, with whom Davout had another violent altercation at Gumbinnen on December 17. At last, on February 14, the sad remains of I Corps reached Magdeburg on the Elbe. The change of sides by Prussia, which Davout had long prophesied,[18] was a final blow to add to almost a half-million casualties sustained since the previous June.

Eugène Beauharnais, who had assumed command from Murat, started the Campaign of 1813 on the wrong foot by abandoning the Oder River line. Davout abandoned thoughts of a short leave in Paris to busy himself with the defense of the Elbe, defending Dresden from March 9 to 19, finally blowing up its bridge. He was then ordered to recapture Hamburg and hold the

Lower Elbe—a subordinate if no less important role. Worse, his own I Corps was awarded to Vandamme, a difficult if valorous officer with whom everybody clashed, yet somehow they collaborated. On May 30 Hamburg was duly occupied. Meanwhile, far away, two good friends had been killed—Bessières and then Duroc—as Napoleon battled the allies at Lutzen and Bautzen, inducing them to accept an armistice on June 2. It held until August 13. Davout used the respite to reorder the administration of his district and to start creating his last command—XIII Corps—from scratch. The formal appointment was dated July 1. Many of his 38,000 men in the 3d, 40th, and 50th Divisions were raw conscripts or unreliable (like the Danish contingent). Apart from Loison, Pecheux, and Vichery, his senior commanders were of unknown worth, although his chief of staff, General Cesar de la Ville, was first class. The new command was somehow licked into shape, while a three week visit from his wife and daughters brought the Marshal some solace.

The renewal of hostilities found Davout ordered to aid Oudinot and the northern group of corps in an onslaught designed to take Berlin. On August 18, XIII Corps brought off a success at Lauenbourg. Soon the troops were approaching Schwein and Wismar, but Oudinot's main advance then foundered at Gross-Beeren. On the southern front, Napoleon's victory at Dresden was spoiled by the defeat of Kulm, where Vandamme's I Corps figured in the disaster. Then Ney's new advance on Berlin was severely checked at Dennewitz on September 6. Davout decided to bring his corps back to the River Stecknitz, and hastened the preparations for the defense of Hamburg whose siege he now deemed inevitable. Provisions for eight months were collected, the defenses improved, and the city's bank taken over. News of Leipzig in October convinced him that he would be fighting alone.

In June Napoleon had informed Davout that he believed it would require 10 years of work and some 40 millions of francs to make the city truly defensible. Nevertheless, the Emperor ordered, "You are responsible to me for Hamburg."[19] The Marshal was about to surpass his instructions. Step by step he fell back toward the Elbe, and by December 3 the last links with the outside world were severed. Within the lines of Hamburg were 34,000 fit troops of all categories besides a further 8,000 sick. They were faced by some 60,000 foes under Bennigsen, to be reinforced by Bernadotte with many more by mid-January. The bitter winter weather saw no lull in operations. Davout destroyed suburbs to improve lines of fire, expelled 25,000 useless mouths from the city, and repeatedly had the ice broken to preserve his water defenses, but the weather swelled his sick returns alarmingly. Careful observation of enemy moves led to each attack being repulsed in turn, often in Davout's presence. Thus, heavy assaults on February 9, 17, and 28 were defeated with loss. On March 23 a major French sortie from the fort of Haarburg surprised the enemy and gained valuable supplies. Meanwhile, the Campaign of France was reaching the climax of Fontainebleau. Twice, on April 15 and 20, Bennigsen sent in messages announcing Napoleon's abdication. Davout replied in style, "The Emperor, of whose downfall I am unaware, is not in the habit of communicating with his general through the enemy."[20] So the manning of defenses continued until, on May 11, General Gérard arrived as Louis XVIII's representative. The restored Bourbon monarch required Davout to give up the city and hand over to his envoy. Negotiations cautiously continued, until on May 27, 26,000 French troops began to evacuate Hamburg's defenses in three columns, leaving 5,000 sick for later repatriation. On the march homeward Davout received a royal order banning him from Paris and ordering him to Savigny-sur-Orge to await further instructions. There the defender of Hamburg was destined to remain until March 1815, enjoying what he could of family life in the country and defending himself in writing—successfully— against trumped-up Prussian charges of having fired on the Bourbon white flag, of having illegally seized the Bank of Hamburg, and of other arbitrary acts of undue severity during the siege. Marshal the Duke of Auerstädt, Prince of Eckmühl, believed he had held his last command. In point of fact, however, he had not performed his last task for Napoleon—or the French army.

The Last Years—and an Assessment (1815-1823)

Although Napoleon had proved decidedly cool toward him since the retreat from Moscow, Davout was one of only two Marshals (the other was Lefebvre) to greet the Emperor at the Tuileries on his return from exile on March 20, 1815. The two men had not seen one another since Smorgoni. Somewhat unwillingly, Davout found himself made minister of war. He would have far preferred a field command—and the history of the Hundred Days' military phase might have ended very differently had he, rather than Grouchy, commanded the right wing of the Army of the North in mid-June. But it was not to be. Instead he busied himself creating a new army—a task undertaken with all his old efficiency and administrative zeal.

The task proved no easy one. Although the frontier garrisons rallied to Napoleon at his minister's summons, there were Bourbon supporters to be dealt with in the south (Grouchy earning his baton in the process) and above all in the west, where Bordeaux and Vendée (from mid-May) constituted serious challenges, absorbing valuable men. The raising and reorganization of a field army were immense achievements. Despite everything being in short supply, some 280,000 men had been collected by mid-May even though the hated conscription was resorted to only in late April. To release trained troops for the fighting armies, the National Guard and the new *fédérés* took over all garrison duties. Everything did not go smoothly. Although old generals hastened to offer their services, the great majority of the marshals were conspicuous by their absence. There were rows and clashes of responsibility. "If you give orders on your part and I on mine," protested Davout to Soult, chief-of-staff to the Army of the North in place of Berthier, "the result will be the utmost confusion, and I will resign my position as Minister of War."[21] He made his point. On other occasions he lost—as when he unwillingly accepted Napoleon's insistence on the appointment of General Bourmont to a field command (an officer who, indeed, deserted to the allies on June 15). Davout's responsibilities were broad. As defined on April 30, he was "Minister of War, Governor of Paris and Commander-in-Chief of the National Guard, the *levées-en-masse* and the troops of the line which will be in the city."[22] That Napoleon was able to take the offensive in mid-June was due largely to the Prince of Eckmühl's unflagging efforts as minister of war. As has been aptly written, "Davout's able defence of Hamburg and loyalty to the Emperor made him the most logical choice [for command of Paris] had he not been needed on the battlefield."[23]

Then came the catastrophe of Waterloo. On the Emperor's return to Paris on June 21, Davout first advised his master to fight on after proroguing the Senate and the Chamber; but when Napoleon hesitated (permitting Fouché to outmaneuver him), he next day accepted the need for the Emperor to abdicate a second time. On June 23 he agreed to inform Napoleon of the need for him to retire to Malmaison forthwith. "The interview was cold," as he admitted of their last meeting. But Davout considered himself absolved from his former allegiance. He saw his role now as being to seek the best possible terms for France and the army from the victorious allies, although this change of attitude has caused some to accuse him of ingratitude and worse.

Although he regarded the continuation of hostilities as pointless, he wished to negotiate from as strong a position as possible. The defenses of Paris were put in the best order that time allowed; and when the allies refused to grant an armistice, Prussian probes to the north of the capital were repulsed on June 30, and on July 1 Sohr's cavalry brigade was drubbed by Exclmans's as it advanced on Versailles at Rocquencourt. The next day there was heavy infantry fighting at Issy, and Davout was about to launch an attack against the Prussian flank with the 60,000 infantry, 25,000 cavalry, and 500 guns at his disposal on July 3, when he agreed to one last diplomatic effort. On July 4, the allies agreed to an armistice. By its terms, Paris would be occupied, and French troops would withdraw south of the Loire. To officers and men—ready for battle—this seemed a betrayal. Morale reached its nadir, and Davout resigned the Ministry of War to take command of the Army of the Loire, and accompanied its 84,000 troops southward, leaving Generals Gérard, Kellermann, and Haxo as a commission to continue negotiations with the allies and (through Oudinot) with Louis XVIII in Paris. By July 11 the withdrawal was completed; and on July 14, on the insistence of Gouvion St.-Cyr, the new minister of war, Davout unwillingly agreed that the army should make an unconditional submission to the king.[24] All this he accepted as being in the best interests of France.

Compliance turned to fury on July 24, when, despite earlier assurances to the contrary, a royal ordinance listed 19 officers to be tried for treason and a further 38 to be arrested pending decisions. Three days later Davout resigned his command in disgust and gallantly offered himself as a substitute for four proscribed generals for whose actions in Vendée and the south he took full responsibility. On August 1 he handed over the army to Marshal Macdonald and retired to Savigny to wait upon events. There he found it necessary to share his sanctuary with a billeted Prussian detachment.

In December he agreed to give evidence on behalf of Ney in Paris, although that officer rashly rejected advice to opt for a court-martial (which would probably have acquitted him) but insisted on a full trial before his peers. Ney was executed on December 8, and Davout was soon aware that his appearance in Paris had attracted the vengeful attention of the Bourbon court. On December 27 he was exiled to Louviers, stripped of all posts and remunerations, and found himself forced to scrape by on 3½ francs a day. As debts piled up, he filled his time walking, studying ancient history, and educating his son, while in Paris his wife did all in her power to intercede for him with the government. For months her efforts were in vain, but thanks eventually to Macdonald's good offices, on June 21, 1816, Davout was permitted to move under precautionary police surveillance to Savigny. His finances remained critical until late August 1817, when suddenly Louis XVIII restored his military salary, even backdating it to January 7, 1816, and followed this up by restoring his baton as marshal of France. In return, Davout swore allegiance to the Bourbons, and little by little began a return to public life—although he shunned the court, preferring the company of the Napoleonic nobility. Nevertheless, as a peer of France (March 5, 1819), he took his place in the Chamber of Peers, but made few speeches.

By 1821 it was becoming clear that Davout's health was failing. Although he agreed to become mayor of Savigny as late as April 1822, he was rarely seen in Paris following the death of his eldest daughter in August 1821, which caused him great grief. He died of consumption, aged 53 years, on June 1, 1823. Marshal Jourdan spoke a fitting eulogy at the Cemetery of Père Lachaise, and old soldiers mourned the passing of "the Iron Marshal," who, despite his severe demeanor and carelessness of popularity, had always had the interests of his soldiers at heart, second only to those of his family and to his unbending concept of duty.

A paragon of virtue is rarely popular, and it is not difficult to understand why Davout was disliked by so many of his contemporaries. His unexpected appointment to the marshalate in 1804 caused resentment among such less fortunate officers as Marmont and Gouvion St.-Cyr. His proven ability as a commander from Auerstädt onward attracted envy, as well as respect, from the less gifted, particularly as Davout was never slow to criticize shortcomings in others in the most forthright terms. At Konigsberg in 1812, a Dutch general recalled, "He treated Rear-Admiral Baste in an indecent fashion in my presence, and spoke to him with such injurious words that I could not conceive how he dared to thus address a senior French commander, nor he to put up with it."[25] The balding, short-sighted marshal had little time for social graces, however exalted his audience. "Marshal Davout's visit has been got over," wrote the duchess of Saxe–Coburg–Saalfeld with evident relief on March 19, 1809. "It was a weary business trying to enliven him, for it is impossible to be more stolid and uncommunicative than was this thoroughly unpleasant man. His face betrays that he can be very harsh and brutal though not specially spiteful."[26] On certain occasions, however, he was known to apologize publicly for undue brusqueness or downright rudeness.

Davout's unflinching sense of duty made him a tricky colleague to serve with. He was forever seeking out evidence of disloyalty or treason; and if a man indulged in any "irregularities," whether of a political or a venal nature, which came to his attention, he could expect short shrift from the austere and unsmiling Burgundian. To his incorruptibility was allied a total, chilling ruthlessness. "If the Emperor told Maret [Minister of Foreign Affairs] and myself to destroy Paris and everyone in it, Maret would keep the secret, but warn his family. I would not even warn my family for fear the secret might leak out."[27] And yet he was an affectionate husband to his second wife and a good and caring father to his children. If his first marriage proved a disaster and served only to increase his introspective isolation, his union to Aimée Leclerc in 1801 proved a great success. It produced eight children, only four of whom survived infancy; and although the exigencies of Napoleonic service made for long absences, the marshal's thoughts were often directed toward his family and the beloved estate at Savigny-sur-Orge they purchased in 1802. From Holland he sent Aimée tulip bulbs "for your garden," and from Germany in mid-1813 "some Saxon linen; the people here are famous for it, and I think you will like it."[28] Her indifferent health often gave him cause for concern, but the happiness of his personal life proved a major solace and support through tempestuous times.

Part of the drive behind Davout was a strong ambition. He enjoyed his ducal title and princedom even if he found the financial concomitants of high social rank difficult to bear—and several times Napoleon had to take steps to ensure his servant's continued liquidity. He may also have aspired to the crown of a re-created kingdom of Poland—an ambition that led to a cool relationship with Jérôme Bonaparte, King of Westphalia from 1810. His particular foes among the marshals were Bernadotte ("the miserable Ponte-Corvo"), Berthier (from April 1809), and Murat, whom he regarded from mid-1812 as a military incompetent, even "a madman." He was not, however, without friends. In early days he was close to General Marceau and then Desaix. Until his death, he got on well with his brother-in-law, General Leclerc, and was friendly with Oudinot (until 1815), Duroc, and Bessières. He was cordial with General Friant, and particularly appreciative of Gudin. But he was always a hard and unbending disciplinarian, bearing down ruthlessly on his subordinates (earning thereby the positive dislike of Lasalle, Morand, and even Gudin, but never forfeiting their respect).

Concerning his relationship with his rank and file, few, if any, among his fellow marshals showed greater solicitude for their welfare. His formations were famous for being equipped correctly down to the last detail, and pay and rations were usually issued on time. In return, Davout expected—and enforced—total obedience and good discipline. Pillaging was severely repressed, and in 1811 it was noted with wonder that "chickens wandered about among the barracks without fear" in the area of the marshal's Corp of Observation on the Elbe. At the same time, no commander was more inflexible in demanding his full measure of regional "contributions," whether in cash or in kind, for the proper maintenance of his formations. But his consistency was appreciated by Poles and Germans alike, and some termed him "the Just."

Davout was also known to his opponents with excellent reason as "the Terrible." His command skills became outstanding, and although he never had the opportunity to demonstrate his ability to wage a full campaign on his own (Hamburg was an exceptional case), only Massena and possibly Suchet rivaled his intellectual and experiential pre-eminence. Murat, Ney, and Lannes may have had more fire and dash in action and been more adulated by their men, but none had more personal courage—both physical and moral—than Davout, peering at the field of battle through his spectacles. He was the quintessential professional soldier of first-rate quality, military skill, and determination; and if his reputation suffered during the retreat from Moscow, his showings at Auerstädt, Eckmühl, and Hamburg placed him in the foremost category of the marshalate even if "no one ever accused 'the Iron Marshal' of being well-liked, much less loved, by his comrades-in-arms."[29]

This cold, appraising aloofness was one characteristic that recommended Davout to Napoleon, who liked to play his marshals off against one another. From 1800 he also appreciated his unquestioning loyalty, which lasted until the second abdication. It is also possible that from Auerstädt onward there was a tincture of envy and suspicion, and Davout's enemies such as Bourienne, Marmont, and Thiébault made determined efforts to besmirch his repute. But Napoleon's declaration on St. Helena that "Davout was one of the purest glories of France"[30] was—despite its hyperbole—not far from the mark.

The Battle of Auerstädt (October 14, 1806)

"This campaign promises to be even more miraculous than that of Ulm or Marengo,"[31] wrote Davout to Berthier late on October 12, 1806, as the French army wheeled westward towards the River Saale and the Prussian army beyond. Before another two days were out, the marshal would have achieved a remarkable battle success that earned him Napoleon's unstinted praise, the privilege of leading the victorious French through the gates of Berlin, and (in 1808) his ducal title.

At the outset of the advance into Saxony in early October, Davout's III Corps had followed Murat's light cavalry and Bernadotte's I Corps through the Thuringerwald passes toward Schleiz, forming, with the reserve cuirassier formations and in rear of all the Imperial Guard, the central column of the three Napoleon had launched north from the River Main. Brushing aside Tauenzien's forces after a stiff fight near Schleiz on October 9, the column forged ahead toward Gera on the Elster, while to right and left the other columns cleared the forested hills and advanced on to the plains beyond. Napoleon believed that the Prussians would be found in strength south of Leipzig, but by mid-morning on October 12 it had become clear that their main forces were well to the west toward Weimar and Erfurt, and the *bataillon carré* of French corps was ordered to alter its line of march radically. So it was that Davout now found himself forming the extreme right wing of the Grand Army near Naumburg, while on October 13 Napoleon rode fast to join Lannes at Jena, some 15 miles to the southwest, summoning Soult, Ney, Augereau, and Murat to join him, expecting to engage the main enemy army in its vicinity early the next day. By the Emperor's orders received early on October 14, Davout was to press ahead westward—ready to cut off the Prussian line of retreat toward Magdeburg or to envelop the foe's flank and rear near Apolda. Bernadotte was supposed to be near Dornburg, halfway to Jena, but, ran the celebrated postscript to the 10 P.M. orders, "if the Duke of Ponte-Corvo is still with you, you can march together. The Emperor hopes, however, that he will be in the position which he has assigned to him at Dornburg."[32] I Corps was still close by when Davout personally communicated this to Bernadotte early on October 14, but he chose to execute the earlier instruction and march for Dornburg. The decision would almost cost him his command, if not his head. He probably revealed his motive to Bourienne in November when he admitted, "I might have felt piqued at receiving something like orders from Davout."[33] For years feeling had run high between the two men.

October 14 was to see some astonishing events. While Napoleon with eventually 96,000 men was to fight only some 55,000 Prussians at Jena in the belief that he was locked in combat with the main enemy army, the commander of III Corps (just 26,000 strong) would be fighting desperately against 63,000 foes near Auerstädt, as the recalcitrant Bernadotte's 20,000 men took no part in either battle.

As he set out to advance through the Kosen defile toward Auerstädt and Apolda, Davout had scant idea of the enemy's strength or positions. As dawn began to break, dense fog shrouded the scene, and although there had been reports overnight of enemy movements in some strength to his front, all details were lacking. In fact, the Duke of Brunswick had ordered his generals to avoid action on October 14 if possible—fearing that Napoleon might be in person at Naumburg; they were to march west of Hassenhaussen toward the River Unstrutt and distant Magdeburg, covered by Schmettau's cavalry and infantry on the flank. By 7 A.M. Davout and Gudin's 3rd Division were passing through Hassenhaussen when Colonel Burke's path-finding cavalry suddenly encountered Prussian horsemen and some guns near Pöppel. Gudin sensibly formed his 8,000 men into square before proceeding further. Abruptly the fog lifted—revealing the Prussians—and Gudin at once opened fire. His divisional artillery soon silenced the rival battery, and the cavalry withdrew, so Gudin advanced again as far as the Lissbach. There he halted to await the arrival of Friant and Morand with their divisions, which were some considerable distance to the rear. Could they arrive in time?

Fortunately for Gudin, the Prussian second and third divisions became badly entangled with north-bound baggage convoys, so by 8 A.M. only Schmettau's nine battalions, Blücher's 12 squadrons, the further four of the flank guard, and 24 guns were in position. Blücher's first hot-headed charges—made before the Prussian infantry had come up—had no impression on the squares formed by Gautier's and Petit's brigades, and the cavalry fell back to reorder its formations. Both the King of Prussia and the Duke of Brunswick were witnesses to this engagement. In order to bring Wartensleben's division into line with Schmettau's formations, the Prussian high command wasted more time, and this just allowed Friant's 2nd Division (7,000 men) to arrive on Gudin's right at about 9.00 A.M. With the brigades of Generals Lister and Lochet came the corps light cavalry under General Vialannes and the 17 12-pounders of the corps reserve park. Judging that the enemy was going to fall upon his right wing in order to keep open the road to Freiburg, Davout redeployed the greater part of Gudin's division to the north of Hassenhaussen, leaving only the 85th Regiment of the Line to the west and south of the village.

Shortly before 10 A.M. the Prussians advanced to the attack. To the north of the village, Schmettau's men were decimated by the crossfire of the two French divisions, but to the south the 85th Regiment was soon routed by Wartensleben's strong onslaught. His left flank in deadly peril, Davout galloped across with his staff and successfully rallied the fugitives behind Hassenhaussen, and then led up two formations from Gudin's second line (the 12th and 21st Regiments) to reoccupy the village. Some stability was thus restored to the French line, but every available soldier was now in action. Morand's 1st Division was still some way distant, while the Prince of Orange's Prussian division was already joining the battle. Nor was there any sign that Bernadotte might be "marching on the sound of the cannon" to the aid of his embattled colleague. Fortunately the Prussians failed to make instant use of their superiority. Instead of turning the open French flank, they wasted more men, time, and effort in launching four vain frontal assaults on the village. These degenerated into an uncontrolled free fight, and Brunswick was mortally wounded at this juncture and Schmettau also became a casualty. Some time elapsed before Frederick William III took over in person. Meanwhile all of 30 Prussian squadrons were massing opposite the unprotected French left flank, but on so restricted a ground that they were unable to maneuver. Another lull descended over the scene.

Both sides received reinforcements at 11 A.M. Morand's three brigades (10,000 men) were all directed on Davout's order to take post on the left of the French line. Covered by some cavalry and the 13th Light Infantry, the columns deployed into line of battalion columns, the divisional guns on the flanks, in time to succor the hard-pressed 12th Regiment and to check a further Prussian infantry onslaught. Most of the French columns then formed into battalion line to exchange volley fire with the Prussian infantry on the Hill of Hassenhaussen, which forced them back. Then, as the 30 enemy squadrons at last charged home, the seven battalions on the extreme left formed square to receive cavalry, while the remainder of the division manned the walls and hedgerows near Hassenhaussen and poured volleys into the Prussian horse at 30 paces' distance. After several charges the Prussians recoiled, whereupon Morand re-formed his division into line of battalion columns and advanced upon the enemy infantry, driving it back over the Lissbach. This had proved a model operation—demonstrating the flexibility of the French tactical system.

The drive, coordination, and energy displayed by Morand were not matched by the Prussians. As Morand appeared on the scene at 11 A.M., so did the tardy Prince of Orange. But instead of going straight into action on one or the other flank—which might have proved decisive—he divided his force in two, sending half to each respective extremity of the Prussian line. This proved a costly mistake. Nor had Morand yet shot his bolt. Wartensleben's men—followed by those of Orange's brigade on the right—recoiled before him, and the Prussian right wing rapidly melted away. Frederick William III still held 14 battalions, five squadrons, and three batteries of guns in reserve, but—yet mesmerized by the thought that he was facing Napoleon—he refused to commit them to stop the collapse of his army. Thus, his superior numbers availed him nothing.

It was now about midday. Davout—squinting to and fro through his spectacles—was scenting victory. Forming up his three divisions, the Marshal ordered a general advance in a

menacing crescent-shaped formation. Numbers of Prussian infantry became trapped in a gully, and a terrible close-order fight
began to rage. "We were within pistol range," the corps commander later recalled, "and the cannonade tore gaps in the ranks
which immediately closed up. Each move of the 61st Regiment
was indicated on the ground by the brave men they left there."[34]
The numerically far superior Prussian artillery was clearly still
taking a heavy toll, but Morand continued to press ahead until he
reached Rehausen, while his opponents reeled back toward
Auerstädt. On the further flank, meanwhile, Friant was in a hard
contest for the village of Pöppel. Succeeding, he soon had 1,000
prisoners of war in his men's hands.

The King of Prussia could only concede defeat, and ordered
a full-scale retreat. Morand rushed his artillery forward to the
Sonnekuppe hill, from which he was able to pour fire into the
flank and rear of Wartensleben's division. By 12:30 P.M. what was
left of the main Prussian army was streaming away to the west
and north. Kalkreuth placed his rear guard in the path of the victorious French near Gemstädt, trying to earn his fleeing compatriots a respite, but he was routed in his turn as Gudin's men
charged frontally and Morand and Friant worked their way inexorably around his flanks. The pursuit continued until 4:30 P.M.,
when Davout, having occupied the last crest above Eckartsberg,
was forced to call a halt. His infantry was by this time exhausted,
but his three regiments of cavalry continued to harass the foe.
Attempts were made to force them southward, but the task was
beyond the horsemen. Summoning Colonel Falcon, Davout
ordered him to ride for Jena to acquaint the emperor with news
of what had happened at Auerstädt. "Your Marshal must be
seeing double," was Napoleon's first, disbelieving, reaction.

The fray had been very bloody. Some 10,000 Prussians lay
dead, and 3,000 more had been taken, along with 115 cannons.
III Corps had lost 258 officers and 6,794 rank and file, killed or
wounded. Gudin's division had suffered particularly heavily—
losing over 40% of its effective strength in the day's fighting.
Miraculously, some units came off unscathed. "Our company
was lucky," wrote Gunner Gaspard Leva. "We lost not a single
man, thank God, although our Army Corps suffered very
much."[35]

In the *Fifth Bulletin of the Grand Army* published on
October 15, Napoleon paid just tribute to Davout and his men.
"On our right, Marshal Davout's corps performed wonders. Not
only did he contain, but he pushed back, and defeated, for more
than three leagues, the bulk of the enemy's troops, which were to
debouch through Kosen. This marshal displayed distinguished
bravery and firmness of character, the first qualities in a war-

rior."[36] A week later Napoleon further decreed through Berthier, in an order to Prince Murat heading the pursuit toward the Prussian capital, "The Emperor, wishing to give a proof of his satisfaction with the 3rd Army Corps commanded by Marshal Davout, intends and wishes that this corps should enter the first into Berlin."[37] Davout had indeed experienced his finest hour, and even his critics could not fault his showing at Auerstädt.

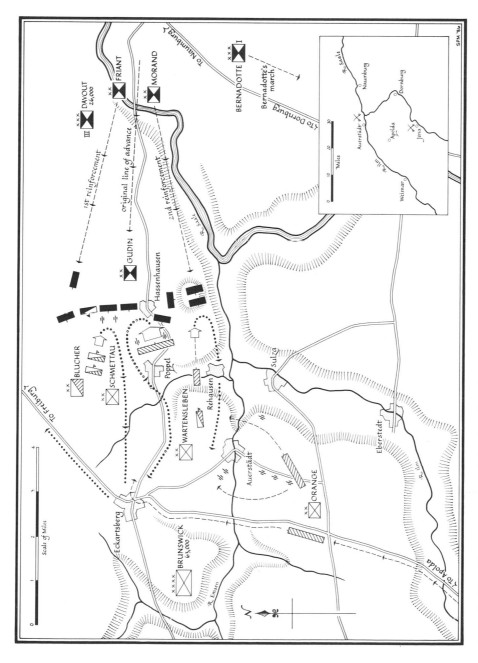

Map 6. The Battle of Auerstädt, October 14, 1806

TEXTUAL REFERENCES

1. F. G. Hourtouille, *Davout le Terrible* (Paris, 1975), p. 7.
2. *Le Moniteur*, No. 233, for August 21, 1790.
3. J. Vigier, *Davout: maréchal d'Empire, duc d'Auerstaedt* (Paris, 1898), Vol. 1, p. 41.
4. D. Reichel, *Davout et l'Art de la Guerre* (Neuchâtel, 1975), pp. 213–16.
5. C. Joly, *Le Maréchal Davout: prince d'Eckmühl* (Auxerre, 1864), p. 15.
6. Vigier, *op. cit.*, p. 64.
7. *Ibid.*, p. 67.
8. C. E. de la Jonquière, *L'Expedition d'Egypte, 1798–1801* (Paris, 1899–1907), Vol. 3, p. 645.
9. *Ibid.*, Vol. 4, p. 444.
10. Cited by P. C. Thiébault, *Mémoires du général baron Thiébault* (Paris, 1895–97), Vol. 5, p. 50.
11. A. L. de Blocqueville, *Le Maréchal Davout, prince d'Eckmühl: correspondance inédites, 1790–1815: Pologne, Russie, Hambourg* (Paris, 1887), Vol. 3, p. 117.
12. E. Fairon and H. Heusse, *Lettres des grognards* (Paris, 1936), p. 98.
13. See D. G. Chandler, *The Campaigns of Napoleon* (New York, 1966), pp. 541–48.
14. *Ibid.*, pp. 727–29.
15. *Correspondance de Napoléon ler*, Vol. 22, letter dated November 24, 1811.
16. P. P. de Ségur, *History of the Expedition to Russia* (London, 1827), Vol. 1, pp. 103–4.
17. *Ibid.*, p. 321.
18. Hourtouille, *op. cit.*, p. 213.
19. Cited in *ibid.*, p. 325.
20. L. N. Davout, *Mémoire de M. le Maréchal Davout au roi* (Paris, 1814), p. 39.
21. *Ibid.;* L. N. Davout, *Correspondance du maréchal Davout, prince d-Eckmühl: ses commandements, son ministère, 1801–15*, ed. by C. de Mazada (Paris, 1885), Vol. 4, p. 554.
22. *Correspondance de Napoléon ler*, Vol. 28, p. 165.
23. J. G. Gallagher, *The Iron Marshal—A Biography of Louis N. Davout* Champaign, Ill., (1976), p. 310.
24. Davout, *Correspondance, op. cit.*, Vol. 4, p. 310.
25. D. van Hogendorp, *Mémoires* (The Hague, 1887), p. 303.
26. Augusta, duchess of Saxe–Coburg–Saalfeld, *In Napoleonic Days*, ed. and trans. by H. R. H. Princess Beatrice (London, 1941), p. 58.
27. Cited by A. G. Macdonnel, *Napoleon and His Marshals* (London, 1934), p. 211.
28. de Blocqueville, *op. cit.*, Vol. 2, p. 46.
29. Gallagher, *op. cit.*, p. 176.
30. Cited by Hourtouille, *op. cit.*, p. 393.
31. L. N. Davout, *Correspondance, op. cit.*, Vol. 1, p. 275.
32. Col. Foucart, *La Campagne de Prusse, 1806* (Paris, 1887), Vol. 1, p. 669.
33. L Bourienne, *Memoirs of Napoleon Bonaparte* (London, 1833), Vol. 2, p. 374.
34. J. Colin, *Les grand batailles d'histoire* (Paris, 1915), p. 110.
35. Fairon and Heusse, *op. cit.*, p. 91.
36. *Correspondance de Napoléon ler*, Vol. 13, p. 357.
37. de Blocqueville, *op. cit.*, Vol. 3, p. 393.

BIBLIOGRAPHICAL NOTE

Apart from John G. Gallagher, *The Iron Marshal—A Biography of Louis N. Davout* (Champaign, Ill., 1976), there has been no comprehensive treatment of the subject in English. Of several in French, F. G.

Hourtouille, *Davout le Terrible* (Paris, 1975), is recent if impressionistic, and Joseph Vigier (Davout's grandson), *Davout, maréchal d'Empire, duc d'Auerstaedt*, 2 vols. (Paris, 1898), is still useful though partisan. The definitive modern work will probably be by Daniel Reichel, the Swiss scholar, whose excellent first volume, *Davout et l'Art de la Guerre* (Neuchâtel, 1975), ends with Auerstädt; Reichel pays valuable attention to the evolution of Davout's military thought and practice, and his second volume is eagerly awaited. Both Gallagher and Reichel contain comprehensive bibliographies.

The basic material for the study of Davout remains the four volumes edited by Charles de Mazada of *Correspondance du maréchal Davout, prince d'Eckmühl: ses commandements, son ministère, 1801–15* (Paris, 1885). The Marshal's prolific letters to his wife were published by his daughter, Adelaide-Louise de Blocqueville, in *Le Maréchal Davout, prince d'Eckmühl: raconté par les siens et par lui-meme*, 4 vols. (Paris, 1879–80), and in *Le Maréchal Davout, prince d'Eckmühl: correspondance inédites, 1790–1815: Pologne, Russie, Hambourg* (Paris, 1887), but once again family partiality is strong.

An introduction to the broader aspects of the period will be found in Gunther Rothenberg's *The Art of War in the Age of Napoleon* (London, 1977), and in David G. Chandler's *The Campaigns of Napoleon* (New York, 1966). Colonel R. W. Phipps, *The Armies of the First French Republic and the Rise of the Marshals of Napoleon I*, 5 vols. (Oxford, 1926–39), is a most useful work for the early career to 1800, but the characterization of Davout is incomplete. The treatment of his conduct in Egypt during 1798–1800 should be supplemented with C. J. Herold, *Bonaparte in Egypt* (New York, 1962). Interesting modern reportrayals of Auerstädt are Reichel (see above) and Col. W. J. Wood, *Leaders and Battles—The Art of Military Leadership* (Novato, 1984), and Davout's conduct at Eckmühl and Wagram in 1809 has been recently treated by Scott Bowden and Charles Tarbox in *Armies on the Danube, 1809* (Arlington, Tex., 1980).

CHRONOLOGY

1764, April 13	—Born in Toul (Merthe et Moselle)
1782	—Leaves home and travels to Italy, then to Paris as artist
1792, September 1	—Enrolls as volunteer in First Battalion of *Chasseurs Republicains* under the name of Laurent Gouvion St.-Cyr
November 1	—Elected captain
1792–1797	—Serves in *l'Armée du Rhin* (later *Rhin-et-Moselle*)
1793, February 1	—Named *capitaine-adjoint* to *adjudant-général* Gay-Vernon
1794, June 10	—Named provisional *général de division* (confirmed September 2)
1795, February 26	—Marries Anne Gouvion
1798, March 6	—Named commander of *l'Armée de Rome* in place of General Massena
1798, July 25	—Removed for political reasons
August 16	—Appointed corps commander of *l'Armée de Mayence*
1799, May 14	—Named commander of right wing of *l'Armée d'Italie*
December 17	—Appointed corps commander of *l'Armée du Rhin*
December 26	—Receives *sabre d'honneur* from Consul Bonaparte
1800, May 9	—Wins Second Battle of Biberach
1801, February 4	—Sent to Spain to oversee Franco–Spanish operations in the war against Portugal, and later as ambassador to Madrid
1803, May 14	—Named *lieutenant-général commandant en chef* of the *Corps d'Observation* of the kingdom of Naples
1804, July 6	—Appointed *colonel-général* of cuirassiers
1805, February 2	—Awarded Grand Eagle of the *Légion d'Honneur*.
December 15	—Named *commandant en chef* of First *Corps de Reserve* (Camp of Boulogne).
1808, May 8	—Named *comte de l'Empire*
September 7	—Named commander of *l'Armée du Catalogne*
1809, November 14	—Suspended from active service for 3 years on possible charges of deserting his command
1812, February 8	—Named commander of Bavarian army corps of *La Grande Armée* (VI corps)
August 18	—Wins First Battle of Polotsk
August 27	—Appinted *Maréchal d'Empire* (twenty-fourth in order of appointment)
1813, November 11	—Prisoner of war after fall of Dresden
1815, July 8–September 25	—Minister of war
1817, August 31	—Named marquis by King Louis XVIII and awarded Grand Cross of the Military Order of St. Louis
1819, September 12–November 18	—Minister of war; successfully implements major reforms in army
1830, March 17	—Dies from heart attack at Hyères

CHAPTER SEVEN

THE OWL

Gouvion St.~Cyr

by

Philipp Coates-Wright

The Formative Years of a Stoic (1764–1799)

The Gouvion family had lived in and around the town of Toul since the sixteenth century. In the seventeenth it had split into two distinct branches. One succeeded in climbing the social ladder to become minor nobility in the 1700s, supplying the French Army with a long line of junior engineer and artillery officers. The other line remained in the traditional family trade of butchers. On February 8, 1763, Jean Baptiste Gouvion, a tanner by trade, aged 21, married by arrangement Anne-Marie Mercier, aged 15, who was of local bourgeois background. On April 13, 1764, their first child, Laurent, was born. Two further sons both died in infancy.[1]

After the birth of a third child in 1767, possibly the most significant event in St.-Cyr's life took place: his mother left home, never to return. She appears to have traveled to Lyons, although this is not certain, where she joined the semi-mystic sect of the Martinistes, an offshoot of freemasonry. St.-Cyr was to retain throughout his life a deep hatred of freemasonry.[2] She took the name of St.-Cyr in place of Gouvion. Deprived of a mother at the age of four, and soon losing both brothers, St.-Cyr's childhood was far from happy. His close friend and biographer of later life, Augustin Cournot, tells how this resulted in a very strong individualism, which even as a child distinguished him from his contemporaries.[3] It left him unsociable and with an air of melancholy. This early depth and power of character and willpower can be judged by his opposition to entering his father's trade. Despite intense pressure from his father, often involving physical violence, St.-Cyr retained an intense disgust for tanning and butchery. He educated himself to a sufficient level to gain admission as a "free listener" to the artillery school of Toul.

Fortunately, here, one of the teachers, the Abbé Siijean, took a personal interest in him. He learned the basics of Greek and Latin and excelled in mathematics and drawing. His cousin, Louis-Jean-Baptiste Gouvion, a career artillery officer, offered to act as his patron if he wished to enter that profession. But rejecting this offer, at 18, feeling suffocated by his provincial home and loathing his father, he left for Italy with dreams of becoming an artist. The drawings that exist from this period display a real talent. Significantly, he traveled via Lyons in an attempt to find his mother, and although he failed, he later adopted the surname of St.-Cyr.

St. Cyr's recent biographer, Christiane d'Ainvil, feels that, although he hardly ever talked or wrote about his mother, this "silent suffering explains the complexity of his character, at one and the same time strong and vulnerable, authoritative and sensitive."[4] It also left him throughout life utterly lacking a gracious self-irony. He was always deeply hurt by even humorous attacks on himself. He could laugh at a joke at another's expense, but never one at his own. Having developed the ability for being totally self-reliant, St.-Cyr found it almost impossible to operate in the normal social sphere. d'Ainvil describes him as a "modern Stoic."

For four years, he wandered up and down Italy, drawing and observing. At aged 22 he traveled to Paris, where he entered the studio of Brenet, a disciple of the neo-classical school of Boucher. He also tried the stage, but the stage manager fired him for being so shy that he stammered his lines.[5]

But the year 1789 radically changed this socially inarticulate and intensely individualistic young artist. He enrolled as a volunteer in the 1st Battalion of *Chasseurs Republicans* on September 1, 1792. Quickly, his comrades recognized his qualities of leadership and administration, and by September 15 he was a sergeant major. At the same time, his almost suicidal insistence on retaining his new name, Gouvion St.-Cyr, at a time when the merest hint of a noble connection could lead to the scaffold, clearly illustrates both the depth of his feeling for his long-absent mother and a high degree of eccentricity. Fortunately, his strongly felt and expressed anti-royalist and church beliefs, plus the knowledge of his true social origins among his comrades, meant he did not suffer. Indeed, by the end of September, he had been elected *sous-lieutenant* and on November 1 captain.

By late November St.-Cyr's battalion had been sent to join the Army of the Rhine, then lying before Mayence under the command of General Custine. St.-Cyr's battalion was soon in action against the Duke of Brunswick's army, and it quickly proved to be highy unruly and full of revolutionary zeal if not discipline. St.-Cyr's experience of company command proved to be very short, a major factor in some of his later failures to appreciate the pressures and needs of troops at company and battalion level. It was St.-Cyr's draftsmanship skills that were to place him on the path to senior command, as one day Custine was riding by and noticed him sketching the position of Hochheim. Snatching the drawing from his hand, he found it an excellent topographical map. After a short series of questions, St.-Cyr was placed on Custine's staff, receiving on February 1, 1793, the rank of *capitaine-adjoint adjudant-général*.[6]

While mapping the area under the direction of General Gay de Vernon, he met Lt.-Colonel adjudant-général Desaix, and a very close and lasting friendship soon developed between two seemingly very different characters. St.-Cyr was always cool, almost glacial in action, careful to conceal his thoughts and socializing little with his staff, while Desaix was always anxious to divulge his ideas and lived cheerily amid his "military family".[7] General Thiébault nicely sums up their characters when he says, "The characters and natures of the two men were such as to give me an aversion for Saint-Cyr proportionate to my intellectual admiration of him, while the more I admired Desaix, the more I felt my attachment and devotion to him increased and strengthened."[8] On some points they did resemble each other: Both were honorable men of clean lives and untainted by corruption, a purity St.-Cyr maintained throughout the temptations of the Empire.[9] St.-Cyr also, at this time, struck up long-lasting friendships with Generals Ney and Davout.

On September 14, 1793, St.-Cyr had his first opportunity to demonstrate his abilities when a sudden Austrian attack at Landremont had to be halted. Serving as assistant to Adjutant-General Montrichand, he was given command of four battalions to defeat the attack. Having been forced by the divisional Representative to accept promotion to lieutenant-colonel adjutant-general (these were the days of the guillotine for failed commanders), he thoroughly defeated the Austrian force. This action demonstrated two of St.-Cyr's major characteristics as a commander: first, his preference for hill and mountain warfare, shown by his skillful dispositions and maneuvers in the hills and valleys around Landremont; and second, his love for spectacular effect, shown here by suddenly opening fire with a concealed gun followed by a decisive cavalry charge.[10] His appreciation of the psychological factors affecting his own and enemy troops was one of his distinguishing abilities. Landremont also illustrated his propensity to eccentricity by his decision to lead the attack with two battalions of raw conscripts armed only with pikes, rather than one of his other battalions of National Guards armed with muskets but composed almost entirely of married men.[11]

Between 1793 and 1797, St.-Cyr remained with the Army of the Rhine (later the Rhine and Moselle), fighting under Generals Kléber, Hoche, Jourdan, Pichegru, and finally Moreau. On June 5, 1794, he was again reluctantly forced by a Representative to become a provisional general of brigade and on June 10 a provisional general of division (confirmed by the Committee of Public Safety on September 2). He was able to take pleasure in these appointments only after the fall of the Committee and the cessation of guillotining defeated generals.

St.-Cyr had less than happy relations with his commanders. His general coolness and habit of speaking with a tone of total authority at briefings had the effect of irritating his seniors; and because of this, throughout his career, St.-Cyr's advice and suggestions were often rejected. The bitter attitude on which contemporaries so often commented was fostered when his projections too often proved correct.

The First Battle of Biberach on October 2, 1796, was St.-Cyr's greatest achievement of this period. The conduct of this battle was almost totally arranged between St.-Cyr and Desaix (proving he could operate as part of a team at times), and saw St.-Cyr advance at the height of the battle in characteristically dramatic style and near-Napoleonic scale, throwing forward 24 guns and advancing under cover of their fire.

The Army of the Rhine helped shape St.-Cyr's personality. Like it, he prided himself on his reserve and self-restraint, disdaining any involvement in politics and concerning himself with serving France and fighting her enemies. It also displayed St.-Cyr's weaknesses, most of which were typical of the staff officer he basically was. While a superb administrator of organization and disposition, he saw his troops as tools, and expected them to be ready for his use, not concerning himself with winning their affection.[12] But it must also be said that he took the greatest care to avoid useless bloodshed, always carefully calculating each move, preparing the movement of his troops down to the last detail, taking into consideration the possible consequences of a maneuver against the possible loss of life. Although prudent, no commentator ever accused him of lacking audacity; his greatest victories, Biberach and Polotsk, were won by daring battle tactics, and it must be remembered that he never lost a battle. The most essential element of his skill was based on psychology. He observed the enemy's bearing so as to know the best way to upset it; and observed his own troops so as to calculate the effort they were capable of, as at Polotsk in 1812, where he began the battle in the late afternoon, knowing his troops were capable of only 4–5 hours of exertion.[13] Contemporaries agree that while his troops never loved him, they trusted and respected him.

Between 1793 and 1797 St.-Cyr had only one short period of leave—in early 1795, when he returned to Toul to marry. He again stands out from many of his contemporaries in that his marriage was not arranged but one of the heart. On February 26 he married Anne Gouvion, his first cousin, aged 19 years. It was a strong match, and throughout their 36 years of marriage not the slightest hint of scandal ever touched the couple. It is interesting that she is described as an extrovert and being full of energy (similar to Desaix's character), unlike her cool and introverted husband. What little is known of their domestic life shows St.-Cyr to have had a very warm and gentle side to his character, and possibly indicates what would have been had he not been deprived of his mother's affection and support, and subjected to the violence and abuses of his father.

After the Peace of Campo Formio, St.-Cyr was dispatched to Italy on March 6, 1798 to take command of the Army of Rome from General Massena. For various reasons the troops in Rome were on the verge of mutiny and the population near revolt. St.-Cyr displayed a considerable degree of psychological astuteness and skill in oratory (he had come a long way since his stage days in Paris) and succeeded in restoring order to the army and preventing any civil disorder, all without spilling any blood.[14] He then spent much time dispatching flying columns into the countryside to counter serious guerrilla activity.

Sadly for St.-Cyr, his love of Italy (from his days as an artist), its people, and traditions plus his own incorruptibility were his undoing. Learning that the French civil consuls had seized a jeweled, gold monstrance from Prince Doria, he immediately ordered it to be returned. Sadly, the Prince, being a remarkably feeble character, handed it back as a "gift," and the consuls used their power to have St.-Cyr recalled to Paris and replaced by General Macdonald.[15] St.-Cyr's stoic code of honor earned the respect of his troops, but none from above.

He was then ordered to the Army of Mayence on August 16, 1798, to command its left wing under the overall command of Jourdan. As before, relations were strained and his counsels rejected, and before long, owing to Jourdan's poor dispositions, his army was soon thrown back to the Rhine. Disillusioned and exhausted, St.-Cyr obtained permission to take leave on April 6, 1799, when he learned that Massena, whom he despised for his greed, was to replace Jourdan.

On June 24, 1799, he was ordered back to Italy to serve under Moreau. At the Battle of Novi on October 16, it was St.-Cyr's superb tactical skill that enabled the right wing under his command to retire in good order and save the remainder of the army from total disaster. He now took command of the troops in Liguria and Genoa, and the autumn of 1799 saw St.-Cyr conduct a notable campaign against considerably superior Austrian forces.

On November 24 the forces in Italy received a proclamation demanding a solemn oath of allegiance to Bonaparte and the Consulate. St.-Cyr obtained the oath from his troops, but, true to his principles, displayed such a lack of enthusiasm due to his disgust at being forced to become involved in a political act that Bonaparte from the outset did not trust him. Yet despite this, St.-Cyr's undeniable brilliance in the field earned him a saber of honor and a proclamation praising his abilities from Bonaparte.

On December 17, 1799, St.-Cyr was ordered back to the Army of the Rhine now under Moreau. Sadly, as ever, St.-Cyr's attitude soon drew Moreau's displeasure, and it is here that the legend of St.-Cyr as a "bad bed-fellow" began. Despite a total lack of evidence, Moreau accused St.-Cyr in his reports of failing to support his brother generals, and Bonaparte was later to use these accusations when he and St.-Cyr came into conflict. Yet, at this time, both Ney and General Baraguey d'Hilliers wrote numerous letters to St.-Cyr thanking him for his support in the field.[16] On May 9, 1800, St.-Cyr won a dazzling victory in the Second Battle of Biberach. But on June 5, unable to bear the strain of serving under Moreau any longer, he obtained permission to return to France on leave.

On his return he was deeply upset to learn of Desaix's death at Marengo, losing probably the most intimate friend he ever had. Bonaparte now made him a councillor of state, and from September 1800 to February 1801 he displayed great ability in the legislature.

A Stoic in the Age of Glory (1800–1814)

On February 4, 1801, St.-Cyr was dispatched to Madrid as ambassador to oversee operations against Portugal. His temperament was totally unsuited to the corrupt and deceitful atmosphere of the Spanish court. Despite successfully concluding a treaty with Portugal to break off relations with England (the aim of the war), and negotiating the cession of Louisiana to France, St.-Cyr was happy to be recalled in May 1803. While in Spain he received Lieutenant Ségur on a mission from Napoleon, who has left an interesting description of St.-Cyr: "This general's appearance was in harmony with his already famous military reknown: tall, and manly, with a serious and noble countenance, and manner of a calm and imposing simplicity."[17]

Unfortunately for St.-Cyr, his next posting brought him no respite, for in May 1803 he was ordered to Naples, where he remained for three years, trying to cope with the intrigues of the Neapolitan court. In addition, he was for a time under the authority of General Murat, and the clash of personalities can be imagined. St.-Cyr's tribulations were increased when, in March 1804, he was expected to sign the proclamation congratulating Napoleon on the declaration of the Empire. He refused to sanction a purely political act; he believed that he as a soldier had no part in political endorsement and did not sign. Napoleon's revenge was soon manifest, when on May 19, 1804, the list of 18 marshals was published, minus St.-Cyr, but including such names as Soult,

Bessières, and Lannes, none of whom had ever held independent commands. As partial compensation he received the position of colonel-general of the cuirassiers and the Grand Eagle of the Legion of Honor. St.-Cyr's stoical silence now masked a deep sense of bitterness. He did, though, swear allegiance to Napoleon and sent a proclamation of congratulation on behalf of the Army of Naples upon Napoleon's coronation, albeit with an obvious lack of enthusiasm.

Yet, despite all his tribulations, St.-Cyr did enjoy some aspects of his years in Naples. His wife was able to be with him, and the many artists, poets, and philosophers who preferred to live in the pleasant southern Italian climate provided him with stimulating and congenial society. As Paul Louis Corne observed: "He is a man of merit, a learned man, perhaps the most learned of men in the gentle art of massacre, a pleasant man in private life, a great friend of mine."[18]

With the approach of war in late 1805, St.-Cyr, having obtained a signed treaty from the Neopolitan court promising neutrality, marched north to support Massena. St.-Cyr's army formed the right wing of Massena's forces, and he proceeded to blockade Venice. The Prince of Rohan led an attempt to raise the blockade, but St.-Cyr defeated him at Castelfranco on November 23 and captured most of his force. St.-Cyr continued to blockade Venice until the end of the war. He then received new orders to prepare to march on Naples where the court had openly cooperated with the British in breach of the treaty. But St.-Cyr found he was to be placed under Massena's direct command; furious at this demotion, he handed over his command to General Perignon, sent a letter of resignation to Massena and Berthier (minister of war), and left immediately for Paris. As St.-Cyr arrived there on January 5, 1806, Napoleon instantly ordered him back to Naples on pain of facing a firing squad for desertion!

Utterly demoralized, St.-Cyr returned to find Joseph Bonaparte on the throne of Naples. After he made very obvious his total distaste for remaining in Naples, Joseph gave him leave to return to France in August. On December 15 he was given command of the Camp de Boulogne and the 1st Reserve Corps. He spent the next 20 months doing little more than maintaining the port facilities and fortifications. He enjoyed this semi-idleness, being able to spend more time with his wife, and executed many drawings of the countryside. He also purchased the beautiful Chateau de Reverseaux, which became his retreat from the strains of active service, and soon developed a love of gardening and farming. In 1808 Napoleon did grant St.-Cyr an endowment of 30,211 francs per annum, but this was paltry when compared, for instance, with the 1 million given to Ney and Davout. Napoleon did not totally deny St.-Cyr recognition, however, for on May 8, 1808, he named him a count of the Empire.

For St.-Cyr, this period of rest ended on August 17, 1808, when he was ordered to Spain to command the Army Corps of Catalonia. This was his most mixed command in regard to success and failure. He succeeded in winning a series of victories over a number of Spanish armies despite having to hold several large cities and maintain the Siege of Gerona. Yet, despite the dramatic victories of Cordadeu, Molinos de Rey, and Valls, he failed to take Gerona. It should be noted that St.-Cyr, appreciating the difficulty of foraging in this barren locality, took great care to ensure his troops were well supplied.[19] (St.-Cyr appears to have operated according to a general rule of thumb that if the countryside was fruitful he left it to his colonels to procure food; while if it was barren, as in Spain, or the troops were poor foragers, for instance, the Bavarians in Russia during 1812,[20] he made great personal efforts to provide supplies.)

St.-Cyr now reached the nadir of his fortunes under the Empire owing to his method of quitting Spain. Napoleon, displeased with St.-Cyr's slow progress before Gerona, announced in May 1809 that he was to be replaced by Marshal Augereau. St.-Cyr believed throughout his life that Napoleon had purposely denied him sufficient troops and equipment to succeed in order to disgrace him.[21] But Augereau, not wishing to hurry to this less than congenial assignment, remained in Perpignan, claiming he was suffering from gout, leaving St.-Cyr responsible for operations until success was near, when he could take over and claim the credit. St.-Cyr could do little until October, when, on the pretext of needing to speak directly about operations to Minister of War Clarke, then at Perpignan, he arrived to find Augereau healthy. He promptly produced a medical certificate from the medical inspector-general of Catalonia as evidence of his own ill health,[22] resigned his command to Augereau, congratulating him on his convalescence, and, without waiting for an answer, left. He was promptly placed under arrest, though soon released to retire to Reverseaux for 18 months while Napoleon asked three commissions to investigate St.-Cyr for possible desertion. Fortunately it was concluded that he was genuinely ill, although he was censured for his method of transferring command. Napoleon signaled the return of St.-Cyr to favor by recalling him to the Council of State on April 14, 1811. But Napoleon soon required his skills for Russia, and on February 8, 1812, St.-Cyr received command of the Bavarian Army Corps, numbered VI in the Grand Army. The year 1812 was to see the rapprochement of Napoleon and St.-Cyr. After attending a long conference with Napoleon on July 22, St.-Cyr appears to have come away totally won over by his magic and enthralled by his personality.[23] Unlike those of other years, St.-Cyr's memoirs for 1812–1813 contain much praise for Napoleon. St.-Cyr was ordered to Polotsk to support II Corps under Marshal Oudinot, where he arrived on August 15. Oudinot barely concealed his dislike for St.-Cyr, while St.-Cyr found himself under an officer he had commanded during the Republic. Many others, though, were glad of St.-Cyr's presence; even Colonel Marbot, a less than favorable witness, comments, "Saint-Cyr was, indeed, one of the most able soldiers in Europe. . . . I never knew anyone handle troops in battle better than Saint-Cyr."[24] When Wittgenstein launched his attack on August 16, Oudinot found himself in serious difficulties, yet St.-Cyr simply followed him around, answering all requests for advice with, "My Lord Marshal";[25] that is, "Napoleon made you the marshal—who am I, a mere general, to advise you?" While no commentator ever accused St.-Cyr of being self-seeking, he had the natural desire of a clever individual to be placed where his talents might have full use. Most accounts of his least pleasing characteristics—for instance, his jealous nature and penchant for solitude—come from the period of the Empire, when, however lacking in personal ambition, he had become soured by seeing himself passed over by men far inferior in talent and experience.

But fate now took a hand, and Oudinot was sufficiently wounded on the evening of the sixteenth, to hand over to St.-Cyr a battle he believed lost. St.-Cyr was also wounded, but not one to flinch from such a challenge. He went on to win a stunning victory (see p. 137).

On August 27 St.-Cyr finally received his long-overdue baton. True to his character, he devoted one sentence to the news in a long letter he wrote to his wife that day.[26]

The next two months were spent fortifying Polotsk, especially as sickness had by mid-October reduced his force to 18,000 men. On October 18 Wittgenstein attacked with 50,000 men, but was defeated and thrown back, despite St.-Cyr being so seriously wounded that he was reduced to being carried around on a stretcher. Unable to maintain his position, he ordered a retreat. On October 30, suffering severe pain from a wound in his left foot, he gladly handed over command to the recovered Oudinot and retired to Minsk to recuperate. On December 29 he was sufficiently recovered to resume command of the Bavarian VI Corps, which had recently received 10,000 reinforcements. On January 16, 1813, he joined Prince Eugène, helping to cover the retreat, falling back on Berlin with VI and XI Corps. But on March 10 he fell dangerously ill with typhus and returned to France.

Fully recuperated, St.-Cyr assumed command of XIV Corps in Germany on August 4. The autumn Campaign of 1813 was St.-

Cyr's honeymoon period with Napoleon. In letters of the time and later memoirs, he enthuses about Napoleon's genius.[27] Napoleon on his side admitted St.-Cyr's skills: "He is the best man among us in the line of defense, though I am superior to him in attack."[28] St.-Cyr's defensive ability was soon put to the grueling test of Dresden, where he held out with a garrison of 20,000 against an allied army of 225,000, throughout August 25 and 26. St.-Cyr had, on August 21, predicted the allied thrust at Dresden if Napoleon advanced on Zittau, but Napoleon disagreed. On August 23, as allied columns threatened Dresden, Napoleon wrote to the marshal admitting his foresight.[29] Allied hesitations and failures to launch an all-out assault enabled Napoleon to arrive with 100,000 troops and win his last major victory. Napoleon's confidence in St.-Cyr's ability to hold Dresden had been fully rewarded. Dresden is the only battle St.-Cyr fought under Napoleon's command, and they each appreciated the other's talents. Throughout September St.-Cyr attended many briefings by Napoleon, but St.-Cyr's advice for a dramatic offensive with a united French army was rejected by Napoleon in preference for a conservative strategy of drawing the allies into a decisive engagement.

St.-Cyr had a most remarkable series of interviews with Napoleon on October 6. In the afternoon Napoleon discussed with St.-Cyr his intention to retire to Leipsig to trigger the decisive battle, and fully agreed with him that it would be military madness to leave a garrison in Dresden when it was vital to concentrate all troops. But 12 hours later St.-Cyr was informed he was to hold Dresden with two army corps. Napoleon gave no reason for this about-face but St.-Cyr made it clear he believed it folly.[30] After Leipsig, Napoleon's order to abandon Dresden arrived too late to prevent St.-Cyr from being blockaded. After several attempts to escape down the right bank of the Elbe, he was forced to sign a capitulation on November 11 owing to imminent starvation. Sadly, the allies refused to honor the agreed-on terms, which would have allowed St.-Cyr's forces to return to France. Faced with a hollow offer to return to Dresden, which meant that he would face starvation, St.-Cyr had to accept total surrender. He spent the remainder of the war as a prisoner at Carlsbad.

A Stoic in the Age of Pragmatism (1814–1830)

Returning to France in June 1814, St.-Cyr found a very different world. He retired to Reverseaux to rest and reflect, while rejecting Louis XVIII's attempts to win him over by making him a Knight of St. Louis and a peer of France. He spent the entire nine months of the First Restoration at Reverseaux. He limited himself to a few letters of advice to Louis on how to win the loyalty of the army: "If you want the army to be yours, leave it its colonels."[31] As usual, his intelligent advice was rejected. On March 7, 1815, believing Louis to be the legitimate head of state, he felt he had no option but to obey orders to proceed to Lyons to organize resistance to Napoleon. He never reached Lyons, for on March 11 he met the Count of Artois fleeing back to Paris after the city had opened its gates to Napoleon. Arriving in Paris on March 14, he found utter chaos, but he reluctantly complied with his new orders to travel to Orleans to organize a new royalist army. But the troops in Orleans soon replaced their white cockades with the tricolors, and learning of Louis's flight to Ghent, St.-Cyr promptly returned to Reverseaux in disgust. Napoleon did not force St.-Cyr to swear an oath of allegiance to him, and allowed him to remain at Reverseaux in peace, where he likewise rejected Louis's offers of service.

The Waterloo episode over, June 22 found St.-Cyr in Paris as adviser to the provisional government. As France was now being invaded, he felt it his duty to assist in her defense. On July 1, during the critical meeting of the provisional government and most of the marshalate to decide whether to defend Paris, St.-Cyr strongly advised fighting. But more cautious voices prevailed, and his plea for national independence and a republic was rejected in favor of a second restoration of the monarchy and allied occupation.[32]

The king re-entered Paris on July 7 among the serried ranks of allied troops, and a totally new career in politics began for St.-Cyr. On Marshal Macdonald's recommendation,[33] Louis offered St.-Cyr the portfolio of minister of war. St.-Cyr accepted, fired with the deep wish to save some form of French army. His tenure as war minister from July 8 to September 25 proved to be unhappy and ultimately tragic. He was unable to prevent the dissolution of the old army, and his very sound plan to re-form a new army of departmental legions based on the early revolutionary composite legions of infantry, cavalry, and artillery was critically weakened by the Ultras. They rejected any form of conscription and ensured the appointment of incompetent royalists. The result was an utterly demoralized force of volunteers and old soldiers numbering less than 80,000 and purged of most able veteran officers and noncommissioned officers. The Ultras also succeeded, despite St.-Cyr's strenuous opposition, in reforming the Royal Guard and replacing blue uniforms with white.

It was the lists of proscribed persons that proved truly tragic for St.-Cyr. When the original list of over 1,000 names was presented in council, he and others succeeded in reducing it and dividing it into two categories. The first contained several hundred names, who faced minor penalties. The second contained 18 names, who were liable to stand trial for treason. It included his old friend, Ney. St.-Cyr tried to assemble a court-martial containing four of Ney's fellow marshals—Augereau, Massena, Mortier, and Moncey—and three other generals, in the hope that they would at worst recommend his dismissal and imprisonment. But Moncey refused even to sit on it, and was disgraced by the king. Five of the remainder declared themselves unable to try the case because of its political nature. At this point St.-Cyr was forced from office by the Ultras and could do no more for Ney. As a peer St.-Cyr attended Ney's trial before the Upper Chamber on charges of treason on November 21. St.-Cyr voted for deportation in the vote that condemned Ney to death, and then addressed a petition for clemency to the king, all in vain. Upset and depressed, he retired to Reverseaux.

St.-Cyr next spent two years concentrating on his family, for on December 30, 1815, his wife gave birth to a son. Many contemporaries noticed at this point a distinct softening in St.-Cyr's temperament. Becoming a father at 51 finally brought to the surface a concealed tenderness, until then reserved for his wife and close friends.[34]

The political history of the period was one of swings between the Ultras and constitutional liberals, with whom St.-Cyr sat in the House of Peers, his speeches being, by the then-contemporary standards, of a "radical left, democratic flavour."[35] On June 23, 1817, with a swing against the Ultras, the king asked St.-Cyr to become minister of marine in the moderate Richelieu government. He accepted, knowing the real aim was to prepare the ground for his becoming minister of war again. Owing to the chronic state of the army, the allies refused to withdraw their army of occupation, fearing further revolution, and only St.-Cyr was judged to have the ability to rebuild an effective new army. With a promise of the king's backing and supported by the entire Richelieu government, St.-Cyr became minister of war on September 12, 1817. To help to prove his sincerity, the king had made St.-Cyr a marquis on August 31, 1817, and awarded him the Grand Cross of St. Louis.

Despite intense opposition from the Ultras, St.-Cyr was now able effectively to implement many of his ideas for a new army that had been thwarted in 1815. His reforms, embodied largely in the Law on Recruitment, stand as his greatest achievement. He believed that the army should be drawn from the nation and should reflect the values, aspirations, and social makeup of French society. A supporter, Guizot, said of it, "An army in his [St-Cyr's] estimate was a small nation, springing from a large one, strongly organized. . . .having defined rights and duties and well trained. . . . Every class in the state was required to assist in the formation of this army."[36] This was a radical departure from the Ultras' ideal of an old eighteenth-century-style volunteer army, separate from the nation. St.-Cyr based his "law" on revolutionary principles and imperial experience.

A limited form of conscription was reintroduced, called *l'appel.* While all adult males (excluding specified skilled artisans) were eligible to draw lots, the purchase of replacements was still permitted to appease the bourgeoisie. Promotion regulations were fixed to prevent favoritism. Non-commissioned officers had to be proficient in reading, writing, and mathematics. To become an officer, one had to have served at least two years as a *sous-officier* or be a graduate of a military school. An officer had to serve a minimum of four years in each grade before promotion to the next grade, up to the rank of lieutenant colonel. The king retained the power of appointment to colonel and above. Interestingly, St.-Cyr would have preferred the revolutionary principle of one-third of all officers being elected, but the king totally rejected the idea.[37] St.-Cyr also established a general staff corps, a staff training school, and an army quartermaster corps.[38]

Finally, a reserve was established, where, after completion of six years of service in the regular army, a veteran was obliged to serve six years in the reserve. St.-Cyr's aim was to provide the standing army of 240,000 with a pool of veterans in time of invasion, for, as he stated to the Chamber of Deputies, "large standing armies, however they are made up, drive nations into wars of aggression. . . .But we have done all in our power to limit the danger by making our regular army as small as possible."[39] As Douglas Porch said, "St-Cyr's reserve embodied the Revolutionary ideal of the citizen soldier, living as a civilian, but ready to defend the nation in time of danger."[40]

St.-Cyr's reforms transfigured the army, and were the foundation for the French army until the late 1860s. But in 1824 the Ultras succeeded in abolishing the reserve as suspect because of its complement of Napoleonic veterans and its negation of the principle of a small, professional royal army. St.-Cyr's concept of a citizen army had to wait until after the catastrophes of 1870–1871, a calamity that might well have been averted if his original ideas had been retained.

Poor health and disgust at the success of the Ultra's in limiting the franchise in November 1819 caused St.-Cyr to resign. He retired permanently to concentrate on his family, farming, and writing his memoirs. By 1829 his health had deteriorated to such an extent he took up residence at Hyères, a renowned spa. On March 12, 1830, he suffered a severe heart attack. After remaining in a near-coma for five days, St.-Cyr died on March 17. His life-long agnosticism was respected; he did not receive the last sacrament, despite his wife's Catholicism, and his tomb bore no cross or religious motif.[41]

The Battle of Polotsk (August 18, 1812)

On the evening of August 16, 1812, the position of St.-Cyr's forces was critical, with many troops scattered among the gardens outside the town walls and others with their backs to the river. But as Marbot says, "Saint-Cyr seized the reins of command with a firm and capable hand, and in a few hours the aspect of things changed entirely—so great is the influence of an able man who knows how to inspire confidence."[42]

St.-Cyr faced Wittgenstein's 30,000 men with 24,000, and he therefore decided on surprise as being his best hope for victory. St.-Cyr judged Wittgenstein would expect him to retreat, so retreat he did, moving most of his troops to the left bank of the Dwina and evacuating the army's baggage and wounded on August 17. During the night he constructed a new bridge and moved the army back to the right bank, concealing the troops among the natural folds in the land around Polotsk. The Russians, still licking their wounds from August 16 and expecting reinforcements three days later, rested in their camp. At 3 P.M. on August 18, calculating that his troops were capable of four to five hours of combat, St.-Cyr initiated the attack, achieving total surprise, with the Russians falling back some distance before they regained their composure. General Wrede's Bavarian division bravely carried the right of the village of Spas, while General Deroy's Bavarian division took Spas itself, supported by a massed battery of 30 guns. Generals Legrand and Verdier's French divisions carried the center between Spas and Polotsk, while General Merle's French division covered the front of Polotsk and the cavalry was deployed on the plain between Merle and the Dwina. Wittgenstein now tried desperately to reverse the course of the battle by throwing in his reserves led by several squadrons of the *Chevalier Garde*, between Merle and General Doumerc's cavalry division. The impetus of the attack carried it into the rear of these formations, where St.-Cyr's carriage (he could not mount a horse owing to his wound of August 16) was overturned and only his plain blue surtout saved him from recognition as Russian and French horsemen swarmed around. Coolly making his way to the Swiss brigade held in reserve in the cemetary of Polotsk, he launched the 3rd Swiss Regiment in a counterattack, supported by the charge of the 4th

Cuirassiers led by General Berckheim. The Russian attack collapsed, and the entire Russian army fell back in utter confusion. The arrival of night and the total exhaustion of St.-Cyr's troops prevented any pursuit. Russian losses were 3,000 killed and wounded, 1,500 prisoners, and 20 guns. St.-Cyr's army sustained less than 1,000 casualties.

It is finally necessary to explode a few myths handed down by Marbot. First, St.-Cyr certainly did spend the whole evening of August 18 writing a long report to Napoleon regarding the battle, listing many officers and men for decorations and promotions, and there is not a shred of evidence that St.-Cyr—as Marbot claims—ever played a musical instrument, certainly not the violin and not that evening.[43] Second, as regards neglecting his men in the two months after Polotsk, both Generals Berthezen and Comeau relate how St.-Cyr visited the troops most days, and carefully ensured the measured distribution of available supplies.[44]

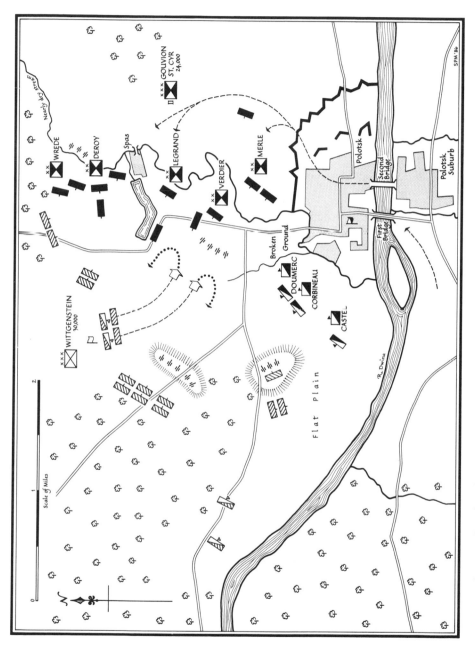

Map 7. The Battle of Polotsk, August 18, 1812

TEXTUAL REFERENCES

1. C. d'Ainval, *Gouvion Saint-Cyr* (Copernic, 1981), p. 29.
2. *Ibid.*, p. 31.
3. *Ibid.*, p. 29.
4. *Ibid.*, p. 31.
5. *Ibid.*, p. 34.
6. R. W. Phipps, *The Armies of the First French Republic and the Rise of the Marshals of Napoleon I* (Oxford, 1929), Vol. 2, p. 41.
7. *Ibid.*, p. 68.
8. D. A. P. F. C. H. Thiébault, *The Memoirs of Baron Thiébault*, English ed., Trans. by A. J. Butler (Smith, Elder & Co., London, 1896), Vol. 1, p. 364.
9. Phipps, *op. cit.*, p. 69.
10. *Ibid.*, pp. 60–61.
11. *Ibid.*, pp. 61–62.
12. *Ibid.*, pp. 445–46.
13. d'Ainval, *op. cit.*, pp. 286–87.
14. Thiébault, *op. cit.*, p. 363.
15. *Ibid.*, pp. 382–83.
16. d'Ainval, *op. cit.*, p. 64.
17. P. de Ségur, *An Aide-de-Camp of Napoleon*, English ed., trans. by H. A. Patchett-Martin (Hutchinson, London, 1896), p. 70.
18. R. P. Dunn-Pattison, *Napoleon's Marshals* (E. P. Publishing, Wakefield, 1977), p. 238.
19. C. Oman, *A History of the Peninsular War* (A.M.S., New York 1980), Vol. 2, pp. 74–75.
20. J. B. A. M. Marbot, *The Memoirs of Baron de Marbot*, English ed., trans. by A. J. Butler (Longmans, London, 1894), p. 560.
21. Oman, *op. cit.*, Vol. 3, p. 17.
22. d'Ainval, *op. cit.*, p. 101.
23. *Ibid.*, p. 110.
24. Marbot, *op. cit.*, p. 530.
25. *Ibid.*, p. 532.
26. d'Ainval, *op. cit.*, p. 116.
27. *Ibid.*, p. 125.
28. *Ibid.*, p. 286, quoted from G. de Vernon, *Vie du Maréchal Gouvion Saint-Cyr* (Paris, 1856), p. 380.
29. F. L. Petre, *Napoleon's Last Campaign in Germany–1813* (new edition, Arms and Armour Press, London, 1974), pp. 188–89.
30. *Ibid.*, pp. 302–5.
31. d'Ainval, *op. cit.*, p. 146.
32. *Ibid.*, pp. 157–58.
33. S. J. J. A. Macdonald, *Recollections of Marshal Maconald*, English ed., trans. by S. L. Simeon (Richard Bentley & Son, London, 1893), pp. 436–37.
34. d'Ainval, *op. cit.*, pp. 180–81.
35. G. de Berthier de Sauvigny, *The Bourbon Restoration*, English ed., trans. by L. M. Case (Philadelphia, 1966), p. 144.
36. D. Porch, *Army and Revolution, France 1815–1846* (Routledge, London, 1974), p. 2, quoting from F. P. G. Guizot, *Memoirs of My Time*, (English Translation, London, n.d.) pp. 166–7.
37. d'Ainval, *op. cit.*, p. 193.
38. de Sauvigny, *op. cit.*, p. 285.
39. Porch, *op. cit.*, p. 3, quoting from J. Monteilhet, *Les Institutions militaires de la France.* (Paris, n.d.), p. 4.
40. *Ibid.*, p. 4.
41. d'Ainval, *op. cit.*, pp. 271, 276.
42. Marbot, *op. cit.*, p. 534.
43. d'Ainval, *op. cit.*, pp. 114–15, 210.
44. *Ibid.*, pp. 114–15.

BIBLIOGRAPHICAL NOTE

For an in-depth analysis of St.-Cyr's personality, Christiane d'Ainval's *Gouvion Saint-Cyr* (Copernic, 1981) is magnificent. While unsatisfactory on the strictly military aspects, the analysis of his personality drawn from his own and family letters and documents paints a very different picture of the man when compared to popular myth. In Marshal Laurant Gouvion Saint-Cyr, *Mémoires*, 4 vols. (Paris, 1831), his own exploits are described in a historical context that is well researched for the time and at times even mildly self-critical. Sadly, the very formal language makes for very dull reading. Colonel Ramsay Weston Phipps, *The Armies of the First French Republic and the Rise of the Marshals of Napoleon I* (describing the Armies *de La Moselle, du Rhin, de Sambre-et-Meuse, du Rhin-et-Moselle*); (Oxford, 1929), Vol. 2, covers St.-Cyr's career from 1792 to 1797 in detail. Phipp's judgments on St.-Cyr are perceptive and free from popular myth. Sir Charles Oman, *A History of the Peninsular War* (A.M.S., New York, 1980), Vols. 2 and 3, is a fair account of St.-Cyr's Catalonian Campaigns of 1808–9, but Oman repeats many of the traditional prejudices as regards St.-Cyr's personality. In Baron Jean-Baptiste-Antoine-Marcellin Marbot, *The Memoirs of Baron de Marbot*, trans. by A. J. Butler (Longmans, Green and Co., London, 1894), the account of Polotsk is surprisingly similar to St.-Cyr's own, and far better written despite his bitter attacks on St.-Cyr's character. Guillaume De Berthier de Sauvigny, *The Bourbon Restoration*, trans. by L. M. Case (Philadelphia, 1966), is useful on the social and political background to both of St.-Cyr's periods as minister of war. Douglas Porch's *Army and Revolution, France 1815–1848* (Routledge & Kegan Paul, London, 1974) gives a good summary of the ideas behind St.-Cyr's army reforms of 1818–19 and their effect in practice. Count Phillip de Ségur, *An Aide-de-Camp of Napoleon*, trans. by H. A. Patchett-Martin (Hutchinson & Co., London, 1896) provides interesting comments on St.-Cyr as ambassador to Madrid. In Baron Dieudonné-Adrian-Paul-Francis-Charles-Henry Thiébault, *The Memoirs of Baron Thiébault*, 2 vols., trans. by A. J. Butler (Smith, Elder & Co., London, 1896), this writer's usual bitter personal attacks are counterbalanced by a very useful account of St.-Cyr in Rome 1797–98. Marshal Stephen-James-Joseph-Alexander Macdonald, *Recollections of Marshal Macdonald*, trans. by S. L. Simeon (Richard Bently and Son, London, 1893), is informative on the period immediately after the Second Restoration. F. Loraine Petre's *Napoleon's Last Campaign in Germany–1813* (Arms and Armour Press, London, 1974) is good on St.-Cyr and Napoleon's relationship in 1813.

CHRONOLOGY

1766, October 23	—Born in Paris
1781, March 14	—*Sous-lieutenant,* Foot Artillery
1784, October 28	—Captain in *Royal-Étranger* cavalry regiment
1785	—Marries Cécile Le Doulcet de Pontécoulant
1787, January 27	—Invalided out of army and supports the Revolution
1791, December 18	—Recalled as lieutenant-colonel in 12th chasseurs à cheval
1793, August–September	—Defends Nantes against Charette; wounded at Sorinières
September 30	—Suspended as a member of the nobility
1794, November 29	—Reinstated and confirmed as *général de division*
1795–1796	—Served under Hoche in *Vendée*, Britanny, and expedition to Ireland
1797	—In Italy; persuaded King of Sardinia to abdicate; fought at Novi and captured at Pasturana
1800, December 3	—Commanded an infantry division at Hohenlinden
1801, September 23	—Inspector general of the cavalry
1805	—Commanded infantry division in Marmont's II Corps
1806, September–October	—Commanded 2nd Dragoon Division in pursuit after Jena–Auerstädt
1807, February 8	—Commanded dragoons at Eylau, where wounded
June 14	—Commanded cavalry at Friedland
1808, May 2	—As governor of Madrid puts down rising in that city
1809, April–May	—Commanded dragoons under Prince Eugène in Italy
July 6	—Coversed right wing of Davout's corps at Wagram
July 31	—Appointed colonel-general of chasseurs *vice* Marmont
1812, January	—Appointed to command 3rd Reserve Cavalry Corps
November	—Commanded *bataillon sacré* in retreat from Moscow
1813, January	—Retired to his estates as no longer physically fit
December	—Returned to duty as commander of the cavalry
1814, February–March	—Fought at Brienne, Vauchamps, Troyes, and Craonne
July	—Handed over colonel-general of the chasseurs to duke of Berry, but made inspector general of the chasseurs and lancers by Louis XVIII
1815, March	—Rallied to Napoleon and put down royalist rising in Midi, capturing the Duke of Angoulême
April 15	—Appointed *Maréchal d'Empire* (26th in seniority)
June 16	—Commanded right of *l'Armée du Nord;* at Ligny
June 17	—Ordered to pursue retreating Prussians
June 18	—Fought at Wavre against Prussian 3rd Corps
June 19	—Breaks off action and slips away via Namur
July 24	—Proscribed; settles in U.S.A. (Philadelphia)
1819, November	—Amnestied and given rank of lieutenant general
1820, June 20	—Returned to France and placed on retired list;
1827	—His wife having died, marries Fanny Hua, (aged 25)
1831, November 19	—Restored to rank of marshal of France
1847, May 29	—Died while returning from a visit to Italy

CHAPTER EIGHT

THE ODD MAN OUT

Grouchy

by

by

Major-General (ret'd.) James D. Lunt

The Making of a Soldier (1766-1805)

There are four reasons why Marshal Emmanuel de Grouchy, who was born in Paris on October 23, 1766, differs from the other marshals of the Empire: first, because he was almost the only hereditary title-bearing noble of France to become one, having supported the republican cause from practically the outset of the Revolution; second, because he was the last of Napoleon's generals to be given his baton (on April 15, 1815); third, because his military reputation was founded primarily as a cavalryman although he had had considerable experience in the command of infantry; finally, because it was Grouchy who was chiefly blamed by Napoleon for his defeat at Waterloo. For too long were Napoleon's strictures accepted uncritically by historians, not least by A. G. Macdonnell.[1]

Grouchy entered the army through the artillery school at Strasbourg, his first commission being in the Foot Artillery on March 14, 1781. His first connection with the cavalry was in 1784 when he joined the *Royal-Étranger* cavalry regiment as a captain. Then after a brief spell with the Royal Bodyguard (the Scottish Company), he was invalided out of the army in 1787.

He rejoined as a supporter of the Revolution on December 18, 1791, as a lieutenant colonel in the 12th Horse Chasseurs, serving with two other cavalry regiments as a colonel during the campaign in Savoy. In 1793, however, he was transferred to the Army at Brest, thereby beginning his connection with Hoche who was to become Grouchy's influential patron. Grouchy served under him in Britanny and Vendée, successfully defending Nantes against Charette and distinguishing himself as Sorinières where he was wounded. But he was removed from the army on September 30, 1793, on account of his aristocratic connections, only being restored a year later when he was confirmed in his rank of general of division. He was then age 29. Grouchy continued to distinguish himself in Vendée under Hoche and served under him as chief of staff and second in command in the abortive expedition to Ireland in November–December 1796.

On his return Grouchy joined Joubert's army in Italy where he secured Piedmont and persuaded the King of Sardinia to abdicate. He fought several successful actions, notably at Valenza where he was wounded and had an aide-de-camp killed beside him. He commanded Joubert's left wing at Novi against Suvorov's Russo–Austrian army on August 15, 1799. Although Grouchy took nearly 2,000 prisoners, he was himself wounded several times in the retreat through the gorge at Pasturana and taken prisoner. During his captivity of nearly one year, he was unwise enough to write protesting against the setting up of the Consulate, an action unlikely to be forgotten by Napoleon.

After his release Grouchy joined Moreau in Germany, serving in the campaign against the Austrians that culminated in the victory at Hohenlinden on December 3, 1800. At that battle he commanded an infantry division, much of the credit for the victory being owed to Grouchy and Ney as divisional commanders. He continued to distinguish himself in the later stages of the campaign, but it was not under Napoleon's eagle eye that he was winning distinction, but under Napoleon's arch-rival, Moreau. He was in the "other camp," and his open championship of Moreau during the latter's trial in 1804 was hardly calculated to endear him to Napoleon. Nevertheless, he had been appointed inspector general of the cavalry on September 23, 1801, an appointment that undoubtedly brought him into close contact with Murat, the leading cavalryman of the age.

However, in the great Campaign in 1805, which included Mack's capitulation at Ulm, Grouchy commanded a line division in Marmont's II Corps. He was placed on the sick list shortly thereafter and did not return to duty until September 1806 when he commanded the Second Division of Dragoons in Murat's Reserve Cavalry of the Grand Army. From then onward Grouchy never looked back, although he still failed to receive the promotion he believed was due to him. This induced him at one stage to contemplate leaving the army altogether, but Napoleon won him over by agreeing that Grouchy's eldest son, Alphonse, could enter the imperial military school. Just as his rank as a noble was a hindrance during his early career, the fact that in later years Grouchy was not included among Napoleon's "inner circle" undoubtedly gave him something of an inferiority complex, although his value as a cavalry general was never doubted by the Emperor.

The Golden Years (1806–1813)

It was in 1806 that Grouchy really began to come to prominence as a leader of cavalry. It was the Golden Age of the horsed soldier, so soon to be banished from the battlefield by barbed wire and the machine gun. Under Napoleon the cavalry was in a class of its own, led by Murat who had all the qualities required to lead cavalry in battle. Napoleon himself had no doubts concerning the value of cavalry. "Without cavalry, battles are without result," he was to write when in exile.[2]

There has never been anything quite like the cavalry of the Grand Army. They set the tone for other European armies to copy: hussars, horse chasseurs, cuirassiers, dragoons, and lancers, all gorgeously appareled, if sometimes less superbly mounted; the French seldom showing to advantage as horsemasters, however good their horsemanship. Their British equivalents were essentially heavy and light dragoons, hussars not being introduced officially until 1811, lancers not until 1816. But official or not, the name "hussar" was taken into use in the summer of 1806, together with the exotic "dolman" and beplumed "kalpak." The British were better mounted on the whole than the French, but they lacked the disciplined élan of Murat's cavalry. Wellington complained on more than one occasion of his cavalry's tendency to gallop away out of control after a charge.

Napoleon had clear views on the organization of his cavalry, writing to his war minister in 1803, "You must consider Cuirassiers, Dragoons and Hussars as forming three different arms, and never put up to me transfers from one arm to the other," and again to Murat, "I am sorry to see your light cavalry and dragoons are intermingled—they are two different arms."[3] When Grouchy returned to duty from the sick list in the autumn of 1806, it was as a general of dragoons.

He led them during the campaign against Prussia in 1806, entering Berlin on October 25 and taking part in the action at Zhedenick on October 26 when Murat caught up with Prince Hohenlohe's rear guard and smashed it. It was there that Queen Louise of Prussia's own regiment of dragoons lost their standard embroidered by the queen herself to Grouchy. He was to distinguish himself again at Prenzlau on October 28 when Prince Hohenlohe capitulated.

The cavalry actions that followed after Jena–Auerstädt have been described as "the greatest sustained pursuit in history." It involved the taking of enormous risks, an ability "to live off the land," and the panache and leadership of Murat and his generals, who included Grouchy. But it failed to bring the Prussians to terms because they knew the Russians were on their way to help them. Napoleon was therefore compelled to advance farther and farther into Poland along tracks turned into morasses by the autumn rains, and soon to be frozen into deep ruts at the onset of winter. The weather was vile, and the French, both horse and foot, were suffering badly from battle fatigue, but Napoleon pressed on to the east, not entering winter quarters until December 29. There had been numerous actions before that came about, one of them at Biezun on December 23, when Grouchy made several successful charges in support of Marshal Bessières's hard-pressed infantry. It made a satisfactory ending to a campaign in which Grouchy's reputation as a commander of heavy cavalry had been greatly enhanced.

Napoleon would have preferred to leave his army in winter quarters until the better campaigning weather in the spring, but his plans were upset by General Bennigsen, the Hanoverian cavalryman who commanded one of the Russian armies, advancing into Poland. Bennigsen suddenly began to move forward, blundering into some elements of Ney's VI Corps on January 23. This led to Napoleon opening a winter campaign, his object being to lure Bennigsen onward until he could completely envelop the Russians.

It did not work out that way. The Russians were far better inured to fighting during the bitter Polish winter than Napoleon's soldiers. They could march farther and faster, even at night. They could survive on scantier rations and forage, and were able to endure without shelter in the dreadfully cold nights. Their cossacks were particularly hardy, seemingly unaffected by the elements, as were their mounts. They were quick to pick up stragglers and officers riding on solitary missions. This served Bennigsen well when they picked up an officer carrying dispatches from Berthier to Bernadotte. Bennigsen was soon in possession of Napoleon's plan for his encirclement and took immediate steps to draw back from the trap.

There followed the pursuit to Eylau, possibly the most pyrrhic of all Napoleon's victories, where Bennigsen stood to fight. The battle took place in a blinding snowstorm, lasting for 36 hours on February 7 and 8. It began sooner than Napoleon had planned, and before he had his troops properly marshaled. Elements from Soult's IV Corps and Murat's Reserve Cavalry became caught up in street fighting with the Russians in Eylau during the afternoon on February 7, the battle continuing until well into the night. At one stage the Emperor's personal baggage and camp were at risk. The battle proper began around 8 A.M. on the following morning, February 8, and lasted all day until around 8 P.M. (see p. 13). Bennigsen decided that enough was enough and withdrew. This left Napoleon as master of the field, although Ney commented later that it had been a massacre without producing any result.[4]

The appalling conditions notwithstanding, it had been a great day for the cavalry. At a critical moment, when the French center was shattered and Napoleon only narrowly escaped capture, he ordered Murat to charge in order to restore the situation. There followed one of the greatest cavalry charges in history as Dahlmann's chasseurs, followed by Murat and the great mass of French horsemen, including Marshal Bessières at the head of the cavalry of the Guard, smashed into and swept over the Russian batteries and the poorly armed lines of Russian infantry, at the same time scattering the Russian cavalry. For the

143

loss of 1,500 men, Murat managed to restore the situation, owing much of his success to the stout Polish horses with which he had remounted most of his cavalry regiments.

Grouchy's dragoons earned their share of the glory. They smashed into the right flank of the Russian cavalry, completely routing them. His horse killed under him, Grouchy was wounded, owing his escape from capture to his aide-de-camp, Lafayette, who gallantly came to his rescue. After remounting, Grouchy rallied his men and led them in a second charge. Then Murat appeared on the scene, assumed command, and led Grouchy's dragoons in a wide left wheel against the Russian cavalry, side by side with the cuirassiers of d'Hautpoul. This great wedge of cavalry, towering over the wiry but undersized Russian horses, hacked and hewed their path through the Russians, driving them from the field.

Eylau may have been won at great cost, but it was at least a victory. Grouchy's part was acknowledged in the *79th Official Bulletin:* "General Grouchy, who was in command of the cavalry on the left flank, rendered important services."[5] He was also awarded the Order of Maximilian-Joseph of Bavaria, after which it was time to return to winter quarters.

The spring Campaign of 1807 began with the investment of Dantzig on March 18 by Marshal Lefebvre. Despite Russian attempts to relieve it, the city fell on May 27. This left Napoleon free to concentrate on the final destruction of the Russian and Prussian armies. There followed two major battles, at Heilsberg on June 11 and at Friedland on June 14. Although Napoleon was very critical of the calvalry's performance at Heilsberg,[6] he was well enough pleased with it at Friedland as to reward Grouchy by the award of the Grand Eagle of the Legion of Honor. This was on July 13, 6 days after Napoleon had concluded peace with Tsar Alexander and the King of Prussia at Tilsit. Friedland will be described in more detail later in this narrative (see p. 150).

After the humbling of Austria, Prussia, and Russia, the eagle eyes were turned south, where a Bourbon still reigned on the throne of Spain. Grouchy found himself commanding his dragoons in the Peninsula, which would prove to be Napoleon's "Achilles' heel," thanks to the inherent dislike of all foreigners by the Spaniards and the tactical skill of a taciturn Anglo–Irish aristocrat, known behind his back to his soldiers as "Old Nosey." Grouchy was governor of Madrid on May 2, 1808, when the mob came out into the streets. It took him three hours, and several charges by his chasseurs and dragoons, to restore order. Napoleon affected to make light of the entire business, but he was fast falling into the error made by all dictators of believing only what it suited him to believe.

Grouchy became a count of the Empire in January 1809, having by then safely quitted Spain and joined Prince Eugène in Italy, still in command of a division of dragoons. He played a prominent part in the Battle of the Piave on May 8, 1810, which ultimately resulted in the Austrians pulling out from Italy. Late in the evening of May 8, when the Archduke John was endeavoring to reestablish his shattered line, Eugène brought up a battery of 24 guns, ordering Generals Grouchy and Pully to charge the Austrian infantry. This turned out to be decisive, leading to the Austrians' retreat, which was to continue until they had cleared Italy altogether. Grouchy continued to distinguish himself during the pursuit, particularly at Raab on June 14, but Italy was very much a secondary theater compared with Germany, where Napoleon himself was in battle against the Archduke Charles. Nonetheless, Grouchy managed to get his toe into the water, taking part in the Battle of Wagram on July 5–6 when he successfully covered the extreme right of Marshal Davout's III Corps.

Although the coveted baton remained elusive, the emperor marked his services with the Cross of Commander of the Iron Crown. More significantly, he was appointed colonel-general of the chasseurs in place of Marmont, an appointment that was likely to bring him into closer contact with Napoleon. But more than 10 long years of campaigning had taken their toll, and Grouchy felt the need of a rest. On October 20, 1809, he was permitted to return to France where he was placed on the semi-active list—a fortunate dispensation in more ways than one, since it saved him from having to endure the hardships and misfortunes of the war in the Peninsula.

Grouchy was back in the saddle, quite literally, when he was given command of a cavalry division in Italy from April 1811 until January 1812. Then he was recalled to take the place of General La-Tour Maubourg in command of the 3rd Corps of Reserve Cavalry. It was in this capacity that he served under Prince Eugène in the Russian Campaign of 1812. Grouchy captured Orcha, and his troops were the first across the Berezina on the road to Moscow. He charged with great success at Smolensk and took part in the assault on the Great Redoubt at Borodino on September 7. His corps was brought up from the rear to exploit the breach made in the Russian line, but he was checked by Barclay de Tolly who had brought up two fresh corps of cavalry. Grouchy had his horse killed under him and was wounded by case shot in the chest. His son, serving alongside, was wounded in the same action, virtually at the same time as his father.

Grouchy was fit enough to participate in the battle at Maloyaroslavets on October 24, and then had to undergo the

horrors of the long retreat from Moscow. Conditions deteriorated so fast, and the Russian pressure was so continuous, that
serious doubts were felt for the personal safety of the Emperor.
Le bataillon sacré was formed, consisting entirely of officers and
commanded by Grouchy. Having successfully brought Napoleon
back to Germany, Grouchy represented that his health no longer
was robust enough for command of cavalry, and requested
instead command of an infantry corps. Napoleon turned down
his request and Grouchy then requested permission to retire
from the army. This was granted and on April 1, 1813, he was
placed on the non-active list.

He was back again within three months, serving brilliantly in
the Campaign of 1814, distinguishing himself particularly at
Vauchamps on February 14, and again at the capture of Troyes
on February 23 where he was wounded. He was wounded again,
in the thigh, at Craonne on March 7.

Grouchy remained loyal until the abdication on April 28
1814, thereafter making his submission to Louis XVIII. He was
replaced as colonel-general of the chasseurs by the duke of
Berry, but was made inspector-general of the chasseurs and of
the lancers in some kind of compensation. But he had still not
achieved his baton.

Waterloo: Confusion Worse Confounded—And Thereafter (1815-1847)

It is surely rather surprising that Grouchy should have rallied to Napoleon after the Emperor's return from Elba, since he
labored under a grievance that his services had not been adequately recognized. It might be thought that he would have had
more to gain by remaining quietly on his estates. But the old
magic still prevailed and on March 31 Napoleon appointed him
to command the army in the Midi where the royalists were in
insurrection under the Duke of Angoulême. Grouchy made short
work of the duke, taking him prisoner and receiving from Napoleon on April 15 a letter appointing him to be a marshal of
France. At last the coveted baton was his. Not much later he was
also made a peer of France.

There is no intention here of describing in any detail the Battle of Waterloo, nor the events preceding it, such as the Battles of
Ligny and Quatre Bras. However, it is intended to examine Grouchy's conduct in command of the right wing of the army of the
North on June 17 and 18 in order to establish whether or not
Napoleon's subsequent criticism of Grouchy was justified. Napoleon's explanation (or apologia?), placing most of the blame on

Grouchy, was swallowed hook, line, and sinker by many historians, most notably by Thiers. It has been repeated since, by A. G. Macdonnell among others, but an impartial consideration of the facts shows that Grouchy, although lamentably slow to get off the mark, was more sinned against than sinning.

But let us first deal briefly with the criticism, supported by some historians, that Grouchy, as a cavalryman, should not have been given command of what was predominantly an infantry force. This overlooks the fact that Grouchy had had experience with all the fighting arms. He began his service in the artillery, although admittedly not for long, and later in his service commanded infantry under both Moreau and Marmont. In any case, specialization of the kind we take for granted in armies of the twentieth century was by no means the case in the past. For example, almost everyone who aspired to become an officer could ride a horse and knew something about horsemastership, just as their modern equivalents can drive automobiles. Moreover, Grouchy was very much a heavy cavalryman, the "shock arm," and as such accustomed to dealing with infantry, if only to charge them.

It has to be admitted that he does not seem to have possessed that lightness of touch, nor ability to seize the fleeting moment, that marked such cavalry leaders as Murat and Lasalle. He might perhaps be best described as a "steady old file," reliable and determined, but cautious and unimaginative, lacking the divine spark that differentiates leaders of mounted troops like Murat and Rommel from the general run of cavalry generals. (Incidentally, Rommel was an infantryman, although admittedly he came from the light infantry.) Whether or not this is a correct judgment is open to argument, but certainly to this writer at least, there was nothing in Grouchy's previous experience and training that unfitted him to command a force of all arms, as he did in the Waterloo campaign.

Then how do we account for Napoleon's strictures? Or for Grouchy's failure to make any contribution to the Battle of Waterloo? There can be little doubt that Napoleon was himself principally to blame, although Grouchy displayed no initiative in sticking so rigidly to the instructions given him by the Emperor before the battle. The sequence of events was as follows.

In the evening after Ligny on June 16, Grouchy waited on Napoleon for instructions for the following day. He was told the Emperor was indisposed and would see him the next morning. When Grouchy returned at dawn on June 17, Napoleon again refused to see him. Grouchy accompanied Napoleon when they rode out to inspect the battlefield of Ligny around 11.30 A.M. that morning. When Grouchy again ventured to ask for instructions, he was curtly told that he would receive them when Napoleon saw fit. Only at 1 P.M. on June 17 was Grouchy summoned and told:

> Proceed to Gembloux with General Pajol's Cavalry corps, the light cavalry of the IV Corps, General Excelmann's cavalry corps, General Teste's division and the III and IV Corps of infantry. You will find out what the position is in the direction of Namur and Maestricht and you will pursue the enemy. It is important to discover the intentions of both Blücher and Wellington. Ensure that the two infantry corps are always within a mile of each other.[7]

Grouchy had sent off his cavalry the previous evening in pursuit of the Prussians, Excelmans heading north-east to Gembloux, Pajol east toward Namur. Thereby they lost contact with the main Prussian force, which was retreating north. Moreover, Pajol, having come up with some stray Prussian artillery, immediately assumed the Prussians were making for Namur, Grouchy informing the Emperor accordingly. A properly coordinated screen of light cavalry hanging onto the Prussians' tail would have been much wiser tactics.

Not that Grouchy acted with the speed into action normally associated with a cavalryman. His leading troops did not set off from Ligny until late in the morning of June 17, reaching Gembloux only by nightfall. By then the roads had been turned into bogs by the thunderstorm, further impeding Grouchy's progress. Meanwhile Excelmanns had lost all touch with the Prussians. Rather than trudge on through the mud to close the gap, Grouchy decided to give his troops a good night's rest, rising himself at dawn on June 18 to receive a report that convinced him that Blücher was making for Wavre. This information was sent to Napoleon, Grouchy meanwhile enjoying a leisurely breakfast before taking to horse.

He was at Sart-à-Walhain eating his lunch when the sound of the cannonade at Waterloo could be clearly heard. Gérard, commander of IV Corps, begged Grouchy to march to the sound of the guns, rather too insistently for Grouchy's taste. No, he said, he had been given his orders. The advance to Wavre would continue. It would have been different if Napoleon's dispatch dictated at 10 A.M. had reached Grouchy by noon on June 18, but it did not reach him until 4 P.M. More battles have been lost as a result of failure in communications than for any other reason. Napoleon had agreed that Grouchy should continue toward Wavre, but he had enjoined him "always to maneuver in our direction." Three hours later another dispatch arrived, with a hurriedly scrawled postscript, "Do not lose a minute to draw nearer and join us.[8] By then Grouchy was 15 miles from Napoleon as the crow flies—much farther by march route. He could never make it. The officer carrying the dispatch had taken two-and-a-half hours of hard riding to deliver it.

These were the facts. Napoleon had sent Grouchy off on his wild goose chase—nobody else. The route he had been given took him *away from* the battle. When Soult suggested early on June 18 that he should be recalled, Napoleon abruptly rejected the advice. None of this excuses Grouchy's failure to respond to Gérard's urgings around noon. A Lannes or Davout would certainly have done so. But Grouchy seems to have stood in considerable awe of Napoleon. The consequences of failing to carry out Napoleon's orders to the letter were too awful to contemplate. His failure to react to Gérard's urgings was certainly not the act of a true cavalryman, whose characteristics should be, according to General Sir Hubert Gough, "a combination of independence of thought, quickness in decision, and boldness in action."[9] Judged by this, Grouchy certainly failed at Waterloo, but his failure was nothing when compared with Napoleon's.

Grouchy displayed great skill in extricating his troops after Waterloo, the result of which he did not know until 10:30 A.M. on June 19. He was then engaged with Thielmann's 3rd Prussian Corps at Wavre. Deciding against surrender, Grouchy slipped away toward Namur. When they caught up with him at Namur on June 20, Grouchy stopped Thielmann dead in his tracks. On the following day, he led his troops into France, heading for Rheims after learning of Napoleon's abdication. Later he brought his troops to Paris and handed them over formally to Davout, the minister of war.

Grouchy could expect no clemency from Louis XVIII after his treatment of the Duke of Angoulême. He was proscribed, taking ship for the United States of America, where he settled in Philadelphia. He was aged only 49 but he spent most of the rest of his life in a battle of polemics to justify his conduct at Waterloo. Napoleon's biased account was published by General Gourgaud in 1818. It was contested in a pamphlet by Grouchy, which brought General Gérard into the fray, insisting that Grouchy should have taken his advice. So the argument went on and on, historians taking sides as they are wont to do, prejudice or bias affecting the judgments of some of them. But the facts are hard to avoid, placing the blame, as they do, for all that went wrong with Grouchy's right wing fairly and squarely on Napoleon himself.[10]

Grouchy was amnestied in 1819, reinstated in the rank of lieutenant general, and placed on the reserve list. Returning to France in 1820, he was formally retired, with the back half-pay due to him, in 1824. The 1830 Revolution restored him to his former honors, Louis-Philippe confirming him in his rank of marshal on November 19, 1831, and raising him to the Chamber of Peers in 1832. He died at St.-Étienne on May 29, 1847. He was twice married, having four children by his first wife who died, and a daughter by his second wife who survived him until 1889, the last widow of a marshal of the Empire to die. There are many descendants living today.

The Battle of Friedland (June 14, 1807)

The battle fought at Friedland between some 50,000 Russians under Bennigsen and some 80,000 French under Napoleon ranks among Napoleon's greatest victories. It also provides an excellent example of Napoleon's ability to size up a situation rapidly, thereafter suiting his tactics to take the maximum advantage from the ground and the enemy's dispositions. The Russians had the advantage in numbers early in the action, but as the day progressed they were far outnumbered by Napoleon.

Friedland is a small town on the left bank of the River Alle in what we once knew as East Prussia. A main highway crosses the Alle at Friedland on the way to Konigsberg, some 35 kilometers distant. Friedland is also connected with Eylau, 20 kilometers to the southwest. The River Alle follows a serpentine course between high banks, being both deep and muddy. The battle took place to the west of the town, on a plain devoted entirely to the growing of wheat and corn, which at that season stood high and provided excellent cover. The cultivated area extended for approximately 6,000 yards from east to west and 12,000 yards from north to south. It was ringed by several considerable forests, extending in a rough semicircle from the Damerau forest in the north, via the Gorgenau and Bothkeim forests in the center, to the Sortlack forest 5,000 yards south of Friedland.

The town itself was bounded on its southern outskirts by the Alle, here flowing from west to east, and to the north by an extensive mill pond. This was fed by a mill stream, which, rising in the area of Bothkeim, roughly bisects the cultivated area, joining the Alle at Friedland; although it is not wide, the mill stream presented a significant obstacle for both horses and guns.

In the immediate vicinity of the town, there are five small villages or hamlets. Henrichsdorff straddles the road to Konigsberg, 4,000 yards northwest of Friedland. Posthenen, about equidistant, is on the road to Eylau. The hamlets of Bothkeim and Grünhof lie south of Posthenen, on one side of the Sortlack forest, the village of Sortlack lying on the other, close to the Alle itself. The only noticeable elevation is immediately behind Posthenen, from where an excellent view can be obtained across the plain to Friedland.

The action began in the early afternoon of June 13 as an encounter battle between the Russian cavalry and a cavalry screen thrown out by Lannes, whose reserve corps was acting as advance guard for Napoleon's main army moving up from Eylau. Bennigsen, the Russian commander, had been retreating down the right bank of the Alle, intending to join forces with Lestocq's Prussians, who were moving up the Alle. Bennigsen gave as his reason for crossing the river his desire to rest his troops for 24 hours before continuing his retreat. He believed he had that amount of time in hand before Napoleon could come up from Eylau. The enemy he had driven out of the town was presumably only part of an advance guard with which he felt confident of dealing. For his part, Napoleon assumed that Bennigsen had crossed the Alle with the intention of making for Konigsberg, then only lightly held by the French.

It was extremely hot and sultry, making marching a torment, while the smoke from the guns lay heavily in the air. Information from prisoners taken by his cavalry satisfied Bennigsen that Napoleon was still far distant, and he sent a division across the river early on June 14. He followed this up during the course of the morning by all but one of his seven divisions, leaving only one on the right bank to protect his rear. He constructed three pontoon bridges across the river to provide Bagration with an escape route were he compelled to withdraw hurriedly.

The reason why Bennigsen found himself sucked into a major battle is easy to explain. Lannes's leading troops under Ruffin and Oudinot arrived on the Friedland plain in the early hours of June 14. Grouchy, with his French and Saxon dragoons, came up shortly afterward. Lannes was hotfoot behind them with the rest of his corps. The fighting began around 4 A.M. when Lannes spotted a Russian force making for Henrichsdorff, from where they were well positioned to turn his left flank. Grouchy was sent off on a 4-mile canter to plug the gap. He charged the Russian cavalry, checked their advance, and drove them out of the village—a smart piece of work, after which he returned to the right flank around Sortlack.

The Russians continued to pour across the Alle until they outnumbered Lannes by as much as four to one, their cavalry being very active. Grouchy had to be sent back to Henrichsdorff to restore the situation there, charging 15 times in all. However, it was clear to Lannes that he would be overwhelmed unless help came soon. He sent messenger after messenger back to the Emperor who was still at Eylau. The first was Captain Marbot who had to gallop across country since the road was clogged with troops hastening to the battle.

Napoleon, already mounted, heard Marbot's report, issued some rapid orders, and then set off with Marbot to gallop to Friedland. As they went he asked the young officer what anniversary it was. "Marengo," was the reply. "That is correct," Napoleon replied, "and I shall beat the Russians as I beat the Austrians." He was in high spirits, calling out as he passed the toiling troops, "Today is a happy day—it is the anniversary of Marengo."[11]

Napoleon arrived with Lannes around noon after a 15-mile gallop. Lannes was under great pressure from the Russians, but already large numbers of French were beginning to debouch from the Eylau road. Ney's corps was in the lead, followed by Mortier's, and then by Victor's and the Imperial Guard. Meanwhile, messages had been sent to Murat and Davout, urging them to hasten to the battle.

Napoleon's first action was to climb the elevation behind Posthenen and survey the battlefield. He saw at once the significance of the mill stream, dividing the Russian left from the center and right. The stream had been bridged at Bennigsen's orders, but it was still an obstacle for the free movement of cavalry and artillery. It was immediately apparent that Napoleon must first destroy the Russian left, forcing it back into the angle made by the mill stream with the Alle, in the meantime holding fast in the center and at Henrichsdorff. Napoleon was puzzled by Bennigsen's selection of the position, with a river to his rear and with every prospect of being outnumbered by his enemy. The reason, of course, was that Bennigsen had not calculated on the stout defense put up by Lannes or on the Emperor's rapid march to Lannes's assistance.

The plan was quickly made. Ney, whose soldiers were already in contact in the Sortlack forest, would be on the right, tasked with forcing the Russians back against the mill stream and Alle. Lannes would hold the center, Oudinot's grenadiers bearing slowly to the left to draw on the enemy. Mortier would hold Henrichsdorff. Mortier and Lannes were not to advance; the right wing was to pivot on the left. Grouchy's and Espagne's cavalry divisions would be with the left wing, maneuvering to do the most harm to the enemy when they, "pressed by the vigorous attack of our right, [would] find it necessary to retreat."[12] The reserve, General Victor, and the Imperial Guard would be in Grünhoff, Boktheim, and behind Posthenen, respectively. Napoleon would be with the reserve. The advance would always be from the right, directed by Ney, who would await the Emperor's orders before moving off.

Nothing could be clearer—or simpler. After allowing a period for rest, and galloping along the line to show himself to his soldiers, Napoleon signaled the start of the action by the firing of salvos by 20 cannons. It was 5.30 P.M.

Ney started off in fine fashion from Sortlack, despite his right flank being threatened by Russian cavalry and cossacks. These were repulsed by reserve cavalry, but chiefly by the fire of the massed batteries. This fire was tremendous, blanketing the battlefield with a pall of black smoke. Afterward the Russians said they had never before experienced such fire. They were forced by Ney back against the mill stream and Alle until Bennigsen's cavalry, successfully negotiating the mill stream, threatened Ney's left flank where a gap was appearing between his corps and Lannes's.

This was filled by Dupont's division, formerly one of Ney's before its transfer to Victor's corps. It fought all the harder to assist its former commander. Dupont not only closed the gap but was enormously helped by Senarmont's battery of 38 guns. Senarmont pushed his guns forward until they were firing grapeshot at 60 yards' range into the packed Russian ranks. It was terrible, the brave Russian infantry falling where they stood, as if cut down by a scythe. Ney kept up the pressure until finally the Russian left was broken, pouring through Friedland in a frantic rush for the bridges. But these had been set on fire by Russian artillery firing from the right bank. The river was too deep to ford and the heavily laden Russian infantry drowned in scores.

Bennigsen, in an attempt to restore his fortunes, sent his two nearest divisions to retake Friedland. They drove the French out of the town, but it was a dying throw. When they tried to retreat, the bridges were blazing. Only the chance discovery of a deep ford some way downstream enabled Bennigsen to rescue part of his army and some of his guns. He left more than 18,000 dead or wounded on the field. The French lost between 7,000 and 8,000.

The Russian losses would have been greater had there been more activity on the left flank of Mortier's corps. If Grouchy and Espagne had charged the Russians as they fell back in disorder, the retreat would have been turned into a rout. But it seems that Grouchy's efforts earlier in the day had drained him of both energy and initiative. The French cavalry remained passive for most of the action. When the moment for *L'arme blanche* arrived, it seems that Grouchy lacked either the will or the sense to perceive it. It is hard to believe it would have been the same had Murat been present, or Lasalle for that matter, and it must cast doubts on the claim that Grouchy was above all "a great cavalry leader." Nevertheless, the satisfied emperor could have borne him no grudge for he conferred on him the Grand Cross of the Legion of Honor on July 13, 1807, for his services at Friedland, seven days after he had successfully concluded peace with Tsar Alexander and the King of Prussia at Tilsit.

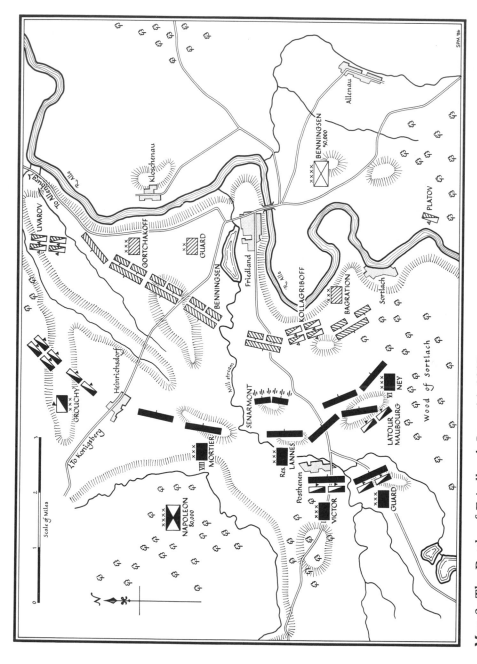

Map 8. The Battle of Friedland, June 14, 1807

TEXTUAL REFERENCES

1. A. G. Macdonnell, *Napoleon and His Marshals* (London, 1934), p. 23 and frequently thereafter.
2. D. G. Chandler, *The Campaigns of Napoleon* (New York, 1966), p. 355.
3. J. D. Lunt, *Scarlet Lancer* (New York, 1964), p. 30.
4. Chandler, *op. cit.*, p. 555.
5. D. Lacroix, *Les Maréchau de Napoleon* (Paris, n.d.), p. 406.
6. F. L. Petre, *Napoleon's Campaign in Poland 1806–7* (London, 1976), p. 304.
7. S. de Chair, *The Waterloo Campaign* (London, 1957), p. 18.
8. H. T. Parker, *Three Napoleonic Battles* (Durham, NC, 1983), p. 147.
9. J. D. Lunt, *Charge to Glory* (New York, 1960), p. vii.
10. D. Fraser, distinguished both as a soldier and as a military historian, in his lecture on *"command"* to the British Army Staff College, has cited Napoleon's instructions to Grouchy before and during the Battle of Waterloo as an example of what *not* to do as a commander in the field.
11. Marbot, *op. cit.* Vol. 1, p. 364.
12. *Ibid.*

BIBLIOGRAPHICAL NOTE

The five volumes of *Mémoires de Maréchal de Grouchy*, published in Paris by the Marquis de Grouchy in 1873–74, do not make for easy reading, and like all examples of filial piety tend to be biased in favor of their subject. *Histoire de la campagne de Waterloo*, 2 vols. (Brussels, 1857) by Jean B.A. Charras puts Grouchy's conduct there in better perspective, as does David G. Chandler in *The Campaigns of Napoleon* (New York, 1966) and Somerset de Chair in *The Waterloo Campaign* (London, 1957). David Howarth's *A Near Run Thing* is also valuable in this regard. Harold T. Parker's *Three Napoleonic Battles* (Durham, NC, 1983) contains an authoritative and very readable account of both Friedland and Waterloo. F. Loraine Petre's *Napoleon's Campaigns in Poland 1806–7* (London, 1976) contains an excellent account of Friedland, together with some very sound observations on the campaign as a whole. Robert Wilson's *Brief Remarks on the Character and Composition of the Russian Army and a Sketch of the Campaigns in Poland in the Years 1806 and 1807* (London, 1860) provides an interesting contemporary account in English, while Marbot's *Mémoires* throw some light on Grouchy's personality.

CHRONOLOGY

1762, April 29	—Born at Limoges (Haute-Vienne)
1778, April 2	—Enlisted at Rhé; posted to *Régiment d'Auxerrois* (December 10)
1779–1781	—Served in West Indies and U.S.A. (Georgia)
1784, July 26	—Discharged from army
1789	—Elected captain, National Guard, Limoges
1791, October 9	—Elected *chef de bataillon*, 2nd Volunteers of Haute-Vienne
1793, May 27	—*Général de brigade; général de division* July 30
September 22	—Commander of *l'Armée du Nord*
October 15–16	—Defeated Coburg at Wattignies
1794, January 6	—Relieved of command and sent to Limoges
March 10	—Commander of *l'Armée de la Moselle* to which *l'Armée des Ardennes* and part of *Nord* were soon added
June 26	—Defeated Coburg at Fleurus
July 2	—Command renamed *l'Armée de Sambre et Meuse*
1795, September 3	—Defeated by Archduke Charles at Würzburg; resigned command
1797, April 12	—Elected to Council of Five Hundred as deputy for Haute-Vienne
September 19	—President of Council of Five Hundred
1798, November 5	—Commander of *l'Armée de Mayence* (renamed *l'Armée du Danube*)
1799, March 2	—Commander of combined *les Armées du Danube, d'Helvétie* and *d'Observation*
March 25	—Defeated by Archduke Charles at Stockach; superseded by Massena
April 27	—Inspector-general of the infantry
November	—Dismissed by Consuls after *Brumaire*
1804, May 19	—Appointed *Maréchal d'Empire* (fourth in order)
1806, March 17	—Governor of Naples
1808, July 17	—Chief of staff to *l'Armée d'Espagne*
1809, July 27–28	—Defeated by Wellesley at Talavera; recalled to France
1811, July 8	—Governor of Madrid and (from October 28) chief of staff to *l'Armée du Centre*
1812, March 16	—Chief of staff to *l'Armée d'Espagne*
1813, June 21	—Defeated by Wellington at Vitoria; recalled to France (12 July)
1830, August 7	—Governor of Les Invalides
1833, November 23	—Died at Paris, aged 71 years

CHAPTER NINE

THE TRUE PATRIOT

Jourdan

by
Michael Glover

General of the Republic (1762–1794)

No one could claim that Jourdan was the brightest star in the galaxy of the Marshals of the Empire, but there can be no doubt that he had a clearer strategic insight than most of his colleagues and that he suffered from several disadvantages that they did not. Alone among the active marshals, he had to learn the art of high command "on the job," and, thanks to a long campaign of deliberate denigration, much of it inspired by Carnot, he had the misfortune to be regarded as a bungling amateur by such men as Soult, Ney, and Mortier who had been fledgling officers under his command in the great days of the *Army of the Sambre and Meuse.* He was also hampered by persistent ill health and by a naive belief in the virtues of republicanism, which made him an object of suspicion both to the violent men of the Committee of Public Safety and later to Bonaparte. Like Bessières he was the son of a surgeon, a calling then low on the social scale, so that there could be no question of his aspiring to a commission in the class-conscious Bourbon army. Hardly had France, in alliance with the American colonies, declared war on Britain than young Jourdan, a month short of his sixteenth birthday, enlisted at the *Dépot des Colonies* on the Île de Ré. After eight months of basic training, he was posted (December 10, 1778) to the Regiment of Auxerrois serving in the West Indies. His first and only experience of active service was on D'Estaing's unauthorized and disastrous assault on Savannah, an attempt that was beaten off by a detachment of the 60th (Royal Americans) leaving 637 French and 264 American casualties in front of the improvized defenses. D'Estaing's dispirited forces sailed back to the Caribbean where the climate was no kinder to the French than to the British, and on January 1, 1782, Jourdan was landed in France prostrated with a fever that was to plague him at intervals for the rest of his life. It was almost two years before he was fit enough to rejoin his regiment and by that time peace had been signed and he was discharged from the army, still a private, on July 26, 1784.

Returning to his birthplace, Limoges, he set up as a haberdasher, marrying in 1788 a dressmaker who bore him five daughters. His detractors were to maintain that he was little more than a peddler, but the probability is that he was in a relatively substantial way of business for when the National Guard was established in July 1789, he was elected captain of the Limoges light company. The new force was essentially a bourgeois body, and it is unlikely that they would have elected to so responsible a position a small-time itinerant whose military experience was limited.

Even in the turbulent peace of that time, it is unlikely that Captain Jourdan would have gained much training in the following two years; but he undoubtedly made himself respected, for, after the flight to Varennes put an effective end to the monarchy, the National Assembly called for 169 battalions of Volunteers and, again by election, he found himself *chef de bataillon* of the 2nd Volunteers of Haute-Vienne. This rapid promotion was fortunate since this first batch of Volunteers, unlike their successors, were good material, many of whom were discharged regulars or trained men from the disbanded militia. Moreover, they were genuine volunteers, very different from the levies of 1792–1793 who, being marked by "indiscipline, ignorance, presumption and cowardice,"[1] were unlikely to bring credit to their commanders. The 2nd Volunteers of Haute-Vienne quickly became reliable troops, and after Jourdan had led them through the victory of Jemappes (November 6, 1792) and the rout at Neerwinden (March 18, 1793), he was recognized as a natural leader and promoted to general of brigade on May 27, 1793, and general of division two months later. Even allowing that the army had lost 5,500 officers out of its peace establishment of 9,578 in 18 months, this was remarkably rapid promotion and it showed no signs of slowing. After six weeks, during which he was first engaged with British troops at Linselles, Jourdan led his division into the scrappy and mismanaged Battle of Hondschoote (September 8, 1793), a tactical victory but a strategic defeat for France. It was a day of mixed fortunes for him, beginning with a triumphant advance. At that stage he called a halt for consolidation, but political pressure forced him to resume his advance and his leading troops were forced back in disorder. Fortunately he was able to cover their rout with a reserve battalion and simultaneously his Hanoverian opponents retired, their covering role completed. In this final phase, Jourdan was wounded in the chest, and, almost before he had recovered, he was nominated (September 22) to the command of the Army of the North.

At a time when his two predecessors, Custine and Houchard, were on their way to the guillotine, the leadership of France's principal army was a daunting prospect quite apart from anything the enemy might do. At his headquarters, as at every other army headquarters, were four Representatives of the People, armed with plenary powers. Their task was to assure themselves of the loyalty of every man in the army and most especially of the loyalty of the commander in chief, since four of them, including Lafayette, had already gone over to the enemy. They were also instructed to bring before the revolutionary tribunal anyone whom they considered to have "engineered the disorganisation of the army." It was not unnatural that losing a battle should be counted as disorganizing the army, but, in the opinion of some of the Representatives, failing to take their advice was equally culpable. Since the majority of them were wholly innocent of military skills, taking the advice of a Representative was very likely to produce disorganization.

Jourdan's first test was not long in coming. In pursuit of his lumbering policy of reducing every fortress within reach, Prince Saxe-Coburg Saalfeld, the Austrian commander, laid siege to Maubeuge. The French garrison of 20,000 was little smaller than the investing force under the lymphatic prince of Orange, and there was a covering corps of 20,000 under Clerfayt, a Belgian of whom the Duke of York wrote, "His lack of resolution and decision is beyond all decision."[2] Jourdan's orders were to relieve Maubeuge without delay, and, to ensure that this was done, no less a figure than Lazare Carnot arrived to add his weight to the advice of the Representatives. Carnot's talents as "the organizer of victory" are beyond dispute, but his tactical skills were minimal, a defect he concealed by a careful rewriting of history. To drive away a poorly led covering force of 20,000 with the 45,000 available to the Army of the North should have posed no great problem, but the business was sadly bungled. Carnot insisted that there should be a double encircling movement, a favorite maneuver of his, combined with a frontal attack, thus carefully dispersing the French numerical superiority. This plan led to a sharp repulse and the loss of 12 guns; so on the following day, that on which Marie Antoinette was executed, Jourdan followed his own judgment, concentrated overwhelming strength on his right, and, not without difficulty, turned the Battle of Wattignies (October 15–16, 1793) into a victory, relieving Maubeuge. Carnot returned to Paris with his own version of events and no love for General Jourdan.

Fresh orders, signed by Carnot and countersigned by Robespierre, soon reached the victorious general and provide a fair sample of Carnot's tactical thinking. The Army of the North was to cross the Sambre, surround the enemy, cut his communications, and burn his magazines. It was unlikely that even the pedestrian Coburg would stand still during this process, but, to make Jourdan's task more difficult, he was instructed to keep his army concentrated, to keep in touch with the fortresses in his rear, and to restrict himself to a war of outposts, engaging in a general action only "when an opportunity offers of fighting with advantage and of putting the enemy's army to utter rout."[3] No explanation was vouchsafed as to how the enemy was to be surrounded while the French remained concentrated.

Jourdan demurred, pointing out that "the infantry have no shoes, the cavalry no forage and the artillery no horses,"[4] and was summoned to Paris where the Terror was at its height. On January 10, 1794, he was arraigned before the Committee of Public Safety, and faced with a document in Carnot's hand and signed by, among others, Robespierre, Collot d'Herbois, and Barère, which demanded that he be "dismissed and put under arrest."[5] Since the committee had only Carnot's account of Wattignies, even his victory would not have saved Jourdan had not a former monk and present exponent of the Terror, Ernest Joseph Duquesnoy, who had been a Representative with the Army of the North in which his brother commanded a division, come to his defense. He rounded on Carnot, contradicted his version of Wattignies, and reduced him to tears. When he ended by offering to vouch for Jourdan's loyalty with his own head, he saved the general's life but could not save him from dismissal and an order to "proceed without delay to your domicile," thus making him the first general to be *limogé*.[*] By January 27 Jourdan was back in his haberdashery business at Limoges, and a week later he was awarded a small pension of 3,000 livres a year.

It was little more than a month later that he was back in favor and appointed to the Army of the Moselle, which was responsible for the frontier with Luxembourg and southern Belgium. He was not to serve there long, for on May 5 he was marching north with four of his divisions as part of the countermeasures to deal with the allied maneuver that culminated in what the British called the Battle of Turcoing (May 17–18, 1794). On his march he took under his command the Army of the Ardennes and four divisions of the North, the whole amounting to 96,000 men—no small command for a man who, 6 months earlier, had narrowly escaped the guillotine. It was to receive the immortal name of the Army of the Sambre and Meuse.

Given the task of taking Charleroi, Jourdan, having detached some flank corps, crossed the Sambre with 70,000 men on June 12 and invested the town. Four days later an Austro–Dutch force of 43,000 attacked in a heavy mist and drove him back across the river with the loss of 3,000 men and eight guns. Urged on by Representative Louis de St.-Just, who, while threatening him with every penalty if Charleroi did not fall immediately, was urging him to detach 30,000 men to the north, Jourdan attacked again on June 18 and found a use for St.-Just since the terror he inspired in the garrison commander induced Charleroi to surrender needlessly on June 26, the day on which Coburg came forward to raise the siege. He had only 52,000 men but he split them into five columns, depriving himself of the chance of even

---

[*]Sent into retirement. Jourdan lived at Limoges—hence the term.

local superiority. Although the French had had time to prepare their positions, the Austrians managed to break through on both wings; while Jourdan's defense was determined, the chief credit for the victory must go to the future Marshal Lefebvre who, assisted by his chief of staff, Colonel Soult, stood and fought it out around Fleurus on the ground where, 21 years later, the French were to batter their way through Blücher's Prussians defending Ligny.

Years afterward Soult was to describe the Battle of Fleurus as "fifteen hours of the most desperate fighting I ever saw in my life,"[6] but in the end Coburg's nerve gave way and he fell back toward Braine L'Alleud and Waterloo. Both the Archduke Charles, who commanded the Austrian left, and Soult believed that Coburg had only to persevere to win, but, as it was, Jourdan gained a victory that was to settle the fate of Belgium for 20 years. Once again, the version of history that circulated in Paris told how Carnot had countermanded Jourdan's orders, substituted his own and led the final charge with his civilian hat waving on the point of a sword. As it happened Carnot was organizing victory somewhere else that day.

Fluctuating Fortunes—The Baton and Spain (1795–1809)

Fleurus, following the defeat of the Turcoing combination, decided the Austrians to abandon the Netherlands, a step that reduced the Dutch to total apathy and forced the British, with their Hanoverian and Hessian auxiliaries, to make the best of their retreat to Emden. The way was open for the Army of the Sambre and Meuse to make spectacular advances. They marched triumphantly into Brussels, took Namur, and, during the autumn, reached the Rhine at Coblenz, Cologne, and Dusseldorf. By that time Robespierre and St.-Just had gone to the scaffold and France was able to consolidate her new-found security from invasion while groping toward a new constitution. It was not until 1796 that Jourdan's war flared into movement again. Paris planned a two-pronged attack across the Rhine, aiming to encircle the army of the Archduke Charles. Carnot, who produced the plan, had still not lost his fondness for double encirclements or learned the perils of operating on exterior lines, and the Sambre and Meuse on the left far outpaced the Rhine and Moselle under the dilatory Moreau. Jourdan was within sight of the Bohemian frontier near Amberg before the archduke concentrated against him. Retreating to Würzburg the French were beaten in a hard-fought action (September 3, 1796) and had to fall back to the Rhine. Jourdan had suffered bouts of illness, part of his Caribbean legacy, at intervals through the campaign and resigned his command in late September.

Within a few weeks he was reappointed to the quiescent Army of the North, but for two years his activities were largely political as he was appointed as deputy for Haute-Vienne and soon became President to the Council of Five Hundred; while he held the latter appointment, the Conscription Law of September 5, 1797, which is usually remembered by his name, was passed.[7] A month later he resigned on appointment to the Army of Mayence, which in the following March was optimistically retitled Army of the Danube. By this time he was also in nominal charge of the Army of Helvetia (Massena) on his right and the smaller Army of Observation (Bernadotte) on the left. This array was to open the new war against Austria by striking through neutral Baden, and Jourdan advanced optimistically, remarking, "If the minister keeps his word, I shall be in Vienna."

The minister did not keep his word and instead of the 124,000 men he had been promised the three armies totaled only 72,000. On March 25, 1799, Jourdan with 34,823 men and 62 guns was confronted by the Archduke Charles with 72,335 men and 114 guns at Stockach at the northwestern end of Lake Constance. Believing that boldness was his only resource, Jourdan attacked and achieved a tactical draw, but his position was untenable and, again beset by fever, he fell back to Strasbourg where he was superseded by Massena. Despite his two serious defeats, he was immediately re-employed as inspector general of infantry.

His next problems were in the political field. Bonaparte sought his help before the coup d'état of *Brumaire* (November 9–10, 1799) but was refused. Jourdan was willing enough to see the government changed—"I was revolted by the incapacity of the Directory . . . and shared the opinion of those who thought it necessary to drive them away and modify the Constitution of Year III"[8]—but he differed fundamentally from Bonaparte on what should replace it. Jourdan wanted to widen the basis of government, Bonaparte to narrow it. He was in consequence an object of suspicion to the newly formed consulate and there was talk of deporting him. Fortunately the residual prestige of Fleurus outweighed both his republicanism and the memory of Stockach, and he was re-employed, though in posts of no great importance, and, rather surprisingly, was among the first creation of marshals of the Empire in 1804. His first significant appointment under Napoleon was the result of Massena's rapacity. When Joseph Bonaparte became King of Naples, the peculations of his army commander, the Duke of Rivoli, were on such a scale that the Emperor found it necessary to send an honest man as governor of Naples. He chose Jourdan (March 1806) and a warm friendship grew up between the king and the 44-year-old marshal, so that when Joseph was translated to the throne of Spain he asked that Jourdan should be his chief of staff.

There was delay in authorizing this appointment and it was not until August 22, 1808, that Jourdan joined Joseph at his temporary capital, Vitoria. The King's stay in Madrid had lasted little more than a week before news of Dupont's capitulation at Bailen (July 19) induced Joseph to retire behind the Ebro. There, there was little for king or marshal to do until Napoleon had brought the Grand Army to Spain, retaken Madrid, and sent Sir John Moore's corps on its way to Corunna. Then, in mid-January 1809, the Emperor set off for Paris, leaving behind a master plan for the subjugation of the Peninsula and proclaiming "the Spanish business is finished."[9] His appreciation of the situation was based on a number of dangerous misconceptions, not least that the British would not dare to intervene again in Spain or Portugal. He was convinced that "we have no need of supplies. There is plenty of everything here."[10] He also presupposed freedom of movement for his armies, in Jourdan's words, "that the roads were as freely passable as those from Paris to Lyons."[11] To Napoleon these last two factors were irrelevant since "he kept on repeating that the whole armed force of Spain could not resist 10,000 Frenchmen"[12] and that, as he wrote to his ambassador in Russia, "there is no longer a Spanish army."[13]

Thus, Jourdan found himself forced to implement a plan in which he had no faith; and, to make matters worse, his nominal subordinates, men such as Bessières, Mortier, Ney, Soult, and Victor, scarcely pretended to conform to his orders. None of them had a high opinion of his military talents, and all soon discovered that they could with impunity appeal to the Emperor over his head and that contrary orders frequently came to them direct from Napoleon. Nor was his position strengthened when, through imperial malice or faulty proofreading, his name was omitted from the list of marshals in the *Almanach* for 1809.

The crunch came in July 1809. An army led by Gregorio Cuesta, with 36,000 Spaniards, and Arthur Wellesley, with 21,000 British, was moving on Madrid on the line of the Tagus, but, thanks to poor interallied cooperation, their advance was halting and uncertain. Jourdan concentrated 46,000 men to block them, while, unknown to the allies, Soult with 50,000 more was marching from the north to cut them off from Badajoz and Portugal. Jourdan's force was under the titular command of King Joseph, but it had only to hold its ground for Cuesta and Wellesley to be driven to an eccentric retreat into Andalusia, leaving Portugal and the all-important naval base at Lisbon unguarded. Unfortunately Victor was among those present and he knew better. On

27 July, having refused three direct orders, he made a public scene, accusing Jourdan in front of the whole staff of incompetence. Then, swinging from lethargy to ill-timed activity, he launched an unauthorized night attack on the British position on the Cerro de Medellin, north of Talavera de la Reyna. It was bloodily repulsed but, still without orders, he renewed his onslaught at dawn with the same result.

Jourdan advised Joseph that the army should do no more than hold its position, keeping the enemy in place, so that Soult, whose arrival was expected within a few days, could take them in the rear. Victor demanded that his own corps with that of Sebastiani should make a final assault on the Cerro. "If," he said, 'we cannot take that hill, we had better give up soldiering." Joseph, knowing that if he sided with Jourdan, Victor would "write to the Emperor telling him that he had been prevented from winning a brilliant victory,"[14] gave the younger marshal his head. The third assault was as ineffective as the others, and, after some pointless cannonading, Victor marched off to the rear, leaving the rest of the army to follow. His arrogance had given the British a tactical victory—the Spaniards had barely been engaged—that became a strategic victory when, Soult being late, Wellesley was able to retreat on Badajoz. Matters were not improved by Joseph's report, a farrago of half-truths implying victory, which infuriated Napoleon who blamed the chief of staff: "Let Marshal Jourdan know of my extreme displeasure." To Victor went a mild reprimand: "When one attacks good troops like the English in good positions, without reconnaissance and without the certainty of beating them, one only condemns men to death without purpose."[15]

Before the imperial displeasure could be conveyed to him, Jourdan was once more prostrated by "nervous troubles, stomach colic and backache." He applied for leave and was allowed to return to France in October.

Return to Spain—And the Last Years (1810-1833)

Two years later Jourdan was posted back to Spain as governor of Madrid, a derisory post for a marshal and one that he received only as part of a bribe to King Joseph to prevent him abdicating his throne. In October 1811, a month after his return, he was made chief of staff to the king, but this only gave him effective control over the small Army of the Center, 15,000 men including a division of dubious Spaniards. It was not until March 1812 that Napoleon, concentrating his attention on the imminent Russian campaign, told Joseph that, with the assistance of Jourdan, he was to have the supreme command of all the French armies in Spain. Typically the Emperor failed to make the king's supremacy clear to the various army commanders, and the Army of the North (48,000 strong), which controlled the roads from France to Madrid, received no orders on this subject. Suchet, commanding the Armies of Aragon and of Catalonia (60,600), claimed that the orders could not apply to Catalonia since most of that province had been annexed to France. As far as Aragon was concerned, he paid only lip service to orders from Madrid, an attitude also adopted by Marmont with the Army of Portugal (52,600). Soult, with the Army of the South (66,000), paid less attention to Madrid than anyone else. In a discerning appreciation of the French situation in Spain, written on May 28, 1812, Jourdan pointed out that their armies were absurdly over-stretched since their total strength of 230,187 was tied down to occupying an implacably hostile country while simultaneously they had to guard against an invasion from Portugal where Wellington, who had already seized the border fortresses of Badajoz and Cuidad Rodrigo, had an Anglo–Portuguese army that Madrid estimated at 60,000 strong. It was significant that Napoleon refused to admit that Wellington had more than 50,000 men,[16] while the actual numbers, exclusive of the detachment at Cadiz, exceeded 66,000 rank and file.

In this appreciation Jourdan pointed out that Wellington was at liberty to strike either south at Soult or west at Marmont with an excellent chance of destroying whichever he chose, since there was no coordination between the two armies. He recommended that if 15,000–20,000 fresh troops could not be provided to form a central reserve, Andalusia should be evacuated.[17] No reinforcements could be sent from France, and Soult refused to obey Joseph's orders to leave his vice-royalty in Andalusia. Jourdan therefore asked him to strengthen his northern flank on the Tagus. Once more Soult refused, and, as a direct result, Marmont was disastrously beaten at Salamanca on July 22. The Army of Portugal was forced back to the Ebro. Joseph and Jourdan had to leave Madrid and seek shelter with Suchet at Valencia, where they were joined by an impenitent Soult, loudly protesting at having to abandon Seville. It took the combined strengths of the Armies of the North, the Center, Portugal, and the South to shepherd Wellington back to Cuidad Rodrigo.

Joseph returned to Madrid on December 2 and for several weeks there was an air of relief and relaxation in the capital. With Andalusia lost the military situation was more secure than it had been for two years since 95,000 men could be deployed on the western frontier to check Wellington. The command situation also looked easier. Marmont had been disabled by a serious wound at Salamanca; Soult had been recalled to act as understudy to Berthier. Jourdan, as the only marshal in western Spain, could hope to exercise undisputed command.

On January 6, 20 days after it had been published in Paris, Madrid received a copy of the *29th Bulletin* telling of the destruction of the Grand Army in Russia. Significantly the news arrived by way of Valencia, since the direct road from the capital to France was blocked by a vast uprising of guerrillas, the inevitable consequence of the concentration of troops that had had to be made to drive Wellington back to Portugal in the previous autumn. So bad was the communication that in mid-March Paris was complaining that no acknowledgment had been received for the Emperor's orders dispatched to Madrid more than 10 weeks earlier. At no stage did the Spanish guerrillas make a more decisive contribution to the allied cause, for Napoleon, intent on resuming his detailed interference in the Spanish campaign, ordered five divisions of infantry to be detached from the force facing Portugal and sent to clear the roads between Burgos and the Pyrenees. He believed that this move could be made with safety since "the English are in no condition to attempt anything."[18] When Jourdan asked whether, if Wellington should attack before the five divisions returned, the remaining troops should "risk battle on the Douro or fall back on Burgos,"[19] the complacent reply came back:

> Bearing in mind the circumstances in which the enemy finds himself, there is no reason to suppose that he will take the offensive. His remoteness, his shortage of transport, his constant and timid caution in any operation out of the ordinary, all demonstrate to us that we can act as seems most suitable without worry or inconvenience.[20]

That letter was signed on June 7. On that day Wellington's headquarters were at Palencia, north of Valladolid, while, as Joseph's master of the household noted in his diary, "the [French] army is in full retreat."[21] In the last week of May, Wellington had struck with 80,000 British and Portuguese in two compact columns. The force available to oppose him consisted of 33,000 infantry, 9,000 cavalry, and 100 guns. The result would be the decisive Battle of Vitoria (see p. 168).

Though small in scale compared with the battles in eastern Europe, Vitoria was disastrous for Napoleon's Empire. Not only was the kingdom of Spain irretrievably lost, but the news played a part in persuading Austria to abandon her neutrality when Metternich was awakened in the night with the words, "Le roi Joseph est foutu en Espagne!" A scapegoat had to be found and

Jourdan was the obvious candidate. He was once more *limogé* and his marshal's pay sharply reduced. For all that, Napoleon, whatever their disagreements, recognized his loyalty to France and, in the desperate days of 1814, appointed him to command the Rouen military district. Always ready to serve the existing government if he was not "revolted by their incapacity," he served Louis XVIII after the first Restoration and was made Chevalier de St. Louis, the first title he had accepted. In the Hundred Days, he continued his unobtrusive service, was returned to full pay, and accepted a peerage. After Waterloo the king made him a count and gave him the St.-Esprit. He was still serving when the Revolution of 1830 occurred. Louis-Philippe made him governor of Les Invalides, a post he held until his death three years later.

He appears to have been happy and content in his private life. Even the Duchess of Abrantes could find nothing unkind to say about him; and although General Decaen accused him of taking a mistress on campaign dressed as an aide-de-camp, no one else mentions this foible and it is probable that Decaen was relaying the true story of Massena with a false attribution. Jourdan was a capable rather than a great soldier, but he was an honest man who served France, whoever ruled it. Napoleon, who frequently behaved badly toward and spoke harshly of him, summed Jourdan up while he was at St. Helena:

> I certainly used that man very ill. . . . I have learned with pleasure that since my fall he invariably acted in the best manner. He has thus afforded an example of that praiseworthy elevation of mind which distinguishes men one from another. Jourdan is a true patriot; and that is the answer to many things that have been said of him.[23]

The Battle of Vitoria (June 21, 1813)

Vitoria was Jourdan's last battle and it was one that he had no hope of winning. Not only was the French army outnumbered throughout the campaign, but the command structure was quite as vicious as it had been when a plethora of marshals had followed their own plans. Even before the allied advance had started, Joseph had complained that "there are four commanders-in-chief who divide the command, argue among themselves and snatch supplies from each other."[23] Three of these competing commanders in chief were Generals Gazan (Army of the South), D'Erlon (Center) and Reille (Portugal), but the fourth was Joseph himself who should have been controlling them all, guided by the advice of Jourdan, the senior officer and his own choice as chief of staff. Instead the King chose to command by committee and, in most cases, disregarded Jourdan's views. As soon as it was clear that Wellington was working round their northern flank, Jourdan advised a thrust into Portugal aiming at the allied communications. The army commanders favored withdrawal and Joseph sided with them, taking up a series of defensive positions all of which Wellington outflanked to the north. By June 16 the royal headquarters was at Miranda de Ebro, but again they were outflanked and forced back to Vitoria within 65 miles of the French frontier. The morale of the army slumped, and officers and men alike demanded to know why they must always retreat, why they could not stand and fight. Now it was the army commanders who were anxious for action while Jourdan advised a further withdrawal so that the full strength of the army could be concentrated. "Sarcasm and jests were showered on the prudence of those opposed to fighting. Their prudence was called by another name."[24] Joseph, believing he had time, delayed a decision.

It would be logical to assume that as the combined armies had been maneuvered back into the area held by the Army of the North, they would not only have regained touch with their five detached divisions but would have been reinforced from the 35,000 men on the strength of that army. In practice only two of the lost divisions had rejoined, with fewer than 1,000 men from the local army. Once again, Joseph was at fault, for his request for the return of his divisions was timorous in tone: "If your operations are sufficiently advanced to make it possible without compromising the issue, send back the troops."[25] Naturally little attention had been paid to this plea, and when, late on June 19, the combined armies assembled near Vitoria, their strength was about 60,000, of whom 11,000 were cavalry. There were 138 field guns.

Vitoria, a road center, lies toward the eastern end of a rough oval of rolling plain through which the little river Zadorra flows in from the northeast and, after many meanderings, flows out through the mountains at the southwestern part of the oval. The positions taken up by the three French armies were such as a force might take up at dusk after a long march when they were not expecting an attack. The fact was that none of the senior officers expected to have to fight there. Since Wellington had turned their right with monotonous regularity for the last four weeks, it was assumed that he would do so again and march on Bilbao. In the ordinary course of events, the positions would have been corrected on the following day, June 20, but Jourdan was once more struck down by fever and had to keep to his bed.

This left the overall command in Joseph's hands and he took no action. He was anxious to stay where he was for at least another 24 hours, since this would give time for the vast convoys of refugees and baggage, which were encumbering the march of the army, to get on their way to France. He also hoped to be joined by General Clausel with 10,000 men of the Army of the North during the night of June 20–21. As it happened this force was 36 hours behind schedule and did not come within sight of Vitoria until June 22.

As far as they were not wholly fortuitous, the positions occupied by the French at dawn on June 20 were designed to resist a frontal attack on the south bank of the Zadorra where it flows out of the plain of Vitoria. The largest of the three armies, Gazan's South, was deployed on a three-division front with its left on the foothills of the heights of La Puebla and its right on the river. An independent brigade was posted as advanced guard and there was a division in reserve. The two divisions of the Army of the Center were in support behind the hill of Arinez, and, in their rear, covering the city of Vitoria, were two divisions of the Army of Portugal and King Joseph's Guard. During the day reports arrived of a Spanish force approaching from the north down the Bilbao road. To counter this threat, which was not highly regarded, Reille was told to move one division of Portugal to the north bank of the river. The rest of the army stayed where it was throughout the day. It was a grotesque deployment since not only were South and Portugal back to back, but the bulk of the army relied on the river as a flank guard. The Zadorra is, in Fortescue's words, no more than "a merry brawling trout stream"[26] and was fordable in many places. Worse than this, it was crossed by five bridges in the areas of the Armies of the South and the Center, and these bridges had not been demolished although some had been barricaded. For all intents and purposes, the bulk of the French army had its right flank in the air.

At 4 A.M. on June 21, Jourdan, restored to health, rode out with Joseph to examine the army's positions. Both believed that an attack was unlikely, a belief strengthened by the arrival during the night of a message asserting that "Lord Wellington with a large body of troops had marched on the Bilbao–Vitoria road."[27] Jourdan realized at once that the deployment was faulty and advised that the front be pulled back to a ridge just in front of Vitoria, behind a small stream that ran from the village of Berosteguieta through Zuazo de Alava to the Zadorra near Crispijana, since this would give a much stronger and more compact position. "This new disposition, which without Marshal Jourdan's illness would have been taken up on the previous evening, might perhaps have avoided the day's disaster; however the officer sent to General Gazan to tell him to come to the king reported that he could not leave his troops who were about to be attacked. It was decided that there was no time to make the change."[28]

As the troops approaching Gazan's position pushed their way through the gorge cut by the Zadorra where it left the plain, they were seen to detach a small division of Spaniards to their right so as to secure the commanding height which the French had occupied with a piquet at company strength. Jourdan's reaction to this was to order Gazan to send three brigades up the heights of La Puebla so that they could strike the enemy in the flank while the rest of the Army of the South attacked them in front. According to Gazan, a hostile witness, the marshal hotly insisted that Wellington had changed his approach and that, instead of turning the French right, he was going to turn their left. Some support is lent to this view by the fact that Jourdan later ordered one of the divisions of the Army of the Center up onto the heights, but the cause of this move was Gazan's extreme slowness in dribbling troops to the heights, which forced Jourdan to draw troops from elsewhere for his planned counterstroke. Whatever the reason, the detachment to the French left was greater than they could afford, for whereas Wellington sent only 4,000 Spaniards, later supported by a British brigade (2,500 men), to the heights of La Puebla, the French committed five brigades, 13,000 men.

Far from trying to turn the French left, Wellington, who had 72,000 men with 90 guns against Joseph's 60,000 with 138 guns, was steadily swinging round their right in four columns of which that at La Puebla was the right-hand one. His right–center and left–center columns crossed the Zadorra behind the front of the Army of the South with scarcely a scuffle, and, having detached so much to their left, neither the South nor the Center could spare the strength to stop them. The extreme left-hand column of the allied array was following the Spaniards coming down the Bilbao road from the north.

As soon as Jourdan grasped that the existing positions were untenable, he ordered a retreat to the Berosteguieta–Crispijana ridge where he had already deployed a powerful artillery defense. Most of the troops on the plain managed to break contact with less trouble than might have been expected, but, once again, the commander of the Army of the South wrecked the plan.

General Gazan, instead of taking his divisions to the positions which had been pointed out to him, strongly secured on his right by the [*Armée du Centre*], continued to retreat following the slope

171

of the heights, leaving the high road and the town of Vitoria far to his left [as he retreated] and a large gap between his own army and that of *Centre.*[29]

Gazan claimed that he received no orders as to the rearward position that he was to take up and that, while retreating, he was "continually outflanked on the right." All the indications are that at least the last part of this was untrue and that D'Erlon had established his remaining division of the Army of the Center at the river end of the new line, while Gazan retreated straight past him leaving his flank in the air. Fortunately for the French, Wellington's right-hand column was unavoidably late and, even when it arrived, was led with less determination than might have been hoped. This enabled Reille's Army of Portugal, although losing control of the main road to France, to hold the northern flank open long enough for the other armies to beat a disorderly retreat on the secondary road to Salvatierra. This was little more than a track "intersected with impassable ravines, ditches, etc." so that no effective cavalry pursuit could be launched, but all the French artillery, except two pieces that were captured next day, had to be abandoned with a vast quantity of baggage and the military chest. The loss in men was only 8,500, of whom 2,500 were returned as missing, 2,000 being taken prisoner. Joseph and Jourdan almost joined the prisoners when British hussars and light dragoons rode in among the staff, but were rescued by Joseph's mounted guard. Nevertheless, king and marshal were separated and did not meet again until 11 P.M. when Joseph was having supper at Salvatierra with D'Erlon and others. Tired and dirty, Jourdan came into the room and looked around, remarking, "Well, gentlemen, you wanted to have a battle and we appear to have lost it."[30]

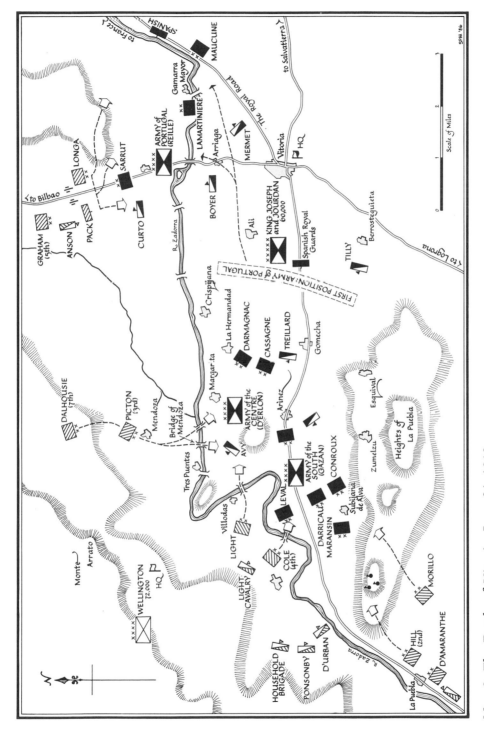

Map 9. The Battle of Vitoria, June 21, 1813

TEXTUAL REFERENCES

1. General Susane, quoted by R.W. Phipps, *The Armies of the First French Republic and the Rise of the Marshals of Napoleon I* (Oxford, 1926–39), Vol. 1, p. 17.
2. A. Aspinall, ed., *The Later Correspondence of George III* (Cambridge, 1968), Vol. 2, Letter no. 1060, p. 203.
3. Phipps, *op. cit.*, p. 26.
4. *Ibid.*, p. 270.
5. *Ibid.*, pp. 272–73.
6. N. J. de D. Soult, *Mémoires . . .* (Paris, 1854), Vol. 1, p. 168.
7. Jourdan's Conscription Law established that every French male had to register for military service at the age of 20. Married men and those with dependents were excepted. If supply exceeded demand, selection was decided by lot.
8. Phipps, *op. cit.*, Vol. 5, p. 454.
9. *Correspondance de Napoléon Ier* (Paris, 1854–69), Vol. 28, No. 14731, to Jérôme, dated January 16, 1809.
10. *Ibid.*, No. 14469, to Dejean, November 13, 1808.
11. J. B. Jourdan, *Mémoires Militaires*, ed. by Vicomte de Grouchy (Paris, 1899), p. 170.
12. *Ibid.*
13. *Lettres inédites . . .* , ed. by Lecestre (Paris, 1897), to Caulaincourt, January 7, 1809, p. 390.
14. Jourdan, *op. cit.*, p. 235.
15. *Correspondance de Napoléon ler* Vol. 18, No. 15694, to Clarke, August 21, 1809.
16. *Ibid.*, Vol. 23, No. 18632, to Berthier, April 3, 1812.
17. Jourdan, *op. cit.*, to Joseph, May 28, 1812, pp. 386–95.
18. *Correspondance, op. cit.*, Vol. 24, No. 19546, to Clarke, February 7, 1813.
19. J. Bonaparte, *Mémoires et Correspondance*, Jourdan to Clarke, May 16, 1813, Vol. 9, p. 274.
20. *Ibid.*, Clarke to Jourdan, May 16, 1813, p. 290.
21. *Ibid.*, Miot's diary for June 7, 1813, p. 467.
22. E. de la Cases, *Memorial of St. Helena* (London, 1823), entry for October 25, 1816, p. 3.
23. Bonaparte, *op. cit.*, Joseph to Clarke, April 1, 1813, p. 240.
24. M. de Melito, *Memoires*, ed. by Fleischmann, trans. by Hoey and Lilley (London, 1881), Vol. 2, p. 598.
25. Bonaparte, *op. cit.*, letter to Clausel, May 27, 1813, p. 280.
26. Sir John Fortescue, *History of the British Army* (London, 1917), Vol. 9, p. 162.
27. Gazan's first account in *Supplementary Despatches of the Duke of Wellington*, ed. by Second Duke (London, 1872), Vol. 14, p. 237.
28. Jourdan, *op. cit.*, p. 476.
29. *Ibid.*, p. 479.
30. de Melito, *op. cit.*, p. 610.

BIBLIOGRAPHICAL NOTE

Jourdan is said to have written a complete history of his part in the campaigns up to 1799, but only his *Mémoires pour servir à l'histoire de la Campagne de 1799* was published in Paris, (1818). For his earlier battles, the most reliable accounts are both by V. Dupuis, viz., *La Campagne de 1793 à l'Armée du Nords et des Ardennes d'Hondschoote à Wattignies* (Paris, 1909) and *Les Opérations Militaire sur la*

Sambre en 1794: Bataille de Fleurus (Paris, 1907). For the English reader, R. W. Phipp's *The Armies of the First French Republic and the Rise of the Marshals of Napoleon I,* 5 vols. (Oxford, 1926–39), is invaluable if confusingly arranged. The political background can be found in R. R. Palmer's *Twelve Who Ruled: The Committee of Public Safety During the Terror* (Princeton, 1941).

The primary source for the peninsular war must be Jourdan's own *Mémoires Militaires,* ed. by Vicomte de Grouchy (Paris, 1899), supplemented by Ducasse's edition of *Mémoires et Correspondance Politique et Militaire du Roi Joseph* (Paris, 1854), Vols. 4–9. For an overall picture of the campaigns, there is *Legacy of Glory: The Bonaparte Kingdom of Spain* by Michael Glover (New York and London, 1971). For the Battle of Vitoria, the French sources are somewhat scattered, but the reports of Generals Reille and D'Erlon can be found in Joseph's correspondence. Two self-exculpatory reports from Gazan are most easily found from British sources. The longer of the two is printed in Wellington's *Supplementary Despatches of the Duke of Wellington,* ed. by Second Duke (London, 1872), Vol. 14, p. 237, while the other, together with a covering letter to Soult, is to be found in *The Dickson Manuscripts,* ed. by J. H. Leslie (R. A. Institution, Woolwich, 1908–09).

CHRONOLOGY

1735, May 28	—Born at Strasbourg
1752	—Enlisted as volunteer cadet in the Lowendahl Regiment
1753	—Became an ensign in the Royal Bavarian Regiment
1756, May 6	—Received rank of lieutenant in the Alsatian Volunteers
1758, April 9	—Became junior captain in a regiment of dragoons
1758–62	—Active service in Germany
1761, April 13	—Captain in the Volunteers of the Dauphiné
1763, April 12	—Captain in the Conflans Legion
1765 and 1766,	—Went on important missions to the Poles and Tartars
1769, March 24	—Became captain of hussars.
1771	—Served in Poland with a corps of volunteers
1772, March 24	—Received rank of lieutenant-colonel in the cavalry
1780, April 2	—Lieutenant colonel in the Colonel-General's Hussars
1788, March 9	—Promoted *maréchal de camp* (major-general)
1791, February	—Commander of the Upper Rhine, later of the Lower Rhine
1792, March 20	—Received rank of lieutenant general
August 20	—Appointed commander of *l'Armée du Centre*
September 20	—Battle of Valmy
November 11	—Commander of *l'Armée des Alpes*
1793, May 20	—Commander of *les Armées des Alpes et d'Italie*
October	—Arrested and imprisoned
1795, January 15	—Reinstated at his former rank
March 3	—Again commander of *les Armées* (as above)
1797, September 13	—Withdrew from service in the field
1798, September 15	—Inspector general of the cavalry of *l'Armée d'Angleterre*
1799, December 24	—Became a senator
1804, May 19	—Appointed *Maréchal d'Empire* (fifteenth in the order of promotion)
1808, June 3	—Created duke of Valmy
1815, June	—Honored as a peer of France
1820, September 13	—Died in Paris; buried in Cemetery of Père Lachaise.

CHAPTER TEN

THE GOOD OFFICER

Kellermann

by

Peter Hofschröer

Background and Early Military Experience (1735-1790)

François Christophe Kellermann was a descendant of an old Saxon family that had been settled in Alsace since the sixteenth century.[1] He was born in Strasbourg on May 28, 1735. Not much more than 50 years earlier, Strasbourg had been a "Free City" in the German Empire, and even today Alsace is a German-speaking province within France's borders. So Kellermann was something of a foreigner within the French Army. Furthermore, he was not of noble birth, unlike many French officers at the time. His family were tailors by profession, and his father, by becoming director of tax collecting in Strasbourg, entered the ranks of the petty bourgeoisie of royal functionaries.[2] Thus, not only was Kellermann of non-French origin, he had also started life rather low down on the social scale. Yet he rose to senior rank in the Royal Army and was one of those lucky men that joined the French Army with a marshal's baton in their knap-sacks. Unlike a number of Napoleon's marshals, Kellermann had advanced most of the way toward being a marshal before the days of the Revolution and Empire. French society of the Old Regime is often said to have been stale and socially rigid, yet the rise of Kellermann and his father before him indicates that with natural ability and hard work it was possible for a "working-class immigrant," as some of his contemporaries may well have seen him, a man who spoke French with a jarring accent and who spelled the language the way he spoke, to become a general of the Royal Army.

He entered military service at the age of 17, joining the Lowendahl Regiment, a German regiment in French service, as a cadet in 1752. As was customary for young men of the middle and upper classes at this time, Kellermann started his military career as an officer aspirant. A year later Kellermann was trans-ferred to the Royal Bavarian Regiment with the rank of ensign. His first experience of warfare came in that global conflict known as the Seven Years' War (1756–1763). Initially, he served as a lieutenant in the Alsatian Volunteers, fighting in Germany. He later became a junior captain in the dragoons, distinguishing himself at Bergen and Friedberg. In 1761 he became a captain of the Volunteers of the Dauphine and earned fame by taking 300 grenadiers and General Scheider prisoner. In 1763 he was trans-ferred to the Conflans Legion.[3] Most of his experience in the Seven Years' War was as a commander of irregular cavalry in the "war of outposts." Many a future general started his military career in the light troops, and Kellermann was one such general.

Once this historic war was over, Kellermann certainly did not fade away into the obscurity of garrison life. In 1765 and

1766 he was charged with important missions in Poland and Russia. In 1769 he became a captain of hussars and he also married in that year. Shortly afterward he became father to a son who himself would become one of the great cavalry generals of history, earning fame at Marengo. In 1771 he was retrospectively awarded the Cross of St. Louis for distinguished cavalry work in the Seven Years' War.[4] Such was his reputation as a commander in the war of outposts that he was sent to Poland in 1771 as an instructor. Here he helped organize and lead various irregular cavalry formations, such as a corps of volunteers under Vioménil and the cavalry in the Palatinate of Krakov. On his return to France in 1772, he obtained the rank of lieutenant-colonel in the cavalry. The days of daring missions seemed to be over, for the time being, at least.

Kellermann now settled down into a military career in peacetime, a time of boring routine and constant parades. For somebody with the energy and ambition of Kellermann, life must have suddenly become rather tedious. Promotion in peacetime came usually as a result of court favoritism. Kellermann's non-aristocratic background would be of no help to him. All that he had to offer was his good organizational ability—and that he put to good use, working his way up through the ranks, step by step. In 1776 he received his own squadron. In 1779 he became a major in the Conflans Hussars, a unit he had served in during the Seven Years War. A year later he became lieutenant colonel in the Colonel-General's Hussars, a rather prestigious regiment. In 1784 he became a brigade commander, and his file in the War Archives reads: "A very intelligent and well informed officer. A good officer." It may well have taken Kellermann over 35 years of service to reach the rank of major general, but to be in such a position in his early fifties was quite an achievement for somebody with his disadvantages of background.

Thus, on the eve of the Revolution, Kellermann had attained the rank of a junior general. In his career so far, he had amassed years of experience in a variety of roles, all of which would stand him in good stead for the fateful year of 1792. He had commanded volunteers and seen their strengths and weaknesses. He had raised, organized, and led raw irregulars. He had spent those long years in routine, painstaking organizational work. He knew how to handle inexperienced troops and, with careful attention to detail, how to make them into good soldiers. Moreover, he knew how to make the most of unfavorable social and political conditions and to rise in rank despite being at a disadvantage. Both the Revolution and the Empire came to need such skills, and Kellermann profited from whatever regime he served.

The Future Marshal's Heyday (1791–1792)

The year 1792 marked the pinnacle of Kellermann's achievements on the field of battle. France was very much in the throes of the Revolution. Nominally still a monarchy, the powers of the king had been severely curtailed. Political instability within the government had its repercussions within the military hierarchy. Any fault, real or imaginary, on the part of a commanding general was likely to end in decapitation. On the other hand, as heads were quite literally rolling, then there were greater opportunities for men of ambition careful enough to survive to make it to the top. Anyone who accepted a senior position in the army was on a knife edge. Success could lead to fame and power, failure to the guillotine.

Kellermann was a man of patriotic sentiment, a well-intentioned old officer who had some sympathy for the first phases of the Revolution. However, he was too good a professional soldier not to object to what the revolutionary leadership was doing to the army.[5] Being of a rather humble background himself and having spent so long climbing to a senior rank, Kellermann no doubt welcomed an end to the exclusive privileges of the nobility. At one stage he was himself placed under arrest and imprisoned. This turned out to be rather a close shave, but being a natural survivor he soon returned to his former position and continued to hold senior rank throughout the Revolution, Empire, and Restoration.

France was in her hour of need and a man of Kellermann's talents did not have long to wait to be called on to serve his country. In February 1791 he was appointed commander of the Upper Rhine. Here his experience in the Seven Years' War, in Poland, and in Russia came into good use. With foreign deserters, the debris of the Saxon hussars and the Royal German Cavalry, he organized a legion that bore his name. He took this legion with him when nominated commander-in-chief of the Army of the Center.[6]

At the end of 1791, three armies were formed to defend France's north-eastern frontier against invasion. The Army of the North held the northern fortresses; the Army of the Center had its headquarters in Metz; the Army of the Rhine was based around Strasbourg. Kellermann, promoted to lieutenant-general on March 20, 1792, had been commanding at Landau. In May he was moved to the camp at Neukirchen and there he commanded the Division of the Saar. His force, consisting of five battalions of regulars, five of volunteers, with five regiments of horses, connected the left of Rhine with the right of Center. Kellermann used the time he had available to get his troops into shape. Here, the experience gained in the years of peace came into good use. He worked and drilled his men; he taught them how to pitch and strike camp and to make fortifications.[7] By linking each battalion of volunteers with one of regulars, he amalgamated the experience and professionalism of the old army with the enthusiasm and patriotic sentiment of the new. In July he was moved to Wissembourg where he served under Lamorlière. On August 20 the Provisional Executive Council appointed him commander-in-chief of the Army of the Center, replacing Luckner. This promotion was owed largely to the friendship of Servan, the minister of war. This appointment was to be his greatest challenge to date, and one that called on all his experience and taxed all his skills. Moreover, it was to provide him with his greatest opportunity to gain fame and renown, and, characteristically, Kellermann's success at Valmy later that year was owed largely to his sheer hard work and organizational ability.

When he arrived at his new headquarters on September 2, Kellermann found a fortress without stores and an army without discipline. He immediately set to work rectifying this lamentable state of affairs and was gladly assisted by the able Berthier, the staff officer who was later to become Napoleon's chief aide. Kellermann's first action was to send home the battalions of volunteers of 1792 who had been arriving in rags and without arms. He selected a few men from each battalion to use as light troops and as sappers. He weeded out the undesirables and drafted reinforcements into his most reliable regiments. In two short weeks of intensive effort, he had entirely transformed his army. It now consisted of 20,000 fighting men capable of bearing arms and achieving success in the field.[8]

On September 12 Dumouriez, commander of the Army of the North, asked Kellermann to join him. This request became a cry for urgent assistance once the pressure of attempting to hold up the advancing Prussians of the Duke of Brunswick in the defiles of the Forest of Argonne became intolerable. He effected the required junction on the evening of September 19. Dumouriez's men consisted largely of panic-stricken volunteers, whereas Kellermann had been sensible enough to send his home. Kellermann's army marched to join Dumouriez as a disciplined body under the command of its leaders. It is rather ironic that the Revolution was saved by the old army under the command of a royal officer. A further twist to this irony is the fact that this officer of the old army was not of the aristocratic mold, but rather a man of a more humble background who by sheer effort had dragged himself up through the ranks. Finding for once an army that was prepared to offer battle, the Duke of Brunswick decided not to waste his men and fell back from the fateful field of Valmy (see p. 184).

It is thus clear that this victory of sorts at Valmy was owed not to the patriotic fervor of the national volunteers of 1792. First, all of Kellermann's cavalry and artillery were regulars. Second, Kellermann had 14 battalions of regulars and 9 of volunteers. Of the latter, six hardly so much as saw the field of battle. Even then, it is likely that the volunteer battalions themselves contained a proportion of experienced soldiers. Finally, most of the officers were old, experienced men.[9] It is with much the same type of army that fought in the Seven Years' War that Kellermann defended the Revolution.

Kellermann's own performance on the field of battle is worthy of comment. By personal example, on horseback in the firing line, he encouraged his men. He rallied them after an exploding ammunition wagon threw several regiments into panic. The remainder of his military career, although distinguished, was not as dramatic and epoch making as Valmy. Kellermann was an organizer of men, a leader on the field of battle, but in no way was he an aspiring and imaginative general of the mould of Napoleon Bonaparte.

The Marshal's Later Years (1793-1820)

The bold stand of Kellermann's men at Valmy soon petered out after a half-hearted pursuit of the Prussians. Kellermann was relieved of his command on November 5 and transferred to the Army of the Alps where he replaced Montesquiou, arriving at his new post on December 21. Almost immediately Kellermann came under political scrutiny. His success at Valmy was due to his use of regular troops and not the politically favored volunteers. The Representatives, the revolutionary government, saw this as opposition to the Revolution. Kellermann was now politically suspect. After a hearing in 1793, common sense won the day and he was declared innocent. That, however, was not good enough for the authorities in Paris, and he was commanded to appear before the Committee of Public Safety, which was soon convinced of his reliability. He returned to command the Army of the Alps. Kellermann was now walking a tightrope, but, as always, he survived this crisis and came out of it with an enhanced reputation.

Given the distasteful task of besieging the rebellious city of Lyons, Kellermann's ability as an organizer still shone. At a time when the armies of the Republic lacked most essential items,

Kellermann had managed to establish stores with clothing for 50,000 men and equipment for 32,000.[10]

Kellermann came closest to suffering the fate of many of his contemporaries when arrested and imprisoned in October 1793. He remained in limbo in the Abbaye Prison in Paris until November 1794. He was fortunate indeed to survive the Terror. Time and again, orders for his trial were passed over, and when he finally did come up for trial on November 8, 1794, the worst excesses of the Terror were over and Kellermann, the survivor, was acquitted. More than that, he was restored to his former rank and, in March 1795, returned to the Armies of the Alps and Italy as their general.[11] With characteristic energy he molded Italy into a fighting force and was on the point of taking the offensive when his command was restricted to the Alps. Gone was Kellermann's best chance ever for obtaining fame as a victor on the field of battle. Bonaparte was to be the man that providence chose to win honor and glory in Italy. The Army of the Alps was disbanded in September 1797 and that marked the end of an important phase in Kellermann's military career. He was first put in charge of the Seventh Military Division in Lyons, then dismissed from service. Never again was Kellermann to command troops in a theater of operations.

A man of Kellermann's talents could not be left out in the cold for long. France needed his experience and organizational ability again. The next phase of his military career gave him every opportunity of utilizing his skills to the full. From February 1798 he worked on a reorganization of the cavalry, the arm of which he had the most experience in his younger days. In April he was appointed president of a military commission examining fortresses. In September he became inspector-general of the cavalry of the Army of England. In 1799 he was moved to a similar post dealing with the cavalry of the Interior and of the Guard of the Directory. In June he was moved again, this time to the Batavian Republic (Holland). Along with his military career, Kellermann also entered politics, first becoming a senator at the end of 1799, then later president of the Senate. Napoleon appointed him a marshal of the Empire on May 19, 1804, although he never commanded troops on the field of battle as such. He was the oldest to be so honored. Bonaparte may well have ousted Kellermann from command of the Army of Italy, but he was not slow to shower this once ambitious Alsatian with honors, and he was continually called upon to command the Army of the Reserve while the ruthless Corsican followed the star of his destiny. On February 2, 1805, Kellermann was awarded the Grand Eagle of the Legion of Honor. During the Austerlitz campaign, he commanded III Corps of the Reserve on the Rhine. While his master was winning honors on campaign against the Prussians in 1806, the old warrior was teaching the National Guard the rudiments of drill. In further recognition of his services, Kellermann was given an estate in Germany, and, on June 3, 1808, was awarded the title of Duke of Valmy. Whenever Napoleon was off abroad pursuing his expansionist policies, Kellermann was always there, right behind him, organizing the recruits and reserves, the cannon fodder of the next campaign. In 1808 he commanded the Army of Reserve of Spain, in 1809 he was on the Rhine, in 1812 he was supervising the National Guard, in 1813 he was again on the Rhine, and in 1814 he was providing Napoleon with badly needed reinforcements. Approaching his eightieth birthday, Kellermann still had his sharp eye for detail. Charged with remounting the troops reunited before Paris, the reports he made show that he still paid close attention to every point—the qualities of the officers, the details of dress and equipment, horsemanship training, etc.[12] He was thorough, a good organizer, and respected by his men.

Surviving the abdication of Napoleon, he was made a peer of France in June 1815. During the Hundred Days, he was sensible enough to keep his distance from his former master, and as an octogenarian he participated in the reorganization of the army made during the Restoration. As far as he was allowed, he applied the fruits of his experience and knowledge to the needs and aspirations of the cavalry.[13] He died in 1820.

Kellermann was thus a man of many talents whose capabilities and sheer hard work allowed him to rise to positions of authority during the Old Monarchy, the Revolution, the Empire, and the Restoration. He was born a survivor, a person who could make the most of any situation and whose eye for detail and great organizational ability did not allow him to be ignored for too long. His fame on the field of battle is limited mainly to Valmy. This fame was not due to attaining a spectacular victory, but rather to keeping his men standing in one spot at a time when everyone else was running away.

The Cannonade of Valmy (September 20, 1792)

Although most historians do not go so far as to describe the encounter between 35,000 Prussians[14] under the duke of Brunswick and the united armies of Dumouriez and Kellermann as a "battle," a number do term it a victory for Kellermann. It is rather questionable that a non-event like Valmy can be defined as a "loss" or "victory," at least in military terms. Rather, it was largely an exchange of artillery fire lasting several hours that, at the time it occurred, decided little. One could go so far as to say it consisted of an exchange of hot air—and much hot air has been made of it since. Militarily it was rather a dull and unimpressive affair and was an indecisive encounter. Psychologically it became a great boost to French morale—at last one of their armies had stood and fought when on earlier occasions the defenders of the French Revolution had been rather inclined to turn tail at the mere sight of the enemy. Politically it marked a significant turning point. What chance Brunswick had ever had, if indeed any at all, of putting down the Revolution was now gone, and Europe was to suffer the ravages of over 20 years of almost uninterrupted war.

An indication of the low state of morale of the French forces at this time comes from an incident on September 15, 1792, when a raiding party of 1,400 Prussian hussars with some infantry and artillery support encountered Dumouriez's vanguard under Chazot at Moncheutin. The mere sight of the hussars caused the French 2nd Dragoons and 12th Chasseurs to flee, and in their panic, they rode down the 5th Grenadier Battalion. This panic spread throughout the entire column and over 10,000 Frenchmen took to their heels to save their skins. Eight officers and 275 men were taken prisoner, and in addition, the Prussians captured four cannons, 36 supply wagons, and the French war chest.[15] With such incidents being not infrequent, how could Brunswick expect any serious opposition to his advance? In fact, the weather and supply difficulties were causing him more problems than the French Army. A somewhat reluctant Kellermann was marching to join Dumouriez. Together they were going to make a stand, a stand that was going to turn the tide and make history. Kellermann himself thought this folly and tried his best to avoid such an encounter so soon, but destiny had chosen another course of events.

The condition of Dumouriez's army was shocking. The 50,000 men, including Kellermann's force, at his disposal may sound an impressive number, but these troops were tired from many long marches in the heavy autumn rains, they were poorly fed, and many lacked proper clothing. Sickness was rampant, the spirit of the men was at a low ebb, and the poorly trained and ill-disciplined volunteers were prone to panic. Any general in his right mind would have been reluctant to face battle with such an army.[16]

Brunswick's men fared little better themselves. The weather had hindered their advance. The muddy roads had held back their supplies and the ammunition trains were well to the rear, leaving the front-line echelons short.[17] The Prussians, too, were suffering from rain-induced illnesses such as exposure and particularly from dysentery. They probably had no more than 35,000 men fit enough to fight. However, the spirit of the troops remained unbroken, there were very few cases of desertion, and Clerfayt's Austrians were only a day's march away.[18]

The allies, however, lacked a clear military aim and an overall plan of war. The King of Prussia, accompanying his army, had the noble intention of liberating his French brother-monarch and the lovely Marie Antoinette, but Brunswick showed little enthusiasm for sliding around in the mud, short of essential supplies and with little chance of getting to Paris and overthrowing the Revolution with the forces available to him. He was clearly not going to advance in the face of any serious opposition.

That was the situation on September 19, the eve of Valmy. Dumouriez was determined to make a stand and looked upon union with Kellermann as his best chance of success. Brunswick was prepared to continue his slow advance only if there was little or no resistance. One resolute stand by the French would be enough to dissuade him from continuing.

On the evening of September 19, Dumouriez prepared to face Brunswick while Kellermann, urging a retreat toward Châlons, bivouacked after crossing the River Auve and awaited the coming dawn shrouded in fog. Dumouriez believed that it was his shaky army that would bear the brunt of any possible attack. Kellermann's intention was to fall back across the Auve the next day. Brunswick was planning to maneuver to the northwest of Dumouriez, thereby threatening his communications with Paris and obliging him to retire. The Duke would then have struck Dumouriez in the plain and destroyed his army, forcing Kellermann to go back the way he had come. However, the King of Prussia intervened and overruled Brunswick. He was ordered to cut the Châlons road. Thus, it was Kellermann's outposts he first encountered and battle was joined with the one army in France that was capable of offering any serious resistance.[19]

At about 6:30 A.M. two columns of Prussians were ordered to march off. The first consisted of hussars and dragoons with a horse battery followed by two battalions of light infantry, a foot battery, two line regiments, and another battery. The second column consisted of a hussar regiment, half a horse battery, a foot battery, three line battalions, and another foot battery.[20]

At about 8 A.M. Kellermann's artillery opened up at the targets they could just make out in the thick mist. A sporadic exchange of fire continued. Thirty-five squadrons of Prussian cavalry under the Duke of Saxe–Weimar drove a French battery out of La Lune. The road to Châlons was now cut and Kellermann's position so threatened that he decided to start a withdrawal toward the Auve. In so doing Kellermann took up the position on the heights around Valmy that Dumouriez had originally wanted him to. Brunswick had not intended to attack Kellermann and Kellermann had not intended to fight Brunswick. Nevertheless, the combat started. Dumouriez moved to support Kellermann's flanks, moving on both Mount Yvron and La Lune. The mist dissipated at around noon.[21]

The Prussians now formed up for the attack. Five companies of riflemen spread out in a skirmish line. Three battalions of light infantry moved up to support them. The Prussian artillery opened up. That of the French replied. Then the sounds of battle were drowned by a massive explosion. Several French ammunition wagons had gone up. The French artillery ceased firing. Three regiments of infantry and the entire ammunition column fled. At this moment of crisis, Kellermann galloped up and stopped the panic from spreading. Now was the best time for the Prussians to press home their attack. However, the cautious Brunswick hesitated.[22] The opportunity was lost, and the French rallied. Kellermann did not lose a moment. He brought up fresh batteries and opened fire again. His men now stood firm. It was 3:30 P.M. and Brunswick uttered those famous words, "We do not have to fight here"[23]—and the battle was over. The exchange of artillery fire continued into the evening through pouring rain. The Prussians had lost 184 men, the French around 300. Both sides had used up so much ammunition that they did not want to continue the fight the next day.

Kellermann had acted coolly and decisively in battle. He did not want to fight in circumstances he saw as being unfavorable, but destiny put him in the firing line. All credit must go to Kellermann for having built up an army of disciplined and reliable men so rapidly. His most significant act that day was to stop the panic caused by the exploding ammunition wagons and holding his men firm. Valmy was not one of the great feats of arms in history and Kellermann was not one of history's great generals, but what he did achieve on September 20, 1792, was to prove to be one of history's decisive events.

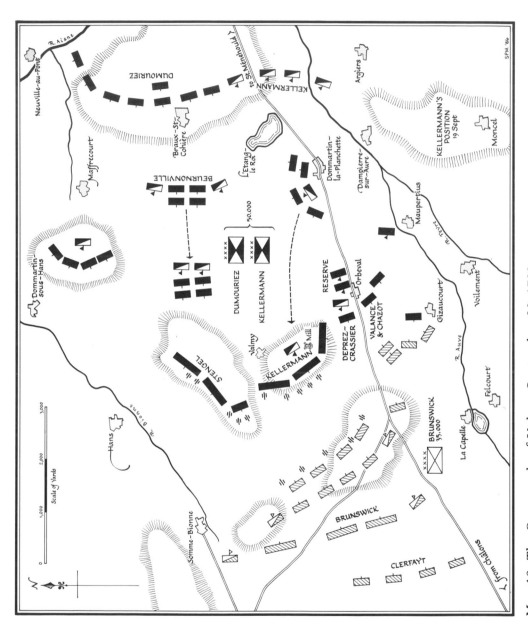

Map 10. The Cannonade of Valmy, September 20, 1792

TEXTUAL REFERENCES

1. R. P. Dunn Pattison, *Napoleon's Marshal's* (Boston, 1909), p. 317.
2. G. Godlewski, *Les Maréchaux de Napoléon*, in the periodical *Le Souvenir Napoléon* No. 328, (March 1983), p. 2.
3. G. Six and A. Lasseray, *Dictionnaire biographique des généraux et amiraux francais de la Révolution et de l'Empire* (Paris, 1934).
4. Dunn-Pattison, *op. cit.*, p. 317.
5. R. W. Phipps, *The Armies of the First French Republic and the Rise of the Marshals of Napoleon I* (Oxford, 1935–39), Vol. 1, p. 52.
6. H. Choppin, *Un Inspecteur général de cavalerie sous le Directoire et le Consulat* (Paris, 1898), p. 7.
7. Phipps, *op. cit.*, p. 9.
8. Dunn-Pattison, *op. cit.*, p. 318.
9. Phipps, *op. cit.*, p. 14; Choppin, *op. cit.*, p. 3.
10. Phipps, *op. cit.*, Vol. 3, p. 98.
11. *Ibid.*, p. 107.
12. Choppin, *op. cit.*, p. 9.
13. *Ibid.*, p. 70.
14. C. Jany, *Geschichte der Preußischen Armee vom 15.Jahrhundert bis 1914* (Berlin, 1928–33), Vol. 3, p. 252.
15. K. and K. Kriegsarchiv, *Krieg gegen die Französische Revolution 1792–1797. Feldzug 1792* (Vienna, 1905), Vol. 2, pp. 158f.
16. *Ibid.*, p. 161.
17. O. von Massenbach, *Memoiren zur Geschichte des preußschen Staats* (Amsterdam, 1809), Vol. 1, p. 99.
18. Jany, *op. cit.*, p. 252.
19. Phipps, *op. cit.*, Vol. 2, pp. 19f.
20. Massenbach, *op. cit.*, pp. 81f.
21. Jany, *op. cit.*, p. 252.
22. Massenbach, *op. cit.*, p. 89.
23. *Ibid.*, p. 98.

BIBLIOGRAPHICAL NOTE

As well as those main reference works listed elsewhere, the following were also consulted: R.P. Dunn Pattison's *Napoleon's Marshals* (Boston, 1909) is not the most reliable of works, but it nevertheless contains several insights into the character and judgment of Kellermann.

H. Choppin, *Un Inspecteur général de cavalerie sous le Directoire et le Consulat* (Paris, 1898), provided one or two snippets of information useful to judge the character of Kellermann. C. Jany's *Geschichte der Preußischen Armee vom 15.Jahrhundert bis 1914*, 4 vols. (Berlin, 1928–33), is the standard history of the Prussian army written by the most renowned historian produced by the Grand General Staff. Volume 3 covers the period 1763–1807. The chapter dealing with the 1792 campaign provided much factual information.

K. and K Kriegsarchiv's *Krieg gegen die Französische Revolution 1792–1797. Feldzug 1792* (Vienna, 1905), Vol. 2, is a history of the wars of the French Revolution produced by the Austrian General Staff. It remains one of the most reliable works on the subject. Also useful is Oberst von Massenbach's *Memoiren zur Geschichte des preußischen Staats* (Amsterdam, 1809), Vol. 1. Massenbach was a member of the Duke of Brunswick's staff at Valmy. His first-hand account of the battle is one that many others derive from. A. Chuquet's *Les Guerres de la Révolution* (Paris, 1887–88), Vol. 1–3, is one of the most thorough on the subject of the wars of the Revolution and is essential background reading. The volumes consulted cover the invasion, Valmy, and the retreat.

CHRONOLOGY

1769, April 10	—Born at Lectoure (Gers)
1792, June 20	—Enlisted in the 2nd Volunteer Battalion of Gers; served in the Pyrenees
1795, March 19	—Married Paulette Méric at Perpignan
1796, April 14–17	—Battles of Voltri and Dego
May 8–10	—Battles of Fombio and Lodi
September 8	—Battle of Bassano
November 15–17	—Wounded three times at Battle of Arcola
1797, March 17	—Promoted to *général de brigade*
1798, July 2	—Siege and storming of Alexandria
1799, March 3–7	—Storming of Jaffa
March 19– May 20	—Siege of Acre
July 25	—Battle of Aboukir
	—Divorced wife because of her infidelity
1800, May 10	—Confirmed as *général de division*
May 14	—Commanded advance guard crossing St. Bernard
June 9	—Battle of Montebello
June 14	—Battle of Marengo
September 15	—Married Louise Antoinette Guéhéneuc
1801, November 14	—Ambassador to Portugal
1804, May 19	—Appointed *Maréchal d'Empire* (tenth in seniority)
1805, October 20	—Capitulation of Ulm
December 2	—Battle of Austerlitz
1806, October 10	—Battles of Saalfeld and Jena
December 26	—Battle of Pultusk
1807, March 18– May 27	—Siege of Danzig
June 10–14	—Battles of Heilsberg and Friedland
1808, March 19	—Named *duc de Montebello*
November 23	—Battle of Tudela
1809, January 9	—Conducts Siege of Saragossa
April 20–23	—Battles of Abensberg, Landshut, Eckmühl, and Ratisbon
May 21–31	—Mortally wounded at Essling, and dies
1810, July 6	—Buried at the Pantheon

CHAPTER ELEVEN

ROLAND OF THE ARMY

Lannes

by

Donald D. Horward

Learning the Profession (1769–1797)

Jean Lannes, born in Lectoure (Gers) on April 10, 1769, was the second son of a Gascon farmer. Although his parents owned a farm and a modest village house, Jean, four brothers, and a sister received little formal education. An older brother, a priest, shared his meager education with Jean, teaching him to read and write. He was apprenticed to a dyer but little is known about his teenage years at Lectoure. When war broke out in April 1792, Lannes, then 23, enlisted in the 2nd Volunteer Battalion of the Gers and, on the same day, June 20, he was elected a *sous-lieutenant* (second lieutenant) by his comrades.[1]

As war spread across Europe, the battalions of the Gers were sent first to camp at Miral near Toulouse where they received their initial military training. There Lannes was fortunate to come under the influence of Lieutenant Pierre Charles Pouzet who instilled in him military instincts and a basic understanding of tactics. The two men would remain close friends until they died. When the Iberian nations joined the First Coalition in the struggle against revolutionary France, the two battalions of the Gers were attached to the Army of the Eastern Pyrenees, posted so as to thwart a Spanish invasion.[2]

Commanded by inexperienced and often incompetent officers without adequate resources, under the meddling eye of Representatives-on-mission, the army experienced few successes. It was in this depressing theater of the war that Lannes was exposed to the rudiments of his chosen profession. He learned quickly and within three months had been promoted to first lieutenant. He took part in the fighting at the unsuccessful combats of Port-Vendras, Collioure, and Banyuls, and on October 21, 1793, he was provisionally promoted to captain of grenadiers. Nine days later he was wounded in the left arm during the fighting at Banyuls. While at the hospital at Perpignan, he was recalled to lead a critical attack on the Spanish positions at Villelongue, thereby earning a promotion to colonel.[3] After returning to Perpignan to recuperate, he met Paulette Méric, daughter of a local banker, whom he married on March 19, 1795.[4]

Upon his return to the army, Lannes was attached to the division of the center under General Dominique Pérignon in time to take part in the bloody three-day Battle of Boulou from April 29 through May 1, 1794. On several earlier occasions, the French had unsuccessfully attempted to seize the great redoubt of Montesquiou. However, with the passionate appeals of the Representative-on-mission, Edouard Milhaud, a swift and bloody assault was made against the position. Lannes commanded his two battalions so effectively that the commander-in-chief of the army, Jacques Dugommier, specifically recognized his efforts.[5]

In June 1794 Dugommier ordered General François Doppet to seize a large Spanish arms-manufacturing center at Ripoll. With almost 13,000 men, an attack was carried out; despite some initial success, a brigade was cut off until Lannes, with 1,200 men, rescued it. After this operation Lannes was attached to General Pierre François Charles Augereau's division where he had the opportunity to improve his understanding of tactics from a master. On June 26, 1795, General Charles Pierre Lamer, chief of staff of the army, wrote of Lannes: "For proof of the great value that he has consistently given since the commencement of the war, this colonel has continued to give his brothers-in-arms the example of the most intrepid and wise actions. All that we are able to say of him is infinitely less than he merits."[6]

When the Convention in Paris decreed the amalgamation of the volunteer battalions with the line troops, the two battalions from the Gers were joined with the 53d Line to form the 105th Demi-Brigade and placed under Lannes's command. It was incorporated into Augereau's division on June 16, 1795, unquestionably the finest division in the army. However, within five weeks the Treaty of Basel was signed, ending the war between France and Spain, and Augereau's division was transferred to the Army of Italy. Lannes, with the division of Augereau, arrived at army headquarters in time to take part in the operations planned by General André Massena to seize Loano. The battle commenced on November 21, 1795, but Lannes did not see fighting until the next night when he replaced a wounded brigade commander and seized four entrenched positions defended by artillery and infantry. In his report Augereau declared, "Colonel Lannes has executed all the movements entrusted to General Banel perfectly, with as much intelligence as bravery. This officer merits the greatest praise and national recognition."[7]

During the winter of 1795–1796, a second amalgamation was proscribed by the new Directory government and Lannes's demi-brigade was incorporated with another, placing him second in command. Nevertheless, soon after Bonaparte's arrival in March 1796, Lannes was given command of the 70th and 79th Regiments of General Jean Baptiste Cervoni's brigade in Massena's advance guard. During the initial operations, Cervoni's brigade was thrust into Voltri to draw the enemy attacks while Massena struck at Montenotte on April 12. Lannes saw little action until April 15 when Bonaparte noticed him for the first time. In the French attack on Dego and the counter-attack by the Austrians, Lannes led a bayonet charge at a crucial moment and was among the first into the town. That night he was assigned a demi-brigade, but Bonaparte placed him in command of three battalions of an élite force of grenadiers and carabineers, organized into an advance guard under the command of General Claude Dallemagne.[8]

After the successful operations against Piedmont and the Treaty of Cherasco on April 28, 1796, Bonaparte made a dash through the mountains and across the Po at Piacenza to surprise the Austrians. Lannes's three grenadier battalions and the advance guard marched 48 miles in 36 hours. As soon as his 900 men reached the Po, they seized several barges and quickly crossed the river only to be attacked by two Austrian cavalry squadrons. Advancing on Fombio, defended by an élite Austrian division, Lannes approached from the left in a coordinated assault and was the first into the town. His forces killed 80 and captured 900 men, several cannons, and three flags.[9]

Advancing from the Po valley, Lannes's troops pursued the retreating Austrians toward Lodi on May 9. After seizing the village the next day, they drove the enemy across the bridge where an Austrian rear guard was posted. Ordered to cross the bridge, the troops appeared to hesitate under the murderous fire of the enemy guns. Lannes quickly joined Massena and several other officers as they led the attacking grenadiers across the bridge. Lannes jumped from the bridge into the knee-deep water and raced for the shore. According to Bonaparte he was the first to reach the Austrian position. With the enemy driven back, the road to Milan was open and half of Austrian Lombardy fell to the French.[10]

Soon after the French occupation of Milan, defiance and insurrection broke out in the neighboring towns. Lannes, accompanied by Bonaparte, undertook the first of a series of minor missions to quell the disturbances, culminating in the suppression of the insurrection at Pavia. Lannes was also sent on special missions to Tortona and Arquat. In June he was sent to Massa and Carrara, but he returned to the Siege of Mantua in time to repulse a determined sortie by 3,000 Austrians on the evening of July 28, 1796, which cost the enemy almost 600 casualties. The next day he led an assault against the left of Mantua.

Lannes did not take part in the operations around Castiglione in August, but on September 8 he led the 4th Regiment of Massena's division in an attack against Austrian General Dagobert Würmser at Bassano. He was slightly wounded, prompting Augereau to request his promotion because he "had continued to give the most striking examples of bravery and in the last affair took two flags from the enemy." This praise was seconded by Bonaparte who wrote to the Directory requesting Lannes's promotion to general of brigade: "He was among the first of those to reach the enemy at Dego, was the first to pass the Po at the bridge of Lodi, and now to enter Bassano."[11] His promotion was not confirmed until March 17, 1797. A few days after being wounded at Bassano, Lannes was more seriously wounded at Governolo during the Battle of St.-Georges on September 15 when he led his 4th Regiment to thwart an Austrian sortie from the besieged fortress of Mantua. Consequently he was sent to Milan to recuperate for several weeks.

When the Austrians advanced on Verona after defeating Bonaparte at Caldiero on November 12, Lannes left the hospital and joined the army. Hoping to outflank Austrian General Josef Alvintzi, Bonaparte collected his forces in the vicinity of Arcola. On November 15 he ordered an attack on the village by Lannes with the 58th Demi-Brigade, supported by three battalions of Augereau's 45th. Sweeping through the village and onto the bridge over the Alpone, the French soldiers recoiled before a withering fire; Lannes was hit and wounded twice. Taken by ambulance to Ronco, where he heard of the continued failures of the French assaults, he mounted his horse and returned to the bridge at Arcola in time to see Bonaparte caught up in the retreat of a French column. As Bonaparte's horse slipped off a dike into the swamp and his aides struggled to protect him from an enemy counter-attack, Lannes quickly led his column in a headlong attack against the Austrians. The enemy was driven back onto the bridge and chased across the span. In the attack Lannes was wounded for the third time that day, but Bonaparte escaped from the quagmire unscathed.[12]

From that day onward, there was a special relationship between Bonaparte and Lannes that was to continue until death separated them. At St. Helena, Napoleon praised Lannes: "Wounded at Governolvo, he was still suffering [but] he placed himself between [me] and the enemy. . . . He received three wounds but he did not wish to retire."[13] To demonstrate his further esteem, Bonaparte later gave the flag he carried on the dike at Arcola to Lannes, declaring, "There was an instant, on the field of Arcola, when victory, uncertain, was in need of the audacity of its commanders. Bloody, covered with wounds, you left the ambulance, determined to die or conquer. I saw you constantly on that day of battle in the first ranks of the brave. . . . You are to be the trustee of this honorable flag which also covers with glory the grenadiers whom you constantly commanded."[14]

Lannes was given special missions to the Papal States in June 1979 while Bonaparte and the main forces of the army drove across Northern Italy and into Austria. Halting at Leoben, he signed an armistice paving the way for the end of the War of the

195

First Coalition. When Bonaparte returned to Milan, Lannes, now commanding a brigade, was given several confidential assignments including an incursion into Genoa. There he came into conflict with the French minister, Flaypoult, who complained of his conduct. Bonaparte responded, "He is unruly but a good and brave man. I am writing to instruct him to behave with courtesy and consideration toward a minister of the Republic especially when the minister is right ten times over."[15]

During the First Italian Campaign, Lannes had seen war waged on a vast scale, and he had begun to develop his tactical abilities under the watchful eye of Bonaparte. He had demonstrated his bravery, loyalty, tenacity, and resourcefulness as an infantry commander. He carried out his orders implicitly in spite of the losses incurred. Perhaps even more significantly, he manifested a personal attachment to Bonaparte that was not shared by the other commanders. He was unpolished, volatile, ill-educated, stubborn, often tactless, and prone to depression and oversensitivity. However, these limitations were overshadowed by a close bond of friendship, respect, and confidence that developed between the two men and continued throughout their careers.

Egypt, Italy, and Portugal (1798–1804)

Soon after Lannes's return to Paris, the Directory decided to strike at England, the last surviving member of the First Coalition, by threatening her interests in the Middle East. Consequently plans were laid for the Egyptian campaign. Bonaparte took Lannes into his confidence. He was sent to Lyons to coordinate troop movements from the east central regions of France and to superintend the shipment of vast quantities of gold from Switzerland for use by the newly formed Army of Egypt.[16]

When the organization of the expeditionary army was completed, Lannes was disappointed to learn that he would be attached to army headquarters. After seizing Malta the expedition arrived in Egypt on July 1. Initially, Lannes was given command of a brigade under General Jean Baptiste Kléber, one of the truly able commanders in the army. When General Jacques François Menou was wounded in the storming of Alexandria, Lannes was named to command his division. During the advance across the desert toward Cairo under the most unfavorable conditions, there was considerable dissatisfaction among the officers and men. General Joachim Murat complained about Bonaparte's plans. When Bonaparte learned of these complaints, Murat became convinced that Lannes had carried his comments to the commander-in-chief, and the two men became bitter enemies and rivals for as long as they lived.

Lannes remained in Cairo where he played a major role in the suppression of the revolt in the city. On February 7 his division marched into Syria with Bonaparte to join the remainder of the army, already completing the Siege of El Arish. Advancing to Jaffa the French opened the trenches before the city on March 5. After brutal abuses were carried out against their dead and wounded comrades, the furious French quickly completed a breach and stormed the city. Led by Lannes's infantry, they seized the towers along the walls and drove into the center of the town while other divisions scaled the walls with ladders. Terrible excesses were committed in the assault, and the remainder of the garrison fled to the citadel and mosques only to be executed several days later on the beaches of the Mediterranean.

En route to St. Jean d'Acre, Lannes's division was involved in a battle against Abdallah Pasha at Quaquoum. In this affray many of Lannes's troops pursued the enemy into the neighboring mountains and were ambushed, resulting in about 60 killed and 300 wounded. Later reproached by Bonaparte for excessive casualties, he claimed that the enemy had defied him.

The Army of Egypt reached Acre on March 19 and two days later the trenches were opened. However, with the capture of their siege pieces en route by sea, Turkish fanaticism, the ferocious energy of Pasha Dejezzar, the efforts of émigré engineer Antoine Phélypeaux, and the continual arrival of reinforcements, French siege work went slowly. Lannes led the first attack on March 28, and although a tower wall was seized, the assault was beaten back. On May 7 another attack was mounted by other brigades but was repulsed with horrendous losses. Early the next morning, Lannes advanced with his division. The column charged into the breach only to find a second wall. Two hundred men broke through it and into the city; they took refuge in one of the mosques, only to be massacred when aid did not arrive. Lannes led a second assault but he was hit in the neck by a ball and fell into the ditch. His column retreated, leaving him near the breach; it would have been only a matter of time until he was butchered by the Turks. One of his captains, leading five or six men, ran into the breach to rescue him. The soldiers were cut down, so the captain, as a last resort, grabbed his leg and dragged the bleeding Lannes across the ground to the safety of the French trenches. Lannes never completely recovered from his wound. Although Dr. Dominique Larrey labored heroically to save his life, thereafter he had difficulty speaking and he carried his head inclined to one side.[17] Following one last assault on May 10, the siege was raised. The same day Bonaparte announced Lannes's promotion to general of division.[18]

With the Siege of Acre raised, Lannes traveled across the desert with his men to Cairo. He remained there recuperating until the British landed a Turkish army at Aboukir on July 14, 1799. Bonaparte attempted to concentrate his force while Lannes and Murat were dispatched to halt the Turks. Lannes formed the right of the attack while Murat's cavalry swept across the first lines of the Pasha of Roumelia, Seraskier, capturing 18 cannons and 40 flags and overwhelming almost 15,000 men, many of whom fled into the sea. Advancing to the Pasha's second line of defense, the French were repulsed. Another attack was ordered as the Turks poured onto the field to cut off the heads of the wounded and dead. Infuriated by this action, Lannes's men attacked the Turkish positions with bayonets, while Murat's cavalry charged along the beach. Lannes's troops seized Aboukir and Murat captured the entire Turkish camp. Lannes's vital role was eclipsed by Murat's brilliant charge at the Battle of Aboukir, but it was Lannes who was given the honor of attacking the citadel. Once again he was wounded, this time in the leg. Menou replaced him and with Davout's assistance seized the citadel. The hospitalized Lannes was further depressed when he learned that his wife had given birth to an illegitimate child.[19]

Brutalized by his physical and psychological suffering, Lannes longed to return to France. He was fortunate to be included among those who sailed for France with Bonaparte on August 22, 1799. After disembarking at Fréjus, Lannes and the other generals set out for Paris. Once there, they joined Bonaparte in the plot to replace the discredited Directory government. Sent to gain the support of infantry officers before he became commander of the troops at the Tuileries, Lannes played no personal role in the coup of 18 *Brumaire*. Yet, two days after the creation of the provisional consulate, Lannes was named commander of the 9th and 10th military districts at Toulouse and Perpignan to garner support for the new government. While in southern France, he visited Lectoure to complete divorce arrangements.

Recalled to Paris to assume command of the 4th Division of the newly formed Army of the Reserve, Lannes was soon appointed commander and inspector of the Consular Guard. As troops were being collected at Dijon to mislead the Austrian forces in Germany, Bonaparte, accompanied by Lannes, left Paris on May 9, 1800, to join his Army of the Reserve near Geneva. Lannes was given the advance guard of the army, a choice command that would demonstrate, for the first time, his full range of talents as an infantry commander. While the Austrians were preoccupied with French troop concentrations along the Rhine, Bonaparte ordered Lannes to climb the narrow road through the high snow to the top of Great St. Bernard Pass. After reaching the pass and collecting supplies at the hospice, he swept down the mountain into Italy, aware that speed and surprise were crucial for victory. Austrian General Michael Melas did not expect an attack across the mountain, so it was hoped that Massena, already blockaded in Genoa for five weeks, could hold out until Bonaparte could defeat Melas and relieve him.

Lannes's advance guard made first contact with the enemy on May 15 at Etroubes; the next day they forced Hungarian troops across the Cluse River at Aosta and on May 18 he drove the enemy out of Chatillon, taking 300 prisoners, two guns, and four caissons. Proceeding down the Dora Baltea valley, Lannes's advance guard reached the impregnable old Fort Bard, high above the road, defended by a garrison of 400 men and 18 cannons. Several unsuccessful efforts were made to seize the fort before a path over Mount Albaredo was discovered to outflank it. Abandoning his artillery, cavalry, and wagons, Lannes led his men over the path to St. Martin where they overthrew an Austrian force barring the route. Supported by a few cavalry, they continued their frantic drive toward the town of Ivrea, which would ensure their successful entrance onto the plain of Piedmont. Town after town fell. At Chiusella the Austrian garrison resisted bitterly but unsuccessfully as the French seized the fortified town.[20]

When the main army reached the plains of Piedmont, a new advance guard was organized with Murat's cavalry. Lannes, meanwhile, pushed on to Pavia, capturing 300–400 cannons. Crossing the Po on June 6, he was attacked by Austrian General O'Reilly with 4,000–5,000 infantry, 1,500 cavalry, and seven guns. Unable to move his cavalry and artillery across the river, a bloody combat ensued before he could seize Stradella. The enemy fell back on Casteggio where they were joined by the troops of General Peter Ott's corps. When Lannes encountered stiff resistance en route to Casteggio, he advanced only to find an enemy force of between 15,000 and 16,000 men, supported by artillery, facing his 5,000 men. A three-column attack was launched, and the second column broke through the Austrian line and into the town. Enemy reserves counter-attacked, reclaiming the village, which changed hands several times. Hard pressed, Lannes's light artillery and cavalry finally arrived, but Austrian superiority was overwhelming his forces. At this point General Claude Victor, marching to the sound of the guns, rushed one of his divisions forward. Although senior in rank, Victor turned his troops over to Lannes who ordered another charge. With the aid of Victor's men, he successively repulsed the Austrian counter-attacks several times and seized Casteggio. The enemy losses were placed at 4,700 killed, wounded, or captured, along with five guns, while the French would admit to only 500 losses. Although the battle was fought at Casteggio, it was labeled Montebello, and it became the basis of Lannes's title, Duke of Montebello, in 1808.[21]

The debris of Ott's corps retired toward Alessandria to join Melas's main army. Bonaparte, unable to determine his enemy's intentions, dispersed his forces while, on the contrary, Melas was uniting his 35,000 men to give battle. Only three divisions of infantry, including Lannes's, and two cavalry brigades, totaling 14,000 men, slept the night of June 13 on the plain of Marengo, which would be transformed the next morning into a living hell. Bonaparte and the division of General Jean Charles Monnier were about 12 miles away at Torre di Garrafoli and 10,000 troops under General Louis Charles Desaix had been sent to Novi in search of the enemy.

The following morning the Austrian forces poured from the bridgehead on the Bormida River and formed into three great columns. While Victor's division retired slowly across the plain of Marengo, Lannes ordered his troops forward on Victor's right. Ott attempted to turn Lannes's position, but he called up all his reserves to halt this maneuver. Simultaneously O'Reilly's column began to turn Victor's flank. Threatened with a double envelopment and short of cartridges, Lannes and Victor retired by echelon while 80 enemy guns played havoc with their men. Bonaparte soon arrived with Monnier's men and the Consular Guard, but they could only delay Melas before being driven back. In a matter of hours, the field at Marengo had been lost. Melas turned over command to General Zach and retired to Alessandria to announce his "victory." Meanwhile, Desaix arrived on the field of battle. After holding a council of war, it was decided to attack again. Lannes's troops advanced to the right of Desaix's column. The conflict was bloody and the losses were heavy; Desaix fell mortally wounded, but the French, with a brilliant cavalry charge by Etienne Kellermann, ultimately drove the Austrians from the field. French losses totaled over 6,000, but the enemy casualties were set at 6,500 dead and 3,000 prisoners, as well as six flags and four cannons. The next day Melas concluded an armistice by which he withdrew from the land west of the Mincio.[22]

After a short visit to Milan, Lannes accompanied Bonaparte, Murat, and Louis Alexandre Berthier to Paris. The trip was not without rancor, for both Lannes and Murat had sought Caroline

Bonaparte's hand. In retrospect Lannes was fortunate indeed, for soon after his return to Paris he married Louise Antoinette Guéhéneuc, the daughter of a senator, on September 15, 1800. She bore him five children. The first was named Napoleon; his godparents were the First Consul and Josephine.

Despite Lannes's personal relationship with the First Consul, friction developed between the two men when Lannes, as commander of the Consular Guard, utilized 300,000 francs from its treasury, without formal authorization, to improve the conditions of the Guard. Bonaparte, apparently wishing to make an example, instructed him to repay the sum within eight days or appear before a court-martial. Lannes did not have the money but his old comrade-in-arms Augereau advanced the necessary funds. As a result Lannes stepped down as commander of the Consular Guard.[23]

This was a period of some embarrassment for Lannes, so his appointment as plenipotentiary to the court of Lisbon on November 14, 1801, was a welcome change from the Paris gossip. His assignment in Lisbon was vital for French interests because Portugal was one of the most active areas of British intrigue in Europe. Lannes was known to have a passionate dislike for the British, and, with his success on the battlefield, it was hoped he could exert a strong influence at court. Finding the Portuguese prime minister, Almeida, firmly under the influence of the British diplomat Ambassador Robert Fitzgerald, the exasperated Lannes asked for his passport after a series of diplomatic confrontations. Bonaparte learned of his action only when Lannes had reached Orleans. Wishing to avert a diplomatic breach with Portugal, Bonaparte ordered his foreign minister, Charles Talleyrand, to reprimand Lannes for leaving his post.[24]

Lannes returned to Lisbon with his vessel laden with duty-free French merchandise, which brought him 300,000 francs to repay Augereau. There may have been some resentment in Paris over this arrangement, but Lannes was received cordially by John, Prince Regent of Portugal. The prince took an instant liking to Lannes, despite his brusque manners. When another son was born to Lannes's wife, Prince John gave him a handful of precious stones for his son, his wife, and himself.[25] In addition to the diplomatic war he carried on with the British ambassador, Lannes faced several problems as a result of Talleyrand's intrigues. He threatened resignation when Talleyrand negotiated a treaty with Portugal through Spain without his knowledge, but Bonaparte came to his defense. Writing to his father-in-law, Lannes declared, "I have done the impossible; I have attained great advantage for our commerce. I have buried English influence in Portugal."[26] This was no idle boast, for the British ambassador complained of the commercial agreement and Lannes's unprecedented treatment.[27] Indeed, Prince John seemed to be unable to deny him any request, and France's influence increased as England's declined. Accordingly he received a letter from Bonaparte praising his achievements and instructing him to remain in Lisbon until recalled.[28]

Lannes with the Grand Army (1805–1809)

Although Lannes remained in Portugal during the spring of 1804, this did not prevent Bonaparte from naming him to the marshalate on May 19. He was recalled to Paris in November to take part in Napoleon's coronation on December 2.[29] With Bonaparte creating the Army of England, Lannes was soon appointed to command IV Corps. He labored at Etaples to organize his new corps for the proposed invasion of England in August 1805. Once Bonaparte realized that his fleet could not gain control of the Channel, he began reorganizing his forces into the Grand Army; he would strike at Austria, which had joined England and Russia in the Third Coalition. Lannes's corps, now redesignated V Corps, was to become one of the most renowned and victorious units in this extraordinary fighting force. Even before the army organization had been completed, Lannes's corps was marching with Murat's cavalry as the advance guard of the army. Crossing the Rhine on August 26, they approached the Black Forest to draw the attention of the Austrian army, commanded by General Karl Mack at Ulm, while the remainder of the army crossed to the north and raced to cut the enemy's retreat route. With the French Army closing the ring around Ulm, the corps of Lannes and Michel Ney seized Frauenberg and Michelsberg, respectively, overlooking Ulm on October 15, sealing the fate of the city. Mack was summoned and five days later he surrendered the entire garrison of almost 30,000 men, 60 cannons, and 40 flags.[30]

Meanwhile, a Russian army of 60,000 men under General Mikhail Kutusov marched to support the Austrians. With the defeat of Mack and the advance of the French, Kutusov fell back to unite with a second Russian army advancing under General Friedrich Buxhowden. Lannes swept across Bavaria into Austria. After overthrowing a Russian rear guard at Amstetten in a bitter bayonet fight, Lannes's infantry raced for Vienna behind Murat's cavalry. Ordered to seize the bridges on the Danube at Vienna, Lannes and Murat, despite their personal animosity, cooperated to convince the Austrian bridge commander, Auersperg, that an armistice had been signed.[31] Both marshals demonstrated unabashed audacity and presence of mind in carrying out a ruse that might have cost them their freedom or lives.

In pursuing the Russians into Bohemia, Lannes fought a five-hour battle at Hollabrunn (Schöngraben) before reaching Brunn on November 19. Less than 20 miles away, the Austrians and Russians had gathered over 96,000 around Austerlitz, but Napoleon, hard pressed, had concentrated only 65,000 troops. For the next two weeks, Lannes's cavalry engaged in skirmishes with the Russians, but on December 1 the allies advanced on Austerlitz to envelop the flanks of the French army.

Lannes was given command of the left wing of the army, anchored to the Santon Hill, supported by Murat's cavalry. He became locked in conflict with General Peter Bagration's corps along the road to Olmütz. Despite an attack by the Russian imperial cavalry, Lannes's infantry, cooperating closely with Murat's cavalry, drove the enemy from Blasowitz and Bosenitz after several powerful counter-attacks. When the Russians' resistance finally collapsed, Lannes halted his pursuit to await orders from headquarters. In five hours of fighting, Lannes's forces, supported by Murat, had cost the Russian 1,500 dead, 7,000–8,000 prisoners, 27 guns, and two flags. Yet, the battle was decided by Marshal Nicolas Soult on the Pratzen heights and Marshal Louis Nicolas Davout at Telnitz. In all the allies lost 27,000 dead, wounded, and captured, and the French losses totaled almost 8,000. The Austrians signed an armistice on December 6, and less than three weeks later the Treaty of Pressburg ended the Third Coalition.[32]

Before the treaty was signed, Lannes left for Paris. Apparently he had a disagreement with the Emperor, but little is known of this controversy. In September 1806, when war seemed imminent with Prussia and the Fourth Coalition was being organized against France, Napoleon sent for Lannes to assume command of V Corps. He rejoined his corps on October 7, the same day war was declared and Prussian territory was violated.

Three days later he encountered a force of some 9,000 infantry and cavalry commanded by Prince Louis of Prussia at Saalfeld near a swampy plain, cut by the Schwarza River. Utilizing his infantry and supported by cavalry, he drove the Prussians into the woods, and during a counterattack Prince Louis was cut down and mortally wounded. All resistance collapsed and Lannes's men took almost 1,800 men, four flags, and 33 cannons. This defeat and death of Prince Louis, along with 900 of his men, had a disastrous effect upon the Prussian army, while the confident French marveled at their meager loss of 172.[33]

The French advance continued and the corps of Lannes and Augereau moved on Jena. The units of Jean Baptiste Bernadotte and Davout marched north toward Naumberg, while the corps of Ney and Soult acted as the army reserve. Lannes drove the enemy out of Jena late on October 12. When he occupied the town, a local priest nursing a Saxon grudge against the Prussians informed him of an obscure road to the heights of Landsgrafenberg, which dominated the village and the surrounding countryside. The heights were quickly cleared of Prussian soldiers, and Lannes began to move his infantry up to the plateau. When Napoleon arrived, he ordered up the Imperial Guard, followed throughout the night by the arriving infantry and supply wagons.

At 4:00 A.M. the following morning, Napoleon issued orders for the Battle of Jena. The V Corps, forming the center of the line, was the first unit to move; it was followed by Augereau on the left and Soult on the right, supported by a reserve under Ney. Driving the Prussian and Saxon troops before him, Lannes pushed through Closewitz on to Verzenheiligen. A gap developed between Augereau and Lannes. Impetuously Ney rushed into the breach with his advance guard, exposing his men to capture. Lannes quickly sent his cavalry to rescue Ney's men. In the fighting Lannes's clothing was shredded and he was grazed by grapeshot, but his pursuit continued. The victory was complete but Lannes's losses were high; one of his divisions had 2,570 casualties and the total for the army must have reached 5,000 men, but the Prussians and Saxons had some 10,000 casualties and 15,000 captured, along with 200 cannons and almost 100 flags.[34] The contributions of his corps were recognized in the army bulletin, but Lannes felt that exaggerated importance had been given to Murat's cavalry. He would not forget this slight. Similarly Davout, nine miles away, had fought the main Russian army at Auerstädt and won a stunning victory, but at first received only grudging praise from Napoleon.

Following the victory at Jena, Lannes was ordered to cooperate with Murat's cavalry in capturing the few Prussian forces that had escaped—a most disagreeable task. Moving quickly to keep pace with the cavalry, his men did not have time to forage for food. Despite Murat's continual complaints to Napoleon about Lannes's delays, V Corps kept pace with the cavalry and took part in the capture of 16,000 men, 45 flags, and 64 guns on October 28 at Prenzlow. Lannes's corps had marched 102 kilometres in 53 hours without sleep or rest. Yet Murat refused to recognize the vital role of Lannes's V Corps. Lannes complained to Napoleon, who wrote in November rectifying the oversight. Lannes replied, "A word from you is sufficient to make the soldiers happy."[35]

After collecting a magazine at Stettin, Lannes's corps marched east toward Warsaw. His troops found movement very difficult in the rain and snow. Nevertheless, he was ordered to advance on Pultusk. Reaching Pultusk, Lannes found a Russian army of perhaps 45,000 infantry, 5,000 cavalry, and thousands of cossacks confronting his 18,000 men. He ordered an attack at 11:00 A.M. on December 26. The French overran the Russians, only to be beaten back by reinforcements sent forward by Russian General Levin Benningsen. Engaged in a desperate battle under trying circumstances with a vastly superior enemy, V Corps was in a critical position. Fortunately, at that moment, one of Davout's divisions arrived to reinforce Lannes's corps. Nightfall ended the struggle that claimed as many as 7,000 Frenchmen and 5,000 Russians, but both sides announced victory. Lannes was again wounded, so he returned to Warsaw to recuperate.[36] His recovery was aided by his wife who traveled from France to care for him. During his convalescence, the Grand Army was engaged in one of its most terrible battles in a blinding snowstorm at Eylau.

During this period Lannes was accused of pocketing funds taken at Stettin. Utilizing the funds he found there, Lannes had paid his troops and gave the remainder to his chief-of-staff for corps expenses. This caused another estrangement with the Emperor, who requested one month's salary immediately in partial payment for the 600,000 francs taken at Stettin. Lannes was dismayed by a series of insulting letters from Alexandre Berthier. He wrote to his wife complaining of political intrigue, perfidy, and revolting treatment by the Emperor.[37]

In May Napoleon gave Lannes command of a reserve corps with instructions to join Marshal François Lefebvre and end the Siege of Danzig that had already dragged on for two months. Although he played the major role in repulsing the Russian and Prussian reinforcements, he was forced to sit by idly while Lefebvre completed the siege, in accordance with Napoleon's instructions.

During the first week of June, Napoleon began to concentrate his forces in response to a Russian attack against his advance corps at Heilsberg. Carefully observing the enemy movements, Napoleon gave Lannes the advance guard of the army with orders to move in the direction of Friedland on June 13. Reaching the village that evening, Lannes's cavalry was repulsed by 3,000 enemy horsemen, sent across the Alle River by Russian General Levin Benningsen.

Lannes moved Nicolas Oudinot's grenadiers and Emmanuel Grouchy's cavalry forward but he halted at Posthenen at 1:00 A.M. Within a few hours, the first rays of the sun began to appear.

Lannes reported to Napoleon that he would try to keep the Russian forces engaged on the left side of the Alle until the army arrived. His force of 10,000 men was arranged to hold a position four miles wide against the mounting Russian forces by utilizing the terrain and shifting several mobile units across the battlefield to contest each enemy advance. After 4:00 A.M. he carried on a grudging defense as his vastly outnumbered French forces were sacrificed to gain time. Reinforcements began to arrive and by 11:00 A.M. Lannes had almost 29,000 men to oppose the 45,000 Russians. Napoleon reached the battlefield at noon and he ordered a general attack on the Russian army at 5:00 P.M. While Ney swept along the Alle River toward Friedland, supported by a massed artillery bettery, Lannes and Oudinot advanced slowly into the burning town, driving the enemy back toward Ney, already moving behind them. The Russians lost in excess of 20,000 men and the morale of their army had been broken. Within a month the Treaty of Tilsit was signed and Tzar Alexander I had formed an alliance with France.[38]

Soon after the battle, Lannes was presented with the principality of Siévres in the department of Kalish for his contributions in the Polish campaign, and on March 19, 1808, he received the title of Duke of Montebello. To this title was attached a donation of 100,000 francs from lands in Westphalia and 50,000 francs from lands in Hanover. Content with that recognition, he returned to France on June 18 where he spent several months with his family.

Despite the superficial tranquility in Europe, the Iberian Peninsula erupted into a widespread insurrection in 1808. French forces were defeated and the loss of Spain seemed probable unless Napoleon intervened personally with units of the Grand Army. As a result the Emperor sent several army corps and the Imperial Guard as well as his most trusted lieutenants, including Lannes, into Spain. Surprised by the suddenness of the orders, Lannes did not have time to collect his baggage. Using an aide's mount he was thrown from the horse while crossing the mountains near Tolosa and seriously injured.

Before he had fully recovered from the fall, Napoleon ordered him to assume command of some 30,000 men, including Moncey's III Corps, and march on Tudela where a Spanish army of 45,000 men commanded by General Francisco Castaños was deployed. Advancing early on the morning of November 23, Lannes's cavalry surprised Castaños at Tudela. The Spanish Armies of Aragon and Andalusia were deployed over 10½ miles. Consequently a gap of three miles developed between the Spanish armies, and Lannes drove into the breach, crushing the Army of Aragon while the Army of Andalusia remained inactive. The

Army of Aragon lost 26 guns, seven flags, and 1,000 prisoners, and 3,000 died or were wounded.[39]

After a false start in late December to surprise and capture the British army under Sir John Moore, Napoleon ordered Lannes to complete the Siege of Saragossa, already under attack for 60 days. On January 9, 1809, when Lannes arrived at Saragossa, defended by Commander José Palafox and a Spanish garrison of 40,000, all the outlying fortified positions had been captured.[40] His artillery fired on the walls for five days and pounded three practicable breaches in the city walls; soon his men broke into the town and seized an area near the walls. Thereafter, a new stage of the siege began with street fighting that was to last for 24 more grueling and bitter days. To avert the slaughter experienced during the first Siege of Saragossa in 1808, Lannes advanced through the city block by block, house by house, barricade by barricade, with artillery and mines to drive the enemy out rather than to sacrifice his men needlessly in bayonet charges. Although typhus broke out among the garrison and civilian population, the fighting continued unabated. Finally, when the center of the town had been mined and the suburbs were a mass of rubble, the exhausted, fever-ridden defenders agreed to capitulate on February 19. The losses were staggering on both sides. The Spanish lost almost 54,000 souls but less than 7,000 fell from gunfire, while the French losses totaled 10,000.[41] Thus ended the siege that paled all others during the Napoleonic wars. It reflected a very substantial tactial achievement on the part of Lannes, but the glory of this siege must be relegated to the extraordinary Spanish defenders who achieved immortality by their struggle.

Lannes left Saragossa on March 26, but little time was spent with his family. In April 1809 Austria invaded Bavaria in the War of the Fifth Coalition. Before leaving Paris to take command of his Army of Germany, Napoleon instructed Lannes to join him immediately and take command of a provisional army corps. Lannes reached headquarters to find Napoleon concentrating the army near Ratisbon. Lannes had to borrow one of the Emperor's mounts because his own baggage had not caught up with him.

To split the advancing Austrian army, numbering about 160,000, Napoleon resolved to attack the Austrian forces in the vicinity of Abensberg. The Emperor posted the Bavarian troops on the right and the Württembergers in the center under his direct command, while Lannes's corps formed the left wing of the army. On April 20, while Napoleon's troops in the center engaged the Austrians, Lannes moved from the left to overthrow General Thierry's Austrian corps, cut its communications with the main army, and force it toward Landshut. On April 21, 1809, while Davout and Lefebvre engaged the main Austrian forces on their front, Napoleon with Lannes's corps and cavalry pushed southward to support Massena's IV Corps and crush the enemy corps under General Johann Hiller at Landshut. Lannes's infantry and the Bavarian cavalry drove to the suburbs, seized the bridge across the Isar, and captured the town. Hiller's force escaped with 10,000 casaulties and the loss of 52 cannons; thus, the left wing of the Austrian army, numbering 40,000 men, had been crushed as a fighting force.[42]

Although the French were victorious at Landshut, Davout was now threatened by the Austrian entry into Ratisbon. After analyzing the various reports, Napoleon decided to march to Davout's aid with all available forces. Early the next morning Lannes, with 40,000 men, including elements of Massena's corps, began advancing northward, accompanied by Napoleon. By 1:30 P.M. Lannes's column and the Württemberger units reached the vicinity of the fighting. Lannes's troops moved east to outflank the Austrian positions near Eckmühl. Aware of his critical position, Archduke Charles withdrew his army from the battlefield with the loss of 6,000 casualties, 1,500 prisoners, 12 flags, and 16 cannons.[43] French losses were heavy with over 5,000 killed or wounded.

The French forces were too weak to continue the pursuit, but the next morning, April 23, Napoleon put the army in motion. He was disturbed since the Austrian army was in full retreat and Ratisbon staunchly held by a rear guard of 6,000 men. Time could not be wasted to undertake a formal siege of the city walls, so Napoleon turned to Lannes for the assault. A partial breach had been blown in the wall, so Lannes called for 50 volunteers to race to the breach, throw up scaling ladders, and climb over the wall. Fifty volunteers accepted the challenge, but they were all killed or wounded. He asked for 50 more volunteers and they suffered a similar fate. The third time he asked for volunteers there were none. Lannes explained, "Well, I will show you that before I was a marshal I was a grenadier, and I am still one." As he prepared to carry a ladder toward the city wall, several of his aides-de-camp seized his ladder, organized themselves, and ran across the field in pairs to escape the enemy fire. They reached the wall and climbed through the breach, followed by 50 grenadiers and other elements of Charles Morand's division.[44] Meanwhile, Lannes led the remainder of Morand's men to the front gate where they broke down the great doors. The Austrians laid down their arms. In this "five day campaign," the French had fought three battles and six combats, taken 50,000 prisoners, 100 cannons, 49 flags, and 3,000 munition wagons. Lannes's contributions were vital for its success. Following the surrender of Ratisbon, he led his corps into Austria; on May 21 he crossed the Danube near Vienna to command French forces at Essling. On the second day of the bloody battle, he was mortally wounded by a chance shot and died on May 31, 1809—the first marshal to fall.

The Battle of Aspern-Essling (May 21–22, 1809)

In pursuit of the retreating Austrian army, Napoleon reorganized his army and a new II Corps was created for Lannes. Advancing with Massena's corps, Lannes's troops swept the Austrians eastward until May 10 when his advance guard reached the suburbs of Vienna. In order to bring the Austrian army to battle, it was necessary to cross the broad Danube. Lannes was sent to reconnoiter a possible crossing site at Nussdorf where the island of Schwarzenlaken, three miles above Vienna, separated two arms of the river. Without instructions from Napoleon, Lannes ordered 500 voltigeurs to be ferried across the river by rowboat; it was soon realized that they had occupied the island of Schwarzenlaken rather than the north bank of the Danube. Two battalions of infantry soon followed, but enemy pickets sighted the expedition and gave the alarm. A large Austrian force was sent to reinforce the island garrison and soon the little band was pushed to the end of the island and forced to surrender. Only 400 of over 1,000 men were able to escape as Lannes, joined by Napoleon, watched the pathetic affair.[45]

Napoleon and Lannes returned to Vienna. It was decided to abandon the Nussdorf site and concentrate on the crossing from Kaiser–Ebersdorf to the island of Lobau and then to the north bank of the Danube near Aspern and Essling. Four bridges were constructed: the first crossed 505 yards to a small sandbar of Schneider Grund in midstream; the second extended 250 yards from the sandbar, across the strongest currents of the river, to the island of Lob Grund; the third passed 30 yards to the large island of Lobau, over a mile wide; and finally the last bridge, 83 yards in length, extended from Lobau to the north bank of the Danube, making the total distance from the right bank to the left just over two miles. The bridge was constructed by Massena and his IV Corps. Boats were used for some segments of the crossing, while building materials found in Vienna were utilized in the construction of the major section of the span.

On May 20 the division of Gabriel Molitor, supported by artillery, quickly crossed to the north shore, followed by Antoine Lasalle's cavalry and the remainder of the corps. Molitor's division occupied Aspern, Boudet's division was deployed at Essling, while the divisions of Claude Legrand and Carra St.-Cyr were moving up; the area between Aspern and Essling was linked by the cavalry of Lasalle and Jean d'Espagne. As these deployments were taking place, Lannes joined Napoleon, who assigned to him the defense of Essling and the public granary, a formidable three-story red-brick structure over 100 feet in length and 30 feet wide. While these preparations were continuing, Archduke Charles concentrated 83,600 infantry, 14,250 cavalry, and 292 guns for the attack on the French enclave. Within four hours the French were well aware of the impending attack. Napoleon considered withdrawing but decided to fight. Aspern and the left wing of the army were placed under Massena, and the right wing, as well as Marshal Jean Baptiste Bessières's cavalry linking Aspern and Essling, was placed under Lannes. French forces totaled 26,300 when the shock of the first attack fell on Massena at Aspern.[46]

Between 1:00 and 5:00 P.M. four columns attacked and were repulsed by Massena's infantry. At 5:00 P.M. Archduke Charles led an attack on the village and, with massive reinforcements, seized part of the town. There was a furious struggle in the streets of the village, which changed hands six times. Legrand's division joined in the fighting that raged into the night with the utmost fury. When the firing ceased, Massena's troops held eastern Aspern, still linked with Lannes's forces. While Massena's corps was fighting for its life, Lannes, with the single division of Boudet, awaited the onslaught. It was only at 6:00 P.M. that General Dedowich launched his column in an attack on Lannes's eastern flank. Napoleon sent d'Espagne's cuirassiers forward and the enemy column was halted. Rosenberg led his corps into Essling, but Lannes's troops, carefully deployed in the village and granary, repulsed them. Three other attacks were sent against Essling during the night, but Lannes's troops also repulsed them. Several times during the day, as Napoleon sought to send reinforcements and munitions to the beleaguered troops, the bridges over the Danube were broken. The French engineers worked frantically to repair them. As soon as possible, supplies were again en route to Lannes and Massena, but the bridge was broken many more times before the battle ended.[47]

Napoleon resolved to reinforce his troops at Aspern and Essling during the night of May 21; then he would launch an offensive early the next morning to break the center of the Austrian army. During the night the troops of Lannes's corps and additional cavalry were moved into Essling, thereby increasing the forces at Aspern and Essling to about 75,000 men. Davout was ordered to cross the Danube early the following morning with the badly needed munitions wagons.[48] Orders were issued for Lannes to break out of the enclave with his recently arrived division and Bessières's cavalry in order to drive the Austrian army westward toward Aspern where Massena's corps would advance to overwhelm its right wing. Similarly Massena was instructed to drive the enemy out of Aspern and move in support of Lannes. Fighting began at 3:30 A.M. at Aspern, and by 7:00 A.M. Massena, with the divisions of Molitor, Legrange, and St.-Cyr, had regained Aspern. Napoleon, noticing a gap in the Austrian forces, ordered Lannes to launch his attack there. With the divisions of Louis St.-Hilaire, Claparède, and Thurreau, supported by heavy cavalry, the Austrians were driven back toward Breitenlee; only the presence of Archduke Charles and his enormous superiority prevented an immediate breakthrough. Nevertheless, Lannes's troops captured an entire enemy battalion, five guns, and a flag.[49]

At approximately 7:00 A.M. the bridge was broken by debris sent down the river by the enemy; this would not have caused a major crisis, but two hours later a massive floating mill, set afire by Austrian engineers, floated down the river and crashed into the bridge, taking out a large section of the structure. The arrival of Davout's corps and the munitions would be delayed indefinitely, so Napoleon ordered Lannes to halt his advance and consolidate his position. Once the extent of the bridge damage was determined, Napoleon ordered Lannes to withdraw to his original position. The marshal skillfully executed the movement despite the overwhelming fire of the enemy artillery.[50]

When Archduke Charles learned of the broken bridge, he resolved to drive the French into the Danube. Renewed assaults were ordered on Aspern and Essling. Hiller's corps attacked Aspern and broke into the village, but he was stopped after a ferocious counterattack by Massena's troops. At 11:00 A.M. a massive assault was made on Essling by Dedowich, Rosenberg, and Rohan. The village of Essling was taken, but Boudet retreated to the granary and continued his fight. In the center Archduke Charles led two massive columns against Lannes at Essling, supported by vastly superior artillery fire. Again Bessières sacrificed with his cavalry to delay the advance, and the musketry of the infantry brought the Austrian attack to a halt. Four battalions of d'Aspre's Austrian grenadiers broke into the town and made a ferocious attack on the granary. Napoleon ordered Mouton into the town with two units of the Young Guard to sustain Boudet at the granary. More Austrian reinforcements were sent into the village, so Napoleon sent General Jean Rapp to reinforce Mouton with two battalions of the Old Guard. By mid-afternoon the French had repulsed the enemy and the battle degenerated into a one-sided cannon duel.[51]

During the thunderous bombardment of the Austrian artillery, hundreds of Frenchmen fell; in fact, each of Lannes's aides-de-camp was wounded or killed, so he reluctantly agreed to move his headquarters out of the direct line of enemy fire. While talking with General Pouzet, who had introduced him to the military life in 1792, a cannonball hit the old general in the head, killing him instantly. Lannes was stunned and grief stricken. Moving in the direction of Enzersdorf, he sat down at the end of a trench and crossed his legs. A few minutes later a three-pound ball fired from Enzersdorf ricocheted along the ground and hit his knees; the left knee cap was shattered and the ligaments and muscles of the right thigh were torn. One of his aides ran over to him; he said, "I am wounded; it's nothing much; give me your hand to help me up."[52] However, he could not rise. He was carried back to the dressing station by the bridge and Dr. Larrey quickly examined him. After a short consultation among three doctors, it was decided to amputate his left leg. Napoleon, who had been awaiting him earlier in the afternoon, came up and sighted him on a stretcher. He hurried to his mortally wounded comrade, embraced him, and uttered a few words of encouragement.

Napoleon returned to Vienna and the next day Lannes was transferred by boat to Kaiser–Ebersdorf. In the first days following his amputation, he seemed to be making a remarkable recovery. However, he then took a turn for the worst and his condition deteriorated as gangrene developed. His fever increased. Napoleon visited him every day and sent the best specialists in Vienna to examine him. They sought to halt his deteriorating condition, but on May 31 he became delirious and died within a few hours.[53] In addition to Lannes, the French suffered at least 19,000 casualties, while almost 20,000 Austrians were wounded or killed. It was a terrible battle that wrought terrible consequences. It snuffed out the life of one of Napoleon's oldest, most loyal, and brilliant field commanders—it was a loss from which Napoleon would never recover. He reflected this in a letter to Lannes's wife: "The Marshal has died this morning of the wounds he received on the field of honor." Expressing the personal pain at his loss, he wrote, "I lost the most distinguished general in my army, and a companion-in-arms for sixteen years whom I considered my best friend."[54]

The Battle of Aspern–Essling ended a few hours after Lannes had been hit. Napoleon turned his forces over to Massena and ordered their withdrawal to Lobau. The results of the battle could hardly be interpreted as more than a moral victory for the French since they had been driven off the north bank of the Danube. It was the first major check for Napoleon personally, and although it was negated at Wagram, the memorials to the battle can still be seen today in the massive "Lion of Aspern" before the village church, in the "1809" room at the Heeresgeschichtliches museum in Vienna, and on Lannes's sarcophagus in the crypt at the Pantheon: *"Blessé à mort à la bataille d'Essling, le 22 mai 1809."*

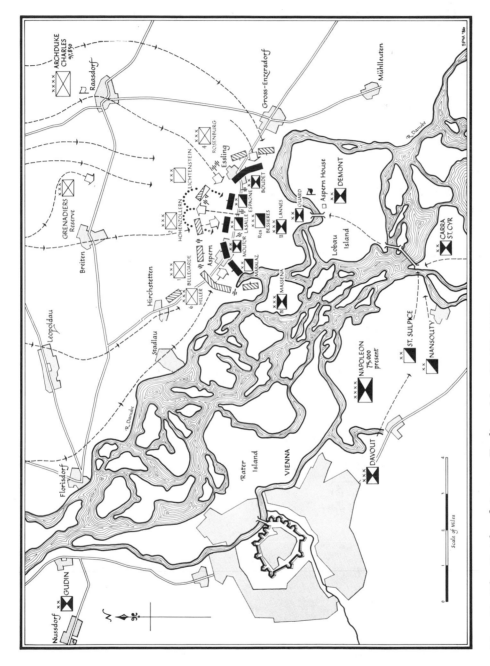

Map 11. The Battle of Aspern-Essling, May 21-22, 1809

TEXTUAL REFERENCES

1. J. B. Marbot, *The Memoirs of Baron Marbot* (London, 1892), Vol. 1, pp. 445–46.
2. C. Thoumas, *Le maréchal Lannes* (Paris, 1891), pp. 4–6.
3. C. L. Lannes, *Le maréchal Lannes, duc de Montebello* (Tours, 1900), p. 17.
4. Thoumas, *op. cit.*, pp. 8–9.
5. R. W. Phipps, *The Armies of the First French Republic and the Rise of the Marshals of Napoleon I* (Oxford, 1968), Vol. 3, pp. 175–77.
6. L. Poussereau, *Histoire du maréchal Lannes* (Nevers, 1910), p. 10.
7. Thoumas, *op. cit.*, p. 356–57.
8. Phipps, *op. cit.*, Vol. 4, pp. 13, 27.
9. Thoumas, *op. cit.*, pp. 17–20; Phipps, *op. cit.*, Vol. 4, pp. 33–34.
10. Phipps, *op. cit.*, Vol. 4, pp. 34–38.
11. *Correspondance de Napoléon Ier* (Paris, 1858–70), Vol. 1, No. 978, pp. 756–58.
12. Phipps, *op. cit.*, Vol. 4, pp. 112–14; Thoumas, *op. cit.*, p. 27.
13. C. Montholon, *Mémoires pour servir à l'historie de France, sous Napoléon* (Paris, 1828), Vol. 3, p. 404.
14. *Correspondance op. cit.*, Vol. 3, No. 2413, pp. 639–40.
15. *Ibid.*, No. 2232., p. 426.
16. Thoumas, *op. cit.*, pp. 33–34.
17. Marbot, *op. cit.*, p. 447.
18. Poussereau, *op. cit.*, p. 36.
19. Thoumas, *op. cit.*, p. 58.
20. J. Adye, *Napoleon of the Snows* (London, 1931), pp. 140–42.
21. Poussereau, *op. cit.*, p. 54; Thoumas, *op. cit.*, pp. 74–75.
22. Thoumas, *op. cit.*, pp. 77–80; Adye, *op. cit.*, pp. 230–39.
23. Poussereau, *op. cit.*, pp. 71–73.
24. Thoumas, *op. cit.*, pp. 361–62.
25. Marbot, *op. cit.*, pp. 447–48.
26. Thoumas, *op. cit.*, p. 98.
27. D. D. Horward, "Portuguese Neutrality and Mobilization: 1801–1810," In *Commission International d'Histoire*, 1976, Acta No. 3, p. 275.
28. *Correspondance op. cit.*, Vol. 9, No. 7689, p. 416.
29. Poussereau, *op. cit.*, p. 94.
30. Thoumas, *op. cit.*, pp. 114–17.
31. C. Duffy, *Austerlitz 1805* (London, 1977), pp. 63–68.
32. Thoumas, *op. cit.*, pp. 137–39; Duffy, *op. cit.*, pp. 123–32.
33. F. L. Petre, *Napoleon's Conquest of Prussia, 1806* (London, 1972), pp. 91–102; Marbot, *op. cit.*, pp. 221–22.
34. H. Houssaye, *Jena* (Paris, 1912), pp. 78–120.
35. Thoumas, *op. cit.*, pp. 167–74.
36. F. L. Petre, *Napoleon's Campaign in Poland, 1806–7* (London, 1908), pp. 90–107.
37. Thoumas, *op. cit.*, pp. 197–200.
38. H. T. Parker, *Three Napoleonic Battles* (Durham N.C., 1983), pp. 11–23.
39. C. W. Oman, *A History of the Peninsular War* (Oxford, 1902–30), Vol. 1, pp. 440–44.
40. *Ibid.*, Vol. 2, pp. 90–114.
41. J. Delmas, *Journaux de siéges faits ou soutenus par les Français dans la péninsule* (Paris, 1836–37), Vol. 2, pp. 203–325; Oman, *op. cit.*, Vol. 2, pp. 115–42.
42. C. Saski, *Campagne de 1809 en Allemagne et Autriche* (Paris, 1899–1900), Vol. 2, pp. 276–331.
43. J. J. Pelet, *Mémoires sur la guerre de 1809, en Allemagne* (Paris, 1824–26), Vol. 2, pp. 77–82.
44. Marbot, *op. cit.*, Vol. 1, pp. 384–87.
45. Thoumas, *op. cit.*, pp. 307–8.

46. Parker, *op. cit.,* pp. 58–59; Saski, *op. cit.,* Vol. 3, pp. 242–46.
47. Pelet, *op. cit.,* Vol. 3, pp. 279–306; Saski, *op. cit.,* Vol. 3, pp. 343–49.
48. Parker, *op. cit.,* p. 59.
49. Saski, *op. cit.,* Vol. 3, pp. 348–53; Pclct, *op. cit.,* Vol. 3, pp. 312–17; Thoumas, *op. cit.,* p. 315.
50. Pelet, *op. cit.,* Vol. 3, p. 318; Marbot, *op. cit.,* Vol. 1, p. 429.
51. F. L. Petre, *Napoleon and Archduke Charles* (London, 1909), pp. 292–93; Saski, *op. cit.,* Vol. 3, pp. 353–54.
52. Marbot, *op. cit.,* Vol. 1, p. 434.
53. Marbot, op. cit., Vol. 1, pp. 431ff.
54. Thoumas, *op. cit.,* pp. 330–31.

BIBLIOGRAPHICAL NOTE

The most complete and probably the most objective of the earlier works on Lannes is Charles Thoumas's *Maréchal Lannes* (Paris, 1891). His appendix includes many valuable official documents. The volumes published by Charles Louis Lannes, *Le maréchal Lannes, duc de Montebello* (Tours, 1900), and by Louis Poussereau, *Histoire de maréchal Lannes* (Nevres, 1910), provide a few additional details but they are less objective. More recent volumes by André Laffargue, *Jean Lannes, maréchal de France* (Paris, 1981), and Luc Wilette, *Le maréchal Lannes, un d'Artagnan sous l'Empire* (Paris, 1979), are both useful but they do not replace Thoumas. Of the primary sources, the most valuable is the memoirs of Marbot, *The Memoirs of Baron Marbot* (London, 1892). Despite his tendency to exaggerate and gossip, Marbot's work is still an extremely valuable source because of the intimate role he played in Lannes's last campaign.

There are a number of valuable studies for each of the campaigns in which Lannes served. F. Loraine Petre's three volumes in English, *Napoleon's Conquest of Prussia, 1806* (London, 1972), *Napoleon's Campaign in Poland, 1806–7* (London, 1908), and *Napoleon and Archduke Charles* (London, 1909), provide interesting details of Lannes's operations. Another useful work is Harold Parker's *Three Napoleonic Battles* (Durham, N.C., 1983), which deals with Friedland and Aspern–Essling. For Austerlitz and Jena there are two volumes by Henry Lachouque, *2 Decembre 1805* and *Jena* (Paris, 1958 and 1961). The all-important 1809 campaign is covered by several important works that must be consulted. Jean Jacques Pelet's *Mémoires sur la guerres de 1809 en Allemagne* (Paris, 1824–26) is an invaluable primary account, and the three-volume study by Charles Saski, *Campagne de 1809 en Allegmagne et Autriche* (Paris, 1899–1900), cites hundreds of original documents from the French *Archives de la guerre.* To locate other works on Lannes and his military career, it would be wise to consult Chapters 4 (Italy), 5 (Egypt), 6 (1805–07), 9 (Peninsular War), 10 (Austria), 13 (Germany), and 20 (Poland) of Donald D. Horward's *Bibliography of Napoleonic Military History* (New York, 1985).

CHRONOLOGY

1755, October 25	—Born at Rouffach (Alsace)
1773, September 10	—Enlisted in the French Guards
1782, June 28	—Promoted sergeant
1783, March 1	—Married Catherine Hübscher
1789, September 1	—Appointed as lieutenant in the National Guard of Paris
1792, January 1	—Promoted captain of light infantry, *l'Armée de la Moselle*
1793, December 2	—Promoted *général de brigade*
1794, January 10	—Confirmed in the rank of *général de division*
June 26	—Served with distinction at Battle of Fleurus
1795–	—Commanded advance guard of *Les armées du*
1799	*Rhin et de la Moselle* and *de Sambre et Meuse*
1796, June 4	—Distinguished service at Battle of Altenkirchen
1797, April 17–18	—Notable conduct during the crossing of the Rhine
1799, March 21	—Wounded at the combat of Ostrach
August 15	—Appointed to command the 17th military district
November 9	—Supported Bonaparte during the *coup d'état* of *Brumaire*
1800, April 1	—Appointed to the Senate by the First Consul
1804, May 19	—Appointed *Maréchal d'Empire* (sixteenth in seniority)
1806, October 5	—Appointed to command the infantry of the Imperial Guard
1807, March 10–	—Commands X Corps at the Siege of Danzig
May 25	
1807, May 28	—Created *duc de Danzig*
1808, September–	—Commanded IV Corps in Spain
January 1809	
October 31	—Defeated General Blake at Battle of Durango
November 10	—Shares in victory of Espinosa
1809, April 20–22	—Commanded VII (Bavarian) Corps at Battles of Abensberg–Eckmühl
May 13	—Victorious over Tyrolean rebels at Mount Wörgl
1812, June–January	—Commanded the infantry of the Old Guard in Russia
1813	
1814, January–March	—Participated with distinction in the Campaign of France
February 10	—Fought at Champaubert
February 18	—Fought at Montereau
March 21–22	—Fought at Arcis-sur-Aube
April 4	—Called for Napoleon's abdication
1815, March–June	—Rallied to Napoleon but took no active part in the Hundred Days
1819, March 5	—Restored to favor and restored to the peerage by the Bourbons
1820, September 14	—Died in Paris

CHAPTER TWELVE

THE HONEST SOLDIER

Lefebvre

by

Gunther E. Rothenberg

Establishing a Reputation (1755-1794)

Posterity has not been kind to Marshal François Joseph Lefebvre, duke of Danzig. Caricatured in Victorien Sardou's play *Madame Sans-Gêne*, he has been dismissed by historians as nothing more than the "complete sergeant-major" who always "remained the complete sergeant-major" and was included among the first eighteen marshals created by Napoleon in 1804 only as a reward for his support on 18 *Brumaire* and to conciliate republican sentiments.[1] Any appraisal of Lefebvre, however, must rest on his performance as a fighting soldier, and here the record speaks in his favor. To be sure, his importance springs entirely from his troop leadership rather than from his strategic talents, which, like those of many of his peers, indeed were limited. But as a commander on the divisional level, he was formidable. If Napoleon occasionally was vexed by his strategic mistakes, he recognized his bravery and loyalty and wrote to his brother that, for all his shortcomings, the marshal was "brave and capable in action."[2] A few years before his death on St. Helena, he repeated these sentiments to General Gourgaud in almost identical words.

The son of a former trooper in the Berecheny Hussars who had become a miller and town constable, the future marshal was born on October 25, 1755, in Rouffach in the Alsace. Following his father's death in 1763, he was brought up by his uncle, Abbé Jean Christophe Lefebvre, but showed no inclination for the Church. Instead, at 17, with little education and a rough Alsatian accent he never lost, young Lefebvre set out for Paris where on September 10, 1773, he enlisted in the French Guards, one of the royal household regiments. Promoted to corporal five years later, he became a sergeant on June 28, 1782, and the following year, on March 1, 1783, he married Catherine Hübscher, an Alsatian washerwoman, two years his senior, a big-hearted and loyal companion in an exceptionally loving union. In April 1788 Lefebvre reached the rank of first sergeant.[3]

With this promotion it appeared that he had reached the apex of his military career. During the last decade before the French Revolution, an aristocratic reaction had ended the practice of allowing deserving noncommissioned officers to rise to commissioned rank. While this restriction alienated many deserving senior sergeants, in the case of the French Guards it was further aggravated in 1788 when the regiment, enjoying better pay and treatment than the line, was threatened with the reduction of its privileges. Disaffected, the French Guards participated in the storming of the Bastille on July 14, 1789. Although there is no evidence that Sergeant Lefebvre participated in this action, it seems clear that he sympathized with the Revolution from the start. Moreover, the new circumstances soon opened the way for advancement. When, on August 31, 1789, the French Guards were disbanded, transferring in large part to the paid National Guard of Paris, Sergeant Lefebvre joined the *bataillon des Filles-Saint Thomas* and on September 1 was elected lieutenant.[4]

As commander of the grenadier company, he gained the respect and affection of his men, while at the same time, though a staunch republican, he also was a determined upholder of good order and discipline. On several occasions he helped to protect members of the royal family from mob violence, and his company furnished part of the escort when the king returned from his ill-starred flight to Varennes in June 1791. Later that year, with war likely, the Constituent Assembly resolved to strengthen the field army and organized active service units from the National Guard. On January 1, 1792, Lefebvre became a captain in the *13th bataillon d'Infanterie legère* in the Army of the Moselle.[5]

The outbreak of the War of the First Coalition accelerated his rise. A captain in January 1792, he was confirmed as general of division in January 1794. He participated in the defense of Thionville in the summer of 1792 and in the engagement at Arlon on June 9, 1793, and was promoted to lieutenant colonel in September. At this point, however, his career was threatened when the Committee of Public Safety directed that all members of the former household troops be removed from the armies. Although the committee's deputies-on-mission effectively nullified this decree, the incident marked the beginning of Lefebvre's aversion to radical Jacobinism. Meanwhile, his rapid advance continued. On December 2, 1793, General Hoche, himself a former corporal in the French Guards, now commanding the Army of the Moselle, promoted Lefebvre to brigadier general in "recognition of his proven talent and bravery" during the fighting around Kaiserslautern on November 28–30. Before the year was out, Lefebvre became acting divisional commander, distinguishing himself during the assault on the Geisberg during the Battle of Wissembourg on December 26, 1793.[6]

Next, Lefebvre was ordered to take Fort Vauban, located on an island in the middle of the Rhine east of Hagenau. When he asked for siege guns, Hoche informed him that "intelligence and above all boldness and patriotism" would suffice and that "courage and the Republic will be your siege train." Lefebvre must have been puzzled by this bombast, but he was elated when on January 10, 1794, the deputies-on-mission, noting that he had "shown sustained bravery and also . . . contributed to the success of the campaign by his skillful maneuvers," confirmed him in rank as general of division.[7] Moreover, luck, an important component of generalship, was on his side. On January 18 the Austrian defenders evacuated the fort.

In April 1794 Hoche temporarily fell from grace with the Committee of Public Safety and was removed from command. Jourdan, his successor, took the Army of the Moselle to join with elements of the Armies of the Rhine and the North in the celebrated Army of the Sambre and Meuse. Moving into southern Belgium, Jourdan suffered a setback on June 16, but 10 days later, on June 26, he defeated the main Austrian force at Fleurus. During the battle the French line was hard pressed and wavered, but Lefebvre's division stood firm and then, with the general at the head of the 80th Line, launched the decisive counterattack. A noted military historian concluded that of the generals of division at Fleurus, Lefebvre had "won most of the credit." At the same time, though formidable in combat, he also was an honorable soldier and, at considerable personal risk, refused standing orders to execute French émigré prisoners taken during the battle.[8]

Consolidation (1794–1804)

Fleurus was a turning point. The victory ended the threat from Belgium and opened the way for the French conquest of the Low Countries and the Rhineland. By the spring of 1795, the British army was expelled from the continent while Prussia treatied for peace and only Austria remained at war. With the danger of invasion banished, there was a reaction against the radicals and their emergency rule, the "Terror" in Paris. In October 1795 the more moderate, if also corrupt, Directory replaced the government of the National Convention and its Committee of Public Safety.

Fighting meanwhile continued. During the Campaigns of 1795–1797 in Germany, Lefebvre commanded the advance guard, the fighting edge of the army, first with the Army of the Rhine and Moselle and then with the Army of the Sambre and Meuse, serving under Kléber, Jourdan, and Hoche. None of these campaigns was decisive, the French suffering as many defeats as they gained victories. Still, Lefebvre did well, distinguishing himself at Altenkirchen on June 4, and again during the battles on the Lahn in July, 1796. On April 17–18, 1797, he led his troops across the Rhine, when, about to win a major victory, he found himself checked by news that preliminary articles of peace had been signed at Leoben. Hoche, the army commander, praised his conduct. "I have to congratulate myself," he wrote, "my dear General, on the numerous and striking successes you gained yesterday. They are a gauge of your talent, of your valor." Clearly, by the end of the War of the First Coalition, Lefebvre had emerged as "one of the first Generals of Division of the Republic," a highly competent, energetic, and steady combat commander.[9] Many years later, during the Restoration, Soult, who had acted as Lefebvre's chief of staff in 1794, wrote that he had learned much from serving under such an excellent commander, while General Jourdan declared that Lefebvre "added to the greatest bravery all the necessary knowledge of a good advance guard commander, maintaining strict discipline, always working to provide his troops with the necessaries, and always manifesting the principles of a good republican."[10]

But if republican principles included civilian control over the military, then Lefebvre's sentiments were changing. As long as France had been threatened, the soldiers, albeit grudgingly, had accepted frequent and arbitrary civilian interference. Now, however, the danger was over and the army was becoming a self-willed "nation of the camps," increasingly professional and not willing to subordinate itself in all matters to a weak and corrupt Directory. To be sure, as a body the generals opposed both a return of the royalists, which would despoil them of their ranks, and equally a return to power of the extreme radicals and their deputies-on-mission. Lefebvre shared these feelings and he already had clashed several times with the radicals. In 1793 he almost had been ousted from the army, in 1794 he had been upset by Hoche's abrupt and unjustified relief, and in 1795 he had on at least one occasion firmly overruled a deputy-on-mission who had tried to interfere with tactical matters. Now, in the summer of 1797, he openly complained that the men who had saved France were not given their due in Paris, but were maligned by politicians and journalists.[11]

Immediately following the signing of peace in October 1797, Lefebvre was left without active employment, and on December 27 he requested to be retired. "The definitive conclusion of peace," he wrote to the Directors, "enables the country to dispense with my services." He continued that he had not become rich by plunder and was asking only for a modest pension. "I want neither carriage nor horses." The Directors, he declared, were acquainted with his deeds. "I shall not enumerate my victories and I have no defeats." He ended by asking for promotions and honors for his subordinates.[12]

The Directory refused his request for retirement, but, exhausted by six years of hard campaigning, Lefebvre went on leave. The next year, when England managed to put together the

Second Coalition, he returned to active duty, but because of poor health asked to be given a less strenuous command, perhaps the Guard of the Directory. Nothing came of this and when early in 1799 Austria appeared to be ready for war, he again assumed command of a division in Jourdan's Army of the Danube. Austria declared war in March, and on March 21 Jourdan's forces met the main enemy body at Ostrach. Fighting a stubborn holding action against superior numbers, the French were pushed back, though the Austrian victory was costly and their offensive blunted.[13] As usual, Lefebvre had exposed himself to rally his troops and, seriously wounded by a musket ball in his right arm, had to be carried from the field.

He now was clearly no longer able to hold field command and returned to Paris to recuperate. That summer Paris was restive. The Directory was detested, its armies defeated, and there was plotting on the right and the left. To shore up its position, the Directors, led by Siéyès, looked for a popular soldier and even briefly considered Lefebvre for a seat in the government. This somewhat unlikely prospect caused the general's wife, always an outspoken woman, to observe that the Directory had to be in poor shape indeed even to consider such a move. In any case nothing came of this, but to restrict the possibility of a radical coup, the directors appointed Lefebvre to command the 17th military district, the capital and neighboring departments, replacing Jacobin General Marbot.[14]

Bonaparte's unexpected return from Egypt in October provided the Directors with the soldier they had been looking for, though it was somewhat naive for them to expect that he would be their subservient tool. Active preparations for a coup began at once. Lefebvre, whose cooperation was essential to silence republican opposition, was not in on the planning, but was invited to visit Bonaparte in his quarters early on the morning of November 9, 18 *Brumaire*. The story that a wily Bonaparte duped him by asking him to save the Republic and offering him the sword he had carried in the Battle of the Pyramids appears to be only a partial explanation. Lefebvre, in any case, disliked the venal civilian politicians and feared a Jacobin resurgence. His reply to Bonaparte's appeal for support, "Yes, let us throw the lawyers into the river," expressed his genuine feelings.[15] He remained at Bonaparte's side during the crucial first days of the coup and found himself well satisfied with the results. Writing to Mortier, a former subordinate, he observed that this "astonishing and salutary revolution has been made without any shock." Bonaparte, he continued, would bring peace, and above all, "the soldier will no longer be the puppet of factious men who mock his privations." Some months later he wrote to Ney that "times are much changed, my dear Ney. Places are no longer given through intrigue, every consideration yields to the public interest."[16]

The establishment of the Consulate brought Lefebvre more advancement. The 15th and 16th military districts were added to his command in order to deal with a flareup of insurgency in Vendée, a mission he accomplished in short order. On April 1, 1800, Bonaparte appointed him to a seat in the Senate with an income of 35,000 francs annually, and when, on May 19, 1804, Bonaparte, now Emperor Napoleon I, created 18 Marshals of the Empire, Lefebvre was included. However, because, as the Emperor had explained when he had nominated him for the Senate, the old soldier had been so gravely wounded that "he no longer [could] take the field in a manner worthy of himself,"[17] he was bracketed with Kellermann, Pérignon, and Sérurier, all deserving republican veterans, as marshals whose main duties would lie in the Senate.

The Marshal's Later Years (1805–1820)

When the War of the Third Coalition broke out in 1805, Lefebvre returned to duty, but initially held only inactive commands. He assembled a reserve corps, composed primarily of National Guard units, at Mayence, which was disbanded after Austerlitz.[18] The next year, following the Treaty of Pressburg, he briefly took over Lannes's V Corps held in reserve in Germany, but when fighting resumed in early summer he asked the Emperor for active employment. On August 5, 1806, Napoleon assured him that he soon would find him a post "worthy of your rank and seniority," and on October 8 he placed Lefebvre in command of the infantry of the Old Guard, a position of much honor and trust but with little independent initiative.[19]

The Emperor's final reserve, the Guard, was not engaged in 1806. Early in 1807, however, with the campaign against the Russo–Prussian forces temporarily bogged down and the Grand Army preparing to renew operations in Poland, Napoleon entrusted the marshal with the Siege of Danzig, a strong Prussian fortress near the mouth of the Vistula. In command of X Corps, a hybrid French, German, and Polish formation, Lefebvre conducted a formal siege from March 11 to May 25, 1807 (see p. 227). Throughout these months the marshal, leaving the technical aspects to his chief of engineers, inspired his indifferent troops by his personal example, always in the trenches, and on one occasion leading a counterattack against a major sortie in person. At long last, after a Russo–Prussian relief effort supported by the Royal Navy had failed, the fortress capitulated. Napoleon rewarded Lefebvre on May 28, 1807 with the title of Duke of Danzig.[20]

Although there were some critics who argued that others had been more deserving of this honor, Napoleon seemed to be well satisfied, and when in the late summer of 1808 he decided to act personally against the Spanish uprising, he appointed Lefebvre to lead IV Corps during the ensuing campaign. Napoleon planned to make a strong central thrust on Madrid, while the two wings of his army closed around the Spanish forces. The right wing was composed of two corps, IV Corps under Lefebvre and VI Corps under Ney. But Lefebvre was not the man to conform patiently to a grand design. Confronted by Captain-General Blake, he immediately engaged him on October 31 at Durango and on November 10 defeated him at Espinosa. Although this battle inflicted heavy casualties on the Spanish forces, Napoleon, apprehensive that his grand plan had been spoiled, was displeased. "The Emperor," Berthier wrote to Lefebvre from Bayonne, "is pained that you have engaged Blake's corps without orders."[21] Napoleon recovered by a series of rapid maneuvers, destroying most of the Spanish army and driving back a British expeditionary force, though Lefebvre once again blundered. In late December he was ordered across the Tagus to scatter the Estremaduran levies and then return to base, but instead he deviated from his set route and marched into Old Castile. This time, Napoleon removed him from command in January 1809, complaining to his brother, Joseph, that the marshal "cannot grasp the meaning of his orders."[22]

Even so, Lefebvre's disgrace was only temporary. Napoleon realized that Lefebvre had no capacity for independent command, but also that he was a loyal and steady troop commander. When the situation in Germany, where Austria was preparing for war, became alarming, he entrusted the marshal with command of VII (Bavarian) Corps, a formation likely to absorb the brunt of an Austrian attack. When the Austrians invaded Bavaria on April 9, the French Army of Germany, somewhat poorly handled by Berthier, was concentrated at Ratisbon and Augsburg, some 76 miles apart, with only VII Corps in the gap. Handling his corps skillfully, Lefebvre, in cooperation with Davout, managed to contain the Austrian offensive, and during the Five Days' Battle that began on April 19 he provided the curtain of maneuver that enabled Napoleon to concentrate his forces to hit the Austrian flank at Eckmühl. This time Lefebvre not only displayed his customary tenacity, but, as one writer commented, "in his first days of the campaign . . . showed himself clearer-headed than Berthier."[23]

After Ratisbon, while Napoleon led the main army in pursuit of the Austrians down the Danube, Lefebvre went to the Tyrol where an insurrection, supported by a small Austrian corps, had expelled the Bavarian garrisons. Beginning his operations on April 28, Lefebvre defeated the Austrians and entered Innsbruck on May 19. Ten days later, however, Tyrolean levies defeated one of his divisions at Mount Isel, compelling him partially to evacuate the country. Moreover, following the repulse at Aspern–Essling on May 21–22, Napoleon ordered Lefebvre to join the main army on the Danube. During the Battle of Wagram on July 5–6, VII Corps saw no action but was deployed on the extreme left wing, opposite Austrian V Corps. Lefebvre returned to the Tyrol in late July and, despite a major setback on August 13 at Mount Isel, managed to defeat the Tyroleans.[24] In these operations he showed considerable skill, managing to divide the insurgents and to gain some popular support, indispensable for successful counter-insurgency, and pacified the country by the end of the year.

In 1810 he returned to his estate at Combault near Paris, but during the Russian Campaign of 1812 he once again commanded the infantry of the Old Guard, taking part in all the hardships of the advance and the horrors of the retreat. Fifty-eight years old, he marched on foot from Moscow to the Vistula, providing security for the Emperor, and then, as the Grand Army fell apart, rallying his men in the fighting around Vilna to drive off the pursuing enemy. But when he heard that his only surviving child, Brigadier-General Marie Xavier Joseph, had been killed around December 15, his spirit broke. He now asked to be relieved, returned to France, and took no part in the Campaign of 1813.[25]

When France was invaded in 1814, the Emperor summoned him on January 26 to the imperial headquarters at Châlons. During the next months, despite his 60 years, Lefebvre again displayed his customary energy and combativeness. On February 11 he personally led a charge by two battalions of the Old Guard on the heights of Montmirail, and at Monterau on February 18 he commanded a small combined force, headquarters personnel and others, against the Russians. On this day he had his horse shot under him, but continued to encourge his troops. As one eyewitness described it, "Foam came out of the marshal's mouth and his saber hardly rested."[26] But it was too late. After Napoleon's repulse at Arcis-sur-Aube on March 21–22, 1814, even Lefebvre began to lose faith. He refused, however, to join any of the intrigues against Napoleon, staunchly supported by his wife who let it be known that "if he were capable of such an infamy I should take him by the hair and drag him to the Emperor's feet."[27]

Even so, Lefebvre was too experienced a campaigner not to

realize that the game was up, and on April 4 he joined the group of marshals pressuring Napoleon to abdicate. This achieved, he went to Paris to plead with Tsar Alexander. Napoleon was gone but France remained, and the marshal convinced the Tsar, perhaps impressed by his good treatment of Russian prisoners of war, that the Alsace, his homeland, should remain French. It was his last service for his country.

From 1814 to his death, Lefebvre spent most of his time on his estate where he devoted himself to helping old comrades who had fallen on hard times. Although created a peer by the restored Bourbons, he rarely attended court. During the Hundred Days he held back, though he accepted a seat in the Senate, for which he was under a cloud during the first years of the Second Restoration. In 1819 he was fully pardoned and restored to rank and offices. But he was tired and in poor health. None of his children had survived him, and many of his old friends were dead. On September 14, 1820, his wife at his side, he died in Paris and was buried in the Cemetery of Pére-Lachaise between Massena and Sérurier and close to Pérignon. His wife raised a monument over his grave, inscribed "Soldat, Maréchal, duc de Dantzick, pair de France: Fleurus, Avant-Garde, Passage du Rhin, Altenkirchen, Montmirail."

The inscription omitted Lefebvre's finest strategic achievement, his handling of VII Corps in the days before Eckmühl in 1809. Of course, he never pretended to great strategic talents and first and foremost remained a combat officer in the mode of the republican armies, inspiring his men by personal example. A strict disciplinarian, his reputation was enhanced by his undoubted probity in his dealings with conquered areas, and it was no empty boast when he wrote to the Directory that he had not amassed riches by plunder. Yet, Lefebvre also was a no-nonsense military conqueror, and one often-repeated anecdote tells that he addressed the people of a newly "liberated" town in Franconia with the statement, "We have come to bring you Liberty and Equality, but don't lose your heads about it; the first one of you who moves without my permission will be shot."[28]

Lefebvre took little part in the frequently ferocious in-fighting among the marshals, though he was quick to assert what he considered his just claims. In 1797, when Hoche stated in army orders that seven flags had been captured at Neuwied, Lefebvre, whose troops actually had captured the colors, was quick to respond that then there had to be 14 because he alone had taken seven. He was proud of his rank, gained by long service and not through connections. When once asked about his ancestry, he replied, "I am an ancestor myself," and when an acquaintance remarked on the splendor of his new marshal's uniform, he replied, "It ought to be, I have been stitching on it for thirty-five years."[29]

Neither the duke nor the duchess had any pretensions and, much to the consternation of the high imperial society, which deplored the couple's lack of sophistication, they tended to preface their remarks by "when I was a sergeant" or "when I did the washing." There were many stories about their scant education and refinement, but this hardly touched the couple who maintained an affectionate and devoted marriage, marred only by personal tragedy. Only two of their 14 children lived beyond the first days of infancy; one died in her early teens, and his surviving son was killed in Russia. Despite their personal grief, Lefebvre and his wife remained as they always had been, honest, truthful, loyal, and spent much of their fortune helping friends, visiting the sick, and supporting charities.

The Siege of Danzig (March 10–May 25, 1807)

Lefebvre's ducal title derived from the Siege of Danzig, one of the relatively few major sieges outside the Peninsula. The capture of Danzig was important on several points. Strategically Napoleon needed the port as a supply base for reopening his campaign in Poland and to eliminate a potential threat in the rear of his army. Politically the Emperor wanted Lefebvre, well known for his republicanism and integrity, to enter the new imperial nobility, and for this he desired Lefebvre to have credit for conducting a major independent operation. "Your glory," he told the marshal, "depends on capturing Danzig."[30]

In late January 1807 a provisional formation, X Corps, was established, comprising two French and one Polish division, some Saxon and Baden contingents, with a siege park and engineer units. On paper the corps numbered almost 20,000 men, but it was not fully assembled until late March. The troops were of indifferent quality; the French were good, but the Poles undisciplined, and neither the Saxons nor the Baden units had seen much combat. Lefebvre, however, was assisted by some excellent officers. General Drouet was assigned as his chief of staff; Colonel François Chasseloup Laubat, a noted engineer, was to supervise the technical aspects of the siege, and Napoleon charged Lefebvre to take his advice on all such matters.[31]

Preliminary operations began in late January, and on February 1, 1807, Polish troops stormed Dirschau, a village on the right bank of the Vistula, massacring 1,500 surrendered Prussians. Lefebvre was very angry indeed.[32] Then, however, progress was interrupted by the Battle of Eylau on February 7–8, a bloody but inconclusive action that, if it had any results, left Napoleon in an unfavorable situation and made the capture of Danzig even more imperative. Therefore, he now prodded the marshal to take immediate action. "There are," he wrote on March 4, "but some 8,000 young troops in Danzig; you have 18,000 men." Lefebvre, he demanded, was to invest the fortress at once and assault it as soon as possible.[33] Napoleon underestimated both the natural position as well as the fortifications of Danzig, actually a strongly defended area, garrisoned by some 16,000 men, mainly Prussians, supported by 349 pieces of artillery, including 20 howitzers and 26 mortars, and commanded by the elderly but energetic *General der Kavallerie* Friedrich Adolph, Count Kalkreuth.[34]

Located on the left bank of the Vistula, some 30 miles from the Baltic, the town occupied a naturally strong position. Just north of the town, the Vistula divided into two branches, forming Holm Island, before continuing northeast into the Baltic. The mouth of the river was protected by a fort at Weichselmünde on the right, while on the left was the entrenched camp at Neufahrwasser, much of its frontage protected by a lake and a channel linking up with the Vistula. Weichselmünde, Neufahrwasser, and Holm Island were well fortified and armed, and several redoubts guarded the stretch between the island and Danzig.

Danzig itself could be attacked only from the west. To the north the fortress was protected by the river and marshy ground, while the south and east sides were covered by inundations created by damming the small River Mottlau that flowed through the town. The west side was approachable, and here the defenders had reinforced the existing works, a casemated rampart with 15 bastions and a wet ditch, with a line of earthworks and palisades stretching from the river in the north to the southwestern edge of the town. This outer line was dominated by the Hagelsberg in the north and the Bischofsberg in the south. At the northern end, between the Hagelsberg and the Vistula, a strong work, the Kalk redoubt, had been constructed. But even so the defenders, some 11,000 in Danzig proper, were not numerous enough to fortify and hold the ridges to the west that overlooked their line. To the east, however, there was a flat, marshy, and in places wooded plain, the Nehrung, stretching along the Baltic coast, which provided for some overland communications with the Russo–Prussian forces near Pillau. Finally, the fortress was well stocked with ammunition and provisions of all kinds.[35]

In early March Lefebvre seized the ridges west and southwest of the town and by March 18 Danzig was partially invested. Two days later General Jean Adam Schramm with some 2,000 men and six guns crossed over to the Nehrung and occupied it, cutting Danzig's eastern approaches.[36] To allow for reinforcements, Lefebvre constructed one bridge north and two bridges south of the city across the Vistula, but continued bad weather and lack of siege materiel hampered further progress. Moreover, there still were light Prussian forces operating in his rear, while the presence of substantial Russo–Prussian forces to the east obliged Napoleon to detach General Nicolas-Charles Oudinot from Lannes's corps to protect the siege in that direction.[37]

Napoleon continued to demand faster action. On April 1 the preliminary movements were concluded and that night the first parallel was opened on the ridge some 1,600 yards from the Hagelsberg. The general plan, designed by Chasseloup, called for the main thrust against the Hagelsberg with diversionary moves against the Bischofsberg and Weichselmünde. During the next night, April 2–3, approach trenches were driven forward against the Hagelsberg, and in a surprise move French troops stormed the Kalk redoubt. The defenders countered with some minor sorties and then, on the morning of April 3, recaptured the redoubt and held it against counter-attacks. Undeterred, the French continued to strengthen the first parallel and the trenches and emplaced some batteries. On April 9 the first trench against the Bischofsberg was opened. During the night of April 11–12, the second main parallel was begun, but Kalkreuth ordered a major sortie, driving the besiegers back some 200 yards, which enabled the Prussians to build some light fieldworks in front of the Hagelsberg. In turn these were stormed by two Saxon battalions the next day, April 13, but Kalkreuth ordered up reinforcements to drive the Saxons back and managed to reach the main French trench. Lefebvre restored the situation, sword in hand, leading a counterattack with the French 44th Line, and succeeded in expelling the Prussians.[38] The next day, April 14, the sappers completed the second parallel and started emplacing batteries. Further north, along the Laake Canal, the eastern branch of the Vistula, General Gardanne established some light works and on April 16, after hard fighting, beat back a sortie from Weichselmünde. The besiegers now had reached the outer edges of the main defenses.

By this time, however, Lefebvre's relations with the touchy allies had become tense. The Hereditary Prince of Baden, who had arrived to take personal command of his contingent, complained about the marshal's brusque manners and excessive demands on the troops. Napoleon, who already had admonished Lefebvre to pay special attention to the sensibilities of the Poles and Saxons, was annoyed and reprimanded him. "You complain," he wrote, "about our allies, yet you treat them without consideration. They are not used to fire, but this will change. Remember that after fifteen years of war we too no longer are the same as in 1792."[39] Perhaps this reprimand revealed more about Napoleon's anxieties after Eylau than it was a true indication of the marshal's shortcomings. When the siege ended, even the Prince conceded that Lefebvre's personal leadership had been decisive in motivating his heterogeneous corps.[40]

The siege continued. The third and final parallel against the Hagelsberg was begun on April 24 and held against repeated sorties during the next three days. The siege artillery, some 60 pieces, now had arrived, but the Hagelsberg defenses remained strong and Chasseloup suggested that Holm Island would have to be taken to provide enfilade and reverse fire against the position. During the night of May 6–7, Drouet crossed the river from the west and Gardanne from the east and landed on the island. After bitter fighting the garrison, comprising 1,200 Russian infantry and some Prussian gunners, surrendered. Also during that night, the Kalk redoubt was stormed. Napoleon, for once, was well satisfied.[41]

The Hagelsberg now was vulnerable and part of its works had to be evacuated. If it fell and the French could bring siege guns there, they could start a heavy bombardment of the main defenses, a prelude to an all-out assault. Aware of Danzig's deteriorating position, General Levin Bennigsen, the Russian commander, was assembling a relief force at Pillau. On May 11 General Kamenskoi with some 8,000 men disembarked at the Vistula's mouth. A crisis seemed at hand, and Lefebvre ordered "every man to defend his post to the death."[42]

Kamenskoi, however, hesitated. Apparently he was surprised to find Holm Island in French hands and he also waited for a Prussian force, some four battalions with artillery, to arrive over land across the Nehrung. This delay gave Napoleon time to order in all of Lannes's corps and to instruct Mortier to march up from Pomerania. On May 15 Kamenskoi, supported by fire from some British men of war, attacked Schramm and Gardanne with 21 battalions and some cossacks, while the Neufahrwasser garrison made a demonstration on the other side. After four attacks the Russians made some progress, but then the advance elements of Lannes's forces arrived and, with a loss of 1,500 men, the Russians withdrew into Weichselmünde. As for the Prussians, they appeared only the next day and were easily driven back by Oudinot's grenadiers. Throughout the fighting the Danzig garrison, normally very combative, had made no effort to support Kamenskoi. All in all, the relief effort was poorly executed and its failure sealed the fate of Danzig.[43]

Even so, the garrison still had spirit. During the night of May 20, Kalkreuth made a major sortie against the siege works opposite the Hagelsberg and inflicted some damage. But this could not halt the inevitable. Mortier's corps began to arrive in strength the next day, and on May 23 Lefebvre, eager to bring the siege to an end without a major all-out assault, summoned Kalkreuth to surrender. Although no breach had yet been made in his main walls, the Prussian decided to negotiate while he still held some cards. He did, however, refuse to negotiate for Weichselmünde and Neufahrwasser. For his part Napoleon was willing to authorize honorable terms. Renewal of major operations was imminent and he could not afford to leave three corps tied up around Danzig. On May 25 terms were agreed upon. The garrison was accorded full honors of war and was to be conducted to Pillau, engaging not to serve against France and her allies for one year. On May 26 the Hagelsberg and the three main gates to the fortress were handed over, and the next day Lefebvre made his formal entry at the head of a unit composed of detachments from all the formations that had taken part in the siege.[44]

Kamenskoi embarked his troops on May 25; and when Lefebvre summoned the Neufahrwasser and Weichselmünde garrisons on May 26, they surrendered, handing over fortifications, stores, and guns in good order.

The defense of Danzig, holding out for 55 days after trenches were opened brought considerable credit to Kalkreuth, who was promoted to field marshal. Lefebvre, of course, was awarded his dukedom. Then and later, some critics have argued that it was Chasseloup and not Lefebvre who deserved credit for the outcome of the siege.[45] Without distracting from Chasseloup's considerable achievements in directing a classic eighteenth-century approach against a bastioned front with outworks, it was Lefebvre who inspired the troops in the face of harsh weather, snow, ice, and later rain, and in heavy fighting and fire. Neither a great strategist or planner, and certainly no director of sieges, Lefebvre as always was the combat leader who, risen from the ranks, inspired his men by personal example.

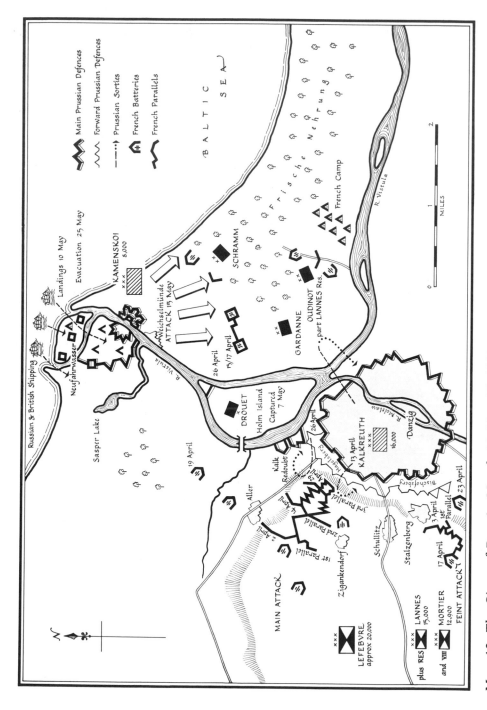

Map. 12. The Siege of Danzig, March 10–May 25, 1807

TEXTUAL REFERENCES

1. A. G. Macdonnell, *Napoleon and His Marshals* (New York, 1934), pp. 23, 90; R. Humble, *Napoleon's Peninsular Marshals* (London, 1973), p. 37; and R. F. Delderfield, *The March of the Twenty-Six: The Story of Napoleon's Marshals* (London, 1962), pp. 119, 186, 196.
2. *Correspondance de Napoléon Ier* (Paris, 1858–70), Vol. 18, No. 14662.
3. J. Wirth, *Le Maréchal Lefebvre, Duc de Dantzig* (Paris, 1904), pp. 32–35.
4. J. P. Bertaud, *La Revolution armée. Les soldats citoyens et la Revolution française* (Paris, 1979), pp. 35, 43; R. W. Phipps, *The Armies of the First French Republic and the Rise of the Marshals of Napoleon I* (London, 1926–39), Vol. 1, p. 105.
5. Wirth, *op. cit.*, pp. 45–46, 50–51, 56, 63.
6. *Ibid.*, p. 63; Phipps, *op. cit.*, Vol. 2, pp. 51–52, 89, 109.
7. Phipps, *op. cit.*, pp. 114–15; Wirth, *op. cit.*, pp. 78, 468–69.
8. Wirth, *op. cit.*, pp. 83–6; Phipps, *op. cit.*, Vol. 2, pp. 160–64, 168–69.
9. Phipps, *op. cit.*, pp. 305–6, 397–98, 428.
10. Marshal Soult, *Mémoires du Maréchal-Général, Duc de Dalmatie* (Paris, 1854), Vol. 1, pp. 206–8; Jourdan cited in R. P. Dunn-Pattison, *Napoleon's Marshals* (Boston, 1909), pp. 323–24.
11. Phipps, *op. cit.*, Vol. 2, pp. 407–9, Vol. 4, p. 273.
12. *Ibid.*, Vol. 4, pp. 115–16; letter in full in Wirth, *op. cit.*, pp. 463–64.
13. Phipps, *op. cit.*, pp. 115–16. See G. E. Rothenberg, *Napoleon's Great Adversaries. The Archduke Charles and the Austrian Army, 1792–1814* (London, 1983), p. 47.
14. Wirth, *op. cit.*, pp. 120–24.
15. Macdonnell, *op. cit.*, pp. 69–71, for the view of Lefebvre as a dupe.
16. Phipps, *op. cit.*, Vol. 5, pp. 462, 464–65.
17. J. E. Howard, ed. and trans., *Letters and Documents of Napoleon* (London, 1961), p. 357.
18. Wirth, *op. cit.*, pp. 138–40.
19. *Correspondance, op. cit.*, Vol. 13, No. 10598.
20. Wirth, *op. cit.*, pp. 158–59, 185–87. D. G. Chandler, *The Campaigns of Napoleon* (New York, 1966), pp. 560–64.
21. Chandler, *op. cit.*, pp. 632–63; Humble, *op. cit.*, pp. 95–97.
22. Humble, *op. cit.*, p. 98; *Correspondance, op. cit.*, Vol. 18, No. 14662.
23. F. L. Petre, *Napoleon and the Archduke Charles* (London, 1909), p. 43; Chandler, *op. cit.*, pp. 1100–1.
24. Petre, *op. cit.*, pp. 247–48, 250, 252.
25. Wirth, *op. cit.*, pp. 220–21, 227; H. Lachouque and A. S. K. Brown, *The Anatomy of Glory* (New York, 1965), pp. 268–69.
26. J. Coignet, *The Notebooks of Captain Coignet*, ed. by J. Fortescue (London, 1929), p. 234; Chandler, *op. cit.*, pp. 972–73.
27. Wirth, *op. cit.*, pp. 240–41.
28. Macdonnell, *op. cit.*, pp. 146–47.
29. *Ibid.*, p. 35; Phipps, *op. cit.*, Vol. 2, p. 436.
30. *Correspondance, op. cit.*, Vol. 14, No. 11826.
31. *Ibid.*, Vol. 15, No. 12600.
32. Wirth, *op. cit.*, pp. 133–34.
33. *Correspondance, op. cit.*, Vol. 14, No. 11921.
34. Details on Danzig's armament are in L. I. von Malinowsky and R. von Bonin, *Geschichte der brandenburg-preussichen Artillerie* (Berlin, 1840–42), Vol. 3, pp. 417–32; on Kalkreuth see Bayrische Akademie der Wissenschaften, *Neue Deutsche Biographie* Vol 11 (Berlin, 1977), Vol. 11, pp. 50–51.
35. F. L. Petre, *Napoleon's Campaign in Poland, 1806–7* (London, 1907), pp. 242–45.
36. *Correspondance, op. cit.*, Vol. 14, No. 11692.
37. *Ibid.*, Nos. 12012, 12088.

38. Wirth, *op. cit.,* pp. 158–59.
39. *Ibid.,* pp. 163–65; *Correspondance, op. cit.,* Vol. 15, No. 12327.
40. Wirth, *op. cit.,* pp. 164–65.
41. *Correspondance, op. cit.,* Vol. 15, No. 12560.
42. Petre, *Campaign in Poland, op. cit.,* p. 256.
43. *Ibid.,* pp. 255–58.
44. *Ibid.,* p. 45.
45. Wirth, *op. cit.,* p. 179.

BIBLIOGRAPHICAL NOTE

Lefebvre is briefly discussed in the various collective biographies of Napoleonic marshals and also appears in the memoirs of some of the leading figures of the revolutionary and imperial periods. Marshal Soult's *Mémoires du Maréchal-Géneral Soult, Duc de Dalmatie,* 3 vols. (Paris, 1854) are highly favorable, while those of Marshal Macdonald, *Souvenirs du Maréchal, Duc de Tarente* (Paris, 1892), tend to make the most of Lefebvre's lack of education and refinement. The frequently cited writings of Baron Marbot, *Mémoires du General Baron de Marbot,* 3 vols. (Paris, 1891), available in numerous translations, are full of splendid anecdotes, but are basically unreliable and biased.

There exists no scholarly life of the marshal. The standard biography by Joseph Wirth, *Le Maréchal Lefebvre, Duc de Dantzig* (Paris, 1904), has a substantial documentary appendix, but lacks detachment and analysis. Even so, it remains the main source for Lefebvre. Some of his papers were published as "Le Maréchal Lefebvre intime—Correspondance inédité" in a special number of *Extrait du Bulletin de la Societé des Sciences et Arts de la Basse Alsace* (Strassbourg, 1900).

Detailed accounts of the Siege of Danzig are General Kirgener's *Précis du siège de Danzig, fait par l'armée française en Avril et Mai 1807* (Paris, 1807), the most frequently cited source, and on the Prussian side the *Belagerung von Danzig 1807, aus General v. Kalkreuths Original Papieren* (Posen, 1809).

CHRONOLOGY

1765, November 17	—born at Sedan
1785,	—Lieutenant in Maillebois's regiment
1792, June	—Aide-de-camp to Beurnonville
November 6	—Captain at Jemappes
1794, November 15	—Appointed *général de division*
1795	—Leads attacks across the Waal
1798, July	—Commander of Rome
1799, February	—Commander of *l'Armée de Naples*
June 17–19	—Defeated at the Trebbia
November 9	—Helps Napoleon to power on 18 *Brumaire*
1800, October 5	—Commander of *l'Armée des Grisons*
December	—Leads the crossing of the Splügen Pass
1801, April	—Appointed envoy extraordinary to the court of Denmark
1803–9	—In rural retirement and disgrace at Courcelles-le-Roi
1809, March	—Recalled to join Prince Eugène's *l'Armée d'Italie*
July 5–6	—Leads central attack at Wagram, and is made *Maréchal d'Empire* (twentieth in order of appointment)
August 15	—Created *duc de Tarante*
1810, April 24	—Commander of *l'Armée de Catalogne*
1812, September	—Commander of X Corps in the Baltic area
1813, May 2	—Corps commander at Lützen
May 20–21	—Corps commander at Bautzen
August 26	—Beaten by Blücher at the Katzbach
October 18	—Corps commander at Leipzig
1814,	—Corps commander in northern France
March	—Tells Napoleon at Fontainebleau to cease fighting
April 4	—Appointed to negotiate terms of Napoleon's abdication
1815, March	—To Lyons to try, unsuccessfully, to organize resistance to Napoleon
July 2	—Appointed arch-chancellor of the Legion of Honor
July 26	—Commander of *l'Armée de la Loire*
1840, September 25	—Died at Courcelles-le-Roi

CHAPTER THIRTEEN

HIS OUTSPOKENNESS

Macdonald

by
Alan Hankinson

Odd Marshal Out (1765–1840)

Macdonald is one of the least-known of the marshals and the reasons are clear. He never fought the British; in one of his rare jokes, Napoleon said he dared not let him within the sound of the bagpipes. He played no part either in other actions that have become the favorites of historians—the First Italian Campaign, Marengo, Austerlitz, the main march on Moscow and its aftermath. Perhaps most important of all, he had none of the flamboyance that made so many of the others such fascinating characters.

He was no great drinker or braggart or swearer. He fought no duels and disdained the tricks of the con-man. He lacked élan. He would not stoop to self-promotion. Although he wrote his *Recollections*, they were for the eyes of his son only and were not published until 1892. And though he admired the military abilities of some of his fellow marshals, there were many whose personal characteristics he despised: Augereau for his dandyism and loud-mouthed cynicism; Lefèbvre for his philistinism; the prickly pride of Victor; the looting, nepotism, and careerist intriguing of others. He liked women and gained a considerable reputation as a lover, but he was no unscrupulous womanizer.

Macdonald was a solid, even a stolid man, careful and decent and conscientious. The thing he prized above all else was his reputation as a man of integrity. In 1825, embarking on his *Recollections*, he wrote: "My conscience during my long and active life reproaches me with nothing, because I always followed three safe guides: honour, fidelity and disinterestedness."[1] He makes this point so insistently that the wary reader grows suspicious. But his contemporaries confirm his claim. The words they most commonly used to describe him were "brave," "upright," "trustworthy," and "unlucky."

Macdonald served many masters in his time—the Bourbons, the Republic, the Directory, the Consuls, the Emperor, then the Bourbons once again. He has been accused of being one of those who could "reconcile their own consciences with any amount of coat-turning."[2] The charge is unfair. Macdonald was a straightforward professional soldier with no strong political attitudes. As he saw it, his first duty was to France, his second to whomever ruled France. When the two came into open conflict—at the *Brumaire* of 1799 and in early 1814 when the allied troops were in Paris—he opted, honorably, for the first.

He took the center of the stage in the Napoleonic drama at two moments only. In July 1809 outside Vienna, it was he who led the attack that clinched the victory of Wagram and won him the baton. And in March–April 1814, it was he—together with Ney—who insisted that the fighting must stop, and it was he again—with Caulaincourt—who negotiated the terms of Napoleon's abdication. "Macdonald does not like me," the Emperor said, announcing his choice as negotiator with the Czar, "but he is a man of his word, of high principles, and he can be relied on, I believe."[3]

It was unfortunate for them both that Napoleon came too late to the realization that he had in Macdonald a man he could trust, but it is not surprising. They never got on together. Their characters were too dissimilar. Macdonald had the highest regard for Napoleon's military skill but no respect for his amoral political methods and, toward the end, little respect for his judgment, political or military. He was not bowled over by the great man's magnetism and not afraid of his wrath. Napoleon did not often hear direct criticism or contradiction, but he heard them both from Macdonald.

Napoleon's mind was perhaps too devious to be able to recognize simple honesty when he met it. Like Talleyrand, another character of Machiavellian complexity who failed to appreciate Macdonald, he was looking for the concealed motivations, the real ambitions that lay behind men's words and actions. If they were not there, he suspected them. When he could not fathom them, he suspected them the more. As a result, throughout their long association, he blew hot and cold upon Macdonald, and mostly cold.

Macdonald's ambition was simply to be a good soldier for France. He sought promotion, naturally, but wanted it to come through merit, not machination. He worked hard, trained his men hard, looked after them, and gave clear orders. He gained their allegiance by proven leadership, never by way of high-flown phrases and promises. As a general he was sensible and thorough rather than nimble-witted or inspirational. He would have been more suited to the more gentlemanly campaigning of the prerevolutionary years.

But when the Revolution came, he chose to stay and serve the new regime. Nearly 40 years later, reflecting on the reasons why he had not emigrated like so many others, he wrote: "Efforts were made to induce me to go too; but I was married, and very much attached to my wife, who was near her confinement. These were surely good reasons! Besides, I cared nothing about politics."[4] There was another reason: the prospect of rapid promotion. It came and carried him, after many years and many setbacks, to the marshalate. He was the only one of the "26" to be awarded his baton on the field of battle by Napoleon in person.

The Road to Wagram (1765–1809)

Macdonald was a Frenchman because his father had to escape from Scotland with the "Young Pretender" in 1746. Neil Macdonald rallied to Prince Charles's cause from his home on South Uist in the Hebrides and after Culloden was one of those—another, Flora Macdonald, was a remote relative—who guided the prince from hiding place to hiding place until they could be taken off by a French ship. Once in France, and promptly dropped by the Stuarts, he settled in Sedan, joined Ogilvy's Scottish Regiment, married the daughter of a French officer, and had two children, a girl first and then the boy who became a marshal.

Etienne Jacques Joseph Alexandre Macdonald was born at Sedan on November 17, 1765, and was brought up by his father—the parents soon separated—at Sancerre. He was intended for the priesthood but at school in Paris, by his own account, he was so impressed by Homer—"I thought myself an Achilles"[5]—that he determined to be a soldier instead. By 19 he was a lieutenant in a regiment that was sent to fight for the Dutch but arrived too late to see action. Disappointed, he joined Dillon's Irish regiment. He studied his profession assiduously but chose his friends from among musicians and draftsmen. He liked art, theater, and music. He played the violin, though never to his own satisfaction, and studied dancing and fencing. He enjoyed polite society.

The Revolution found him avid for action. Married in 1791, his career took off more dramatically than either of them could have dreamed possible. In three years he rose from the obscurity of an infantry subaltern to command of a division. At Jemappes he showed great coolness under fire. He served with distinction on the staffs of Generals Beurnonville and Dumouriez. He played an active part in driving the Austrians out of the Low Countries. In November 1794 General Pichegru promoted him to general of division. Pichegru was soon succeeded by Moreau. The friendship, and respect of these two served Macdonald in excellent stead at the time. Eight years later it was to endanger his career.

In the harsh winter of 1794–1795, Macdonald led the crossing of the frozen River Waal at Nijmegen. The breakthrough was doubly fortunate. As he freely admitted at the time and later, the victory owed as much to good luck as to good generalship. And it was important to be known as a man of victories, for the political commissioners from Paris were in sharp-eyed attendance, eager to equate failure with treachery. Macdonald had no time for mob rule and hated the endless complications and suspicions that sprang from political surveillance in what he called "those horrible times of revolutionary crises." He would not play the political game himself and despised those who did. It was well for him that the march into Holland continued without serious interruption.

In the years that followed, he went to Walcheren and caught fever, then to the Rhineland, then back to Holland. In July 1798 he succeeded St.-Cyr as commander of Rome. He fought a lively, aggressive campaign against Neapolitan insurgents, winning victories against the odds and acquiring a profound contempt for the enemy's cowardice and brutality: "I was dealing not with regulars but with assassins,"[6] he said when he saw the way they dealt with prisoners. Years later he felt insulted when it was proposed he might command a Neapolitan force.

Until this time he had gotten on well with his commanders but he regarded General Championnet as a jealous incompetent. In return, Championnet thought Macdonald rash and independent, not charges that were leveled at him in later campaigns. They rowed continuously until the Directory announced in Macdonald's favor and gave him command of the Army of Naples.

It was an unpropitious moment to get one's first army command. In northern Italy the French were under pressure from Austro–Russian forces and there were many local insurrections. Macdonald was ordered to march north and join the Army of Italy under Moreau. He had to fight most of the way and in June 1799, after taking Modena, was nearly killed by Austrian cavalry. He received saber cuts to the head and hand and was still recovering five days later when an outnumbering force of Russians and Austrians, under Suvorov and Melas, severely mauled his army in three days of fighting along the Trebbia River. Macdonald believed he had been let down by the sluggish reactions of Victor. He told him so and was not forgiven.

In the upheavals of this campaign, he suffered a great loss. His personal collection of paintings, marbles, Etruscan vases, and frescoes from Pompeii disappeared en route for Genoa and France. It was an invaluable hoard but none of it, he claimed, was loot: He had bought some of the things, others were legitimate gifts, most had come to him as part of a French government distribution: "I had no reason to blush for that or for anything else in my long military career."[7]

He returned to Paris to find the capital alive with plots against the Directory. He was, he says, offered the military leadership of the uprising. The offer was then made to General

Moreau, who also declined. Then, right on cue, Napoleon landed back from Egypt. Macdonald was already on friendly terms with Josephine and other members of the Bonaparte family, and on 18 *Brumaire,* in the coup that ended the Directory, he helped Napoleon to power by controlling Versailles and the approaches to St. Cloud.

He was rewarded by an army command in the Rhineland, then by command of the Army of Grisons. In an epic march in December 1800, he led this army across the Alps by way of the Splügen Pass, north of Lake Como. It was a desperate time of the year to attempt such a thing. Several hundred men and more than 100 horses and mules were killed by avalanches and the cold. One of his staff, Count Mathieu Dumas, wrote:

> An unerring *coup d'oeil,* prompt resolution, much boldness and perseverence under the most trying circumstances, are the principal traits of character which General Macdonald manifested in this campaign. . . . The avalanches had in several places blocked the path; the guides declared that the passage was entirely closed up. . . . General Macdonald rallied the guides and, himself sounding first of all, made them pierce and clear away the walls of snow in which many men were entombed.[8]

By the first days of the new year, they were over the pass and into the Adige valley. They rapidly drove the Austrians from Bolzano and Trento. There was little fighting—the weather was crueller than the Austrians—and it was to be more than eight years before Macdonald saw fighting of any kind again.

First he was sent to be envoy extraordinary to the court of Denmark. He was no diplomat and knew it, and spent most of his time pleading for recall to the army. By the time his pleas were heeded, the Peace of Amiens was in force. Then in 1803 his former commanders and friends, Pichegru and Moreau, were accused of treason. There were moves to implicate Macdonald. He believed they were inspired by Foreign Minister Talleyrand to whom he had spoken rather too forcefully on his return from Copenhagen: "I know that he did me serious injury in the eyes of the First Consul by prejudicing him against me, and suggesting that I was a foe to his authority."[9]

Nothing could be proven against Macdonald. He retired to his recently acquired château at Courcelles-le-Roi near Bourges and devoted himself to estate management and his family. His first wife had died in 1797, leaving two daughters. In 1802 he married again—the widow of General Joubert—and she gave him another daughter. But this wife died after only two years of marriage. Macdonald had no more luck in his domestic life than in his professional.

Aware that Fouché's spies were watching, he kept a low profile. He was saddened but not surprised when the first 18 marshals were announced in 1804 and his name was not among them. He found it hardest of all to sit in his country retreat and read of the triumphs of his old comrades at Ulm, Austerlitz, Jena, and Friedland: "My military ardour blazed up at the accounts of every fresh victory."[10] He must have almost given up hope when the recall to arms came at the end of March 1809.

The French were deeply involved in Spain, the Danube valley, and north Italy. There was a serious shortage of experienced commanders. Macdonald was ordered to join the Army of Italy, which had a fledgling commander, the Emperor's stepson, Prince Eugène Beauharnais. The historian Thiers says:

> Macdonald, one of the most intrepid men that ever graced our army, experienced, skilful, cool, with the power of making himself obeyed, was received with confidence by the soldiers, with displeasure by some of the generals who beheld a firm hand about to be laid upon them.... But a man of Macdonald's character was not to be trifled with, and he soon drew back to their allegiance such as had been tempted to stray from it.... Prince Eugène, as modest as he was discreet, never failed to consult him on all important occasions, and always had reason to be satisfied with his counsels.[11]

When Macdonald arrived, Eugène had just been beaten by the Austrians at Sacilio. It was his first army command and he was glad to have Macdonald's steadying support. Before long they were friends and marching forward again. It was clear by this time that the decisive engagements would be fought in the Danube valley, and both opposing armies were ordered to make their way there as expeditiously as possible. In his *Recollections* Macdonald claims that his corps marched the last 60 leagues in three days, which means they averaged over 43 miles a day in the midsummer heat. It was, if the figures are reliable, a magnificent march even by the French standards of the time. But from the point of view of Macdonald's career, the effort was justified for it ensured his presence on the field of Wagram. The course of that battle and the award of the baton to Macdonald will be described below (see p. 247).

After Wagram (1809-1840)

Five weeks after Wagram, on the Emperor's birthday, Macdonald was made Duke of Taranto and given a pension of 60,000 francs a year.

In April 1810 he was given command of the Army of Catalonia. He was not pleased: "I had a very strong objection to the manner in which war was carried on in Spain; my objection had its root in the dishonesty—or what in high places is called policy—which caused the invasion of the country: however, the noble and courageous resistance of its inhabitants triumphed over our efforts and our arms."[12]

He took over from Augereau, whose policy had been one of repression. Macdonald tried a gentler approach, but the Spaniards would not be wooed. Like many others he hated his time in Spain and was relieved to be back in Paris in July 1811 even though the cause was an attack of gout so fierce that he could move only on crutches.

Macdonald was fortunate to be spared the full horrors of the Russian Campaign of 1812. His role was to protect the left flank of the main French force by controlling the Baltic provinces. His command, X Corps, consisted chiefly of Prussian troops with additional contingents of Poles, Bavarians, and Westphalians. The only Frenchmen with him were his headquarters staff. They had a comparatively quiet and comfortable time of it until mid-December when, with what was left of the Grand Army perishing on the long retreat from Moscow, they were ordered to fall back from before Riga on Tilsit. Macdonald went ahead to establish crossings over the Niemen. There he waited for his Prussians, 17,000 men commanded by General Yorck. After five anxious days he heard that Yorck had made a separate armistice with the Russians. Emboldened by recent events, Prussian nationalism was asserting itself. Macdonald described it, with understandable exaggeration, as "an act of treachery unparalleled in history."[13] He conducted a fast, fighting retreat to join up with Ney at Königsberg. It was his opinion that the French should now evacuate Poland and Prussia altogether, and word of this probably reached Napoleon, for when Macdonald arrived in Paris he was given a glacial reception.

He was actively involved throughout the campaign in Germany in 1813. At Lützen in May he led his XI Corps, another heterogeneous group, in the attack that forced the enemy's retreat. Two weeks later they were in action at Bautzen. In late August his army, reinforced to a strength of more than 75,000 men, was badly beaten, almost routed, by Blücher's Army of Silesia. Macdonald, in an aggressive vein, pushed his force across the Katzbach River. Almost immediately a fierce summer downpour rendered the tracks beyond virtually impassable, the river itself dangerous, and much of their ammunition too damp for use. Blücher, much stronger in cavalry, saw his chance. Macdonald's retreat became a shambles. French casualties numbered more than 13,000 killed, many of them drowned in the river. Blücher took 15,000 prisoners and 100 cannons. It was the worst defeat of Macdonald's career. In his *Recollections* he blames the weather and the ineptitude of some of his subordinate generals. At the time he took the blame himself. One of his officers at the Katzbach, Baron de Marbot, wrote:

> Marshal Macdonald, whose miscalculation from a strategic point of view had brought about this irreparable disaster, though he had lost the confidence of the army, was able to preserve its esteem by the honest and straightforward way in which he admitted his mistake. On the following day he called a meeting of all the generals and colonels, and after inviting us all to help maintain order, said that every man and officer had done his duty, that the loss of the battle was due to one man only, and that was himself. . . . This noble confession disarmed criticism, and each man did his utmost to contribute to the safety of the army during its retreat to the Elbe.[14]

Marbot admired Macdonald but thought the army at the Katzbach was too large for him and that he was "too limited and too exclusive in his strategy. Before a battle he could chalk out a plan which was nearly always good, but he should have modified it according to circumstances, and this he was too slow-witted to do."[15]

Macdonald and his men acquitted themselves well at the Battle of the Nations in October. Under repeated attack from superior numbers, they fell back on Leipzig in a controlled manner, then fought a dogged rearguard action through the city streets. Macdonald was shocked by the disorder around him— the defection of Saxon and Hessian units in mid-battle, the precipitate withdrawal of Augereau, the failure to secure a line of retreat across the Elster. Macdonald had to swim the river under fire with the cries of his drowning soldiers in his ears. When he reached Napoleon's headquarters, soaked, exhausted, and angry, he made his feelings known.

The months that followed were full of marching, fighting, and argument. Macdonald saw himself as Kent to Napoleon's King Lear—loyal and reliable but ever ready to point out the folly of his master's ways. They disagreed on questions tactical, strategic, and political. Often when they disputed, Macdonald says, the Emperor's staff would stop work in astonishment that anyone should address Napoleon so. The discussion over, however, Macdonald would obey his orders to the utmost of his ability, although in the final weeks his health was almost broken.

Macdonald was one of the handful of marshals still at the Emperor's side in March 1814 when the cossacks were in Paris and Napoleon, although hopelessly outnumbered, wanted to fight on. There are varying acounts of the scenes at Fontaine-bleau, but there is no doubt that it was Macdonald and Ney who played the leading parts in persuading Napoleon to stop. "We have decided to make an end of this," Macdonald told the Emperor, who, seeing his marshals united, agreed to abdicate.

Napoleon appointed three men to negotiate his abdication terms—Marshal Ney, General de Caulaincourt, and Macdonald. The man they dealt with was Tsar Alexander I, who was impressed with the combination of Caulaincourt's diplomatic skills and Macdonald's palpable honesty. Caulcaincourt, who had been ambassador in Moscow for two years, was also impressed with Macdonald:

> But for him, and for the Tsar's respect for his own word, I know not what would have happened to the Emperor or what he could have secured, for, excepting the Duke of Taranto and myself, His Majesty had not a single defender in Paris. This fact ought to be an aid to reflection on the part of princes whose whole trust is in their flatterers; for Macdonald and I, in our respective capacities, were certainly the two men whom the Emperor loved the least, to whom he had shown the least favour, and who repeatedly had shown him the most opposition.[16]

It was at this time that Napoleon finally recognized Macdonald's worth. On April 11 he told Bausset, "Macdonald is a brave and true soldier. . . . Only during these recent circumstances have I brought myself to appreciate the full nobility of his character."[17]

Two days later, the agreement signed, Macdonald went to say farewell. It was the morning after Napoleon's attempted suicide by poison. In the *Recollections* Macdonald says merely he found the Emperor abstracted in manner, "yellow and greenish" in complexion. Finally Napoleon roused himself to thank Macdonald and express regret that he had come to appreciate him only when he was no longer able to reward him adequately. Macdonald said his actions had been "entirely disinterested." Napoleon acknowledged this but sent for the sword he had won from Murad Bey, the Mameluke leader, and presented it to Macdonald. They embraced. It was their last meeting.

With the restoration of the Bourbons, Macdonald served Louis XVIII as an adviser. His frank disapproval of many of the things the royalists did earned him a nickname from the King of which he was proud: "His Outspokenness." But he did not turn against them when Napoleon returned from Elba. He hurried to Lyons and made strenuous efforts to persuade the army to stop Napoleon's northward march. Failing in this, he helped to escort the King to safety across the frontier. Back in Paris he ignored Napoleon's summons. He wanted to retire to his château but an agonizing attack of gout kept him in the capital until the final Napoleonic convulsion was over.

On the King's return Macdonald was appointed Arch-Chancellor of the Legion of Honor. He refused the secretaryship for war but accepted temporary command of the Army of the Loire in succession to Davout, which meant, in effect, presiding over the disbanding of the last remnants of the Grand Army. It was a sad and delicate task and he strove to make it as painless as possible for his old comrades in arms. He helped a group of senior officers, who had fought for Napoleon at Waterloo, to escape arrest. This was his last military command. His final years were devoted to his country estate, his children, and his duties as arch-chancellor.

In 1821 he married for the third time and three years later a son was born, Alexandre, who was to be the second Duke of Taranto. His joy in this was great but soon overshadowed by the death of his wife in 1825. In the summer of that year, he visited the Hebridean home of his father, then sat down to write his *Recollections*, hurriedly, from memory. They reveal him as a man of no subtlety and little humor, a simple, serious, conscientious, considerate, honourable man. Of medium height, well built and muscular, he was still—despite the recurrent gout—in good physical condition. Macdonald died in 1840, in his seventy-fifth year, at his château at Courcelles-le-Roi.

The Battle of Wagram and the Baton (July 5-6, 1809)

Immediately east of Vienna the Danube follows a twisting and complicated course with many islands and channels. On its northern bank stands a wide and fertile plain, the Marchfeld, which is overlooked by a line of hills some six miles to the north. This area, visible from the ramparts of Vienna, was the scene for two great and bloody battles within six weeks in the summer of 1809.

By mid-May Napoleon had taken Vienna and was assembled on the southern bank of the river and on the big, wooded island of Lobau. On May 21, after perfunctory planning and reconnaissance, he moved into the attack across a single pontoon bridge from Lobau. The Austrians, commanded by their best general, Archduke Charles, and much improved since the humiliations of 1806, waited until the French army was partly across, then attacked in overwhelming force, at the same time sending logs and floating mills downstream to smash the bridge. There were two days of intense fighting, centered on the villages of Aspern and Essling, before the French—having lost more than 20,000 men—were back on Lobau.

The battle of Aspern–Essling was Napoleon's first real defeat in the field. Luckily for him the Austrians did not follow up and he was given time to make sure it did not happen again.

In the weeks that followed, he brought up reinforcements, including the Army of Italy and Macdonald. He went to elaborate pains to persuade the Austrians that his next attack would follow much the same route as the first. Hidden by the woods, engineers prepared bridges to be swung into positions when the moment came. Detailed movement orders were issued for a night river crossing, not north of Lobau but to the east where the Austrians were thin on the ground and unprepared.

It went like clockwork. Macdonald's corps arrived on the south bank, after their three-day marathon march, on July 4. That night they crossed to Lobau in a violent thunderstorm. Soon after first light—the storm over—they were on the Marchfeld.

The coming battle was the biggest Napoleon had fought. The French had 154,000 men and 554 guns, the Austrians 142,000 men and 480 guns. Although the statistics were marginally in the Emperor's favor, he was aware that the balance could be changed at any moment by the arrival of the Archduke John and his army of 13,000.

The French advanced north and west, with Davout on the right flank and Massena's corps on the left with the job of rolling up the Austrian defenses on the Aspern–Essling line. As these two corps diverged, others—including the Army of Italy—filled the widening gap between them. By late afternoon the French formed a compact semicircle with Massena on the extreme left, then Bernadotte with his Saxons, Eugène in the center and facing the slopes below Wagram, then Oudinot, then Davout on the right flank at Glinzendorf.

The main Austrian force, more than 90,000 men, had taken up hastily prepared positions on the high ground between Wagram and Markgrafneusiedl. At the foot of the slope ran a stream, the Russbach, which was shallow and manageable by infantry but whose marshy confines made it awkward for cavalry and worse for artillery.

Napoleon was still worried about the whereabouts of the Archduke John and anxious to strike a telling blow before he could join the enemy. He ordered an attack across the Russbach. Macdonald objected on the grounds that the Austrians were entrenched above and there was little daylight left—it was about 7 P.M. The attack went ahead but it was poorly coordinated. Macdonald dismounted to lead his men across the stream, sword in hand, and they quickly gained the high ground east of Wagram. But they found themselves under heavy fire, organized by Archduke Charles himself, not only from the front but from both flanks as well. Gradually, they were forced back and then—as darkness fell and French units were shooting at each other in the confusion—the retreat became a rout. Macdonald struggled to hold the tide, but his men bolted down the hill and back across the stream and did not stop until they came up against the bayonets of the Imperial Guard.

Macdonald was relieved that the Austrians did not attempt pursuit: "A few squadrons would have sufficed to disperse us, for the night had come on, and we should have imagined ourselves charged by the entire Austrian army, and the result would not be difficult to imagine."[18] He spent the night reorganizing his corps.

Before dawn on July 6 the Austrians surprised Napoleon by attacking his right flank. But this was diversionary. The Archduke's main plan was to smash through the French left, cutting them off from the river and threatening their rear. The Austrians were helped in this by the eccentric conduct of Bernadotte who, during the night, on his own initiative, had withdrawn from the village of Aderklaa. Napoleon was furious when he heard this, and a fierce battle developed for the village. At one point Bernadotte's Saxons were routed and Massena's corps was increasingly drawn in to stabilize the position.

Macdonald, who had been preparing to repeat his attack of the previous evening, swung to face west and support his embattled colleagues. The Emperor, much in evidence, now heard of the Austrian advance further south, threatening his access to the river. It was the moment of crisis and he rose to it. In the center a battery of 112 guns was organized to pour shot into the massed enemy formations. Under cover of this fire and a series of cavalry charges, Massena was able to redeploy to hold the river line. On the other wing Oudinot and Davout were advancing steadily. The time had come for the knockout blow.

Macdonald was the man on the spot and his particular abilities were suited to the job. One of his strengths was his mastery of drill movements, the formation and reformation of large bodies of men:

> I therefore ordered four battalions, followed by four others which I deployed in two lines, to advance at the double; and while my artillery opened fire, my two divisions formed themselves into attacking columns. The enemy, who were still advancing, halted; and redoubling their fire, caused us terrible loss. However, in proportion as my ranks became unserviceable, I drew them up closer together and made them dress up as at drill.[19]

In this great, wedge-like formation, Macdonald's force of 8,000 men repulsed a cavalry charge, then began a controlled advance with leveled bayonets. Eight battalions, each in two lines, formed the front of the square: On the right nine battalions marched in column, on the left four in column. Each flank had cavalry protection, and three more infantry battalions brought up the rear.

The historian F. Loraine Petre argues that such compression was needed because so many of the soldiers were conscripts: "With the armies of Jena or Austerlitz it would have been simple waste of men to send them to the attack in such a formation; with the army of Wagram the close association of large numbers was the only way to keep together the deteriorated infantry."[20] It was expensive but effective. Despite their heavy casualties—and their panic of the night before—Macdonald's men moved forward, sweating and cursing in the midday heat, closing ranks as their comrades fell. Napoleon watched and more than once exclaimed, "*Quel brave homme!*"[21]

Macdonald was angry with the cavalry commanders. Had they charged then, he believed, the Austrians would have broken. But his orders went unheeded. When his force was reduced to 1,500 men, he called for reinforcements, then resumed the advance. By 3 P.M. he had taken the village of Süssenbrünn.

The Archduke Charles realized that victory was beyond his grasp. Before long he ordered withdrawal. Macdonald did not know this, though, and he and his weary troops spent another night on stand-to. At dawn, with no sign of the enemy, he sent his cavalry out and snatched a few hours' sleep. He was awakened with the news that the Emperor was asking for him:

> I saw the Emperor surrounded by my troops, whom he was congratulating. He approached me, and embracing me cordially, said: "Let us be friends henceforward." "Yes," I answered, "till death. . . ." "You have behaved valiantly, and have rendered me the greatest services, as indeed throughout the entire campaign. On the battlefield of your glory, where I owe you so large a part of yesterday's success, I make you a Marshal of France. . . . You have long deserved it."[22]

There were many who agreed. Napoleon's former private secretary, De Bourienne, wrote: "The general opinion was that the elevation of Macdonald added less to the general's military reputation than it redounded to the honour of the Emperor."[23] And the army soon had a chant about the three men who won their batons in 1809:

La France a nommé Macdonald,
L'armée a nommé Oudinot,
L'amitié a nommé Marmont.[24]

Napoleon's later judgment, pronounced on St. Helena, was not so flattering to Macdonald. He conceded his courage and loyalty but thought him slow and even lazy, able enough with a small force (up to 20,000 men) and under supervision, but no more than that. General Dumas, however, remembered when Macdonald arrived to take over the Army of Grisons in 1800:

In my first communications with my new General-in-Chief, I foresaw how easy and agreeable I should find the duties that I had to perform about him; easy, because his foresight and activity left nothing to the Chief of Staff, besides the care of well directing the execution of orders, always precise, always clearly expressed; and agreeable, because his frank and military manner was tempered and set off by a tone of the most pleasing urbanity, and by lively and instructive conversation, which invited and inspired confidence.[25]

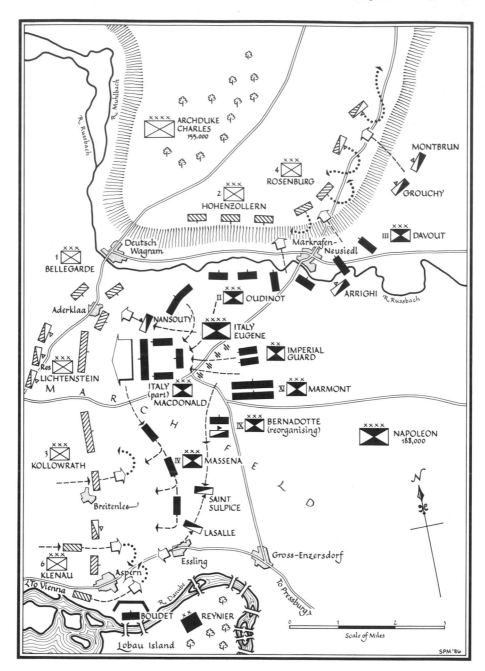

Map 13. The Battle of Wagram, July 5–6, 1809

TEXTUAL REFERENCES

1. Marshal Macdonald, *Recollections*, ed. by C. Rousset (London, 1892), Vol. 1, p. 345.
2. A. G. Macdonnell, *Napoleon and His Marshals* (London, 1934), p. 199.
3. A. de Caulaincourt, *Memoirs* (London, 1935), Vol. 2, pp. 171–72.
4. Macdonald, *op. cit.*, p. 136.
5. *Ibid.*, p. 128.
6. *Ibid.*, p. 200.
7. *Ibid.*, p. 276.
8. M. Dumas, *Souvenirs* (Paris, 1839), Vol. 2, p. 162.
9. Macdonald, *op. cit.*, p. 289.
10. *Ibid.*, p. 291.
11. M. A. Thiers, *History of the Consulate and the Empire* (Paris, 1851), Vol. 10, pp. 100–1.
12. Macdonald, *op. cit.*, Vol. 2, p. 16.
13. *Ibid.*, p. 28.
14. Baron de Marbot, *Memoirs* (London, 1892), Vol. 2, pp. 384–85.
15. *Ibid.*, p. 378.
16. Caulaincourt, *op. cit.*, p. 267.
17. L. F. de Bausset, *Mémoires*, quoted in *ibid.*, p. 172 n.
18. Macdonald, *op. cit.*, Vol. 1, p. 334.
19. *Ibid.*, p. 338.
20. F. L. Pctrc, *Napoleon and the Archduke Charles* (London, 1909), pp. 22–23.
21. J. Thiry, *Wagram* (Paris, 1966), p. 184.
22. Macdonald, *op. cit.*, Vol. 1, pp. 345–46.
23. F. de Bourienne, *Memoirs of Napoleon Bonaparte* (London, 1836), Vol. 3, p. 109.
24. R. Christophe, *Le Maréchal Marmont* (Paris, 1968), pp. 140–41.
25. Dumas, *op. cit.*, p. 162.

BIBLIOGRAPHICAL NOTE

The key work is Macdonald's own *Recollections*, published in Paris in 1892 (edited by Camille Rousset). A two-volume English translation by Stephen Louis Simeon was published in London the same year, and the following year the same publishers brought out a revised edition in a single volume. Macdonald wrote hurriedly and chiefly, it seems, from memory, and he was no stylist. It is a work of plain narrative, setting out—without guile—his own view of the story of his life. It is not particularly self-revealing, but it is a readable account and more reliable than most memoirs of its kind. For the rest I have relied mainly on the published memoirs of those who fought with him.

Two works were of particular help in dealing with Wagram. F. Loraine Petre's *Napoleon and the Archduke Charles* (London, 1909) gives a detailed, thoroughly researched, and sometimes exciting account of the whole Danube Campaign of 1809 with all its military and political complications and implications. *Wagram* by Jean Thiry (Paris, 1966) covers much the same ground in a racier and more personalized manner with some additional detail.

CHRONOLOGY

1774, July 20	—Born at Châtillon-sur-Seine (Côte d'Or)
1792, September 1	—Gazetted lieutenant in 1st Foot Artillery
1793, November 12	—Promoted captain during Siege of Toulon
1796, February 8	—Promoted *chef de bataillon* of artillery and aide-de-camp to Bonaparte
March 27	—Accompanied Bonaparte to Italy; fought at Mondovi, Lodi, Castiglione, and Arcola
1797, January 1	—Appointed to command Second Regiment of Horse Artillery; chief aide-de-camp to Bonaparte
1798, May 19	—Accompanied Bonaparte to Egypt; fought at Malta and, as *général de brigade*, at Alexandria and the Pyramids
1799, November 9–10	—Participated in coup of 18 *Brumaire;* appointed councillor of state (December 25)
1800, June 14	—Commanded artillery at Marengo
September 9	—Promoted *général de division*
1802, September 16	—Appointed inspector general of artillery; responsible for major reforms
1803, June 14	—Appointed commandant-in-chief of artillery for *la Grande Armée*
1805, February 1–2	—Appointed colonel-general of hussars and chasseurs; created Grand Eagle of the Legion of Honor
August 30	—Appointed to command II Corps of *la Grande Armée;* present at Ulm
December 23	—Appointed to command I Corps of *l'Armée d'Italie*
1806, July 7	—Appointed governor-general of Dalmatia by Napoleon; raised Russian Siege of Ragusa
1808, April 15	—Created *duc de Raguse*
1809, May 17	—Wounded at Gradschatz while commanding XI Corps
July 5–6	—In reserve at Wagram; censured for over-enthusiastic pursuit of defeated Austrians at Znaim (July 10)
July 12	—Appointed *Maréchal d-Empire* (twenty-second in order of appointment)
October	—Appointed governor of the Illyrian provinces
1811, May 7	—Succeeded Massena as commander of *l'Armée de Portugal*
1812, June–July	—Outmaneuvered Wellington between the Duero and Tormes Rivers
July 22	—Defeated by Wellington at Salamanca; badly wounded
1813, May–October	—Fought at Lützen, Bautzen, Dresden, and Leipzig as commander of VI Corps
1814, February–March	—Fought at La Rothière, Champaubert, Vauchamps, Laon, La Fère-Champenoise, and Romainville during defense of France
April 5	—Betrayed Napoleon by surrendering his corps
1815, April 10	—Struck from the list of marshals by Napoleon; refused to join the Emperor in the Hundred Days
1830, July	—As governor of the 1st Military District at Paris, failed to prevent Revolution; fled into exile
1852, March 3	—Died in Venice

FRIENDSHIP'S CHOICE

Marmont

by
John L. Pimlott

La France a nommé Macdonald.
L'armée a nommé Oudinot.
L'amitié a nommé Marmont.[1]

The Making of a Marshal (1774-1811)

Marmont is remembered for his failures. His tactical error at Salamanca (July 1812) and his lethargy at Laon (March 1814) seem to condemn him as a field commander, while his actions outside Paris in April 1814, when he surrendered his entire corps to the advancing allies, mark him down as the arch-traitor of the Napoleonic era. Indeed, the verb *raguser*, derived from his title, still means "to betray."

Yet this is hardly a balanced view, for despite his shortcomings Marmont did display a range of capabilities in both military and civilian affairs. As a soldier he was undoubtedly brave, resourceful, and professional; as a general he was occasionally skillful and successful more often than not; as an administrator he was innovative and efficient; as a man he was intellectually curious and extremely well read. The result is a paradox—a marshal who deserved his baton but did not fight consistently, a man who owed his advancement to Napoleon yet betrayed him in the end—and it is this that makes his career a particularly interesting one to study.

Marmont was born in Châtillon-sur-Seine on July 20, 1774,[2] and from an early age expressed an interest in military affairs. In 1790 he joined the garrison battalion at Chartres as a volunteer, using the experience to gain entry as a cadet to the artillery school at Châlons two years later. On September 1, 1792, he was gazetted a lieutenant in the 1st Foot Artillery; he could not have made a better choice of unit, for it was within its officer ranks that the young Bonaparte had already served.[3] The two men met for the first time in late 1793, when Marmont was promoted to captain during the Siege of Toulon, and their common interest in the tactics and impact of artillery ensured a lasting friendship. Its importance was shown initially in early 1796, when Bonaparte chose Marmont as one of his aides-de-camp and appointed him *chef de batallion* (or Major) of artillery in the force being gathered for war against the Austrians and Piedmontese in Italy.

During the subsequent campaign, Marmont gained invaluable combat experience and showed to his chief the latent abilities that were to be exploited to the full in later years. At Mondovi (April 21, 1796) Marmont participated in the frontal attack that broke the resistance of the Piedmontese; at Lodi (May 10) he personally captured an enemy battery and was constantly under fire; at Castiglione (August 5) he concentrated a force of 18 guns to batter enemy positions on the Medelano knoll, enabling infantry units to advance and throw the entire enemy left flank into disarray. The rewards came thick and fast: in early October Marmont was afforded the honor of carrying dispatches (and 22 captured colors) to the Directory in Paris and, after rushing back to Italy just in time to fight at the Arcola bridge (November 17), was given command of the 2nd Regiment of Horse Artillery and appointed chief aide-de-camp to Bonaparte. He was not yet 23 years old.

By now the relationship between Marmont and the future Emperor was deep rooted, and it was no surprise when, in May 1798, he was chosen to accompany his friend and mentor to Egypt. It was an opportunity for further glory and was not wasted: at Malta in June Marmont seized the banner of the Knights of St. John, earning himself promotion to general of brigade in Bon's division; at the Battles of Alexandria (July 2) and the Pyramids (July 21), he fought well. Indeed, in the latter action it was his seizure of a defile behind the village of Embibeh that trapped the Mamelukes with their backs to the Nile, forcing them to swim to safety under the murderous fire of French guns. Marmont's reward in this instance was to be appointed commandant of Alexandria, securing Bonaparte's rear while the incursion into Syria took place. His successful control of a huge province, achieved through a mixture of reform and repression, ensured that he stayed firmly in Bonaparte's mind, with the result that Marmont was one of only a select band chosen to return to France in August 1799. He repaid the compliment by supporting his chief in the coup of 18 *Brumaire* (November 9–10), accepting in its aftermath a seat as councillor of state (section of war).

This appointment did not mean an end to active campaigning, for when the new First Consul set out again for northern Italy in May 1800 he chose Marmont to command his artillery. The subsequent campaign was hard, particularly in its approach march across the Great St. Bernard Pass, and Marmont soon showed a remarkable resourcefulness that, for a time, made his reputation. As the expeditionary force approached the pass, it was obvious that the artillery pieces could not be towed forward in the normal way, presenting Marmont with a problem for which he easily found two solutions:

> The first was to hollow out tree trunks in the form of troughs, into which were laid the eight pounders and the mortars. One hundred men were harnessed to each gun, and took two days to drag them over the St Bernard. The second measure was to use sledges on

rollers. . . . The carriages were taken to pieces and carried in sections, except for the mountings of the eight pounders which were carried by ten men apiece on stretchers.[4]

Nor was this all, for once across the Alps, the French had to advance past the Austrian stronghold at Fort Bard. After two attempts to move the guns forward had failed, Marmont came up with an ingenious solution. Late on May 24 he drew his cannon "in the dark through the town, close under the guns of the fort, by spreading straw and dung on the streets, and wrapping the wheels up so as to prevent the slightest sound."[5] Without such success Bonaparte would have been unable to defeat the Austrians at Marengo (June 14), for during the crucial phase of the battle it was Marmont's dramatic concentration of artillery fire, followed by his prompt dispatch of light guns to support Desaix's infantry, that broke the enemy line. By September Marmont had been promoted to general of division.

Two years later his career took another turn when, on September 16, 1802, he was appointed inspector-general of artillery, for under Bonaparte's guidance it was Marmont who modernized and reformed this important arm. Under the "System of the Year XIII," the number of guns available was considerably increased, the unsatisfactory 4-pounder was replaced by the 6-pounder, and, together with the 8- and 24-pounders, the mobility and impact of the artillery were significantly enhanced. Similar improvements to ammunition limbers and wagons ensured a smoother process of battlefield supply and repair, enabling Marmont to introduce a more efficient force capable of carrying out the sort of massed concentration of firepower that both he and his chief had been advocating for some time. To ensure that the reforms were carried out to full advantage, Marmont was appointed commandant-in-chief of artillery for the Grand Army in June 1803.[6]

With such a record of command and administrative success behind him, Marmont clearly expected to be included in the list of marshals appointed on May 19, 1804. It was not to be. He was extremely young, and, as Napoleon confided to him, he still had "plenty of opportunities of gaining distinction,"[7] but there was no disguising his disappointment. Promotion to colonel-general of hussars and chasseurs and elevation to Grand Eagle of the Legion of Honor (February 1805) were small recompense, although his appointment to command II Corps of the Grand Army (August 1805) did seem to promise future action. Even in this, however, Marmont was denied his opportunity, for in the campaign that culminated at Ulm (October 21) his new command, comprising the infantry divisions of Boudet, Grouchy, and Dumonceau, together with Lacoste's light cavalry, played a relatively insignificant part. For much of the time, II Corps was held in reserve, and after Ulm Marmont was transferred to I Corps of the Army of Italy (December 23). It was a frustrating time.

He found fulfillment in an unusual theater and in a totally unexpected way. On July 7, 1806, he was suddenly appointed governor general of Dalmatia, covering the Balkan areas recently ceded to France by Austria, and almost immediately he enjoyed success, forcing the Russians under Admiral Siniavin to raise the Siege of Ragusa and retreat as far as Cattaro. The next five years were among the most satisfying of Marmont's life. In April 1808 he was elevated to the peerage with the appropriate title of Duke of Ragusa, and this was indicative of his close association with Dalmatia. His rule was stern, guaranteeing continued French control of a sensitive area, but at the same time he introduced a number of reforms that undoubtedly improved the life of the local people and ensured his popularity. He built roads, established industries, increased trade, and founded schools, creating a framework of civic improvement that outlasted his term of office. In 1817 the Emperor of Austria summed up the achievement when he remarked to Metternich, "It is a great pity that Marshal Marmont was not two or three years longer in Dalmatia."[8]

But not all his time was spent on administrative matters, for in 1809 he was called on to contribute to Napoleon's latest campaign. At first, as the Emperor advanced toward the Danube, the Army of Dalmatia (newly entitled XI Corps of the Grand Army) was expected to tie down Austrian forces in the south, but after Napoleon's setback at Aspern–Essling in May, Marmont was called forward with his troops as reinforcement. Despite a slight wound sustained in a clash with Austrian units at Gradschatz in Croatia (May 17), Marmont pushed north to join Napoleon in time for the epic Battle of Wagram (July 5–6). Once again, he had to face the frustration of acting as reserve—XI Corps was not committed until the tail end of the engagement, when Marmont supported Eugène's Army of Italy in its occupation of Wagram village—but once the battle was over, he was directed to conduct a part of the pursuit. By now he was desperate for glory, and this may explain his rush of enthusiasm, leading to overextension on the Thaya River at Znaim (July 10). Marmont was lucky not to be defeated by the Austrian rear guard and, as Napoleon censured his actions, extremely fortunate not to jeopardize his promotion to marshal, announced on July 12. The Emperor's comments must have taken the edge off his euphoria:

I am afraid I have incurred the reproach of listening rather to my affection than to your right to this distinction. You have plenty of intelligence, but there are needed . . . war qualities in which you are still lacking, and which you must work to acquire. Between ourselves, you have not yet done enough to justify entirely my choice.[9]

It must have been a bitter message to take back to Dalmatia (soon to be renamed the Illyrian provinces) and it undoubtedly increased Marmont's desire for a fighting command in which he could prove his worth. His chance came in spring 1811: on April 9 he was appointed to succeed Ney as commander of VI Corps of the Army of Portugal, and less than a month later he was ordered to replace Massena as army commander. It was now up to him.

Marmont in the Peninsula (1811–1812)

When Marmont arrived to take up his new command, he faced a difficult strategic situation. Although French forces in the Iberian Peninsula—Dorsenne's Army of the North in Asturias, Leon, and Castile; Soult's Army of the South in Andalusia; Suchet's Army of the East in Aragon; King Joseph's Army of the Center around Madrid; and Marmont's Army of Portugal on the borders of Beira—vastly outnumbered the Anglo–Portuguese forces under Wellington, they could not afford to concentrate. Guerrilla activity kept each army dispersed and its commander fearful of the consequences of "out-of-area" operations, while the need to live off the land restricted the time and place of coordinated campaigns. Moreover, as recent operations against Massena had shown, Wellington was well aware of his enemy's limitations and more than willing to exploit them by subsidizing guerrilla groups and concentrating his divisions against individual French commanders once they had been weakened.[10]

Marmont's first priority was to allow his army to recover from its recent defeat at Fuentes de Oñoro (May 3–5, 1811), and for this reason he authorized a withdrawal to Salamanca, out of Wellington's reach. This was a sensible move, but one that left the initiative firmly in British hands, and Wellington was not one to miss an opportunity, opting to concentrate next on Soult in the south. To do so, he had to ensure the defense of Portugal against a countermove from the east, and this he did by laying siege to the border fortresses of Ciudad Rodrigo and Badajoz. Marmont has been criticized for allowing both to fall[11]—a process completed by early April 1812—but with his divisions dispersed against guerrilla activities or spread out in winter quarters, there was little alternative. In the event a scratch force of four divisions was put together, taking advantage of Wellington's absence in the south to cross the border into Portugal, but the effects were disappointing. Any hopes of coordinated action with Soult were dashed when the latter's forward units under Drouet were mauled at Villafranca (April 11), and the Army of Portugal soon found itself overextended. By April 15 Marmont had managed to probe forward as far as Sabugal on the Coa River; by April 24 he had withdrawn to the line of the Agueda, inside Spain.

Once again, the initiative lay with Wellington and he used it to alter his strategic priority, sending a strong force to capture the bridge of boats at Almaraz on the Tagus River, cutting Marmont's communications with Soult, and deciding "to move forward into Castile . . . to bring Marmont to a general action."[12] The circumstances certainly seemed right: Marmont's withdrawal from the Coa implied a lack of decisiveness, while diversionary raids by guerrillas and by British seaborne forces on the nothern and eastern coasts of Spain promised to keep the enemy dispersed. On June 13, 1812, seven Anglo–Portuguese infantry divisions, a Spanish division, two independent Portuguese brigades, four cavalry brigades, and 48 artillery pieces (a total of 48,000 men)[13] crossed the Agueda River and advanced on Salamanca. Marmont was facing the ultimate test of his generalship.

At first he displayed remarkable skill: having clearly absorbed the lesson of his previous foray, he refused to be drawn forward until his army had been concentrated, preferring to abandon Salamanca (leaving the strategically vital bridge to be guarded by three fortress garrisons) to give his scattered divisions time to gather. Wellington entered Salamanca on June 17 on the horns of a dilemma: If he ignored the fortress garrisons and pursued Marmont northward, he would run the risk of being caught between two enemy forces; if he delayed to take out the garrisons, Marmont's strength would inevitably increase. In the end he chose to conduct an extemporized siege of the Salamanca forts, and this gave Marmont the chance he had been wanting. By June 20 six of his eight divisions were concentrated at Fuente Sauco, with the other two en route. It was a neat move.

The French immediately began to push toward Salamanca, hoping to tempt Wellington to battle with reduced strength, but Marmont did not rush into an engagement. Indeed, when the Anglo–Portuguese army temporarily abandoned its siege operations and occupied prepared positions on the heights of San Cristobal to the north of Salamanca (June 21), Marmont refused to be drawn, preferring maneuver to confrontation. It was a wise decision, denying Wellington his preference for set-piece battle on favorable ground; and when Marmont pulled back to his own prepared positions on the Duero River, the British commander followed, gradually extending his line of communications and supply. By July 4 both armies faced each other on the Duero, with neither prepared to mount an attack but with Wellington beginning to feel stretched.

By now, Marmont was convinced that he was facing a defensively minded enemy, reluctant to experience battle, and this led him to mount an immediate offensive. To begin with, all went well. On July 16 Marmont conducted a brilliant feint attack, pretending to cross the Duero at Toro and then shifting the emphasis further east once Wellington had started to withdraw. For five days (July 16–21) the French successfully probed the Anglo–Portuguese right flank, gradually forcing Wellington to abandon prepared positions. The maneuver developed into a "race," with both armies marching, often in parallel, to secure or escape an outflanking move. By July 21 Wellington had fallen back as far as Salamanca and, with most of his divisions already across the Tormes River, seemed set for a rapid retreat, at least as far as the supply base at Ciudad Rodrigo. Marmont, growing more confident with every move, crossed the Tormes further east at Huerta and Encinas, aiming to swing round Wellington's flank on the Zurguen River and, if possible, mount a spoiling attack on his rearguard units. Neither side was expecting a major battle.

When the two armies did clash on July 22, in what is known to the British as the Battle of Salamanca and to the French as the Battle of the Arapiles, serious flaws in Marmont's generalship were revealed (see p. 265). His failure to control the uncoordinated movements of his divisional commanders gave Wellington the opportunity to mount a series of attacks that broke the back of the Army of Portugal, sending it into headlong retreat. There was little Marmont could do to save the situation; before the main engagement had even begun, he had been badly wounded by cannon fire and forced to quit the field. It was a crushing blow to his military reputation.

The Road to Dishonor (1812–1852)

Marmont's wound kept him out of action for the rest of 1812, and, with the Emperor's anger echoing in his ears,[14] he must have thought that his career as a field commander was at an end. But Napoleon could not afford to lose the services of an experienced marshal, regardless of his lack of recent success, and in March 1813, as France faced a growing threat from the east,

Marmont was given command of the newly reconstituted VI Corps on the Main River. His regiments were weak—although they contained some veterans, a significant proportion of their manpower comprised ill-trained recruits[15]—and his confidence cannot have been high as he set out on May 1 as part of the Emperor's advance on Dresden. Nevertheless, the corps fought well, occupying key positions in the center at both Lützen (May 2) and Bautzen (May 20–21) while other units conducted out-flanking moves, and Marmont's relationship with Napoleon gradually improved. By August, as the second phase of the 1813 campaign began, Marmont even felt bold enough to criticize the Emperor's proposed plan for simultaneous advances in both the Dresden and the Berlin sectors, recognizing the potential for dis-aster contained within it: "I greatly fear lest on the day on which Your Majesty gains a great victory, and believes you have won a decisive battle, you may learn you have lost two."[16]

This turned out to be a remarkably accurate prediction, for despite a successful defense of Dresden (August 27), during which Marmont's corps was badly mauled, a concurrent defeat of Oudinot on the road to Berlin left the French in danger of concentric attack from both north and east. As this materialized Marmont conducted a series of marches and countermarches, acting effectively as Napoleon's reserve, until on October 12 he found himself deployed to the northwest of Leipzig as the allies closed in. During the subsequent Battle of the Nations (October 16–19), Marmont was heavily engaged around the village of Möckern, coming under repeated attack from the Prussians under Blücher, and although he managed to hold on with com-mendable tenacity, events elsewhere rendered his efforts useless. As the French forces were gradually overwhelmed, Marmont had no option but to pull back to the eastern outskirts of Leipzig, from where he acted as part of the covering force as Napoleon withdrew toward the Rhine. It must have been a demoralizing affair.

In an ideal world, this retreat should have been followed by a period of rest and recuperation, but the allies showed no sign of halting their advance, even with the onset of winter. VI Corps, hastily reinforced with raw recruits, was thrown in to a desper-ate defense of France, marching and fighting under appalling weather and supply conditions. By now, Marmont was beginning to feel the strain. His wound had never properly healed—his arm was still in a sling for much of the 1813 campaign—and, as the pressures mounted, his grasp of military skills seemed to slip. At first this was not obvious—he fought well at La Rothière (Febru-ary 1, 1814), where he rallied his corps despite a strong enemy attack; at Champaubert (February 10), where he smashed a superior Prussian force; and at Vauchamps (February 14), where he skillfully maneuvered Blücher into a trap[17]—but by March 1814 he had clearly had enough.

Called up to support Napoleon at Laon on March 9, Marmont arrived late, at the head of tired and dispirited troops, and although he managed to seize the village of Athies on the extreme left of the enemy position, he did nothing to consolidate his gain or to coordinate his actions with those of the Emperor. Indeed, once the village had been captured, Marmont personally left the field to spend the night at a nearby château and was not present when, at 7:00 P.M. Blücher suddenly attacked. The VI Corps was smashed, losing a third of its strength and most of its guns, and Napoleon was forced to withdraw from what had seemed to be a promising tactical position. He never forgave Marmont this error, accusing him of behaving "like a second lieutenant."[18] Their friendship was at an end.

This may help to explain Marmont's subsequent actions, for as he, Mortier, and Moncey fell back toward Paris, fighting bitter rearguard battles at La Fère-Champenoise (March 25) and Romainville (March 30), it was obvious that his loyalty and enthusiasm were waning fast. Early on March 31 Marmont negotiated a local truce that enabled the allies to occupy Paris, and five days later he took his entire corps—some 12,000 men—over to the allies' camp. It was a spectacular act of betrayal that broke Napoleon's resolve. "That Marmont should do such a thing; a man with whom I have shared my bread,"[19] was the exasperated cry.

Marmont's future was blighted by this single act. Although he was welcomed by the allies and showered with honors by a grateful French monarchy, he never again commanded troops in the field. Even the Royalist Army (many of whose soldiers were inevitably veterans of the Empire) distrusted him, particularly after he sat as one of the judges who condemned Ney to death in 1815. By then Marmont had shown where his loyalties lay by refusing to participate in the Hundred Days campaign—a decision that led Napoleon to strike his name from the list of marshals—and thereafter he held few effective posts. In 1830 he faced the revolutionaries in his capacity as governor of the 1st Military District at Paris, but his powers of command had clearly deserted him. Forced into exile with the king, he never set foot in France again, spending the remainder of his days compiling his memoirs, conducting scientific experiments, and traveling. He died in Venice on March 3, 1852, unmourned by his fellow countrymen.[20]

The Battle of Salamanca (July 22, 1812)

As dawn broke on July 22, 1812, Marmont appeared to hold a strong tactical advantage over his Anglo–Portuguese adversaries.[21] His one cavalry and eight infantry divisions were south of the Tormes River, swinging through wooded hills toward the Algabele stream and a distinctive plain beneath the Arapiles heights. So far as could be ascertained, Wellington had left a single division (the 7th) to occupy rearguard positions opposite the village of Calvarrasa de Arriba, with skirmishers deployed forward to the east of the Algabele, around the ruined chapel of Neustra Señora de la Pena. Dispatching Foy's division, with Ferey and Sarrut in support, to tie down these forces, Marmont took the bulk of his army—the infantry divisions commanded by Brenier, Clauzel, Thomières, Bonet, and Maucune, with Boyer's cavalry in support—to the south and west, aiming to occupy high ground to the south of the Arapiles plain preparatory to a flank assault on Wellington's rear. By 9:00 A.M. Marmont had joined his forward units on the Greater Arapile, from which he could see behind what he took to be the enemy's defensive line and westward along the plain, with its scattered villages and low rolling ridges leading eventually to wooded hills beyond the Zurguen. As he watched a cloud of dust could be seen rising from the Ciudad Rodrigo road to the north, suggesting that Wellington's main force was already in retreat.

Unfortunately Marmont's appreciation was wrong on two counts. On the one hand, Wellington was not withdrawing—the dust had been raised by his baggage train, escorted by a regiment of light cavalry—and, on the other, the folds of ground west of the Algabele were hiding much of the Anglo–Portuguese army from French observers. Although the 7th Division was in full view, what Marmont could not see was the 6th and Light Divisions to its left, the 4th Division to its right, and a substantial reserve, comprising the 1st Division, Carlos de España's Spanish Division, Pack's Portuguese Brigade, and two brigades of cavalry, around the village of Carbajos. The 5th Division was completing its crossing of the Tormes, while the 3rd Division and most of D'Urban's cavalry were still to the north of the river, but Wellington had no intention of pulling back. Indeed, when he realized that Marmont was advancing well south of the Tormes, he consolidated his hold on the high ground, ordering the 3rd Division and its cavalry support to move south to the village of Aldea Tejada and extending his line westward, hinging on the Lesser Arapile. By midday what had been a line facing due east across the Algabele had developed into a dogleg: as the Light and 1st Divisions maintained the defense of the heights opposite Calvarrasa de Arriba, the 4th and 5th Divisions, with the 6th, 7th and Spanish Divisions and most of the cavalry in reserve, ranged westward to cover the Arapiles plain, even pushing forward to occupy the village of Los Arapiles.

Marmont was clearly unaware of all this, spending most of the morning leisurely redeploying his divisions, for he did not issue orders to prepare for an attack until about 1:00 P.M. Directing Foy to hold on the right, distracting what was still regarded to be the main enemy force, Bonet was ordered to seize the Lesser Arapile while Thomières and Maucune, with Clauzel in reserve, moved west toward the village of Miranda de Azan. Once in position, with cavalry protecting both flanks and up to 50 artillery pieces interspersed along the new line, the French force would attack northward across the plain in a solid phalanx, taking the Anglo–Portuguese in the flank.

Technically this was a sound plan, but it was based on poor intelligence, and Marmont, to his discredit, did nothing to prevent the problems that quickly developed. At about 2:00 P.M. Thomières and Maucune moved off, filling the plain with soldiers and alerting Wellington to the plan. He rushed forward to a vantage point on the Lesser Arapile, from where it soon became apparent that Thomières was tracking too far to the west, leaving his flank overextended and opening up a gap between himself and Maucune. With a muttered cry of "By God, that will do,"[22] Wellington hurriedly ordered the 3rd Division and its cavalry to advance onto Thomières's exposed left flank and prepared the 4th and 5th Divisions for a frontal assault across the plain against Maucune.

The 3rd Division began to move at 3:45 P.M., emerging from the hills to the north of Miranda de Azan about an hour later in two brigade columns, flanked by cavalry. Their appearance caught Marmont completely by surprise, and, suddenly realizing the weakness of his left wing, he rushed down the slope of the Greater Arapile, shouting orders for the reserve divisions to come up. As he was about to mount his horse, a British artillery shell exploded beneath him, shattering his right arm and two ribs. He was lucky to survive, but was in no condition to continue his command, which devolved first to Bonet and then, when he too was wounded, to Clauzel. For a critical 20 minutes, the French command chain was in chaos.

The main part of the battle therefore took place without Marmont, although there can be no doubt that his failure to prevent Thomières's overextension was a prime cause of his army's defeat. As Marmont was being carried from the field to begin a slow and painful journey back to France,[23] Wellington's 3rd Division, aided by D'Urban's cavalry, smashed into Thomières's left flank, sending it reeling back toward Maucune, himself under attack from across the plain. The 5th Division broke into Maucune's first line, opening the way for a stunning cavalry charge by Le Marchant's heavy brigade, and by 5:00 P.M. the whole of the French left was in disarray. Wellington immediately ordered the 4th Division forward against the Greater Arapile, and although elements of Bonet's division prevented a breakthrough and even forced the 4th to retreat, they soon fell victim to the 6th Division coming up in reserve. As the Light and 1st Divisions advanced across the Algabele against Foy, the Army of Portugal collapsed, losing an estimated 14,000 men and 20 guns.[24] It was a resounding defeat.

Events such as these make an overall assessment of Marmont's career extremely difficult, for the paradox remains. There can be no escaping his errors at Salamanca and Laon, both of which resulted in major French defeats, and his betrayal of his master is, by any code of ethics, difficult to forgive. But this does not alter the fact that Marmont could command and fight well—his use of artillery at Castiglione and Marengo, his tactical sense at the Pyramids, his feint attack on the Duero, and his tenacity at Leipzig all provide ample evidence—and there is no denying his personal bravery on countless occasions. Nevertheless, he did owe his promotion and survival as a marshal to his close friendship with Napoleon, and once that had been destroyed, his weaknesses were highlighted for all to see. In the end, one has to acknowledge that he was occasionally prone to fatigue and lethargy, human characteristics that had no place in the demanding world of Napoleonic warfare.

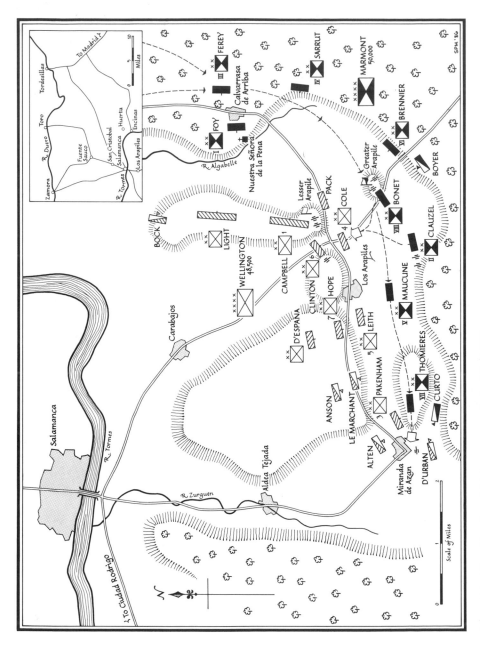

Map 14. The Battle of Salamanca, July 22, 1812

TEXTUAL REFERENCES

1. A contemporary soldier's saying, quoted in R. Christophe, *Le maréchal Marmont, Duc de Raguse* (Paris, 1968), p. 141.
2. Accounts of Marmont's life may be found in R. P. Dunn-Pattison, *Napoleon's Marshals* (Boston, 1909), pp. 200–18; and P. Young, *Napoleon's Marshals* (London, 1973), pp. 163–68. Dunn-Pattison cites an incorrect date of birth.
3. The First Foot Artillery had been known formerly as the *Régiment de la Fère*.
4. *Correspondance de Napoléon Ier* (Paris, 1858), Vol. 6, No. 4846, p. 314.
5. A. H. Jomini, *Life of Napoleon* (Kansas City, 1897), Vol. 1, p. 247.
6. D. G. Chandler, *The Campaigns of Napoleon* (New York, 1966), pp. 356–63.
7. Dunn-Pattison, *op. cit.*, p. 207.
8. *Ibid.*, p. 209.
9. *Ibid.*, p. 210.
10. J. P. Lawford and P. Young, *Wellington's Masterpiece. The Battle and Campaign of Salamanca* (London, 1973), pp. 15–32.
11. *Ibid.*, p. 133.
12. Wellington to the Earl of Liverpool, May 26, 1812, quoted in *ibid.*, pp. 166–68.
13. J. Weller, *Wellington in the Peninsula* (London, 1962), pp. 227–29.
14. Dunn-Pattison, *op. cit.*, p. 213.
15. *Ibid.*
16. E. d'Odeleben, *Relation de la Campagne de 1813* (Paris, 1817), Vol. 1, p. 250.
17. For details, see Chandler, *op. cit.*, pp. 953–76.
18. *Correspondance, op. cit.* Napoleon to Joseph, March 11, 1814, Vol. 27, No. 21461, p. 301.
19. Dunn-Pattison, *op. cit.*, p. 215.
20. For details of Marmont's later life, see Christophe, *op. cit.*, pp. 239–83.
21. Lawford and Young, *op. cit.*, pp. 199–278, contains an account of the battle.
22. *Ibid.*, p. 224.
23. B. T. Jones, ed., *The Memoirs of Charles Parquin* (London, 1969), pp. 149–50.
24. Weller, *op. cit.*, p. 230.

BIBLIOGRAPHICAL NOTE

Robert Christophe's *Le maréchal Marmont, Duc de Raguse* (Paris, 1968) is the only modern biography of Marmont, readable and accurate. Richard Humble, *Napoleon's Peninsular Marshals* (London, 1973), is a useful overview of the peninsular campaign from the French point of view, but is rather superficial in parts. *The Memoirs of Charles Parquin*, ed. by B. T. Jones (London, 1969), is one of the few contemporary French accounts readily available in English of life in Napoleon's army. Parquin was also wounded at Salamanca and accompanied Marmont back to France. Lt.-Col. J. P. Lawford and Brig. Peter Young's, *Wellington's Masterpiece. The Battle and Campaign of Salamanca* (London, 1973) is by far the most exhaustive account of the Salamanca campaign. Although written from the Anglo–Portuguese point of view, it contains much of relevance to Marmont's strategic and tactical moves in 1811–12. The *Mémoires du maréchal Marmont, duc de Raguse, de 1792 à 1841*, 9 vols. (Paris, 1857 et seq.) are long winded and highly selective in terms of evidence, but valuable reading for an understanding of the man. Finally Jac Weller's *Wellington in the Peninsula* (London, 1962) provides a good overview of the peninsular campaign, particularly in terms of strategy and tactics. It is useful for placing the Salamanca action in its context.

CHRONOLOGY

1758, May 6	—Born at Nice (then belonging to Piedmont)
1775, August 18	—Enlisted in *Régiment Royal-Italien*
1789, August 10	—Marries Rosalie Lamarre at Antibes
1791, September 17	—Joins 2nd Battalion, *Volontaires du Var*
1797, December 20	—Promoted *général de division*
1795, November 22-24	—Defeats the Austrians at Loano
1796, April 12-21	—Defeats Austrians at Montenotte, Dego, and Mondovi
August and November	—Plays major role at Lonato, Castiglione, and Arcole (Arcola)
1797, January 14	—Fights with distinction at Rivoli
March 23	—Defeats the Archduke Charles at the Tarvisio Pass
April 23	—Sent to report to the Directory on the Austrian campaign
1798, February 19	—Arrives in Rome to command French troops; faces a mutiny
December 10	—Appointed to command *l'Armée d'Helvetie*
1799, April 5	—Appointed to command *l'Armée de la Danube*
June 4-5	—Attacked unsuccessfully by the Archduke Charles at Zurich
September 26	—Defeats Suvorov at second Battle of Zurich; completes success by October 6
1800, June 4	—Capitulates at Genoa after 60-day siege; repatriated
August 13	—Relieved of command; retires to Rueil estate; unemployed
1804, May 19	—Appointed *Maréchal d'Empire* (fifth in seniority)
1805, August 23	—Appointed to command *l'Armée d'Italie*
October 20-31	—Defeats the Archduke Charles at Verona–Caldiero; occupies Laibach
1806, July 18	—Captures Gaeta
1808, March	—Created *duc de Rivoli*
1809, May 21-22	—Commands IV Corps at Aspern–Essling with distinction
July 5-6	—Injured by horse fall at Wagram; IV Corps pursues foe to Znaim (reached on 12th)
1810, April 17	—Appointed to command *l'Armée de Portugal* of three corps
August	—Invades Portugal and captures Almeida
September 27	—Defeated at Busaco; Wellington withdraws to Torres Vedras
October 10	—Halted by lines of Torres Vedras
November 14	—Withdraws to defensive position at Santarem-Rio Maior
1811, May 3-5	—Defeated by Wellington at Fuentes de Oñoro; subsequently recalled
1815, March 9	—Transfers his allegiance to Louis XVIII
April 10	—Transfers his allegiance to Napoleon
July 3	—Appointed governor of Paris by the provisional government
1816, January 1	—Retired without pension by the Royal Council of Ministers
1817, April 4	—Dies in Paris; buried in Cemetery Père-Lachaise (April 10)

CHAPTER FIFTEEN

DEAR CHILD OF VICTORY

Massena

by
General (ret'd)
Sir James Marshall-Cornwall

Early Years and First Italian Campaign (1758–1797)

Andrea Massena was born at Nice on May 6, 1758.[1] That county then formed part of the kingdom of Sardinia, so he was not a French citizen but a Piedmontese, his native language being Italian. His father was a small shopkeeper, but he was orphaned at the age of six and spent an unhappy childhood. In 1775, at the age of 17, he enlisted in the French *Régiment Royal-Italien*. Massena showed an early aptitude for soldiering and in two years was promoted to sergeant. At the age of 26 he was promoted to sergeant-major. In 1789, after 14 years of service, he took his discharge from the army. The French Revolution had broken out a month earlier, and Massena joined the revolutionary army, enlisting in a battalion of the *Volontaires du Var* as a warrant officer. In 1792 his fellow soldiers elected him to command the battalion as lieutenant colonel.

The revolutionary government then declared war against Austria and the allied kingdom of Sardinia. The French troops crossed the Var and annexed Nice, so that Massena acquired French nationality. In 1793 he was promoted to brigadier general and took part in the recapture of Toulon. For his distinguished service there, he was promoted to divisional general. In January 1794 he was given command of the right wing of the Army of Italy, then invading the Genoese Republic, occupied by the Austrians. The French offensive opened early in April, and Massena gained the crest of the Maritime Alps, dominating the plain of Piedmont. Further advance was held up by logistic difficulties, and the Austrians, strongly reinforced, opened a counteroffensive on June 23, 1795. Massena commanded one of the three divisions forming the right wing of the Army of Italy, now commanded by General Schérer.

The Directory ordered Schérer to attack, despite the approach of winter. This was launched on November 22, 1795. Massena was placed in command of two divisions. The Austrians were taken completely by surprise and retreated. Massena's corps captured all its objectives and entered Savona on November 26, having killed or wounded 1,500 of the enemy and taken 4,000 prisoners and 92 guns. His own corps had lost 1,150 casualties. Loano was Massena's first major victory and established his reputation.

After Loano Schérer withdrew to his base at Nice, where he tried without success to replenish his famished army, whose pay was two months in arrear. Schérer resigned in disgust on February 4, 1796. Massena, the victor of Loano, seemed to be his obvious successor. But Paul Barras, the predominant Director, was a friend of the young Brigadier-General Bonaparte, who had commanded the artillery of the Army of Italy until May 1795. On March 2, 1796, the Directory appointed Bonaparte as army commander. He arrived at Nice on March 26 with his chief of staff, Alexandre Berthier, aged 42. Massena was 37. The new army commander was 26.

The Army of Italy now numbered 47,000, organized under Massena and Augereau, Massena forming the advanced guard. They were opposed by 25,000 Austrians and 20,000 Sardinians under the overall command of 71-year-old Austrian General Beaulieu. The Piedmontese contingent was commanded by an Austrian general, Colli. Bonaparte's first objective was to separate these two forces. On April 10 he met Massena at Savona. Their meeting was cordial and Bonaparte gave Massena his orders. The attack started on the evening of April 11. Massena's two divisions crossed the Cadibona defile and advanced on Montenotte. One division held Argenteau frontally while the other, having marched all night through the foothills, fell upon his flank at dawn on April 12. The rout was complete, 2,000 prisoners and five guns being captured and about 3,000 Austrians killed or wounded.

On April 14 Massena's leading division drove the Austrians out of Dego, capturing 6,000 prisoners and 30 guns. Bonaparte, having now separated his two opponents, turned to drive the Sardinians northward. Colli retired to Mondovi. The French had reached the open plain, and their cavalry pursued the Sardinians to Turin, where on April 28 they signed an armistice. Massena had played a leading role in the campaign and received the special thanks of the Directory.[2]

Bonaparte now turned on Beaulieu's Austrian army, 24,000 strong. After crossing the Po, Massena's advanced guard on May 10 forced the passage of the River Adda at Lodi, which was strongly defended. The whole of Lombardy was now in French hands. Bonaparte decided to invade the supposedly neutral Venetian Republic and drive the Austrians beyond the Adige. On May 21 Massena left Milan, commanding the advanced guard. Unopposed, he entered Brescia on April 27, and on April 30 forced the River Mincio at Valeggio. On June 1 he entered Verona. Massena held the northern sector with his left flank on Lake Garda.

The Austrian army, 47,000 strong, was now commanded by the elderly Field-Marshal Count Würmser. On July 29 he launched an attack in four columns on the French holding the Adige. Massena on the left commanded six infantry brigades extended southward from Lake Garda, but was driven back 12 miles to the Mincio. On August 5 Bonaparte launched Massena and Augereau's divisions in a strong counterattack at Castiglione, which regained their previous position. Würmser retreated northward to Trento, having lost 70 guns and 14,000 prisoners, besides 6,000 killed and wounded. Massena's casualties were 2,590. In Bonaparte's dispatch to the Directory, he described Massena as "active, tireless; has audacity, a good eye for country and promptitude in decision."[3]

On September 2 Bonaparte ordered Massena and Augereau to advance northeastward. On September 8 they defeated the enemy at Bassano, taking 5,000 prisoners and 32 guns. Würmser, now reinforced, crossed the Adige at Legnago and joined the Austrian force blockaded in Mantua by Serrurier's division. At the end of September, Field-Marshal Alvintzy, an elderly Hungarian, was given a fresh army of 40,000 with orders to relieve Mantua and free Würmser. In November Alvintzy advanced southward and pushed Massena and Augereau out of Bassano. On September 11 hard fighting took place at Caldiero, 10 miles east of Verona, Massena's troops suffering fairly heavy casualties. Bonaparte then withdrew to Arcole* on the Adige, where heavy fighting took place on September 15. On September 18 Massena delivered a strong counterattack and Alvintzy withdrew. In three days of fighting, he had lost 18 guns and 13,000 men. The French casualties amounted to 4,600, of which Massena's were 1,400.

Although the ground was thickly covered with snow, Alvintzy renewed his offensive on January 12, 1797. Advancing down the Adige valley east of Monte Baldo, he attacked the French left sector, held by Joubert's division, 9,700 strong, centered on the Rivoli plateau. Alvintzy's corps numbered 23,000. Joubert resisted strongly under heavy attacks, and appealed to Bonaparte at Verona for reinforcement. Bonaparte at once sent Massena with seven infantry battalions and cavalry and artillery to support Joubert at Rivoli. There then took place the most brilliant achievement of Massena's career (see p. 294).

Zurich and Genoa (1798–1800)

On December 29, 1798, Austria joined Britain, Prussia, Russia, Portugal, and Turkey in the Second Coalition against France. On March 1 war was declared. Four days later the French occupied Berne and the western Cantons of neutral Switzerland. The possession of Switzerland was of vital importance to the security of France's eastern frontier, and it was the

*Commonly, but wrongly, called 'Arcola'

deliberate policy of the Directory to annex that country. The eastern Cantons in particular stoutly resisted joining the Helvetic Republic, which the French had set up forcibly in April 1798.

In order to meet the threat of the Second Coalition, the Directory in December redistributed its forces on the eastern front in the four Armies of the Rhine, Mayence, Switzerland, and Italy. Jourdan at Wiesbaden commanded the Army of Mayence. On December 10 Massena was appointed to command the newly formed Army of Switzerland with headquarters at Zurich. It was his first appointment as an independent army commander. His army numbered nearly 34,000, forming six infantry brigades, each of six battalions. Allowing for garrisons and guarding his line of communications, only 25,000 would be available for field operations. The first thing that Massena did was to order his two engineer companies to construct a strong entrenched camp just north of Zurich, the most important road junction in eastern Switzerland, controlling all communication from east to west as well as from north to south. The approaches from east and south were well covered by the Lake of Zurich, 23 miles long and two miles wide.

Although an armistice was still in force, the Directory decided to strike before the spring, as a corps of 20,000 Russians was due to arrive shortly to reinforce the Austrians. The Army of Switzerland was to drive Hotze's corps out of the Grisons Canton and invade the Austrian Vorarlberg. The Army of Italy, commanded by Schérer, was to advance up the Valtellina on Massena's right.

Massena accordingly moved his troops forward and assembled them near Sargans in the upper Rhine valley, where he established his headquarters on March 2, 1799. The upper Rhine divides Switzerland from the Vorarlberg, the river varying from 80 to 120 yards in width, with very few bridges. After reconnoitering the possible fords, Massena ordered Ménard's division to force a crossing between Ragaz and Vaduz.

Two days of warm sunshine had melted the snow and the selected fords were impassable. Massena had no pontoon equipment, but he collected timber and supervised the construction of a trestle bridge two miles north of Sargans. This involved some difficulty as the sappers had to work in icy cold water in a snowstorm. Massena launched his attack at dawn on March 6. Fortunately the crossing was unopposed. Having gained the right bank, his troops stormed the St. Luzisteig fort, Massena himself leading the assault. The Austrian battalion commander was killed with 250 of his men; 800 prisoners and four guns were captured. The next day, advancing upstream, Massena drove the Austrians out of Chur, capital of the Grisons Canton. The garrison's retreat was cut off, and on March 9, 2,980 prisoners, three colors, and 16 guns fell into the hands of the French.

Owing to defective commissariat arrangements, the French troops were left without rations and other supplies. An orgy of looting took place. Massena was so exasperated that on March 18 he wrote a strongly worded letter to the Directory, threatening to resign his command. Meanwhile on his right and left flanks, disasters were taking place that seriously threatened the safety of his army. On March 1 Jourdan's army on his left flank, 41,000 strong, had crossed the Rhine and advanced eastward through the Black Forest. On March 18 he encountered Prince Schwarzenberg's corps forming the advanced guard of the Archduke's army. On March 22 Massena received from Jourdan an urgent appeal for help. On the following day Massena, with 6,000 men, crossed the marshy Rhine valley. But the Austrians confronted him in strongly entrenched positions. After five hours of stiff fighting, the French were repulsed with heavy loss, leaving 1,500 dead and 300 prisoners. Massena's effort to help Jourdan was fruitless. Two days later at Stockach, the Archduke routed Jourdan's army completely. Jourdan suffered 5,000 casualties and was driven back behind the Rhine.

The following day a further disaster occurred. The Austrians under Kray defeated Schérer's Army of Italy near Verona and drove the French back to the Mincio. Schérer was again defeated on April 5 at Magnano and driven back behind the Adda. Ten days later the Austrians were reinforced by 24,000 Russians under Field-Marshal Suvorov, who now took over the joint command. The French continued their retreat and Suvorov entered Milan on April 27.

Massena's situation was now extremely exposed. The armies on his two flanks had melted away, leaving him in a salient open to encirclement. A man of less courage would have abandoned Switzerland and withdrawn to the Jura Mountains. Not so of Massena. On April 5 the Directory merged the remnants of the defeated armies with the Army of Switzerland. Massena thus became responsible for the defense of the whole French eastern frontier. He was fully equal to the task. Fortunately the Austrians did not follow up their victory at Stockach, so Massena was given a breathing space to reorganize his forces. He now had 113,000 men under his command, of whom 60,000 were available for mobile operations.

The Archduke made no forward move until the beginning of May. He had three strong corps: Nauendorff in the Black Forest, Jellachich on the Lake of Constanz, and Hotze in the Grisons Canton. The first to move was Hotze, who on May 1 attacked Ménard's division at Feldkirch, driving it back over the upper

Rhine and recapturing Chur. The next attack was made three weeks later, when Nauendorff crossed the Rhine on May 24 and reached the River Thur, thus threatening Massena's line of communications. The latter withdrew from Zurich to Winterthur and counterattacked with Oudinot's and Soult's divisions, driving the Austrians back with the loss of 2,140 killed and wounded and 1,000 taken prisoner. The total French loss was under 800.

Massena now felt that he could no longer keep his forward troops in the exposed salient east of Zurich, so on May 26 he withdrew his center sector to the entrenched camp that he had organized to cover the town. This gave him a strong defensive position with a continuous water line in front of it. The Austrian advance was renewed on May 29, when they closed up to the new French line. In the center Jellachich was opposite Zurich, while further south Hotze advanced to the Zurich and Walen lakes. Their main attack was delivered on the morning of June 4, with the Archduke's three corps converging on the Zurichberg, over 2,000 feet high, which was the key point of the entrenched camp. Heavy fighting continued, Hotze himself being wounded. By nightfall the Austrians had failed to break the French defense and had suffered 3,430 casualties, the French losses being 1,730.

Massena felt that he could not continue to fight with the town of Zurich containing 11,000 inhabitants actually in the firing line. So on June 5 he withdrew his center to the Ütliberg, 2,850 feet high, two miles southwest of the town. This feature dominated the whole country north and west of Zurich, making his position stronger than before. In mid-August a second Russian corps, 30,000 strong, under General Rimski-Korsakov, arrived to reinforce the Austrians. It had been agreed between the Tsar Paul and the Emperor Francis that all the Russian and Austrian forces should be placed under the supreme command of Field-Marshal Suvorov in order to crush Massena's army. The field marshal, a remarkable character, aged 69, was energetic, tireless, and regardless of any personal comfort, although not particularly intelligent.

Suvorov issued his orders on September 3. Hotze and Korsakov were to attack Massena frontally between Zurich and Glarus, while his own army would ascend Lake Maggiore to Bellinzona, cross the St. Gotthard Pass, and by following the Lake of Lucerne take Massena in rear. The tactical methods to be employed were based on extreme concentration, attacks being made in close column, using the sword and bayonet. These tactics were quite unsuited to the narrow Alpine valleys through which the troops would have to march.

Massena decided to attack before the Austro–Russians completed their maneuver. On September 25 he attacked and drove the enemy back to the walls of Zurich. Korsakov retired within the town walls, but realized that his position was indefensible and evacuated the town during the night. Massena pursued him and a complete rout followed. The Russians abandoned 6,000 dead, wounded, and prisoners, besides all their artillery and baggage. Simultaneously Soult also launched an attack. Crossing the Lake of Zurich at its eastern end, he attacked Uznach, at the junction between the Austrian and Russian corps. Hotze, the Austrian corps commander, with his chief of staff galloped down with reinforcements, but both were shot dead. After two days of stiff fighting, the Austrians withdrew, leaving 3,500 prisoners and 2,000 dead and wounded.

Meanwhile Suvorov threatened Massena's southern flank by his pincer operation. Crossing the St. Gotthard Pass, he moved northward to join the Austrians near Glarus, reaching the Vierwaldstätter Lake on September 26. The following day he heard of the disasters suffered by Korsakov and Hotze. Massena then brought Mortier's division down from Zurich to bar Suvorov's advance. The Russians were now caught in a trap as their supply line was cut. On October 4 heavy snow began to fall and they suffered severely. On October 5 Suvorov broke out eastward and on October 10 managed to collect the remnant of his army behind the upper Rhine at Chur. Two months later he was recalled by the Tsar. The second Battle of Zurich was a master stroke of strategic conception and tactical execution on the part of Massena. It was his finest achievement as an army commander. On October 14 he received a special commendation from the Directory.[4] On November 25 Bonaparte, now returned from Egypt as First Consul, gave him command of the Army of Italy.

Throughout the greater part of 1799, the Army of Italy had been commanded by General Schérer. He had been ordered to attack the Austrians at Verona at the end of March. His attack failed and he again attacked on April 5, but with still less success. His troops became demoralized and insubordinate. Schérer's health broke down and he handed over the army to Moreau, whose shattered 27,000 troops were defeated on April 27 by an Austro–Russian army of 70,000 under Suvorov. On August 4 the Directory sent Joubert to replace Moreau, but he was also defeated by Suvorov and killed at Novi on August 15, when his army retreated to Genoa.

In November the defeated Army of Italy withdrew to the crest of the Maritime Alps. The troops were in a shocking condition. The men's pay was five months in arrear. They were without boots and their clothing was in rags. Discipline no longer existed. Massena was thus confronted with a formidable task, which he tackled with vigor. Having been assured by Bonaparte and the two other consuls that his troops would be adequately paid, provisioned, and equipped, he left Paris on December 27 for his new command at Nice. He found that several battalions had mutinied, and ordered a number of mutineers and deserters to be shot. Although on paper his army numbered 150,000, he found only 28,000 fit for service. It took him a month to clear up his Augean stable. On February 5, 1800, he received from Bonaparte the following commendation: "I have seen with much pleasure, Citizen-General, the firmness which you are showing to restore order in your Army."[5]

On February 10 Massena moved his headquarters up to Genoa to deal with the strategic and tactical problems confronting him. The front held by the Army of Italy was extensive and precarious. From Recco on the coast 12 miles east of Genoa, the line followed the crest of the Ligurian Apennines across the Savona gap, continuing westward along the Maritime Alps and northward to the St. Bernard Pass. The French had no control of the Gulf of Genoa as it was patrolled by a squadron of the Royal Navy, commanded by Vice-Admiral Lord Keith. On the landward side Massena was opposed by an Austrian army under the elderly von Melas.

The Republic of Genoa was an independent neutral state, but in 1797 Bonaparte had bullied the Genoese into accepting a French garrison for their "protection." The population was about 70,000. The city and harbor are protected on the landward side by a steep semicircular ridge of hills with a continuous masonry rampart. The town itself was surrounded by an old dilapidated wall. On the seaward side the most important battery was sited on a promontory with a lighthouse, *La Lanterna*, at the western entrance to the port. If an active defense could be maintained, the city could be reduced only by blockade and starvation.

Massena's main problem was to keep the enemy as far as possible from the fortress while securing the vulnerable line of communication with Nice along the Riviera coast, 127 miles in length. It was almost impossible for supply ships to penetrate the close blockade maintained by Lord Keith's squadron. Massena at once started to repair and rearm the outer forts. He appointed General Miollis as fortress commander. The bulk of his 35,912 troops formed a mobile striking force under Soult's command. In spite of Massena's efforts, the equipment of his troops was still unsatisfactory.

The Austrian offensive opened on April 5. Melas launched 60,000 men from their assembly area in four columns. The two left columns under Ott and Prince Hohenzollern attacked the Genoa section, while Melas himself attacked the Cadibona Pass in the Savona gap in order to reach the coastal supply line to Nice. All attacks made rapid progress. The two left columns captured Recco, forcing the French right wing back to Nervi, only 5 miles east of Genoa. In the center Hohenzollern stormed the important Bochetta Pass north of Genoa. Melas's main drive broke through to the coast at Vado, separating the divisions of Soult and Suchet. After three days of stiff fighting, Melas had gained all his first objectives. On April 7 Massena personally led a counterattack on the northeastern sector, capturing the commanding peak of Monte Fascie and driving the enemy 3 miles further northeast, taking 200 prisoners. On April 8 Massena organized a strong counter-offensive, to join up with Suchet's division and restore communication with Nice.

Massena commanded the operation in person. Leaving Genoa on April 9, he set up his command post at Cogoleto, 18 miles west of Genoa, but met with stiff resistance. General Gardanne, one of Soult's divisional commanders, was severely wounded and Massena took command of his division. In the day's fighting 1,000 Austrians were captured and heavy casualties inflicted. Massena himself narrowly escaped capture. Austrian pressure continued and the French were gradually driven back. By April 20 their left flank was withdrawn to within three miles west of Genoa. On April 24 Admiral Keith, from his flagship HMS *Minotaur*, sent a parlementaire to Massena suggesting that he should surrender in view of the hopelessness of his position. Massena promptly replied that Genoa would be defended to the last extremity.

The Austrians now prepared to launch a final offensive. Ott was to attack from the west, while Hohenzollern was to capture the vital northern ridge. This was launched on April 30. The Austrians made some progress, but most of the ground was recovered by French counterattacks. The enemy lost 3,200 men, including 1,340 prisoners, the French casualties being half that number.

On May 2 Colonel Reille, one of Massena's staff officers, who had been sent to Bonaparte, slipped through the British blockade and reached Genoa, with 1 million francs to pay the troops and a letter from Carnot, the war minister, outlining Bonaparte's plan to cross the Alps with his Reserve Army and relieve Genoa.[6]

The French garrison and the civilian population were now subjected to severe privations. The enemy had cut the aqueduct that supplied water power for the flour mills and flour was running short. All foodstuffs were commandeered and rigorously rationed. There were 8,000 prisoners of war, whose rations had to be reduced to a quarter of that of the French troops.

On May 11 and 13 Massena ordered further counterattacks, which collected some much needed supplies, but Soult was severely wounded and taken prisoner. On May 29 an insurrection by the Genoese was suppressed with difficulty. There was only enough food left for three more days. On May 30 General Ott and Admiral Keith realized that the garrison must be at its last gasp. They sent an officer under a flag of truce repeating Melas's previous offer of an honorable capitulation. But Massena still temporized as he felt that Bonaparte must now be invading Italy. On May 31 a number of French troops deserted to the enemy and the civilian population was getting out of control. Hundreds were dying daily of typhus and starvation. On June 1 Massena sent his chief of staff to Ott's headquarters to discuss terms for an exchange of prisoners. Ott sent him back with the suggestion that Massena send a representative that evening to discuss terms of capitulation. Ott was now in command of the besieging force, Melas having gone north with the bulk of his troops to encounter Bonaparte, who had now crossed the Alps and was approaching Milan.

An hour later Ott received orders from Melas to raise the siege immediately and march northward to join him. Ott ignored the order. On the morning of June 2, the armistice delegates met at Rivarolo. No agreement was reached before nightfall. The conference was resumed at noon on June 3 and continued for eight hours. That evening Massena's chief commissary reported that only one more day's food ration remained. The delegates met again at 9:30 A.M. on June 4 to settle the final terms. It was agreed that 8,000 French troops should leave Genoa by road for the frontier with all their arms, artillery, and baggage. The Royal Navy would transport the remainder of the garrison to Antibes. On June 6 the garrison marched out.

Massena's dogged defense of Genoa had contributed materially to the success of Bonaparte's Reserve Army, which had already occupied Milan. On June 14 Bonaparte defeated Melas on the field of Marengo. The defense of Genoa had been justified.

Final Campaigns and Last Years (1805–1817)

The two-month Siege of Genoa had imposed excessive strain on Massena, both physical and mental. He had reached the zenith of his career. Bonaparte realized this. On August 13, 1800, he relieved Massena of command of the Army of Italy and sent him into temporary retirement on full pay. Massena purchased a handsome château at Rueil, 10 miles west of Paris, and settled down there with his wife and their three children for the next five years.

On March 25, 1802, the Treaty of Amiens brought a short cessation of hostilities in Europe. On May 18, 1804, Bonaparte was proclaimed Emperor of the French as Napoleon I. On the following day Massena and 17 other generals were created Marshals of the Empire. On August 9, 1805, a Third Coalition was formed against Napoleon and hostilities broke out.

On March 1, 1807, Napoleon, then engaged in defeating the Russians and Prussians in Poland, gave Massena command of V Corps of the Grand Army. Massena's corps, forming the left flank, saw little fighting. On June 14 Napoleon won the final Battle of Friedland and a peace treaty was signed at Tilsit on July 9. The climate of Poland had seriously impaired Massena's health and he contracted lung trouble. He was on sick leave throughout 1808.

In March 1808 Napoleon created 15 dukedoms for his most distinguished field commanders. Massena was appropriately created Duke of Rivoli to comemorate his most successful battle. In September, having been invited by the Emperor to attend a shooting party at Fontainebleau, he was peppered in the face by Napoleon, a notoriously bad shot, and lost the sight of his left eye. Berthier loyally pleaded guilty.

On April 6, 1809, war again broke out between France and Austria. The Archduke Charles invaded Bavaria with an army numbering 300,000. Napoleon, who was then trying to eject the British from the Peninsula, hurried back to Paris and organized a new Army of Germany. Massena was given command of IV Corps and took over command at Strasbourg on March 17. Napoleon arrived on April 17 and ordered Massena to push down the Isar valley to Landshut. Heavy fighting took place and the Austrians were driven back to the Danube valley on the April 23. Massena's corps led the pursuit and entered Vienna on May 11.

On May 13 Napoleon ordered Massena to prepare a bridging operation to cross the Danube 6 miles below Vienna. Massena accomplished this successfully and by May 20 Napoleon had 20,000 men across. On May 21, however, the Archduke counter-attacked with 80,000. The French ran out of ammunition and withdrew into Lobau island. Their retreat from the villages of Aspern and Essling cost them 20,000 casualties. The Austrians lost 23,400.

After his repulse at Aspern–Essling, Napoleon decided to make more careful preparations for another Danube crossing. He planned to bridge the river 5 miles further downstream. Massena was again charged with assisting the bridging operation.

Napoleon assembled an army of 150,000 on the large island of Lobau to cross the main river on July 4–5. The Archduke's army held a semicircular defensive position, 12 miles in extent, with its right flank at Aspern and its center at Deutsch-Wagram.

From dawn onward on July 6 the French drove back the Austrian outpost screen. Massena's corps of four divisions held the left sector, 7,000 yards long, from Aspern northward facing west. The battle now raged all along the front. It was the heaviest artillery engagement ever recorded, with 446 Austrian guns in action and 544 French. Before nightfall the Archduke decided to retreat northward. The French troops were too exhausted to pursue them. The Austrians had lost 37,000, the French 27,000.

On the following day Massena's corps led the pursuit. On July 11 he caught up with the Austrian rear guard at Znaim in Moravia, 50 miles north of Vienna. There a delegation from the Archduke asked for an armistice. A peace treaty was finally signed at Schönbrunn Palace in Vienna on October 14. On the same day Massena was created Prince of Essling. He was now 51 years old and in need of a long rest after a severe horse-fall.

The peace treaties of Tilsit and Schönbrunn had enabled Napoleon to dominate the whole of eastern and central Europe. Only Spain and Portugal, supported by Wellington's Anglo-Portuguese army and the Royal Navy, remained unconquered. The bulk of the Grand Army was now transferred to the Iberian Peninsula. Napoleon had intended to command this campaign in person, but on April 2, 1810, he married the Archduchess Marie-Louise of Austria. On April 17 the Prince of Essling was appointed to command the Army of Portugal and, as soon as the harvest had been carried in the autumn, to capture Lisbon. Massena protested that he was feeling his age and was crippled with rheumatism,[7] but the Emperor insisted.

On May 10 Massena took over his new command at Valladolid and met his subordinates: Marshal Ney (VI Corps), General Reynier (II Corps), General Junot (VIII Corps), and General Montbrun (Cavalry Corps). Massena meant to be comfortable during the coming campaign, for he brought with him no less than 14 aides-de-camp. One of them was his eldest son and another was Captain Renique, whose attractive sister, Henriette, was another aide-de-camp and also his mistress. She was disguised as a cornet of dragoons, and insisted on accompanying him throughout the campaign. This aroused the indignation of his corps commanders, who refused to talk to her at meals.[8]

At the end of May, Massena moved his headquarters up to Salamanca. His physical and mental powers had declined since the Danube campaign, and made an unfortunate impression on his new subordinates. Brigadier-General Foy, for instance, who had served under him at Zurich, has recorded: "He is no longer the Massena of the flashing eyes, mobile face and alert figure whom I knew in 1799. He is only 52, but looks more than 60. He is thinner and begins to stoop. His glance, since the accident when he lost his eye by the Emperor's hand, has lost its keenness."[9] The critical Marbot, one of his senior aides-de-camp, was still less complimentary: "The Marshal's character, formerly so firm, had become completely lacking in resolution."[10]

Ney's VI Corps had already been watching the Spanish fortress of Ciudad Rodrigo, which barred the road into Portugal. Ney was faced by Wellington's Light Division, commanded by Robert Craufurd, strung out on a front of 30 miles along the left bank of the River Agueda. The fortress of Ciudad Rodrigo was held by 5,500 Spanish troops under Don Andrés Herrasti, a determined veteran aged 69. From June 24 the fortress was subjected to an intense bombardment for 16 days. One of the main powder magazines exploded, causing a large breach. On July 9 the garrison capitulated. The way into Portugal was now open. On Massena's order Ney advanced on July 21 and drove Craufurd back 10 miles, leaving the fortress of Almeida completely isolated.

Almeida was held by 4,500 Portuguese under a British commander, Brigadier-General William Cox. The French siege train did not arrive until August 26, when an intense bombardment opened. On the following day a leaking powder barrel left a trail of powder to the main magazine. This was ignited by a French shell and the magazine with 70 tons of gunpowder blew up with terrific force, killing half the gunners. Cox had to capitulate.

On September 15 the French advanced 30 miles to Celorico, Wellington's previous headquarters. The premature fall of Almeida was a blow to Wellington, who was playing for time. His chief engineer was completing the lines of Torres Vedras protecting the British main base at Lisbon. But Massena was in no hurry, for he was waiting until the harvest had all been threshed, when his army could live on the country. Massena had not reckoned with Wellington's foresight. On entering Portugal he found that not an animal or a sack of grain remained in the frontier villages. Wellington's scorched-earth policy had been faithfully carried out in at least some areas, but not all.

Massena's army of 65,000 slightly outnumbered Wellington's 59,000, but there was a lack of harmony between the Prince of Essling and his corps commanders. Brigadier-General Foy, commanding an infantry brigade in Reynier's II Corps, recorded in his diary on September 19, 1810: "Our Army of Portugal seethes with discordant elements. Ney is anxious to get moving, but never obeys orders and is always lacking in the respect due to the Prince. Junot heartily hopes that the campaign will prove a failure. Reynier plays straight, but the Prince dislikes him."[11] The Army of Portugal was out of step when it moved off.

Wellington expected that the French would follow him down the direct Celorico–Coimbra road, but on September 11 Massena made a more westerly detour through Viseu, where he halted for six days. The road taken by Massena was a much worse one and 10 miles longer than the direct one. Baron de Marbot, his senior aide-de-camp, gives the following explanation for this detour and the long halt there: "The fatigues experienced by Madame X contributed largely to delaying Massena and holding him up there, for with the country in a state of insurrection it was impossible to leave her behind without exposing her to the risk of capture."[12] Massena's adoption of this circuitous route and his lengthy halt there were a godsend to Wellington, who knew that the French army was committed to a road that led across the Serra do Busaco, an ideal defensive position where Wellington decided to give battle. On September 21 he established his command post in the Carmelite monastery at the north end of the Busaco ridge, and stationed his six infantry divisions along that ridge, hidden just behind the crest.

The French advance guard moved slowly southwestward from Viseu and reached the village of Mortágua on September 26, 6 miles from the Busaco ridge. This feature was 9 miles long. The Coimbra road crossed the ridge by a col, just north of the Carmelite monastery. Wellington held the ridge with 50,000 infantry and 60 guns. The two leading French corps now deployed, Ney's VI Corps on the right astride the main road, with Reynier's II Corps on his left. A mysterious delay then occurred, which Marbot explains as follows: "Precious time was now wasted while lodging was found for Madame X, so that Massena and his staff did not leave for the front until 2 p.m."[13] Massena did not arrive until the late afternoon of September 26. After viewing the position he ordered both corps to attack at dawn the next day. He made no attempt to reconnoiter a means of outflanking the Busaco ridge.

At dawn on September 27 Reynier launched his attack on a two-division front with 15 battalions in close column. It was an exhausting climb up a gradient of one in three. As they reached the crest, the French were met by a terrific hail of musketry and grapeshot. As the smoke cleared they were swept downhill by a bayonet charge. As soon as Ney saw that Reynier's leading troops had reached the crest, he attacked with two divisions astride the Coimbra road toward the monastery. Here they were met by Pack's Portuguese Brigade and Craufurd's Light Division, 6,400 in all, concealed in an ideal defensive position. Ney's massed columns advanced steadily up the valley under a hail of musketry and shrapnel. As they reached the crest of the col, Craufurd launched a counterattack with the bayonet. Ney's attack failed with a loss of 2,400 casualties.

By 4 P.M. Massena realized that the attack of both corps had failed, so he called off the fight. The French had suffered 4,486 casualties, while the total Anglo–Portuguese loss was 1,269. But the Prince of Essling was not thrown off balance by an initial reverse. He sent for Montbrun, his cavalry commander, and ordered reconnaissances to be made to find a way of outflanking the Busaco position. A rough hill road was found by an unguarded pass through the hills north of the Serra. Massena issued orders for his army to follow this road. Leaving their campfires burning, the French slipped away during the night.

Wellington left Craufurd's Light Division and a cavalry brigade to form a rear guard, and led the rest of his army to Coimbra, where they crossed the River Mondego, and then, practically unmolested, marched southward to the fortified lines of Torres Vedras.

Completely unknown to the French, Wellington had constructed a vast fortified zone in the Lisbon Peninsula, its left flank on the sea and its right on the Tagus. The lines consisted of a triple chain of mutually supporting masonry forts, armed with 12- and six-pounder guns. The forward line was 28 miles long. The second and main defensive line ran about 5 miles behind the forward line, with a length of 24 miles. The third line was quite short, covering the port of embarkation, 11 miles west of Lisbon.

The French pursuit was beset by many difficulties. On October 8 the autumn rains began. Massena's army was now completely cut off from its communications with Spain and France by the Portuguese militia under British officers. On October 11 Montbrun, leading the advanced guard, found his squadrons held up by the lines. On October 14 Massena arrived to make a personal reconnaissance. He was amazed by the powerful fortifications confronting him and also by the tangle of hill country between his army and Lisbon. He sat down facing the lines for a whole month, hoping that Wellington would come out to attack him, which Wellington refused to do. The French army had now exhausted all the local supplies, so Massena's only hope was to move up the right bank of the Tagus and join with Soult's Army of Andalusia. On November 14, therefore, he moved his army 20 miles eastward to Santarém, where he found a good defensive line in fresh country where provisions had not been removed.

Massena held his Santarém position for over three months.

His starving army was now losing many men from sickness. On March 1, 1811, he ordered a retreat northward to regain his base at Salamanca by Almeida and Ciudad Rodrigo. The retreat was skillfully planned and executed, Wellington pursuing him closely. The French marched north-eastward at 20 miles a day, subsisting entirely on the country, and reached Celerico on March 22. Massena then amazed his corps commanders by ordering them, instead of continuing to Almeida, to turn eastward and invade Spain by Coria and Placencia. This extraordinary move so infuriated Ney that he wrote to Massena refusing to obey his orders. That evening Massena sacked Ney, ordering him to return to Paris.

Two days later, following Massena's orders, his army turned eastward from Guarda into the mountains, but soon got into trouble. The roads were so bad that the guns could not follow the infantry, and no supplies existed in that desolate region. After four days Massena realized his mistake and turned northward. On April 3 he crossed the Spanish frontier to Ciudad Rodrigo, reaching Salamanca on April 8. At Salamanca Massena found General Paul Thiébault, his former aide-de-camp, installed as district governor. He asked Thiébault to arrange a dinner party for himself and his lady aide-de-camp. She had been badly hurt by a fall from her horse during the retreat and had been carried out of Portugal by a stretcher party. She was now relegated to the lines of communication. As he himself admitted, "What a mistake I made in taking a woman to war with me!"[14]

Massena had now to reequip and reinforce his exhausted army, but he received scant assistance from the local commander in chief, Marshal Bessières, recently appointed to command the Army of Northern Spain. Massena felt that he must relieve the French garrison in Almeida, now closely blockaded by Wellington. He was very weak in cavalry and artillery, having lost 6,500 horses during the Portuguese campaign. He applied to Bessières at Valladolid, who replied that he could spare him only some cavalry and gun teams.

On April 19 Massena received a letter from Berthier, conveying the Emperor's disapproval of his conduct of the campaign and informing him that Marshal Marmont, Duke of Ragusa, was being sent to take over Ney's corps.[15] On April 25 Massena moved his command post up to Ciudad Rodrigo and his four corps were deployed east of the River Águeda. On May 1 a convoy of grain and flour at last reached Ciudad Rodrigo, and Marshal Bessières arrived with 1,500 cavalry, one six-gun battery, and 30 gun teams. On the following day the French crossed the Águeda and drove the Anglo–Portuguese outposts over the Dos

Casas brook. A road from Ciudad Rodrigo crossed this brook at the village of Fuentes de Oñoro. Wellington's army was deployed along a slight ridge west of this village.

On dawn on May 3 the French attacked the village, their left flank covered by Montbrun's cavalry. Their attack was made frontally with 10 battalions and the village changed hands several times, but the British retained possession of the greater part of it. The action died down at nightfall. The French had suffered 650 casualties, the British only 260. Massena then realized that he had made the same mistake as at Busaco, by attacking Wellington frontally. On the following morning he reconnoitered the position more carefully and ordered three divisions to attack his enemy's right flank. At dawn on May 5, Montbrun's three cavalry brigades were to turn the enemy's right flank, cutting off their retreat. Wellington had foreseen Massena's move, so he ordered his 7th, 1st and 3rd Divisions to face southward, having Fuentes de Oñoro on their left flank instead of in front of them. He held Craufurd's Light Division in reserve.

The French attack opened at dawn. The British cavalry charged repeatedly to cover their infantry, causing the French serious losses. The village of Fuentes de Oñoro again changed hands frequently, but the French commanders delivered their attacks piecemeal. In the late afternoon Massena's artillery commander reported that only four rounds per man remained in the small arms ammunition park. Bessières, who had lent Massena the ammunition wagon teams, refused to allow them to be further employed, owing to their exhausted condition. The battle came to an end.

In the two-day battle, the French had suffered 2,844 casualties, the Anglo–Portuguese only 1,786. Massena withdrew to Ciudad Rodrigo, where he received a letter from Berthier, dated April 17, which ended as follows: "The Emperor charges me to inform you that he expected more from your energy. He has repeatedly indicated his intentions to you. At this distance he can add nothing to them, but His Majesty is distressed, as we all are, to see his army retire before a British force so inferior in numbers."[16] That same evening a second letter, dated April 20, arrived from Berthier: "The Emperor having thought fit to give the command of the Army of Portugal to Marshal Marmont, Duke of Ragusa, His Majesty intends that, as soon as you have handed over your command, you should return to Paris."[17] It was the close of Massena's active career.

Massena had to wait several weeks before Napoleon granted him an audience. He greeted the marshal with the cutting words: "Well, Prince of Essling, so you are no longer Massena."[18] On April 14, 1813, the Emperor appointed Massena to be governor of the 8th military district at Toulon, the most important naval base in the Mediterranean.

A year later, on April 4, 1814, Napoleon abdicated, having been driven back to Paris by the converging allied armies, thus releasing his marshals from their oath of allegiance. On April 26 Louis XVIII was proclaimed King of France. Most of the marshals retained their appointments. On May 4 Napoleon retired in exile to Elba, from which he escaped and landed at Golfe-Juan on March 1, 1815. Massena, rather reluctantly, transferred his allegiance back to Napoleon, and on April 10 issued a proclamation to that effect to the 8th Military District. But his health had now broken down and he resigned his post, being replaced by Marshal Brune.

The Prince of Essling died on April 4, 1817, a month before his fifty-ninth birthday. He was buried with ceremonial honors in the Cemetery of Père-Lachaise in Paris. The white marble obelisk surmounting his tomb bears the single name Massena with the date of his death. Above are the names of his most celebrated battles: Rivoli, Zurich, Gènes (or Genoa), Essling.

The Battle of Rivoli (January 14, 1797) and the Invasion of Austria

The little village of Rivoli stands on a low plateau between Lake Garda and the narrow gorge of the River Adige, known as La Chiusa. Massena held a 12-mile center sector of the French front at Verona. At 5 P.M. on January 13, 1797, Bonaparte, to meet Joubert's appeal for help, ordered Massena to march with a detachment so as to reach Rivoli by dawn on January 14. Leaving five battalions to hold his Verona sector, Massena started at dusk. It was a bright moonlit night and they covered the 15 miles to Rivoli by daybreak. Joubert's men had been fighting hard for two days and their flanks were now being turned.

By 9 A.M. the whole situation was transformed. Massena had arrived at the head of his column, his 10 guns leading. The Austrians were blasted off the two hills that outflanked Joubert's left, Monte Pipolo and Monte Brunizzi. Massena swept northward along the Rivoli perimeter and drove the Austrian center column off Monte Trambasore through Caprino. Thanks to Massena's timely intervention, the whole French line was able to counterattack and recover the ground and the guns lost by Joubert's division. When dusk fell Alvintzy's corps was in full retreat, leaving 3,376 killed and wounded, 7,000 prisoners, and nine guns. Alvintzy himself narrowly escaped capture. The French loss was 2,180 killed and wounded. It was a brilliant victory.

Meanwhile General Provera's corps of 19,000 Austrians in the Padua area had outflanked Augereau's division holding the French right, and crossed the Adige in order to relieve Würmser's corps besieged in Mantua by Sérurier's division. Bonaparte ordered Massena to move south and attack Provera. Although exhausted by his Rivoli battle, Massena started at 5 A.M. on January 15 for his 30-mile march. At dawn on January 16 he attacked Provera just northeast of Mantua. Provera was defeated and Mantua capitulated on the same day, 7,000 Austrians and 22 guns being captured. In front of the troops, Bonaparte acclaimed Massena as *"l'enfant chéri de la victoire."*[19]* The double defeat of the enemy at Rivoli and Mantua was due to Massena's relentless marching powers and dynamic tactical skill.

Bonaparte, now reinforced, decided to invade Austria. On March 10, 1797, the Army of Italy began its advance. Massena's division, now 12,000 strong, formed the advance guard and pushed northeastward by Belluno and Cadore, heading for Vienna by the Tarvisio Pass, Villach, and Klagenfurt. The Austrians, under their best commander, the Archduke Charles, put up a stiff resistance, but Massena drove their rear guard from the Tarvisio Pass on March 24 and entered the mountainous Austrian province of Carinthia, reaching Klagenfurt on March 28.

After a stiff fight at the Dürnstein gorge in Lower Austria on April 2, Massena reached Bruck, 100 miles from Vienna, on April 9. On April 18 the Austrians gave in, and a preliminary peace treaty was signed at Leoben. On April 23 Bonaparte sent Massena to Paris, carrying to the Directory his dispatch on the campaign. On May 9, three days after his arrival in Paris, he was accorded a state reception by the Directory at the Palais du Luxembourg. The president embraced Massena and presented him with a sword of honor. At the end of June, Massena left Paris to spend a few days at Antibes with his wife and their two children, aged five and four, whom he had not seen for two years. He then traveled by Genoa to Milan, where he reported for duty to his army commander.

Bonaparte was now given by the Directory the task of negotiating a final peace treaty with Austria. On August 24 he and Berthier arrived at Padua on their way to Udine. After long and acrimonious negotiations, the Treaty of Campo-Formio was signed on October 17. It was a triumph for Bonaparte's forceful diplomacy. The Austrian Emperor recognized the Rhine as France's eastern frontier, in compensation for which the independent Venetian Republic was given to Austria. Lombardy was recognized by the Emperor as an independent "Cisalpine Republic" under French protection.

*In fact Napoleon did not call Massena "the *dear* child of victory" but used the word *"spoilt"* (or 'gaté') according to most reliable authorities.

While Bonaparte recognized Massena's outstanding qualities as a commander in the field, he had also detected two major blemishes in his moral character, namely, his insatiable greed for money and his inordinate passion for women.

As regards his avarice, Massena was aided and abetted by his chief of staff, Colonel Jean-Baptiste Solignac, an inveterate gambler. On capturing the town of Leoben in April 1797, Solignac extorted from the burgomaster a substantial cash payment, which he pocketed. A complaint was made to Bonaparte, and on April 24 Berthier sent him the following order: "The Commander-in-Chief orders Colonel Solignac to repay immediately the contribution of 1000 Venetian ducats which he levied at Leoben. Within 24 hours he will forward the receipt for it, which is required by the Commander-in-Chief."[20] On November 15 Bonaparte received the following report from his deputy in Milan: "The people of Padua claim that at various times they have given Massena three millions of Venetian currency for the benefit of his division. The division says that only 300,000 francs have been spent on their behalf, and the remainder must have been employed in winning popularity for himself."[21] After the final peace treaty in October, Solignac and Massena's aide-de-camp Paul Thiébault, traveled together to Paris on leave. Thiébault was amazed to discover that in Solignac's luggage was a trunk containing 400,000 francs in gold.[22]

Regarding Massena's weakness for women, he quickly acquired a mistress when the Army of Italy overran Piedmont. On May 11, 1796, the day after the battle of Lodi, Bonaparte issued the following army order: "It is expressly forbidden for any officer, of whatever rank, to have women with him. Consequently the Commander-in-Chief orders that those who have them must send them away beyond the river Po within 24 hours."[23] Massena was certainly one of the culprits. He had brought with him his mistress, Silvia Cepolini.

But certain senior officers appear to have ignored Bonaparte's previous orders regarding women in the Carinthian campaign. On April 5, 1797, he issued the following army order:

The Commander-in-Chief observes with the greatest displeasure that, in spite of his order dated March 28, women continue to follow the army. He notices that it is principally the officers who persist in this abuse. He warns all officers that within five days they must arrange to send their women back. Any officer who has not done so within that period will be provisionally cashiered and his name reported to the War Minister.[24]

Presumably Silvia Cepolini no longer accompanied Massena in the field.

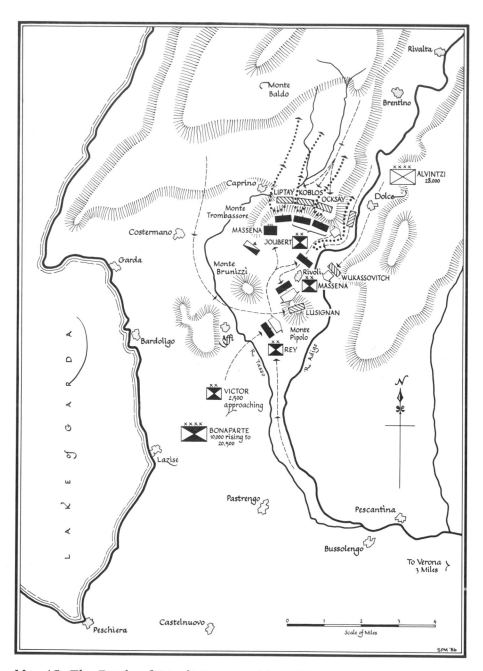

Map 15. The Battle of Rivoli, January 14, 1797

TEXTUAL REFERENCES

1. P. Sabor, *Massena et sa famille* (Aix-en-Provence, 1926), pp. 269–172.
2. Gen. Koch, *Memoires de Massena* (Paris, 1848–50), Vol. 1, p. lxxxvi.
3. *Correspondance de Napoléon Ier* (Paris, 1858–70), Vol. 2, No. 890.
4. Document in the Prince of Essling's archives.
5. *Correspondance, op. cit.,* Vol. 6, No. 4565.
6. *Ibid.,* No. 4795.
7. G. de l'Ain, *Vie militaire du General Foy* (Paris, 1900), Vol. 2, p. 100.
8. M. Marbot, *Mémoires du Général Baron de Marbot* (Paris, 1892), Vol. 2, p. 336.
9. G. de l'Ain, *op. cit.,* p. 101.
10. Marbot, *op. cit.,* p. 384.
11. de l'Ain, *op. cit.,* Vol. 2, p. 101.
12. Marbot, *op. cit.,* p. 384.
13. *Ibid.*
14. *Ibid.,* p. 435.
15. Koch, *op. cit.,* Vol. 7, pp. 490–91.
16. *Ibid.,* p. 604.
17. *Ibid.,* p. 558.
18. *Ibid.,* Vol. 1, p. lv.
19. E. Gachot, *Histoire Militaire de Massena* (Paris, 1898–1908), Vol. 1, p. 290.
20. *Correspondance, op. cit.,* Vol. 2, No. 1731.
21. *Correspondance inédite de Napoléon Ier* (Paris, 1912–13), Vol. 4, No. 460.
22. P. C. Thiébault, *Mémoires du Général Baron Thiébault* (Paris, 1893–95), Vol. 2, p. 102.
23. *Correspondance, op. cit.,* Vol. 1, No. 400.
24. *Ibid.,* Vol. 2, No. 1697.

BIBLIOGRAPHICAL NOTE

Standard accounts of the subject include Auguste Amic, *Histoire de Massena* (Paris, 1864). A fine treatment of his Swiss campaign is by Captaine L. Hennequin, *Zurich: Massena en Suisse* (Berger-Levrault, 1911), and the Comte de Beauregard, *Le Maréchal Massena* (Nice, 1902). A good account of Wagram and the marshal's role during and after the battle is Baron Binder's *Der Krieg Napoleons gegen Oesterreich,* 2 vols. (Berlin, 1906). Interesting if spiteful remarks about Massena are to be found in *Mémoires de Madame la Duchesse d'Abrantes* (Paris, 1831). Care is needed in reading Edouard Gachot, *Histoire Militaire de Massena,* 5 vols. (Paris, 1898–1908), as it was sponsored by the family and overlooks its subject's failings. Other books, laudatory but of value, are General Koch's *Mémoires de Massena,* 7 vols. (Paris, 1850) and the recollections of a sometimes aide-de-camp, *Mémoires du Général Baron Thiébault,* 5 vols. (Paris, 1893–95). René Valentin's *Le Maréchal Massena, 1758–1817* (Paris, 1960) is overpartial. On the other hand, the *Mémoires du Général Baron de Marbot,* 3 vols. (Paris, 1892), also available in English translation, are highly readable but bitterly critical of Massena's ability and moral failings, as seen by another aide-de-camp in 1810.

Reliable treatments of Massena's family background and his home life are, respectively, Pierre Sabor, *Massena et sa famille* (Aix-en-Provence, 1926), and A. Augustin-Thierry, *Massena, l'enfant gâté de la victoire* (Paris, 1947).

Editor's Note: The best English-language life of Massena to date is General Sir James Marshall-Cornwall's *Massena* (Oxford, 1965). The works of Prof. Don Horward, *Bussaco* (Gainesville, Fla., 1965) and *Napoleon and Iberia* (Gainesville, Fla., 1984), together with his edited version of the *Pelet Papers* (Oxford, 1975), throw much new light on the campaigns in Spain and Portugal, 1810–11, and the marshal's role in them.

CHRONOLOGY

1754, July 31	—Born at Palise (Doubs)
1769, September 15	—Enlists in *Régiment de Champagne-infanterie*
1773, June 30	—Purchases discharge
1774, April 8	—Reenlists in *Gendarmerie-Anglais*
1776, August 15	—Dismissed for misconduct
1779, August 16	—Commissioned in *Corps d'infanterie de Nassau-Siegen*
1788, June 1	—Transfers to *5th Bataillon de Chasseurs*
1793, June 26	—Appointed to command *5th Demi-Brigade Légère*
1794, February 18	—Appointed *général de brigade*
June 9	—Appointed *général de division*
August 17	—Appointed to command *l'Armée des Pyrénnées Occidentales*
1795, September 15	—Appointed to command 11th Division at Bayonne
1797, October 26	—Denounced as a royalist
1800, March 24	—Appointed lieutenant to Moreau, *l'Armée du Rhin*
June 20	—Commands corps in *l'Armée d'Italie*
1801, March 8	—Appointed to command *l'Armée d'Italie*
December 3	—*Inspecteur général de la Gendarmerie*
1804, May 19	—Created *Maréchal d'Empire* (third in seniority)
1807, December 16	—Commands Corps *d'Observation des Côtes de l'Océan*
1808, July 2	—Created *duc de Conegliano*
1809, January 2	—Recalled from Spain
September 5	—Commands *l'Armée de la Tête-de-Flandre*
1813, November 16	—Commands *l'Armée de Réserve des Pyrénnées*
1814, January 8	—Major-general of the *Garde Nationale de Paris*
1815, August 29	—Refuses to preside at Ney's court-martial
1823, February 12	—Commands IV Corps, *l'Armée des Pyrénnées*
1833, December 17	—Appointed governor of Les Invalides
1842, April 20	—Dies at Paris

CHAPTER SIXTEEN

AN HONEST MAN

Moncey

by

Ian F. W. Beckett

"Creation" of the Republic (1754-1800)

Moncey was born at Palise in the Doubs region near Besançon on July 31, 1754. His father, François-Antoine de Jeannot, was lawyer to the parliament of Besançon but appears not to have practiced once he acquired an estate at Moncey in 1789, at which time the surname of Moncey was adopted. At 15 Moncey ran away from his law studies at Besançon and enlisted as a volunteer in the Périgord (later Conti) Regiment. His father purchased his discharge, but on September 15, 1769, Moncey again enlisted, this time as a grenadier in the Champagne Infantry Regiment. Following anti-invasion duties in Brittany in 1773, Moncey purchased his discharge on June 30, 1773, apparently through dissatisfaction at not being offered a commission. However, he once more re-enlisted on April 8, 1774, in the elite *Gendarmes-Anglais* quartered at Versailles and ranked second only to the *Maison du Roi.*

Moncey was a tall man and was later noted for his stately bearing, and this, in addition to his father's income, must have enabled him to enter the *gendarmerie* despite his discharge from two former units. However, on August 15, 1776, Moncey was dismissed from the corps for misconduct. As the corps roll expressed it, "He has left the service on account of ignorance and fickleness; he has a good appearance, but is not really to be regretted; not to be re-enlisted."[1] Nevertheless, Moncey subsequently secured a commission as sub-lieutenant on August 16, 1779, in a battalion of the Nassau–Siegen corps, a body of both infantry and artillery raised for naval service. It was later named the Montréal Regiment.

As so often in the Royal Army, promotion for one of Moncey's class was slow. Under the old 1760 regulations, for example, only nobles presented at court could progress beyond the rank of colonel. Some reforms had been introduced after the Seven Years' War, but the Ségur decree effectively turned back the clock by requiring at least four generations of nobility as qualification for a direct commission in the regular army. Moncey gained the confirmed rank of second lieutenant only on August 30, 1782, and that of first lieutenant on July 1, 1785. Transferring on June 1, 1788, to the 5th Chasseur Battalion, a regiment recruited and stationed in the Garonne, Moncey eventually reached the rank of captain on April 1, 1791.

By this time, however, the army and its officer corps were being rapidly transformed. Indiscipline and desertion among the rank and file increased significantly after July 1789, while, following the king's unsuccessful flight to Varennes in June 1791, large numbers of aristocratic officers also began to refuse to take the newly instituted oath of loyalty and to desert. At least 6,000 officers or approximately 60% of the officer establishment had fled by the end of 1791 to be replaced largely by former non-commissioned officers. The outbreak of war between France and Austria in April 1792 brought a further wave of officer desertions, a process encouraged by the beginnings of the summary justice administered to those who were deemed to have failed. Some 2,000 officers were removed during 1792 and three-quarters of the pre-war officers corps had gone by the end of 1793. Of 200 general officers serving in 1789, only five remained by 1793, while in the course of 1792–1793 no less than 593 general officers were appointed or dismissed.[2] In such circumstances a dedicated soldier such as Moncey without discernible political preferences beyond perhaps a certain regard for moderate royalism (as evinced by his friendship with men like Moreau, Pichegru, Willot, and Cadoudal) could aspire to that upward social mobility that the new army now conveyed. In short, the army was now "a career open to talent," as Napoleon later expressed it.

By contrast, therefore, with his slow rise to the rank of captain over 22 years of continuous service, Moncey's promotion after 1791 was positively meteoric, the catalyst being his service with the Army of the Western Pyrenees after France's declaration of war on Spain in March 1793. The army itself consisted of some 14½ battalions of line infantry, of which only two were regular battalions; 18 locally raised companies; five companies of artillery; a regular dragoon regiment; and Moncey's own regular light infantry battalion. Moncey soon distinguished himself, while commanding the French outposts at Château-Pignon on June 6, 1793, by putting to flight Spanish forces attacking his position and then, when forced to retire, trying to prevent volunteers in other units from fleeing in disorder. For his efforts he was rewarded with promotion to command the 5th Light Demi-Brigade on June 26, 1793, demi-brigades being the mixed regular and volunteer formations introduced for both the practical reason of stiffening the conscripts and the ideological reason of exposing surviving regulars to the volunteers' revolutionary spirit. In the case of the Army of the Western Pyrenees, five demi-brigades were formed while two more cavalry regiments were added.

Moncey led his new command in engagements at Aldudes in June 1793, at St. Jean de Luz on July 23, 1793, and at Hendaye on February 5, 1794. His efforts had caught the attention of the Representatives, those individuals appointed to all the republican armies as a means of countering royalist tendencies among the commanders. As a result Moncey jumped a rank, being promoted to command a brigade in the 1st Division on February 18, 1794. His appointment was confirmed on February 23, 1794, but within a few months he was promoted again to command of a division on June 9, 1794. Moncey led his division at St. Jean Pied de Porte, where he rallied his men in the face of a cavalry charge led by the Spanish commander Bonaventura Casa; defeated a force at Arquinzu led by the Marquis of St.-Simon on July 9, 1794; and stormed the Spanish entrenchments in the Baztan valley between July 27 and 30, 1794. He then successively seized the Spanish positions at Haya and Fuenterrabia before capturing the port of Pasajes on August 2 and both the town and citadel of San Sebastian with 200 artillery pieces on August 3, 1794. Further service at the Siege of Tolosa brought a recommendation by the Representatives of the People that he succeed to the command of the Army of the Western Pyrenees on August 9, 1794. Despite his lack of seniority, Moncey was confirmed in the command by the Committee of Public Safety on August 17, 1794.

His command of the Army of the Western Pyrenees was undoubtedly the most successful period of his military career, although one historian has dismissed this force as the least significant of all the Republic's armies.[3] In many respects, too, Moncey was fortunate in finding his Spanish opponents consistently tardy in their responses to his movements. The Spanish, indeed, were far more preoccupied with the campaign in the eastern Pyrenees. Some 52,000 men were at Moncey's disposal, but, in common with other republican armies, they were frequently kept short of supplies. The Representatives were, in theory, those responsible for maintaining such logistic support, but a siege train destined for Moncey's planned siege of Pamplona was diverted to Strasbourg while muskets were diverted to Lyons. Moncey owed all to the Representatives, describing himself on one occasion as their *ouvrage* or "creation,"[4] but although he enjoyed better relations with them than his immediate predecessor, Muller, his operational plans were equally obstructed. Minor engagements were won at Lecumberry on October 16 and at Villanova on October 17, 1794, leading to the capture of important foundaries at Eugui and Orbaiceta and the Spanish navy's mast store at Irati. However, major operations were not authorized until November, by which time winter and the outbreak of disease prevented the advance to Pamplona.

Moncey took advantage of the winter to reorganize his forces and complete the brigading of his battalions. A new siege train reached him, and in June 1795 some 12,000 men from Vendée arrived to replace the 3,000 lost through disease during the winter. Moncey commenced his advance on June 28, 1795. Moncey always had a particular penchant for encircling movements. He had attempted them with his division at Arquinzu and in the Baztan valley and was now to attempt them again with his army. Much, however, depended upon those subordinates entrusted with the encircling movement itself. In the Baztan valley one of Moncey's columns under Digonet had attacked too soon, while in the autumn campaign of 1794 Delaborde had failed to close the Spanish escape route from the same valley. In the new operations Moncey's subordinates again failed him when the Spanish commander, Crespo, eluded the junction of the columns of Willot and Dessein at Salinas. However, Moncey's operations did result in the capture of Vitoria on July 17 and of Bilbao on July 19, 1795. Undoubtedly, too, his army's successes placed additional pressure on the Spanish, who had begun negotiations in May. When news of the Treaty of Basel, signed on July 22, 1795, reached Moncey in August, his army had crossed the Ebro and was poised to begin the siege of Pamplona.

With the disbandment of the Army of the Western Pyrenees, Moncey was offered command of the Army of the Coasts of Brest on September 1, 1795. But he pleaded ill health and was appointed instead to the command of the 11th Division at Bayonne on September 15, 1795. There is little doubt that Moncey infinitely preferred such a local command to waging war in Vendée, which was the responsibility of the Brest army. By nature he was a kindly and sensitive man of decency and honor. His troops had been responsible for some outrages, mostly committed by the troops of Delaborde who had previously served in Vendée, but Moncey had no liking for the prospect of guerrilla war. Indeed, he remarked, "It is very cruel to have to fight against Frenchmen who are defending their opinions."[5] Dessein, whose division was posted to Vendée, also subsequently wrote to Moncey that his "extreme sensibility" would have prevented Moncey serving the Republic to the best of his ability in that particular theater. Moncey's sensibility was also seen in his decision not to report adversely on Delaborde's failures in the Baztan valley, which might conceivably have led to the latter's execution.

To some extent Moncey's sensitivity also derived from a nervousness enhanced by his rapid promotion. At the time of his appointment to the army command, Moncey had complained, "This sensibility has affected my spirit in such a way as to render it stupid."[6] He had pleaded to both Muller and the Representatives that he was too irresolute and undecided to serve the Republic well. The Representatives chose to regard Moncey's protestations as proof of his modesty, but in reality he well knew that his promotion would make him enemies. Former subordinates such as Frègeville and Marbot, both dismissed by the

Representatives for the excesses of their troops in June 1795, intrigued against him prior to his dismissal from command in October 1797.

That dismissal itself followed the coup of 18 *Fructidor* on September 4, 1797, by which Carnot and Barthélemy were ousted by their fellow Directors. While commanding the 11th Division, Moncey had become popular for the suppression of local brigandage and had been offered a seat in the Council of Ancients. He had declined but was widely spoken of as a possible ambassador to Spain, or as a possible minister of war, or even a possible member of the Directory. That in itself may well have been sufficient condemnation, but Moncey was also suspected of royalism through his friendship with Carnot, and particularly with Pichegru and his former subordinate, Willot, now a leading member of the opposition to the Directory. When Pichegru's correspondence was seized, Moncey's regular contacts were exposed. His opposition to suppressing Vendée was also recalled, and, having been denounced by the adjutant general, Juncker, Moncey was dismissed from his command on October 26, 1797. He was only reinstated on September 20, 1799.

His precise part in Napoleon's coup on 18 *Brumaire* (November 10, 1799) is uncertain, since he was not allocated a specific role, but Moncey clearly approved of the overthrow of the Directory. He was rewarded for his support by appointment with Macdonald and Sérurier to the commission of general officers on November 15, 1799, charged with examining the employment of auxiliary battalions. Moncey was then appointed to the 12th Division at Nantes on November 30, 1799, and to the 19th Division at Lyons on December 3, 1799. On March 24, 1800, he was appointed lieutenant to his old friend Moreau, now commander-in-chief of the Army of the Rhine.

In the Service of the Consulate and Empire (1800–1814)

Moreau had not actually requested Moncey's services but regarded him highly and, given Moncey's experience of mountain warfare, sent him to command a detachment of 15,000 men in Switzerland on April 16, 1800. Moncey was transferred to the Army of the Reserve on May 9 and ordered to bring his men— consisting of the divisions of Lapoype and Lorge—across the St. Gotthard Pass to support Napoleon's campaign in Italy. Moncey's force was pitifully weak in artillery with only 11 small-caliber cannons, but he set out on May 28 with a total of 11,510 men, forming the flank guard to the main army crossing the St. Bernard Pass under Napoleon's watchful eye. Only bad road conditions arrested his progress, and, after rejoining the Army of the Reserve on June 7, Moncey was detached to defend Lombardy. He occupied Valteline on June 20, 1800, and linked with Macdonald's Army of the Grisons crossing the Splügen Pass. Moncey was then used as the left wing of Brune's Army of Italy, forcing the Mincio Pass at Monzembano on December 26, 1800. Moncey was deceived by the Austrian general, Laudon, into believing that Brune had accepted an armistice—another indication of Moncey's own honesty and belief in the honesty of others—and Laudon made good his escape. Brune demanded his removal on January 7, 1801, but Moncey was retained in his command and actually succeeded Brune as commander of the Army of Italy on March 8 that year. However, he held the appointment only until June 19, when he took command of French forces in the Cisalpine Republic. He was subsequently offered a subordinate command to Murat of French forces in Ancona, the Papal States, and Etruria, but he declined and left his command on August 28.

After the Peace of Lunéville, Moncey was appointed senior inspector-general of the *gendarmerie* on December 3, 1801, a post he continued to hold until December 1807. It was not primarily an active post, although it involved him in the Enghien affair, and between 1801 and 1807 his most noteworthy activities were accompanying Napoleon on his visit to Holland in 1803 and carrying Frederick the Great's sword in the triumphal procession in Paris after the victory at Jena three years later.[7] It was therefore somewhat surprising that Moncey was raised to the marshalate on May 19, 1804. He had never personally served under Napoleon, nor participated in any of Napoleon's early victories, nor held any high office between 1799 and 1804. In theory, he was senior to many of Napoleon's other marshals, although he was not the oldest—Kellermann, Sérurier, Berthier, and Pérignon were all older although the latter two by only one year. The assumption must be that Moncey's appointment was a political gesture to associate former republican generals with the Empire.[8]

What brought Moncey back to active service was the prospects of war in Spain, with which Moncey was thoroughly familiar. Thus, at the age of 53, he was appointed to command the Corps of Observation of the Coasts of the Ocean on December 16, 1807, and led it into Spain on January 9, 1808. Initially his troops occupied Biscay and Navarre, but his 30,000 men, mostly conscripts of the class of 1808, were then strung out from Madrid to Aranda in occupation of the countryside. With the outbreak of insurrection in May 1808, Moncey's men came under attack on the streets of Madrid and he was reinforced by Frère's division. He was then detached on June 4, 1808, with 9,000 men to capture Valencia and the naval arsenal at Cartagena, his failure to do so reflecting not only the difficulties in which he was placed by his superiors but also his own shortcomings as a military commander.

There is little doubt that 9,000 men were wholly inadequate for the task, especially when they comprised eight provisional battalions and two provisional dragoon regiments in addition to two Spanish corps that promptly deserted. The luck Moncey had experienced in his earlier campaigns fortunately repeated itself, however, since the Spaniards chose to block the longer and easier route to Valencia while Moncey struck across the difficult but lightly defended defiles of Cabriel and Cabrillas. Similarly, the Spaniards chose the wrong road to defend when Moncey retired from Valencia through San Clemente and La Mancha to link up with Frère on July 15, 1808. To say that Moncey struck through the defiles is perhaps something of an exaggeration since he compromised his slim hopes of success by halting for seven days after taking Cuença on June 11, 1808. He was spurred into movement only by Savary's orders, the latter deputizing for Murat in Madrid. By the time the advance resumed on June 18, the Spaniards had had time to inundate the approaches to Valencia, throw up new defenses, and bring in reinforcements to raise the garrison to some 20,000 men although only 8,000 were regulars. Moncey summoned the town without success on June 26 and, with virtually no artillery, was forced to launch a frontal assault on June 28. He clearly underestimated the determination of the defenders and suffered between 1,200 and 2,000 casualties, forcing his retirement.

Napoleon did not hold Moncey entirely responsible for the failure despite Moncey's slowness after seizing Cuenca; indeed, the Emperor remarked, "One does not take a town of 80,000 souls by the scruff of the neck."[9] Further evidence of Napoleon's confidence was Moncey's assumption of the title of Duke of Conegliano on July 2, 1808. On September 7 Moncey was appointed to command III Corps of the Army of Spain, securing a minor victory at Lérrin on October 3 but then being subordinated to Lannes for the action at Tudela on November 23. Ney and Moncey were ordered to pursue the defeated Spanish commanders, Palafox and Castaños, Ney following the latter toward Borja and Moncey pursuing the former to Saragossa. Again Moncey found himself faced with a well-defended city with inadequate forces for a siege, and on November 30 he fell back to await reinforcement by Mortier. The two marshals then commenced the siege of Saragossa on December 20, 1808, after Palafox rejected Moncey's offer of terms. No sooner had the first parallel been opened than Moncey was recalled on January 2,

1809, and replaced by Junot.[10] Ostensibly, he had been dismissed for his slow progress in conducting the siege, but he had never been an intimate of the Emperor and that same humanity apparent in his reluctance to coerce Vendée had again surfaced in Spain, even the Spanish *junta* of Oviedo praising Moncey for his humane conduct of the war.[11] In particular, the offer of terms to Palafox appears to have rankled with Napoleon or his circle.

Only rear appointments followed: command of the Army of Flanders in Belgium from September 5, 1809; command of the reserve divisions of the Belgian National Guard from September 11, 1809; appointment as inspector-general of National Guard units in the 12th, 13th, 14th, and 15th Divisions in 1812; and command of the Reserve Army of the Pyrenees from November 16, 1813. His appointment as major-general of the newly formed Parisian National Guard on January 8, 1814, was also intended as a virtually non-active command, but in March 1814 Paris itself became the front line as the allied armies surged across France. Moncey, well used to motivating amateur soldiers or conscripts throughout his career, played a gallant role in the defense of the Clichy Gate on March 30, 1814 (see p. 306). After the fall of the city, he withdrew his men to Fontainebleau where, as blunt as always, he was one of the eight marshals to demand Napoleon's abdication and, with Ney and Lefebvre, confronted the Emperor with their decision.

Doyen of the Marshals (1814–1842)

As Berthier and Murat were sovereign princes, Moncey had become the doyen of the marshals in 1809 and continued to be so until 1813. With Berthier's death in June 1815, he once again ranked first among the surviving marshalate, but the postwar years were far from easy for Moncey.

Moncey accepted the provisional government on April 11, 1814, and joined its council on April 16. Louis XVIII retained him in his office as inspector-general of the gendarmerie and he became a peer of France on June 4, 1814, only to be given the same honor by Napoleon on June 2, 1815, during the Hundred Days. Moncey was thought to be too old for active command and played no active part in the last campaign. However, his punishment for deserting the Bourbons was to be appointed to preside over Ney's court-martial. Rather than make excuses as others did, Moncey wrote to the king declining the appointment. As far as he was concerned, Ney had saved the army and countless lives in Russia, a campaign Moncey had actually opposed. He could not, therefore, now condemn Ney: "No Sire, if I am not allowed to save my country, nor my own life, then at least I will save my honour."[12] His frankness brought his dismissal on August 29, 1815, and three months of imprisonment in the fortress of Ham.

Reinstated on July 3, 1816, Moncey was once more made a peer of France on March 5, 1819. He was then given command of the 9th Division on April 5, 1820, and continued in that appointment until November 5, 1830, with the brief interval of February 12 to November 1820, when the old soldier was once more sent on active service to Spain, this time when the French intervened on behalf of the royalists in the civil war. Moncey took command of IV Corps of the Army of the Pyrenees and occupied Catalonia, defeating the former Spanish guerrilla leader, Espoz y Mina, and capturing Barcelona. His career culminated with his appointment as governor of Les Invalides by King Louis Philippe on December 17, 1833, Moncey receiving the body of Napoleon on its return from St. Helena on December 15, 1840. Two years later, Moncey himself died on April 20, 1842, and, at his own request, was buried in the "aisle of the brave" close to the Emperor's tomb.

Moncey was not a great general, but his courage both in his early career in Spain as well as at the age of 60 in defending the Clichy Gate was undeniable. He had also displayed considerable moral courage in his consistent refusal to wage war as ruthlessly as some of his contemporaries. Such honest convictions, again displayed in the refusal to try Ney, undoubtedly damaged his career, but his long-term survival is perhaps suitable testament to the ultimate strength of his personal honor that struck a chord in others. He was never afraid to speak his mind. As Napoleon himself remarked on St. Helena, Moncey's behavior toward him had been fitting and proper to the end. In short, Moncey was *"un honnête homme."*[13] It was Moncey's misfortune that others were not as honest toward him.

The "Barrière" (or Gate) of Clichy (March 30, 1814)

There had been little expectation of danger when Moncey had been appointed to command the Parisian National Guard in January 1814. Indeed, through fears of arming the general population, membership was severely restricted, with the result that by March 16 there were only 11,500 men instead of the proposed 24,000. Moreover, weapons were in such short supply that some 3,000 men had only pikes. But then Paris as a whole was totally unprepared when, on March 24, the allied armies of Silesia and Bohemia managed to get between Napoleon and his capital and gambled on taking Paris rather than pursuing the French field army. Through the lack of initiative of King Joseph, charged with the defense of Paris; the disbelief of the minister of war, Clarke, that any threat existed; and Napoleon's own failure to decide between alternative plans of fortification, no serious attempt was made to put the city into a state of defense until as late as March 23, 1814. In all, only 38,800 men could be found, including Moncey's National Guard, hastily armed depot troops, and the remnants of the corps of Marmont and Mortier. By contrast, the allies mustered 111,300 men when they closed on Paris on March 29.

Moncey, who was nominally Joseph's chief of staff, took post at the vulnerable Clichy Gate, one of no less than 56 entries to be defended, and opposite the key high ground of Montmartre upon which available artillery was stationed. Moncey's men were called to arms at 4 A.M. on March 30, 1814, but, in practice, their services were restricted to the defense of the city walls or their immediate vicinity through their inexperience. By 10 A.M. the French right at Vincennes had been driven in, but the allies held back to allow Blücher to attack Montmartre with the Army of Silesia. At 11 A.M. Joseph, who had been observing the action from Montmartre, decided to abandon the city and sent messages to Marmont and Mortier to seek terms before riding down to tell Moncey of his departure. With Joseph gone the defense of Montmartre all but collapsed, but Moncey was determined to hold on, just as Marmont similarly resolved initially to fight on when he received Joseph's message.

Moncey's situation was desperate and he was of immense encouragement to his untrained citizen soldiers. At one point he ordered them to take cover, but his own courage had so impressed them that they, too, refused to do so until one of Moncey's subordinates, Allent, cried, "Do you think that the oldest of the Marshals would advise you to do anything cowardly?"[14] Sending his aides to encourage the defense at other points, Moncey ordered a second barricade built behind the gate, women and children helping to pile up carts, paving stones, and blocks of wood. The allies, however, were anxious to avoid street fighting and ultimately contented themselves with exchanging fire with Moncey's men from the suburbs. With the conclusion of terms between Marmont and the allies at 2 A.M. on March 31, 1814, the French troops marched out, although the National Guard was allowed to remain to keep order. As the allies entered Paris, Moncey led off his forces to the west and reached Fontainebleau where the Emperor had belatedly arrived.[15] The Emperor might well have had reason to criticize Joseph or even Marmont but of the gallant conduct of the 60-year-old doyen of his marshalate there could be no question.

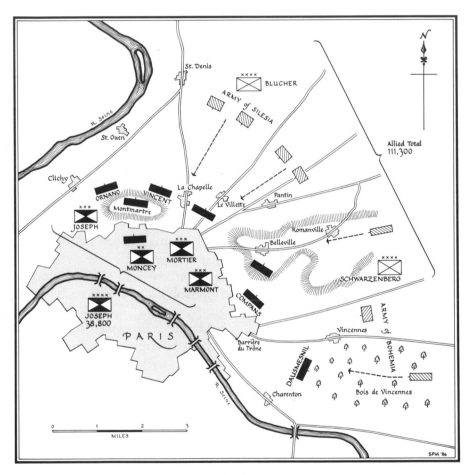

Map 16. The *Barrière* (or Gate) of Clichy, March 30, 1814

TEXTUAL REFERENCES

1. R. W. Phipps, *The Armies of the First French Republic and the Rise of the Marshals of Napoleon I* (Oxford, 1931), Vol. 3, pp. 136–37.
2. S. F. Scott, *The Response of the Royal Army to the French Revolution* (Oxford, 1978), *passim*.
3. Phipps, *op. cit.*, p. 133.
4. *Ibid.*, p. 188.
5. *Ibid.*, p. 210.
6. *Ibid.*, p. 188.
7. J. Hanoteau, ed., *Memoirs of General de Caulaincourt* (London, 1938), abridged, one volume edition, p. 394; E. Fraser, *The War Drama of the Eagles* (London, 1912), p. 149.
8. G. Godelewski, "Bon-Adrien Jeannot de Moncey," in *Le Souvenir Napoléon*, (No. 326, November, Paris 1982), pp. 14–15.
9. J. Read, *War in the Peninsula* (London, 1977) pp. 77–78; C. Oman, *A History of the Peninsular War* (Oxford, 1902), Vol. 1, pp. 136–38.
10. R. Rudorff, *War to the Death: The Siege of Saragossa* (London, 1974), pp. 173–267.
11. R. P. Dunn-Pattison, *Napleon's Marshals* (Boston, 1909), pp. 248–49.
12. Godelewski, *op. cit.*, pp. 14–15; R. F. Delderfield, *The March of the Twenty Six: The Story of Napoleon's Marshals* (London, 1962), p. 262.
13. Hanoteau, *op. cit.*, Vol. 3, p. 371.
14. H. Houssaye, *Napoleon and the Campaign of 1814* (London, 1914), p. 411.
15. F. W. O. Maycock, *Invasion of France, 1814* (London, 1914), pp. 174–92; A. H. Atteridge, *Napoleon's Brothers* (London, 1909) pp. 393–410.

BIBLIOGRAPHICAL NOTE

Moncey has not been the subject of any books in the English language, although the third volume of R. W. Phipps's *The Armies of the First French Republic and the Rise of the Marshals of Napoleon I* (Oxford, 1931) has a comprehensive treatment of Moncey's command of the Army of the Western Pyrenees. Similarly, Moncey's Peninsular campaigns are well covered in C. Oman, *A History of the Peninsular War* (Oxford, 1902), Vol. 1. The best treatment of his role in defense of Paris is H. Houssaye's *Napoleon and the Campaign of 1814* (London, 1914). For the reader of French, there are three biographies of Moncey. Two are contemporary with his death: General Ambert, *Notes sur le Maréchal Moncey* (Paris, 1842), and L. J. G. Chénier, *Éloge historique du Maréchal Moncey* (Paris, 1848). Neither is easy to find, and this applies equally to the best account of his career by the third Duke of Conegliano: C. A. G. Duchesne de Gillevoisin, *duc de Conegliano, Le Maréchal Moncey* (Paris, 1902).

CHRONOLOGY

1768, February 13	—Born at Cateau-Cambrésis (Nord); today Le Cateau
1789–1791	—Served with Dunkirk and Le Cateau National Guards
1791, September 6	—Elected captain in 1st Battalion, *Volontaires du Nord*
1792, April 28–30	—Saw first action at Quiévrain in Austrian Flanders
1793, October 15	—Wounded at Battle of Wattignies
1795, June 13	—Promoted staff colonel
1796, May–August	—Commanded advance guard (under Lefebvre) of *l'Armée de Sambre et Meuse*
1797, December 17–30	—Negotiated the surrender of Mainz
1798, January 4	—Promoted colonel of the 23rd Cavalry Regiment
1799, January 25	—Marries Anne-Eve Himmies at Koblenz
February 23	—Promoted *général de brigade*
September 25	—Promoted *général de division* by Massena at Zurich
1800, April 15	—Appointed to command 17th military division (Paris)
1803, May 3	—Made lieutenant-general for the occupation of Hanover
July 5	—Took the surrender of the Hanoverian Army on the Elbe
1804, February 2	—Made colonel-general of artillery, the Consular Guard
May 19	—Appointed *Maréchal d'Empire* (eleventh in seniority)
1805, November 7– December 13	—Commanded a corps north of the Danube; victor of Dürrenstein
December 15	—Commanded V Corps in Moravia and south Germany
1806, October 1	—Commanded VIII Corps in north Germany
1807, January 28	—Invaded Swedish Pomerania and blockades Stralsund
April 16–17	—Victor of Battle of Anclam
June 14	—Commanded left wing at Battle of Friedland
1808, July 2	—Created *duc de Trevise*
September 8	—Led V Corps in advance into Spain
1809, November 19	—Wounded at Battle of Ocaña
1812, June–December	—Commanded Young Guard in invasion of Russia
September 14– October 24	—Governor of Moscow
1813, February– November	—Commanded Young Guard in Germany
1814, January–April	—Commanded Old Guard in Campaign of France
June 21	—Appointed to command 16th military division (Lille)
1815, March	—Sends Louis XVIII into Belgium; rejoins Napoleon
June 14	—Appointed Guard cavalry commander, but falls ill
1816, January 10	—Appointed governor of 15th military division (Rouen)
October 4	—Elected a deputy for *Département du Nord*
1828, February 1	—Appointed a member of the Superior War Council
1830, December 6	—Appointed ambassador to Russia (and again in 1832)
1834, November 18	—Appointed minister of war and council president
1835, March 12	—Retired from public life
July 28	—Murdered by Fieschi's "infernal machine"

CHAPTER SEVENTEEN

THE BIG MORTAR

Mortier

by

Randal Gray

Early Service up to the Occupation of Hanover (1768–1804)

The tallest, most loyal, most generally liked, and the only English speaker or writer among the Napoleonic marshalate bore the names Adolphe-Édouard-Casimir-Joseph Mortier. Genial, unflamboyant, and not self-seeking, he was to give 46 years of service to France, as valuable in administration as in battle. Born on February 13, 1768, at Cateau-Cambrésis (now Le Cateau) in northwest France, the sixth child of the wealthy cloth merchant and farmer Charles Mortier and his English wife, Marie-Anne Joseph Bonnaire, Édouard Mortier was educated at the famous English College in Douai. There his future opponent at Saragossa, José Palafox, was a contemporary. Much later Mortier modestly and tantalizingly told an English officer prisoner, "I could have spoken it [English] tolerably: I resided in England a good deal while, when very young, I went there only to spend money for my father."[1]

Édouard was put into a Lille merchant's office but lost this job when he failed to do up the moneybags properly. The year of the Revolution called Charles Mortier to the States-General as deputy for Cateau-Cambrésis and enabled his younger son to join the Dunkirk National Guard. He soon transferred to his hometown's unit and, on September 6, 1791, at Cambrai was unanimously elected captain of the 6th Company in his uncle and godfather's, (François Mortier's), 1st Battalion, Volunteers of the North. The 23-year-old officer even received 10 votes standing for command of the battalion.

Captain Mortier's baptism of fire came in the very first fighting of 1792, at Quiévrain on the Belgian border. Leading Lieutenant-General de Biron's 10,000 men, his 550-man volunteer battalion took the frontier village on April 29, 1792, and defended it for some time during their column's panic-stricken rout next day. The Austrians killed Mortier's horse but did not cool the 6-foot 4-inch officer's revolutionary zeal. His company served at Jemappes and joined in taking Namur only to re-enter France after Dumouriez's defeat at Neerwinden. At the camp of Famars (May 23, 1793), Mortier held his position six hours longer than anyone else and got 150 men back to the main army.

Switched north to help relieve Dunkirk, Mortier's battalion attacked Esquelbecq on the Yser, taking a Hanoverian post and forcing their eventual retreat on September 6. Joining the Dunkirk garrison, they made two sorties against the Duke of York's besieging army during the Battle of Hondschoote on September 8. There, at Army of the North headquarters, Mortier received promotion to staff major dated September 3. His minimum regimental service of two years received a glowing testimonial from his brother officers.

The new staff officer reported to advance-guard headquarters on September 20, 1793, beginning notes of his daily movements from that date until April 15, 1800. Major Mortier led the miller Thibaut into Carnot's and Jourdan's council of war before Wattignies (October 15–16). During that victory he dismounted and calmly began to set fire to the village of Dourlers under Austrian musket fire that eventually wounded him. Staff duties clearly did not appeal, for he had requested transfer to the cavalry before the battle. However, General Antoine Balland kept his chief of staff: "Citizen Mortier being of the very greatest use through his activity and by his knowledge of the country . . . has an ardent patriotism, is very exact in carrying out his duties and an even higher qualification is the confidence he inspires in me."[2]

In April 1794 Mortier received a second wound, in the right leg, during vain efforts to break out beyond the Sambre. Balland's 13,400-strong division came under Kléber's command, and Mortier saw the decisive day of Fleurus (June 26), which soon took him through Brussels a second time. His staff-work contributed to Kléber's crossing the Meuse in bad weather to encircle Maestricht (September 28–29). During its three-week siege, Major Mortier was chief of staff for the attack on Fort St. Pierre, which succumbed to mining and bombardment.

That winter Mortier had his first leave and returning received promotion to colonel (June 13, 1795) in a year of much hardship and little action. It did, however, see the start of his lifelong friendship with Soult and featured a September Rhine crossing (although this ended in a retreat and armistice).

Hostilities resumed in May 1796 with Colonel Mortier leading the light infantry of Lefebvre's elite division, advance-guard to the whole Army of the Sambre and Meuse. Having been divisional chief of staff since October 1795, Mortier probably asked for a more active role from his fire-eating chief. He was to fight 15 times in three months. At Altenkirchen (June 4) he rode his horse *Le Favori* for the first time when 3,000 Austrians were taken prisoner in two hours. On June 16 he saved his detachment from capture.

By June 29 he was leading a small formation of all arms that became Lefebvre's central column at Wilnsdorf (July 4), where he charged through a Tyrolean battalion with a squadron of chasseurs.

After storming two villages in the Battle of Friedberg, Mortier negotiated the Austrian surrender of Frankfurt (July 14).

Schweinfurt fell to the young colonel's three battalions, three squadrons, and four four-pounders on July 22. Kléber wrote of the cavalry action at Hirscheid (August 6): "Adjutant General Mortier, who replaced General Richepanse, gave this day in the midst of the struggle proof of great sang-froid. With such leaders a general need not count the number of his enemies."[3] The next day Mortier's smaller force took only an hour to drive 1,500 Austrians out of Ebermannstädt.

The summer's successes ran out just when Mortier relieved General Ney's force in Nabburg. The colonel now took the rear guard, even finding himself temporarily commanding Lefebvre's division before it was last to recross the Rhine. Kléber chose Mortier to command the Neuwied bridgehead through the winter. Despite an armistice, leave "to settle his family affairs" did not begin until January 24, 1797, so he missed the year's brief Rhine campaign. Nonetheless, not only was Augereau, at Lefebvre's prompting, to name him commander of the 23rd Cavalry, but his next temporary commander in chief, Hatry, selected him to secure the surrender of Mainz, invested but untaken since September 1795. Within two weeks Mortier's diplomatic handling of the Elector yielded up the fortress to French occupation.

He took the news to Paris and the Directory gave him the 23rd Cavalry for 1798. They would have made him a general of brigade, but with unfashionable modesty he declined. Younger than all but three of his new officers, Édouard reluctantly obeyed Kléber's summons to join the Army of England. He spent two weeks in Paris only to discover that its real destination was Egypt and that he had missed his berth. Despite Kléber's regrets it was probably a blessing in disguise.

Almost a year's exacting but administratively satisfying cavalry duty still left the colonel time to court and marry 20-year-old Ann-Eve Himmies at Koblenz. Their February 1799 honeymoon at Cateau-Cambrésis was ended with the news of Mortier's promotion to general of brigade, aged 31. En route for the Army of the Danube, he gaily hailed Chasseur Dupuy, "This is the first dispatch I have received as general: dismount, and let us drink some brandy."[4] Mortier plunged into the fray at Stockach (March 25), leading Soult's advance guard, and the day left his "vedettes ten paces from the enemy's"[5], but the outcome was another retreat to the Rhine.

Nonetheless, General Mortier's activity during it earned him transfer to a brigade in Soult's new division under Massena in Switzerland. On August 26 he took over its command and was first to fight the Russians in this theater. "These famous soldiers do not intimidate us,"[6] he wrote to Lefebvre, and his 100th Demi-Brigade took Wollishofen with the bayonet on the night of Septcmbcr 8, killing or wounding 300 Russians. At the second Battle of Zurich, Rimski-Korsakov mauled his division, but thus fell deeper into Massena's trap, and a grateful commander in chief promoted Mortier general of division on the field.

The pursuit of Suvorov was to be sterner yet. It took all Mortier's efforts to check a rout on September 30, and the next day Prince Rosenberg drove his 3,000 men back in disorder, inflicting 817 casualties. His pursuit resumed only on October 3, yielding Suvorov's supposed carriage "a wretched trap not worth a crown."[7] Mortier felt the Alpine march on October 6 was "the most painful we have made in the war."[8] By October 31, despite all the obstacles, his brigade forced the Austrians across the Rhine, for which achievement he received the Directory's thanks and Massena's acknowledgment for "essential services."[9]

The new century began frustratingly. His mother's and a brother's deaths did not move General Lecourbe to grant leave despite three appeals. Mortier's preference for the Rhine rather than Italy meant he did not leave the 3rd Division and Switzerland until March 1800. He spent an unsanctioned week over family affairs at Cateau-Cambrésis, but while in Paris, expecting to go on to Italy, the First Consul appointed him commander of the capital (17th military division) on April 15, adding the 15th division (Rouen area) on April 21. Prompted by the outgoing Commander Lefebvre, Bonaparte was obviously impressed with Mortier's administrative talents, for he wrote during the Marengo campaign, "Thanks to your activity and surveillance, I am happy with Paris."[10]

For the next three years, General Mortier directed the capital's multifarious military business from six offices in the Rue des Capucines off Place Vendôme. His staff numbered 27 and the garrison increased from under 3,000 to nearly 24,000. He rejoiced at the peace and the transformations wrought by the First Consul. In July 1801 Mortier's suggestion of different ration scales for different types of cavalry horses was instituted.

His late but now close association with Bonaparte made him an automatic choice to seize the electorate of Hanover, England's only continental possession, when war resumed. Lieutenant-General Mortier left Paris at 1:00 A.M. on May 3, 1803, after going to the opera with the First Consul. At Nimeguen he concentrated 11,833 infantry, 1,732 cavalry, and 20 guns, warning them on May 16, the day England declared war, that "it is only discipline which prepares success and assures the fruits."[11] Berthier's orders stressed taking as many prisoners as possible to exchange for French sailors.

On May 30 Mortier invaded Hanover, marching 145 miles to the Weser in five days. His advance guard under Drouet fought two small skirmishes with a retreating 17,000-strong Hanoverian army. By the Convention of Suhlingen (June 4), it retired behind the Elbe and Mortier entered Hanover next day. To Berthier he frankly admitted the bluff involved: "At the moment the capitulation was signed, I was without bread, without the means of procuring it, without ambulances, having behind me a desert of 45 leagues separating me from Holland, all my infantry ammunition was reduced to 100 rounds a man."[12]

The lieutenant general's diplomacy was fully exercised after King George III's refusal to ratify the Convention of Suhlingen. From Lüneburg Mortier wrote to Field-Marshal Count Wallmoden, "It is evident, Field Marshal, that England unworthily sacrifices your troops whose bravery is known throughout Europe . . . but it is no less true that any defensive move . . . will be illusory and . . . [will] bring new evils on your country."[13] The capitulation of the Elbe was signed by the two commanders on July 5 aboard a raft in that river, a miniature foretaste of Tilsit.

Mortier's Army of Hanover, increased to 38,000 by troops from Holland, had obtained everything except taking the Hanoverian prisoners to France. On July 21 he reported demobilization complete with 14,000 muskets, 80 guns, and 3,867 horses in his hands. He governed Hanover from the Duke of Cambridge's hotel until February 1804, keeping the civil administration under a five-man Hanoverian executive council and refusing to make his own army responsible for getting its pay. He obtained loans from neighboring German states to ease the burden of its two million-franc monthly upkeep, likewise obtaining cavalry remounts rather than remove yet more horses from the electorate. A 1,000-strong French Hanoverian Legion existed by the time he left. Although an occupier and an exploiter under orders, he was popular. Madame Mortier received a farewell poem of thanks from two Hanoverian ladies and certainly the electorate had cause to compare him favorably with later governors.

It signaled Bonaparte's satisfaction with Mortier's first active independent command ("You have struck a deadly blow at England.")[14] that he was recalled to be one of the four generals commanding the Consular Guard, and its artillery at that. The imperial baton that soon followed in May 1804 was recognition for steady, often thankless service in more than just combat and his ability to speak English. "Any officer would be proud to serve under him!"[15] wrote an Englishman who had met him during the Peace of Amiens. At age 36 Édouard Mortier was younger than all save five of his 17 colleagues. He and Sérurier were the only marshals to come from north of Paris. His father typically commented, "Tell him to continue to be an honest man."[16] Édouard's income was already four times his parent's.

Corps and Imperial Guard Commander (1804-1815)

It spoke volumes for Mortier's imperial allegiance that his first son (born August 7, 1804) was named Napoleon. The new marshal accompanied his Emperor to the Channel invasion ports, the Rhine, and Italy. For that last visit he began a second daily journal (May 10, 1805) that would be kept until 1820, and before leaving presided at his father's nomination to the Senate.

Mortier embarked the Imperial Guard with 10 days of rations in 154 craft amid the Army of England at Boulogne on August 21, 1805, the nearest he ever again got to his mother's homeland. A week later the guns were disembarked and Napoleon instructed Mortier to have the 5,500-strong Guard at Strasbourg within a month. He did so. But while Bessières led the troops, he remained on the imperial staff, a mere spectator to the Ulm campaign. Mortier's chance at last came on November 6. The astonishing Battle of Dürrenstein (see p. 325) was to remedy his lack of action since 1799.

Mortier garrisoned Vienna from November 19 until after Austerlitz whence came 10,000 Russian prisoners for escort across the city. On December 11 he took over Lannes's V Corps at Brünn, occupying Moravia up to the armistice line and evacuating it in January 1806. Garrison and occupation duties in south Germany followed, under Bernadotte's command. They often stayed together and went hunting. Bernadotte replied to congratulations on his princedom, "Nobody is more your friend."[17] Mortier was recalled to Paris on September 9 and departed with Napoleon for the Prussian war on the twenty-fifth.

This time Mortier was to have a command. VIII Corps, formed at Mainz from October 1 to cover the Rhine confederation, lacked cavalry, staff, administration, and even the marshal's own horses. Mortier appointed Empress Josephine's elderly father as second aide-de-camp. Jena–Auerstädt enabled him to advance from Frankfurt with just 5,500 light infantry and 6 guns, enough to occupy Hesse–Cassel and disarm the elector's 20,000-strong army on November 1. Mortier confidently reentered Hanover on November 11, a day ahead of his troops, and found that "the Prussians are generally detested."[18] Still having only 150 Dutch cavalry, he occupied Hamburg with Dupas's division on November 19. All English-made goods were requisitioned and English bankers sent prisoner to Verdun. Mortier and the French consul Bourrienne persuaded Napoleon to keep the Bank of Hamburg open.

After VIII Corps occupied Schwerin and Mecklenburg, the Emperor wrote, "I do not disdain, in the chances of fortune, 16,000 men commanded by you."[19] In fact, Mortier could concentrate only 8,900 men at Anclam on December 12 to watch Stralsund and Sweden's German province of Pomerania. His corps, lacking food, shoes, and greatcoats, overstretched between the Baltic and the Weser, might still have to reinforce the Grand Army. On January 20, 1807, Mortier received orders to invade and take Stralsund by March 1.

Anticipating normal winter ice for occupying Rugen Island and 36 siege guns from Stettin, Mortier invaded on January 28. After two successful skirmishes, he reached Stralsund on the thirtieth. Try as he might, the marshal could not obtain the guns. "The time we lose here is precious," he wrote on February 10. "It is truly terrible that the season has been so mild."[20] Supported by 20 gunboats, General Baron Essen's 15,000 Swedish troops made dozens of sorties, nearly all unsuccessful, but from March 5 Mortier lost three regiments to make good the losses of Eylau.

To crown his frustrations the marshal was authorized to conclude a truce, was told Stralsund was never meant to be taken, and was sent instead to besiege stubborn Colberg, held by Prussia's Gneisenau. In the week he did so, Essen sortied and drove Grandjean's covering division to Stettin. Mortier returned hot foot with 13,000 men, including Dutch and Italian troops. Throughout April 16–17 he attacked Essen relentlessly in constant hail and rain, taking 1,052 prisoners and six guns. This running Battle of Anclam left Essen ready to negotiate and by the twenty-ninth they had a satisfactory armistice.

Mortier's corps was now free for the Siege of Danzig's last week. At Friedland VIII Corps, reinforced to 18,000 men by Dombrowski's Polish division, helped Lannes sustain the morning's delaying action and then, as left wing formation in the evening, to pin down 40,000 Russians. Mortier had a horse killed under him, and the reward for this first battle under Napoleon was the governorship of Silesia. A pleasant 14 months, in which his family joined, saw him created Duke of Treviso (July 2, 1808) with an income of 100,000 francs fittingly drawn from Hanover's electoral lands.

In September 1808 the Duke departed with the veteran V Corps for Spain. His largest force yet, 21,000 infantry, 1,500 cavalry, and 30 guns, joined with Moncey's III Corps in beginning Saragossa's second siege on December 20. Alone of the 16 peninsular marshals, Mortier was to experience hardly a reverse, let alone a defeat. Much hard work (for which his superior and old friend Soult took the credit and profit) was the Duke of Treviso's. At Saragossa V Corps covered the siege with Suchet's division and so avoided its worst horrors, suffering perhaps one-fifth of the 10,000 French casualties. In any case, as Mortier admitted to

Berthier, Lannes "nearly always"[21] gave orders direct to his officers without telling him. The city's cathedral clergy offered the marshal a diamond flower worth 100,000 francs, but he quietly returned it to the church.

After Talavera, Mortier's caution missed a fleeting chance to attack the retreating allies, but his treatment of 1,500 English wounded left there earned Wellesley's letter of thanks.[22] At Arzobispo (August 8, 1809) his troops crossed the Tagus to maul the Spanish rear guard. V Corps formed 40% of Soult's strength for winning Ocaña (November 19). Grapeshot slightly wounded the marshal in the arm. He led one of four columns overrunning Andalusia during January 1810.

On February 12 Mortier, with 9,000 men, summoned Badajoz to surrender, but 13,000 Spanish troops were too close and he got no reinforcements. The duke won three more actions that year but lacked the strength to reinvade Estremadura until January 1811. He successfully summoned Olivenza for Soult after an 11-day siege, and they again advanced to Badajoz. Mortier identified the dangerous Spanish sortie on February 7 and sent four battalions to help repulse it. On February 19 Soult gave him tactical command of the Battle of the Gebora in which 7,000 men and 12 guns forded that river on a foggy morning. The duke of Treviso synchronized a surprise cavalry flank attack with an infantry frontal assault on the San Christobal heights. The 12,400-strong Spanish relief army lost 5,000 men and all 17 guns in the rout. Mortier's 403 casualties represented the war's most cost-effective French victory.

Badajoz fell on March 10, Mortier being left to exploit its capture. On the fourteenth, the marshal's 7,000 men marched 9 miles to besiege the Portuguese fortress of Campo Mayor the same day. He took it in a week before Marshal Beresford's Anglo–Portuguese army appeared. And on March 25 Mortier neatly sortied from Badajoz with 2,500 men to rescue his siege train and General Latour-Maubourg's escort from Beresford's pursuing cavalry. A recall to Paris had already come, but it is interesting to speculate whether Mortier would have swayed Soult's Battle of Albuera.

Mortier was recalled for the year-long task of recruiting, organizing, and training the Young Guard for the invasion of Russia. It took him as far as Lyons, Nîmes, Avignon, and the tip of Holland.

On the long march to Moscow, Mortier's 17,700-strong Young Guard helped bridge the Dvina and lost one man in seven to tropical heat, desertion, scanty rations, and fatigue. No wonder the marshal lost his usual cheerfulness: "From the Niemen to the Vilia I have seen nothing but ruined houses and abandoned carts. . . . Ten thousand horses have been killed already by the cold rains and by eating unripe rye. . . . The smell . . . is perfectly horrible. But that is not so bad as the shortness of rations. Several of my Young Guard have already starved to death."[23]

At Borodino Mortier's three divisions stood watching the slaughter; their commander is not recorded as having joined the vain appeals to commit his force, but he was soon thereafter in bitter dispute with Murat over the conduct of the pursuit. A week later Napoleon appointed him governor of Moscow: "Above all, no looting! You will answer for it to me with your head. Defend Moscow against all comers."[24] Employing at least two Franco–Russian interpreters, the duke did all he could to stop the looting and fires (he had to move quarters five times), as well as collect supplies.

On October 18 the Emperor left his governor, 8,500 men, and 49 guns in the capital with orders to blow up the Kremlin. The duke lamented, "Why me rather than another?"[25] Obediently his sappers dug 183,000 pounds of gunpowder under the Kremlin and Mortier stayed to see the detonations in the early hours of October 24. Rain wet the fuses and so spoiled the full effect. Nor was the Lubianka Palace demolished: "Had Mortier wanted to spare one of the few untouched districts and the Church of Saint-Louis-des Francais?"[26] The Young Guard carriages took all but 400–500 of the wounded, and after eight days on his own the marshal rejoined the main retreat. Mortier survived on biscuits and brandy, taken with horse's liver and snow on November 8. That day he also asked a sentry in to share his fire.

At Krasnöe, to extricate Davout's corps on November 17, Mortier promised Napoleon, "Sire, I shall hold the enemy back throughout the day."[27] His 5,000-strong Young Guard, deployed in two long lines rather than three, fought their first full battle in knee-deep snow as he promised retiring "at an ordinary pace." On the west bank of the Berezina, down to 1,500 men, Mortier helped drive off 34,000 Russians from the Grand Army's path, losing half his survivors. Told of Napoleon's imminent departure for France, the marshal calmly informed his divisional general, Delaborde, "A most unexpected event is about to occur, but in my opinion a necessary one. Let us resign ourselves and not be discouraged."[28]

An undiscouraged marshal was rare enough to be back in Paris on February 1, 1813, and a fortnight later training the new 1st Young Guard Division at Frankfurt. Within 11 weeks Mortier led General Dumoustier's 10,000 men in four four-battalion columns to deliver the decisive attack on Lützen. The marshal was pinned under a wounded horse during Kaja's storming, but for 1,069 casualties "the Young Guard has fulfilled our expectations."[29] (Napoleon). It was the same at Bautzen after which Mortier narrowly escaped the Russian cannonball that killed Duroc.

During the summer armistice the duke was back in Silesia forming the 32,000-strong Young Guard into four divisions. He proposed Napoleon's forty-fourth birthday toast in Dresden and ran a shooting competition with lavish prizes. Mortier's elite force, having marched 125 miles in four days, stopped the allied right at the city gates, and the next morning, with Ney, drove it relentlessly back in pouring rain. The Guard suffered a fifth of the French casualties. Justly or not, Mortier and St.-Cyr were blamed for failing to save Vandamme's I Corps at Gross Beeren later in the campaign.

After Dresden Oudinot took over half the Young Guard, but Mortier led his two divisions into Leipzig. The first day almost repeated Dresden. Seeing enemy cavalry, Mortier formed 3,000 men of the 7th and 8th *Tirailleurs* into squares, shouting, "Don't make a sound, and don't fire until orders."[30] They stopped the horsemen at 50 paces. That night Napoleon ordered Mortier's command back to secure and increase (by 30) the Elster bridges. They led the retreat, a model one until the Lindenau bridge was prematurely blown, by then Oudinot's responsibility. The two marshals alternated as rear guard, marching at night and combining at Eisenach to check the Prussian pursuit before the Thuringian defiles. Mortier detoured around hostile Hanau using a route he knew from 1796 and reached Mainz.

Late in November he recrossed the Rhine and, at Trier, began again reforming the Young Guard. Madame Mortier and his children joined him at the Bishop's Palace. The Prussian invasion of Holland took Mortier and the 6,000-strong Old Guard north to Belgium. In driving snow they entered Namur on December 26: "There was Marshal Mortier, sword in hand, his roan charger almost hidden by the voluminous skirts of his greatcoat. His eyes were large and keen under arched eyebrows and he had a straight nose, thin lips, and a firm chin. His greying hair receded from the temples. All his features radiated vigour as well as tact and kindness."[31] He was 45.

Alone of the marshals, Mortier did not despair and obeyed Napoleon's orders in January 1814. His 1st Old Guard Division marched 200 miles in 15 days to save Langres from Schwarzenberg's Army of Bohemia. By brilliant delaying actions, the largest in fog on January 24 at Bar-sur-Aube with 13,000 men and 12 guns, he kept the enemy out of Champagne until Napoleon himself took the field. Mortier continued to contain Schwarzenberg while the Emperor struck at Blücher and then arrived at Montmirail with 9,500 Old Guard to turn the battle in Napoleon's favor. Mortier joined Marmont on February 26. Reinforced to 16,500 men, they won four successive days of fighting against Blücher's Army of Silesia on the Ourcq. Only Soissons's premature surrender allowed the enemy to escape. Mortier's hat was shot through during a vain March 5 recapture attempt.

At Craonne and still more at Laon, Mortier's 6,000 Guards fought flawlessly, a Young Guard company getting nearest the latter town. Afterward his command took its final form of three Guard infantry divisions (8,500 men), 2,480 dragoons and light cavalry with 30 guns. Marmont had only 5,800 line troops, yet Napoleon gave the junior marshal command of their containing operations against Blücher. Berthier blithely told Marmont on March 19, "You will concert and direct the movements, without upsetting the Duke of Treviso. Keep up the appearance of agreeing with him."[32] It was a recipe for discord. Late on March 18 Mortier reluctantly obeyed Marmont's summons to evacuate Rheims and join him. The two marshals met next morning and Mortier won his argument to return, but 5,000–6,000 Russians could not be dislodged from Rheims and so the allied armies could make their fatal junction unopposed.

Napoleon's March 20 orders required the two marshals to join him even if not via Rheims. Mortier's troops marched 62½ miles in 60 hours only to lose all their guns and worse than one man in three to the allied cavalry before La Fère-Champenoise (March 25). Marmont's memoirs blame Mortier for late arrival, but the duke of Ragusa stood to fight at seven-to-one odds on cavalry terrain, still unconvinced that the allied objective was Paris. Late on March 29 the two marshals reconnoitered the capital's slender outer defenses as their troops still approached.

At daybreak Mortier was in a 24-pounder gun redoubt at La Villette, telling his staff: "We have not enough troops to resist their large armies for long; but today, more than ever before, we are fighting for our honour. We must think first of Paris and hold our advance positions as long as we can." Through his telescope he saw 20 cossacks coming down the Le Bourget road and ordered the first shot in Paris' defense since 1652: "Gunners, let us see if your big piece caught cold last night."[33] Mortier's 6,500 men could not reach their positions until 8:00 A.M. on the thirtieth, but they fought for eight hours against up to 30,000 Russians and Prussians before retiring unit by unit into the city.

Although both marshals were authorized to negotiate by Joseph Bonaparte, Marmont did not so inform his colleague from 4:00 P.M. A little later Napoleon's aide-de-camp, General Pierre Dejean, prompted Mortier to send his chief of staff to Schwarzenberg, only to return with a demand for unconditional surrender. Eventually Mortier joined Marmont's peace talks for a half-hour or hour in the Petit Jardinet Café near La Villette gate. He left, saying, "I leave Marshal Marmont to continue the negotiations, and to decide as he may think best. As for me, I am obliged to take steps for the defence of Paris."[34] That meant evacuating his troops across the Seine to join Napoleon, and it was Mortier's cavalry under General Belliard that the Emperor met 10 miles from Paris. Marmont signed the capital's surrender at 2:00 A.M., still invoking his senior colleague's name.

By April 4 Mortier, unlike his Emperor, suspected Marmont enough to leave his aide-de-camp, Captain Paul de Bourgoing, at VI Corps headquarters. Bourgoing reported its defection at 5:00 A.M. on April 5 and Mortier sent him forthwith to Fontainebleau with assurances "of my constant loyalty and the devotion of the Young Guard." Napoleon's thanks ended significantly: "Tell him we shall fight no more."[35] The Duke of Treviso was not present at the abdication and said a proper farewell to his ex-sovereign.

The day after giving his allegiance to the new regime (April 8), he wrote to his sister, Victoire:

> The Emperor Napoleon must go to Elba. . . . I shall probably accompany him. If I can be of any use I shall go with pleasure. We hope the peace will last. Having done my duty as an honourable man, I have no anxiety for myself. . . . So long as my wife and children have bread and are happy, I care little what happens to me. . . . We have been sitting on top of a volcano. When I was summoned to Fontainebleau [on April 4] my troops came near to deserting. . . . Calm was restored only on my return.

A postscript added:

> Everyone is trying to feather his own nest. I desire only to preserve my honour and merit the esteem of friends and foes alike. All my colleagues have been pushing themselves forward.[36]

By June 21, 1814, having disbanded the Young Guard, the marshal was a Chevalier of St. Louis, a peer of France, and governor of the 16th military division at Lille in his home region. Mortier quashed Count Drouet d'Erlon's attempt to take the city's 16,000-strong garrison to Napoleon in early March 1815 by arresting his subordinate on the road. Ignoring Davout's repeated orders to arrest the Bourbons, he did not end his royal allegiance until Louis XVIII had left France via Lille and gave his staff freedom of choice. Both sides found his conduct impeccable. Napoleon greeted him in the Tuileries with "Ah! Here you are, Monsieur le Blanc."[37]

On April 29 the Emperor sent him on a special month-long and grueling inspection tour of the frontier fortresses and National Guard from Calais to Landau. On June 9 Mortier took command of the 4,000-strong Imperial Guard cavalry at Soissons. In pouring rain late on June 14, walking with difficulty, the duke of Treviso chose camps for the Guard artillery, field hospital, and train.

It was Napoleon's intention to give him the Young Guard again, when three divisions strong, but Mortier's journal explains why he missed Waterloo:

> The attacks of sciatica that began at Strasbourg have increased daily in severity. During the night of the 14th I had violent pains accompanied by chills and all next day I was confined to bed. M. Percy examined me and warned me that this would continue for 40 days. Since I could not possibly mount a horse, I sent my regrets to the Chief of Staff [Soult] for my inability . . . to share the glory and dangers of the Army. . . . I left Beaumont on the 16th.[38]

He had sold two of his fine chargers to Marshal Ney on June 15. From Napoleon on St. Helena onward, it has been said that Mortier would not have let the Prince of the Moscova ruin them or the Guard cavalry against Wellington's squares on June 18.

Politics, Family, and State Duties (1815–1835)

On July 1, 1815, Mortier was among the 10 marshals invited by Davout to give the provisional government military advice before Paris' second surrender. Reluctantly roped in to try Marshal Ney, he prevented anonymous letters being read to the court and told Ney's defense counsel that he would become a farm laborer rather than condemn his client. If the military court had convicted him, Mortier's written withdrawal from it was already in his pocket.[39] The October death of his second son, Édouard, grieved him more than all 1815's upheavals.

Although the marshal's ducal title and decorations were not restored until 1819, the 15th military division (Rouen) was again his in January 1816. In October he was handsomely elected to the Chamber of Deputies for the North Department. Estates at Plessis–Lalande and his stud farm (both near Cateau-Cambrésis), established in 1805, took up much time. Caroline Mortier, his firstborn, married a marquis in 1819, and two of his other three daughters found counts for husbands. The Mortier masculine line died out only in 1946 with the fifth duke.

In 1826 Mortier delivered the funeral oration for his younger colleague Suchet, once his divisional commander in V Corps. The

Duke of Treviso fittingly carried the hand of justice royal insignia during the coronations of Charles X and Louis Philippe. The latter had known him since the 1792–1793 campaigns and showed special favor. Twice ambassador to Russia (1830 and 1832), the marshal loyally stepped into the 1834–1835 political vacuum as both president of the council and minister of war. He served less than four months before thankfully retiring, no rival to Soult or Wellington in high politics.

At age 67 peaceful retirement with a growing number of grandchildren was not to be his. On July 28, 1835, the marshal rode behind Louis Philippe in the National Guard review as he had insisted, despite his family's warnings. Soon after noon he fell dead, shot in the left ear, one of 18 to be murdered by the volley from the Corsican terrorist Fieschi's "infernal machine" of 25 rifles at No. 50 Boulevard de Temple. The Citizen King survived and continued his review. A week later he tearfully said, "Goodbye, my old friend," over the marshal's coffin in Les Invalides.[40]

Mortier was more than a good corps commander or an ideal subordinate, "the big mortar with a short range,"[41] as Bonaparte punningly called him in 1800. Seldom given independent command for long or with many troops, he consistently showed his unfulfilled potential in Germany (1796, 1803, 1805–1807), Spain (1810), Russia (1812), and France (1814). He still achieved results with small forces and successfully administered conquered territories. From 1802 he only had five chiefs of staff, the last (General Delapointe) being an aide-de-camp from Hanover onward. As a trainer, disciplinarian, administrator, and particularly carer for horses, he was ahead of most of his colleagues. As an honest and modest human being, Mortier surpassed them all.

The Battle of Dürrenstein (November 11, 1805)

Mortier's journal describes his bloodiest and most dramatic battle in a single laconic sentence: "On November 11 memorable affair against the Russians near Stein; the 4th Light, 100th and 103rd Line Regiments hold off 25,000 Russians and they open, in the evening, a passage through their ranks."[42] Only four days earlier he had taken command at Linz of an ad hoc corps strung out north of the Danube.

The idea was Murat's, and Mortier came under his orders to forestall the Russians by reaching Krems first. On paper the marshal had over 15,000 men and 23 guns, but on November 6 two of his three divisions (each from different corps) were starting from Passau not Linz. There was no corps staff and only 11 boats to keep in touch with the main army on the south bank. And Mortier never was clear if General Klein's dragoon division on his left flank came under his command or not. By November 10 Klein was out of touch, having reluctantly left the 4th Dragoons as Mortier's only cavalry.

Nonetheless the marshal made good progress along the narrow, winding river road with the 5,500 infantry (nine battalions) of Gazan's division. He used his 11 boats to embark two regiments and three guns on the Danube, landing them near Dürrenstein[43] at 3:00 P.M. on November 10. The dragoons and 103rd Line Regiment reached the walled town that evening. There was no intelligence from the inhabitants and only scattered enemy parties visible. Mortier knew from Soult only that some Russians had crossed at Krems with artillery on the ninth. It was Kutuzov who learned from sore-footed French prisoners, captured when they disobeyed orders and landed to forage from the boats beyond Dürrenstein, that Mortier was pursuing with one division only.

At 8:00 A.M. the 4th Light Infantry was attacked by a heavy Russian column (Miloradovitch's 16 battalions) from Stein, which Mortier still hoped to take that day. Snow lay on the ground and it was bitter cold. The marshal had confidence in Gazan, a general of division from the same battle against the Russians as himself (Zurich, 1799). Over a third of his line infantry had at least 10 years of service, including Hanover under Mortier, and two-thirds had seen action before 1805.[44] Leaving one battalion and the three guns to cover Dürrenstein, Mortier counterattacked with five battalions of the 100th (veterans of Zurich) and 103rd Regiments. Three times the villages of Ober and Unter Loiben were taken and retaken until Gazan stormed a plateau above them, taking four guns and 400 prisoners. Miloradovitch was pushed back almost to Stein.

In Mortier's words, "Towards 2:00 P.M. , the firing diminished sensibly in all quarters, the affair appeared to be entirely ended; I proposed . . . to remain in my new positions until the arrival of . . . Dupont and Dumonceau [divisions] . . . whom I have given the order to force march to rejoin me."[45] Two hours later the marshal had lost Dürrenstein to Doctorov's outflanking column descending late from the mountains. And he soon galloped back with escorting dragoons from a vain effort to reach Dupont. Gazan's division was surrounded, cut off from the Danube and running short of ammunition. One cartridge-less company stood the enemy's fire for 1½ hours.

At this juncture Mortier called together his senior officers to propose a breakout. Major François Henriod of the 100th offered to lead his grenadiers seven abreast down the narrow road, and

the troops shouted that "they were not the soldiers of Ulm."[46]
Mortier and Gazan rode between the first two battalion columns
in this unstoppable bayonet charge. The heroic division stabbed
its way to, through, and beyond Dürrenstein, eventually linking
up with Dupont.

That commander had halted at Spitz during the afternoon
lull but sent on light troops. They were found at grips with 6,000
Russians. After nearly an hour's fighting here, 400 Russians flung
themselves into the Danube. Firing ceased around 9:00 P.M.
Loiben village, set alight by the Russians, had blazed in the darkness, consuming both sides' wounded.

Mortier had personally to cut down tall Russians in his way
out of a trap born of Murat's preoccupation with Vienna and the
Emperor's lax supervision. All the next day, while Vienna fell, the
marshal ferried his weary survivors back across the Danube. On
November 13 he recrossed at Spitz and reoccupied Dürrenstein,
but Kutuzov had gained two days on his pursuers. Mortier took
1,200 Russian wounded at Stein and Krems with another 132
prisoners in his pursuit lasting until the eighteenth when Gazan
and Dupont were ordered to Vienna and completely replaced
by Bernadotte's I Corps.

Mortier had been "exposed to bear all the Russians' efforts
and ought to [have been] crushed."[47] He had been given inadequate orders, communications, or cavalry and artillery. Yet
veteran troops, "his eyes and his thoughts fixed on all points of
the field of battle,"[48] had produced a tactical victory over four-
fold odds. For his probable 2,300 casualties (only 106 were
Dupont's), including perhaps 1,000 prisoners, Mortier estimated
the Russian loss at 6,000, including five guns, two flags, and
700–800 prisoners.[49] The marshal declined busts to himself in
Cambrai or Cateau-Cambrésis; he replied that he owed the day
to his troops' valor.

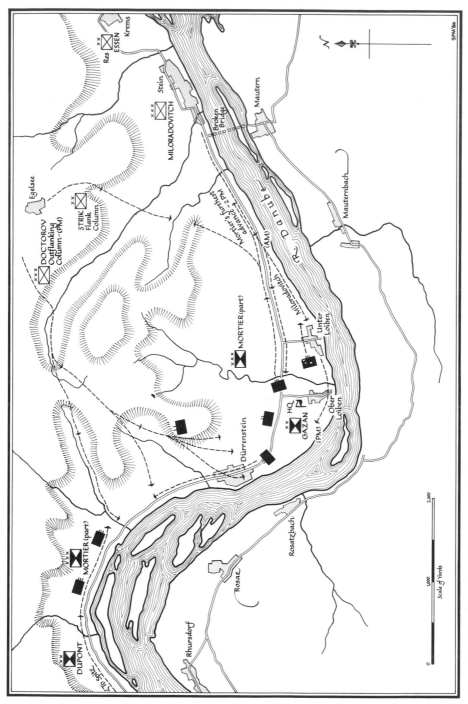

Map 17. The Battle of Dürrenstein, November 11, 1805.

TEXTUAL REFERENCES

1. R. W. Phipps, *The Armies of the First French Republic and the Rise of the Marshals of Napoleon I* (Oxford, 1926), Vol. 1, p. 80.
2. General Balland to minister of war, December 13, 1793, quoted by F. Despréaux, *Le Maréchal Mortier*, (Paris, 1913), Vol. 1, p. 170.
3. General Kléber to Directory, August 7, 1796, in *ibid.*, p. 345.
4. Phipps, *op. cit.*, Vol. 5, p. 39.
5. Despréaux, *op. cit.*, Vol. 2, p. 59.
6. Mortier to Lefebvre, August 16, 1799, in *ibid.*, p. 100.
7. Mortier to Soult, October 3, 1799, in *ibid.*, p. 140.
8. Mortier, *Notes*, October 6, 1799, in *ibid.*, p. 144.
9. Massena to Mortier, November 29, 1799, in *ibid.*, p. 163.
10. Bonaparte to Mortier from Aosta, May 24, 1800, in *ibid.*, p. 196. Napoleon told Caulaincourt on April 16, 1814, before leaving for Elba, that Mortier was "an honest man, incapable of intrigue; I sized up his character in Paris during the Consulate." *Memoirs of General Caulaincourt, Duke of Vicenza*, (London, 1938), Vol. 2, p. 363.
11. Mortier general order, May 16, 1803, in Despréaux, *op. cit.*, Vol. 2, p. 292.
12. Mortier to Berthier, June 8, 1803, in *ibid.*, p. 329.
13. Mortier to Field-Marshal Count Wallmoden, June 30, 1803, in *ibid.*, p. 354.
14. Bonaparte to Mortier from Bruges, July 11, 1803, in *ibid.*, p. 374.
15. British officer comment, quoted by R. F. Delderfield, *The March of the Twenty-Six: The Story of Napoleon's Marshals* (London, 1962), p. 130.
16. Charles Mortier's remark at home in Cateau during May 1804, in Despréaux, *op. cit.*, Vol. 1, p. 5.
17. Bernadotte to Mortier, June 14, 1806, in *ibid.*, Vol. 3, p. 221.
18. Mortier to Ney in Magdeburg, November 12, 1806, in *ibid.*, p. 293.
19. Napoleon to Mortier from Posen, November 29, 1806, in *ibid.*, p. 334.
20. Mortier to General Thouvenot (Governor of Stettin), February 10, 1807, in *ibid.*, p. 386.
21. Mortier to Berthier, March 20, 1809, in *ibid.*, Vol. 1, p. 8.
22. Wellesley to Mortier, August 22, 1809, in Lieutenant-Colonel Gurwood, ed., *The Dispatches of Field Marshal the Duke of Wellington* (London, 1838), Vol. 5, p. 74.
23. Quoted by A. G. Macdonnell, *Napoleon and His Marshals* (London, 1934), p. 240.
24. Napoleon to Mortier, September 14, 1812, quoted in Daria Olivier, *The Burning of Moscow 1812* (London, 1966), p. 52.
25. Mortier as originally quoted by E. F. Berthèzene, *Souvenirs militaires de la République et de l'Empire*, published by his son (Paris, 1855).
26. Olivier, *op. cit.*, p. 183.
27. H. Lachouque and A. S. K. Brown, *The Anatomy of Glory: Napoleon and His Guard* (London, 1961), p. 257.
28. *Ibid.*, p. 265.
29. *Ibid.*, p. 294.
30. *Ibid.*, p. 315, quoting P. de Bourgoing, *Souvenirs militaires 1791–1815* (Paris, 1897).
31. Lachouque and Brown, *op. cit.*, p. 333, quoting J. Delhaize, *La Domination Française en Belgique* (Brussels, 1912), Vol. 6, p. 152.
32. Marshal Marmont, *Memoires* (Paris, 1857), Vol. 6, p. 328.
33. Lachouque and Brown, *op. cit.*, p. 396, quoting de Bourgoing, *op. cit.*, n. 30.
34. H. Houssaye, *Napoleon and the Campaign of 1814* (London, 1914), p. 425.
35. Lachouque and Brown, *op. cit.*, p. 407, quoting de Bourgoing, *op. cit.*, n. 30.
36. Lachouque and Brown, *op. cit.*, p. 411, and partially in Despréaux, *op. cit.*, Vol. 1, p. 9.
37. Despréaux, *op. cit.*, Vol. 1, p. 10; anecdote from the author's father, Mortier's nephew.

38. Lachouque and Brown, *op. cit.,* p. 475.
39. André Dupin *Memoires de M. Dupin* (Paris, 1855), Vol. 1, pp. 34–36. Dupin had acted for Mortier in civil cases before 1815.
40. T. E. B. Howarth, *Citizen King: The Life of Louis Philippe King of the French* (London, 1961), pp. 232–34. A statue of the marshal (unveiled September 16, 1838) stands in the main square of Le Cateau. Mortier's wife died in 1855.
41. Lieutenant-General Baron Thiébault, *Memoirs,* English ed. (London, 1896), Vol. 2, p. 54. Thiébault heard this at a Tuileries audience with the first consul in late 1800 at which Bonaparte was blaming Mortier for stagecoach robberies (despite military escorts) outside Paris. The phrase later became a Grand Army joke.
42. Mortier, *Journal,* in Despréaux, *op. cit.,* Vol. 3, p. 97.
43. Diernstein (the French pronunciation and spelling), Dürnstein, and Dirnstein are all variations. King Richard the Lionheart of England was kept prisoner there by the duke of Austria in 1191. The battle is sometimes known as the Action of Krems.
44. Figures taken from Captain Alombert, *Le Corps d'Armée aux ordres du Maréchal Mortier: Combat du Dürrenstein* (Paris, 1897); see Annexe II, parts V and VIII, at the end of the book, for notes and statistics on the regiments.
45. Mortier to Berthier from Vienna, November 26, 1805, in Despréaux, *op. cit.,* Vol. 3, p. 104.
46. *Ibid.,* p. 104.
47. *Ibid.,* p. 119, quoting Napoleon's order to Murat of 7:00 A.M., November 11, 1805, from Melk Abbey.
48. *Ibid.,* p. 109, quoting Colonel Talandier, *Relation de la bataille de Diernstein* (Strasbourg, 1835).
49. Despréaux, *op. cit.,* Vol. 3, pp. 103, 105–6. French casualties are often given as 3,000, but a comparison of Gazan's division's strengths (November 1 and 22) in Alombert, *op. cit.,* n. 44, yields the figure of 2,300, which is also Talandier's estimate. Russian losses are often given as only 4,000, but Mortier was seldom prone to exaggeration and his estimate includes 1,500–2,000 Russians scattered in the mountains.

BIBLIOGRAPHICAL NOTE

Colonel Frignet Despréaux's *Le Maréchal Mortier,* 3 vols. (Paris, 1913–20) is a monumental, exhaustively documented biography by the marshal's great nephew, complete with maps picking out in red Mortier's daily itinerary, but unfortunately goes only up to the end of March 1807. It draws on the Duke of Treviso's archives, the national and war ministry collections, as well as family tradition. Léon Moreel's *Le Maréchal Mortier duc de Trevise* (Paris, 1958) is a one-volume popular life with more illustrations, ordered but unhappily not obtained by this contributor.

General Charles de Cosse-Brissac, "Le Maréchal Mortier pendant la Campagne de Russie 1812," in *La Cohorte, Société d'Entr'aide de la Legion d'Honneur,* 1974, includes his role as governor of Moscow. Percy Cross Standing, "Marshal Mortier and the Cavalry Arm," in *The Cavalry Journal* No. 74 (1929), pp. 648–656 belies its title by being a very inaccurate account of his life. The limelight was seldom on this reticent marshal, so many anecdotes about him have to be quarried from memoirs and more general works of the period.

On the Dürrenstein campaign, there is Captain Alombert's *Le Corps d'Armée aux ordres du Maréchal Mortier: Combat du Dürrenstein* (Paris, 1897), a record in documents of November 7–19, 1805. It has many fascinating details of officers, divisions, and units under Mortier's command as well as the Danube flotilla, but missed the marshal's own reports, which are in Despréaux's work.

CHRONOLOGY

1767, March 25	—Born in La Bastide, department of Lot
1787, February 23	—Joined the army
1792, April 29	—First appointed non-commissioned officer
October 15	—First appointed officer
1795, October 4	—First met Napoleon
1796, May 10	—Promoted *général de brigade*
April 14	—Led his first cavalry charge
1799, July 25	—Battle of Aboukir
August 2	—Confirmed as *général de division*
1800, January 18	—Married Caroline Bonaparte
1801, September 11	—Army commander in Italy
January 21	—Achille Charles Louis Napoleon Murat born
1802, April 24	—Marie Laetitia Josephine Annunziade Murat born
1803, May 16	—Napoleon Lucien Charles Francois Murat born
1804, May 19	—Appointed *Maréchal d'Empire* (second in seniority); awarded the Collar of the Legion of Honor
July 13	—Governor General of Paris
1805, March 22	—Louise Julie Caroline Murat (fourth and last child) born
August 28	—Lieutenant of the Emperor
1808, February 20	—Appointed Lieutenant of the Emperor in Spain
July 15	—King of Naples
October 16	—Captures Capri
1812, December 4	—Lieutenant-general of *la Grande Armée*
1814, January 11	—Treaty with the allies; commander of the 7th Army
1815, May 2	—Battle of Tollentino
May 21	—Quit Naples for France
August 24	—Arrived in Corsica
October 7	—Expedition arrived at Pizzo
October 13	—Executed by firing squad

Murat

by

Tim Pickles

From Cloister to Cavalry Commander (1767–1803)

Murat was born in La Bastide, sometimes known as La Bastide Fortoniere or La Bastide en Quercy. Nowadays it is called La Bastide Murat after its most famous son. Murat's mother and father kept the posting house in the village, which also served as the inn. His father, Pierre, was far from being a rich man but was certainly prosperous in the terms of La Bastide because, apart from his business, he was the intendant for the Tallerand family who were the largest landowners of that area. He was of the better class of simple country folk; he was described, in his marriage document, as a *travailleur* (itinerant landworker). In terms of offspring his marriage was also prosperous. His wife, Jeanne Loubière, had 12 children (six of whom died at birth). At the time of Joachim's birth, the youngest, on March 25, 1767, he had two elder brothers and three elder sisters. He was given his name, Joachim, in honor of his godfather, one Joachim Vidieu. It is also interesting to note that on his baptismal register, he is given the name Joachim Murat-Jordy, the legitimate son of Pierre Murat Jordy. It is the only document that gives the family this second name.

His parents decided that he should be educated for the Church, and, with the help of the Tallerand family, he received a scholarship at the age of 10 to attend the College of St. Michael in Cahors. He did sufficiently well to be sent to the Archiepiscopal Seminary of the Lazarites at Toulouse, where he also sang in the choir. In February 1787 he left the seminary. While no definite details are available as to why, the popular supposition is that he fell in love. He ran off with the girl, fought a duel over her, and, when all his money was gone and the affair at an end, decided to join the army as being the only life he had felt fit for from the start. It was, perhaps, sheer chance that the *Chasseurs à Cheval du Champagne* had halted in Toulouse en route from Auch to Carcassonne.

Murat approached a sergeant of the company of one Captain Neil, clean shaven and somewhat unsoldierly: He was 5 feet, 6½ inches,[1] had quite a swaggering manner, black hair, and dark eyes. The next day he marched out of Toulouse as a trooper in the service of his king. In the old Royal Army, educated men in the ranks were rare, and so Murat rapidly won promotion, obtaining the rank of sergeant-major. His regiment, meanwhile, moved away into the northeast of France, to Schlestadt in Alsace. What happened next is somewhat unclear. Some authorities say that he obtained a long leave of absence to return to La Bastide; others, that some misdemeanor in the regiment caused him to be dismissed. Whatever happened, he returned home and, it is said, spent some while working in a draper's shop. However, he was also extremely useful in the area of organizing the local National Guard. Now that the old aura was being swept away, there was a real chance of promotion.

In 1790 the Republic ordered a great ceremony. At this, Louis the King was to swear his allegiance to the constitutional monarchy, as were representatives of every department in France. The Federal National Guards of Montfaucon, in which Cahors is situated, were commanded by Murat, on special leave from his regiment.

The period following the ceremony was a heady time but expensive, and Murat was short of funds, principally because the departmental authorities had not yet set his allowance of expenses; finally in 1791 a notice from the War Office arrived, saying that his leave was at an end and he must immediately rejoin his regiment at Schlestadt. On January 4, 1791, he wrote to the Department at Lot that, owing to unforeseen circumstances, the expenses incurred had been higher than expected, and he included certificates from the Paris municipality to prove his point. In spite of the decree of the National Assembly stating that the provinces were bound to provide all the necessary funds for delegates, he was very disappointed to receive only 100 livres from his Department before quitting Paris and rejoining his regiment near the Rhine.

In June of that year, troops of the eastern district, commanded by Marquis de Bouille, were being concentrated and strung out along the roads to and from Paris. Rumors of a treasure convoy moving eastward from the capital were the ostensible reason for this, and a detachment from the *chasseurs à cheval* was ordered from the barracks at Schlestadt to Mont Medi as part of the arrangements and concentration. The actual reason for the concentration of troops was far more important than mere treasure. Along the road guarded by the detachment came a traveling carriage carrying King Louis and Queen Marie Antoinette. The arrangements were not as efficient as de Bouille had intended and the Mont Medi detachment never found the traveling carriage. Finally, news came to Schlestadt that the king and queen had been arrested trying to escape the country and had been taken back to Paris under guard. The fact that the chasseurs had been merely following orders, and that de Bouille, who had been their immediate commander, was fleeing the country himself, cut little ice with the Paris authorities. Colonel Joseph Francois Jean Batiste D'Urre de Molans, who was commander of the regiment and a thoroughgoing aristocrat, had decided that his best course would be to throw in his lot once and for all with the revolutionaries. He decided to send two men to Mont Medi, find out how his detachment was getting along, and see if there would be some way of them rejoining the regiment. The two members of the regiment chosen for this mission were the adjutant and their sergeant-major, Murat. We know something of their mission from a letter written by Murat from Toul on July 5, 1791, to his brother, which reads:

> I have just come from Mont Medi, three leagues from Varennes, where the King was arrested. I was deputed by my comrades to go to Mont Medi to obtain information as to the position of other comrades of mine who were sent there on detachment. Mont Medi was to have received the King and our regiment was to have guarded him. I saw the apartments prepared for him there and I send you two speeches that we delivered, I made one and our adjutant the other.[2]

Pierre had mentioned in a letter to him that he was considering leaving his post as a member of the municipality. Murat urged him not to—perhaps more out of a sense that, being implicated in the proposed escape of the king, it might reflect badly on himself, rather than out of a concern for Pierre's future.

On February 8, 1792, Murat was chosen to be a member of the Constitutional Guard of Louis XVI. Nominally a Royal Guard of Honor, the purpose of the body was, in fact, to ensure that no future escapes by the king were planned. The nominations to the unit were made by the various departments of France. One other member nominated by Murat's department was Jean Baptiste Bessières—another future marshal. On March 4 he was absent from roll call and put in the guardroom for this offense. Rather than be punished, Murat preferred to leave the Guard, but when he wrote to his departmental council at Lot to explain, he said that his real reason was not this trifling incident but the fact that officers of his unit had been urging him to join a regiment of émigrés being formed at Coblenz and indeed that he had been offered 40 gold francs as traveling expenses to go and join them. This testimony was passed on by the department to the Legislative Assembly and used as part of the evidence to disband the regiment later that year. Murat returned to his old regiment, which was now termed the 12th Horse Chasseurs. He, of course, came out of this with glowing colors, a fact reflected in the swiftness of his promotion. Although he had to rejoin his regiment as a private, he became a brigadier (corporal) on April 29, 1792, a regimental-sergeant-major on May 5, and a *sous-lieutenant* (Cornet or 2nd Lieutenant) on October 15, and a full lieutenant on October 31.

There is a letter existing, sent by Murat to his brother, Pierre, dated November 19, 1792, first year of the Republic (which is a strange mixture of old and new styles of calendar), that says:

> I have presented a memoir to the Minister. A General is to get me his reply, and this General is himself going soon to be the Minister. If this happens, then my lot will be a very fortunate one. I am a Lieutenant and, if my Colonel is made a General, about which there is no doubt, I am to be his Aide de Camp and a Captain. At my age and with my courage and my military talents I may go still further. God grant that I may not be disappointed in my expectations.[3]

A different translation of this letter puts that particular phrase in a more florid, and perhaps more apt, way (knowing Murat's poetical bent), as "I intend to make my way if God and the bullets allow." It is interesting to note that when this letter was written, Pierre had already been in his grave for a month, and Murat himself must have been irked that his regiment was now serving under General Dumouriez in Flanders and, although they had seen action, that he had not been there to share the glory with them. Upon his death on October 8, Pierre had left his pregnant widow with three children still to care for. As soon as he learned what had happened, Joachim immediately took responsibility for them.

Murat had rejoined his regiment, but even though he was now on active service, he did not see any action. Although between November 1792 and February 1793 Dumouriez had all but captured Belgium, Murat and the chasseurs were on the French border in Artois on garrison duty and forming lines of communication. In January 1793 the king was executed. By February 25 Murat was back in Paris. He wrote two letters, one official to the authorities of La Bastide and a second to his brother, André, saying, "I expect I shall have to leave Paris in ten days for Holland. I have been appointed Aide de Camp to a General. I have a horse that cost me 60 Louis and I have to buy another—they are very dear." He continues his letter telling André that there was talk of him being elected to the Convention, although admitting, with uncharacteristic modesty, "I have not much talent, but with my good intentions and my courage I would do more than many who are there."[4] He also suggested that his brother should advise any of the locals who had enlisted in the new levy to come to him at Arras, where he would attempt to get them positions as cavalrymen—pointing out that for the brother of the curé at La Bastide he had been able to obtain promotion as quartermaster sergeant in his own company.

Shortly afterward Murat took up his position once more as aide-de-camp. But things were not going well for the revolutionary armies. In March Dumouriez was in full retreat, and on March 18 the Austrians defeated him at Neerwinden. Also Custine had failed on the Rhine. The Spaniards were coming over the Pyrenees and the English were preparing an expedition to cross the Channel and join the Austrians in the north. In Paris the tribunal was panicking and new powers were given to the revolutionary committees that were formed in every city and town to hunt out any hint of disloyalty to the fatherland. Dumouriez, with a prince on his staff and never a keen supporter of the execution of the king, now decided that his setbacks were not going to sit well with the Convention and deserted to the Austrians with his staff. The immediate effect of this on Murat was that Dumouriez's replacement was General Dampierre, who had been Murat's host at a supper at Valenciennes in February. One of his first acts was to promote Murat to the rank of captain, a fact that Joachim reported to his brother, André, in a letter from Atois on April 22. In a typical piece of Murat oratory, he states, "Our armies have abandoned the infamous Dumouriez the moment they recognised him as a traitor and everywhere our republican soldiers are giving new proofs of their courage in fighting against those infamous satellites of tyrants."[5] The situation at the frontiers was getting still worse: The allies were destroying the French fortresses and the English army, under the Duke of York, was besieging Dunkirk. Murat at Hesdin was not having to advance on the fighting—the fighting was coming to him. But soon he was to leave his staffwork and the chasseurs for more active service. Because of the changed situation, an irregular cavalry corps, known as the "Poacher Hussars," was being formed in order to act against the enemies of the Republic. It had been in existence in small numbers for some time, but the new situation meant reorganizing armies and, indeed, the organization of new armies against the allies. A vital part of this was a serviceable cavalry regiment. Jean Landrieux, the organizer, proposed that Murat join the corps with a step in rank to that of cavalry major, as his military training and experience would be useful in converting the somewhat undisciplined unit into a respectable regiment. Murat accepted and on May 1, 1793, Landrieux wrote to Paris requesting his promotion. Murat's official notification did not arrive until September, but on May 8 Landrieux wrote to Murat,

> I beg to inform you citizen that in virtue of the order of the Minister now in my hands and at the request of General Dampierre you have been named, provisionally, second *Chef d'Escadron* of the

regiment which I command. Will you be so good as to inform the General, to whose staff you are attached, of this arrangement, so that he may send you to your post as soon as possible. Let me know of his decision.

The reorganized cavalry was first termed the 16th Horse Chasseurs, and later the 21st Horse Chasseurs. Murat's commission as cavalry major of the 21st Chasseurs is dated September 23, although by this time he had served for some months with the regiment in that rank. However, the very role that brought him into the regiment was almost his downfall.

In trying to form the "Poacher Hussars" into a real regiment, he earned the enmity of his colonel, who was more concerned with lining his own pockets. After a blazing row, Landrieux accused Murat of disloyalty to the Republic, stating that not only was he the protégé of an aristocrat, but was an aristocrat himself. Never was Murat more pleased of his father's occupation, clearly stated on his birth certificate, which brought the investigation to a grinding halt. To help emphasize his devotion, he even took to signing his name "Marat" (after the murdered politician) for a while. When Robespierre fell, Landrieux tried to prove that Murat had supported the Terror by showing documents in which he had signed himself "Marat." Although Murat was arrested once more, he again defended himself with skill and thoroughly discredited his accuser.

Murat rejoined his regiment in Paris where it had been moved when the insurrectionist parties had begun to show their hand. When the Jacobins and Sansculottes invaded the assembly, Murat was at the head of the first party of cavalry to put itself at the disposal of the civil power. The Directory was formed and Paul Barras was appointed to put down the revolt. He chose as his "sword" Napoleon Bonaparte. At midnight on October 4, 1795, Murat, still a squadron commander, was ordered with his 260 men to take possession of the artillery of the National Guard parked at the Place de Sablons. He arrived at the same time as a party of National Guard that was also trying to secure the guns, but he threatened to cut them down if they tried to stop him, and under this threat they retreated. Horses and carts were requisitioned and shortly after the guns were safely delivered to the Tuileries without a drop of French blood being spilled. So General Bonaparte had his guns, the opposition had none, and with his "whiff of grape" literally swept the streets clean of insurrectionists. Napoleon had used his guns skillfully, but it was Murat who had armed him, and his immediate reward was to return to his regiment as its colonel. On February 2, 1795, he was given the honorific rank of *chef de brigade* whereby, although he might still rank as colonel, his field of command would be a cavalry brigade. He asked for, and received, an appointment on Napoleon's staff in the first Italian campaign. The gradual giving to him of more and more command responsibility and his commission to report on operations by other commanders show Napoleon's increasingly high opinion of his judgment. Finally, at Dego on April 14, 1796, Joachim Murat led his first cavalry charge in pitched battle.

In the first Italian campaign, Murat found many other occasions to prove his worth. In his time there, he was given the opportunity to lead both infantry and cavalry and distinguished himself to such a degree that when the captured standards were sent back to France, Murat was the officer appointed to present them to the Republic. With north Italy placed under various pro-French republican governments, Napoleon's eyes turned toward "British" India and the land route via Egypt. Murat was appointed general of brigade on May 10, 1796, and on March 15, 1797, to the command of a brigade of dragoons (14th and 18th) in the cavalry division of General Baraguay d'Hilliers in the expedition. On the voyage he was unwell. The expedition made a stop at Malta, capturing the castle from the Knights of St. John with very little trouble—the great days of the Knight Hospitallers were long since past. A severe bout of sickness detained General d'Hilliers on the island with the occupation forces, thus promoting Menou to overall command of the cavalry.

In pitched battles, sieges, and any set-piece action in Egypt, the French usually came out on top. In spite of everything, the French adapted to the country as well as they could. Many officers affected Arab dress in varying degrees including the scimitar (which is still carried by general officers to this day), Murat having his cavalry augmented by a camel corps. At the Battle of the Pyramids, the cavalry spent most of its time sheltering in the squares of the infantry, while the cream of the Mamelukes died in futile attempts to break them; but at Aboukir Murat showed what cavalry, horse artillery, and camels could do (see p. 352). His brilliant flank attack put the entire enemy force to rout, Murat ending up in single combat with Säid Mustapha Pasha, the enemy commander, receiving a wound in the mouth from a pistol shot and taking two fingers from his opponent as he struck the pistol from his hand with his saber.

At the end of the campaign, France had lost several thousand men and an able general or two and Murat had set his seal on being the leading cavalry commander of the army—far too valuable a man to be left behind when Bonaparte gathered to him the men who would accompany him home for his bid for power.

The ship avoided the British blockades and arrived to the wild enthusiasm of the French people who even brushed aside the quarantine laws—so pleased were they to have the heroes back. In these turbulent times Napoleon's first job was to make sure he was accepted by the army as its *de facto* commander, and Murat's promotion to general of division came on July 25, 1799, and was confirmed on October 19, 1799. When the crunch came on November 9, the 18 *Brumaire*, Murat's quick thinking again saved the day in the Council of Deputies when there were calls for Napoleon's execution as a traitor, and, in the uproar, some deputies actually advanced on him brandishing knives. It was Murat who rushed from the chamber in order to bring in the grenadiers who were waiting outside, and who gave the simple but direct order, "Grenadiers forward, throw them out!."[6] Later, Murat was appointed commander of the Guard of the Consuls. The basis of the future Empire was being established. It was also about this time that Murat first met Caroline Bonaparte who, in spite of her youth, was probably (after Napoleon) the most intelligent member of the Bonaparte clan. She was once described by Talleyrand as having "the head of Cromwell on the body of a pretty woman." She and Joachim married in January 1800 (when she was 16 years old and Joachim 30) at the home of Napoleon's brother, Joseph. Shortly after, in April of that year, Murat was nominated commander-in-chief of the Cavalry Reserve.

The new appointment was to occupy much of his time from the outset, as Napoleon had decided to commence the re-invasion of Italy by crossing the Alps and surprising the Austrians by appearing at their rear. The logistics of the accompanying cavalry must have been complicated in the extreme, but the cavalry arrived in good order, and in the decisive Battle of Marengo (along with the corps of the ill-fated Desaix)[7] was decisive in turning the tables. But their commander also had some illusions shattered. Murat had believed that in being appointed cavalry commander he would have some hand in organizing the mounted arm of the French forces and helping to plan campaigns. Napoleon had made it very clear to him that he was a figurehead and field commander and that all grand strategy was the province of the First Consul alone.

For the Marengo campaign Murat won a Sword of Honor and a still greater reputation as a cavalry commander of rare perception, as well as consolidating his place among the new ruling family of France.

From Soldier to Sovereign (1804–1811)

The year 1804 saw the final official confirmation of what had actually been in force since 1800, the transformation of the Republic into the first French Empire. The pomp and glory to which Murat had been addicted since childhood were now offered to him, loaded with titles and honors, including the honorific court appointment of Grand Admiral of the Empire. His name was also among the first creation of the Marshals of the Empire, being second in seniority to Berthier and sharing with him the privilege of access to the Emperor at any time, never being challenged by the bodyguard.

The year 1805 saw the first great challenge to the Empire, with an Austro–Russian force advancing on France. The army formed to invade England was diverted to central Europe to counter the threat. Murat, under the *nom de guerre* of Colonel de Beaumont, traveled ahead of the army, making assessments of the terrain and plotting lines of march. The effectiveness of his groundwork was evident in the total encirclement of the Austrian army under Mack at Ulm where the cavalry screen organized by Murat was basic to the victory. His magnificient charge at Austerlitz is well known. Perhaps the most interesting aspect of the campaign was the first "Murat myth," the sort of story that bolsters the vision of Murat as a foolish featherbrain—his capture of the bridge at Vienna, when he and Marshal Lannes pretended that an armistice had been signed in order to prevent Prince Auersperg from destroying it. The incident is often quoted as an example of his vainglorious desire to be first into Vienna. However, in his memoirs General Rapp, aide-de-camp to the Emperor quotes the order sent to Murat from Napoleon urging him to capture the bridge intact using any means necessary.

The year 1806 saw Murat created Grand Duke of Cleves and Berg, joining the marshals who had been made sovereign princes of vassal states in the Empire, although, of course, he outranked his fellows, being created "prince imperial" at the time of the coronation. Caroline rankled at being of inferior status in the court to her sisters.

The important campaign of the year was against the new Fourth Coalition, and the crushing of the Prussian army at Jena–Auerstädt and the brilliant cavalry actions following it. Under Murat the cavalry performed as never before, completely destroying the army built up by Frederick the Great (and even, in the case of La Salle's division, capturing towns) until, on November 7, he entered Warsaw. The population were ecstatic: for the first time in living memory, here was a possibility of Polish independence. Murat was presented with the Sword of King

Stephen by Prince Poniatowski and there were even elements in Poland who thought he should become king, a dignity for which Murat had no doubts about his suitability. He took up residence in Warsaw and ordered 26,000 francs worth of plumes to replace those he had lost. The campaign continued into 1807, this time against the Russians, and at Eylau, on February 8, in the midst of a snowstorm, he executed a quite brilliant cavalry charge that showed his unerring instinct for battle and the unsurpassed discipline of the French cavalry. The rest of the campaign was not quite so happy, particularly at Heilsberg where he was almost captured just before the final capitulation of Koenigsberg negotiated between June 14 and 16. On June 19 the great Conference of Tilsit began, and while Napoleon and the Tsar were reshaping Europe, former enemies were giving one another orders of knighthood; Murat, who was already a holder of the Collar of the Legion of Honor and Grand Cross of the Iron Crown, received from Tsar Alexander I the Orders of St. Andrew and St. Alexander Nevski, from Prussia the Black Eagle, from Saxony the Red Crown, and from Wurtzbourg the Order of St. Joseph.

Marshal Murat had only until February 1808 to enjoy his grand duchy and his official residence in Paris (the Elysée Palace), for on February 20 he was appointed Lieutenant of the Emperor and commander-in-chief of the Army of Spain. In spite of what was to follow, it would be wrong to suppose that the French army was hated from the beginning in Spain. Indeed, it was universally welcomed; even Spain's chief minister, Godoy, sent Murat the Order of the Golden Fleece, hoping to win the French to his cause. The reason for this welcome was the turmoil in Spanish politics at that time. The king and the crown prince were at odds. The king had appealed to Napoleon (who had been non-commital) to settle the dispute, and as the army marched in both sides were convinced that the French were coming to their assistance. When he finally reached Madrid, Murat recommended that the prince attend Napoleon at Bayonne where the Emperor was in conference with Ferdinand, and that while they were both out of the way an effective pro-French king be appointed (hinting at his own suitability).

Soon after the French arrival, the mood of the Spanish people began to change as the volatile population realized that the French would support neither side, but were, in effect, an army of occupation. All sides united against a common enemy. Feelings finally boiled over on the same day that Murat was appointed lieutenant-general of the kingdom. On the second day of May, a band of insurgents attacked a party of mamelukes and dragoons in Madrid; mamelukes were fired on from a house and they retaliated by killing everyone inside. The insurrection was put down effectively but in a manner that appears quite brutal for such a naturally fair-minded and chivalrous man as Murat; but one must remember that at this time it was still considered that any civilian who presumed to interfere in military affairs had forfeited all claims to the protection of law or mercy. For the previous few weeks, Murat had been unwell with a bout of fever and so was not displeased to be recalled to France on June 15.

On July 15, as Joseph Bonaparte was proclaimed King of Spain, Murat was appointed to rule Joseph's former kingdom of Naples. In many ways, one of Napoleon's worst moves (as far as he was concerned) was to make Murat a king. The two men looked on the appointment in completely different ways. To Napoleon he was merely a district governor with a grand title, emphasized by the fact that every member of his family whom he raised to the kingly dignity was also expected to adopt the name Napoleon. To Murat a king was a king, however that kingdom was obtained. Throughout history countries had been won by the sword, but once won, the king was as much an independent sovereign ruling by the will of God as any other. Joachim Napoleon of Naples saw himself as an ally of Napoleon, not a vassal. However wrong a view Napoleon might have thought this to be, he bolstered it himself (though perhaps unintentionally) by pointing out to his brother-in-law that as he was now a sovereign in his own right it would be wrong for him to maintain property in France; and in the treaty granting Murat his kingdom, all his French property reverted to the state. In fact, only personal items were supposed to be taken to Naples. Palaces, furniture, paintings—all were to be left in France. Murat evaded the treaty in only one respect: he managed to take his war horses out of the country before the document took effect. The acceptance of his kingdom cost Murat some six million francs; worse still, on his arrival in Naples, he found that Joseph had bled the country white, taken all the cash he could lay his hands on to Spain, and left unpaid levies to the Empire, which Napoleon was now demanding from the new king.

There were, of course, compensations. The people loved their new swaggering, dashing king. The glitter and pomp beloved by Murat was just the sort of thing that the Neapolitans loved. He proclaimed a general pardon with many convicts being released, reequipped and uniformed the army (such as it was), and embarked on a ship-building program. A previous King of Naples said, when new uniforms were proposed for the army, "Dress them in whatever you like, they will still run away."* So it

*D. G. Chandler, *The Campaigns of Napoleon* (New York, 1966) p. 46.

is a great testament to King Joachim Napoleon's leadership that he was able, on October 16, 1808, only two months after his arrival, to use his new army along with the French army stationed in Naples to conclude a successful attack on the Isle of Capri. The enemy troops were Anglo–Sicilian—commanded by the future jailer of Napoleon, Sir Hudson Lowe. Having been lulled into a false sense of security by Joseph's inactivity and secure in the knowledge of British naval superiority, they were amazed by the surprise attack when supplies were running low. The garrison surrendered and was transported back to Sicily. The following year an even more amazing battle took place in the Bay of Naples. An Anglo–Sicilian invasion fleet was prevented from landing their troops by Murat's one and only frigate, the *Ceres*, and some half-dozen gunboats, for which action the king decorated *Ceres'* captain and crew on the deck of the vessel the instant it docked. But there was one very sour military note in 1809. Naples was the kingdom of the two Sicilies in name only as the island of Sicily was held by Ferdinand, Bourbon ex-King of Naples. Murat planned to rectify the situation with an invasion. It was to be a joint operation by the Neapolitan army (native) and the Army of Naples (French). All went well with the Neapolitans, who were to commence the invasion; but when the time came for the French to embark, the commander merely stated that as he had received no orders from the Emperor he could not do so. The invasion was, of course, a complete and utter failure. Murat now realized that he had in fact an army of occupation that he had to feed, clothe, and pay, but that would not necessarily obey his orders. It is said that he was so furious at this time that he tore his Cross of the Legion of Honor from his breast and threw it across the room; whether or not this is true, it is certainly the case that most pictures of Murat painted after this date show him wearing his order of the two Sicilies to the right of that of the Legion of Honor in the superior position.

The next three years saw King Joachim in the military backwater of Naples, possibly because of two quite major arguments with the Emperor. First, Murat turned a blind eye to the export of certain goods to England, which was, of course, in contravention of the Continental System, although essential for certain areas of the Neapolitan economy. Second, when on an official visit to Paris for the christening of the King of Rome, it was intimated to him by Napoleon that he should give up his throne. Asked to wait until the following day to discuss it, Murat immediately rode nonstop back to Naples and virtually dared Napoleon to depose him. In all matters concerning the retention of the throne, he was enthusiastically encouraged by his Queen, and it has to be said that Caroline was by far the better statesman of the two. This did lead to more than a little domestic strife, as there were definite "king's" and "queen's" factions in the court, each trying to use their influence to oust the other; but as the king and queen were genuinely in love, the arguments between them, though spectacular, were usually short lived. Of much more importance to Joachim was making time to spend with his four children on whom he doted, playing with them like any bourgeois father. The domestic life of the couple could not be better explained than the breakfasts described by General Thiébault who was their guest: "After an excellent breakfast served on handsome china, a coarse earthenware pot was brought in containing some *raisin* (dried fruit). 'This is one of our provincial tit-bits', said Murat. 'My mother makes it and sends it to me'".[8]

From Moscow to Pizzo (1812–1815)

Suddenly, Napoleon softened his attitude toward his brother-in-law. The reason soon became clear: Russia was to be tamed once and for all. The largest army the world had ever seen was to be assembled and Murat was to command the cavalry. In spite of past disagreements, Napoleon knew he had to have Murat to command the cavalry, and for his part Murat was seduced by the sheer glory of the command and the full knowledge that his wife was perfectly capable of running the kingdom.

The plan for the Russian campaign was meticulous, with every aspect taken into account; that is, all but one: the speed of retreat of the Russians. The Grand Army was equipped with herds of cattle, traveling bake houses, and every necessity for the campaign. King Joachim Napoleon conducted this campaign in a manner that astonished even those who knew him of old, with a household to rival Napoleon's own. Because of the Russian refusal to give battle, Murat had a stiff piece of work cut out as commander of the advance guard. He was ordered to keep contact with the enemy and to order troops that were in the forefront to be ready for action at a moment's notice, the practical result of this being that the leading troops were unable to unsaddle their horses. Murat was his old self, dressed more gorgeously than ever, tiring out five horses a day, and so astonishing the cossacks that at one point a group of troopers asked him to change sides and become their *Hetman* (or headman). At the Battle of Borodino, he was largely responsible for the capture of the redoubt by dismounting and daring the retreating French troops to leave him to the enemy. He, along with Marshal Ney, had urged Napoleon not to advance further than Smolensk, but to wait for supplies and consolidate the position. However, spurred on by the lack of food in the city (which had been destroyed by the Russians) and the frustration of no decisive battle, Napoleon pressed on to Moscow. Soon thereafter the notorious retreat began.

By December 5, 1812, the Russian campaign had gone disastrously wrong and Napoleon was leaving the army to its fate in the snow after appointing Murat to command what was fast disintegrating into an indisciplined mob. Nearly all of Murat's personal guard died of frostbite after insisting on wearing only full dress uniform when escorting the Emperor. The whole of the 7th Neapolitan Infantry, exclusively black men, was soon to follow. In honor Murat could not leave his command until he considered it safe; on the other hand, he had disturbing reports of events in Naples. He felt Queen Caroline was exceeding her authority in certain matters and he had received several requests from his ministers for his immediate return. When the army was at last out of hostile territory, Murat could justify his stay with it no longer. Handing the command to Prince Eugène, whom he knew was more than equal to the task, he left the army on January 18, 1813.

Napoleon now used his knowledge of Murat to try to win him back despite his fury at his brother-in-law's leaving the army. The Emperor was quite aware that he was negotiating with the allies, but he was still the best cavalry commander at his disposal. The allies were delighted at the prospect of Naples joining them; but not unreservedly so, as for years they had been supporting Ferdinand's claims to be reinstated as king. No treaty had been signed when Napoleon sent his final letter asking for the help of an allied sovereign and a "dear brother and comrade-in-arms." He had judged his man well—the final call to honor had its effect and in August 1813 Marshal Murat rejoined the army of the Emperor Napoleon.

The Battle of Leipzig finally turned him against Napoleon. He now believed that even if Napoleon could make peace, he would not. All the Emperor would accept was total victory, and for that he would sacrifice everything and everyone to preserve an empire that the rest of Europe was determined to destroy. As king, Murat's first concern was Naples, and the allies would not wait forever. If he did not do something soon, they would no longer need him. Murat requested permission from Napoleon to return home to levy new troops and organize the defense of his kingdom. The two men were never to meet again.

Back once more in Naples, he commenced negotiations in earnest with Austria and Great Britain. A treaty was agreed upon guaranteeing him Naples and compensating Ferdinand. This was signed by Austria, though only initialed by Great Britain, whose representative, Lord Castlereagh, was not at all enthusiastic. So on January 11, 1814, King Joachim Napoleon of Naples became commander of the 7th Allied Army and marched north with 30,000 men to face the French under Prince Eugène, encouraging his men with a proclamation that read in part: "So long as it was possible for me to believe that the Emperor Napoleon was fighting to bring peace and glory to France, I fought loyally at his side; but now I can deceive myself no longer; I know that the Emperor's sole desire is war."[9] When he reached Bologna, he was greeted with cries of "Long live the King of Italy." For the first time he saw the possibility of an Italy united by the desire of the people. The idea appealed to him greatly, though it should not be imagined that Italian troops flocked to his banner in quite the numbers he might have wished. He advanced on the Franco–Italian army under Prince Eugène, which was on the Adige, but as the Neapolitans reached the Po, Prince Eugène retreated to the Mincio. At this stage, despite demands from Austria and England that he engage the enemy, neither country had fully ratified the treaty. Murat sent a secret letter to Napoleon.

When Murat's letter reached Napoleon, he showed that he still did not understand that, because of his own act creating him king, Murat had not been a Frenchman since 1808. He wrote to Eugène, "Make a treaty with him in my name—you may go as far as you like—after such ingratitude and in such circumstances no obligation is binding."[10] On March 15 Lord William Bentinck[11] arrived at Murat's headquarters and demanded that he evacuate Tuscany. Murat countered with a demand that England ratify its treaty with him. Bentinck then stated that if he did not evacuate he would use his Anglo–Sicilians to drive him out and then invade Naples and proclaim Ferdinand king. The situation was sorted out only by the good offices of General Wilson[12] and the Austrians pointing out to Murat that his insistence on Italian unity might lose him everything, and to the British government that if Bentinck's blustering caused Murat to join forces with Eugène the Austrians might be forced out of Italy. On April 15 Murat received news that he never anticipated: The allies were in Paris and the Emperor had abdicated. This news was devastating. That the Greater Empire was doomed had been obvious to him; that the Emperor would be forced to abandon France was inconceivable, and Murat had little choice now but to take his troops back to Naples and hope the allies would keep their word.

Austria was solidly behind the treaty, Russia unfavorable, and Britain still wavering. Not withstanding this, Murat continued his Anglophile tendencies. He employed English nurses for his children and English grooms for his horses, drank "English port wine," and had his sporting guns made in London.[13] He also entertained many English visitors during the year, including Lord John Russell and later on the princess of Wales. But when the Congress of Vienna was convened, not only was Naples not represented but Metternich persuaded Lord Castlereagh not to bring up the subject of Italy until later, as it could lead to a revolution. The reason for this was that in August Castlereagh had asked the Duke of Wellington about the feasibility of an invasion of Naples, which had gone so far as to work out how many troops would be needed and from where they coud be drawn. All that was needed was to present the plan for the agreement of the Emperor of Austria. In some ways King Murat played into their hands. When his delegation returned from Vienna after being refused recognition, he mobilized almost immediately. On November 26, Lord Oxford was arrested on his way to Naples with unauthorized letters for the king and queen. In his eagerness to curry favor with Austria, Murat offered to loan troops to the Austrian commander in Tuscany, which was seen in some quarters as another sinister attempt at Italian unification. Of one thing Murat was now certain: he could trust no one—not Napoleon and certainly not the allies. His one hope was to raise Italy to his banner and force whoever was in power in Europe to accept him as king. Just as the time appeared to be right to remove Murat, "either by negotiation or by force,"[14] as it was put to Wellington, the whole situation changed. Napoleon landed in France from Elba and the nation rallied to him. Once more Murat had to be courted. But by this stage he was in no mood to listen to political promises that were good only as long as he was useful. He gathered together his army and invaded Italy. In Italy the campaign was successful, the Austrians were defeated at the River Panaro, and the nationalists, through Piedmont, raised the cry, "Long live the King of Italy! Independence or death!" Then came the disastrous Battle of Tolentino. It was Marengo in reverse. So confident was Murat of victory that he left the field before the Austrians retreated and inside two hours the tables were turned and the Neapolitans defeated. Britain had also declared war, and Murat knew his reign was over.

King Murat entered his capital for the last time on May 18, 1815, and remained only long enough to take farewell of his family and court, departing from Naples the following day. On May 21, after disguising himself by shaving off his famous whiskers and concealing a quantity of diamonds about his person, he left for France—no longer a king but now a Frenchman, and intending to offer his sword to the Emperor.

Napoleon not only refused to give Murat a command in the forthcoming campaign, he would not even receive his brother-in-law, ordering him to remain in Toulon until he had made up his mind about what was to be done with him. No good news reached Murat in all his time in Toulon. First, his wife and children, whom the British had originally promised to send to France, were now in Austria. Second, he learned of the defeat of the Army of the North at Waterloo, which was followed by severe retribution from royalists humiliated by the cowardly conduct of Louis XVIII on Napoleon's return. Finally, having used his diamonds to buy a passage to Corsica after hearing that a reward of 40,000 francs had been offered for his capture, he failed to locate the boat waiting to take him on board and had to find refuge in the countryside. Here he remained until hunger drove him to beg at a humble cottage where he was recognized by an old soldier. Notwithstanding the offered reward, the man and his wife counted it an honor to be able to serve "His Imperial and Royal Majesty," and even concealed him from a systematic search of their property. He finally left France on August 22 with three friends who had managed to obtain a small skiff in Toulon, and it was in this small craft that they sailed for Corsica. It was their good fortune during the rough crossing that they met the packet boat heading for the island, for no sooner had the party been taken on board than the skiff sank like a stone. Although bearded and disguised as a common soldier, he was instantly recognized in Ajaccio by the mayor and became the center of adulation, being greeted by cheering crowds wherever he went. Passports had arrived for him to enter Austria with assurances from the Emperor that he and Caroline could live unmolested in any part of Bohemia as the Count and Countess of Lipona (an anagram of Napoli that Caroline was already using). But Murat had determined to attempt a landing in Naples. The "invasion" force consisted of 250 soldiers, and the little fleet set sail on September 28, sighting Calabria on October 6. That very night a severe storm arose, and in the morning Murat's ship was the only vessel in sight of land; though two more joined him during the day, one deserted during the night. This last disaster was the end. Murat determined to sail for Trieste and use his Austrian passports. The captain of his ship would not sail without reprovisioning and would not go on shore without the passports to prove why the journey was being made. Murat, however, would not allow the passports out of his possession. So in the end Murat and 30 companions (28 soldiers and two servants) landed at the fishing port of Pizzo wearing full dress uniform. On recognizing him some fishermen shouted, "Long live King Joachim," but the troops drilling in the town square were not quite so impressed. The unfurling of his banner and a cry of "Joachim forever!" brought only stunned silence. An ugly crowd had gathered, and although the party made a break for the beach, the mob caught them before they were able to reach the boats. Murat was imprisoned and then tried by court-martial. He conducted himself bravely throughout, insisting that none of his companions was guilty of anything but faithfulness to him. He stated that if the court (which insisted on calling him Marshal Murat) considered him a Frenchman, then they were not competent to try him. If, on the other hand, they accepted him as Neapolitan, then he was king and they were his subjects and still not competent to try him. The argument was not unlike that used by King Charles I of England and just as effective: His sentence of death had already been ordered by Ferdinand under a law enacted by Murat himself to discourage insurrection.

His last day on earth, October 13, 1815, Murat rose and dressed in white shirt, waistcoat, stock and breeches, black hussar boots, and a plain blue civilian tunic. He made his confession to a priest (who remembered him from their last meeting when, as king, Murat had made a generous donation to his church), wrote a last letter to Caroline, enclosed some locks of his hair, and, stating that his only regret was not being able to bid farewell to his family, signed it Joachim Napoleon. He then gave his watch to his valet and, declaring himself a faithful member of the Church, went to the place of execution. The firing party was drawn up in a courtyard so small that the muzzles of the muskets almost touched Murat's chest. He was offered a chair and a blindfold, both of which he refused. He kissed a cameo bearing a portrait of his wife that he held in his hand, and urging the squad, "If you wish to spare me, aim at the heart," offered himself for death by giving the word "Fire!"[15] The volley crashed out and Murat's body fell to the ground; and to deny his last request, he was shot in the head three times. What happened to the body is not known for sure. Some say he was buried in the local churchyard in a common grave; others that he was thrown into the sea; and last, most gruesome of all, that the body was thrown into the sea but only after the head had been cut off and sent to Ferdinand as proof of his death.

If Napoleon was a man ahead of his time, Murat was of a past age when chivalry and courage were all. He even used to relate in later life how a vision of the transfiguration of Jesus sustained him at the Battle of Mount Tabor. Many Italians consider Murat the founder of the movement for unification and hail Tolentino not as a defeat but the first spark of fire later fanned by Garibaldi. His descendants are numerous and played a prominent part in the restoration of Napoleon's nephew to the Third Empire in 1852, and even include a British general who served during World War II. It is interesting that when the troopers of Lord William Bentinck's old regiment, the 11th Hussars (formally Light Dragoons), wished to praise Lord Cardigan their colonel, they took to referring to him as "the Murat of the British Army."

The Murat line still continues, which I am sure would be all that the king would ask. Perhaps the epitaph that would please him most was Lord Byron's in a letter to Tom Moore dated November 4, 1815: "Poor dear Murat, what an end! You know I suppose that his white plume used to be a rallying point in battle, like Henry IV's."*

The Battle of Aboukir (July 25, 1799)

On July 12, 1799, the British squadron of Sir William Sidney Smith arrived in Aboukir Bay and landed an invasion force of 18,000 Turks at Aboukir town to join forces with Murad Bey's mamelukes. General Bonaparte immediately advanced from Cairo to meet the threat, giving General Murat command of the vanguard consisting of his own cavalry brigade (3d and 14th Dragoons and 7th Hussars), four guns, and the brigade of General Destaing, 3,000 men in all. When the French army began its attack on July 25, this force had been joined by the divisions of General Lanusse (2,400 men and six guns) and Lannes (2,700 men and five guns). The Turkish army was drawn up in two entrenched lines, the first line having as its flanks two fortified hills, and the second having as its center the old redoubt. The old village and fort of Aboukir were also occupied, the whole being supported by some 30 artillery pieces and gunboats in both the Mediterranean and Lake Aboukir. The French army was drawn up with Lanusse and Destaing on the left flank, Lannes on the right with Murat and his cavalry, and horse artillery in the center. Both flanks began with cannonades against the fortified hills and followed this up with a frontal assault with the bayonet. Seeing that the Turks had taken troops from the center to meet the challenge on the flanks, Murat immediately charged through the gap unopposed. He wheeled his cavalry right and left and unlimbered his guns, pouring canister into the Turkish emplacements in support of the infantry. As the Turks broke and ran, the cavalry charged again, and those who were not cut to pieces were driven into the sea. Within an hour the French had the first line in their position, and Murat had pressed on to the forward position of the second line where the defenders had been foolish

*Lord Byron, *Byron's Letters and Journals* (London, 1899) p. 265.

enough to leave their entrenchments to try to aid their comrades. They only succeeded in sharing their fate.

Napoleon had managed to bring forward artillery to a position where it could be brought to bear on the extreme left flank of the second line so as to support a frontal infantry assault on the position. The infantry was generally unsuccessful and the cavalry was coming under fire from both the second line and the gunboats. The Turks were confident enough for some to venture out of their defenses to massacre French wounded and decapitate the dead for the bounty they had been promised. But the French artillery forced the left flank to withdraw to a mere 200 yards from the sea, and Murat immediately charged for the gap rolling up the second line. The French infantry counter-attacked and joined in the melee, the cavalry being left free to press on to the tents of Säid Mustapha Pasha and his janissary guard numbering some 200 men. The final act of the battle was pure romantic fiction brought to life. With the French cavalry and Turks battling around them, Murat galloped up to Säid Mustapha Pasha and demanded his surrender. In reply the enemy commander leveled a pistol at him and fired, wounding him in the jaw. Murat slashed down with his saber, knocking the pistol from his hand and taking two fingers with it. Two hussars accompanying the general dismounted and took the Pasha prisoner. Although the Turks' reserve in Aboukir town and the fort held out until August 2, the battle was over. Of the total of Turks involved (8,000 in the first line, 6,000 in the second, and 4,000 reserves), 2,000 were killed, 10,000 drowned trying to escape, and 3,000 were taken prisoner, for a loss to the French of 150 killed and 750 wounded. In reporting the battle to the Directory, Napoleon wrote, "The winning of the battle, which will have such an influence on the glory of the Republic, is due chiefly to General Murat. I ask you to grant this General the rank of General of Division. His cavalry brigade has achieved the impossible."[16]

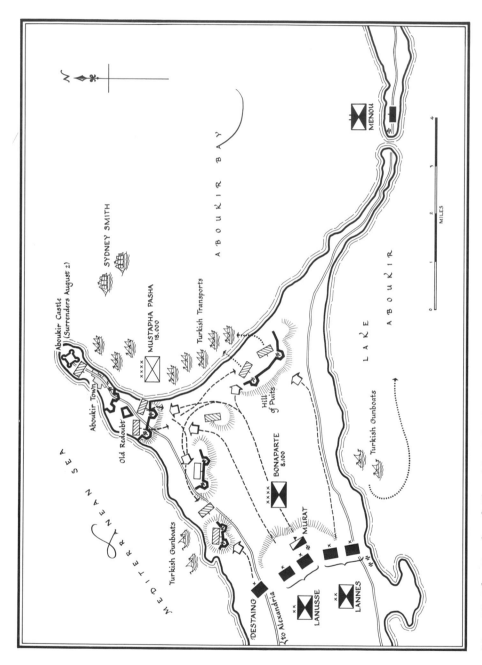

Map 18. The Battle of Aboukir, July 25, 1799

TEXTUAL REFERENCES

1. French measurement, approximately 6 feet in English measurement.
2. *Letters et Documents pour Servir à L'Histoire de Joachim Murat*, pub. by S. A. le Prince Murat (Paris, 1908–10), Vol. 1, quoted in A. H. Atteridge, *Marshal Murat* (London, circa 1945), p. 15.
3. Atteridge, *op. cit.*, p. 18.
4. *ibid.*, p. 21.
5. *ibid.*, p. 24.
6. L. Bonaparte, *Memoirs*, Sect. 1, p. 74.
7. Desaix was one of the most able generals of the revolutionary army, rivaling Bonapart in his brilliance. He arrived from Egypt just in time to take part in the Battle of Marengo and led a brilliant counterattack during which he was tragically killed.
8. R. M. Johnson, *The Napoleonic Empire in Southern Italy and the Rise of the Secret Societies* (London, 1904), p. 194.
9. A. Espitalier, ed., *Napoleon and King Murat* (London, 1912), p. 397.
10. *Napoléon I: Lettres inédites à Marie-Louise* (ed. L. Madelin) (Paris 1935) Vol. 10, p. 215.
11. Lord William Bentinck was colonel of the 11th Light Dragoons and commander of the Anglo–Sicilian troops in Italy. In an attempt to curry favor with him, Murat presented him with a diamond-hilted sword.
12. The same General Wilson who had served on the Russian staff during the 1812 campaign as British observer.
13. F. Macerone, *Interesting Facts Relating to the Fall and Death of Joachim Murat, Etc.* (London, 1817).
14. Arthur Wellesley, Duke of Wellington' *Supplementary Despatches* (ed. Second Duke of Wellington, 1858–72), (London, 1858–64), Vol. 9, p. 593.
15. Princess Caroline Murat, *My Memoirs* (London, 1910), p. 23.
16. *Correspondance de l'Emperor Napolèon I*, Vol. 5, p. 537., letter dated Alexandria, July 27, 1799.

BIBLIOGRAPHICAL NOTE

A splendid basic account in English is A. Hilliard Atteridge's *Marshal Murat* (London, *circa* 1945), which has some interesting sidelights but is particularly valuable for a "no frills," highly readable account of Murat's life. Essential to the understanding of Murat's time as king is R. M. Johnston's *The Napoleonic Empire in Southern Italy and the Rise of the Secret Societies* (New York, 1904)—not the easiest book to read but a treasure trove of the political intrigues that beset Naples, which shatters forever the view that ruling Naples was a simple matter; it is also invaluable for the bibliography, 466 titles with the author's assessment of their value in relation to Naples (some of the comments are very "pithy"). Although Francis Macerone's *Interesting Facts Relating to the Fall and Death of Joachim Murat, Etc.* (London, 1817) is written off as almost a fiction by some historians, I have found it generally trustworthy when dealing solely with Murat. However, be sure to cross-check information with other sources before putting too much faith in it. Hubert Cole's *The Betrayers* (London, 1972) is a splendid, if sometimes complex, account of the personal lives and thoughts of King Joachim and Queen Caroline without forgetting the wider picture, and Joan Bear's *Caroline Murat* (London, 1972) fills in many gaps left by other accounts. *Napoleon and King*

Murat compiled by Albert Espitalier (London, 1912) uses original sources but is in every respect a character assassination of Murat and justificaton of Napoleon in the way the material is presented, and certainly the financial dealings have been "doctored" by the editor. Nonetheless, much valuable information is to be gleaned, but rather after the fashion of gold nuggets among the dross. Not to be forgotten is Job's (Jaques Onfidy Bréville) *L'Album Murat* (Paris, *circa* 1900). Although produced as a child's picturebook, it is one of the finest references for Murat's uniforms and needs no recommendation to anyone with the slightest knowledge of this remarkable artist's work; it simply has never been bettered.

There are also many sources in French and Italian that could be cited, but the titles given above are more accessible to the general reader. However, I must mention the *Murat Papers* in the possession of Prince Louis Murat and also record the invaluable assistance given to me over the years by H. H. Joachim, Eighth Prince Murat, Prince Napoleon Murat, the Baroness de Chassiron, M. Jean Vanell, and Mr. Malcolm Harper.

CHRONOLOGY

1769, January 10	—Born at Sarrlouis (Moselle)
1787, February 12	—Enlisted in *Colonel General des Hussards* Regiment
1792, April 1	—Promoted regimental sergeant major
October 29	—Commissioned as sublieutenant in the 5th Hussars
1794, April 12	—Elected captain; subsequently serves under Kléber
October 15	—Appointed adjutant general brigade commander
December 22	—Badly wounded in left shoulder at the Siege of Maastricht
1796, August 1	—Promoted *général de brigade* after fall of Würzbourg
1797, April 21	—Taken prisoner at Giessen by the Austrians
1799, March 28	—Promoted *général de division*
1800, December 3	—Fights at Hohenlinden under Moreau
1802, August 5	—Marries Aglaée Louise Aiguiée
1804, May 19	—Appointed *Maréchal d'Empire* (twelfth in seniority)
1805, October 14	—Commands VI Corps at Elchingen
1806, October 14	—Commands VI Corps at Jena
November 8	—Captures Magdeburg
1807, February 8	—Commands VI Corps at Eylau
June 14	—Commands VI Corps at Friedland
1808, June 6	—Created *duc d'Elchingen*
August 2	—Summoned to join *l'Armée d'Espagne*
1810, April 17	—Posted with VI Corps to *l'Armée de Portugal*
July 10	—Captures Ciudad Rodrigo
July 24	—Fights at the combat of the Coa
September 27	—Commands VI Corps at Busaco
1811, March 23	—Dismissed by Massena for insubordination
1812, August 17	—Commands III Corps at Smolensk; wounded
September 7	—Commands III Corps with distinction at Borodino
November 3	—Given command of the rear guard during the retreat from Moscow
1813, March 25	—Created *prince de la Moskowa*
May 2	—Commands III Corps at Lützen
May 20–21	—Commands French left wing at Bautzen
October 18	—Severely wounded at Leipzig; returns to France
1814, April 4	—Leads group of Marshals to secure Napoleon's abdication at Fontainebleau
May 20	—Given command of the cavalry by Louis XVIII
1815, March 12	—Declares for Napoleon; joins him at Auxerre
June 16 and 18	—Fights at Quatre-Bras and Waterloo
December 7	—Shot by firing squad after trial by Court of Peers

CHAPTER NINETEEN

THE BRAVEST OF THE BRAVE

Ney

by

Brigadier (ret'd.) Peter Young

From Hussar to Marshal (1787–1804)

My name is Michel Ney. I was born at Saarlouis on 10 January 1769. I am the Duke of Elchingen, Prince of the Moscova and Marshal of France, a *Chevalier* of the Order of St.-Louis,[*] I wear the Grand Cordon of the Legion of Honour, also the decorations of the Iron Crown of Italy and the Order of Christ.[*]

Thus spoke Ney at his court-martial on November 10, 1815. The officer who could claim these bravely earned distinctions was one of those who, beginning life in humble circumstances, owed his advancement to the opportunities offered by the upheaval of 1789—opportunities that the young man, eager for glory, seized with the utmost ardor.

On the occasion of Ney's wedding (August 5, 1802), Jean-Baptiste Isabey organized illuminations commemorating his successes with the armies of the Republic. The general, who had been under fire a score of times, chose but six engagements to celebrate his career: Mainz (November 29, 1794), Altenkirchen (June 4, 1796), Winterthur (May 27, 1799), Würzburg (July 15, 1799), Mannheim (December 1799), and Hohenlinden (December 3, 1800).[1] Doubtless these were the actions that, for one reason or another, Ney remembered with most pride. Promoted to general of division at the age of 30, he had paid for his advancement with the blood of five wounds, one at least being severe, and a spell in the hands of the Austrians. He had served with several of the great soldiers of the Armies of the Rhine and of the Sambre and Meuse, Lamarche, Kléber, Colaud, and Marceau among them. Ney owed his first step to old Lamarche, who commanded the regiment when he became regimental sergeant major. The Colonel-General Hussars Regiment was one whose officer corps showed a remarkable devotion to duty, at the time when other corps were emigrating wholesale.[2]

Michel Ney was born on January 10, 1769, the second son of Pierre Ney, master barrel-cooper. His father had served in the Seven Years' War. Ney was bilingual, for Saarlouis, now in West Germany, was then a French city in German-speaking Lorraine. Ney received, at the Collège des Augustins, an education that fitted him to work for a notary at Sarrelouis and subsequently as an overseer of mines and forges. But the life of a civil servant had no appeal for Michel Ney, and on February 12, 1787, more than two years before the outbreak of the Revolution, he enlisted voluntarily as a hussar in the army of the Old Regime.

[*]See R. Horricks: Marshal Ney—*The Romance and the Real* (Turnbridge Wells, 1982) p. 258

Promotion was slow, but when he had 4 years of service he was promoted to corporal quartermaster, and by the time (April 20, 1792) the Girondins, who were then in power, declared war on Austria, Ney, age 23, was already regimental sergeant major. No doubt by this time he was an accomplished horseman, a first-class *sabreur*, and a good drill-master.

From October 19, 1792, to July 4, 1793, Ney, now a lieutenant, was aide-de-camp to Lamarche. The general gave him a most favorable "confidential report," praising his intrepidity, activity, and courage as well as his rare tactical skill.[3]

After a spell as aide-de-camp to General Colaud, Ney was given command of 500 cavalry under Kléber in the Army of the Sambre and Meuse, and it was here, in his first command, that he made his name.

Ney was not destined to see action under Bonaparte until 1805. Yet, though thought to be a friend of General Jean-Victor Moreau (1763–1813), he was one of the only three senior officers of the Sambre and Meuse who were singled out by the Corsican to be marshals of his Empire.[4] In Ney's case this new friendship was cemented by a dynastic marriage. On August 5, 1802, at the age of 32, Michel Ney espoused a charming young protégée of the future Empress Josephine. This was the 20-year-old Aglaée Louise Auguiée, whose father had been a senior financial official under Louis XVI. It could be said that Ney married above his station, but Aglaée was of a sweet and tractable disposition, while her husband was, if one may be forgiven such a vulgar expression, a self-confident bastard, and 12 years older than she. Their's seems to have been a happy marriage, and the evidence for Ney's having a German mistress, or a liaison with Moreau's friend Ida St.-Elme,[5] seems but thin. Algaée is described as tall, slender, and pretty. Gérard's portrait shows a typical ornament of the cultivated court of the Empress Josephine. Her family had been devoted to the Old Regime, and she has been described as in effect an unofficial lady-in-waiting to Josephine. Her mother, on hearing of the execution of Queen Marie Antoinette, had thrown herself from a high window.

During Napoleon's preparations for the invasion of England, Ney, in command of VI Corps of the Grand Army, was quartered at Montreuil. It was at this period that Ney became acquainted with the Swiss theorist Antoine-Henri Jomini (1779–1869). Jomini had studied the posthumous works of Frederick the Great, as well as the events of Bonaparte's first Italian campaign (1796). The fruit of these studies was his *Treatise on Grand Military Operations*. This work he offered to various French and Russian generals, without finding a Maecenas. Murat, for one, did not feel that he had anything to learn from the military history of his own or the previous generation. Ney, however, had a rather more inquiring mind. He read Jomini's manuscript and was sufficiently impressed not only to take the Swiss major on his staff, but to advance him the money required to publish it.

By imperial decree of May 19, 1804, 18 senior commanders of the French Army were made marshals of the Empire. In this first promotion, the name of Ney came twelfth. In 17 years the hussar had fought his way to marshal and to command of a corps.

Corps Commander in Central Europe and Spain (1805–1811)

Ney opened a glorious spell with the Grand Army with the victory that gave him his ducal title: Elchingen (see p. 375). It was his misfortune to miss the Battle of Austerlitz. At Jena, Ney, at the head of his corps cavalry, attacked prematurely, and was perhaps fortunate not to be cut off. General Savary tells us that the Emperor was very much displeased and said a few words to Ney on the subject—"but with delicacy".[6] Ney made amends with the capture of Erfurt and Magdeburg: valuable contributions to the success of Napoleon's most skillful and devastating campaign.

The indecisive Battle of Pultusk (December 26) left the French depressed and exhausted. The Emperor was compelled to send his men into winter quarters. Ney found himself in a thinly populated frontier district, where the imperial method of making war support war simply did not work. In the first week of January 1807, Ney, using his initiative, marched his corps 60 miles into East Prussia, ran into L'Estocq's Prussian corps, and was compelled to retire. Benningsen, misinterpreting Ney's foraging raid as a full-scale offensive, advanced with the intention of clearing the French from the Lower Vistula.

The Emperor was not pleased with Ney for provoking this Russian offensive, but, as Bennigsen seemed to be exposing his left flank, engaged him in the sanguinary Battle of Eylau, truly described as a check to the Grand Army. But Ney's corps arrived opportunely, and his pressure on the Russian right compelled them to withdraw.

The campaign ended with the glorious Battle of Friedland (June 14, 1807), in which VI Corps played the decisive part. "That man is a lion,"* said the Emperor, as Ney marched past him at the head of the right wing. By 8 P.M. the marshal had stormed

*Horricks, *op. cit.*, p. 83.

Friedland, and Napoleon had celebrated the anniversary of Marengo with one of his most brilliant tactical successes. "How glorious it is to be a Frenchman," Ney wrote to his wife, while Berthier paid a generous tribute to his "brilliant courage— equalled only in the age of chivalry."

Ney, now in high favor, was showered with financial rewards and—to him far more important—was created Duke of Elchingen. But if the Emperor valued his prowess in battle, a fellow marshal, Davout, had some hard things to say of VI Corps' administrative indiscipline, and *les desordres affreux* that its men had committed while passing through Warsaw. Not only pillage, but murder, it is alleged, blemished their conduct.[7]

> Most important, perhaps, of all the arrivals was that of Marshal Ney, the toughest and most resolute of all the Emperor's fighting-men, who brought with him a spirit of enterprise and confidence which had long been wanting in the army of Spain.[8]

On August 2, 1808, the duke of Elchingen was summoned to the Army of Spain. He was to spend nearly two-and-a-half years in Spain and Portugal, a period of misfortune for the French arms and one that revealed Ney in a bad light: thoroughly insubordinate to any commander but the Emperor himself, besides being unreasonably touchy, quarrelsome, and uncooperative.

Napoleon opened his campaign with a complicated combination. On November 23, 1808, Marshal Lannes defeated General Castaños at Tudela. The Emperor expected the routed Aragonese to find Ney cutting off their retreat.

To his brother, Joseph, Napoleon wrote on November 27: "Ney has allowed himself to be imposed upon by the Spaniards, and rested for the twenty-second and twenty-third at Soria, because he chose to imagine that the enemy had 80,000 men and other follies. If he had reached Agreda on the twenty-third, according to my orders not a man would have escaped."[9] From this one could not suppose that in order to succeed VI Corps would have had to cover 120 miles in four days, crossing a rugged mountain range on the way. However, Napoleon was not one to appear as anything but infallible.

The death at Caçabellos (January 3, 1809) of General Auguste Colbert (1777–1809) deprived Ney of a trusted friend. "I sleep peacefully, when Colbert commands my outposts," the marshal had said. Although Colbert was serving in Soult's corps at the time of his death, Ney sent one of his own aides-de-camp to collect his possessions. "His wife and children will one day attach value to having what belonged to him. Besides it is the only and final proof of friendship that I could give to this brave young man."[10] Ney is sometimes said to have been distant with his generals and his staff. It may be that this aloofness has been exaggerated.

On January 16 Soult fought Sir John Moore at Corunna. Among the casualties was Major Charles James Napier,* who received five wounds and was taken prisoner. The marshal treated him with the kindness of a friend rather than the civility of an enemy, and set him at liberty on parole not to serve again until exchanged.[11]

But if the marshal was a generous foe, he could be the most uncooperative of colleagues. Both Soult and Massena were to discover this to their cost, the former after his ignominious retreat from Oporto and the latter during his disastrous campaign in Portugal. Soult, who had extricated his army only by abandoning his artillery and baggage, found Ney reluctant to give him so much as a gun team.

It might have been well for Napoleon had he entrusted command of the Army of Portugal to someone other than Massena. The prince of Essling, despite the fresh laurels on his brow, was in no mood for campaigning. General Foy thought that Massena at 52 looked 60, while the marshal himself declared that, tired and ill, he was feeling his years. Ney, who by this time detested the lecherous old miser, felt that he himself, still only 41, was the man to drive the English leopard into the sea.

Massena entrusted Ney with the Sieges of Almeida and Ciudad Rodrigo. The former, tenaciously defended by 5,000 Spaniards under General Andrés Herrasti, held out for 24 days. Leaving the Siege of Ciudad Rodrigo to his chief sapper, Major Conche, Ney set up his headquarters at Salamanca, conducting operations by remote control. At this juncture Colonel Valazé (1780–1838), a very experienced engineer officer belonging to Junot's corps, reported for duty. Ney sent him back to Valladolid with an unworthy gibe: "I don't want the Duc d'Abrantès to bother me with his protégés. If they are so good, let him keep them for himself."

Massena lost no time in sending the unfortunate sapper back to Ney, who took up his pen and produced a letter that, while protesting his esteem for his commander, was so extraordinarily insolent that it provoked an outburst from Massena. "So I am no more than a fake commander-in-chief! I mean that this young man shall conduct the siege, and by the Devil in hell Monsieur Ney shall bow the knee before my will, or my name is not Massena!" The temptation to relieve Ney of his command must have

---

*1782–1853; major in 1st. Battalion of the 50th Regiment of Foot; elder brother of the historian of the Peninsular War.

been almost insuperable, As it was, the patient Massena had his way insofar as Valazé did indeed conduct the siege operations at Ciudad Rodrigo from June 29 to July 10, when he was severely wounded by a grenade.[12] When at length the French advance began, the high command made a fine old muddle of their first battle: the attack on the ridge of Busaco.

With Montbrun and 7,962 cavalry at his command,[13] Massena failed dismally in his "forward recce," and was quite satisfied with the ill-grounded opinion of his corps commanders that the position was held by little more than a rear guard. No marks to Ney or to Reynier, but the responsibility was Massena's, and he, eight miles to the rear, was currently concerned with Venus rather than Mars.

When on September 27 the French infantry, laden with their heavy packs and pouches, toiled up the steep slopes that concealed Wellington's position, *Le Rougeaud* (the "Redhead"), perfectly properly, if uncharacteristically, directed operations from the "Start Line"—the foot of the hill. It was, of course, quite sufficient that generals of brigade and division should lead the assault. When the attack crumbled before the British musketry, there was nothing that Reynier or Ney could do to restore the situation. Massena, who could recognize disaster when he saw it, very sensibly called off the action. Only then did the cavalry explore Wellington's left flank and discover the way to outflank his position.

The French now advanced on Coimbra, which, though it offered no resistance, was sacked. Massena helped himself to scientific instruments found in the university. He presented one of the telescopes to Ney, who sent it back saying that he was not a receiver of stolen goods.

Thus far Ney had shown himself sullen, critical, and unhelpful, but when at long last Massena was compelled to retreat, Ney, entrusted with the conduct of the rear guard, showed his best side: great tactical skill, coupled with inexhaustible energy. "It was a dress rehearsal for Ney's *tour de force* in Russia."[14] Even so, when, during the retreat, false rumor reported the capture of Massena, Ney cried out "Pardieu! Tant mieux!" ("By God! So much the better!") But if Ney was "critical," we may suppose that Reynier and Junot were not much better.

The retreat ended, Ney's insubordination showed itself once more, and Massena, who had an iron will as well as seemingly endless patience, finally ordered him home. At first Ney would not accept his dismissal, but Massena had his way.

The Emperor does not seem to have been unduly upset by Ney's misconduct. After a pleasant stay at his country estate, Ney was given command of the camp of Boulogne,[15] while poor old

Massena found himself replaced by Marmont. One is tempted to suspect that the Corsican liked to see his marshals at daggers drawn: divide and rule . . .

The Empire in Decline (1812–1815)

The camp of Boulogne proved a dreary place: a waste of barrack huts abandoned when the invasion of England was called off. But in January Ney received orders that were to prove the first step on the long road to Moscow. "I intend," he told Aglaée, "to restore my good name and my honour as a general with France's army in this, the coming clash between the two Emperors who at present divide Europe."[16] He was as good as his word. In hard fighting at Smolensk (August 17) where he was wounded in the neck, at Valutino, and especially at Borodino, where he stormed the Russian center, he showed that he was still the man who had made the decisive attack at Friedland. But it was by his noble conduct during the retreat that Ney rendered his name immortal.

Napoleon left Moscow on October 19, but he did not give Ney command of his rear guard until November 3. By this time it had begun to snow. Of 100,000 men who left Moscow, about 40,000 reached Smolensk. Ney still had 6,000 infantry, a squadron of cavalry, and 12 guns. On November 18 General Miloradovich, one of the more enterprising of the Russian generals, managed to cut him off and sent an officer to demand his surrender. Ney's answer was worthy of Bayard: "A Marshal of France does not surrender. One does not parley under the fire of the enemy. You are my prisoner."

Throughout the retreat Ney's energy and courage were equaled only by his tactical ingenuity. Musket in hand, he led countless charges. On one night march, a wagon went through the ice, and a survivor could be seen still clinging to the edge. Ney himself crawled to pull him out of the icy water. Recognizing the rescued officer, he said in a matter-of-fact way, "Ah . . . de Briqueville, I'm glad we got you out!"

On November 20 near Orcha, Ney with his last 2,000 men found themselves cut off by a mass of cossacks. *"Tambours! La Charge!"* the marshal cried, and once more led his men in a desperate attack.

A Polish officer got through to headquarters. The tidings that Ney had almost broken through seemed to the Emperor "like that of a famous victory."[17] "At last, I have saved my eagles!" he cried—rather inaccurately—"I have three hundred millions in francs at the Tuileries. I'd give the lot to save Ney.

What a soldier! The army of France is full of brave men, but Michel Ney is truly *the bravest of the brave.*"[18] Next day Prince Eugene broke through to the 925 survivors of III Corps. It was an emotional and tearful moment, as they embraced: *"Monsieur le Maréchal!" "Monsieur le Vice-roi!"*

The Emperor was able to reinforce Ney to a strength of 4,000 and with these he continued to cover the melting remains of the Grand Army as it trudged westward. The marshal's tactics were simple and practical. Toward the end of a day's march, he would find a defensive position, a knoll or wood or small ravine. Then he would close his ranks and light fires. Such food as was available would be cooked and the men were given five hours rest. About 10 P.M. they would follow the army's route, halting at first light and repeating the process all over again.[19] Not far ahead of the rear guard, some 10,000 stragglers, some wounded, others frostbitten, moved slowly westward. Ney did his best to keep them going—orders, entreaties, blows. It was not for nothing that he had been regimental-sergeant-major of the *Colonel-Général* Hussars!

Meanwhile Berthier, true to his trade of chief clerk, continued to churn out "bumf" by the ream. Ney was not harassed only by the cossacks!

The Grand Army dwindled away, starving and frozen. By December 2 only 13,000 men remained in the ranks. By December 13 Ney had only 100 left. With these the marshal and General Baron Gérard held the bridge of Kovno. That brave veteran, Jean-Roch Coignet, describes the scene. "Marshal Ney effected a retreat at nine o'clock at night, after having destroyed all that remained of our artillery, ammunition, and provisions, and having set fire to the bridges. It may be said in praise of Marshal Ney that he kept the enemy at bay at Kovno by his own bravery. I saw him take a musket and five men and face the enemy. The country ought to be grateful for such men.'"* And so after five months the wreckage of the Grand Army quit the soil of Russia.

On December 15 Ney reached Gumbinnen in East Prussia. He wore a ragged brown coat over his tattered and filthy uniform. From behind a long beard, his red-rimmed eyes glared out of his darkened face. This apparition burst in on the intendant general of the Grand Army, Count Mathieu Dumas (1753–1837), who was at breakfast.

Ney: Here I am then.
Dumas: But who are you?

---

*Captain J. R. Coignet—*The Notebooks of Captain Coignet, Soldier of the Empire, 1799–1816 *England trans. (London, 1928) p. 241.

Ney: What! Don't you recognize me? I am Marshal Ney: the rear-guard of the *Grande Armée.* I have fired the last shot on the bridge at Kovno. I have thrown the last of our muskets into the Niemen. I have made my way here across a hundred fields of snow. Also I'm damnably hungry. Get someone to bring me a bowl of soup.

None can tell how many of Napoleon's men got back from Russia. But every man that did owed his freedom, indeed his life to Michel Ney of Saarlouis, who could swear at them in both French and German.

On March 25, 1813 Napoleon bestowed upon Ney the title of Prince of the Moskova. Of the many honors awarded under the Empire, none was better deserved. It recognized Ney as being on the same level as Davout and Massena. In addition, Ney received an annuity of 800,000 francs and a month's leave, during which the Emperor took the opportunity to show him off in Paris as a reminder that the Russians had not defeated him, declaring that the "good effect our Brave Ney is having" struck him as "better than a *champ de mai.*"[*] To be the Lion of the Hour was not a role that appealed to "the Redhead," whose martial pride should not be confused with vanity. The end of his leave was marred by the news that Aglaée's sister, Adèle, had been accidentally drowned while in attendance on Queen Hortense at Aix-les-Bains.[20]

All too soon Ney found himself summoned to Germany to command the new III Corps. He was far from happy about the strategy of the coming campaign. He could not believe that the Emperor could be so mad as to recommence hostilities when he no longer had an army: "the machine no longer has either strength or cohesion: we need peace to reorganize everything. . . . It would be folly to ensconce ourselves in Germany."[21] Ney's views cannot be faulted from a strategic point of view.

General Van Dedem van der Gelder (1774–1825), a Dutch brigadier, has some interesting comments on his corps commander under whom he served for eight months in 1813. Ney "was a man of much courage and energy on the battlefield"; otherwise "he was feeble and indecisive, permitting himself to be led by others' counsel.[†] Deeply detesting Napoleon, on bad terms with the Prince of Neuchâtel, jealous of other marshals, he was on good terms only with Macdonald. Uncommunicative, reserved, he saw little of the generals who served under him." Van der Gelder goes on to say that Ney was tormented with jealousy

---

[*]Horricks *op. cit.,* p. 152. A *champ de mai* was a parade and festival held periodically on a large open space of that name in Paris.
[†]*See Mémoires du Général Baron de Dedem der Gelder, 1779–1825.* (Paris, 1900)

over his wife and had a poor opinion of the ladies with whom she was intimate, particularly Queen Hortense. In addition, Ney "foresaw early on the unfortunate end of the 1813 campaign."

Ney's new formation took part in the Battle of Lützen (May 2, 1813). It proved a hard struggle, and an indecisive victory. Ney received a shot in the right leg and his chief of staff, General Baron Gouré (1768–1813), was mortally wounded. He had been with Ney since April 1, 1812, and proved difficult to replace. Eventually Jomini was appointed in his stead.

Napoleon planned his next operation, Bautzen (May 20–21), as a battle of envelopment. Three corps were to pin the allied left. Ney with four others was to turn the allied right. All went well at first, but one of Napoleon's hastily scribbled pencil notes was misunderstood by Ney, who halted when, by pushing on, he might have cut the allies' line of retreat. Once again the Emperor had won, but it was a fruitless victory. Ney had clearly demonstrated that he was not really capable of commanding more than a single corps. There were those who said that Ney had taken a village—Prostitz—and lost an empire.

Ney chose this moment to recommend Jomini for promotion to general of division, but the jealous Berthier managed to prevent this by arresting the Swiss pundit for not submitting his strength returns on time. On August 15 the wily Swiss went over to the Tsar, who promoted him to lieutenant-general and made him an aide-de-camp.

Ney fought at Dresden (August 26–27) and greatly distinguished himself. His old friend Moreau, serving on the Tsar's staff, was mortally wounded, possibly by a gun laid by the Emperor himself.

Hoping to exploit his success, Napoleon sent Ney to attack Berlin. Ney drove back the Prussian corps under General Tauenzein and, not expecting a fight, failed to carry out a proper forward reconnaissance. Bülow was able to attack him at Dennewitz, 40 miles south-southwest of Berlin. Ney, who had lost 24,000 men and 50 guns, fell back behind the Elbe.[22] He was so upset by this reverse that he actually contemplated suicide. To the Emperor he wrote, "The spirit of generals and officers is shattered and our foreign allies will desert at the first opportunity."[*]

Ney's dislike of Napoleon, which, in view of his changeable nature, should not be exaggerated, dates from the days following the disaster at Dennewitz. The Emperor's Corsican suspicions were aroused when he learned that Bernadotte had corres-

---

[*] Delderfield, *March of the Twenty-Six* (London, 1962) p. 174.

ponded with Murat, Berthier, Ney, Oudinot, and Macdonald. There was a furious row. At first Ney spoke for them all, but the others came to his support. Napoleon called his brother-in-law a traitor, whereupon Murat laid his hand on the hilt of his saber. Berthier tried to speak of his duty as a French prince, and Napoleon turned on him savagely: "You too, old imbecile, what are you meddling in? Be quiet!" To such a pass had things come!

Ney fought at Leipzig where he and Marmont held the big village of Schönefeld. Langeron found them powerful opponents. On October 18 Ney received a severe contusion in the shoulder and was given leave to go home. Ney recovered from his Leipzig wound in time to ride at the Emperor's side throughout the Campaign of France. When the army concentrated at Châlons-sur-Marne in January 1814, Ney commanded the Young Guard, 16,000 strong.

An incident of the Battle of Montmirail shows that Ney had lost nothing of his old dash. At the height of the battle, the Emperor gave Ney the task of driving the enemy out of the farm of Les Greneaux, which they had turned into a stronghold with heavy artillery support. Ney dismounted—from one of his more fortunate horses—and, drawing his sword, put himself at the head of six battalions of the Young Guard. He ordered his men to empty the pans of their muskets and take out the flints. This done, he led the men forward with fixed bayonets. Ney's resolute charge was altogether too much for the enemy. Russians and Prussians fled from the farm, abandoning their guns, their limbers, and even their cooking pots.[23]

When at last the corps commanders found that they could no longer hold the allies with the few exhausted men that remained, it was Ney who spoke for the other marshals at Fontainebleau, demanding the Emperor's abdication.[24]

On May 29 the divorced empress, Josephine de Beauharnais, died. Doubtless the Neys felt that she had been ill-used.

With the departure to Elba of the Emperor Napoleon, Marshal Ney found himself the foremost soldier in France. The Bourbon government did not hesitate to employ him. He was a member of the Council of War and commander of the cavalry, which he reorganized with a zeal and efficiency that won the praise of Marshal Soult, who became minister of war on December 3, 1814.

But life under the Ultras of the Old Regime soon proved irksome with émigré officers looking for unearned rewards and courtiers reviving their tedious etiquette. One November evening the sensitive Madame Ney, finding herself insulted by the Duchess of Angoulême, went home in tears. There followed an explosion of "the Redhead's" uncontrollable temper. He stormed into the Tuileries in his riding boots, burst into the presence, and delivered a broadside, which began: "I and others were fighting for France while you sat sipping tea in English gardens." He went on to air his views on the manners and ancestry of the duchess and her circle, bluntly ending with: "You don't seem to know what the name Ney means, but one of these days I'll show you."* And he stormed out as unceremoniously as he had come.

Louis XVIII, timid by nature, was for placating Ney by making him a gentleman of his bedchamber, but found himself no match for the implacable duchess. Still, when the dread news came that the Eagle had flown from Elba, it was to Ney that they turned. Before the marshal took leave of King Louis—for the last time—he declared, "France must not have another civil war. Bonaparte's enterprise is sheer madness. I am leaving at once for Besançon, and if need be I will bring him back to Paris in an iron cage!"

"I did not ask him to say all that," said the monarch faintly as the marshal withdrew. "Napoleon in an iron cage, eh? Well. I would not like such a bird in my room!"

There were but few troops at Besançon when on March 10 Ney arrived there. Still full of fight he pushed on to Lens-le-Saulnier, whence he wrote to Marshal Suchet at Strasbourg asking for reinforcements: "We are on the eve of a tremendous revolution. Only if we cut the evil at its root is there any hope. But I fear many of the troops are infected."[25]

On March 13 Ney was visited by emissaries of Napoleon, who brought a letter that said, "Execute Bertrand's orders and join me at Châlons. I shall receive you as I did after the Battle of the Moscova."[26] This evidently struck the right note with Ney. It was not the Bourbons who had made him a marshal, a duke, and a prince, but the magnetic Corsican with all his detestable and tyrannical qualities. Instead of simply retiring as Moncey, Oudinot, and Macdonald did, the impetuous Ney went over to Napoleon in an emotional scene at Auxerre (March 18). His desertion put an end to royalist resistance. It was an act that did nothing for the marshal's reputation as a man of honor. Why could he not simply have retired? "The frontier was not far away."

That Napoleon welcomed Ney does not prove that he trusted him—during the Hundred Days he did not employ him. But at the last moment (June 11), Napoleon wrote to Davout, now minister of war: "Send for Marshal Ney and tell him that if he wishes to be present for the first battles, he ought to be at Avesnes on the fourteenth." Ney lost not a moment in accepting this belated

---

*For both quotations: Horricks, *op. cit.* p. 544.

invitation. Deeply conscious of the trust that the French soldiery had in him, he simply could not let them take the field without him. On his arrival the Emperor invited him to dinner and entrusted command of his left wing to him. But we may suppose that neither had forgotten Dennewitz, or the first abdication, or that ill-conceived iron cage. Ney's first mission was to seize the crossroads at Quatre-Bras. It should have been possible to pin one ally while turning the other's flank. The Emperor, who, evidently forgetting Bautzen, had put 45,000–50,000 at Ney's command, hoped to arrive in Brussels on the morning of June 17.

June 16 was a day of hard fighting, both at Ligny and at Quatre-Bras. Several urgent messages failed to make Ney break away from Quatre-Bras and fall upon Blücher's right flank. At Ligny it was not until 7:30 P.M. that a determined onslaught by the Guard smashed through the Prussian center. At Quatre-Bras Ney went about his task in leisurely fashion. By 10:00 A.M. Wellington himself was present and ready for Ney's tardy attack. Reille, who like Ney himself had fought the British in the Peninsula, advanced cautiously until by 4:15 P.M. he was heavily engaged. Ney sent for d'Erlon's corps to reinforce Reille, and to his astonishment and fury found that it had vanished. It seems that d'Erlon spent the afternoon marching and countermarching between the two battlefields of Quatre-Bras and Ligny: Exactly why is uncertain, but it seems that, unknown to Ney, a strongminded aide-de-camp (Labédoyère) had brought d'Erlon a note in the Emperor's more or less illegible hand.

By nightfall Ney had gotten d'Erlon back under his command, but it was now too late. Wellington's reinforcements had arrived, and Ney, who had lost 4,000 men, retired two miles to Frasnes. His men rested throughout the morning of June 17, while Wellington was quietly falling back on Waterloo. At about 2 P.M. the Emperor arrived and Ney told him—incorrectly—that the reason for his not being at Quatre-Bras was that "it was occupied by the whole of Wellington's army."[27]

At 11 A.M. on June 18 Napoleon gave his orders to his corps commanders. At about 1 P.M. he intended to give the order to Marshal Ney to capture the village of Mont-St.-Jean at the intersection of the roads.

The Emperor had devised nothing more subtle than a massive frontal attack against a skillfully chosen position. Napoleon entrusted the conduct of this attack to Ney, though there was no apparent reason, except indifferent health, to prevent the Emperor running the battle himself. The first French attacks were repulsed by about 2:30 P.M., and in the distance beyond Plancenoit the Prussian advance guard could be seen.

Foiled in his infantry attacks, Ney, now acting without

orders, put himself at the head of Milhaud's 5,000 cuirassiers and hurled them at the squares between Hougoumont and La Haie Sainte. The valiant horsemen flowed between the rock-like squares, galloping over some of the battery positions, and then, countercharged by Lord Uxbridge's well-mounted regiments, ebbed back down the slope. Undaunted, Ney now led Kellermann's corps to the charge; but since he failed to provide any infantry support, the result was no more successful than before.

At about 6 P.M. the Emperor ordered Ney to make another assault on La Haie Sainte, and this was successful, for the garrison had almost run out of ammunition. Since Ney had exhausted the heavy cavalry, he was virtually unable to exploit his success. But, eager to do so, he asked the Emperor for more troops. The allied line opposite La Haye Sainte was now but thin, nor was it entirely steady. Now if ever was the time to launch the superb battalions of the Guard, but Napoleon, his cavalry massacred and his command post exposed to Prussian roundshot, turned on Colonel Heymès, Ney's messenger, with "Troops? Where do you wish me to take them from? Do you want me to make them?"[28] A little later Napoleon decided that he would play his last card: he would send in the Guard. Once more he entrusted Ney with the tactical conduct of the battle. Gallant and headstrong as ever, the marshal led five battalions in two huge columns, not against the gap he had made near La Haye Sainte, but more or less where he had earlier led the heavy cavalry. The British had had time to reorganize and, though suffering severely from the French artillery, held their fire until the Imperial Guard was within 20 yards, when they delivered their volley. It was shattering.

But the Third Foot Chasseurs, who received the devastating volley, were stern veterans. They held their ground and even tried to deploy, but after 10 minutes Wellington detected a wavering in the French lines and sent in the 1st Foot Guards with bayonets. From the French ranks arose the cry *"La Garde recule."* ("The Guard retreats . . .") By this time, it seems, four horses had been killed under Ney. "Come, and see how a Marshal of France can die!"* he cried as he tried to rally some of Durutte's division for yet another desperate charge. The marshal owed his escape to Major Schmidt of the Red Lancers, who obtained a horse for him—apparently the fifth he had ridden that day. It was pitch dark now, and the routed army was in no mood to rally: not even for the hero of the retreat from Moscow.

Ney, too, had had enough. Arriving in Paris on June 20—the day *before* Napoleon—he was in the Chamber of Peers on June 22 and delivered an extraordinary tirade exposing the weakness

---

*A. Brett-James, *The Hundred Days* (London, 1966) p. 153.

of what remained of the army and venturing to reproach the Emperor for putting in the Guard too late.

Ney, unable to make up his mind to go into exile, lingered in Paris until July 6. Eventually he took refuge at the isolated château of Bessonie, near Aurillac (Cantal), which he reached on July 29. There on August 3 he was arrested.[29]

The restored Bourbon government lost no time in bringing him to trial. His lawyers tried to make the point that Sarrlouis, the marshal's birthplace, was no longer French. Ney sprang to his feet and cried out, "I am French, I shall know how to die like a Frenchman!" And so it proved. On December 7, 1815, condemned by his peers, he appeared before a firing squad at the Carrefour de l'Observatoire in the Jardins du Luxembourg. "Soldiers," he said, "when I give the command to fire, fire straight at the heart. Wait for the order. It will be my last to you. I protest against my condemnation. I have fought a hundred battles for France, and not one against her." General Count Leon Rochechouart, who was in charge of the proceedings, remembered that Ney's demeanor was "noble, calm and dignified beyond reproach." The marshal gave the order to fire, and fell struck by 11 bullets. "One of the soldiers had the good taste to hit the top of the wall."[30]

Thus, true to himself, died Michel Ney. With a little foresight, and something of the energy that he displayed when he mounted his white charger at Borodino, he could very easily have escaped.

Ney was at his best under the eye of the Emperor, for the talents of a dashing hussar complemented those of a clever gunner. Napoleon in his last four campaigns was sometimes handicapped by ill health, while Ney was extraordinarily hardy and rugged. They were practically the same age, but in Russia Napoleon suffered terribly from the cold, while the marshal proved not only the bravest of the brave, but the toughest of the tough.

It is perhaps not too much to suggest that the successes of 1814 were to some extent achieved because with Ney always at his side Napoleon had a paladin at hand to carry out great strokes, as at Montmirail. Ney with his proved valor and his quick *coup d'oeil* was a formidable weapon.

It has been suggested that after Russia the marshal had something akin to "shell shock," and that this accounts for his unpredictability. This to my mind is absurd. If so, why did the other marshals—Davout, Macdonald, Mortier, Lefebvre, Oudinot— not suffer from the same malady? It cannot be denied that Ney was temperamental and changeable, but this may be attributed to obstinate disagreement with the policies of both Bonaparte and Bourbon. Ney was insubordinate and quarrelsome, proud and touchy, but this should not be confused with shell shock. In action Ney was undaunted. His tactical skill might fail him, but never his courage. As a disciplinarian and an administrator, he was probably rather better than Davout and others would have us believe, though it may be that he left these matters to be attended to by his officers. He needed the spur of action to make him show his war-like talents to the best advantage.

Napoleon was a strategist and an organizer. Ney, the tactician, was like a sharp saber ready to his hand when, as at Elchingen or Friedland or Montmirail, he had some special tactical move to execute. Their qualities were complementary.

The Battle of Elchingen (October 14, 1805)

Officers and [noncommissioned officers] must strive to be as well-informed as possible. Our national genius offers enormous resources in this field, especially now when promotion is open to all. But two conditions remain absolutely imperative: the infantry must be good, swift marchers, accustomed to fatigue; also their fire-power must be effective.

NEY, 1805.*

On August 23, 1805, Emperor Napoleon abandoned his plan to invade England and determined to crush Austria before the Russians could reinforce her. The Grand Army was launched on an operation such as Europe had never before seen. It was to end with the capitulation of "the unfortunate Mack" and 30,000 Austrians at Ulm, and in this denouement the splendidly trained VI Corps was to play a leading part.

Although the 1805 campaign was the first in which Ney served directly under the orders of Napoleon, the marshal had the greatest confidence in the Emperor at this period. When Jomini ventured to suggest a possible line of withdrawal should things go wrong, Ney turned on him: "How can you imagine that French troops led by the Emperor would ever retreat? People who think of retreating before a battle has been fought ought to have stayed at home."[31]

On August 29 orders were given for the 375-mile march of the Grand Army from the Channel coast to the Rhine. The move was completed by September 26. On September 20 a report from Murat informed Napoleon that the Austrians were approaching Ulm. By crossing the Danube lower down, the Emperor could cut their communications with Vienna and intervene between them and their Russian allies. The corps of Lannes (V) and Ney (VI) were ordered to march by Stuttgart, Ludwigsburg, Heiden-

*Cited by Horricks, *op. cit.*, p. 71.

heim, and Gundelfingen so as to find the Austrians' northern flank. The other four corps[32] were to move in a southeasterly direction, crossing the Danube between Donauwörth and Ingolstadt, and march on Augsburg and Munich.

Lannes crossed the Rhine at Strasbourg and Ney near Karlsruhe. The Emperor arrived at Strasbourg on September 26. The Imperial Guard was there already. Mack now had 50,000 men around Ulm, while General Kienmaier was watching the Danube between Donauwörth and Ulm. On October 8 Murat, supported by II and IV Corps, attacked Kienmaier and compelled him to fall back southward toward Munich. Murat, wheeling westward, ran into General Auffenberg at Wertingen (October 8), where he and Lannes took 1,469 prisoners, four colors, and six guns. Lannes and Ney were now to approach Ulm from the east, on either bank of the Danube, so as to complete the encirclement of the fortress.

On October 12 Napoleon gave Murat command of the force that was to give the *coup de grâce*: V and VI Corps and the Reserve Cavalry. "There is no question," wrote the Emperor, "of just beating the enemy, not a man must escape."[33] But some did escape.

Lannes would have been a much better choice than Murat to command such an operation. The latter, who had not grasped the Emperor's intention, ordered Ney, who was on the left bank near Günzburg, to cross to the south bank. Ney, prompted it seems by Jomini, argued against this, but in vain. Mack, using his initiative for once, took advantage of Murat's blundering to send General Werneck's corps away northeastward. This led to a sharp action at Albeck (October 11) with General Dupont's division of Ney's corps. This cost the Austrians heavy casualties, including 3,000 prisoners. Thanks to Murat's stupidity the Austrians still held the bridge over the Danube at Elchingen, 6 miles northeast of Ulm. Here the Emperor planned to stage a dramatic conclusion to his brilliant campaign.

"Soldiers," he proclaimed, "tomorrow will be a hundred times more famous than the day of Marengo; I have put the enemy in the same position. The most remote posterity will recall your deeds on this memorable occasion."*

The Austrian defensive position, held by Field-Marshal Count Riesch and 8,000 men (32 battalions, and 12 half-squadrons of cavalry) was a strong one, but they were already contemplating withdrawal and had partially demolished the bridge.

Phase 1. At 8 A.M. Ney in full uniform rode up to the Elchingen bridge at the head of Loison's division. Elite companies of Villatte's brigade, despite a brave resistance, drove back the Aus-

---

*Le Correspondence de l'Emperor Napoléon I, Vol. XI, letter No. 9381.

trians, so that the bridge could be repaired without delay. Riesch, watching from the village, sent down two battalions supported by four guns, but they were easily repulsed.

Phase 2. Ney crossed with his leading battalions and himself led the 1st Battalion of the 6th Leger toward the abbey, the 2nd Battalion of the 6th toward Ober–Elchingen, and the 1st Battalion of the 39th Regiment toward St.-Wolfgang. Ten guns supported this attack. Colbert drew up the 10th Chasseurs and the 3rd Hussars, ready to exploit any infantry success. The 1/6th Légér stormed the abbey and an Austrian battalion (Spork—800 strong) was taken. The village was overrun, except for the brickworks, which held out. Riesch fell back toward Gottingen.

Phase 3. The attack of Loison's division led by 1/39th Line, too isolated, was driven back by Austrian cavalry, but the rest of Loison's division came to its support; while Colbert, after charging the enemy infantry, swiftly redeployed to ward off the threat from 150 cuirassiers.

Phase 4. The crisis of the battle came when Ney ordered Roguet to take the wood on which the Austrian right rested. Colonel Brun (69th Line) outmaneuvered the enemy, who, dismayed by their boldness, fell back into the Grosser Forest, abandoning their artillery.

Phase 5. Threatened by the 18th Dragoons, the Austrians formed square. The 76th Line opened fire on them, and Colonel Lefèbvre-Desnoettes led the 18th Dragoons to the charge. The square was broken and two guns taken. Colonel Caulaincourt led the 19th Dragoons in pursuit toward Unter–Elchingen.

Phase 6. The Austrian withdrawal now began in earnest. Villatte took Kesselbronn, and Roguet, pushing on, had to repulse a last great charge by the enemy cavalry. Colbert and his light cavalry took them in flank. Reisch fell back on Ulm. Ney still had Malher's division in reserve. He had taken 4,000 prisoners. His losses amounted to 737 killed or wounded.

The French ring round Ulm was complete. With the eye of the Emperor upon them, Ney and his well-trained corps had fought brilliantly. Napoleon, congratulating Ney on his success, said, "True, we have paid dearly for it, but to be called Duke of such a nice town is not to be sneezed at. What do you think of it?" Three years later Ney was duly made Duke of Elchingen.

On October 20 Ulm surrendered with 16 generals, 20 guns, 40 colors, and 32,000 men.

Ney's next task was the pacification of the Tyrol. He entered Innsbruck on November 5, and so missed the great victory at Austerlitz (December 2). It was some consolation to Ney when he was told that on the eve of the battle Napoleon had said, "Oh! If only I had my Ney here now. He would soon give these ruffians a drubbing!"

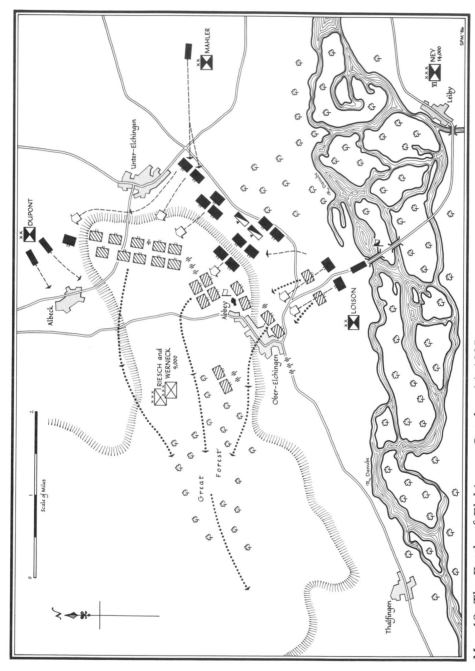

Map 19. The Battle of Elchingen, October 14, 1805

TEXTUAL REFERENCES

1. R. Horricks, *Marshal Ney: The Romance and the Real* (Tunbridge Wells, 1982), p. 48.
2. Among those who chose to be true to their salt were the two Kellermanns, Francois Drouot, Baron de Stengel, Henry-Jacques-Guillaume Clarke, and General Corbineau.
3. Horricks, *op. cit.*, p. 21.
4. The other two were Mortier and Soult.
5. See F. G. Hourtoulle, *Ney, le Brave des Braves* (Paris, 1981), p. 15.
6. As recounted by General Rapp in L. Bourienne, *Memoirs* (London, 1833), Vol. 2, p. 384.
7. Hourtoulle, *op. cit.*, p. 54.
8. C. Oman, *A History of the Peninsular War* (Oxford, 1902–30) Vol. 1, p. 341.
9. *Correspondance de Napoléon Ier*, Vol. XVIII, No. 14,518
10. See J. Ojala, *Auguste de Colbert* (Salt Lake City, 1979), p. 182.
11. Horricks, *op. cit.*, p. 94.
12. Ney does not seem to have held a grudge against Valazé, who commanded the engineers of his corps in 1813.
13. Oman, *op. cit.*, Vol. 3, pp. 540–43.
14. R. E. Delderfield, *The March of the Twenty-Six: The Story of Napoleon's Marshals* (London, 1962), p. 141.
15. From August 31, 1811.
16. Horricks, *op. cit.*, p. 113.
17. General A. A. L. de Caulaincourt. *Memoirs,* Eng. trans. (London, 1950), Vol. 2, p. 89.
18. A title that Napoleon had bestowed earlier, with equal justice, on Marshal Lannes.
19. Horricks, *op. cit.*, p. 144.
20. *Ibid.*, p. 153.
21. Hourtoulle, *op. cit.*, p. 136.
22. A. Brett-James, *Europe Against Napoleon* (London, 1970), pp. 34, 35.
23. C. Parquin, *Military Memoirs*, ed. by B. Jones (London, 1969), p. 172.
24. Namely, Lefebvre, Macdonald, Moncey, and Oudinot.
25. Horricks, *op. cit.*, p. 194.
26. *Ibid.*, p. 196.
27. J. Marshall-Cornwall, *Napoleon as Military Commander* (London, 1967), p. 274 fn.
28. A. F. Becke, *Napoleon and Waterloo* (London, 1939), p. 216.
29. Horricks, *op. cit.*, pp. 250, 251.
30. P. Young, *Napoleon's Marshals* (London, 1973), p. 119.
31. Horricks, *op. cit.*, p. 73.
32. Augereau (VII Corps) was watching the roads into the Black Forest.
33. To Soult, October 12, 1805, *Correspondance op. cit.*, Vol. XI, No. 9375.

BIBLIOGRAPHICAL NOTE

There are two excellent modern biographies of Marshal Ney, by Dr. Francois-Guy Hourtoulle, *Ney, le Brave des Braves* (Paris, 1981), and Raymond Horricks, *Marshal Ney: The Romance and the Real* (Tunbridge Wells, 1982). Other works that I have found revealing include R. F. Delderfield, *The March of the Twenty-Six: The Story of Napoleon's Marshals* (London, 1962); General Sir James Marshall-Cornwall, KCB, CBE, DSO, MC, *Napoleon as Military Commander* (London, 1967); Sir Charles Oman, *A History of the Peninsular War*

(Oxford, 1902–30); and Lt.-Col. Charles Parquin, *Miliary Memoirs*, ed. by B. Jones (London, 1969).

Standard sources include Ney's *Mémoires*, 2 vols. (Paris, 1833) and *Documents inedits du duc d'Elchingen* (Paris, 1833). Older biographies include E. Bonnal, *La vie militaire du maréchal Ney*, 3 vols. (Paris, 1910–14), and Piers Compton, *Marshal Ney* (Leipzig, 1937). Of great value for its study of the end of Ney's life is Harold Kurtz, *The Trial of Marshal Ney, His Last Years and Death* (London, 1957). See also, for 1815, Antony Brett-James, *The Hundred Days* (London, 1964).

CHRONOLOGY

1767, April 25	—Born at Bar-le-Duc (Mense)
1784–87	—Private in Médoc Regiment at Peripignan
1789, July 14	—Captain of a company of regular cavalry
1790, November 7	—*Chef de légion* of *Garde Nationale de la Meuse*
1791, September 6	—*Lieutenant-colonel en seconde* of Third Battalion of Meuse Volonteers
1795, June 13	—Confirmed in rank of *général de brigade*
1795–96	—Wounded and taken prisoner at Neckerau; exchanged
1796, September	—Wounded storming Ingolstadt bridge
1798, March 7	—Victory at Feldkirch, followed by two setbacks
1799	—*Général de division* (April); replaces Suchet as Masséna's chief of staff (July)
1799–1800	—At Siege of Genoa
1800	—Chief of staff to Brune; fights well at Monzembano
1801, December 18	—Inspector general of the cavalry
1803, August 30	—Command of 1st Infantry Division at Bruges
1805, February 5	—Takes command of Grenadier Reserve Corps at Arras
August 29	—Takes command of 1st Division (*grenadiers réunis*) of V Corps
October 8	—Victorious at Wertingen
1807, February 16	—Victorious against Russians at Ostrolenka
May and June 14	—At Siege of Danzig; important role at Friedland
July 12	—Succeeds Lannes in command of Soult's reserve
1808, July 2	—Made *comte d'Empire*
1809, April 19	—Victorious at Pfaffenhofen under Massena
May	—Wounded at Essling; succeeds to II Corps; disobeys orders at Wagram and secures victory
July 2	—Appointed *Maréchal d'Empire* (twenty-second in order of appointment)
1810, April 14	—Created *duc de Reggio*
1812, January 15	—Commands II Corps, on the Elbe
June–July	—Victorious at Wilkomir; is repulsed at Jakowo
August	—Victorious at Oboiartsina; badly wounded at Battle of Polotsk; hands over II Corps to St.-Cyr
November 28	—Badly wounded at the Berezina
1813, April–May	—Commands XII Corps and extreme right at Bautzen
August 23	—Defeated by Bernadotte at Gross-Beeren
1814, February–March	—Commands VII Corps in Champagne
April–June	—Government commissioner for armistice; made Chevalier of St. Louis and peer of France
1815, March 24	—Fails to save Metz for Louis XVIII; retires
September–October	—Major general of Royal Guard; member of Privy Council; commander in chief of Paris National Guard
1823	—Commands I Corps; governor of Madrid
1830, August 11	—Suspended after dissolution of the Royal Guard
1839, May 17	—Grand Chancellor of the Legion of Honor
1842, October 21	—Governor of Les Invalides, where he dies, September 13, 1847

CHAPTER TWENTY

THE FATHER OF THE GRENADIERS

Oudinot

by

Paul Britten Austin

Emergence of a Leader (1767–1801)

Oudinot, duke of Reggio, was Napoleon's most wounded marshal. This did not prevent him from living to a ripe old age and dying, doyen of them all, at the age of 81. He owed neither his baton nor his dukedom to any single brilliant exploit—unless possibly to his brilliant disobedience to imperial orders at Wagram. Yet in all other respects he was the very type of his kind. On St. Helena Napoleon would call him *un brave homme, ma poca testa*, "a decent fellow, but not very bright."[1] He was neither a politician nor an intellectual. If he survived five regimes "without fear and without reproach," it was solely by virtue of his military and administrative abilities and his personal integrity.

Son of a brewer, Nicolas-Charles Oudinot was born on April 25, 1767, in the plebeian district of Bar-le-Duc, on the borders of Champagne and Lorraine. An affectionate, good-natured child, he was also an unruly one. Aged 17, having no taste for business, he (like Bernadotte) ran away and enlisted as a private soldier, in the Médoc Regiment. Bought out three years later by his father, he was at Nancy, again unwillingly studying bookkeeping, when the Revolution broke out. Elected captain of a company of Bar-le-Duc volunteers, he was promoted a year later to *chef-de-légion* (approximating to Major) of the department's national guard and thereafter colonel of the 3rd Battalion of the Volunteers of the Meuse. For three dramatic years he fought with them in the fluxes and refluxes of war between the Moselle and Rhine, on the plains of Alsace, and in the Vosges. On September 20, 1793, while pursuing the fleeing Austrians at Bitch, he sustained his first wound—a saber cut on his head. Promoted a fortnight later to command the Fourth Demi-Brigade, formed from the famous Picardy Regiment, the 27-year-old republican colonel soon attained the same ascendancy over its aristocratic officers as he clearly did over everyone else. "How I loved those men," he would exclaim in later years. "I loved them so, I got them all killed!"[*]

On November 27 of that year, Oudinot's "bullet head," which, according to Napoleon, had so few ideas in it, was hit by a musket ball during a hot affray in the woods around Hagenau in Alsace, and he was invalided home, not for the last time, to Bar where he had already married. But Oudinot's wounds were as remarkable for the speed with which they healed as for their frequency. On June 2, 1794, he distinguished himself by saving a division of Ambert's Army of the Vosges at Morlautend, and was

---

[*]Cited by G. Stiegler in *Récits* (Eng. trans., 1896), p. 12.

promoted to provisional general of brigade; after conducting the brilliant retreat from Kaiserlautern in front of the advancing Möllendorf, he was confirmed in the rank. After a fall from his horse while leading a charge at Treves, and a badly broken leg, it looked as if his tempestuously active career was at an end. Moreau gave him a glowing certificate. But after only six months, he was ready to cross the Rhine with Pichegru's victorious army. Mannheim surrendered, but the enemy counterattacked vigorously; and during a night action at Neckerau, Oudinot suffered five saber cuts and next morning was picked up by the Austrians and interned at Ulm. Three months at Ulm ended with his being exchanged for an Austrian general. After several months' rest and having briefly been governor of the captured fortress of Phalsburg (June 2, 1796), he rejoined Moreau in Bavaria. Occupying Nordlingen, Donauwörth, and Neuburg, he was ordered to invest Ingolstadt and, on September 14 while sustaining the enemy's furious attack, suffered four saber cuts on the neck and a ball in his thigh. A month later, his arm still in a sling, he was the hero of Moreau's brilliant retreat at Ettenheim. Another year's fighting in Alsace led to the conquest of the Palatinate, where he pushed on as far as to Oggersheim, opposite Mannheim, where, on November 7, 1797, he thoroughly defeated the Austrians and was able to winter his troops at Grunstädt, deep inside enemy territory.

During the truce that followed the Treaty of Campo Formio, he returned to Mayence. Thence in late 1798 he was ordered to Switzerland to serve under Massena. The Army of Switzerland had advanced, rather rashly, as far as Lake Constance. An attempt was to be made to support Jourdan on the Danube. But to do this, the Vorarlberg first had to forced at Feldkirch. The whole terrain presented a stupendous obstacle: sheer cliffs, narrow defiles, the Ill's swampy banks. On March 7, 1799, Oudinot, entrusted with this impossible task, attacked, took 600 prisoners, and almost managed to break through. Two more attempts also failed under a massive Austrian fire of grape and musketry and with the peasants on the heights rolling down rocks onto the assailants' heads. But Massena, realizing what kind of an officer he had under him, promoted him to general of division and made him his chief of staff.

Calling off his offensive, Massena entrenched himself in a strong position behind the Limmat River where it flows out of Lake Zurich. While defending this line (June 4, 1799), Oudinot was hit in the chest by a musket ball; and on August 14 at Schwitz, while halting the Austrians and an enraged peasantry that were trying to turn the French position as it was being frontally assaulted by the Russians, by yet another, this time on the shoulder blade, while charging at the head of a dragoon regiment.

Massena was now in an increasingly critical situation. Bonaparte was in Egypt. The fleet had been destroyed at Aboukir. Republican France was threatened from all sides—by Suvorov's Russians in Italy and Korsakov's in Switzerland, both coordinating their movements with de Hotze's Austrians. Switzerland had become at once a salient and the bastion of the Republic.

Massena began by attacking Korsakov on the right bank of the Limat, and occupied Zurich itself. It was to Oudinot, commanding a corps of 15,000 men, that he entrusted the crucial river crossing, with orders to march up the right bank and envelop the town. Oudinot carried out his orders with such secrecy and effect that he seized the Russians' camp at Houg by a *coup de main*, got ahead of them on the Winterthur road, and cut off their retreat. The next day, doubling back, after a furious fight and despite being hit yet again by a musket ball in his chest, he burst into the city where he rejoined his commander-in-chief. It was the end of Korsakov's offensive (September 26).

Two weeks later Oudinot marched into Constance. The town was defended by Austrians and the last debris of Condé's army. About 200 of the latter, taken prisoner, expected to be shot as traitors. But Oudinot avoided applying the rigor of the law by sending them off to Massena under so weak an escort that half escaped en route. Massena took the hint and in the same fashion forwarded the rest to Besancon. Only the escort arrived. Massena had saved France from invasion. He wrote: "I owe the very greatest praise to Gen. Oudinot, my chief of staff, who can subordinate his ebullient ardour to office work, yet whom I always find to his advantage on the field of battle. He has followed me in all my movements and seconded me to perfection."[2]

After five months of recuperating from his latest wounds, Oudinot shared with the Army of Liguria the horrors of the Siege of Genoa. In a small boat Massena's do-it-yourself chief of staff personally ran the British blockade to liaise with Suchet on the Var, and then returned the same way to the starving city. Repeatedly he offered to return the 3,000 prisoners, for whom there was no food at all—an offer as often rejected. "In the end," Oudinot would relate in afteryears, "these unfortunates, shut up in an anchored ship, had begun by eating their ropes and shirts, and ended by eating each other."[3] Dwindled to half its numbers, the ghost army after its honorable capitulation joined Suchet 10 days before Marengo. After another spell of domesticity, recuperating at Bar, Oudinot was seconded to Brune, who was busy pushing the Austrians out of Lombardy. At Monzembano (December 26, 1800) with a handful of the 14th Chasseurs, he charged and silenced an enemy battery that was paralyzing French attempts to cross the Mincio. Sabering the gunners at their pieces, he himself took one of the guns. Sent to Paris with the text of the armistice of January 16, 1801, he was received in the most flattering matter by the First Consul, who presented him with a saber of honor—and the cannon he had captured.

General of Grenadiers (1802–1811)

The Peace of Amiens was followed by two years of organizational work as corps commander under Davout. The two men would always remain close friends. It was at Bruges, too, that Oudinot seems to have taken on the batman to whose pen and watercolor brush we owe so much. "Grenadier" Pils was an Alsatian whose devotion to his patron knew no bounds. Since he could virtually count on his master being wounded, Pils, besides his journal and box of watercolors, always had with him a first-aid kit.

The ever-famous Grenadier Corps, with which Oudinot's name would always be associated, had originally been formed by Junot out of the elite of the elite of the infantry. It was in command of this crack corps that Oudinot, on August 16, 1805, marched for Germany, sharing with Murat the honors of "the unfortunate General Mack's"* first defeat at Wertingen (October 8); but when Mack capitulated at Ulm 10 days later, the Grenadier Corps was already hot on the retreating Archduke Ferdinand's heels, taking 12,000 of his men prisoner and then harrying the Russian rear guard toward Vienna. At Amstetten, without artillery and preceded only by their light cavalry and 200 carabiniers, they first flung themselves on the enemy rear guard and then on the entire Russian army. The ferocious struggle was crucial to the campaign's outcome. It forced the enemy off the right bank of the Danube and opened the road to Vienna.

It was Oudinot who led his grenadiers over the 1,800-foot-long Thabor–Brouke bridge as they flung Austrian powder barrels and fascines into the Danube, while at its far end Lannes and Murat chatted up the elderly and unsuspecting Austrian commander. In the days leading to Austerlitz, the grenadiers were always in the van. In the intense fighting at Schoengraben (November 16), their commander, though shot in the thigh, continued giving orders until the end. Telling him "your courage is greater than your strength"[4] and ordering him back to Vienna to recuperate, Napoleon proposed to give his grenadiers to Duroc.

*See D. G. Chandler, *The Campaigns of Napoleon* (New York, 1966) p. 400.

But Oudinot rejoined two days before Austerlitz, where they were in reserve, in support of Soult.

After only two weeks convalescence in France, Oudinot was entrusted with his first civil mission. So well did he carry out the occupation and administration of Berthier's new principality that, when he left, the Neufchâtelois made him an honorary burgher of their ancient city, and a local monk presented him with a sacred relic.

At Jena, too, the Grenadier Corps was in reserve. On February 15, 1807, Suchet and Oudinot saved a critical situation at Ostrolenka, where they were guarding the Grand Army's right flank as it marched slowly and painfully toward East Prussia. The Russians tried a surprise attack; driven off, they lost two standards and seven guns. The next day Oudinot—it would not be the only time—was himself nearly taken prisoner by pillaging cossacks. After his men, while besieging Danzig, had carried out the singular exploit of capturing a British corvette that was trying to run victuals to the besieged Russians under cover of a dense morning mist—the fog lifted suddenly and the ship, becalmed in the sea canal, surrendered after only a token resistance—Oudinot had a horse shot under him while valliantly resisting a last breakout attempt by 8,000 Russians in four columns.

After the city's surrender, Lannes and his 10,000 men, among them the Grenadier Corps, were marching eastward when, in the afternoon of June 13, they made contact near the little village of Friedland with the rear guard of the main Russian army retreating toward Königsberg. An immediate onslaught being out of the question, Oudinot put off his pinning-down operation until the next morning, but then promptly seized the village of Posthenen, the Sortlack Wood, and the high ground dominating the River Alle, thus barring the Königsberg road and forcing the Russians to await Napoleon's arrival and fight a full-scale battle with their backs to the river.

The fighting had started at 3 A.M. By 7 A.M. the Grand Army's advance guard was already beginning to dwindle. But Mortier's arrival raised their numbers to 26,000—not much, even so, to do battle against 75,000 Russians. The advance guard hung on until midday, when Napoleon, after a nine-hour forced march, arrived on the scene with the whole army. By that time Oudinot's coat was torn by musket balls, his horse drenched in blood, and his men dead beat. Even so he offered, if reinforced, to throw the Russians into the river. Since Napoleon's corps were also all in, it was not until 4 P.M. that the battle was resumed in earnest. Friedland was carried. The bridges were destroyed, and the Russians, forced to ford the river, were flung into full retreat. Though now in reserve, Oudinot's men had meanwhile been gravely exposed to Russian artillery fire. Oudinot's horse had a leg broken. And a round shot passed so close to him that one of his aides-de-camp fell dead, stifled by its wind.

It is at Danzig, after the Peace of Tilsit, that we read of Oudinot passing jolly evenings in Mortier's company, blowing out candles with pistol shots—and paying handsomely for the damage. But not even in peace could Oudinot keep out of harm's way: one of his "unofficial" wounds had been sustained in a café brawl in Paris at the time of the *Fructidor* coup. This time it was his horse that, on December 12, 1807, refused to jump a ravine and fell on top of him, again breaking his right leg. So it was not until March 1808 that Oudinot, still limping badly, was again active. It was on the occasion of his rejoining his command that we hear of a party at which Rapp, Napoleon's favored aide-de-camp, lifting the lid off a magnificent paté, unleashed a volley of birds with tricolor garlands tied to their necks and legs. On the ribbons was written: "To the glory of General Oudinot!"*

According to Napoleon, Oudinot, like Ney (whom he in some respects resembled and therefore hated), never opened or closed a campaign without asking for money. He had a vast family of dependants and was always running up debts. Already, a year after Friedland, he had been given 33,000 francs annually. On July 2, 1808, Napoleon made him a count of the Empire and settled on him an estate worth one million francs, at Inoclavo. Oudinot used the income to purchase a confiscated abbey near Bar-le-Duc. On festive occasions the Monzembano cannon, set up in its vast park that Oudinot loved to embellish, would fire a salute in his and everyone else's honor. He also established there a papermill to provide employment for the locals.

When Napoleon met the Tsar at Erfurt in 1809, his star was at its zenith. Oudinot was appointed governor of the city. It was then that Napoleon, presenting him to Alexander, said, "Sire, I present to you the Bayard of the French Army. Like that valiant knight, he is without fear and without reproach"[5]—a sobriquet he had to share with Bessières.

Lucky enough not to fight in Spain, in 1809 Oudinot commanded Massena's advance guard against the Austrians, arriving on the Isar in time to secure victory at Landshut (April 20) and throw Archduke Charles across the Danube. On May 1, marching into Upper Austria, he was again successful against the enemy at Ried. Three days later, amid frightful scenes of slaughter that shocked even Napoleon, he seized Ebersberg. On May 9 he was at the gates of Vienna. The city was disposed to resist, but Oudinot flung his men into the Maria–Hilf suburb and forced a capitulation.

*Included in Steigler, *op. cit.*, p. 52.

This time it was not so easy to get across the Danube. After the first crossing, from the Isle of Lobau on the night of May 21–22, Oudinot's II Corps occupied the center. It had already advanced so far into the Austrian center that it was in danger of losing touch with Lannes and Massena, when news came that the bridges behind them were broken. During a withdrawal even more costly than the attack, Oudinot, hit in the arm by a musket ball, had to return to the Isle of Lobau in his carriage.

After Lannes's death a few days later, the *10th Bulletin* announced that command of II corps had been given to "Count Oudinot, a general tested in a hundred combats, where his intrepidity has equalled his knowledge."[6]

The offensive being resumed, it was Oudinot who effected the surprise crossing before Wagram. Taking the Austrians off their guard, II Corps seized a fort and a hamlet, and by dawn had forced the enemy troops in Sachsengang Schloss to surrender. At 7 A.M. it was mounting the first slopes of the plain and by 9 A.M. was in line opposite Archduke Charles's troops, occupying high ground. By evening, with Davout to its right and Massena to its left, it had reached Grosshofen. Although ordered the next day not to attack unless himself attacked, Oudinot saw his advantage. Flouting imperial orders, he crossed the Russbach stream and carried Baumersdorf and the Wagram heights. Neither a musket ball that carried away his ear nor a horse shot dead under him could stem his ardor. He was just entering Wagram itself when yet another musket ball hit him in the thigh. By 3 P.M. the Austrians were retiring at all points. Oudinot had made a decisive contribution to an otherwise most uncertain victory. The next day Napoleon said to him:

"Do you realise what you did yesterday?"
"But Sire, I hope I didn't do my duty too badly."
"You deserved to be shot."*

On July 19, 1809, Napoleon wrote from Schoenbrunn Palace, "It was General Oudinot who took Wagram on the 6th, at midday"; and on August 5, in his order of the day, "His Majesty owes the success of his arms to the Duc de Rivoli and to Oudinot, who pierced the enemy centre at the same time as the Duc d'Auerstaedt turned his left."[7]

Clearly, Oudinot was by now standing not merely in the line of fire, as always, but also next in line for a marshal's baton. In fact, on July 13 he was resting (wounded as usual) on some straw at Znäim, where the armistice had just been signed, when

*See Steigler, *op. cit.*, p. 105.

the handsome Colonel Flahaut entered his tent and delivered an imperial dispatch. It appointed him marshal of the Empire, with a further annual income of 60,000 francs. He received the title of duke of Reggio (in Calabria, where he had never been), together with yet another annual endowment of 36,000 francs.

The next year the duke of Reggio's faculties as administrator and conciliator were again needed. After incorporation of the Netherlands in the Empire, he was sent in with the Army of the North to explain as tactfully as possible to the Dutch that they were indeed part of the Continental System. It was at Utrecht (February 1810) that his son, Victor, a second lieutenant in the Chasseurs of the Guard, accompanied by the mayor of Bar, brought him the sad news of the death of the first Duchess of Reggio, a very fat woman, never seen at court. On July 1 King Louis abdicated, and the Army of the North entered Amsterdam.

If ever a people had won its independence with blood, sweat, and tears, it was the Dutch: "Oh come, M. Cambier, don't cry like that," said Oudinot, as the mayor of Amsterdam, in tears, handed over the keys of the city, "or, *ma foi,* I'll do the same; and then we'll both look silly!"[8]

Despite the rarity and brevity of his stays at Bar-le-Duc, Oudinot had produced a large brood of children—the final count would be 11. Feeling the necessity of a new wife to head this big family, he decided to remarry. His new bride, the 18-year-old Eugénie de Coussy, came from an ancient aristocratic and military family at Bar. "Tell Mlle. de Coussy that I'm forty-four and have 500,000 frs in rents," he wrote to a go-between. "As for my social position, it is well-known; and I'd be happy to share it with her."[9]

More urgent matters put off the wedding. As satrap he had to prepare Napoleon and Marie Louise's tour of their new kingdom. The tour's success was a tour de force by Oudinot. Little though the Dutch liked being part of the French Empire, there is no doubt they appreciated its representative: in 1815, after Waterloo, the House of Orange would honor him with the grand cordon of its highest order. A more immediate reward was Napoleon's agreement to his marriage. Perhaps no wedding of a Napoleonic marshal has been described so vividly.

Russia and After (1812–1842)

But already it is 1812. The very day before his wedding, Oudinot had again been posted to command II Corps, this time in Westphalia. The supreme effort, as Napoleon would afterward call it, was already under way.

On February 12 a cavalcade of carriages left Bar with the duke and Duchess of Reggio and General Lorencez, his chief of staff who had married his second daughter. Making for the frontier, they were welcomed by an enthusiastic staff at Munster, "ten to twelve generals, all in the prime of life, not one of whom is on this earth today."[10] Despite an irascible temper, Oudinot, unlike Davout, seems to have been popular with his staff. Kindly little reconciling gestures made up for frequent injustices and a punctiliousness not second to his friend's. As for the rank and file, this rough-mannered marshal who, in a café or at the theater, would as soon knock a man down as look at him—still less be looked at—was wholly to their taste.

Prussian resentments, Oudinot knew, ran high, and he slipped unobtrusively into Berlin. But then a flea in his ear from Berthier ordered him to make another triumphal entry with all his 40,000 men. As the King of Prussia reviewed them, Oudinot observed protocol by riding on the king's left, but broke it by ensuring his own horse's head was a few inches ahead of his companion's. Napoleon was still top dog.

On June 24, II Corps crossed the Niemen with the main body and marched for Kovno. Pursuing Wittgenstein's rear guard, it formed the extreme left wing, if not of the Grand Army as a whole—Macdonald's X Corps had crossed still farther downstream—at least of its central body (Davout, Ney, Murat), which, under Napoleon's direct orders, would ultimately reach Moscow. It was Oudinot's first really independent command.

"For the first three days," Pils writes in his journal, "the marshal marched without encountering a single Russian soldier."[11] Then, at 10 A.M. on June 28, just as the army had halted at the village of Develtowo, it ran into the Russians. Marbot, who had applied for a position on Oudinot's staff and been turned down, gives an extremely scathing, not to say funny, account of what he regards as Oudinot's unpreparedness to meet the enemy, who however, after two hours of fighting, retired. It was the first real action of the campaign. According to Pils, Oudinot had to wait three days for an acknowledgment of his report to reach him from Vilna, 30 miles away. Already this unprecedentedly far-flung theater of operations was widening dangerously.

Through blazing heats such as they had never known even in Italy, II Corps marched northeastward, mounted the Dwina's left bank, and took the entrenched camp at Dwinaborg. Ordered by Napoleon to push Wittgenstein back toward Petersburg, Oudinot crossed the Dwina at Polotsk and, fording the Drissa at Sivotschina, ran unawares into the Russians at Jakoubowo (July 29). After the appalling losses en route, his corps was already at only half-strength, while Wittgenstein's was being steadily reinforced. Feigning retreat Oudinot withdrew across the Drissa and arranged a large-scale ambush. On July 31 the Russians fell into it. Thrown back into the river, they lost 14 guns, 13 ammunition wagons, and more than 2,000 prisoners.

Even when reinforced (August 6) by what was left of St.-Cyr's route-weary Bavarians, Oudinot was no longer in a position to take the offensive. The complicated series of operations, advances, and withdrawals that were to prelude the first Battle of Polotsk (August 17) followed. Perhaps it would have been "Oudinot's battle" if it had not been for his penchant for himself rushing into the fray. A few weeks earlier, at faraway Bar, his young wife had just received delivery of his bust, commissioned at Berlin. When opened, the left shoulder fell off. "A fatal thought seized on my imagination. It came only too true. A few days later the marshal's shoulder was shattered by grapeshot."[12] In reality, it occurred as he had rushed forward to sustain a wavering battalion of *voltigeurs*. So it remained for St.-Cyr to win the first Battle of Polotsk—and his marshal's baton.

For Oudinot it meant a long, painful journey in his carriage back to Vilna. There he was joined by his intrepid young wife who, against Napoleon's strict orders that no woman was to cross the Niemen, had come to nurse him. But already on her arrival in early October he was able to sit on his horse, and by the end of the month he was having more and more frequent tête-à-têtes with Maret, the foreign minister. A new word had made itself heard: retreat. And the marshal, his wife said, was seized with an indescribable agitation.

At the very earliest moment, he rejoined his corps, via Minsk, Borissov, and Orcha, on November 4. Finding Marshal Victor's strategies "as dangerous as they are useless,"[13] he was often tempted, according to Lorencez, to flout Napoleon's orders to coordinate with IX Corps in front of Wittgenstein and instead to secure the crucial Borissov bridge at an early stage, "but he believed himself chained to the Emperor's will."[14] In the event IX Corps made tracks southward for the Smolensk high road and II Corps for Borissov. For Oudinot's part in the dramatic events that followed (November 22–29), see p. 395.

In 1813 Oudinot, loyally subordinating himself to the senior marshal, commanded the rearmost division of Ney's corps in its abortive march on Berlin. Running head-first into Bernadotte at Grossbeeren, it was heavily defeated. Oudinot was so far in the tail that he could not deploy. The retreat into France followed. He was in all the final battles. At one moment Napoleon seems to have seriously considered his proposal for a breakout to relieve the German fortress garrisons. At Arcis, in 1814, he saved the army by containing the Wurtembergers and Badeners.

At Fontainebleau the abdicating emperor ordered him to offer his services to Louis XVIII, which he did. The Bourbons made him a peer of France, a minister of state, and governor of Metz. Nor did he break his new oath of fealty. The day Napoleon re-entered Paris, he, in the king's name, declared Metz in a state of siege (the intense drama of those days can be read in Eugénie de Reggio's memoirs). When troops and population declared for the tricolor, the Oudinots quietly left for Bar, but not before he had written to his friend Davout, minister of war:

> Not wishing to play a double role, I am leaving Metz for Bar, my home. . . . Only one thing I recommend to you, my dear Minister, and that is not to enquire into my means of subsistence. I shall sell the little I own to pay the most sensitive of my debts. Above all prevent my household being spied on, and reply that Oudinot, in his poverty (!), is incapable of an act of perfidy.[15]

Davout's appeal to him to side with Napoleon had no effect: "I am faithful to my new master. . . . I shall always remain the Grenadier Oudinot, a title I delight in.—Your old friend, Marshal Oudinot."[16] At first Napoleon dismissed him to his estates; then, on second thought, recalled him and in a tone of voice "half ironical and half severe" twitted him: "Well, M. le Duc de Reggio, what have the Bourbons done for you that I haven't that you should have wished to defend them at my approach?" Whereto Oudinot: "Since I shan't serve under you, Sire, I'll serve under no one."[17]

During the rest of the Hundred Days, Eugénie describes her marshal going for donkey rides in the countryside near Paris. It seems not unlikely that, all beknown to himself, the bluff, politically not very bright soldier had let himself be manipulated by her. That at least would be Napoleon's view from faraway St. Helena: "Recently he has fallen under the influence of his wife, a woman of an old family."[18]

After Waterloo Oudinot accepted the command of the Seine National Guard, resumed his position as minister of state, and for 11 years commanded the Paris National Guard. He also took turn and turn about with Marmont, Victor, and Macdonald in commanding the Royal Guard. Both he and his wife had, in fact, become confirmed legitimists. Louis XVIII stood godfather to their daughter and the formidable (Eugénie calls her "the saintly") Duchess of Angoulême, godmother. In 1823 Oudinot commanded I Corps when it marched into Madrid and rescued the King of Spain from the Cortez. "If he wasn't wounded it was because he didn't fight."[19] Louis Napoleon, too, hastened to court this veteran of the Empire, who in 1845 exchanged his rank of

Grand Chancellor of the Legion of Honor for Governor of Les Invalides. Now 81 he was determined to die there, and did.

Napoleon, congratulating him on his valor, had once said, "Even so, in the life of even the bravest man there comes a moment when he's afraid." To which Oudinot replied, "Sire, I haven't had the time."[20] In his 22 campaigns he had been allegedly wounded 36 times on some 23 occasions.

The Battle of Berezina, Before and After (November 26–29, 1812)

The Berezina was Napoleon's own battle. But more perhaps than any of his fellow marshals, except perhaps Victor, Oudinot played a crucial role in it. On November 20 he had written to Berthier that in two days he hoped his advance guard would be at Borissov, and the rest—in all some 5,000 men, in good fighting trim—the day after. But the aide-de-camp he had sent ahead to liaise with Dombrowski at Minsk ran into his defeated corps, retreating hastily toward Borissov. At 5 P.M. on November 21, he wrote to the Pole: "No matter what forces are threatening you, don't abandon the bridgehead. I insist you cling to it, even to the extinction of all your troops, and await the arrival of II Corps, whose cavalry, at least, should be there some time tomorrow."[21] But it was too late. Of the 4,000 Poles whom 14,000 Russians had flushed out of Borissov, only 300 infantry and 500 cavalry remained to put at the tail of II Corps. But now it was the Russians' turn to be taken off guard. Driving back Tchichakov's men pell-mell into Borissov, Castex's brigade, supported by Doumerc's cuirassiers, "made an extremely brilliant charge . . . and we should have entered the town at the same time as the enemy, if he hadn't fired a small bridge at the entrance. . . . This obstacle lost us some minutes at a moment where the least instant was precious."[22] Dismounting, three-quarters of Castex brigade, armed only with their carbines, tried to rush the 200-yard-long Berezina bridge; but the Russians, commanded by the French émigré General Lambert, repulsed them with artillery fire and grenadier bayonets and broke it, irreparably, at three points. Castex's men, Marbot says, consoled themselves by methodically dividing up the badly needed food, boots, and clothing in the Russians' 1,500 carriages and transport wagons abandoned in the town. When at 3 P.M. Oudinot arrived on the scene, he found the bridge in flames.

The catastrophe would have been complete but for a stroke of luck. After a long cross-country march eastward to rejoin II Corps, Corbineau's light cavalry brigade had found Borissov in Russian hands and been obliged to ford the half-frozen river at a point nine miles upstream. Oudinot, "impatiently" requesting further orders, immediately informed Berthier, and, sending Corbineau's brigade back to Studienka with an infantry regiment and a company of pontooneers, arranged the feint to throw Tchichakov off the track. "Minutely interrogating" some Borissov Jews about the Veresino–Ighumen–Minsk route, now out of the question, he released them like carrier pigeons, ostensibly as spies, in the direction of their Russian outposts. At nightfall (6 P.M.) on November 25, while the cuirassier division marched "pompously" downstream to Oukholada, there to draw Tchichakov's cannon fire by ostentatiously making soundings and amassing materials, the rest of II Corps, "in the most profound silence," set off for Studienka, even the drivers of the train being "forbidden to shout to encourage their horses."[23] Suspecting his Jewish guide of trying to mislead him, he had him shot.

Summoned to Napoleon's headquarters at Locnicza, Oudinot found Berthier in tears and a troubled Emperor, with whom he had a 45-minute interview. It was the first time he had seen anything of the shattered Moscow army. On returning to his own headquarters, he clapped his hand on his chief-of-staff's shoulder and uttered only one word:" Poltava!"[24]

By the time Eblé and Lariboisière arrived with six wagon loads of broken cannon wheels whose iron fellies could be turned into clamps, II Corps' pontooneers had already been at work on the bridges for 12 hours. One of Oudinot's aides-de-camp (Jacqueminot) swam the river with some Polish lancers, and, driving away a handful of cossacks (Pils saw only four), and brought one back for Napoleon to interrogate. Napoleon was delighted to find II Corps in such good shape. Unaware of the state of the Moscow army, their morale, says Marbot, was excellent. Oudinot still had more than 60 guns plus 14 captured Russian ones. All were harnessed to good horses. Rubbing his hands, Napoleon exclaimed, "*Eh bien!* You will be my locksmith to open this passage for me!"[25]

Immediately on the first bridge's completion (11 A.M. on November 26), Oudinot himself, against Napoleon's advice, crossed on foot at the head of II Corps. Tchichakov, he knew, would soon be back in force; and his vital task, supported by the Guard, was to keep open the sole escape route along the Zembin causeway.

November 27 passed quietly enough, under heavily falling show. But at 7 A.M. the next morning, a Russian shell fell on the shack that a moment before had been Oudinot's headquarters as an officer came galloping up to report Tchichakov's approach.

With visibility at only 30 paces, Oudinot was advancing with his infantry through enfilading Russian gunfire, had just seen one of two guns he had called up to protect them carried off under his nose, and was standing "furious" (according to Pils; Eugénie says he was "humming a little tune") in the middle of the Minsk road. He had just sent off his last aide-de-camp to fetch up Dumerc's cuirassiers and recapture it, and was asking Pils for a drop of brandy to warm him when Pils, as he later wrote,

> . . . saw M. le Maréchal put his hand to his side and fall from his horse, which immediately bolted. I was the only person with him. . . . He showed not a sign of life. I tried desperately to dismount, but my right shoe was stuck in the stirrup; but a young *voltigeur* who had lost his right hand at the wrist and was holding his musket in the other, came to my aid. We made a kind of stretcher out of pine branches. The Emperor . . . sent his own carriage with an escort of Horse Grenadiers; but M. le Maréchal, who had regained consciousness said he couldn't stand any jolting.[26]

Although Napoleon ordered Desgenettes to attend to him, his own surgeon (Capiomont) insisted. Oudinot refused to be tied down, and Pils gave him a wad of cloth to bite on. But "though the surgeon's probe went in six or seven inches, he couldn't find the ball, which was never extracted." "If he vomits," murmured Desgenettes, "he's a dead man."[27] He did not.

The following afternoon (November 29) the greviously wounded marshal's carriage had gone on ahead of its infantry escort and had reached the hamlet of Pletchnitzy, where Capiomont was dressing his wound in a Jew's house, when Victor Oudinot came rushing in: "My dear father, I've sad news. We're all prisoners."* Oudinot's reply to his son is only partly printable. Half-naked, wearing only a fur pelisse, the marshal, saying, "If they get me, at least they'll know what they've got!" ordered Pils to bring him his Grand Cordon of the Legion of Honor and his pistols and set him on his horse. A momentary distraction among the cossacks gave the little party time to join the Italian General Pino and 10 of his grenadiers in a nearby house. There they sustained a veritable siege—this time the cossacks had a cannon, which, bringing down the roof, again wounded Oudinot with one of its splinters. Finally the Westphalian General Hamerstein came to their rescue. But Oudinot's private battle with cossacks is legendary.

Sent on ahead to Vilna, his senior aide-de-camp (Tellier) was the first man to bring news from the Berezina. The duchess thought she saw a ghost. Worse was to come. Arrived at last at Wilna, the little party seemed frozen to the carriage:

---

*See Steigler, *op. cit.*, p. 220.

The door was open, but no one got out. It was sinister. Finally, with great trouble, gently supported by his zealous entourage, the Marshal, broken by suffering and stiff with cold, could be got out. We wanted to carry him upstairs, but he refused, and bent double, unrecognizable from head to foot, he arrived, annihilated in front of the fire that was waiting for him."[28]

Nursed by his wife, his gaping wound rejected—if not the musket ball—at least the bits of "shirt, flannel, uniform, astrakhan fur" that had preceded it.

Up to then, the Duchess tells us, "I'd never known him anything but cheerful. . . . [But] the word disaster was so new to him, he couldn't understand it."[29] Only after he knew Napoleon had passed Vilna by en route for France would Oudinot, rage in his heart, consent to leave. The account of how the wounded marshal and his party, squeezed into his wife's traveling carriage, finally reached Germany must be read in her unforgettable memoirs.

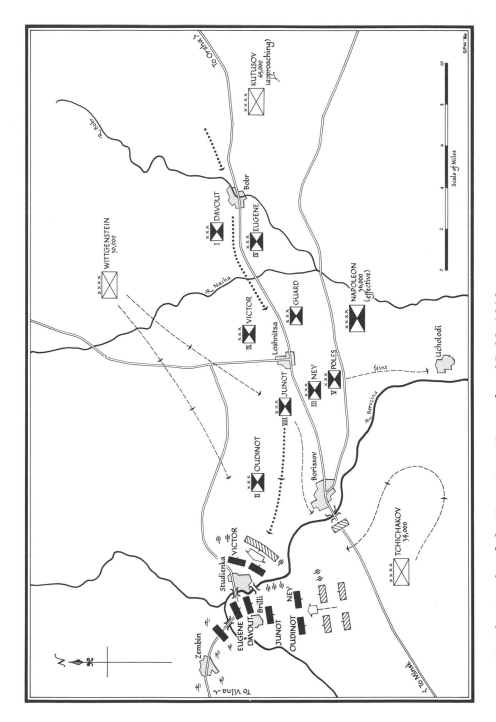

Map 20. The Battle of the Berezina, November 25–29, 1812

TEXTUAL REFERENCES

1. G. Gourgaud, *Journal de Sainte Hèlene*, (Paris, 1947 edition), p. 222.
2. G. Stiegler, *Le Maréchal Oudinot, Duc de Reggio* (Paris, 1894), p. 22.
3. *Ibid.*, p. 24.
4. *Ibid.*, p. 39.
5. *Ibid.*, p. 92.
6. *Ibid.*, p. 102.
7. *Ibid.*, p. 105.
8. *Ibid.*, p. 114.
9. *Ibid.*, p. 123.
10. *Ibid.*, p. 146.
11. F. Pils, *Journal de Marche du Grenadier Pils* (Paris, 1895), p. 105.
12. Stiegler, *op. cit.*, p. 162.
13. Pils, *op. cit.*, *Pièces Justificatives* (cited documents), p. 317.
14. *Ibid.*, Lorencez's letter to Ségur, May 8, 1823, p. 314.
15. Stiegler, *op. cit.*, p. 365.
16. *Ibid.*, p. 367.
17. *Ibid.*, p. 371.
18. Gourgaud, *op. cit.*, p. 238.
19. Stiegler, *op. cit.*, p. 440.
20. *Ibid.*, p. 536.
21. Pils, *op. cit.*, *Pièces Justificatives*, (cited documents), p. 320.
22. *Ibid.*, p. 313, and Lorencez's letter to Ségur, p. 313.
23. *Ibid.*, *Pièces Justificatives*, p. 313, and Oudinot's order, p. 326.
24. *Ibid.*, *Pièces Justificatives*, p. 313, and Lorencez's letter to Ségur, p. 313.
25. *Ibid.*, p. 113.
26. *Ibid.*, p. 147. Eugénie says it was her marshal whose foot got caught in the stirrup, so that his bolting horse dragged him some distance before being halted by an aide-de-camp. But since Pils was actually there . . .
27. *Ibid.*
28. Stiegler, *op. cit.*, p. 225.
29. *Ibid.* She adds that her husband could not stem "the flood of imprecations" against Napoleon "except among those nearest to him." But by the time she had come to write her *Récits* she was an ardent royalist. None of the other 87 memoirists, not even Labaume, reports anything of the sort.

BIBLIOGRAPHICAL NOTE

Oudinot's career and domestic life can be studied quite comprehensively in two works: G. Stiegler's *Le Maréchal Oudinot, Duc de Reggio* (Paris, 1894) and J. Pils's *Journal de Marche du Grenadier Pils* (Paris, 1895). Both are packed with vivid detail, the more so as the former comprises Eugénie Coussy's, duchess of Reggio *Récits de Guerre et de Foyer*, a work that she wrote for her grandchildren but that has gone into at least 28 editions. A third work, Marbot's *Memoirs*, useful for 1812, should in all respects be read with caution. He commanded one of the chasseur regiments in the Castex brigade.

CHRONOLOGY

1754, May 31	—Born at Grenade (Haute-Garonne)
1780, July 6	—*Sous-lieutenant* in *Régiment du Lyonnais;* transfers to *Grenadiers Royaux du Quercy* (1782)
1786, February 14	—Marries Hélène-Catherine de Grenier at Montech
1789, July	—Lieutenant-colonel, *Garde Nationale,* at Montech
1791, September 5	—Elected deputy to the Legislative Assembly
1792, September 16	—Lieutenant-colonel in the *Légion des Pyrénnées*
1793, September 18	—Promoted *général de brigade* (provisional); wounded in the thigh
December 7	—Promoted *général de division;* confirmed on 23rd
1794, November 18	—Appointed commander in chief after the death of Dugommier at La Montagne Noire
November 27	—Captures Figuièras and besieges Rosas
1795, February 3	—Captures Rosas
May 6	—Defeated at Bascara and replaced by Schérer (30th)
September 15	—Appointed commander-in-chief of *l'Armée des Côtes de Brest*
November 26	—Appointed ambassador of the French Republic at Madrid (until December 1797)
1798, October 14	—After short retirement, sent to *l'Armée d'Italie*
1799, August 15	—Commands the left wing at Novi; severely wounded and prisoner for a year
1801	—Commands the 10th military division in Toulouse and becomes a senator (April 12)
1802, September 11	—Appointed *Commissaire Extraordinaire*
October 27	—Appointed vice president of the Senate
1804, May 19	—Created *maréchal d'Empire* (seventeenth in order of appointment)
1806, September 18	—Made governor general of Parma and Plasencia
1808, March 19	—Created *comte d'Empire;* governor of Naples
1813, March 27	—Retired
1814, April 22	—Appointed *Commissaire Extraordinaire du Roi* in the 1st military division
May 31	—Made president of a commission appointed to examine the situation of former officers
June	—Made Chevalier of St. Louis, then a peer of France
1815, April 10	—Dismissed from the dignity of Marshal by Napoleon
July 24	—Restored by Louis XVIII and made governor of the 1st military division (January 10, 1816)
1817, August 2	—Created marquis; Grand Cross of the Order of St. Louis from August 24
1818, December 25	—Died in Paris, aged 74 years

CHAPTER TWENTY-ONE

THE UNKNOWN MARSHAL

Pérignon

by

Dr. Georges Ostermann

Officer and Gentleman: The Early Years (1754–1792)

The family de Pérignon has been known in the southwest of France since the middle of the sixteenth century. In 1569 Antoine Pérignon was a *consul* of Grenade-sur-Garonne, and the hereditary nobility of the family was confirmed at the beginning of the eighteenth century. Bernard-Nicolas de Pérignon (1755–1826), the marshal's uncle, was commissioned in the *Dragons du Dauphin* and in the *Régiment de la Reine*. Jean-Bernard de Pérignon, the marshal's father (1729–1775), was provost in command of the *gendarmerie* in St.-Domingo. In 1752 he married Marie Dirat, the daughter of a notary. Dominique-Catherine was born in Grenade-sur-Garonne in May 1754.

The family of the future marshal, if not really rich and aristocratic by the standards of the time, was comfortably off and influential in the parliament of Toulouse. They owned lands and enjoyed the life of country squires with responsibilities in local administration and relatives in the army, the law, and trading. His education was traditional, and, after sound military studies, Pérignon was commissioned in 1780.

Sous-lieutenant, first in the *Régiment du Lyonnais*, then in the *Grenadiers Royaux du Quercy* in 1782, he became aide-de-camp to Brigadier-General Count de Preissac. Far from the theater of operations, he never saw any action. Garrison duties did not interest him for long, and after the Peace of 1783 he resigned and returned to the country. In 1786 he married Hélène-Catherine de Grenier (1764–1816), the daughter of a former grenadier officer and mayor of Montech. The bride brought a dowry of property and Pérignon could have ended his life as a gentleman-farmer in one of France's wealthiest regions.

In a family so involved in local administration, it seemed natural to reach positions of responsibility, and in July 1789 Pérignon became lieutenant-colonel of the National Guard. In 1790 he was elected justice of the peace, assuming military and civil duties until the National Guard was dissolved on March 30, 1791. On September 5 he was elected deputy to the Legislative Assembly, the sixth of the 12 deputies of the Haute-Garonne. At the age of 37, with a disappointing military career but undoubted electoral successes, Pérignon seemed conclusively turned toward political life and became a member of the Military Committee.

Instead, in May 1792, he resigned his position of deputy and enlisted in the Legion of the Pyrenees and four months later he was a lieutenant-colonel. From this modest but highly dangerous position, he started one of the most amazing and quick rises at a time when rapid careers were so common. Most men who rose to supreme honors were usually either soldiers or politicians and began sooner. They also usually served Napoleon when he was Bonaparte, in Italy, in Egypt, in Paris. And last but not least, they had rich lives full of adventures, resounding victories, love affairs, debts, or aborted religious promises. For Pérignon, history has recorded neither mistress nor scandal—only an exceptional marital fidelity that saw the birth of 11 children in 19 years.

Pérignon had nothing behind him but the prolific life of a well-educated gentleman, with some slight military experience in a remote town close to Spain when the war broke out.

"A Sombre Kind of Energy": War in the Pyrenees (1792–1794)

Over the centuries, Catalonia and Roussillon, on opposite sides of the eastern Pyrenees, had changed kings so often that their inhabitants developed a way of life based on suspicious distrust of all authority. They especially hated the armies, whether French or Spanish, as they never succeeded in protecting their interests but were always ready for looting, in advances or during retreats, knowing no friends or foes. They always had, and still have, a spirit of independence based on their history and culture. Being one of Spain's richest provinces, with its own language, Catalonia was especially desirous to recover its sovereignty.

The Pyrenees look like an impassable, inhospitable natural barrier between two rich plains. The only places to cross them in force were at the extremities, close to the shore. But the mountains were not uninhabited, and the locals were feared on both sides: as *Miquelets* or *Soumatens* they provided light troops for the French as well as the Spanish crowns. They soon found their place in the armies, which were, once again, preparing to invade each other's country. But this time, they looked really different.

Since Spain was ruled by a Bourbon, it was eager to join the coalition against the French Republic, but the Spanish army was not ready and the French declared war in anticipation. They were weak and ill-armed but expected some support from the population of Catalonia. Facing the professionally-drilled but obsolescent Spaniards, there were 18,000 line infantry backed by four volunteer battalions and a handful of gunners. Supplies were non-existent, muskets were old and unreliable, and underfed horses were too weak to draw the guns. Above all, the ubiquitous People's Representatives, with almost limitless power, watched the French generals and sent every suspect to the guillotine at the first sign of weakness. This practice was not unknown in the other revolutionary armies, but it was probably in the eastern

Pyrenees that it reached its peak, as here the men were often defaulters sent for punishment.

Facing General François Doppet, an incompetent former physician, Lieutenant-General Count La Union was probably the best Spanish general of the time, and when he took command after the death of two short-lived commanders-in-chief, the Spaniards advanced to within sight of Perpignan. This period, when Pérignon joined the army with his Legion of the Pyrenees, was one of the worst experienced by the revolutionary armies: marching day and night, in storms of torrential rain or freezing winds, they suffered the cruelty of guerrilla warfare. This foreshadowed the form of war the Imperial Army had to endure from 1808: fanatical monks leading *Soumatens* and criminals (some French), mutilating and killing stragglers and wounded, as Goya depicted later.

Pérignon began his ascending career under these circumstances. Noticed at Truillas, he was promoted to provisional general of brigade on September 18, after being wounded in the thigh. Three months later he was general of division, confirmed in this rank on December 23, 1793. But the position was not one of security, for many a general had "sneezed in the basket" of "Madame Guillotine" as quickly as he earned his honors, and the French were still retreating in a state of starvation and misery.

At last the French government reacted. Replacing Doppet by Dagobert, a former royalist officer, they began to send reinforcements. Dagobert was an experienced soldier and a leader. He soon advanced on his right, taking Belver and Urgel where he could feed his men. Urgel was his last victory as he died from fever, giving command to Dugommier.

This was the general the Army of the Eastern Pyrenees badly needed: the victor of Toulon, he was liked by the soldiers and feared by the politicians. His first measures were to put some order into the mess and confusion of the camps, to feed and equip the men (with what was available), to end the wasting of the few remaining supplies, and to take care of the many sick and wounded. In this task he was unreservedly seconded by Pérignon, himself a man of order.

The work completed in the winter of 1794 was impressive. Stores, hospitals, roads, even arms factories were established as far away as Toulouse and Albi. The troops, reinforced by seasoned veterans from Toulon, were instructed and reorganized with a freshly mounted cavalry and an effective artillery. In April the army was 28,000 combatants strong, backed by 20,000 garrison troops and 9,000 inexperienced volunteers. Their morale was now fair and they were ready for the counteroffensive to free French soil.

The Army of the Eastern Pyrenees currently comprised three divisions: on the right, Augereau, the future duke of Castiglione; in the center, Pérignon; on the left, La Borie. Labarre, one of the finest cavalry leaders of the time, commanded 2,500 horsemen. Perrin "Victor," the future Duke of Belluno, commanded the reserve, and the Count of Lamartillière, an able professional, the artillery.

Covered by the River Tech, the Spanish army was resting in its winter quarters from Céret to Collioures and Port-Vendre, underestimating completely the French reorganization. Ordered to besiege Collioure, but without the siege train expected from Toulon, Dugommier launched a series of bold swift blows on the Spanish positions.

On April 30 Pérignon led his division across the Tech and captured the field works commanding the main road to the fortress of Bellegarde. On May 1, the Spanish camp of Le Boulou was captured and the troops routed, pursued by Augereau up to the Muga. St. Laurent fell on May 6 and Dugommier turned his forces to the coast: Port-Vendre and Fort St.-Elmo were evacuated on May 23 and Collioure surrendered on May 29, ending the Spanish occupation of French soil.

The French could now see the rich plain of the Lampurdan at their feet. The 20,000 Spanish left in Bellegarde were tightly surrounded and besieged by Pérignon. They began to starve while the French pushed south to Figuièras via la Junquera. Ordered to reconnoiter and demonstrate with his division, Pérignon advanced boldly up to the positions held by La Union, stretching in front of Figuièras, at Pont-des-moulins. Convinced he was dealing with the whole French Army and underestimating its strength, La Union left a good position to attack. In the ensuing fighting, Pérignon was menaced on his left wing by the charge of 1,200 regular cavalrymen, but was saved by a daring counter-charge of the 250 troopers led by Labarre who died in the action. Anyway, the French had driven back the Spanish center with heavy losses and their advance was checked. La Junquera (June 7) was the first victory for Pérignon acting as an independent commander. The way to Figuièras was now open before Dugommier.

Unfortunately the offensive had to be halted: once again, supplies, the nightmare of Dugommier, did not materialize. La Union strengthened his position astride the valley leading to Figuièras and prepared his 45,000 men with 4,000 cavalry for the relief of Bellegarde. Their attack, on August 13, was bloodily repulsed by Augereau and Pérignon, and La Union fell back to his lines covered by the Portuguese Division of Don Juan Forbes. The garrison of Bellegarde was soon in the most dire straits, starving and suffering from an epidemic. The governor, the Marquis of Val-Santaro, surrendered after a blockade of 134 days. The French found 68 guns and 40,000 rounds of shot at the place.

Indeed they needed guns, as La Union had established a fortified line of 90 redoubts from St.-Laurent to the coast, in successive lines covered by earthworks and abattis, with Spanish and Portuguese batteries on the heights. At night on November 16, Augereau advanced on the right; Pérignon with the center and Dugua's cavalry were held in reserve on the main road; Victor and Sauret were ordered to mount deceptive attacks on the left, then advance to the lines. Augereau's night advance on the Muga was highly successful, routing the Spaniards and the French émigrés with them. But the line held. In the morning Dugommier, overlooking the battle from the top of La Montagne Noire with Deputy Delbrel, was struck by a Spanish shell and was killed.

Pérignon was immediately put in command. He reinforced Sauret at once on the left, then came back to the right to help Augereau defeat Courten, who withdrew to Figuièras. The next day the army was reorganized by Pérignon. Eager to avenge his beloved general, he advanced swiftly up to Notre-Dame-Del-Roure—a strong redoubt containing 25 guns—where La Union made a courageous last stand against Bon and Guillot. His death, the loss of two other generals, and the storming of most of the strongholds completed the Spanish defeat. They were soon fleeing in panic, allowing Pérignon to invest Figuièras without delay.

The citadel of San Fernando, a Vauban fortress, was a formidable place housing 10,000 men with 200 guns, commanded by Governor Valdes. A scouting party, entering the town at night, was acclaimed by the inhabitants. Pérignon acted then with a noteworthy diplomatic skill: knowing he had little chance of taking such a place by force of arms, he succeeded in bluffing Valdes by a combination of intimidation and promises. On November 27 the Spanish garrison surrendered. More than a victory, it was a providential godsend as the stores were filled for a six-month siege. Pérignon could now turn to Rosas, the last stronghold of the demoralized Spaniards.

Master of the Lampourdan, a rich country with enough resources to feed his army and rest the exhausted men, Pérignon now looked southward to the heart of Catalonia, across the Fluvia. The new Spanish commander, Urrutia, was not very active: he did little to relieve Rosas but wisely reorganized his reinforced army, seconded by Major-General O'Farill. Across the Fluvia, up to Campredon in the east, the two armies fought a number of small-scale battles without any useful effect as no one had a marked advantage now. Meanwhile, the Spanish government (also defeated in the western Pyrenees) discreetly began peace talks. This did not mean idleness for the men, as Pérignon intended to maintain the efficiency and readiness of his troops. They had also to fight the hated *Soumatens* in their rear areas and watch the regulars over the river.

In the words of C. A. Thoumas: "the products of a harsh school used to privations and misfortunes, the soldiers of the Army of the Eastern Pyrenees had a sombre kind of energy which marked them out from the other troops."[1] It was not Pérignon who led them to the peace, signed on July 22, 1795. Having failed to cross the Fluvia at Bascara, he had been replaced by Schérer on May 30.

The Fighting Ambassador and Honorary Marshal (1795–1818)

One of the most interesting facets of Pérignon's personality was his ability to consider military affairs as a politician and vice versa. Even in the harsh winter of 1794–1795, he corresponded with Urrutia and the Spanish government.[2] Uncompromising, he was always fair and acted with humanity as long as circumstances permitted. His name was always respected by his adversaries and civilians.

When Schérer replaced him, he was promoted to the rank of commander-in-chief of the Army of Brittany on September 15. But he was soon returning to the political side of things and was elected (on October 16) deputy to the council of Five Hundred by his countrymen of the Haute-Garonne. Although once again promoted, this time to commander-in-chief of the united Armies on November 13, he never took up his command. Instead, on November 26 he was appointed as ambassador to Spain.

In Madrid he played an important part in the negotiations that ended in the Treaty of St.-Ildefonso, signed on April 19, 1796. His position as a victorious—but generous—commander of the forces that had defeated the Spanish army made him a personage. His aristocratic origins and education were appreciated at the Spanish court where he had to operate amid the intrigues of Charles IV, Godoy, and Marie-Louise de Parme. He succeeded so well that Spain entered into an alliance against England, which lost the use of the Spanish ports.

In December 1797 he was replaced at Madrid by a new ambassador, Truguet, who soon proved his clumsiness. Meanwhile, Pérignon had been put on the retired list (August 24, 1798) and enjoyed some rest; but not for long, for on October 14 he was sent to the Army of Italy. In 1799 he was in command of the French troops in Liguria, trying to save what he could of a starved army in which bribery and incompetence flourished. The events in Italy during 1799 showed once again the weaknesses of the Directory and exasperated the army as well as civilians. Eventually, they led to the fall of the government.

The Army of Italy was commanded by Joubert, a young general (30 years old) who had fought in Italy since 1794 with distinction. With 35,000 men he was ordered to block the massive Russo–Austrian advance north of Genoa. Pérignon was given command of the left wing, with Grouchy and Lemoine as divisional commanders and General Richepanse with 1,000 cavalry. General St.-Cyr commanded the right wing. The whole army contained only 2,087 cavalry.

The advancing forces were impressive: outnumbering the French by two to one, they enjoyed an overwhelming superiority in cavalry and artillery, and their morale was high. They were commanded by one of the most revered generals—and one of the best outside France—Alexander Vassilievitch Suvorov. For the French, whose army was in a shocking condition, lacking food and ammunition and with only a handful of cavalry, there was no choice but to retreat cautiously into the mountains. There, the Russian cavalry and the feared cossacks could be checked.

Unfortunately the Directory desperately needed a victory and ordered Joubert to stand at Novi and win or die. So, by late on August 15, 1799, despite the utmost gallantry of the troops and their officers, the French army had almost ceased to exist— at least 11,000 were casualties. Among them, Joubert had been killed in the morning. The young general was leading a charge when an ill-prepared Austrian attack offered the only opportunity of the day. But Suvorov soon regained control and the slaughter continued for 16 hours, until the French gave up after inflicting some 8,000 casualties on the attackers. Side by side Pérignon and Grouchy attempted to cover the retreat. They were both wounded, Grouchy countercharging with the cavalry and Pérignon rallying the routed rear guard. Savagely attacked, he received wounds in the head, arms, and body and was taken prisoner for a year.

On January 5, 1801, Pérignon was given command of the 10th military division in Toulouse, but on April 12 he became a senator. On November 18 he retired once again with a pension of 6,000 francs awarded by the Consuls. But he did not rest for long as France and Spain were involved in difficult negotiations to draw definitive borders in the Pyrenees. The knowledge he had of the region and the inhabitants, and his successes in Madrid, singled out Pérignon for this task. On September 11, 1802, he was appointed commissioner-extraordinary. On October 27 he was made vice-president of the Senate.

When Napoleon re-created the marshalate, Pérignon was selected in order to honor the Army of the Western Pyrenees and acknowledge his personal value. He was one of the four honorary marshals, the seventeenth on the list. He received the Grand Eagle of the Legion of Honor on February 2, 1805, but was never again employed in an active military capacity.

On September 18, 1806, he was appointed governor-general of the states of Parma and Plasencia. For seven years he lived in Italy and began to enjoy a family life. On July 23, 1808, he became governor of Naples, where he commanded the French troops, under Murat, "King Joachim". In this appointment he was probably also Napoleon's private informer.

In Naples his children were the young people about the court, the last born, Léopold, being only two years old. The family did well: Germaine (1787–1844) married General Baron Lanusse; Mélanie (1788–1858) married Baron Darayon, treasurer general; Caroline (1799–1819) married Baron Duprat; Irma (1803–1849) married General Baron Cavaignac; and Octavie (1804–1847) married General Baron Rogniat in 1826. All served with distinction, the last-named having been commander of the engineers in the Grand Army.

The eldest son, Pierre, an officer in the Horse Carabineers, was killed at Friedland: but Henri (1793–1841) was a lieutenant in the Light Horse of the Royal Neapolitan Guard and followed Murat to Russia. He was a major in 1814.

Grand Dignitary of the Order of the Two Sicilies, Pérignon was also, from March 1808, a count of the Empire with financial grants drawn on Westphalia and Hanover worth 20,000 francs each. A rich old gentleman now, he was not after adventures and did not interfere in the rivalries between King Joachim and Napoleon. He was chief-of-staff in 1809, in the interim between Lamarque and Pamphile de la Croix; he then became interim minister of the army and navy until the nomination of Campredon.

In the crisis of 1811, Murat dismissed him as governor, whereupon his son-in-law, Lanusse, Grand Marshal of the Palace, and Cavaignac, lieutenant-general, resigned in protest. Their loyalty to the Empire was never in question although their position was now exposed. In 1812 Napoleon gave Pérignon command of the French troops (Corps of Grenier) in Naples, but he was once again put on the retired list on March 27, 1813.

Pérignon did not participate in the marshals' plot and had no responsibility for the fall of the Empire. A loyal soldier, he remained faithful until the end of the regime. Once the Bourbons were legally installed, he again agreed to serve king and country. Appointed extraordinary-commissioner in the first military division on April 22, 1814, he was next (May 31) made president of the commission appointed to examine the qualifications of former officers. He resigned on October 10, but was made Chevalier of St. Louis and a peer of France. In 1815 the Duke of Angoulême appointed him as governor of the 10th military division in Toulouse.

On April 4 that year, he resigned and returned to his estates at Montech, refusing to serve Napoleon after giving his oath of allegiance to the king. On April 10 his name was struck from the list of marshals.

After the Hundred Days, Pérignon was restored to his dignities and received a new marshal's baton from the king on July 14, 1816. He was made governor of the first military division (January 10) and Commander of St. Louis (May 3) and awarded the Grand Cross of St. Louis (August 24). He was created a marquis on August 31.

He died in Paris on December 25, 1818, two years after his beloved wife. His name figures on the west side of the Arc de Triomphe.

Opinions on Pérignon are ambiguous: he was probably leaving France to join the émigrés[3] when he was persuaded to fight in the Army of the Pyrenees, where "he was hiding his moderation among the soldiers."[4] He was certainly honest, but in Naples his family was quite intrusive.[5] He served Napoleon loyally but played a dubious role in the commission of 1814.

Once he had taken "the King's Shilling," he did not go back on his oath, but his worst action, which should not be forgotten, was to vote, as a peer, for the execution of Ney. "M. de Pérignon ended his life under Louis XVIII as if the Revolution he served well, without liking it, had never existed."[6]

The Siege of Rosas (November 28, 1794–February 4, 1795)

After the victories in the valley of la Muga and the capture of Figuièras, the French army was exhausted, but the spoils of the Spanish garrison and its full warehouses improved supplies while the continuous advance had boosted its morale. Conversely the Spaniards were in complete disarray. One of their last strongholds was the fortified town and harbor of Rosas, which allowed the reinforcement as well as the resupply of the last Spanish field army by sea. For the French army, therefore, Rosas was a threat and had to be captured before any further advance could be contemplated.

Pérignon acted swiftly. Without consideration of the circumstances, he brought up his 10,000 tired men,[7] through terrible winter weather, and began the siegeworks the day after the surrender of Figuièras. His stubborn determination allowed the first French batteries to open fire on the fortress as early as November 29.

But Rosas was a tough nut to crack and could not be taken by a simple bold advance and sheer intimidation, as Figuièras had been. With its double surrounding walls, citadel, and fort, it housed a 4,800-man garrison commanded by General Isquierdo. In the harbor Admiral Gravina with 13 ships of the line and 45 other ships—including bomb vessels—stood ready to support and supply Isquierdo.

As Pérignon soon discovered, the key position was the Fort of la Trinité—nicknamed *le Bouton de Rose* ("the Pimple") by the troops—which commanded the harbor from the east. The fort was overlooked, to the north, by Mt. Puy-Bois, a steep hill some thousand feet above sea level. When engineers objected that it was impossible to climb this with heavy guns, Pérignon replied, "I want nothing but the impossible."[8]

Meanwhile, on the western side, the guns began to shell the citadel and the fleet, setting some stores on fire. By December 7 six new batteries had been established and trenches surrounded the city against which the Spanish launched weak counterattacks without any useful effect. The fire coming from "the Pimple" was far more effective, and Pérignon hurried his exhausted, frozen men to haul a battery up Mt. Puy-Bois

In six days they had cleared a way through boulders and up cliffs. On December 25 three batteries were pounding the fort and shelling the fleet from the heights. Although the weather was so cold that sentries froze to death on duty, the French kept a high morale while the Spanish will to resist began to break. Fire from the fort ceased on January 1, 1795. Their walls breached, the small garrison escaped at night on the sixth with rope ladders just before the storming.

The guns of the fort were soon turned against the town, but on January 25 the siegeworks were brought to a halt because of the weather. Time was vital to Pérignon as the threat of Spanish reinforcement by sea, or land attack by General Urrutia, was increasing. So he had little choice but to win before the enemy could regain the initiative. On February 1 he boldly stormed their advanced positions with an immediate effect on the Spanish governor's morale. Conspicuously Pérignon ordered 3,000 ladders from Figuièras and ostentatiously prepared the final assault in full sight of the garrison.

This psychological blow was decisive. At night on February 3, Isquierdo and the remaining defenders withdrew to the safety of the fleet. A rear guard of 300 men was supposed to cover his retreat and leave on smaller vessels early the next morning, but they were abandoned by the sailors and taken prisoner.[9]

The 70-day siege thus ended in a decisive victory, despite the escape of the garrison, as it gave a good supply post to the French and, above all, shattered Spanish morale. Although the latter won some further minor battles, their fighting spirit was lost and peace was close. Pérignon, bold and resolute in battle, wise and generous after, was to be one of its negotiators.

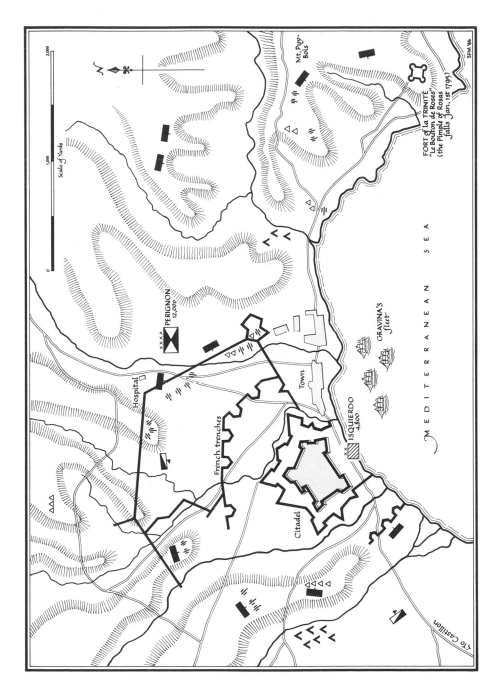

Map 21. The Siege of Rosas, November 28, 1794–February 4, 1795

TEXTUAL REFERENCES

1. C. A. Thoumas, *Le Maréchal Lannes* (Paris, 1895), p. 68.
2. A. Hugo, *La France Militaire, Histoire des Armées Françaises de 1792 à 1833* (Paris, 1833), Vol. 1, p. 311.
3. H. Lachouque, *Aux armes, Citoyens! Les soldats de la Révolution* (Paris, 1969), p. 377.
4. L. Chardigny, *Les Maréchaux de Napoléon* (Paris, 1946), p. 142.
5. P. Carles, *L'Armée du Royaume de Naples,* unpublished doctoral dissertation, Library, University of Montpellier, p. 52.
6. Chardigny, *op. cit.,* p. 146.
7. According to Hugo, *op. cit.,* pp. 287–90, the French army had an estimated strength of 15,000 men at Figuièras. Some were allowed to rest for a short period, garrisoning the city and exploiting the various supplies found in the Spanish stores. Figuièras also provided guns and ammunition for the siege. By the end of February, the Spanish army of Urrutia was 35,000 strong with some 10,000 more *Miquelets* and other irregulars. The Army of the Eastern Pyrenees was less than 25,000, all along the Fluvia. The French forces besieging Rosas were probably never above 12,000 with about 100 guns. The losses are not recorded.
8. *Ibid.,* p. 297.
9. *Ibid.*

BIBLIOGRAPHICAL NOTE

Obviously Pérignon is the least known of the marshals and he has not attracted scholarly biographies. The *Archives des Maréchaux de France* at the Defense Ministry contains 70 pieces referenced as Carton VI, Dossier 17. The *Fonds Pérignon* in the *Archives Departmentales de la Haute-Garonne* (Toulouse) has 49 parts referenced 14J.

All the studies mentioned in this biography are general works. Of special interest for the period 1795–99 is *La France sous le Directoire* (Paris, 1977), the masterly study by Georges Lefebvre. The war in the Pyrenees is well covered by A. Hugo, *La France Militaire, Histoire des Armées Française de 1792 à 1833,* 5 vols. (Paris, 1833), which includes some useful maps, and by J. N. Fervel, *Campagne de la Révolution Française dans les Pyrénnées Orientales* (Paris n.d.). V. Fanet's article In *Les Carnets de la Sabretache* (Paris, 1902) is a very interesting study on Dugommier's command and the state of the Army of the Eastern Pyrenees, drawn from the letters of Dugommier (*Carnets* 116–118). *Aux Armes Citoyens! Les soldats de la Révolution* (Paris, 1969) by H. Lachouque is highly readable but somewhat romanticized, although well documented. The unpublished thesis of Colonel P. Carles (University of Montpellier) is an essential work for the kingdom of Naples and its armies. Among the studies on the marshalate, *Les Maréchaux de Napoléon* (Paris, 1946) by Louis Chardigny is an original short work, clear and accurate with personal assessments of value.

CHRONOLOGY

1763, May 7	—Born in Vienna
1773	—When father died, came under the supervision of his uncle, the king of Poland
1780	—Entered the Austrian army
1786	—Transferred to Joseph II Light Horse as lieutenant-colonel
1787	—Visited the court of Catherine the Great at Kiev
1788, April 24	—Wounded at Sabatch, on campaign against the Turks
1789, August	—Recalled to Warsaw to be major-general of the Polish army
1792, June 18	—Won the Battle of Zielence against the Russian General Markov
July 30	—Formally resigned in protest at armistice with the Russians
August	—Banished from Poland
1794, August	—Joined the insurrection in Poland
November	—Went into retirement after insurrection defeated
1798	—Visited Petersburg by invitation of Czar Paul
1807, January	—Appointed minister of war in the Polish Directory
1809, April 19	—Defeated by the Austrians in Battle of Raszyn
May	—Invaded and overran Galicia
July	—Seized Krakow; became a national hero
1811	—Rejected approaches from the Czar
1812, June 4	—Led V Corps of *la Grande Armée* into Russia
August 17	—Took part in the assault on Smolensk
September 5-7	—Took part in the Battle of Borodino
October 18	—Took part in the Battle at Spass Kouplia
November 3	—Engaged in rescue of Davout's Corps at Vyazma.
December 25	—Reviewed remnants of V Corps at Warsaw
1813, February 5	—Led the Polish army into Galicia
March	—Nominated commander of VIII Corps of Napoleon's army
October 9	—Wounded in rearguard action
October 15	—Received his baton as a *Maréchal d'Empire* (twenty-fifth in date of appointment)
October 16	—Fought in battles to the south of Leipzig
October 19	—Fought in the city of Leipzig; drowned in the River Elster

CHAPTER TWENTY-TWO

TRAGIC PATRIOT AND RELUCTANT BONAPARTIST

Poniatowski

by

Nigel de Lee

Political and Military Apprenticeship (1763–1794)

Prince Josef Anton Poniatowski was the second to last of the marshals, and the most incongruous. He was an enlightened reformist nobleman of Lithuanian, Czech, and Italian descent, a hereditary prince of Bohemia and of Poland. He was familiar with the court circles of Vienna, Berlin, and St. Petersburg. But he was also a Polish patriot, and political necessity drove him to serve the parvenu Emperor Napoleon, whom he neither liked nor trusted. His motto, *Bog, Honor, Ojczyzna* ("God, Honor, Fatherland"), imposed commitments that were impossible to uphold and reconcile. The prince was brave and honest, sensitive and melancholic; he lacked the subtlety essential to the successful practitioner of national politics in an age of turmoil. He was tormented by the inner contradictions imposed by external circumstances. By 1813 the demands of personal honor and national interest had reduced him to suicidal desperation. He resolved his difficulties by finding a heroic death at the Battle of Leipzig, so discharging his debt of honor to his unworthy creditor and false friend Napoleon and adding luster to the martial reputation of Poland.

He was born in Vienna on May 7, 1763. His father was André Poniatowski, who claimed descent on his mother's side from the Czartoryskis. In 1764 André's brother, Stanislaus Augustus, was elected king of Poland and made all his brothers hereditary princes of the kingdom. Josef's mother was a Kinski, of Czech and Italian blood.

André Poniatowski died in 1773. Josef's mother was an invalid, and took only intermittent interest in him. His upbringing, welfare, and education were arranged by his uncle, the King of Poland. At that time Poland was disturbed by radical and nationalist ideas and menaced by the threat of partition. Stanislaus was inspired by ideas of enlightenment, but enfeebled by years of futile struggle and personal dissipation. He hoped Prince Josef could take up the cause of Poland with the vigor of youth. Josef was carefully educated by a team of tutors, with particular attention to the study of history and military affairs. He was not taught Polish, but learned it from his household, and was encouraged by his uncle to think of himself as a prince of Poland. In 1780 Josef was commissioned into the 2nd Carabineers, and embarked upon the usual life of a young cavalry officer: regimental duty, long leaves, a busy social life, and escapades. But he was not frivolous, and it was zeal and application in the performance of duty, as well as lineage and connections, that won him promotion to squadron commander by 1781 and lieutenant-colonel in Joseph II's Light Horse by 1786. He was an enthusiastic cavalry officer with a natural eye for ground and a real interest in training recruits. His own studies of tactics and strategy were directed most strongly by Mack, who inculcated in him the lessons and principles derived from the Seven Years' War. Meanwhile, he was being groomed for a political and diplomatic life in the service of his uncle. He spent most of 1787 on a mission to Catherine of Russia in Kiev. This long sybaritic interlude was terminated by rumors of the possibility of war against Turkey and the opportunity for real military activity.

Josef was anxious to get into action, but was frustrated. Having served with a regiment of Polish uhlans in 1784, he offered to raise a *Freikorps* in Galicia and lead it into Serbia. His offer was refused, and he was ordered to serve at imperial headquarters as aide-de-camp to the Austrian Emperor. His first experience of action was painful and almost fatal. In spring 1788 the army was besieging the fortress of Sabatch on the River Sava. On April 24 Josef volunteered to lead a column of infantry in the assault. He reached the foot of the rampart of the citadel, and was there severely wounded in the thigh by a shell-burst. He was reckoned fortunate to survive the wound, and in November the Emperor promoted him to full colonel in recognition of his gallantry. However, he was out of action until the end of the year, and did not regain his full health for several years. In January 1789 he volunteered to return to the war and was given command of the Regiment of Modena, but never led it into the field, for at this moment he was recalled to Poland.

The return to Polish affairs was not welcome, but he was aware of his patriotic duty and also of his personal obligations to his uncle. These duties were imperative, but he was reluctant to abandon Emperor Joseph, and took great care to have himself released from the customary oath never to bear arms against Austria. He might have to fight the Emperor, who had favored him, but he was determined not to be foresworn. He believed in honesty, goodness, loyalty, and courage, and was not prepared for the political role his uncle had devised for him. He was disgusted by the proceedings of the Diet, and appalled by the intrigues of leading politicians. But for most of 1789 he was required to stay in Warsaw and play the political game. The government had decided to create an army of 100,000 in 1788 and was in need of trained officers. Josef, who had never commanded a substantial body of troops in action, was made major-general and appointed to the Commission on Military Regulations. When not occupied by business, he took an active interest in the sensual delights of fashionable society, drinking, and womanizing to the delight of the city and detriment of his health.

In spring 1790 he was sent to command the 4th Division,

encamped at Braclaw, despite his objection that he was competent to command no more than a regiment. Out in the field he showed a particular interest in the training and handling of cavalry, but clearly had little practical knowledge of infantry or artillery work. His obvious talent was as a leader of light horse. He knew his limitations, and was aware that he could not escape responsibilities way beyond his competence owing to the royal connection. He also knew enough to recognize the obvious deficiencies of the Polish army, short of trained men, experienced officers, and all kinds of material.

The test of this army came in 1792. On May 3, 1791, Poland proclaimed a new, modern constitution that was absolutely unacceptable to Catherine of Russia. The Empress duly recruited a party of Polish and Lithuanian nobles who formed the Confederation of Targowice. In May 1792 the confederation denounced the Polish constitution, and the Russian army invaded the Ukraine. Josef was in command of the Polish army in the Ukraine, with his headquarters at Tulczyn. From the beginning he had no confidence in his own ability to command or in his army's ability to fight the Russians. The Russian army, commanded by Kakhowski, consisted of some 60,000 men, of whom 40,000 had been seasoned in recent campaigns against the Turks. Josef led some 20,000 green troops, untried in battle and lacking in discipline. The Polish army was desperately short of money, weapons, ammunition, transport, clothing, and food. The Prince had no general or logistic staff to help him overcome these difficulties. The local people of the Ukraine were uncooperative, through fear of the Tsarina and political uncertainty, so it was impossible to rely upon them for supplies or intelligence. Josef himself was inexperienced in the arts of higher command, and was easily outmaneuvered by his opponent.

Initially he concentrated his forces in a fortified camp at Polona, and relied upon support from the Corps of Reserve commanded by Lubomorski to cover his flanks. But Lubomorski had been suborned by the Russians, and failed to move forward in time. The Russian army advanced in parallel columns, outflanking Polona, and Josef was forced to withdraw. His urgent pleas to the king to send supplies and reinforcements went unanswered; in fact, his pessimistic assessments of the situation reinforced Stanislaus's inclination to reach an accommodation with Catherine.

On June 18 Josef scored his first victory in battle at Zielence. More by luck than judgment, his army accomplished an ambush of General Markov. In the press of battle, the Prince proved his personal leadership by charging at the head of the *Potocki Infantry Regiment*. He was, however, unable to seize the initiative and exploit the opportunity presented to him. His courage was quick but his judgment was slow; General Markov extricated his column, checked and mauled, but not destroyed. On that very day the king had decided to accept the Convention of Targowice and allow Poland to pass under Russian tutelage. Josef was horrified by the king's decision. He considered that the king could have inspired a national uprising to resist the Russian army. He wrote to his uncle, "If, since this war was not militarily prepared, your Majesty had mounted a horse together with the gentry, armed the townsmen, proclaimed the peasants free—we then should have either perished with honour, or Poland would be now a power."[1]

These exhortations were futile. For a while the Prince inclined to join a conspiracy to kidnap the king, take him to the army, and fight on in his name, but family piety overcame patriotic sentiment. He went out to seek death on reconnaissance, but did not find it. In a mood of resignation he obeyed the royal order to move the army to the left bank of the Vistula, and on July 30 handed in his resignation. He left the army to return to Warsaw, where he led a political agitation for the salvation and reform of the army. As his popularity grew the king was alarmed. In August the Prince published a pamphlet promising to take revenge for the bitter humiliation of July, and was promptly banished by his uncle.

He went abroad to Vienna and then to Brussels. Despite the pleas of Stanislaus, he refused to subscribe to the Convention of Targowice or to give up his 1792 military insignia. He replied by urging Stanislaus to prepare for a national resurgence, but the king remained pessimistic and inert. His conduct reflected badly on all the Poniatowskis, and the Prince became unpopular, blamed by patriots for the conduct of the king. So, when the resurgence occurred in 1794, it was led by the radical Kosciuszko, Josef's deputy in 1792, and Josef had no part in the planning of it. When the patriots rose to seize Krakow and Warsaw in the spring, Josef was surprised and hurt by his exclusion, but was impelled by duty to return home to serve the insurrection.

He went, in disguise, through Galicia to report to Kosciuszko, refused to take command in Lithuania, and volunteered to serve as a soldier in Mokronowski's division. In that capacity he fought in the successful action against the Prussians at Blonie, then took part in the withdrawal toward Warsaw. He was unwilling to take a command owing to his inexperience and his political unpopularity. The 1794 insurrection was strongly influenced by Jacobin ideas that made all aristocrats suspect, and the failure of the 1792 war made all Poniatowskis particularly disliked. But Kosciuszko had faith in him, and in August he was persuaded to take over Mokronowski's division, holding a defensive line from Powonski to Mlociny. He hoped to prove his loyalty and to improve the reputation of his family by a successful campaign, but once more lack of experience was his undoing. Initially his agressive defense was successful, and the Prussian outposts were driven back. But in late August the Prussians made a surprise attack at night in superior numbers, and his troops, caught unprepared, were overwhelmed. Overcome with shame he handed over command to the more experienced Dombrowski. For most of September he was employed in the perilous business of reconnaissance work, but in October was given a detachment of some 2,500 to command. This column was supposed to act as a liaison force, but the Prince was unable to maneuver it to avoid enemy forces and rendezvous with friendly ones. His apprenticeship was terminated in November, when Suvorov stormed the fortress of Praga and the revolt collapsed. The Prince handed over his column to Kaminiencki and returned to Warsaw. So far, he had proved himself a heroic leader in the field, but had not mastered the art of command.

In the Service of Poland and France (1794–1812)

The prince avoided any further active part in military affairs up to 1807. Until the death of the Empress Catherine in 1796, he lived, an ailing and impoverished exile, in Vienna. In 1798 he visited Petrograd at the invitation of Tsar Paul, but eventually returned to settle in Warsaw, which was at that time under Prussian occupation. For the next eight years, he enjoyed the life of a landed nobleman, occupied by extravagant and ostentatious social activity and affairs of the heart. The Tsar and the King of Prussia honored him with titles and appointments in attempts to win his favor. He resisted their efforts, and remained an enlightened patriotic reformer, aloof from active politics.

The situation changed dramatically in 1806. After the defeat of the Prussian army at Jena, there were spontaneous uprisings in western Poland, and soon the French arrived in Warsaw. The Prince had been influenced by his French mistress, Madame de Vauban, and was convinced that the best means of advancing the Polish cause would be close cooperation with France. Accordingly, he decided to return to political and military life. Early in 1807 he met Murat in Warsaw, presented to him the sword of Stephen Bathori, and disclaimed any personal interest in the crown of Poland.[2] This theatrical gesture won him a friend at court, but at first his relations with Napoleon and Davout were more difficult. Napoleon did not share Murat's enthusiasm for the Prince and referred to him as "an inconsequential light-weight" of no particular talent, influence, or value.[3] Davout suspected him of military incompetence and of leading an underground political movement. However, he could not be ignored. In autumn 1806 he had reluctantly taken overall command of the militia raised by the provisional government. In January 1807, with the support of Murat and Talleyrand, he was appointed minister of war in the Polish Directory set up by Napoleon's decree. He was also commander of the First Legion of the Polish army, but Napoleon gave command of the Second and Third Legions to Zayoncek and Dombrowski, both implacable political enemies of the prince. It is certain that the Prince was suspicious of Napoleon. He was afraid that the Emperor would use, exploit, and abandon the Poles, and repeatedly demanded that Napoleon publicly commit himself to a full restoration of Poland. The Prince regarded the Treaty of Tilsit of July 1807, which gave the Grand Duchy of Warsaw to the king of Saxony, as a betrayal. But it still seemed that cooperation with France offered the best prospects of a national resurgence. In October 1807 the prince accepted the post of commander-in-chief of the Polish army, under the overall authority of Davout, and with a Saxon corps in Poland to keep him in check.

Once he had been nominated as commander-in-chief, the Prince reorganized the army. His intention was to make it an expression and symbol of the national will and a school for the nation, as well as a military instrument. In 1808 he replaced the three legions with a unified structure, and imposed a universal system of conscription in order to weaken the barriers of social class. He founded schools of engineering and artillery. The infantry was trained in French tactics and to execute battlefield maneuvers at a run. The cavalry based its tactics and training on principles devised by the Prince himself.[4]

In 1807 the army mustered some 30,000 soldiers; by 1810 it consisted of 56,000 men organized in 17 regiments of infantry and 16 squadrons of cavalry, supported by artillery, engineer, and transport companies, formed into six divisions. All this was accomplished despite an empty treasury and stiff competition for recruits from the French Army. Davout and Napoleon were impressed by the achievements of the Prince. In 1808 Napoleon promised, through Davout, that he would restore Polish independence if the Poles furnished him with 40,000 good troops. Prince Josef ensured that the Poles kept their side of the bargain.

In 1809 the Prince proved that he could handle an army in the field. In the spring war was brewing between Austria and France. Napoleon ordered the Prince to demonstrate against Galicia, believing that the Polish army would be supported by a

Russian corps under the command of Prince Golitsyn. In fact, the Russians were in secret accord with the Austrians, intent on the suppression of Poland. In April the Archduke Ferdinand advanced on Warsaw with a corps of 32,000. The Poles, taken by surprise and reduced by the provision of garrisons to fortresses, met the invasion with a field army of 17,000. On April 17 the Austrians attacked the Polish army at Raszyn. Eventually the Poles were outflanked and forced to retreat; but they had stood firm for some hours against an attack by larger numbers of seasoned troops, and this gave them confidence and self-respect. Throughout the battle the Prince exposed himself to danger in order to inspire his soldiers.

The defeat at Raszyn made Warsaw indefensible, and the Prince negotiated the surrender of the city. He then decided on a bold radical strategy; rather than attempt a defensive campaign that was certain to fail owing to lack of numbers, he would mount a counteroffensive. As the Archduke moved north toward the fortress of Thorn, the Poles set off southward to Galicia. This took the Austrians by surprise. The Poles took the fortified town of Sandomierz on May 19 and seized the fortress of Zamosc by a *coup de main* on May 20. By the end of May, the Prince held Lublin. There was a general nationalist rising in Galicia in response. The Archduke, held at the fortress of Thorn, was alarmed and turned back.[5] On June 2 the Austrians gave up Warsaw on their way south. The Archduke invested and recaptured Sandomierz, but was unable to catch the Polish army, now swollen with partisans. In late July, in the face of direct obstruction by the Russians, the Prince seized Krakow and became a national hero. By the end of the war, his campaign had doubled the territory of the Grand Duchy, and Napoleon sent him a saber of honor in recognition of his accomplishments.

The years 1810–1812 brought a return to the business of politics and military administration. Napoleon had a better opinion of the Prince's military ability, but still regarded him as politically dangerous. He was afraid that the Prince's vigorous and persistent nationalism might compromise his own relations with the Tsar or his father-in-law, the Austrian Emperor. While Napoleon sought to conciliate and cajole the Tsar, the Tsar attempted to suborn the prince and subvert the Polish army, with offers of an extensive and autonomous Polish kingdom under the Russian crown. In 1811 the Prince reported these approaches to Napoleon, and used them to extract permission and funds for improvements to the Polish army. In particular, the infantry regiments were given reserve companies and integral field artillery. Some efforts were made to rectify glaring deficiencies in stores, equipment, and matériel.

By 1812 the Polish army consisted of 74,000 regulars supplemented by 15,000 mobile National Guards. News of Napoleon's intention to invade Russia was received with great enthusiasm, the enterprise being regarded as a war of national liberation. Napoleon's own proclamation named it "the Second Polish War."[6] The Polish army raised 10 regiments of infantry, 12 of light cavalry, and 1 of cuirassiers, 30,000 men in all, as a contribution to the Grand Army. These units were formed into the 16th, 17th, and 18th Divisions and the 4th Light Cavalry Division, and together they constituted V Corps of Napoleon's army. Throughout the campaign in Russia, this corps performed the most arduous service, as advance and flank guard on outposts beyond Moscow and as rear guard during the retreat. Very few of its soldiers returned from Russia, but those that did saved their guns and their Eagles.

In spring 1812, V Corps was deployed around Warsaw, Modlin, and Plock. On June 4 it moved forward to take post on the right of the Grand Army to act as part of the flank guard. On June 28 the corps entered Wilna; on June 30 it encountered the enemy for the first time, and pushed Platov's cossacks out of Grodno. The advance continued via Igumen and Mohilev. There was plenty of hard marching and little contact with the enemy. On July 9 at Mir, and on July 14 at Romanovo, Platov took advantage of the impetuosity and inexperience of Rozniecki's cavalry and mauled the leading elements.

In mid-July the corps did a long forced march in a futile attempt to trap Bagration's army at Bobruisk. The exertions and privations of the campaign took effect. On July 9 Napoleon wrote to Berthier complaining that the Poles lacked the right spirit, because the Prince had demanded money and supplies for his corps.[7] By July 27 the corps was reduced to a strength of 23,000, and went into cantonments around Mohilev to recuperate. On August 10 Dombrowski's 17th Division was detached to watch routes from the south. The rest of the corps advanced via Orsha to Smolensk.

V Corps fought vigorously in the fighting at Smolensk, but was only partially successful, and did not play a decisive part in the battle. This was typical of their role throughout the campaign. The Poles arrived at Smolensk late on August 16 and took a position on the right of the French army, with their own right resting on the Dniepr. The morning of August 17 was taken up with skirmishing and reconnaissance. To the front lay the Malakova Gate on the left and the Nikolska suburb on the right. In the afternoon they took part in the general assault on the city. The 16th Division attacked and forced the Malakova Gate, but was ejected from the interior of the city by ferocious counterattacks. The 17th Division cleared and held the Nikolska suburb, but was stopped by the ramparts and could not break into the city. The cavalry, having swept the Russian dragoons from the ground before the city walls, forded the Dniepr to attack a Russian battery. Their charge was halted by a countermove of Barclay de Tolly's own escort, and they fell back. Meanwhile, the Prince and Murat brought up their own guns to cover the bridges over the Dniepr beyond Smolensk. These guns were forced to fall silent and withdraw by the Russian battery, which was much more strongly emplaced. By the time that nightfall stilled the fighting, the Poles had lost some 2,000 casualties. Early on August 18, the Russians evacuated Smolensk by stealth.

Napoleon ordered a resumption of the advance on August 22, to the surprise and consternation of many in his army. They had expected the Emperor to settle into winter quarters in Smolensk and Witebsk, reinforce and repair the weary regiments, and move off in spring 1813.[8] But the Emperor was determined to trap and fight the Russian army. V Corps moved off to form the left flank of Murat's advance guard. It marched down the Old Smolensk Road, and on August 23 turned an enemy position at Dorogobuzh, forcing the Russians to evacuate. The Prince kept his cavalry active, scouring the country ahead by deep reconnaissance patrols. On September 3 he himself was surrounded by cossacks and cut his way out to safety. These forward patrols were very effective; all through August and September, the Russian commanders were never sure of what Napoleon's movements and intentions were.

Having fought at Borodino (described on p. 433), the Prince continued to move on the right of the Grand Army and approached Moscow from the direction of Kaluga. V Corps entered Moscow in good order, and maintained a strict discipline while in the city. After two days the Prince was ordered to join Murat in pursuit of the Russian army. V Corps pressed on, skirmishing with the rear guard of the enemy. At Tcharigov, on the Kaluga road, the Prince was involved in a night action lasting six hours, and was injured by a fall from his horse.[9] Eventually the advance guard came to rest at Winkovo to watch Kutuzov's encampment across the Narew. By now V Corps had been reduced to a strength of 4,000 infantry and 1,000 cavalry, partly by battle casualties but mainly by privation and disease. The soldiers lived in primitive shelters and food was very short, but morale was well sustained.

On October 18 the Russians launched an attack on Murat's force, hoping to trap it by seizing the pass at Spass Kouplia on the French line of retreat. The attack proceeded by stealth and surprised Murat, who was in bed when the Russians appeared.

But V Corps, on the right center of the French position, was on the alert and stood to arms in time to meet the Russian infantry. The Poles held their ground, so the Russians were unable to occupy the pass with their infantry.[10] Murat dispersed the Russian cavalry, which had taken the vital ground, and the advance guard withdrew to safety.

The next day Napoleon decided to abandon Moscow and fall back to the southwest. The Prince considered this course of action unnecessary and dangerous, but his advice was ignored.[11] V Corps was ordered to protect the southern flank of the army by marching along the old road from Moscow to Smolensk. On October 22 the Poles set off to probe the route from Trotskoie to Vereia and Medyn. They were not engaged in any major action until they reached Vyazma, but their maneuvers imposed on Kutuzov a persistent sense of insecurity and inhibited his pursuit of the French army. Their presence on the flank was his excuse for failing to press hard at Malo-Yaroslavets when he might have trapped a substantial portion of Napoleon's army. But the withdrawal was enlivened by numerous brief encounters with the Russians. Near Vereia the Prince was involved in "a desperate charge of cavalry. . . . Poles and Russians, animated by a mutual hatred, fought with the utmost fury. Excited by the ardour of combat, they gave no quarter."[12] On October 30 the advance guard led by Tyskiewicze was ambushed by a brigade of cossacks and cut to pieces. These small actions imposed their steady attrition. By early November the corps was reduced to a strength of 3,500.

On November 3 the Poles turned back from Vyazma to help the Viceroy Eugène rescue Davout's corps from encirclement and annihilation by the pursuing Russians. This was their last important action as a distinct corps. Thereafter, they always acted in conjunction with Ney's corps. On November 5 the snow began to fall, but the Poles kept going and made better progress than the rest of the Grand Army because they had prepared their horses for the winter. Near Krasnoie the prince fell from his horse and was put into a carriage to continue the journey. On November 26 he watched the army crossing the Berezina, and was observed to weep at the ruin and misery of the soldiers.[13]

He continued on his way, and reached Warsaw. On Christmas day he reviewed the survivors of V Corps. The great war of national liberation had failed. The prince was inclined to suicide, but the catastrophe in Russia was not of his making. His troops had fought skillfully and bravely, although always short of food, forage, ammunition, and equipment. He had again proved himself a bold and fearless leader in battle. He had also shown that he was a sound corps commander and capable of acting in coordination with other corps, in battle and on campaign. He had remained loyal to Napoleon, despite the failings of the Corsican upstart and the constant entreaties and blandishments of the Tsar. Now that the political game was lost, it remained only to uphold the honor and reputation of Poland, and seek a good death for himself on the battlefield.

The Baton and Death (1813)

In spring 1813 the Prince was in Warsaw with his army, beset by political difficulties. The Austrians and Prussians wanted to destroy the Polish army, for they saw it as a symbol of the nation and an inspiration to national resistance. The Tsar tried to persuade the Prince and his army to desert Napoleon and support the establishment of a Polish state under the Russian crown, such as had been imposed upon Finland. The Prince contemplated suicide, defied Prussian threats, evaded Austrian intrigue, rejected Russian approaches, and decided he must continue to serve Napoleon. He sent a personal challenge to the Austrian Schwarzenberg, whom he considered to have acted in a deceitful and dishonorable manner. In the face of Prussian threats and the advance of the Russian army, he left Warsaw on February 5 and led his army into Austrian territory. There he was safer, as Austria was still nominally an ally of France. However, everything possible was done to obstruct and harass the Polish army, and prevent it from moving to join up with the main body of Napoleon's forces. In March 1813 the Prince had assembled some 8,000 men, seven regiments of infantry, and two of cavalry at Krakow. He reported himself to Napoleon, who was surprised to have his support, and was named commander of VIII Corps. The Emperor awarded him the emoluments and status of a Marshal of the Empire, but not the title or baton. In July VIII Corps moved to Zittau to screen the southern flank of Napoleon's intended area of operations.

On August 15 active hostilities started after a summer truce. Until late September VIII Corps, still based on Zittau, covered the Bohemian passes. Napoleon praised the skill with which these masking operations were conducted. In late September VIII Corps slowly fell back toward the main body of the army, holding and delaying the Austrians by a succession of rearguard actions. As usual, the Prince was in the thick of the fighting, particularly as the corps approached Leipzig in early October. He got his customary reward; on October 9 he was wounded by a lance thrust, and he got another wound while leading a lancer regiment in a charge on October 12.

On October 14 the prince had his corps deployed in positions to the south of Leipzig around the villages of Markkleeburg, Dolitz, Losnig, and Connewitz, with the right flank resting on the Pleisse. On October 15 Napoleon came to inspect VIII Corps and gave the Prince his baton. He had little time left to enjoy his new status.

The Battle of Leipzig commenced on October 16. Napoleon had planned to employ VIII, V, and II Corps to make a general advance from the line Connewitz–Liebertwolkwitz–Wachau. This was intended to pin Schwarzenberg's army and force him to commit his reserves. Once this maneuver had paralyzed the enemy, Macdonald was to lead XI Corps and II Cavalry Corps southeastward to outflank and envelop their right, moving through Taucha, Holzhausen, and Seifferheim. When the enemy had been thoroughly disrupted and shaken by this move, the Imperial Guard and the 1st and 5th Cavalry Corps would strike the decisive blow to annihilate them. On the day this plan failed. The enemy attacked first, Macdonald moved too late, and VIII Corps had to cling on grimly all day in the face of a superior enemy force.

The allies' plan was for Barclay de Tolly to attack along the line Liebertwolkwitz–Markkleeburg in order to hold the French VIII, V, and II Corps while Klenau's corps moved against their eastern (left) flank and Meerveldt enveloped the west. Meerveldt was to advance across the soft ground between the Elster and the Pleisse, then cross the latter to fall on the flank and rear of VIII Corps via Connewitz and Dolitz. The allies' attack started at 9:00 A.M., with six huge columns advancing all along the line. Kleist, with 18,000 men, pushed the Prince, with his 6,000, out of Markkleeburg. The Poles fell back until supported by Augereau and a brigade of Young Guard Cavalry. At noon Kleist overran Liebertwolkwitz, and the left flank of the French line fell back. But the allies' attack was exhausted. At 2:00 P.M. Napoleon ordered a general advance. VIII Corps went forward and pushed Kleist back, recovering most of Markkleeburg. Unfortunately for the French, Macdonald did not start his maneuver until 4:00 P.M., by which time the main infantry attack had lost impetus. The Poles were exhausted. At 5:00 P.M. Meerveldt attacked across the Pleisse and seized Dolitz. VIII Corps could not hold this attack, and Napoleon had to send two reserve divisions to push Meerveldt back across the river. As darkness fell, VIII Corps, now reduced to 4,000 men, settled down to rest on the battlefield.

The fighting resumed on October 18 and once more the Poles held their own in the face of superior numbers. VIII Corps stood on the line from Connewitz to Losnig, with Lefol's division covering their right and Augereau in support. In the morning they were attacked by a column under the command of the Prince of Hessen–Homburg. The villages of Dolitz and Losnig changed hands several times in severe fighting, and were eventually secured by the allies. By noon Hessen–Homburg had fought his way forward to the outskirts of Connewitz, but the French and Poles were still in reasonable order. At 2:00 P.M. the Prince and Augereau launched a fierce counterattack. Although the Poles were by now reduced to 2,500 men, they drove the enemy back from Connewitz. Although greatly inferior in numbers to the enemy, VIII Corps had imposed a grand tactical stalemate for two days of heavy fighting.

At 5:00 P.M. on October 18, Napoleon gave orders for a general retreat. The main force was to prepare to withdraw westward along the Lindenau Causeway on October 19. During the night of October 18–19, VII, VIII, and XI Corps were to fall back into the city of Leipzig and prepare it for defense. Napoleon hoped that with these depleted and weary formations, Macdonald would be able to hold the city for a day to cover the retreat.

The withdrawal into the city began at 2:00 A.M. on October 19 and was accomplished successfully. The Poles, reinforced by two battalions of the Old Guard, were to hold a sector extending from the windmill to the Munz Gate, near the Pleisse. The situation in the city was confused, and there was little opportunity to prepare for defense. Early in the morning, Colleredo attacked the sector held by the Prince. The Poles fought hard, but were steadily pushed back into the city by weight of numbers.

Just before 1:00 P.M., the Lindenau bridge was demolished prematurely, and panic reduced the troops in the city to a state of chaos.[14] The prince had suffered a number of severe wounds during the desperate struggle of the morning, but refused to contemplate surrender, despite the invitations of his enemies and pleas of his subordinates. He drove his horse into the Pleisse, but was too weak to grip the reins and was swept from the saddle. A French officer, Captain Bléchamp, rescued him and hauled him onto the west bank of the river. He was so weak that he could hardly speak, but, whispering "Poland" and "honor," had himself lifted onto another horse, which he rode into the Elster. This time there was no rescue. As he plunged into the water he was shot yet again, and slid into the torrent to be carried away.

His death was much admired and much regretted by both friends and enemies. On October 22 General Wilson wrote, "Prince Poniatowski's death is universally lamented; he deserved a better fate. His conduct of the Polish contingent, and their corresponding conduct, has been splendidly distinguished."[15]

His death signified an end to hopes of Polish independence. The Polish elements in the French army melted away in despair.

But his memory lives on, especially as an example to the Poles of the value of heroic and hopeless struggle: "Polish youth looks neither to Lenin nor to Leftism, but to Pilsudski, Poniatowski and the Pope."[16]

He died a prince of Poland, a prince of Bohemia, and a Marshal of the Empire. He did not esteem the baton that was given to him so late, for it represented an attempt to buy loyalty that was already firm. His conduct was determined by his personal honor, not influenced by a gesture that was cynical, empty, and superfluous.

The Battle of Borodino (September 7, 1812)

The Polish corps played an impetuous but inconclusive part in the Battle of Borodino. The Poles were handled well and fought hard, but Napoleon did not recognize or exploit the opportunities that they created for him. It is this quality of disregarded and lost opportunity, of heroic effort rendered futile by neglect, that makes the part the Prince played at Borodino typical of his military career as a whole.

On September 5, V Corps was advancing along the Old Smolensk Road on the right flank of the Napoleonic army. The ground in front of the Poles was not strongly held, because Kutuzov anticipated that the main attack on his position would be made along the New Smolensk Road to the north.[17] As the troops of the Grand Army marched on the Russian positions at Borodino, they encountered the Shevardino redoubt, a fortified observation post on a knoll, well in advance of the enemy's main line of resistance. The Prince was ordered to use his corps to clear the woods to the south of the redoubt, while other formations prepared to assault it from the west and the north. V Corps deployed on both sides of the Old Smolensk Road and pushed on eastward. While V Corps was advancing, the redoubt was attacked and changed hands several times. The issue was settled when the Prince's troops debouched from woods southeast of the redoubt to support an attack from the west by Compans's division. The Polish cavalry gave direct support to Compans's assault; the advance of the infantry prejudiced an attempt to relieve the redoubt by a Russian division under Karl of Mecklenburg. Kutuzov decided that the redoubt had been compromised and ordered Bagration to abandon it. The Russians fell back on their main position. The skilful maneuvering of V Corps attracted the attention of Napoleon, who visited the Prince the next day to commend him.[18]

The Russian commander was also impressed by the advance of V Corps. Late on September 5 Kutuzov sent a force consisting of Tuchkov's corps of 8,000 infantry, 7,000 of the Moscow militia, and 1,500 cossacks to defend the Old Smolensk Road on the southern flank of his position. This deployment extended the front held by Bagration's army by about one mile. Most of the newly arrived troops were put into thick woods to the southeast of the village of Utitza. Three regiments of light infantry took post in an area of scrub northwest of the village. This deployment was changed on September 6, when Tuchkov was ordered to forsake the cover of the woods and go forward to hold Utitza, giving more immediate support to the light infantry. This shift of position meant that instead of facing an unknown force in ambush, V Corps was opposed by an exposed and over-extended formation on the southern extremity of the Russian line.[19] Davout observed that this wing of the Russian army was weak, and wished to take advantage of it. He proposed that his corps and V Corps carry out a wide turning movement to the south to outflank Bagration's army and cut off its line of retreat to Mojaisk. But Napoleon rejected this plan as being too risky, to the disgust of Davout. Instead, while Davout's corps took part in a frontal onslaught on the left center of the Russian line, the Prince was to attempt a limited tactical outflanking movement by pushing through Utitza and along the Old Smolensk Road.[20] By now V Corps was only 5,000 strong,[21] much inferior to the enemy it confronted before Utitza. But it seems that Napoleon did not appreciate the strength of the enemy forces in that sector.[22] The result was that the task set for the Prince was tactically difficult, and of limited strategic importance.

On September 7 the Prince sent his corps forward at about 6:00 A.M., as the divisions of Desaix and Compans to his north commenced their approach to attack the Bagration flèches. At 8:00 A.M. the Poles engaged Strogonoff's division before Utitza and drove it back into the village. Strogonoff's men fired the village and then fell back on Tuchkov's corps, which was firmly positioned on the Utitza mound. The Poles pushed on through the village but were stopped by artillery fire from batteries on the mound to their front and rifle fire from the light infantry in the brush to their left and rear. The Prince halted his men, pulled them back to reorganize, summoned his own artillery, and asked for reinforcement.

The call for assistance was answered by Junot, who sent his Westphalian *jaegers* into the brush to drive out the Russian chasseurs. Meanwhile, the Prince organized his 22 guns in a battery to play on the Utitza mound. The commencement of this bombardment alarmed the Russian headquarters. Kutuzov was concerned for the security of his southern flank, and aware that the mound controlled the Old Smolensk Road and commanded the rear of Bagration's army. He feared that Tuchkov was in danger of annihilation, and sent Baggavout with his II Corps all the way from the extreme north of the Russian line to reinforce him.[23] It was impossible to send reinforcements from any other part of the line, because at that time the Bagration *flèches* and Raevsky redoubt were being attacked and in danger of being lost. Because he had so far to go, Baggavout was only just in time to save Tuchkov's corps from collapse.

At noon, with his flank now clear and aware that attacks on the Russian center were making ground, the Prince decided to attack the mound. His attack employed two elements in a pincer movement. To the north two columns of infantry advanced to attack the mound. Shortly after they had set off, three columns of infantry supported by cavalry moved to assault the south side. The two columns from the north drew the attention of the Russians, and forced them to commit four regiments of infantry. Then the southern force assaulted the mound, and forced its way up to the military crest of the feature. Baggavout was forced to throw in all his reserves to meet this attack, and after a counterattack by two divisions of infantry and a horde of cossacks, the Poles were slowly forced back down the slope.[24] The Prince pulled his exhausted troops back to Utitza to rest and reorganize.

At about 4:00 P.M. the Russians evacuated the Utitza mound and fell back to conform to the movement of their center, forced back from the main line of resistance by the persistent thrusts of Davout, Ney, and Eugène. As the rest of the Grand Army ground to a halt, the Poles moved forward to occupy the mound. The Russians made a late and feeble attempt to recapture it, but were repulsed with ease. The Prince pushed on down the Old Smolensk Road, anxious to exploit his opportunity and envelop the left flank of the Russian army. But he was too late; the Russians were in full retreat and already well beyond his grasp.

By his conduct at Borodino, the Prince demonstrated that he was a competent, vigorous, and obedient corps commander, well able to handle his formation in battle. No doubt he sympathized with Davout's scheme for a wide strategic outflanking movement to the south, but he conformed to Napoleon's less inspiring plan of battle. He had insufficient forces for the task assigned to him, but worked hard in his attempts to accomplish it. He coordinated his initial advance with that of Desaix and Compans to his left, to assist their attacks on the Bagration *flèches*. He assaulted and cleared Utitza, then exercised prudence and self-discipline in waiting for his flank to be cleared before attacking the mound. In his attack on the mound, he coordinated the efforts of infantry, artillery, and cavalry to such good effect that the Russians were almost beaten, even although they enjoyed superior numbers and held the high ground. The prospect of this attack and its possible consequences disconcerted the Russian commanders, and induced them to make a very awkward redeployment in the middle of the battle. The Prince continued to maintain pressure on the enemy long after the main battle was over. Had he been given more substantial forces, he might well have destroyed much of Bagration's army.[25] At Borodino, as in other cases, the Prince showed his fine qualities to advantage, but failed to achieve his aim because he received insufficient support from Napoleon.

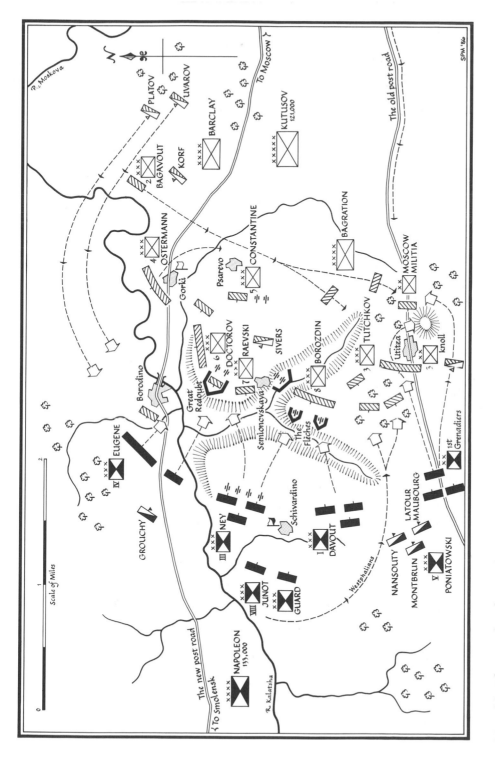

Map 22. The Battle of Borodino, September 7, 1812

TEXTUAL REFERENCES

1. W. F. Reddaway, *The Cambridge History of Poland* (Cambridge, 1941), Vol. 2, p. 154.
2. A. H. Atteridge, *Joachim Murat* (London, 1911), p. 157.
3. S. Askenazi, *Le Prince Joseph Poniatowski, Maréchal de France* (Paris, 1921), p. 216.
4. R. H. de Montmorency, *Proposed Rules and Regulations for the Exercise and Manoeuvres of the Lance* (London, 1820), *passim.*
5. A. von Horsetzky, *The Chief Campaigns in Europe Since 1792* (London, 1909), p. 167.
6. R. Wilson, *The Invasion of Russia* (London, 1860), p. 14.
7. *Ibid.*, p. 121.
8. E. Labaume, *A Circumstantial Narrative of the Campaign in Russia* (London, 1815), pp. 107–8.
9. A. de Caulaincourt, *Memoirs* (London, 1980), Vol. 2, p. 291.
10. E. Foord, *Napoleon's Russian Campaign of 1812* (London, 1914), p. 258.
11. O. Halecki, *A History of Poland* (London, 1978), p. 223.
12. Labaume, *op. cit.*, p. 261.
13. Reddaway, *op. cit.*, p. 233.
14. F. L. Petre, *Napoleon's Last Campaign in Germany, 1813* (London, 1974), p. 380.
15. A. Brett-James, *General Wilson's Diary* (London, 1964), p. 204.
16. N. Davies, *Heart of Europe* (O.U.P., 1984), p. 402.
17. C. J. Duffy, *Borodino and the War of 1812* (London, 1972), p. 72.
18. Caulaincourt, *op. cit.*, p. 236.
19. Duffy, *op. cit.*, pp. 74–75.
20. *Ibid.*, p. 85.
21. P. de Ségur, *Napoleon's Russian Campaign* (London, 1959), p. 65.
22. Foord, *op. cit.*, p. 204.
23. Duffy, *op. cit.*, pp. 99–100.
24. *Ibid.*, pp. 131–32.
25. Wilson, *op. cit.*, p. 152.

BIBLIOGRAPHICAL NOTE

The standard biography of the Prince is S. Askenazi's *Le Prince Joseph Poniatowski, Maréchal de France* (Paris, 1921), but it is a history of the man and the politician, not of the soldier. The Prince's ideas as a theorist of cavalry tactics are reflected in R. H. de Montmorency, *Proposed Rules and Regulations for the Exercise and Manoeuvres of the Lance* (London, 1820), and the context is covered in F. Masson, *Cavaliers de Napoleon* (Paris, 1902). The Polish political background is well covered in W. F. Reddaway, *The Cambridge History of Poland* (Cambridge, 1941), O. Halecki, *A History of Poland* (London, 1978), and N. Davies, *Heart of Europe* (London, 1984). Davies's *God's Playground* (Oxford, 1981) is also most useful in this context. A Hilliard Atteridge's *Joachim Murat* (London, 1911) and Marshal Davout's *Correspondance inédite* (Paris, 1816) make some references to the early stages of the Prince's relations with Napoleon and his senior commanders. A. von Horsetzky's *The Chief Campaigns in Europe Since 1792* (London, 1909) provides a brief but unique account (in English) of the Polish involvement in the war of 1809. The 1812 campaign is well covered by E. Foord in *Napoleon's Russian*

Campaign of 1812 (London, 1914), which gives a basic outline of the part played by the Polish corps. There are also occasional references to the Prince and his corps in A. de Caulaincourt, *Memoirs* (London, 1980); E. Labaume, *A Circumstantial Narrative of the Campaign in Russia* (London, 1815); P. de Ségur, *Napoleon's Russian Campaign* (London, 1959); and R. Wilson, *The Invasion of Russia* (London, 1860). C. J. Duffy's *Borodino and the War of 1812* (London, 1972) is the best source for the battle, being based on a careful analysis of Russian and French documents, checked by a personal inspection of the ground. F. Loraine Petre, *Napoleon's Last Campaign in Germany, 1813* (London, 1974), describes the actions of the Prince and his corps in 1813, and gives an account of his death at Leipzig. H. Lachouque's *Napoleon's Battles* (London, 1966) gives a very clear account of the Battle of Leipzig. A. Brett-James's *General Wilson's Diary* (London, 1964) provides contemporary observations on the 1813 campaign.

CHRONOLOGY

1742, December 8	—Born at Laon (Aisne)
1755, March 25	—Joined the army; commissioned into the Laon militia
1760, July 31	—Wounded at Siege of Warburg in Seven Years' War
1762	—Took part in expedition to Portugal
1770	—Commanded chasseurs in expedition to Corsica
1789, March 17	—Promoted major in Médoc infantry
1791, January 1	—Promoted lieutenant-colonel
1792, October	—Deprived of rank and arrested, but later reinstated
1794, December 22	—Promoted *général de division*
1796, March 27	—First meeting with Napoleon at Nice
April 12	—Battle of Montenotte
April 14	—Capture of Dego; loss and recapture
April 21	—Victory of Mondovi—his greatest triumph
April 28	—Treaty of Cherasco, dictated by Napoleon to Piedmont
May 5	—Crossing of the River Po at Piacenza
May 30	—Battle of Borghetto; Beaulieu's Austrian forces driven north to the Tyrol
June 4	—After failure of attack on Mantua, in charge of siege
August	—Battle of Castiglione; invalided out
1797, January 16	—La Favorite; failure of breakout; Mantua surrenders
	—Took captured Austrian colors to Paris
	—Governor of Venice, followed by posting to Rennes
1798	—Return to Northern Italy for campaign under Schérer
1799, April 27	—Surrendered to Suvorov at Verderio
November	—Took part in coup d'état *Brumaire*
1801, August 13	—Retired and shortly became vice-president of Senate
1804, April 23	—Appointed governor of Les Invalides
May 19	—Appointed an honorary *Maréchal d'Empire* (eighteenth in seniority)
1808	—Created *comte*
1814, March 31	—At Les Invalides destroyed trophies of Frederick the Great and captured colors as allies approached Paris
1819, December 21	—Died, age 77; buried at Cemetery of Père-Lachaise.

CHAPTER TWENTY-THREE

THE VIRGIN OF ITALY

Sérurier

by

David D. Rooney

Early Life (1742–1796)

On March 27, 1796, General Philibert Sérurier, a battle-hardened warrior with years of campaigning experience, was summoned to Nice, along with his colleagues Generals Augereau and Massena, to meet the 27-year-old Napoleon. The three veterans showed deep suspicion at the summons, even though word of the Paris mob and the Tuileries had already reached the Army of Italy. Their suspicions were quickly allayed by the incisiveness and confidence of their new commander, and soon they embarked on a campaign of foreign adventure that was to lay the foundation of French conquest from Lisbon to Moscow and that in the future would secure for the three generals their marshal's batons.

At 53, nearly twice the age of Napoleon, Sérurier had as much military experience as any officer in the Revolutionary armies. Having survived the upheavals of the years after 1789, he was now a solid, widely respected, but unexciting leader, and probably, like any soldier of his age, hoping for a few more years with the colors. A fierce disciplinarian, matured in the age of Frederick the Great's drill book, his tall, angular figure and scarred, lop-sided face had won respect, if not affection. His face wound, caused by a bullet at the Siege of Warburg on July 31, 1760, when he was only 18, gave him an air of distinction, and on one occasion saved him from premature retirement.

His father, a mole catcher at the royal stud at Laon, owned a small manor near Vervins, and as a royal official considered himself a member of the minor nobility. This enabled him to gain for his son, Philibert, a commission in the Laon militia, in 1755 at the age of 13. Philibert served in Germany as an ensign in the *Régiment d'Infanterie d'Aumont,* and in April 1762 was promoted to lieutenant before taking part in an expedition to Portugal later that year. Here he took part in the capture of Almeida. The Peace of Paris in 1763 brought a reduction in rank and a period of doubt and uncertainty about a military career. In the next 20 years, many as an infantry and drill instructor, with scant chance of promotion, he established himself as a conscientious and hard-working officer who would not neglect the more tedious duties and responsibilities. He was rewarded with the opportunity to command a detachment of chasseurs in an expedition to Corsica from 1770 to 1774. In 1779 he was at last promoted to captain, and he then married Louise Marie Itasse, the daughter of a minor official from Laon. There were no children of the marriage, though he later adopted the child of a wounded non-commissioned officer. He was appointed a Chevalier of St. Louis in 1781, and by the critical year 1789, with 34 years of service behind him, he was finally promoted to major in the *Régiment d'Infanterie de Médoc.*

For an officer of his experience, the Revolution brought new opportunities for promotion, but with so many years in the royalist armies, it also brought the grave hazard that, coming from the minor provincial nobility, he might be suspected of royalist sympathies. The Directory, or the civilian committees at a lower level, could make or break a commander through political intrigue or personal malice, as Sérurier was to find. Promoted to lieutenant-colonel in 1791, as garrison commander in Perpignan, he tactfully handled the situation when his soldiers revolted and seized the regimental colors and chest. Having survived this crisis, he was promoted to colonel of the 70th Line and engaged actively in the search for royalist sympathizers. Just as suddenly he was himself arrested and deprived of his rank for suspected royalist sympathies; but Paul Barras, who also played a critical role in the early career of Napoleon, intervened, and Sérurier was reinstated. He was back in action at Utelle on February 28, 1793, and the Representatives of the People—again influenced by Barras—confirmed Sérurier as general of brigade in the Army of Italy from June 25, 1793. His wide experience both of military administration and of action in the field now brought him due recognition, and again the Committee of Public Safety confirmed his appointment as general of division on June 13, 1795.

From this point Sérurier's career falls into two parts: the dramatic years from 1796 to 1799, when he was one of Napoleon's staunchest commanders in the Italian theatre; and then, after his retirement from active service in 1799, and after receiving his marshal's baton in 1804, when he filled with distinction some of the high offices of state—above all, a figure of massive integrity.

Italian Campaign—First Advance (1796)

Only two days before his first critical meeting with Napoleon on March 27, 1796,[1] Sérurier had had to deal with a mutiny in one of the battalions in his division—an indication of the hunger, neglect, and lack of supplies that made the Army of Italy a mutinous rabble. In spite of this Napoleon announced April 15 as the deadline for an attack, and authorized an issue of pay. The terrain and the enemy dispositions dictated that the fighting would take place in the coastal mountains and valleys between Nice and Genoa.

Austrian General Beaulieu, with his Piedmontese colleague,

Colli, had 50,000 troops, but they were weakened by political distrust and disloyalty. Napoleon therefore decided to attack the Piedmontese in force, in order to knock them out of the war and to be able to feed and equip his starving troops in the lusher valleys of the Po.

The first move in the campaign was a French feint along the coast toward Genoa. This deceived General Beaulieu into thinking that the main attack would be in this direction. In fact, the main French forces were already moving rapidly into the mountains toward Montenotte and Dego. The Battle of Montenotte (April 12, 1796), in which Napoleon directed Massena and La Harpe while he held Sérurier in reserve on the left flank, was a vital and significant victory. Napoleon achieved a local superiority of 9,000 to 6,000, he captured substantial supplies of arms and ammunition, he gained valuable ground, and above all he gave an immense boost to the morale of his troops. The resounding victory of Montenotte led directly to the Battle of Dego and the French pursuit of General Colli and the Piedmontese forces.

Massena, strongly reinforced, captured the town of Dego on April 14, taking 5,000 prisoners and 19 guns, but even such a formidable figure as Massena could not prevent his men from going off foraging. It was to cost them dearly. The Austrians under General Wukassovitch attacked that night, nearly capturing Massena himself, who escaped in his nightclothes from a woman's bedroom. He also lost his guns, and it cost 1,000 casualties to recapture Dego the following day—a savage price for poor discipline.

Sérurier with his fresh division, and backed up by Augereau, now led the advance. As the French advanced, Colli with 13,000 Piedmontese abandoned a useful defensive position and fell back on Ceva. By April 16 Sérurier and Augereau were probing the defenses of Ceva. Augereau put in the first attack and was repulsed.[2] Napoleon therefore rapidly concentrated more troops to make a major attack on April 18. Sérurier advanced on to the defenses of Ceva only to find that Colli had withdrawn to a defensive position on the way to Mondovi, leaving a battalion to garrison Ceva. Here Sérurier showed more initiative than Augereau, and forced a crossing over the Corsaglia River; but once again discipline broke down, and while the troops dispersed looking for food and loot, Colli counter-attacked and drove the French back over the river, with heavy losses. On the twenty-first there followed the Battle of Mondovi (see p. 452).

The victory of Mondovi—rightly attributed to Sérurier alone—not only restored the morale of all the French forces but totally changed the strategic situation. A well-stocked arsenal fell into Sérurier's hands, but, even more important, the Army of Italy, ill-armed and half-starved up to that moment, could advance more confidently into the more generous and fertile lands of Piedmont. The victory of Mondovi was the key to Napoleon's advance into Piedmont. After a hurried reorganization, he set out for Turin on April 23. His gratitude to Sérurier was not to be forgotten. Massena and Augereau led the new advance, while Sérurier covered the left flank, in closer proximity to Colli, the Piedmontese leader, who still held the fortress of Fossano and Cherasco. The armies, their morale high after the victory of Mondovi and the rapid withdrawal of the enemy, had advanced for less than a day when Colli sent a letter asking for an armistice. Napoleon refused to consider this unless several fortresses were handed over. The advance continued. On April 25 Massena brushed aside some feeble resistance and occupied Cherasco, and then, on April 27, Napoleon received the reply from the Piedmontese. The reply was not satisfactory and Napoleon brusquely dictated his own terms: the surrender of the fortresses of Coni, Tortona, and Ceva and the right for French armies to march across Piedmont and to cross the River Po. This was a vital factor in planning the next advance against the Austrians. These harsh terms were accepted by Turin on April 28. This was a critical moment in the career of Napoleon: the first major foreign victory, and Piedmont the first foreign country to accept an armistice after military defeat. Napoleon's incisive leadership had galvanized the wretched Army of Italy into action, but this first success was really achieved by the brilliant exploit of Sérurier personally leading his men at the double into the half-occupied town of Mondovi.

Although Napoleon continued his headlong advance, he had to make a number of both tactical and strategic decisions. He still had Sérurier and a strong division holding his left flank facing Colli and any threat from the Piedmontese, while Massena and Augereau were now in the lead. La Harpe, on the right hand, facing Beaulieu and the Austrians, could not advance because his troops lacked boots, ammunition, and food and were mutinous—not having enjoyed the orgy in Mondovi.

Strategically Napoleon could consolidate in Piedmont and wait for a peace treaty, or advance as quickly as possible and destroy Beaulieu's forces before they could be reinforced via the Brenner Pass and Lake Garda. France was at war with the Papacy and with Austria, which controlled the Milanese, but not with the independent states of Venice and Genoa or the duchies of Parma, Modena, and Tuscany. The greatest danger to the French position would arise if Beaulieu were substantially reinforced from Austria, and therefore Napoleon decided to advance and attempt to destroy Beaulieu's existing forces. He was not immediately successful.

Because La Harpe could not advance quickly enough, Beaulieu, virtually unmolested, reached Valenza, where he crossed the Po. Napoleon realized Beaulieu had escaped and had made the vital Po crossing, and he therefore ordered up his main forces—now 37,000 strong to Beaulieu's 26,000—to the area southeast of Valenza, where the River Tanaro joins the Po.

Beaulieu had moved all his forces across the Po by May 2, and decided to await reinforcements and to hold his forces ready to defend Milan. To save Austrian territory in the Milanese from the depredations of his army, he kept his forces in the area of Valeggio in Piedmontese territory.

Beaulieu's new position presented Napoleon with two new problems: He urgently needed to destroy Beaulieu's forces before they could be reinforced, and now there was the difficult problem of crossing a major river in the face of a substantial enemy army. There were three possibilities. The Po, as it flowed past Valenza, was fairly shallow, but the far bank was held in strength by Beaulieu's main forces. Another possible crossing point lay further east at Pavia, but this was also fairly close to Beaulieu's army. A third possible crossing point lay at Piacenza, 50 miles east of Valenza. Napoleon, relying on his greater efficiency and more rapid movement, decided to cross at Piacenza, so that he could get a substantial force across the river before Beaulieu's armies appeared. In order to deceive Beaulieu, Sérurier and Massena made ostentatious preparations to cross the river at Valenza.[3]

On May 5 La Harpe's and Augereau's divisions were made ready, with a rapidly moving advance guard of 5,000 grenadiers and cavalry under Dallemagne. By a brilliantly swift march, Dallemagne's advance guard reached Piacenza by the morning of May 7 and, commandeering boats and rafts, crossed the river. La Harpe with his division reached Piacenza by late morning and also crossed. Soon after crossing Dallemagne was attacked by an advance guard of an Austrian division, and, to his amazement, it withdrew. Beaulieu had begun to suspect Napoleon's plan, especially as Sérurier's forces had made no actual moves to cross at Valenza, but the Austrians made a major mistake in dividing up their forces into small groups of about 5,000 men. On the evening of May 8, Beaulieu's advancing forces stumbled on La Harpe's outpost, and in a brief skirmish La Harpe was accidentally killed by his own men. In spite of this stroke of good fortune for Beaulieu, he failed to press his advantage, and instead of attacking the relatively small French forces on the north bank of the river, he decided to withdraw all his forces northward towards Lodi and to cross the River Adda, which joins the Po east of Piacenza. This gave him another defensive line as he retreated toward Lake Garda, but it left Milan undefended.

By May 9 the divisions of Massena and Sérurier—which had covered 60 miles in three days—arrived at Piacenza. The crossing was now complete, but Beaulieu by his withdrawal had shortened his lines of communication and still had not been mauled. This phase of the campaign was completed with Sérurier and his division holding Piacenza, while Napoleon took part in the sharp action at the bridge of Lodi prior to occupying Milan; meanwhile Beaulieu moved slowly southeastward to the major fortress of Mantua.

Beaulieu, relying on reinforcements coming through the Brenner Pass and the Tyrol, drew up his forces between Peschiera, on the southern tip of Lake Garda, down the line of the River Mincio to Mantua.[4] Napoleon, having briskly crushed some opposition in the Milanese, advanced toward the River Mincio from the west. Beaulieu, trying to hold the whole line from Lake Garda to Mantua, easily fell for Napoleon's deceptions. Pretending to make a major assault on Peschiera, Napoleon launched his real attack toward Borghetto at 2 A.M. on May 30.[5] Augereau in the vanguard marched rapidly toward Peschiera, but the main body under Sérurier and Massena, and with Murat commanding the cavalry, veered off and attacked the bridge at Borghetto, some seven miles south of Peschiera. The French moved so quickly that the Austrians were even prevented from destroying the bridge at Borghetto. While Massena held Borghetto, Sérurier and his division fanned out northeast of Villafranca, but failed to catch up with Beaulieu's main forces, which made a very rapid retreat to the safety of the Tyrol. Napoleon once again, by speed of movement and concentration of force, had won another battle and had conquered substantial territory, but Beaulieu had still managed to withdraw with much of his army—except the abandoned garrison of Mantua—still intact.

Further Service in Italy (1796–1799)—and Retirement (1800–1819)

Between April 12 and May 30, 1796, Napoleon had defeated Piedmont and had driven the Austrians from most of Northern Italy, but, while containing the forces of Beaulieu, still had to subdue the fortress of Milan and Mantua and anticipate an Austrian counter-attack. On June 4 a surprise attack on Mantua narrowly failed; Napoleon then left Sérurier to command the siege, while the only available siege guns were used to subdue Milan. During June and July Sérurier held firm in the bogs and lakes around Mantua, while rapid developments took place elsewhere.

Naples, which could raise 60,000 troops, sought an armistice, signed on June 5, 1796. A mobile column under Murat forced Genoa to eject the Austrian ambassador and to safeguard French troops and convoys. A swift strike taking Bologna and Ancona frightened the Papacy temporarily into submission, and an armistice was signed on June 23. Another detachment attacked and drove out the English garrison at Leghorn on the west coast. Finally on June 27 Milan gave in.

Early in June 1796 Napoleon had discovered that because the southern French army on the Rhine had made no move, the Austrians had decided to withdraw 30,000 troops under Field-Marshal Würmser from the Rhine army and bring them to the relief of Mantua.[6] Napoleon estimated that there would be no threat from these forces until mid-July—and this accounts for the frenetic activity all over Northern Italy in June. By July 29 Würmser, with 60,000 troops against Napoleon's 40,000, was advancing southward on both sides of Lake Garda and was about to threaten both Brescia and Mantua, where Sérurier remained doggedly at his post.

From July 19 to August 7, 1796, there were a series of battles between Napoleon and his veteran commanders and troops, on the one hand, and Würmser and Quasdanovitch with their slow-moving Austrian troops, on the other. For the first few days, Sérurier remained in command at Mantua, but when Napoleon, reading the battle correctly, decided to abandon the siege of Mantua, it fell to Sérurier to destroy the careful work of weeks and to withdraw with his forces southwesterly toward Cremona. This was to safeguard the French lines of communication should the Austrian commander, Quasdanovitch, advance effectively from Brescia, which he had captured. In contrast, because of Napoleon's rapid decisions and the rapid marching and countermarching by the French troops, Quasdanovitch was defeated at the two Battles of Lonato and driven into the mountains northwest of Lake Garda, while Napoleon was able to bring overwhelming strength to attack Würmser's main force at the Battle of Castiglione on August 5.[7] At this critical moment Sérurier was struck down by malaria, but General Fiorella led the division with determination. The sound of his guns advancing from the south was the sign for the main attack at Castiglione, which defeated Würmser and drove him northward—like Beaulieu before him—toward the northern haven of Trente. The rapid French advance, which gave Würmser no time to regroup on the

Mincio and which resulted in the immediate capture of Peschiera, was led by Sérurier who, accompanied by Napoleon, entered Verona.

During the lull that followed these hectic days of almost continuous fighting, Sérurier was invalided home. Thus, he missed the hard-fought September battles and the failure of Morceau to advance from the Rhine to Innsbruck. He also missed the great November Battle of Arcola, when the Austrians made another desperate attempt to relieve Würmser and his 30,000 troops in Mantua. Early in 1797 Sérurier returned to the front and resumed command of the forces investing Mantua.

At the same time the Austrians attacked again—their main thrust going down the east side of Lake Garda, with a diversionary column making a left hook to attack Verona from the east. This was the final attempt to relieve Mantua, and since the Frence knew from a captured dispatch that Würmser would try to break out southward and join up with the papal forces, Sérurier, in charge of the siege, had a key role to play.[8]

In a hard-fought battle at Rivoli on January 14, 1797, the French forces under Napoleon's direct control defeated the main Austrian armies advancing by Lake Garda and forced them back to Trente. Simultaneously Austrian Commander Provera outwitted Augereau and made a surprise lunge at Mantua with 7,000 men. He reached Mantua from Legnano by midday on January 15. Provera was able to contact Würmser inside the city and they arranged a breakout through a northern gate of Mantua—La Favorite—the next morning. Unfortunately for the Austrians, Napoleon with strong elements of Massena's division arrived during the night, and bivouacked between La Favorite and Provera's forces. When the breakout started, Sérurier's forces stood firm, while Provera, surrounded by Massena and Augereau, was quickly forced to surrender, together with 7,000 Austrian troops. Würmser retreated into Mantua again. Würmser soon realized that his position was hopeless—with no prospect of help from Austria—and he agreed to surrender. Sérurier, who had commanded the blockading forces for so long, was given the privilege of accepting the surrender on February 2, 1797. In a brief further campaign prompted by the papal intrigues with Austria, Napoleon defeated the papal forces and dictated extremely harsh terms.

In recognition of his outstanding service throughout the campaign, and especially at the Siege of Mantua, Sérurier was sent by Napoleon to take 22 captured Austrian standards to the Directory in Paris. In a highly complimentary report, Napoleon referred to his firm discipline and reliability. His own troops echoed the admiration of Napoleon. They respected his firm discipline and fairness and the rigorous standards of behavior he set for himself. In a licentious and lecherous age, and recalling Massena's episode at Dego, there was an element of respect and awe in the nickname his troops gave to Sérurier: "The Virgin of Italy."

During 1797 he was dogged by ill health, probably from his continued exposure to the fevers of the marshes around Mantua, and this may well have prevented him from gaining any higher command than a division. In the summer of 1797 when the Army of Italy was resting on its laurels, there was serious discontent and grumbling among many of the generals, including Bernadotte and Joubert, but not Sérurier. A contemporary account describes him as being 55, tall and distinguished looking, honest, estimable in every respect, considered to be an aristocrat, but supported by Napoleon who valued and admired him.

His reputation for integrity and probity brought him one of his most unpleasant and testing appointments.[9] Sérurier was personally selected by Napoleon to be governor of Venice, while the French took over all the war-like stores in Venice and also most of the works of art. This caused bitter clashes with his colleagues, but Napoleon and Berthier supported all he did. He kept his hands clean in a dirty business, and he was glad to go back to France to command a division at Rennes.

During 1798 he returned to Italy into an unhappy situation in which many areas were being ravaged by the French commanders and their men. Sérurier was sent on one such expedition to Lucca to extort a heavy ransom in money and clothing and to set up a small republic. Early in 1799 campaigning started again. The incompetent Schérer, who had made so many blunders in the Army of Italy before being replaced by Napoleon in March 1796, was again put in command and quickly exhibited his qualities of pathetic dithering. The battlegrounds were as before—Verona, Villafranca, Lake Garda, and the River Adda—but the magic ingredient of Napoleon's leadership was missing. In March 1799 Schérer attacked Verona while Sérurier's division, using boats on Lake Garda, captured Rivoli. Next Sérurier had to make a feint attack on Verona and got heavily mauled, though he personally came out of it with credit. On April 5 Sérurier with the remnants of his division captured Villafranca, but the demoralization caused by Schérer increased very rapidly. Because of a succession of defeats, insubordination and insolence spread everywhere. Sérurier, renowned for his firm discipline, demanded to be replaced. The murder of officers became common throughout the divisions, and Sérurier quoted an incident in which two of his excellent colonels had been threatened by their own men. He concluded, "This manner of serving cannot be suitable for a man of my age."*

Before the end of April, Schérer had begged to be replaced by Moreau, in whom the troops had some confidence, but Moreau took over 27,000 broken troops to face the Russian Commander Suvorov, who commanded 70,000 fresh and experienced troops. In this dangerous situation Sérurier was posted, with a widely scattered division to hold the western sector, which stretched almost to Lake Maggiore. Under heavy attack he held out at Verderio on the River Adda, until all his ammunition was spent, then with the ragged remains of his division he surrendered. Later he was criticized for failing to go to the help of Moreau, but the real reason for the debacle was the chaos, confusion, and demoralization of the whole army.[10]

As a captive he was insulted by the Milan mob, but his captor, Suvorov, treated him courteously, while gently chiding him for supporting a republic. Sérurier replied, "My father in giving me my sword expressly ordered me only to use it to defend my country."† He was allowed to return to Paris on parole, but was not well received by the Directory. Understandably he was soon caught up with his former colleagues and supported the coup d'état of *Brumaire*, in which he commanded a detachment at Pont du Jour.

Again Napoleon showed his gratitude for reliable help at a critical time. Sérurier was granted an honorable retirement and became vice-president of the Senate. In 1803 he enjoyed a nostalgic interlude as president of the commission to decide the border between France and Piedmont. Appointed governor of Les Invalides in 1804, this honor was quickly followed on May 19, 1804, by his appointment as an Honorary Marshal of the Empire. As a marshal he received further awards, the Grand Eagle of the Legion of Honor and the Grand Cordon of the Iron Crown, and in 1808 he was created count and awarded 40,000 francs per annum.

He had one further dramatic act to contribute to the history of France. On March 31, 1814, as the allies approached Paris, Sérurier at Les Invalides, in front of the assembled pensioners, took 1,417 captured colors and had them burned, and he personally burned the sword and sash of Frederick the Great—to the dismay of subsequent historians.

In 1814 the restored Bourbons made him a peer—confirmed by Napoleon during the Hundred Days—but in 1815 he was

---

*See R. H. Phipps, *The Armies of the First French Republic*, Vol. V, p. 259.
†See Phipps, *op. cit.*, Vol. V, p. 264.

removed from Les Invalides and he lost his marshal's salary until shortly before his death. As a peer he was involved in the tragic trial of Marshal Ney, and voted for his execution. In 1819 he was restored as a marshal of France, but he died on December 21, 1819. He was buried at the Cemetery of Père-Lachaise, but his body was brought to Les Invalides in 1847.

Not the ablest or most brilliant of the Napoleonic marshals, Sérurier nonetheless achieved great things because of his reliability and his unshakable integrity.

The Battle of Mondovi (April 21, 1796)

After General Colli's counterstroke on April 19, there followed urgent consultations between Napoleon, Sérurier, and Augereau, which illustrate another side of the campaigning. Napoleon demanded an attack the next day (April 20), but Sérurier argued that his men were at the end of their tether, and unless they were allowed a day to forage for food, they would not attack—indeed could well disperse altogether. This argument, together with the expected arrival of artillery the following day, convinced Napoleon, and he agreed to postpone the attack for one day. The twentieth was used to regroup the forces, with Massena joining Sérurier on the central and southern arc, and Augereau facing the northern sector.

Colli, again facing overwhelming odds, withdrew from his fortified position during the night of April 20–21 and fell back to Mondovi. Stengel, the most experienced French cavalry leader, led a vigorous pursuit, but was killed. Sérurier did not allow this to curb the momentum and was determined to attack Mondovi before Colli had time to organize its defense.

Here Sérurier was to play a brilliant and decisive role—one that confirmed his position and led to his eventual promotion to the highest honors. He had always had the respect of both his troops and his fellow officers, but he also had his critics who considered him stuffy and old fashioned, too strongly influenced by the rigid drill and limited flexibility of the prerevolutionary armies. Now he showed initiative, bravery, and brilliant tactical sense.

From his years of experience, he had had time to weigh up which were his seasoned and reliable troops and which were raw and unseasoned. The less reliable were rapidly formed into three columns, while the better units were thrown out in front as skirmishers. Smarting under the rebukes and failures of the previous three days, Sérurier put himself at the head of the central column, drew his sword, and led his troops at the double into the attack. The troops responded to this daring leadership, and advanced rapidly into the town against ineffective and patchy defenses. The momentum was kept up, and the Piedmontese, bluffed into thinking the French were being reinforced, were hustled out of the town. The troops, which had responded to Sérurier's positive leadership in mounting the attack, indulged in an orgy of pillage and destruction as soon as the Piedmontese under Colli had withdrawn. This could now be tolerated, for a critical victory had been won, and much of the credit was Sérurier's.

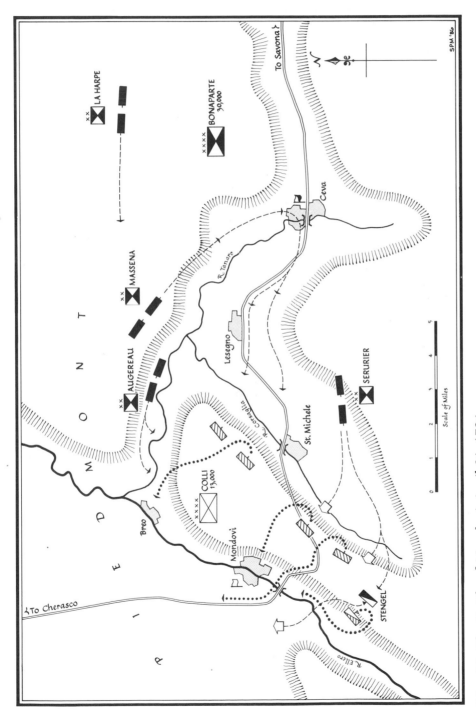

Map 23. The Battle of Mondovi, April 21, 1796

TEXTUAL REFERENCES

1. D. G. Chandler, *The Campaigns of Napoleon* (New York, 1966), p. 53.
2. W. G. F. Jackson, *Attack in the West* (London, 1953), p. 72.
3. *Ibid.*, p. 102.
4. V. J. Esposito and J. R. Elting, *A Military History and Atlas of the Napoleonic Wars* (New York, 1964), p. 11.
5. D. G. Chandler, *Dictionary of the Napoleonic Wars* (New York, 1979), p. 64.
6. Jackson, *op. cit.*, p. 130.
7. Chandler, *Dictionary, op. cit.*, p. 253.
8. Jackson, *op. cit.*, p.211ff.
9. R. W. Phipps, *The Armies of the First French Republic and the Rise of the Marshals of Napoleon I* (Oxford, 1926–39), Vol. 4, p. 200.
10. *Ibid.*, p. 263.

BIBLIOGRAPHICAL NOTE

Correlli Barnett's *Bonaparte* (New York, 1978) is a controversial view, critical of some aspects of Napoleon's leadership. D. G. Chandler's *Campaigns of Napoleon* (New York, 1966) and *Dictionary of the Napoleonic Wars* (New York, 1979) are the most scholarly and up-to-date accounts of the Napoleonic wars.

R. F. Delderfield, *The March of the Twenty-Six: The Story of Napoleon's Marshals* (London, 1962), is a fascinating description of the lives of the marshals by an author with a sensitive feel for the period. V. J. Esposito and J. R. Elting, *A Military History and Atlas of the Napoleonic Wars* (New York, 1964), has some very good maps but sometimes a rathe confusing narrative. W. G. F. Jackson's *Attack in the West* (London, 1953) is an excellent book covering the Italian Campaign. A. G. Macdonell's *Napoleon and His Marshals* (London, 1934) is readable but flawed.

R. W. Phipps's *The Armies of the First French Republic and the Rise of the Marshals of Napoleon I,* 5 vols. (Oxford, 1926–39) is an invaluable source book covering the period. P. Young, *Napoleon's Marshals* (London, 1973), is a useful brief outline.

CHRONOLOGY

1769, March 29	—Born at St.-Amans-Labastide (Tarn)
1785, April 16	—Enlisted in *Régiment Royal Infanterie*
1792, January 17	—Elected drill instructor, First Battalion, *Volontaires du Haut-Rhin*
1793, November 19	—Appointed staff captain in the divisions Taponier then Lefebvre
1794, June 26	—Serves at Fleurus; soon promoted to command a brigade in *l'Armée de Sambre et Meuse*
1796, April 26	—Marries Louise Berg at Solingen
1798, May 19	—Fights at combat of Ostend in Championnet's division
1799, March 21–25	—Serves at Stockach
April 21	—Promoted *général de division;*
June and September	—Serves in battles around Zurich under Massena
1800, April 6–May 13	—Fights around Genoa; wounded and taken prisoner
1801, February 13	—Served under Murat in Italy (until early June 1802)
1803, August 28	—Appointed to command St. Omer camp
1804, May 19	—Appointed *Maréchal d'Empire* (eighth in seniority) and colonel general of the Imperial Guard
1805 to 1807	—Commands IV Corps in Austria, Prussia, and Poland
1808, June 29	—Created *duc de Dalmatie*
November 3– September 16, 1809	—Commands II Corps at Corunna and Oporto
1809, September 16	—"major-general" to King Joseph
1810, June 14	—Commands *l'Armée d'Andalousie*
1811, May 16	—Fights General Beresford at Battle of Albuera
1813, January 3–July 1	—Commands Old Guard, then Imperial Guard, ultimately IV Corps in Saxony
July 6	—Commands armies in the Pyrenees (mid-April 1814)
1814, December 4	—Appointed Bourbon minister of war (until March 1815)
1815, May 9–June 26	—Appointed "major-general" in *l'Armée du Nord*
1816, January 12	—Banished from France (until late May 1819); starts memoirs in Germany
1830, November 17	—Appointed minister of war (until mid-July 1834)
1832, October 11	—Appointed president of Council of Ministers (until mid-July 1834)
1839, May 12	—Reappointed President of Council of Ministers (until early March 1840)
1840, October 29	—Reappointed minister of war (to November 10, 1845) and president of Council of Ministers (until late October 1847)
1847, September 26	—Appointed *Maréchal-Général de France*
1851, November 26	—Dies at St.-Amans-Labastide

CHAPTER TWENTY-FOUR

KING NICOLAS

Soult

by

Dr. Paddy Griffith

From Wissembourg to Genoa (1789–1800)

Marshal-General Nicolas Jean de Dieu Soult, duke of Dalmatia, shared many things in common with Field-Marshal Sir Arthur Wellesley, Duke of Wellington. They were born within a year of each other, rose to high command at a comparable pace, and enjoyed successful second careers in politics and as the "grand old men" of their respective armies. Both were present at the coronation of Queen Victoria in 1838, just as they had often both been present in the same battles in the Peninsula and then at Waterloo. They died within a year of each other, leaving extensive estates and art collections to their heirs.[1]

There, however, the similarities end. Whereas Wellington was the archetypal officer "descended from the gentry," Soult was the classic case of an officer "risen from the ranks." From the age of 16, his education had been the *Régiment Royal Infanterie*, which he had joined upon the death of his father, a small-town notary. Although Soult apparently wanted to earn enough to set up his own village bakery, he never succeeded in breaking from the army, and the habits of the barrack room entered his blood. By the time of the Revolution, he had grown into a hard-bitten drill sergeant: coarse and bullying but energetic and precise. From there he rose rapidly and discovered—perhaps to his own surprise—that he also had a natural flair for administration. Thus, at the peak of his powers, about 1800, he combined the manners and leadership qualities of a non-commissioned officer with the intellectual achievements of a general.

Unfortunately this happy combination could not long survive the temptations of high command, and especially after his wound at Genoa, Soult often allowed himself to be swayed by avarice and self-indulgence. He shunned the dangers of the front line, yet failed to coordinate his strategies effectively with those of the other marshals. Despite a close understanding of Napoleon himself, Soult's record during the Empire was that of a man who could not quite live up to his early promise.

Sergeant Soult's introduction to the wars of the Revolution was his transfer from his old regiment to serve as a drill instructor (acting second-lieutenant) with the grenadier company of the First Battalion of *Haut-Rhin* (or Upper Rhine) volunteers in the Army of the Rhine. This was a new unit of raw troops formed for the emergency, with elected officers who were for the most part just as green as their soldiers. The battalion belonged to a force tasked with the defense of the middle Vosges—the classic military frontier in France's northeast corner. Thus, Soult, who hailed from the Cevennes in the deep south, found himself about as far from home as it was possible to be without leaving the country. Not for eight weary years of war was he to be posted nearer to the Mediterranean: it was on the Rhine that he was destined to make his name.

Fortunately there were several months available for training in the spring of 1792, before operations began in earnest. Soult's experience appears to have been much in demand among the untutored men of his battalion, and he was able to take a lead and show all ranks how to drill and maneuver. At one point he even took over from the colonel since (as he put it) although he knew as little about battalion drill as the colonel himself, he did at least have more of a military manner and self-confidence.[2]

In July his personal ascendancy was recognized when he was confirmed in his rank and given command of a company. There was even a whiff of action in a few small outpost skirmishes around the fortress of Wissembourg. Soult's first major action, however, did not come until almost a year later, at Ueberfelsheim on March 29. Custine's bloodless victory at Mainz had suddenly been shattered by a Prussian counterstroke, and there was some desperate rearguard fighting as the French withdrew. Soult's battalion lost no less than 50% of its strength to shot and shell,[3] although it did effectively prevent a total collapse. Soult was personally commended by Custine for his part in the action, and he emerges as an effective regimental officer—staunch under fire and presumably sharply reprimanding his men when they were tempted to retire from the line.

Soult's next battle was at Bodenthal camp, in the hills west of Wissembourg, on September 13–14. In this battle Soult actually controlled two battalions as part of Gouvion St.-Cyr's convergent assault on a strong Austrian position. Soult's role was in the pursuit phase, where he appears to have done well. The total balance of losses amounted to over 700 Austrians as against less than 100 French—a most impressive final result in the first true offensive battle that Soult had witnessed. In his memoirs he shows us something of his enthusiasm for actions of a similar type,[4] and it is perhaps from Bodenthal that we may date his penchant for enveloping attacks made on more than one axis of advance.

Soult was next thrown into a desultory war of outposts, which culminated in the Battle of Saverne on October 18. He was hotly engaged and lost a cousin killed and a brother wounded in the affair; but once again he witnessed the triumph of offensive tactics. The Austrian onset had been halted by a resolute firing line, and then put to rout by a counterattack in massed column.[5] This must have reinforced such lessons as he had already learned, and we detect a growth in his professional confidence in tune with that of the army as a whole. This feeling must have been strongly reinforced when he applied for, and was granted, an appointment on the staff of Hoche's Army of the Moselle, attached to the headquarters of Taponier's division. As the tempo of the campaign accelerated, he found himself increasingly employed on special missions on the outpost line for Hoche and Taponier. He enjoyed a position of trust that, despite one serious misunderstanding, he appears to have fulfilled admirably. During the successful offensives in mid-December around Niederbronn and Le Pigeonnier, he was constantly at the heart of the action, particularly specializing in rapid, unexpected attacks and in scouting work. Although he was still only a substantive captain, he was on occasion placed in command of a full brigade. There simply were not sufficient reliable officers of the appropriate rank available for the tasks that had to be performed,[6] so the hierarchy of command suffered, but Soult's career benefited.

In January 1794 there was a pause in campaigning and a reorganization of the Army of the Moselle. Soult gained a plum job as chief of staff to Lefebvre's strong vanguard division, and promotion soon followed. Then a little later this division was moved west to join Jourdan's new Army of the Sambre et Meuse, which was assembling for the invasion of Belgium. Soult's association with Lefebvre was to be a long and fruitful one, and indeed the Army of the *Sambre et Meuse* itself was soon to become an exceptionally effective fighting force, quite comparable in *esprit de corps* to Bonaparte's Army of Italy a couple of years later.

The *Sambre et Meuse* was first seriously engaged at Fleurus, where it narrowly succeeded in beating off both the internal and the external enemy. Soult later learned that if the battle had been lost, he and a number of his colleagues would have been singled out for execution by the odious Representative on mission, St. Just[8]—so it is fortunate that the Austrian attacks abated in the nick of time. As it was, Fleurus was one of Soult's most grueling trials in the front line, as he raced back and forth plugging gaps and rallying waverers. He had no less than five horses shot from under him,[9] which is a fair indication of the extent to which he was ready to expose himself to danger during this phase of his military life.

Lefebvre's men next went into action, curiously enough, at Mont St. Jean on July 6, 1794. When they arrived they found that a combined Dutch and Austrian force had beaten off all attacks on this famous position for several hours—but the appearance of the fresh French troops was enough to break their line, and they retreated hastily through Brussels.[10] How Soult must have wished that history could have repeated itself when he came to refight this battle 21 years later!

During the next year the *Sambre et Meuse* was employed in securing Belgium and Luxembourg, reducing their fortresses and closing up to the Rhine. For a young staff officer whose experience had previously been centered on outpost work and the infantry battle line, this campaign must have opened up a whole new vista of professional expertise. Soult tells us that he never worked harder than at this period, and he noticed that the administration and regularity of the whole army were improving rapidly.[11] His apprenticeship to arms can be considered to have been rounded off when in October he was taken out of Lefebvre's division and given command of a brigade on a permanent basis. He was now a fully-fledged general, less than 3 years after he had been a sergeant.

As a general Soult started to realize that he could express preferences that had an effect upon his future life. Thus, when invited by Hoche to join him in the suppression of the Vendée insurgency, he refused on the grounds that he abhorred such police work within his own country.[12] On the contrary, he maneuvered to rejoin Lefebvre's staff, where he obviously felt at home. Most important of all, however, was his decision to marry. In April 1796 he won the hand of Louise Berg of Solingen, near Düsseldorf, in whose mother's house he had been quartered. Soult's new wife was a Protestant while he was a Catholic, but otherwise they appear to have had much in common. They came from similar social backgrounds, and to all accounts both displayed a formidable outward manner. Their 55-year marriage appears to have been as successful as it was long lived, even if not quite entirely free from infidelities on either side.

Meanwhile, on the Rhine Soult saw combat many times, and with Lefebvre he even sometimes returned to his old duties on the outpost line. In both attack and in defense he normally acted with decision and flair, and could certainly now be called a "tactician" in the full sense of that term. One of his finest achievements was the withdrawal of his brigade from Herborn on June 16, 1796, in the face of overwhelming numbers of enemy cavalry. For six hours Soult's men retired in an echelon of squares, occasionally halting to repulse a charge, until the arrival of Ney, Soult's rival at this time, with a handful of his hussars finally persuaded the Austrians that French reinforcements were at hand. Soult reports that in this action he suffered no casualties at all, although the main body of the army had entirely given him up for lost.[13] A somewhat similar operation was his breakout from encirclement near Bamberg on August 30 of the same year. This stands out as a particularly bold stroke as well as a neat technical maneuver; and Soult was later to use it to illustrate his aphorism that in war anything may be attempted provided one retains one's own *sangfroid* and continues to give inspiration to one's subordinates.[14]

Early in 1797 Soult transferred to vanguard work in Championnet's division, where he had many opportunities to feed his growing animosity toward Ney. A year later, however, the division was moved to the Channel coast as part of the "Army of England" intended for an invasion of the British Isles. In the event, however, the boot turned out to be on the other foot, since in May it was the British who raided Ostend. A hectic battle was joined around the lock gates on the Bruges canal, which the British were trying to destroy. Soult noted with some disgust that if it had been successful this scheme would have flooded and destituted many innocent civilians, yet at the same time he could not help marveling at the intricate time bomb that the raiders had brought for the demolition. The French defenders eventually forced the British to surrender, although, despite Soult's extravagant claims, it is not quite crystal clear that he was actually present in person at the time.[15] We are perhaps looking here at an early example of his self-publicity outrunning his real achievement. We can at least state that he was in error when he claimed Sir John Moore among the prisoners. Sir Henry Burrard—the man who spoiled Wellesley's victory at Vimeiro—was certainly captured, but not Moore.

After Ostend Soult returned to Lefebvre's vanguard in the Army of Mainz, later renamed Army of the Danube, which included many of the former members of the old *Sambre et Meuse*. It was soon in action around Stockach in a series of rather ill-considered battles against a superior enemy. For Soult, however, these actions were a great opportunity for his talents to shine. At Ostrach (March 21) he took over the vanguard division when Lefebvre was wounded, and energetically rallied the troops to make a counterattack that saved the position.[16] This was a bloody affair, however, and the division lost some 1,800 men in the day. There was more action on the twenty-fourth, and the fiercest fighting of all on the twenty-fifth, when Soult's vanguard division was used at Liptingen in a frontal attack against the whole of Archduke Charles's army. Mortier, now a brigadier under Soult's command, performed splendidly at the spearhead of the attack, but the adverse odds soon threw the whole division onto the defensive. By the end of the day, it had lost some 2,000 men, making a total of about 50% casualties in the division within a week; in fact, it was saved from annihilation only by the Austrians' lack of urgency in pursuit.[17] Nevertheless, Soult could fairly claim that he had fought with success and skill, carefully handling his reserves, directing attack and defense with equal understanding, and maintaining the morale of his subordinates by his example. Stockach was certainly the biggest battle he had fought thus far in his career, and it represents an important milestone in his progress as a commander. During the retreat that followed, he was entrusted with command of two divisions, and soon confirmed in his rank as a two-star general some five and a half years after he had started to command brigades.

After Stockach this army was united with Massena's Army of Helvetia. Soult was moved up to the Bâle area, and thence detached for a lightning campaign of counterinsurgency in the Reuss valley. It is to his credit that in this very successful operation he always insisted upon the most lenient treatment for the insurgents.

Soult's next role was in reserve for Massena's battles to the east of Zurich, and then at the center of the defense of the strongly fortified Zurichberg. Repeated attacks on this position between June 2 and 4 were all beaten off skillfully, as Soult acted as energetically as ever in the front line and won the high praise of Massena.[18] There were nevertheless some 1,250 casualties in Soult's division, leaving approximately 7,000 men in the ranks. A few days later the contest was renewed and again Soult was successful, although at one point he was forced to commit his final reserve of newly arrived raw recruits. Telling them not to lose impetus by stopping to fire in the attack,[19] Soult sent them forward in a victorious column assault that stabilized his position.

There was now a lull in the fighting as the Austrians awaited the arrival of Suvorov's reinforcements. Soult launched a telling local probing attack on August 14 and then, on September 25, played a spectacular role in Massena's preemptive assault, known as the Second Battle of Zurich. In this operation Soult was posted at the eastern end of the Zurich lake, and had to bridge the Linth at a particularly unpromising spot. The plan adopted involved a complex mixture of swimming assault pistoleers, roadways constructed on fascines, and then the bridging itself, but above all it was based upon the principle of surprise. It worked like clockwork, and both the enemy's lake flotilla and a large magazine of stores were captured.[20] The enemy counterattacks were beaten off and Austrian General Hotze was killed. This set the seal on Massena's victory around Zurich itself, and the allied forces withdrew hastily to the Rhine.

Soult was now dispatched to gather forces to meet Suvorov's advance from the St. Gotthard, and we gain an impression that he was able to apply a sophisticated technique of coordination to the march maneuvers of several separate columns. In the first week of October, Soult was moving backward and forward from one to another of his three divisions, trying to direct them to the best position to hem in the errant Russian force. First Mortier was sent forward, and when he headed off the enemy around Schwyz a new force had to be gathered in the next valley. Gazan came up and a battle was planned at Glarus, but the enemy managed to slip away in the nick of time. Finally two separate columns were sent out to pursue Suvorov down the Rhine, while Soult himself turned back to the north to help Massena chase Korsakov and the remaining Austrians. Through all of this very fluid sequence, Soult was acting as a strategist and an administrator of considerable forces, rather than in his usual role as a local or tactical leader in the front line. It therefore marks a vital new stage in his military development, namely, his mastery of the art of commanding an army corps.

Brumaire saw the veterans of the Sambre and Meuse disappointed, perhaps, that Hoche had not done the deed, but flattered at the recognition given in Paris to Lefebvre and Mortier. Soult's blossoming strategic gifts were also acknowledged by his appointment as a wing commander, under Massena, in the Army of Italy. This promotion was doubly welcome since it gave Soult his first opportunity since the start of the wars to go home and visit his mother.

Upon their arrival in Italy, Soult and Massena were soon forced back into the fortress of Genoa and the toils of a debilitating siege. Soult was often active in sorties against the Austrians, again displaying his command of minor tactics by the shrewd timing and direction of his assaults, as by his prohibition on firing until after the enemy positions had been carried.[21] In one of these sorties, however, he finally paid the price for his unstinting leadership from the front. He was seriously wounded in the leg and captured by the Austrians as his aides attempted to move him away on a stretcher improvised from muskets. He suffered all the indignities of being robbed by his captors and then having to endure pain-wracked days and nights in the grisly surroundings of an emergency field hospital. Reading between the lines of his memoirs as he describes this torment,[22] we can well believe that Soult was unwilling to undergo such an ordeal a second time, if it lay within his power to avoid it.

From Genoa to Toulouse (1800-1814)

Partly as a result of his wound and the terms of his parole, and partly because the war itself was running down after the Battle of Marengo, Soult now experienced a long period without a major combat command. After nine hectic years of battle, the whole tempo of his life suddenly changed. He first became military governor of Piedmont, where, apart from a little enlightened counterinsurgency against the Barbets, he had little to do beyond the peaceable arts of recruiting, hospital administration, and logistic reorganization. Then as commander of Murat's vanguard division, he led the occupation of southern Italy and tasted the delights of privileged rank in a rich land with a Mediterranean climate. We may speculate that his nervous energy, which had been coiled and tense in the gloomy forests of the Rhineland and the bleak valleys of Switzerland, was suddenly relaxed and unwound by this brightly illuminated military promenade. Here Soult first tasted the rewards of office, as opposed to its responsibilities; and he did so under the personal tutelage of the two finest plunderers in the whole of the Napoleonic pantheon—Massena and then Murat in quick succession. The influence of Jourdan and Lefebvre was pushed to one side. For Soult the meridional drill sergeant, the glorious possibility of a baton, a fortune, even a gilded throne in the sun suddenly seemed to be within his grasp. None of that was a prospect that had been offered to him in all his long years on the Rhine, and he revelled in it all the more as a result.

Soult's Italian temptations were scarcely dimmed by the sequence of events that followed. Recalled to Paris on Massena's recommendation, he became colonel-general of the Light Infantry of the Consular Guard, then commander of the Camp of St. Omer, and then, in quick succession, Marshal of the Empire, colonel-general of the Imperial Guard, and finally commander of the biggest army corps of the new Grand Army at Boulogne. We should scarcely be surprised that this welter of recognition left him wedded firmly to Napoleon's cause, or that in his gratitude he erected a spectacular monument to Napoleon's glory. Visitors to Boulogne today can still see it on the heights overlooking the harbor—a giant column surmounted by Napoleon's statue and inscribed with honeyed words in eulogy of the invasion of England, which did not, as it turned out, actually occur.

In late 1805 Napoleon marched forth from Boulogne with his new acolytes to capture Vienna and defeat the power of Austria and Russia. Soult was to play an important role in this campaign, both for his essential preliminary work in training and drilling the army at Boulogne itself—surely the crowning glory of his work as a drillmaster—and then for his maneuvers at the head of IV Corps in the field. Marching in the center of the great wheel that encircled Ulm, he was to capture Augsburg, Landsberg, and Memmingen to emerge in a blocking position some 30 miles to the south of the main target at Ulm.[23] Thus, without actually having to perform any serious feat of arms himself, he was nevertheless able to claim that he had materially helped the success of the campaign as a whole.

Something similar could be said of Soult's role in the Battle of Austerlitz. He was intensely active in the maneuvers that led up to the combat, and showed all his old fire in pushing forward his exhausted troops in their relentless march to the east; but when it came to the battle itself, he went strangely quiet. Thiébault, one of his brigadiers who fought at the forefront of the action, tells us that a few days before the armies clashed, Soult was all for calling off the battle and retreating, and that this nearly led to a duel with Marshal Lannes.[24]

Again, when "the sun of Austerlitz" finally dawned on December 2, it was Soult's corps that was chosen for the decisive central attack upon the Pratzen and Soult who was at Napoleon's side advising him on timings and tactics. Yet when the assault was actually ordered, Soult was nowhere to be seen. Thiébault complained that no reserves were sent forward by the corps commander and nothing at all was done to "read the battle" or to intervene in it by anyone higher than a divisional commander:

> In spite of the critical position in which St. Hilaire's troops were for the space of three hours, Marshal Soult never appeared either to direct them in case of need, to encourge them by his presence, or to judge if it was necessary to reinforce them. . . . In the battle of Austerlitz Marshal Soult had fulfilled none of the functions of a soldier or shared the danger of any of the men of his corps. I was told, indeed, that that morning he had complained of inflammation of the eyes, and had put on a green silk shade just when the battle began. . . . Thus it is clear that Marshal Soult took no personal part in the battle of Austerlitz, unless one can consider the transmission of a few orders at points where fighting was no longer going on as the part of the commander of an army corps.[25]

Thiébault goes on to suggest that Soult was later created Duke of Dalmatia rather than Duke of Austerlitz because Napoleon realized that he had been absent from the storming of the Pratzen. Against this opinion we have the conventional polemic that Soult did in fact win the battle, that he was (in Napoleon's words) "the *premier manoeuvrier* in Europe," and that he was deprived of the Austerlitz title simply because Napoleon wished to reserve that particular laurel to himself.

After Austerlitz Soult maintained his activity as an organizer and an administrator. We also read that he sought to make good the gaps in his interrupted education by using his aides-de-camp as a sort of "evening class." After their supper he would quiz them on historical, scientific, or literary subjects about which they were better informed than he. In this way he would absorb the level of general culture that he felt was appropriate to one of his rank.[26]

In the Jena campaign Soult's art of war remained as "managerial" as it had been in 1805. He commanded from his corps headquarters by remote control, using couriers and staff officers to relay his orders to the front line. One of these, St. Chamans, was fully appreciative of Soult's meticulous preparations, his depth of perception, and his firmness, but he added that "in war he loved vigorous enterprises, but only on condition that he did not expose his own person too far. He was far from sharing the brilliant courage of Marshal Ney and Marshal Lannes; one could even reproach him of the opposite excess, of sheltering himself from danger too carefully. This defect came to him with the great fortune he had amassed."[27] Fortunately, at the Battle of Jena IV Corps was only partially engaged. St. Hilaire's division played an important role in the victory, but Soult himself was not called upon to make excessive exertions.

In Poland Soult made the same system work with success in the combats leading up to Eylau and then in the battle itself. Despite the frosty disapproval of Berthier, Soult was on excellent terms with the Emperor, and on a number of occasions almost read his mind. Both of them understood the strategic situation rather better than most of the other marshals, and it would not be too much to say that Napoleon relied on Soult's advice as much as he ever relied upon anyone's. Yet in the especially murderous battles of the campaign, Soult kept himself well to the rear and failed to exercise the minute tactical control that perhaps he ought to have. Especially at Heilsburg in June this failure backfired upon him, since the front line troops, including Murat's cavalry, started a battle unnecessarily and then let it run out of control. The cavalry was routed and Soult was forced to take shelter in an infantry square until nightfall finally restored the situation.

After the Polish campaign came the time for rewards, and Soult was especially showered with orders, decorations, and incomes. Quite apart from his pay and private sources of income, he collected numerous official titles that gave him a total of well over 300,000 francs per annum (the annual pay of a foot soldier at this time was around 250 francs before stoppages). He was also created Duke of Dalmatia, which was a rank appropriate to his importance in the imperial hierarchy, but displeasing to him because it did not specifically commemorate any of his feats of arms.

Also after Poland came Spain. At first Soult continued in his role as a corps commander under Napoleon's direct command, but after the start of the new Austrian war, when the Emperor absented himself from the Peninsula, Soult's authority grew much wider. By September 1809 he had become King Joseph's major-general, or chief military commander, displacing his own former superior, Jourdan. Soult thus controlled not just one army corps, but several. With the Emperor distant some thousands of miles, Soult suddenly had to bear rather more of the responsibility for what happened in Spain than he was really ready to embrace. Alas for France, he was ultimately to prove unequal to that heavy burden.

Soult was always highly penetrating in his strategic assessments, and he excelled at maintaining his armies in good shape and then bringing them face to face with the enemy. When that enemy was a ramshackle Spanish force that ran away almost at the first shot—as it did, for example, on the Gebora outside Badajoz in 1811[28]—the action naturally redounded spectacularly to Soult's credit. When the enemy was made of sterner stuff, however, he would either back down from the contest or make a half-hearted attack that he failed to carry through.

The list of Soult's "non-battles" against the Anglo–Portuguese army is impressive: Almaraz in 1809, when he failed to cut off Wellington's retreat from Talavera; Badajoz in 1810, when he signally failed to lift a finger to help Massena's invasion of Portugal; the Caia in 1811, when neither he nor Marmont dared to push forward against a markedly inferior force; Second San Christoval in 1812, when Soult had a defeated and dispirited British force in his power but made no move to destroy it; and several further occasions in the Bayonne area during 1813–1814.

Whenever he did actually fight a battle against the Anglo–Portuguese forces, Soult left the tactics to his subordinates, with the result that matters ran out of control—just as they had at Heilsburg. Thus it was that he lost the Battle of Corunna against Moore's ragged and defeated army; he was taken entirely by surprise at Oporto when Wellington placed a mere 600 men in a key position; he allowed himself to be entrapped at the Siege of Cadiz in a far greater strategic *cul de sac* than ever Massena endured before the lines of Torres Vedras; he threw away the decisive victory that he might have won at Albuera; he failed utterly to push home his brilliant strategic surprise of Wellington on the Pyrenees; and he lost the Battles of Nive, Nivelle, Orthez, and Toulouse. Admittedly in these last four cases he had a very inferior and demoralized French army under command, and he could claim that between the end of 1812 and the summer of 1813 some irreparable mistakes had been committed in his absence by Joseph and Jourdan. Yet even with this excuse it is a trifle excessive for Soult's apologists to claim that the campaign from the Pyrenees to Toulouse was a victory.[29]

It could be argued that by this time in his career Soult was no longer a tactician or a drillmaster but a strategist and army commander. By keeping out of the front line, he was simply following Napoleon's own style of leadership and keeping his keen brain clear for the higher calculus of politics and war. He was leaving the physical and charismatic side of the business to a rising generation of more junior but more active men.

This argument would be convincing were it not for three important considerations. The first is that a good strategist has a responsibility to ensure that his battles come to a successful conclusion, and Soult in his years of glory was no longer doing this. The second is that Soult allowed his ambitions to divert him from his duty—both in the ignominious Portugal campaign, where his intriguing to become king earned him the satirical nickname of "King Nicolas,"[30] and then in the enchanted garden of Andalusia, from which he plundered works of art valued at 1.5 million francs.

The third problem was that Soult allowed his relations with other marshals to deteriorate badly at this period. He had never enjoyed warm relations with Ney, but now they got worse still. He also fell out badly with Joseph and Jourdan, with Victor at Cadiz, and in fact with every other commander whom Soult failed to support from his sumptuous palaces in Seville. Admittedly the extreme difficulties of command, control, and communication in the Peninsula[31] worked strongly against close cooperation between the French armies at the best of times, but we must also attribute some of the difficulty to Soult's prickly exterior and self-contained personality. It was at this time that Saint-Chamans, his aide since 1803, finally fell out with the marshal, of whom he wrote, "Soult's character is hard, and above all egotistical. He takes no more than a passing interest in those around him, and I have had to perform very important, and fully-attested, services for him before he has given me rewards."[32] Soult's manner as a gruff sergeant-major was doubtless appropriate to his duties when he commanded a regiment, a brigade, or even an army corps—if it was under the direct supervision of the Emperor. When he was set loose with a wide independent brief and a vast territory to manage on his own, however, Soult found that he needed more sociable and more diplomatic skills than he actually possessed.

Revolutions and Restorations (1814–1851)

In 1814 at the Battle of Toulouse, Soult fought for Napoleon to the very last, and even for a few days beyond the end of the Empire. Being essentially a non-political soldier, however, he was soon persuaded to transfer his allegiance to Louis XVIII, for which he was duly rewarded with a new military command. Indeed he went further still, and displayed such zeal for the government that he was invited to become part of it. As minister of war from December 1814, he was responsible for some of the changes that were bitterly resented in the army and that helped to fuel the military reaction in favor of Napoleon.

In the nick of time, Soult realized that the tide of opinion was flowing against him, and he resigned his office with sufficient dexterity to offer his services once again to the Bonapartist cause. The offer was accepted and Soult was given the highly responsible post of chief-of-staff to the Grand Army during the Waterloo campaign.

The result was a disaster. Accustomed to command-in-chief, the strong-willed Soult was ill equipped to play the office clerk to an even stronger-willed master. Whereas Berthier had been raised and groomed for this role through decades of campaigning, it was entirely out of keeping with most of Soult's experience. Even his strongest qualities—his meticulous attention to detail and his skill as an organizer—were overriden and nullified by his newly subordinate role.

In the Waterloo campaign many of the mistakes were committed by Ney, but we cannot help speculating that if the chief-of-staff had been on good terms with that marshal, he might have intervened to correct them. Soult could not do this, and the Empire duly fell. Equally the advice that Soult gave Napoleon himself was not always the best, particularly in relation to the timing of the French attack on Wellington's Mont St. Jean position. Soult apparently recommended caution and delay—as in his "non-battles" in the Peninsula—when the crying need was actually for haste and boldness. Thus, it may be that Soult was directly instrumental in preventing an early morning assault that might have swept the allies away.

After Waterloo Soult was energetic in rallying the fugitives at Laon before retiring to his estates in his hometown of St.-Amans-Labastide. On this occasion, however, he was to be less fortunate than he had been the previous year. The White Terror now fell far more heavily upon Bonapartists than it had in 1814, and this was particularly true in the south of France. Soult was proscribed and narrowly escaped a lynching.[33] He was forced to flee to his wife's home in Germany, where he stayed until pardoned in the political thaw of 1818–1819. During the 1820s he gradually insinuated himself back into favor, although it was only after the Revolution of 1830 that hard-line Bonapartists—as he was still assumed to be—were fully welcomed back to the corridors of power.

Apart from his early battlefield glories in Switzerland and on the Rhine, Soult's most effective work for his country probably came in the course of the July monarchy. He became minister of war at a moment of international tension in 1830, and then again at another in 1840. He also served at various times as foreign minister and president of the Council of Ministers, although in the constitutional structure then in force these last two offices were largely honorific. The War Ministry was certainly not honorific, however, and Soult plunged into it with his customary energy, astonishing the permanent staff by his daily routine of work, which started at 5 A.M.[34]

Promotion, pay, recruiting, military justice and prisons, stud farms, regimental education, drill and service regulations—all were shaken up in the course of Soult's two ministries. Sometimes the impetus for these changes came from Soult, who favored moderate reform, and sometimes it came from others with more radical views, notably the Duke of Orleans and Thiers in the early 1840s. Of the projects that enjoyed Soult's personal backing, perhaps the most successful was his drive to create a more spiritually united army after the disturbances and mutinies of 1830.

A major reform for which Soult worked hard, but which was not actually implemented, was the organization of a trained reserve. He was acutely aware of the army's manpower shortage upon mobilization, and wished to extend the recruiting base by shortening the length of service. In the event he could achieve only minor and quasi-unofficial steps toward this goal in his recruiting law of 1832 and subsequent tinkering with it, since antiliberal opinion in Parliament was too strong. It is worth noting, however, that not even Soult's original proposals envisaged a mobilized strength of more than a half-million men, which was considerably less than the liberal extremists desired and a great deal less than Chancellor Bismarck was eventually able to mobilize.[35]

Other failures might be cited in the details of Soult's reforms, and we notice with little surprise that the man who had no solution to the guerrilla menace in Spain was equally devoid of proposals for a satisfactory remedy to the endemic guerrilla war in Algeria. Nor, perhaps, ought we to be surprised to read that certain "scandalous markets" in supply contracts flourished under his ministry. Nevertheless, the main bulk of his administrative work for the army was constructive and beneficial, and if he was never to become a politician of outstanding brilliance we can hardly blame him for that. He had on at least a few occasions shown himself to be a soldier of outstanding brilliance, and on many others to be one of solid competence. He had certainly come a very long way indeed since his days as a sergeant in the *Royal Infanterie.*

The Battle of Albuera (May 16, 1811)

Soult's finest battlefield performances were those in which he led from the front, under the higher direction of a superior officer. When it came to battles that he himself commanded, we find much less sureness of touch—at least in the tactical phase of close combat. On the other hand, we do find that Soult's battles were often pre-planned with great skill and insight. They gave his subordinates the necessary pre-conditions for victory, if only those subordinates could rise to the challenge. Sometimes they did so magnificently—Austerlitz itself is the classic case—but more frequently they did not. The "typical" Soult battle is therefore one in which the context is perfect but the content is badly flawed.

Albuera was just such a battle.[36] Soult's aim was to relieve the garrison of Badajoz, which was undergoing a siege conducted by Beresford's combined army of British, Portuguese, and Spanish troops. The Duke of Dalmatia had collected some 25,000 men from his Army of the South—all he could spare without denuding half of Andalusia—and was marching to the attack. Beresford had lifted his siege and concentrated his force on the gentle slopes behind Albuera village—a well-concealed and reasonably strong blocking position in the path of the French Army. Soult's problem was therefore to find a way to drive off the allies and open the road to Badajoz.

Soult made his plans as his army closed up to the position toward the end of May 15. He believed that Beresford had about 20,000 men and was therefore numerically inferior to the French, but that Blake's 12,000-strong Spanish troops would shortly arrive from the south to reinforce him. Soult therefore felt confident that a blow against the southern flank of Beresford's line on the morning of May 16 would serve the double purpose of breaking the defense at Albuera itself at the same time as it cut off Blake's advance to join in. Thus, the battle would locally be a flank encirclement reminiscent of Bodenthal's camp in 1793, but if viewed with a higher perspective it would be a central breakthrough as at Austerlitz in 1805.

Soult's plan was well conceived and finely coordinated in its details, including a diversionary frontal atack on Albuera village and skillful exploitation of terrain to conceal the swinging left wing from the allies. Unfortunately, however, the fundamental intelligence upon which the plan had been based proved to be faulty, since Blake had already joined Beresford and was arrayed upon the precise ground that Soult's outflanking movement was destined to cross. It is quite possible that the French attack would never have been launched at all if Soult had realized that the allies actually outnumbered him by some 10,000 troops—and we can certainly say that when the news of Blake's arrival trickled through to him in the course of the battle, Soult recognized that he had been severely strategically surprised.

Before this realization dawned, however, Soult had seen his plan achieve a major surprise of its own. His swinging left wing arrived on Beresford's flank like a bolt from the blue. The allied commanders had been utterly deceived by the French demonstration to their front, and no one had noticed the heavy columns creeping up on them until it was almost too late. Indeed, the first intimation that the frontal attack was no more than a feint seems to have been given by the French themselves. They broke it off and marched to join the main body at a moment previously fixed in Soult's timetable, rather than waiting for the moment at which the allies had divined their true purpose. If the diversionary forces had not broken off the engagement in this way, it is quite conceivable that the allies would never have understood that the real threat lay on their right flank, and Soult would thus have won game, set, and match.

As it was Soult's assault forces gained the plateau to Blake's right and advanced boldly along it, expecting a walkover such as they had achieved against so many Spanish armies in the past. Soult himself does not appear to have had any hand in this part of the action, and he may be assumed to have sat back, confident of the result. He had placed some 14,000 massed infantry and 3,000 cavalry against the unprepared flank of a Spanish army of which less than 5,000 infantry were detailed to meet the threat. It is true that he had not known that those Spanish troops would be present; but once the attack was under way, there is no particular reason to suppose that he ought to have considered them a major obstacle until they showed themselves to be one.

In the event, however, Zayas's division of Blake's army defeated Soult's overwhelming massed attack. It stood on the high ground without breaking, and threw the French spearhead into such confusion that it could never recover. The French utterly destroyed the first British brigade sent to succor the Spaniards, but they could not crack the Spaniards themselves. Eventually some more British did arrive on the scene and took over the burden of the combat, but by that time Zayas had so thoroughly disorganized Soult's spearhead that launching a coherent assault had ceased to be an option for the French. All that remained was for Beresford to gather together yet another segment of his superior force and make a flanking counter-attack. He eventually did this in grand style, and chased off the French most convincingly.

Where Soult lost the battle was in the initital clashes between his leading troops, under Girard, and the gallant Spanish of Zayas. Girard failed to arrange his assault correctly, and Soult apparently failed to intervene to mend the mistake while he still had a chance to do so. This was the crucial event that decided the outcome at Albuera, and we should not be blinded to it by Soult's later explanation that he gave up the contest because he realized Blake had united with Beresford. The battle had already been lost before that moment of strategic insight arrived, and the reason was the customary one for all Soult's defeats—his personal failure to lead from the front.

At Albuera each side lost some 6,000 men, or a quarter of the French force as against less than a fifth of the allies'. Beresford has been condemned for losing so many, and a number of faults may indeed be detected in the details of his response to Soult's unexpected flank maneuver. Nevertheless, the fact remains that the allies met an exceptionally dangerous situation head on and acted energetically to control it, whereas the French did nothing constructive at all once the initial assault had been committed. The majority of the French casualties can thus be seen as helpless and passive victims of their own commander's inactivity.

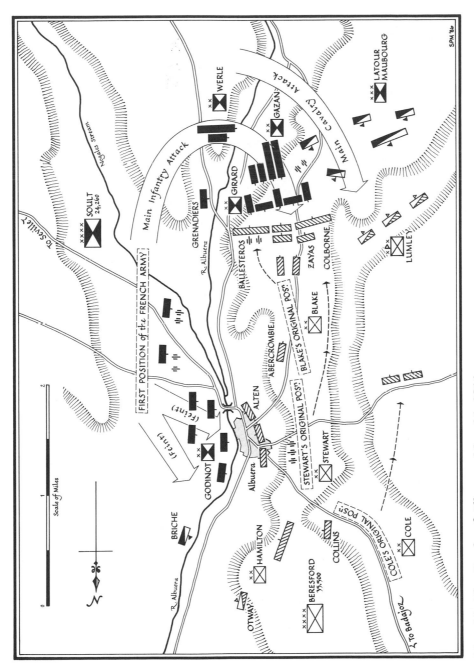

Map 24. The Battle of Albuera, May 16, 1811

TEXTUAL REFERENCES

1. Wellington's military career is covered in *Wellington—Commander*, which I edited in 1985 (London). For his later influence see H. Strachan, *The Reform of the British Army 1830–54* (Manchester University Press, Manchester, 1984).
2. Marshal Soult, *Mémoires du Maréchal-Général Soult, publiés par son fils* (Paris, 1854), Vol. 1, pp. 7–8.
3. *Ibid.*, pp. 25–26. Soult attributes these losses to *mitraille*, which strictly translates as "grapeshot" but is more normally used for a "hail of shot" of any type. In this case it may well mean musketry.
4. *Ibid.*, pp. 60–61.
5. *Ibid.*, pp. 71–78.
6. *Ibid.*, pp. 90–91.
7. R. W. Phipps, *The Armies of the First French Republic and the Rise of the Marshals of Napoleon I* (Oxford, 1926–39), Vol. 2, p. 137ff.
8. Soult, *op. cit.*, p. 157.
9. *Ibid.*, pp. 168–73.
10. *Ibid.*, pp. 180–81.
11. *Ibid.*, p. 199.
12. *Ibid.*, p. 208.
13. *Ibid.*, pp. 298–99.
14. *Ibid.*, pp. 312–16.
15. *Ibid.*, pp. 355–59.
16. *Ibid.*, Vol. 2, pp. 18–24.
17. *Ibid.*, pp. 31–47.
18. *Ibid.*, pp. 100–8.
19. *Ibid.*, p. 188. This seems to have been Soult's favorite tactic; see p. 213 for another example.
20. This was Soult's first set-piece battle, and we note the aggressive blitzkrieg conception behind it. *Ibid.*, p. 219.
21. *Ibid.*, Vol. 3, p. 103.
22. *Ibid.*, pp. 130–34.
23. C. Duffy *Austerlitz 1805* (London, 1977), pp. 47–50.
24. Baron Paul Thiébault, *Memoirs of Général Thiébault*, (trans. by M. Butler) (London, 1896), Vol 2, p. 146.
25. *Ibid.*, p. 178.
26. Général Brun, *Les Cahiers du Général Brun*, ed. by Louis De Saint-Pierre (Paris, 1953), p. 38.
27. Général Comte de Saint-Chamans, *Mémoires du Général Comte de Saint-Chamans* (Paris, 1896), p. 35.
28. Brun, *op. cit.*, p. 121.
29. This claim was made by, among others, L. Fayol (lecture on Soult at Les Invalides, Paris, 1970).
30. Saint-Chamans, *op. cit.*, p. 162; Brun, *op. cit.*, p. 116.
31. Both Brun and Saint-Chamans spent much of their time with Soult as couriers between Seville and Napoleon's headquarters. Their memoirs are crammed with descriptions of what these journeys entailed.
32. Saint-Chamans, *op. cit.*, p. 203.
33. Brun, *op. cit.*, Ch. 11 and appendix, p. 287.
34. Bardin's comments in Soult's manuscript dossier in the *Archives Administratives de la Guerre*, Château de Vincennes.
35. These debates may be followed in Soult's Report to the Crown, May 1, 1833 (official paper), and the periodical *Moniteur Universel* 1831, pp. 1988 and 2044, and 1841, p. 186.
36. For Albuera I have used Sir C. Oman, *A History of the Peninsular War* (Oxford, 1902–30), Vol. 4, pp. 362–403, although I have doubtless used the evidence that he presents in a sense different from that intended.

BIBLIOGRAPHICAL NOTE

As Jean Tulard remarks in his excellent *Napoléon* (Paris, 1977), p. 263, there is "no serious work on Soult." We are left to glean what we can from his memoirs [*Mémoires du Maréchal-Général Soult, publiés par son fils*, 3 vols. (Paris, 1854–55)], which were planned (while he was in exile after Waterloo) to appear in four separate parts: the revolutionary wars, Boulogne to Tilsit, the Peninsula, the First Restoration and Hundred Days. Unfortunately Soult's return to office in 1830 interrupted his work and the first part appeared only in 1854, edited by his son. Part three appeared a century later (Paris, 1955)—and we are still waiting for parts two and four, let alone additional sections covering his career under the July monarchy. We are told that the manuscripts are "well guarded" by the family—but it would be helpful to see more of them in print.

Among other materials available, R. W. Phipps's *Armies of the First French Republic and the Rise of the Marshals of Napoleon I* (Oxford, 1926–39), vols. 2 and 5, give a useful commentary on the *Mémoires* up to *Brumaire*. Soult's thoughts in the crucial three years that followed are not, however, well covered. For the Boulogne camp and the wars of the Empire, we have many accounts of Soult's activities, both friendly and hostile, from diarists and general historians. Three colorful views come in Baron Thiébault, *Mémoirs*, trans. by Butler, 2 vols. (London, 1896), Vol. 2; Général A. Brun, *Les Cahiers du Général Brun*, ed. by Louis De Saint-Pierre (Paris, 1953); and Général Comte de Saint-Chamans, *Mémoires du Général Comte de Saint-Chamans* (Paris, 1896). A useful British view of Soult in 1813 is in F. W. Beatson's *With Wellington in the Pyrenees* (London, n.d., about 1914), while a British view of Soult in the July monarchy is in my "Military Thought in the French Army 1815–51," unpublished D.Phil. thesis, Oxford University, 1976.

CHRONOLOGY

1770, March 2	—Born at Lyons
1792, May 12	—Joined a volunteer company in the Ardèche
1793, September 20	—Lieutenant-colonel of 4th Battalion of the Ardèche
December	—Participated in the Siege of Toulon
1796, April	—Serves in *l'Armée d'Italie* (to September 15)
1797, January	—Serves at Rivoli
April 2	—Wounded at Neumarkt
1798, March 23	—Promoted to *général de brigade*
August 22	—Chief-of-staff in *l'Armée d'Italie*
December 27	—Relieved of duties by the Directory
1799, July 10	—Made *général de division* and chief of staff to Joubert, *l'Armée d'Italie*
August 15	—Served at the Battle of Novi
1800, May 22–26	—Defended the bridgehead of the Var River
1801, July 24	—Named inspector general of infantry
1805, August 26	—Appointed to command 4th Division of I Corps; serves at Ulm, Hollabrunn, and Austerlitz
1806, February 8	—Awarded the Grand Eagle of the Legion of Honor
October 14	—Participated in Battle of Jena
1808, March	—Granted the title of *comte de l'Empire*
November 16	—Married Honorine Antoine de St.-Joseph
1809, April 5	—Given command of III Corps in Spain (later designated *l'Armée d'Aragon*); made governor of Aragon
June 15–18	—Defeated General Blake at Maria and Belchite
1810, April–December	—Besieged and took Lerida, Mequinenza, and Tortosa
1811, May 4–June 28	—Siege and capture of fortress of Tarragona
July 8	—Appointed *Maréchal d'Empire* (twenty-third in order of appointment)
1812, January 9–10	—Valencia seized
January 24	—Granted the title of *duc d'Albufera*
1813, April	—Named commander-in-chief of *l'Armée de Catalogne et d'Aragon*
November 18	—Made colonel general of the Imperial Guard
1814, April 15	—Transfers allegiance to King Louis XVIII
1815, March 26	—Actively supported Napoleon; given command of V Corps of Observation at Strasbourg
April 4	—Sent to Lyons in command of five military divisions
April 26	—Commander in chief of VII Corps of Observation
July 12	—Concluded a convention with the Austrians at Lyons
December 27	—Struck from the list of peers of France
1819, March 5	—Named new peer of France
1826, January 3	—Died at his château near Marseilles

CHAPTER TWENTY-FIVE

THE PENINSULAR MARSHAL

Suchet

by

Professor Jeanne A. Ojala

Early Years and the Italian Campaigns (1770–1804)

Louis-Gabriel Suchet was born on March 2, 1770, at his father's country house, La Mignonne, on the banks of the Saône River near Lyons, son of a well-to-do silk manufacturer. He attended the small college of l'Ile-Barbe near his home, and began training for a commercial career at age 17. However, only a few years later the fervor of revolutionary feelings induced Suchet to join the Lyons National Guard. It is not clear why Suchet left the Guard and joined a volunteer company of the 4th Battalion of the Ardèche as a simple soldier in 1792. Sixteen months later the ardent young patriot was elected lieutenant-colonel of the 4th Battalion and participated in the blockade of Lyons until the city capitulated to the armies of the Convention in October 1793. Later that same month the 4th became a part of the future celebrated Army of Italy.

In December 1793, during the Siege of Toulon, Suchet distinguished himself in an attack on the formidable battery of Malbousquet, which failed in its purpose but which brought the 23-year-old Lyonnaise officer to the attention of Bonaparte. Suchet also took the wounded English General O'Hara prisoner; his generous, kindly treatment of the general foreshadowed his admirable conduct amid the horrors of the war in Spain. Years later Napoleon wrote to Suchet, "You know the esteem which I have always felt for you since the siege of Toulon."[1] However sincere Napoleon's flattery might have been in 1815, it did not influence his decisions at this time regarding promotions for Suchet. Of those who served with Bonaparte at Toulon—Marmont, Junot, and Victor—each was promoted and rewarded by his grateful commander much more rapidly than the equally capable Suchet. The slow recognition of Suchet's contribution to victories in Italy was remarked on by several of his colleagues. Suchet did not have a very high opinion of Bonaparte at this time, but whether this affected relations with his commander is not known. However, Suchet was named governor of Toulon and remained there for some time before leaving to join the Army of Italy.

Revolutionary passions reached ferocious levels in early 1794. Insurgents were being hunted down and ferreted out by Representatives of the People appointed by the National Convention. Citizen Maigret singled out the commune of Bédouin in the Vaucluse to suffer a terrible fate for the outrageous crime of cutting down a tree of liberty. Houses were destroyed and the culpable inhabitants put to death. Suchet not only condoned Maigret's deplorable actions, he wrote him a letter praising his patriotic zeal. The letter began, "Equality, bayonet forward, Liberty." The young republican soldier commended the miserable Maigret and even offered to shoot the anti-revolutionary rebels if the People's Republic so desired. Suchet ended his eulogy to citizen Maigret, "Fearing not to express our satisfaction in a warm enough manner, we deputize you our brother. . . . I swear to you, tears of joy ran from our eyes as we said, 'It is a representative of the French people who speaks; oh! how much does the Nation owe to him'."[2] There is no evidence that Suchet was actually involved at Bédouin, but he had volunteered without being asked or ordered to commit himself. Perhaps one could excuse his youthful eagerness and revolutionary rhetoric by blaming the uncertain times, but his zealous approval of Jacobin excesses was probably sincere. Suchet had left the comfortable bourgeois life and the security of his father's business to serve his country, and he believed fervently in the ideals of the Revolution for which he was fighting. However, much can be forgiven as the mature man—equitable, compassionate, and always patriotic—began to emerge and win acclaim.

With the completion of the amalgamation of the Army of Italy, Suchet's 4th Battalion became part of the future renowned 18th Regiment, composed of two regular and 14 volunteer battalions. Only one important engagement, that at Loano, occurred in 1795. But after Bonaparte took over as commander of the Army of Italy in March 1796, a series of conflicts was fought. At Dego the Army of Italy was in a deplorable condition; 1,000 of Suchet's men did not even have arms, and their futile assault against the Piedmontese occupying the château on the hill of Cossaria was beaten off. The colonel of the regiment was killed, and Suchet assumed temporary command. Suchet and his regiment served with distinction at Dego, Lodi, Borghetto, Castiglione, Peschiera, and Bassano. The army was still in a truly miserable condition, an undisciplined and unruly rabble. "Misery has sanctioned indiscipline, and without discipline, [there is] no victory," Bonaparte declared.[3] Suchet firmly believed this, and from his experience among the neglected French soldiers in Italy the future commander of the Army of Aragon learned a vital lesson: care for your men and they will respond with gratitude and tremendous effort. Four days after victory at Bassano, Suchet was wounded at Cerea on September 12. The 18th was fatigued from their long, swift march, and when Bonaparte rushed them into action against Würmser's troops, they were broken and thrown back. In spite of his wound, Suchet served valiantly at St.-Georges. Nothing is heard of Suchet from October to November; presumably he was recuperating in Milan. By December he had joined Massena in Verona, commanding the 1st Battalion of the 18th Regiment.

The rigorous campaigns of 1796 substantiated the fighting ability and valor of the young battalion commander. He performed well and did his duty without great display or flashy feats of bravado. He was not once singled out for rewards or promotion. Suchet remained unheralded, though not unappreciated. Individuals and regiments competed for recognition from Bonaparte who encouraged rivalry among his officers and corps; his words were proudly carried into battle on the colors of the 18th Regiment: "Brave 18th, I know you, the enemy will not stand before you." They had earned the epigram, as had Suchet. It is obvious that Suchet was not a member of Bonaparte's inner circle. Having known Bonaparte since Toulon, Suchet's rather critical attitude toward him persisted. After Bonaparte had addressed the 18th one day, Suchet caustically remarked, "This Corsican has no reputation beyond what he acquired at the siege of Toulon—that of a good general commander; as a general officer he is known only to the Parisians. This intriguer has no support"[4]—harsh words from a level-headed, ambitious officer, the future Duke of Albufera.

As part of Massena's division, Suchet's battalion took part in the celebrated French successes at Arcola and Rivoli. In February 1797 the French took the offensive and advanced into Austria, with Suchet leading the advance guard. Hard marching and savage fighting tested the most seasoned men. Suchet was wounded a second time at Tarvis, but not seriously enough to prevent him from continuing the advance. The day before capturing Neumarkt, Suchet was again wounded. At last his efforts were acknowledged, and he was named provisional *chef de brigade* (Brigade-Major) on the field of battle, confirmed on October 28, 1797.

In early 1798 Suchet was appointed chief-of-staff to General Brune and accompanied him to Switzerland. Following successful engagements at Fribourg, Guimine, and Berne, Suchet was dispatched to Paris to present the 19 flags captured by the French. On March 20 Suchet was presented to members of the government by the minister of war and made a fiery, patriotic speech to the assembled officials. "You have heard the courageous address from the armies; their agreement is no less unanimous at present against the tyrants of the Seas than it was against the partisans of Louis XVIII. . . . Count on them, count on success."[5] Director Merlin presented Suchet with a pair of small pistols while everyone embraced and an orchestra played the "Hymn to Liberty." Three days later the long-overdue promotion to general of brigade was announced. Suchet replaced Leclerc as chief-of-staff of the Army of Italy, and when Joubert succeeded Brune the new commander requested that the Directory allow

Suchet to remain with him. Joubert valued Suchet's knowledge of the country and saw that he had talents for organization and administration.

In December 1798 Suchet was ordered to return to France or be designated an émigré. Amazingly Suchet was accused of political intrigue both in Switzerland and in Italy. Director La Reveillière-Lepeaux was violently anti-Jacobin and a severe critic of both Brune and Suchet. He described Suchet as "a very insolent soldier, and one of the most shameless plunderers."[6] Moreover, he accused Suchet of being an evil influence on Joubert. There is no doubt that political intrigue and outrageous plundering were rampant in these areas, but Suchet claimed that he had neither the time nor the inclination to meddle in politics. Curiously a vague charge of being aristocratic was made against him. Suchet also was accused of misappropriating funds intended for supplies of the army in Italy and political intrigue. Joubert supported Suchet and in fact resigned his command in protest. Suchet expressed deep concern about civilian suspicions, even fear, of the military. He viewed himself as a citizen, a loyal supporter of the Republic, the enemy of despots and tyranny. On December 27, 1798, Suchet was relieved of his duties. Nevertheless, Massena wrote the minister of war requesting Suchet as his chief-of-staff.

Although he had been listed among the officers to accompany Bonaparte on the expedition to Egypt earlier in the year, Suchet inexplicably left the 18th Line to rejoin General Brune. When reminded that the 18th was Suchet's, Bonaparte retorted, "I saw Suchet in Paris; he considers himself well off where he is, and I do not think he will return to us."[7] Suchet missed a singular opportunity in not joining Bonaparte. He would never be one of Napoleon's intimates; only after long and dedicated service would he receive his rewards.

As commander of the First Brigade of the Third Division in Massena's Army of the Helvetic Republic, Suchet saw action in the area of Grisons where he resolutely defended the French positions at Davos, Bergen, and Splugen. Miserable roads, famine, and attacks by local peasants plagued Suchet's troops. The Austrians under Bellegarde captured the fort of Luciensteig, separating Suchet from the rest of the army. Surrounded by superior forces, Suchet made a bold and resolute move: in late May he crossed the frozen lake of Ober Alp, losing 100 men, and rejoined the main body of the army. Massena was most impressed with Suchet's bravado in what appeared to be a hopeless situation. "I felt quite confident that Suchet would bring me back his brigade," he exclaimed.[8] Shortly thereafter Suchet replaced Chérin, who had been killed, as Massena's chief-of-staff.

After the coup of 12 *Floréal,* Joubert was assigned to command the Army of Italy. He immediately requested Suchet as his chief-of-staff and that he be promoted to general of division. There is no explanation for Suchet's removal from Massena's staff, although Joubert may have made Suchet's appointment a condition for his assuming command in Italy. On July 10, 1799, Suchet received his commission and joined Joubert at Nice. From there they sailed to Genoa.

The French had suffered several defeats in Italy and would unfortunately fare no better at Novi. In spite of insufficient forces and advice from his officers, including Suchet, Joubert disregarded their counsel to retreat and await reinforcements from Championnet. The self-effacing, hesitant Joubert changed his mind several times, but finally resolved to fight. His force of 35,000 tired, hungry, and thirsty troops met the numerically superior Russian forces under the formidable Suvorov. The Russians delivered a stinging defeat to the French, who lost over 6,600 men. Early in the battle Joubert fell, mortally wounded, and died in Suchet's arms. Moreau took command and withdrew to Genoa.

The last months of 1799 were a time of intense suffering for the army. Even Suchet, the master organizer and provider, could not supply the needs of the desperate soldiers who slowly wound their way toward the frontiers of France. He never forgot the misery and deprivation endured by these brave soldiers of France.

A change in fortune was anticipated after Bonaparte became First Consul, but not everyone in the Army of Italy was enthusiastic about the new government. Suchet, however, believed that the interests of the army would now be better served. With the deaths of Joubert and then Championnet, Suchet was free from all military duties and left for France. At Fréjus Suchet met Massena who had just been appointed commander in Italy, and the latter persuaded Suchet to remain with the army. Suchet's knowledge of and experience in Italy would be extremely valuable as the French prepared for a major Austrian offensive. Suchet, with the center of the army totaling 12,000 men, was engaged in almost daily struggles against a numerically superior enemy. In April 1800 Massena was blockaded in Genoa, Soult (commanding the right wing) was an Austrian prisoner, and Suchet was moving toward Nice. By early May, Melas's army threatened the Var River and Suchet evacuated Nice, sending on all his provisions and cannons to Antibes. Melas entered Nice on the thirteenth, and Elsnitz and Lattermann attacked the French lines along the Var. For ten days Suchet with only 7,000–8,000 determined men held their position. When the Austrians began their retreat, Suchet vigorously pursued them, re-entered Nice on May 29, and moved into the Tenda Pass in early June. By attacking and defeating Elnitz several times, Suchet reached the Genoa River, crossed the mountains, and moved into the Bormida valley. He had captured 15,000 men, 30 cannons, and six standards. Suchet received an especially laudatory letter from Carnot, minister of war: "The entire Republic had its eyes fixed on this new passage of Thermopylae. You have been not less brave, but more successful, than the Spartans."[9] In fact, Suchet and his small force had saved the south of France from invasion. Suchet could command, and he could win.

By this time Massena was barely holding on to the starved, typhus-ridden city of Genoa, while Bonaparte was crossing the Alps. When Massena disembarked at Finale, Suchet met and congratulated him on his glorious defense. Massena, exhausted and wounded, now thought only of returning to France to rest, but Suchet was still eager for glory and for further victories against the beleaguered Austrians. He wanted to join Bonaparte with troops from the Var and from Genoa. In the face of Massena's adamant objections, Suchet continued with his plans. Suchet was unhappy about not being allowed to pursue victory. Unfortunately he sent his chief-of-staff to inform Bonaparte that if he and his troops from the Var did not arrive before the battle, it was not his fault, but Massena's. The messenger had not yet reached Bonaparte when he learned of the victory at Marengo. A furious Massena sought to punish the over-eager Suchet who was trying hard to please the First Consul; in retaliation Suchet was assigned the unhappy task of negotiating with the British over Genoa. On June 24 Suchet occupied the city, but this did not end the dispute with his commander. When he met Massena later in Milan, Suchet was curtly informed that the First Consul meant him to have command of a simple division, citing the need for Suchet to rest after his long, arduous campaign. An abject Suchet wrote to Bonaparte, "I am ignorant of how jealousy, perhaps even perfidy, can mislead certain people." He then gave excuses for not being present at the Battle of Marengo. "I am young, my general. Your example and the sentiment of my own esteem teach me to cherish glory. I have done too little to quit the battlefields so soon."[10] Suchet had revealed his personal ambition and realized where future glory lay. Once again he had been thwarted of being near the great Bonaparte at a moment of triumph, and was concerned lest he be left behind in the scramble for recognition and rewards.

Suchet remained with the Army of Italy when Brune took over as commander. The only action seen in late 1800 was at Pozzolo where Suchet unselfishly came to the aid of Dupont, trying desperately to hold his ground against a massive Austrian attack. Appointed governor of Padua, Suchet remained there until April the next year. The Treaty of Lunéville finally permitted Suchet to return to France in May 1801. Of all the future marshals of France who served in the Army of Italy, only Suchet remained with it until 1801. But in spite of his solid achievements, perseverance, and personal ambitions, Suchet's career progressed very slowly. Raised to the rank of lieutenant-general before age 30, and having demonstrated his loyalty to France and to Bonaparte, Suchet arrived in Paris expecting further recognition of his services. Once there Suchet received a gracious and appreciative welcome from the First Consul, was invited to dinners and fêtes, and engaged in conversation with Bonaparte at a grand parade, which made it appear that Suchet was close to him. This in fact was not true; he would always remain an outsider.[11] Though he assiduously courted Josephine and talked with Bonaparte about military subjects and the administration of Italy, Suchet won no special favors or friends. Not as flamboyant as Murat, as avaracious as Massena or Soult, or as enigmatic as Bernadotte, Suchet did not attract attention. Compared with some future marshals, he appeared solid and able, but not outstanding, a man who did his duty without a great deal of fanfare. One wonders why Massena was described by Napoleon as *l'enfant chéri de la victoire* after the Battle of Favorita, while Suchet was given no particular recognition for his brave, tenacious, and successful defense of the Var. Massena destroyed the Russians under Suvorov at Zurich, but Suchet not only saved Provence from invasion but drew a large Austrian force toward Nice while Bonaparte won the crucial Battle of Marengo. Massena garnered more praise for holding out for months at Genoa than Suchet did for beating the Austrians in a decisive campaign. In February 1801 Suchet was made inspector-general of the infantry, an honor surely, but not commensurate with the achievements of the thrice-wounded veteran of the Army of Italy.

The German and Polish Campaigns (1804–1808)

Suchet remained in France during the years of relative peace. In June 1804 he was raised to the dignity of Grand Officer of the Legion of Honor, which at last placed him among the select in Napoleon's France. When Napoleon organized the Grand Army and prepared for the invasion of England, Suchet anticipated being chosen to head an army corps. After having served as general of brigade, general of division, lieutenant-general in command of a wing of an army, and chief of staff, Suchet possessed all the qualities and experience requisite in a corps commander. However, this was not to be. Instead, Suchet was named a divisional commander at Boulogne under his former colleague, Soult, who had been awarded a baton by the Emperor. Suchet wrote to Joseph Bonaparte that he deeply resented this assignment, which he considered a setback in his career.[12]

In August 1805 Suchet dutifully assumed command of the 4th Division of IV Corps under Marshal Soult. The 4th Division was particularly distinguished by its professional appearance and excellent discipline, conspicuous even among the future immortals of the Grand Army. But when the camp of Boulogne was raised and the Grand Army made its orderly march toward Austria, Suchet led the 3rd Division of V Corps (due to reorganization in October 1805) of Marshal Lannes. At Ulm Suchet's division boldy attacked enemy entrenchments on the Michelsberg. At the Battle of Austerlitz, V Corps occupied the Santon hill overlooking the route from Brünn to Olmutz along which the right wing of the Russian army advanced. Suchet and Caffarelli, supported by a division of cuirassiers, routed the enemy and gathered up around 10,000 packs discarded by the Russians. What appeared to be an immense booty yielded only a paltry prize—a few images of St. Nicholas in reliquaries and some bits of black bread. Suchet added to his distinguished record by the outstanding performance of his division, and in February 1806 he was awarded the Grand Eagle of the Legion of Honor. Whether this helped to assuage his rancor at being "demoted" in 1804 is not known, but one can assume that his ambition would never have been satisfied with baubles and ribbons. And more certainly the mere allowance of 10,000 francs for the Grand Cordon did not impress the already wealthy general of division.

Suchet observed at the beginning of the German campaign that the Prussians were not arrogant or insolent in their contacts with the French advance posts; they were ill-prepared to meet the victors of Austerlitz. At Saalfeld Suchet's 1st Division formed the advance guard of V Corps and delivered the initial blow to the corps of the Prussian army led by Prince Louis-Ferdinand of Prussia. The Prussians broke and fled, abandoning their baggage and caissons and mourning the loss of Prince Louis. Three days later, on the eve of the Battle of Jena, the 1st Division secured the French position at the entrance of a narrow plateau. Napoleon spent the night in bivouac with Suchet's division, and they discussed the lines of his advanced posts. Early on October 14 the 1st Division opened the attack against the enemy advance guard, fought in the second attack, and captured 28 cannons. At the end of the day, Suchet supported Murat's cavalry in pursuing the defeated prince of Hohenlohe in full retreat toward Wiemar.[13]

In October 1806, V Corps crossed the Elbe River and occupied Lowicz, located on the road from Posen to Warsaw. The wretched, bleak winter campaign against the Russians now commenced. The day after Christmas four of Suchet's regiments and General Beker's cavalry attempted to hold off 40,000 Russians commanded by General Kamenskoi at Pultusk. Suchet's division suffered tremendous losses in this unequal struggle. Toward evening he received reinforcements and was able to hold his position and compel the Russians to retreat. The valor and skill evidenced that day earned no great victory for the French, no great event to be memorialized, because Napoleon's maneuver against Buxhowden failed. Eight days of incessant rain had made the roads impassable, and the Emperor could not reach the Russians. Pultusk was an incomplete victory.[14]

Winter quarters were established on the right bank of the Vistula: Lannes was at Warsaw, and Suchet's division occupied the area between the city and the suburb of Praga. When Russian movements along the Passarge River compelled Napoleon to march, V Corps remained to cover Warsaw and observe the Russian corps of General Essen. Lannes fell ill and was replaced by Savary, and later by Massena. Though outnumbered by the Russians, V Corps displayed a renewed confidence and prevented the Russians from advancing during the winter months. At Ostrolenka Suchet's division fought a rigorous battle and put the enemy to flight. Minor skirmishes continued into June without a significant shift in positions on either side. Suchet had not participated in the murderous battles of Eylau or Friedland, but his contribution to the Polish campaign did not go unnoticed. After peace was arranged at Tilsit, Suchet took over as provisional commander of V Corps in cantonment in Silesia; it was called to active duty in Spain on September 8, 1808.

General Louis-Gabriel Suchet, reserved, methodical, and dependable, would now receive the recognition so long due him. By a decree of March 10, 1808, Napoleon granted him the revenues from three dependencies, which amounted to 24,000 francs per year: the estates of Siegersleben and Hartbourg, formerly belonging to the duke of Brunswick, and that of Luysbourg, from the royal house of Prussia.[15] In the same month he was named Chevalier of the Iron Crown, Commander of the Order of St.-Henry of Saxony, and Count of the Empire. Suchet had without question earned his place among the celebrated soldiers who were granted titles and incomes from French-controlled Europe. He had waited longer than many for recognition from the Emperor, and he deserved it more than many. After 13 years of campaigning, Suchet had solid experience in diverse forms of warfare: in pitched battles from the mountains

of Italy and Switzerland to the swamps of Poland, in siege warfare at Toulon where he first encountered the English, in defending the Var where his valiant men starved and stragglers were
killed by hostile local inhabitants. He had conceived the idea of
units of mountain chasseurs, and though this was never realized,
it indicates that Suchet could be innovative. His knowledge and
abilities were superior to those of many who were awarded the
military dignity of the marshalate long before he. He was an able
tactician and was respected by his men. He learned in Italy that
an army lives off the land and what neglect could do to otherwise confident and inspired soldiers. A large part of his reputation in Spain was based on his almost unrivaled ability to provide
and care for his troops in a country with few resources and a
hostile population. Three principles guided Suchet's conduct and
command: First, discipline was the foundation of a strong army.
Second, success and discipline depended on good administration
(regular pay, adequate provisions, clothing, and hospitals). And
last, officers must display integrity and not live ostentatiously,
which would be offensive to the common soldier.[16] While other
generals would have agreed with these principles, Suchet lived
by them—this alone set him apart from the majority of Napoleon's great commanders. Suchet was pragmatic and humane; he
knew his soldiers and what he could expect of them. In his
memoirs the marshal wrote, "The French soldier distinguishes
himself by a brilliant quality which no other soldier in Europe
possesses in so eminent a degree; he has a soul-stirring spirit
within him. His bravery is not that of a mere automaton."[17] Hardened through years of military service, the soldier was still a
fragile being, subject to inclement conditions and disease. And a
good commander did not waste human beings. In fact, Suchet
was sparing of the lives of his men—experienced soldiers were
"precious capital" to him.[18] Neglect and poor medical treatment
could decimate an army. With no possibility of receiving large
numbers of reinforcements in Spain, Suchet was especially cautious in preserving the health and fighting spirit of the soldier.
His talent as an organizer and administrator added to his already
recognized ability as a tactician. Of all Napoleon's marshals, only
Suchet achieved a modicum of glory in Spain; only he won a
series of decisive battles and earned the respect of the Spanish.
Moreover, by the end of the Empire, the glory of many marshals
was tarnished, but that of Suchet increased through his actions in
Spain and during the last days of Napoleon's rule.

By the time he left Silesia for Spain in 1808, Suchet had
gained the admiration of his peers and his Emperor, but his place
among the great of the Empire was yet to be captured beyond
the Pyrenees.

Before rejoining his division at Burgos, the handsome, 38-year-old bachelor decided to get married. Suchet was not acquainted with his future wife, but her family and his brother, Gabriel-Catherine, negotiated the arrangements. Honorine Antoine de St.-Joseph was 18 years old, the niece of Julie and Desirée Clary. Her father, Ignace Antoine de St.-Joseph, was a rich industrialist and mayor of Marseilles. He had been ennobled by Louis XVI in 1786. Negotiations did not proceed smoothly at first because Honorine was hesitant to marry a man she did not know and whom she thought was 45 years old. With the aid of her mother and Aunt Julie, she was finally persuaded that the match would be a good one. On his side Suchet was also a little uncertain about marrying and somewhat distressed by all the wrangling that preceded the engagement. Understandably his pride was hurt by Honorine's uneasiness about him. In a touching letter to his brother, Suchet revealed a sensitivity not often evident. He said he hoped Honorine would accept him and that he had a sincere desire to find happiness in having someone to love. It is clear, too, from his letters to his brother that military life could be lonely and he longed for more time to spend with his family. Despite concerns about an arranged marriage, by both Suchet and Honorine, the couple was married on November 16, 1808, at the Luxembourg Palace in Paris, home of Joseph Bonaparte, in the presence of Queen Julie.[19] All hesitancy was dispelled after the couple spent their honeymoon at Gabriels' country house, Morfontaine, near Vernon in the department of the Eure. This was a marriage of love on both sides, of respect and happiness. By this alliance with the Clary family, Suchet was now related to the royal house of Spain and —later—to that of Sweden. His future was full of promise; domestic felicity and military triumphs in that graveyard of reputations beyond the Pyrenees were at hand.

The Peninsular War and the End of the Empire (1808–1815)

On December 1, 1808, Suchet regretfully left his young wife and his brother and sister-in-law (Adèle Arnautizon) for Bordeaux. Slowed by bad weather, he finally rejoined his division at Burgos. He was prepared to march on Madrid when he received an order to go to Saragossa. Suchet and his men were disappointed that they would not be with Napoleon. To be separated from his beloved family and from the Emperor was disheartening, and Suchet wrote to his brother, "Bear in mind that I am in this place for glory and for my friend [Napoleon]."[20] In fact, Suchet would never again be near the Emperor. While the future marshal won laurels where so many others failed, the Emperor marched inexorably toward his destiny.

Suchet was at the fullness of his military talents, self-assured and confident of victory. His division was incorporated with Mortier's V Corps, which with Junot's III Corps was besieging Saragossa under the direction of Lannes. However, Suchet did not actively participate in the action; he was directed to Cala-tayud, 20 leagues to the south-west of the city, charged with maintaining communications with Madrid. For the first time Suchet came in contact with guerrilla forces. It did not take him long to conclude that the best way to neutralize the support and strength of the partisans was to win the confidence of the local populations: respect their lives, property, and religion and grant them a large degree of autonomy. He never underestimated the redoubtable force of a fanatical, insurgent population that detested the godless French invaders and preferred death to rule by these foreigners. As the French devastated the country, the Spanish retaliated with all the furor of religious crusaders. War was to nourish war, which meant the army had to live off the countryside. Widespread pillage brought cruel reprisals from the local people, and unrelieved misery came full circle. Lack of resources forced the soldier to maneuver over extended areas and left him prey to ambush. Suchet was very aware of the critical problems he faced and made plans to rectify the situation.

He was appalled by the rivalries among the French generals, their lack of success in battle, and their seeming inability to provision their men. They were mediocre, and Suchet chaffed at being subordinate to men such as Junot whom he did not regard highly. He was anxious to be a commander-in-chief, to be totally responsible and determine the fate of his men. Napoleon recognized Suchet as among the best 12 or 15 divisional generals, a fine tactician with imperturbable *sangfroid*, but he was not yet convinced that Suchet had what it took to be a great commander.[21]

After a nine-month siege, Saragossa surrendered on February 20, 1809, and Lannes was recalled to France to prepare for the Austrian campaign. Both Lannes and Duroc recommended to Napoleon that Suchet replace Junot. This was done, and on April 5, 1809, Suchet took over three mediocre divisions that he forged into the invincible Army of Aragon. His task was to secure the French hold on Aragon after V Corps departed. Suchet could now show the full measure of his abilities, both civil and military, for he was also designated governor of the province. All power was in his hands. He used it well and earned the gratitude of his Emperor and, amazingly, that of the Spanish people. "He proved to be an outstanding selection, and without question he became the most capable of the French military governors."[22]

The III Corps had made an honorable showing during the Siege of Saragossa. However, the troops were neither disciplined nor obedient, owing largely to irregular pay and provisioning. There were three divisions of infantry, eight squadrons of cavalry, a solid corps of engineers, and good artillery, about 20,000 men. The sick and wounded, deserters, and those conducting prisoners to France and returning with recruits had cut their ranks by half. Suchet found the corps in terrible shape.

Aragon was not secure by any measure, the French controlling only "the ground in the shadow of their bayonets."[23] Suchet was surrounded by serious threats from General Blake and his army, from the partisans, and from a hostile population in Saragossa. He wasted no time in moving against Blake. He planned to destroy his army and then crush the troublesome partisans who continually stirred up the Aragonese. On May 23, 1809, Suchet had his initial experience with the poorly disciplined III Corps. At Alcaniz, for the first and only time, regular Spanish forces defeated Suchet. After seven hours of fighting, Suchet retreated toward Saragossa under cover of darkness. One officer was shot; more officers and men were reprimanded, a junior officer dismissed, and court-martials and the firing squad were used to restore order. Without employing unduly draconian measures, Suchet began to reorganize and rebuild his corps into a first-rate fighting force.

Blake's army and the partisans were still a menace to the French position in Saragossa. Suchet could not remain there and be starved out, nor could he wait for reinforcements. With inferior numbers Suchet fought and defeated the Spanish second army under Blake on June 15 at Maria. Three days later he dislodged Blake's army at Belchite. In a period of two weeks, the French had extended their control to the borders of Catalonia and Valencia. From Alcaniz on June 19, Suchet issued a proclamation to his soldiers in which he praised their newfound valor, singling out several units for special recognition: "Soldiers! What beautiful results have you obtained in four days by your courage." Obviously Suchet was well pleased with his men, and he went on to reassure them that they would be cared for. "I will look after your well-being. The country will furnish your subsistence, and you, by your discipline, will give security to the inhabitants; you will restore to submission and peace the lost men [the Spanish], victims of ambitious leaders and English intrigues. You will make them, by your conduct, care for the government of the worthy brother of our great Emperor."[24] The return of a victorious French army to Saragossa impressed the inhabitants, and Suchet had a *Te Deum* sung in his presence in the cathedral.

The stunning victories over Blake opened the way for Suchet to conquer and pacify Aragon. King Joseph had invested Suchet with the overall governance of the province on June 9, three days before being so instructed by minister of war Clarke. Only one month later the king wrote to Napoleon praising Suchet's handling of affairs in Aragon and adding that he "worked for Joseph's interests, not his own."[25] To administer the province Suchet had to persuade the Aragonese that it was to their advantage to cooperate, to convince them that the French were not barbarians and that they were in Aragon to stay. Suchet had already begun to take his troops in hand. After their amazing victories at Maria and Belchite, Suchet was able slowly to inculcate each unit with the idea that they were part of an elite corps and could accomplish great feats. He established better coordination between arms and artillery, and successfully incorporated German, Polish, Italian, and even Spanish units into III Corps. Suchet expected cooperation from his subordinates, and he got it. He proved to be a man of his word and could be trusted.

Suchet as military and civil governor did not enjoy complete independence of action. King Joseph, though ineffective, was a presence not to be ignored. Local juntas made demands on the populations for contributions and men, and the guerrilla bands incited rebellion, competing with the French for resources and the loyalty of the people. Orders from the Emperor had to be executed, though Suchet took liberties in interpreting them according to existing conditions. He soon realized that the Aragonese had to be administered according to their own customs and ways. In a proclamation he tried to reassure the Aragonese of his intentions. "My troops will not impede your harvests nor overcrowd your cities, they will live in the countryside ready to protect you. . . . The maintenance of the army will be distributed equally. . . . A deputy from the chief place of each area will form a committee to assure just reparation charges. . . . Religion and clergy will be respected."[26] This latter was adhered to as long as priests confined themselves to preaching; clergy who were captured while armed were shot. Notables were encouraged to accept posts in the local administration, including a central junta for the whole province, but "there are hardly any of them who want to serve us," Suchet lamented to Clarke.[26] This was not surprising since the French could not protect them, but the Spanish officials proved to be generally competent and were treated with more respect than was usual among the French in Spain.

Suchet deserved the reputation he made in Spain. Deeds, not high-sounding rhetoric, created a fairly efficient administration in Aragon and a well-cared-for army. He restored law and order through the use of an Aragonese gendarmerie and civil guard, which was preferable to employing French who were not familiar with the inhabitants. He was actually able to present an annual budget to the junta, and they, rather than Suchet, fixed the contribution exacted from each district. Further, he made an accounting to the junta of income, expenditures, work accomplished in the province, and work under way. By strict financial accounting, Suchet paid his soldiers regularly, which was almost unheard of in the French armies. Requisitions were promptly settled, the Aragonese officials received salaries, and widows of Spanish military collected pensions and retirements. Suchet realized that brutal repression would bring brutal retaliation; he sought instead "a peaceful coexistence." There were "two alternatives available to the Aragonese—submission or death. . . . This kind of idea clearly placed Suchet ahead of his contemporaries and went far in allowing Aragon to remain more passive for a longer time than any other occupied province."[28]

As money circulated more freely, so the economy revived. Better rapport with the Aragonese was achieved when Suchet refused to confiscate the treasury of Notre Dame du Pilar and protected the convent of St.-Jean de la Peña near Jaca, which contained the tombs of former kings of Aragon. The achievements of the last half of 1809 were impressive. A fairly efficient administration staffed by local notables was in place, and regular collection of taxes provided the foundation for further military exploits. In Aragon war nourished war, as Napoleon insisted it must.

During this period of pacification and administrative work, not all military operations ceased. The border between Aragon and Navarre was insecure, constantly troubled by partisan activities that called for immediate attention. Coordination among French commanders in Spain was notoriously bad. And here Suchet was as guilty as any of them. Navarre was not his problem and he flatly refused to aid General d'Agoult; but it was eventually placed under Suchet's orders, and he attempted to implement the same reforms as in Aragon. Little could be done here, however, because in February 1810 Napoleon ordered Suchet to concentrate on the conquest of Catalonia and Valencia. Napoleon's decision to rule the north-eastern provinces as imperial military districts had an immediate effect on Suchet's career: In February he was appointed to head the second military government, responsible for all civil and military affairs for the government of Aragon.[29]

Suchet's unequaled record in Aragon was due to four factors: the Siege of Saragossa and the victories at Maria and Belchite, which blunted the people's opposition to the French; guerrilla forces not yet effective enough to damage seriously the French position; Suchet's utilization of his entire corps to pacify the province before the partisans could become firmly entrenched there; and his policies of using local notables in administration, respecting religion and Spanish customs and governing by intimidation and moderation, achieving a degree of success not found elsewhere in Spain.[30]

The pacification and exploitation of Aragon were never total, however. Suchet simply could not engage in protracted campaigns at any great distance from his base at Saragossa and hope to keep the province under strict control. His 20,000 troops constituted a proficient force, but 4,000–5,000 men were needed to garrison Aragon. As the counterinsurgents became more adept tactically and won greater support from their countrymen, the French base in Aragon eroded. But Napoleon placed prime emphasis on conquering Lower Catalonia and Valencia, and Suchet had no alternative but to carry out his orders. The second military government ultimately failed to retain its hold on the province, and sufficient supplies to sustain III Corps were increasingly difficult to obtain. Suchet did better than most governors, but as partisan strength and tactical abilities improved and fewer reinforcements and materials were available from France, the French cause was irrevocably damaged.

Suchet commenced preparations for taking the strongholds of Lerida, Mequinenza, and Tortosa in Lower Catalonia as the Emperor had ordered. These actions would strengthen the French position in that province, protect the borders of Aragon, and allow Suchet to turn his attention to liquidating the partisan bands operating in Aragon, Navarre, and Castile. Before he could put his plans into action, Suchet received orders from King Joseph in Madrid and from Berthier, chief-of-staff of the Grand Army, to occupy Valencia. This decision was not fully supported by Count Suchet, but he had no recourse except to obey. On reaching Valencia, Suchet soon realized that the people had no loyalty or sympathy for the French regime in Madrid, and more importantly there was no sign of the promised reinforcements from King Joseph or from Andalusia. Uncertain about how to proceed, Suchet finally decided to withdraw; after two months of futile maneuvers, in March 1810 he began an orderly, deliberate retreat to avoid the impression that the French were fleeing or withdrawing under duress. Napoleon was furious. Precious time and 500 men had been lost with no discernible gains. He was especially angry with Suchet, not realizing that his commander had never received his counter-order. Berthier knew the truth but dared not tell Napoleon; but Duroc did, thus avoiding a painful reprimand for Suchet.

It was still imperative for the French to secure their position in Catalonia, and Suchet prepared to capture Lerida. He be-grudgingly provisioned Macdonald's army, which was to cooper-ate in conquering and pacifying Catalonia. Leaving a third of his troops in Aragon, Suchet invested Lerida on April 12, stormed the city on May 13, and received the surrender of its garrison on May 14. While besieging Lerida, Suchet's army also defeated the forces of Henry O'Donnell, who had advanced to relieve the city, and captured 5,700 of the enemy. The French took over 7,000 prisoners, 133 guns, 10,000 rifles, and 10 flags.[31] In less than a month, Mesquinenza capitulated (June 8, 1810) without putting up great resistance. Morella, on the extreme north-east of Valen-cia, was occupied on June 13.

The first week of July, the Army of Aragon advanced on Tor-tosa, and Macdonald's Army of Catalonia prepared for an assault on Tarragona. Neither commander could engage the enemy, however, until Macdonald's soldiers had been provisioned. Suchet was critical of Macdonald's inability to feed his own men and of causing a delay in commencing operations.[32] This was a typical reaction on Suchet's part to requests for supplies or aid from his fellow commanders. One division from Macdonald's army assisted in the blockade of Tortosa. After six months of semiblockade, two weeks of trench fighting, and five days of bombardment, the fortress and more than 9,000 men surren-dered on January 2, 1811.[33] A diversionary attack was made on Fort St.-Philippe in the Balaguer Pass. Suchet and his valiant corps reentered Saragossa in triumph on January 10, and a *Te Deum* was sung to celebrate the recent victories and to impress the inhabitants of French invincibility.

After years of failures and setbacks in Spain, Napoleon at last had a man who could defeat the Spanish regular armies and prevent the guerillas from immobilizing him. Berthier wrote to Suchet in February 1811, modifying Napoleon's orders of the previous year. Suchet was invested "with all the necessary pow-ers, whether for the command of the province, or for its adminis-tration; and [he was] only to correspond with [Berthier] on this subject."[34] In March Lower Catalonia was incorporated into the second military government, and nine infantry regiments were transferred from Macdonald's corps to Suchet's Army of Aragon.

There is no doubt that Suchet was satisfied with his perfor-mance and relished the admiration showered on him. His preg-nant wife, Honorine, had been living with him in Aragon for almost a year, contrary to an emphatic injunction against this practice. Her confinement was imminent, and Suchet's *"bonne amie"* traveled to Paris in April. "She has embellished my life and made me suffer a sharp sorrow at our momentary separation.-... See her often, you will love her more everyday," Suchet wrote to his brother, Gabriel.[35] A daughter, Louise Honorine, was born in Paris in May. There was little time to devote to personal sentiments, however, for Napoleon told Suchet that his marshal's baton awaited him inside the walls of Tarragona (see p. 503).

The fall of Tarragona and destruction of partisan bands completed the conquest of Lower Catalonia. In one action 228 guerrillas were taken prisoner "and Suchet ordered these men branded with a painfully long inscription, *'traitres à la patrie'.*"[36] Fighting the guerrillas adversely affected the morale of the French soldiers, many of whom were recent conscripts. Inadequate rations and long, sometimes fruitless pursuits of Spanish insurgents led to some desertions. Yet Suchet had largely achieved his civil and military objectives; only Valencia remained to be subjugated. The Spanish strategy of relying on fortresses for defense and security was a major factor in Suchet's string of successes. Fifteen years of fighting under various conditions all over Europe had prepared Suchet well for meeting the challenges and obstacles encountered in Spain. He knew his officers and had a good rapport with them; he did not shirk responsibility or hesitate to commend or punish. In short, he commanded.[37]

Suchet had done as Napoleon ordered, and he could take pride in his administration of Aragon and the state of his army. However, the Emperor was not completely satisfied with Suchet's tax collection in the province. In May 1811, while Suchet was besieging Tarragona, Baron Lacuée arrived in Saragossa to assume his duties as intendant-general of the provincial administration. Suchet would retain full civil and military control in Aragon, but from the very beginning Suchet viewed the intendant-general as an adversary. Moreover, he hated Lacuée and tried to persuade Berthier to recall him. The marshal's chief complaint was that Lacuée was "stupid and incompetent," that he alienated the Aragonese and threatened the welfare of the army. In spite of Suchet's aversion to Napoleon's civilian agent, Lacuée remained in Aragon until the end of the war.[38]

Aragon was the most powerful French base in the Peninsula at the time, for which Suchet must receive full credit. In recognition of his achievements, Napoleon made Suchet a Marshal of the Empire on July 8, 1811. At last, this pertinacious, dedicated "old" veteran of the Army of Italy stood among the elite echelons of the most powerful army in Europe. Suchet earned his baton in a field of operations where many of the celebrated French commanders faltered and sullied their reputations, the only French general to receive it for the campaigns in Spain.

There was no slackening of military action in the last half of 1811. Napoleon ordered Suchet to seize Valencia and complete the destruction of Spanish regular forces in eastern Spain. Between July 24 and October 11, the French occupied Mont Serrat and Murviedro, defeated General Blake at Puebla de Benaguaril, and seized the fortress of Oropesa. The French crossed the frontier of Valencia on September 15 with 25,000 men and 2,000 horses. In late October Blake moved from Valencia to Sagunto where the French won an important victory on October 26. Suchet was seriously wounded in his shoulder during this engagement. The French continued their advance toward Valencia, strengthened by two divisions from Navarre. Suchet could now control Aragon, protect his rear and supply routes, and react to a possible English landing on the coast. Unfortunately, with more men to feed, the harvest in north-east Spain that autumn was a disaster. Valencia was not a grain-producing area, and the poor harvest in France prevented Lacuée from importing grain.

On January 2, 1812, the trenches were opened before Valencia, and seven days later the city surrendered. Owing to Blake's bad judgment, he had allowed his forces and the inhabitants to be shut up in a city that could not be defended or provisioned. The French captured 18,219 Spanish prisoners, including General Blake. It was a disastrous defeat for the Spanish. On January 24, 1812, Napoleon named Suchet Duke of Albufera (the name of a large pond south-west of the city of Valencia). In addition, Napoleon sent his surgeon, Baron Boyer, to attend to Suchet's serious shoulder wound; only two months later could he ride again.

While recuperating Suchet began organizing the administration of Valencia along the same lines as in Aragon. Taxes were collected fairly regularly and the vital irrigation works were maintained to ensure the continued prosperity of the region and to provision the occupying army. Local notables were encouraged to cooperate, the population was more or less conciliated, and fanatical priests, monks, and students were dispatched to France.

Harassed from all sides and faced with increased partisan activity in Aragon and Lower Catalonia and a serious Anglo–Spanish threat in Valencia, Suchet was suddenly confronted with receiving King Joseph, his court, and 14,000 men of the Army of the Center. After defeating Marmont at Salamanca, Wellington had driven Joseph from Madrid. In September 4,000 from Decaen's Army of Catalonia along with Soult and the ragged Army of Andalusia added to the marshal's burdens. With his usual efficiency Suchet fed, clothed, housed, and re-outfitted his presumably less than welcome guests. After their departure in early November, he turned his attention to the Hispanic–Anglo–Sicilian army concentrated to the south around Alicante.

In mid-April 1813 the French were dealt a serious blow at Castella, which Suchet considered vital to his position. The French underestimated the strength of General John Murray's forces there and were compelled to retreat, leaving their wounded behind. Suchet returned to Valencia, and Murray marched to Alicante and embarked on the English ships ready to carry him and his diminished forces to Tarragona. Sixteen thousand Anglo–Sicilians, supported by artillery, landed on June 3, immediately invested Tarragona, and made contact with local Spanish regulars and Catalan guerilla bands. Balaguer Pass to the north and Fort St.-Philippe in the south fell into enemy hands. Conditions were deteriorating rapidly, but Suchet responded in his usual unflappable way. Leaving 7,000 men with General Harispe in Valencia, the marshal and 9,000 men advanced by forced marches on Tarragona. General Maurice Mathieu and his division meanwhile pushed down from Barcelona. The governor of Tarragona, Bertoletti, refused to capitulate; he strengthened his advanced works and made it appear that he had a strong garrison at hand.[39] The English were deceived by these stratagems, and Murray hastily re-embarked, abandoning 18 pieces of artillery on shore. The situation had been retrieved one more time.

Back in Valencia Suchet had to contend with increasing numbers of Spanish regulars, the English threat of coastal landings, and Catalan partisans operating along the Ebro River. As the counter-insurgents expanded to divisional strength, the French had to fight to collect the harvests. Bread mixed with corn and chaff already had been rationed. Morale suffered and sickness and desertions increased. News of the French defeat at Vitoria on June 21 and the evacuation of Madrid forced Suchet to return to Aragon in July 1813. Highly disciplined, still intact, and always prepared for combat, the Army of Aragon retreated in faultless military order. In his typical, reasoned efficiency, the Duke of Albuera left solid, tough, well-commanded small garrisons with abundant provisions in Valencia. Optimistically Suchet also anticipated using these seasoned veterans in a possible resumption of hostilities by the Emperor in the Peninsula. In the end Suchet exerted great effort to have all these detachments returned to their homeland after the collapse of the Empire. In this, as one might expect, he was successful.

The situation in Aragon was desperate. Partisans now controlled almost the entire province and could count on the fidelity of their countrymen. Suchet wrongly blamed the defeat at Vitoria for the loss of Aragon; actually the French hold began to deteriorate when Suchet moved into Valencia.[40] There was little time for regrets or recriminations. In August Suchet, in command of the Army of Catalonia and Aragon, once again relieved the fortress of Tarragona and was appointed governor of Catalonia and colonel-general of the Imperial Guard, replacing Bessières who had been killed at Lutzen. His adored wife was at his side; she had given birth to a son, Louis-Napoleon, in Paris in May 1813. As in Aragon, Suchet and the duchess won the respect of the Catalans.

Regardless of his immense efforts to hold Catalonia and his victory at Molina del Rey in January 1814, events on both sides of the Pyrenees destroyed any hope of continuing the struggle in Spain. Suchet's army was drastically reduced in numbers and effectiveness as Napoleon ordered whole divisions to France to defend the homeland. With two divisions of infantry and a cavalry reserve, Suchet reached Gerona on February 1, ready to march and defend the frontier. A major concern was to reach an agreement with the Spanish to evacuate French troops from garrisons in northeast Spain. When King Ferdinand arrived in Peripignan on March 19, Suchet met him and attempted to negotiate the return of the French garrisons. However, Ferdinand would not commit himself, claiming that the *Cortès* had to agree to any formal arrangement. The king also graciously thanked Suchet for his benevolent conduct in Spain. His reputation and a weak force were all that remained to Marshal Suchet; he had fought his last battle, but he had not forgotten his men left behind.

Meanwhile, Marshal Soult was fighting Wellington on French territory. Like Suchet, he had lost troops and was simply unable to prevent an invasion from Spain. During March the two marshals often communicated with each other; on the night of April 4–5, Soult, for the first time, asked Suchet for help. The request, no matter how urgent, had to be refused, for Suchet's small forces were at Figueras and Perpignan, guarding the eastern Pyrenees. Suchet could not abandon this critical area owing to the threat of an English attack on Languedoc and Roussillon. In any event Suchet could not have reached Toulouse in time for the battle that occurred on April 10.

While at Narbonne on April 13, Suchet received word of the unhappy events in Paris. Before he concluded an armistice with Wellington, Marshal Suchet had already pledged his loyalty to the new government there. From Narbonne on April 14, Suchet wrote to the president of the provisional government, "In our camps, we are ever faithful to France; we have shared the suffering of our *patrie*, today we share its hope: we comply with its wishes and we join our voices to her's."[41] The pragmatic warrior was not a traitor to his Emperor. He was a loyal Frenchman and a realist. His new allegiance was rewarded: Suchet was made commander-in-chief of the Royal Army of the Midi and a peer of France.

His acceptance of the situation and his pride in his army are evident in an order of the day in late June: "The king comes to give peace to France; he has proclaimed aloud that *the glory of the armies has not been damaged in the great struggle that is ending.* Thus your constancy and your valor have attained the goal for which France has fought for so many years: independence and peace."[42]

Suchet was far from a defeated, broken man. He had served France faithfully and well, under all its governments. There was no reason to retire; he had earned his ranks and titles, and he would continue to serve his country. In straightforward manner he informed his brother, "I only want to serve France, and I will serve the Bourbons, French princes, with whole-hearted devotion and with more satisfaction than I have had to this day."[43] Shortly thereafter, Suchet was appointed governor of the 14th military division at Caen by Louis XVIII, later of the 5th military division at Strasbourg, and made Commander of St. Louis.

The calm was suddenly shattered in March 1815. Napoleon in Paris meant war in France, and Suchet prepared himself for this eventuality. He set about maintaining order in his military government at Strasbourg, visited the garrisons, and inspected the fortifications on the eastern frontier. Without knowing that the king had issued an order on March 23 dismissing all who joined "the revolt" in France, Suchet committed himself and his troops to Napoleon. On that same day he wrote to the prefect at Colmar, "Napoleon will assure to France her Constitutions, her independence and peace. The foreigner will never be able to influence our form of government. . . . We will not cross our borders, but we will fight to the utmost those who would enter our *belle* France to dictate the laws. . . . *Vive l'Empereur!*"[44] Suchet had not changed sides; he would still fight for France, for her "independence and peace." Louis XVIII had fled to the allies, the enemies of France, and Napoleon's triumphal march to Paris convinced Suchet to support the golden eagles once again. The French people welcomed him back, and Suchet would uphold and defend their wishes. After an absence of seven years, the marshal met Napoleon in Paris: "Marshal Suchet, you have grown greatly since we saw one another last," the Emperor remarked, adding later that Suchet was one "whose spirit and character had increased surprisingly."[45] Napoleon put Suchet in charge of the Isère and the Rhône, and on April 8 the dutiful marshal arrived in Lyons to take command of five military divisions. Volunteers poured in to supplement Suchet's meager 6,000 regulars of the Army of the Alps. They lacked uniforms and arms but not patriotic fervor. The fortifications at Lyons were readied for the expected invasion by the Austrians, Piedmontese, and Swiss. On April 10 Suchet could report to Minister of War Davout that the royalist troops of the Duke of Angoulême had been beaten and a capitulation signed. Some of the more zealous imperial officers hoped the Duke would be sent to Lyons rather than be allowed safe conduct out of the country. Marshal Suchet, Duke of Albufera, bristled at the ungentlemanly behavior of his staff. "I declare to you . . . that if the Duke of Angoulême arrives in this city, we will go to see him together, and we will render to him all the honors due to his rank and his qualities."[46] Suchet was a man of honor and treated a defeated enemy, whether foreign or French, with all the courtesy due a fellow officer.

While Napoleon was gathering his forces for his final struggle for survival, Suchet was not among those chosen to accompany him. The Emperor saw the threat of foreign invasion on the eastern frontier of France as a serious menace to his campaign in the north; Suchet knew the area, was capable of independent command, and had had two Italian divisions in his army in Spain. One can assume that the outcome of this tragic gamble would not have been different even if Suchet had been present at Waterloo. As it turned out, Austrian and Italian attacks had to be repelled, and during the months of May and June, Suchet coordinated actions against the enemy and moved into Savoy. On June 22, Davout informed the marshal of the Emperor's total defeat, and Suchet immediately sent negotiators to treat with the Austrians. Only on July 12 was a convention concluded. Suchet's energetic, well-conceived plans could not alter the final outcome, but he was able to save Lyons from savage plunder and reprisals. Suchet also tried to save Marshal Michel Ney. He encouraged the fiery prince of Moskova to emigrate and offered to provide him with money, a passport, and an escort. Few men at this time would have been willing to compromise themselves; though unable to rescue Ney, Suchet had done the honorable thing.

Marshal Louis-Gabriel Suchet was struck from the list of peers of France and deprived of his position in the 5th military division. At the age of 45, his career at an end, Suchet retired into private life. But not everyone had forgotten Suchet. On St. Helena Napoleon was asked which of his generals was the most skillful: "That is difficult to say, but it seems to me that it is Suchet; previously it was Massena, but one can consider him as dead: Suchet, Clauzel and Gérard are in my view the best French generals."[47] In 1819 Suchet was named a new peer of France. The years of disgrace must have been difficult for a patriot like Suchet. He had given his entire adult life to serving his country, and he deserved much from it. His final years were spent in obscurity, living quietly with his family far from Paris. Marshal Suchet died, almost forgotten, at his château near Marseilles on January 3, 1826; in February the inhabitants of Saragossa attended a mass for the repose of his soul at the cathedral where Suchet had had Te Deums sung to celebrate the victories of

French arms. Suchet's beloved Honorine, Duchess of Albufera, died in Paris in 1884, aged 94 years. The descendants of Louis-Gabriel and Honorine Suchet have reached the seventh generation. As late as 1912, Napoleon-Marie-Joseph Suchet was born at the family home near Vernon (Eure) where the first duke and his bride spent their short honeymoon in 1808.

The Siege of Tarragona (May 4–June 28, 1811)

On March 10, 1811, Berthier informed Suchet that Tortosa, Lerida, and Tarragona were to be placed under his governance, and he would receive reinforcements (about 17,000) from the Army of Catalonia, increasing his forces to 40,000 men. With half his army, Suchet began his preparations for the siege of Tarragona, which, as Berthier concluded, "will crown the military glory which you have won in this campaign, and give you fresh claims upon the Emperor."[48] From the outset Suchet anticipated a long, costly struggle. Tarragona was the last stronghold in Catalonia still in Spanish hands, and the Catalans surely would be as tenacious as the Aragonese. This kind of warfare was familiar to Suchet by now, and he foresaw victory in this important venture. "Experience, moreover, had proved that to destroy the Spanish armies, it was necessary to besiege them in their fortresses; it was there only that any considerable number of prisoners could be made." This, in fact, was the formula for so much of Suchet's success in Spain.

Suchet reorganized his army, putting different regiments together so they would "consider themselves as forming a whole, to lend each other mutual support, and to absorb all rivalry in a general desire for acquiring glory." Adequate and secure provisioning was essential to maintain the army far from its supply centers. Wheat, siege materials, and equipment were procured from local resources, all at no expense to the imperial treasury. The aqueduct that supplied water to the area of Tarragona was repaired and guarded. Suchet resolved to keep up the morale of his men and to ensure their well-being. A medical staff and hospital facilities, "organized in the military way, appeared for the first time in the army." The soldiers knew of Suchet's exhaustive efforts on their behalf, and Suchet knew he could count on them. "The French soldier is grateful; he returns in zeal and affection all that is done for him." Suchet was always a good judge of his men and their abilities, and they did not disappoint him.

In April Figueras fell to the Spanish. General Maurice Mathieu requested troops from Suchet to retake this vital link to France, but the latter refused. If he delayed his actions against

Tarragona, provisions and reinforcements could be collected inside the fortress and thus prolong the siege. "In war all depends on opportunity," Suchet wrote, and "the most valuable of all things is time."

On May 2 Suchet reached Reuss, his major supply depot. Two days later he invested Tarragona with his 20,000 men. The remainder of the army was employed in securing supply routes, holding off enemy advances, and ensuring the pacification of Aragon. From May 6 to 28 trenches and batteries were readied under ceaseless artillery and musket fire from the Spanish: "A battle indeed it was, both obstinate and bloody." Throughout the two-month siege, the French lost about 60 men a day. The governor of Tarragona, Juan Senen de Contreras, refused to surrender, and Suchet hastened to attack. Siege preparations were not his only concern; he faced a fierce, numerous foe within the walls of Tarragona; Spanish relief armies (those of Valencia and Murcia) were moving toward his position; and the English fleet landed Spanish troops and 2,000 of their own in the vicinity.

The besiegers opened fire on Fort Olivo on the twenty-eighth and made a successful assault the next day. On June 7 they took Fort Francoli in the lower city. Spanish resistance was ferocious; unable to bury the enemy dead piled up in the trenches, the French burned 1,354 corpses under the gaze of their comrades inside the walls of Tarragona.

The morning of June 28 the batteries were ready; at noon a breach was well under way, and at 5 P.M. the troops left the trenches and dashed onto the breach. Spanish artillery and musket fire was intense, and for a moment the French wavered. The Spanish resistors kept up an intense fire that could not stop the French but threw the exasperated soldiers into a frenzy of killing. When resistance collapsed it was nearly impossible for the French officers to restrain the men. A furious rage had driven them to conquer; words and pleas were not enough to halt the killing. Suchet admitted "their uncurbed fury would listen to nothing." The carnage was terrible, which Suchet blamed on the frustration built up among the attackers after a long siege. The majority of the civilian population had evacuated the town before or during the two-month siege and thus escaped the murderous assault by the French. Spanish and English accounts of the taking of Tarragona stress the atrocities committed by the uncontrolled French soldier. A Colonel Jones published a work (in 1817) on the war in Spain in which he attributed 4,000 civilian deaths to the French attackers and blamed Suchet for not preventing the massacre. Suchet admitted that the obstinancy of Contreras and his men had infuriated the French, and one could not expect the victors to spare the armed resistors. There is little evidence, however, to support the claim of heavy civilian casualties among the dead.

This victory earned the marshal's baton for Louis-Gabriel Suchet, the only marshal to have won it in Spain. With Tarragona in French hands, Lower Catalonia came under French administration. Owing to Suchet's solid preparations and tactical ability, another Spanish army had been broken. Nearly 10,000 prisoners were captured along with 337 pieces of ordnance, 15,000 muskets, 40,000 cannon balls and bombs, four million cartridges, and 50,000 weight of powder. French losses were less but still serious—924 dead and 3,369 wounded, about half of whom would never fight again.

Napoleon is said to have remarked that if he had had two marshals like Suchet in Spain, he not only would have conquered the country but retained possession of it.[49] High praise indeed from the man who set the standard for military success. Undoubtedly Suchet would have relished this accolade; his performance at Tarragona was the capstone of a brilliant career.

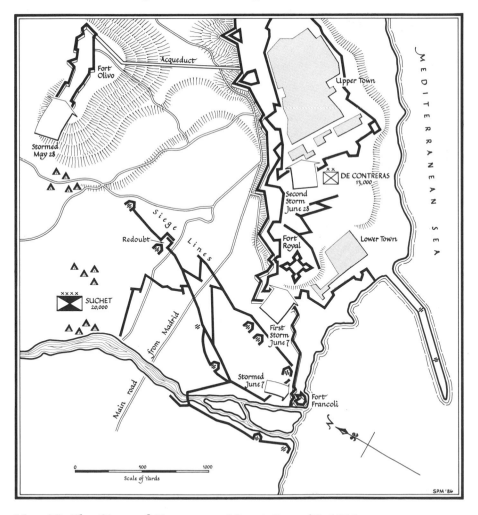

Map 25. The Siege of Tarragona, May 4–June 28, 1811

TEXTUAL REFERENCES

1. R. W. Phipps, *The Armies of the First French Republic and the Rise of the Marshals of Napoleon I* (Oxford, 1926–39), Vol. 3, p. 123.
2. F. Rousseau, *La carrière du maréchal Suchet, duc d'Albufera* (Paris, 1898), pp. 3–4.
3. Phipps, *op. cit.*, Vol. 4, p. 6.
4. *Ibid.*, pp. 10–11.
5. C.-H. Barault-Roullon, *Le maréchal Suchet, duc d'Albufera* (Paris, 1854), pp. 223–25.
6. Phipps, *op. cit.*, Vol. 5, p. 229.
7. *Ibid.*, p. 70.
8. Marshal Suchet, duke of Albufera, *Memoirs of the War in Spain, from 1808 to 1814* (London, 1829), Vol. 1, p. xx; Rousseau, *op. cit.*, p. 21.
9. Barault-Roullon, *op. cit.*, p. 248.
10. Rousseau, *op. cit.*, p. 37.
11. *Ibid.*, pp. 39–40.
12. *Ibid.*, p. 44.
13. Barault-Roullon, *op. cit.*, pp. 252–57.
14. *Ibid.*, pp. 258–59.
15. Rousseau, *op. cit.*, pp. 302–3.
16. G. Spillmann, "Le maréchal Suchet, stratège et pacificateur," in *Souvenir Napoléonien* (1977), No. 292,
17. Suchet, *op. cit.*, p. lix.
18. Spillmann, *op. cit.*, p. 4.
19. Rousseau, *op. cit.*, pp. 56–62.
20. *Ibid.*, p. 62.
21. Spillmann, *op. cit.*, p. 8.
22. D. W. Alexander, *Rod of Iron: French Counterinsurgency Policy in Aragon During the Peninsular War* (Wilmington, 1985), p. 9.
23. Spillmann, *op. cit.*, p. 9.
24. Barault-Roullon, *op. cit.*, pp. 262–63.
25. Alexander, *op. cit.*, p. 50 fn.
26. Spillmann, *op. cit.*, p. 11.
27. Alexander, *op. cit.*, pp. 50–51.
28. *Ibid.*, p. 54.
29. Suchet, *op. cit.*, pp. 330, 376.
30. Alexander, *op. cit.*, pp. 60–61.
31. Suchet, *op. cit.*, pp. 352–61.
32. Alexander, *op. cit.*, pp. 352–61.
33. G. de Raimes, *Soldats de France; actions heroiques* (Paris, 1892–95), pp. 99–101.
34. Suchet, *op. cit.*, p. 377.
35. Rousseau, *op. cit.*, p. 315.
36. Alexander, *op. cit.*, p. 97.
37. Spillmann, *op. cit.*, p. 15.
38. Alexander, *op. cit.*, pp. 103–5.
39. Suchet, *op. cit.*, Vol. 2, pp. 440–42.
40. Alexander, *op. cit.*, pp. 222–23.
41. Rousseau, *op. cit.*, p. 299.
42. Barault-Roullon, *op. cit.*, pp. 316–17.
43. Rousseau, *op. cit.*, pp. 319–20.
44. Barault-Roullon, *op. cit.*, pp. 328–29.
45. Spillmann, *op. cit.*, p. 20.
46. Raimes, *op. cit.*, p. 161.
47. Spillmann, *op. cit.*, p. 20; Suchet, *op. cit.*, Vol. 1, p. xlix.
48. Suchet, *op. cit.*, Vol. 2, pp. 4–5. All information on Tarragona is from Suchet's *Memoires.*
49. Suchet, *op. cit.*, Vol. 1, p. xlix.

BIBLIOGRAPHICAL NOTE

There are few recent works devoted to the life and career of Marshal Suchet. Standard works include a flattering biography by C.-H. Barault-Roullon, *Le Maréchal Suchet, duc d'Albufera* (Paris, 1854), which merely catalogs the early years of his military service, concentrating on the Peninsular War where the author served in the Army of Aragon and Catalonia. This biography was selected from eight entries in a competition sponsored by the Imperial Academy of Sciences, Belles-lettres and Arts of Lyons to pay homage to their local hero. It contains a wide selection of documents that are very useful. Francois Rousseau's *La Carrière du Maréchal Suchet, duc d'Albufera* (Paris, 1898) is one of the few works covering Suchet's entire career, but it does not put much emphasis on Suchet the man. The book is laudatory, placing Suchet among the most talented of the marshals. Rousseau also includes a good collection of documents from public archives and private holdings. A short, concise article by General Georges Spillmann, "Le Maréchal Suchet, stratège et pacificateur," *Souvenir Napoléonien*, No. 292, March 1977, pays tribute to Suchet's military and administrative achievements. The author considers Suchet among the best of the imperial marshals and also a decent, humane commander and conqueror. Suchet's *Memoirs of the War in Spain, from 1808 to 1814*, 2 vols. (London, 1829) concentrate on the most illustrious period of his career. The two volumes shed light on his governance in Spain, reasons behind his decisions, and problems encountered by the French in pacifying and administering a hostile population. Suchet avoids bombast and denunciation of the conduct of other French commanders in Spain. The tone of the work is muted, often understated, and actually less self-serving than one finds in other memoirs of this great period. The documents included in each volume are essential for understanding the private man, husband, brother, and leader of his soldiers that is not always evident in the text. *Napoleon's Peninsular Marshals* (London, 1973; New York, 1974) by R. Humble is valuable for comparing and contrasting the strengths and weaknesses of the marshals who served in Spain. Suchet comes off quite well despite "the fact that he could be as factious and bloody-minded—with headquarters or his fellow army commanders—as any of them." Gaston de Raimes's *Soldats de France* (Paris, 1892–95) provides a substantial overview of Suchet's entire career but lacks analysis. The most recent study of French policies in Spain and why they ultimately failed is *Rod of Iron: French Counterinsurgency Policy in Aragon During the Peninsular Wars* by Major Don W. Alexander (Wilmington, 1985). Thoroughly researched and well written, the book describes the enormous efforts made by commanders to govern Aragon, defeat Spanish regulars, and annihilate the partisan bands. Alexander relates the French military failure in Aragon to the overall lack of a political solution to partisan insurgency and pacification. Suchet is credited with accomplishing a great deal in the face of mounting pressures from English and Spanish forces and of Napoleon's unreasonable demands. This is an excellent study on the ravages inflicted on French regular forces by guerrilla fighters and the French failure to forge firm policies in Spain.

The *Atlas des Campagnes du Maréchal Suchet* (Paris, 1834) is a good companion to the several biographies of the marshals, which contain few, if any, maps. The family history of the marshals can be found in J. Valynseele's *Les Maréchaux du Premier Empire, leur famille et leur descendance* (Paris, 1957).

CHRONOLOGY

1764, December 7	—Born at Lamarche (Vosges district)
1781, October 16	—Enlists in Grenoble Artillery Regiment as a private
1791, October 12	—Re-enlists as grenadier in 3rd Battalion, Drôme Volunteers
1793, December 1	—As lieutenant-colonel distinguished himself in storm on Mount Faron, Toulon
December 17	—Gravely wounded leading decisive attack at Toulon
December 20	—Promoted provisional *général de brigade*
1796, September 15	—Distinguishes himself (wounded) repelling an Austrian sortie from Mantua
1797, January 14	—Leads elite reserves at Rivoli; promoted provisional *général de division* (18th), confirmed March 10
1799, June 18	—Wounded at Trebbia in Italy under Macdonald
1800, April 21	—Appointed corps commander, *l'Armée du Réserve*
June 9	—Rescues Lannes at Montebello by "marching on the sound of the cannon"
June 14	—Distinguished service at Marengo
1802, August 9	—Named captain general of Louisiana, but does not go
1806, October 7	—Appointed chief-of-staff to Marshal Lannes; wounded at Jena (October 14)
1807, January 20	—Captured in Poland by Prussian partisans
June 14	—Commands I Corps at Friedland with distinction
July 13	—Appointed *Maréchal d'Empire* (nineteenth in order of appointment)
1808, September 18	—Created *duc de Bellune;* posted to Spain
1809, March 28	—Commands an independent corps and wins Medellin
July 27 and 28	—Commands night attack, then defeat, of Talavera
1811, March 5	—Defeated at Barossa by General Graham
1812, November 27 and 28	—Commanding IX Corps in Russia, saves the army at the Berezina
1813, August 27	—Commands II Corps at the victory of Dresden
1814, February 18	—Relieved of command by Napoleon after poor performance at Montereau
March 7	—Given an Imperial Guard command; wounded at Craonne
1815, March 22	—Accompanies Louis XVIII into exile at Ghent
October 12	—Appointed president of a commission investigating veterans' activities during the Hundred Days
1821, December 14	—Appointed minister of war
1830, August	—Declines all further duties on political grounds
1841, March 1	—Dies in Paris, aged 77

CHAPTER TWENTY-SIX

LE BEAU SOLEIL

Victor

by

James R. Arnold

From Earliest Years to Toulon and Marengo (1764–1800)

Advancing through the dark toward the British-held fortification, 29-year-old Claude-Victor Perrin urged the assault column onward. He knew that his army rewarded individual gallantry; if he could distinguish himself again, he might earn the next step up the promotional ladder. What he did not know was that his soon-to-be exhibited bravery would be noted by a man with an eye for conspicuous courage, and that this man would one day be in a position to grant great rewards. Accompanying the assault was a certain Captain Bonaparte.

In 1793 the great French port of Toulon had risen in support of the Bourbons. Backed by a British fleet, this event presented a mortal threat to struggling, Revolutionary France. An army was sent to lay siege to Toulon. The force included a lieutenant-colonel of volunteers, Claude-Victor Perrin, who called himself Victor. The siege progressed poorly. But one high point occurred when Victor led his men in a nocturnal assault against Mount Faron. He stormed the fort, but a command mixup forced his battalion to stand alone against a vicious counterattack. Victor held despite overwhelming odds until it became evident no friendly forces would support him. Having lost half the battalion, he retired in order with the survivors. The army honored him by naming him full colonel.[1]

Victor had prepared for this honor since boyhood. Born in 1764 to humble parents (his father was the local bailif), he had no early advantages. His father groomed young Victor to follow in his footsteps. But at age 17 he entered the Grenoble Artillery Regiment instead. During times of turmoil and corruption, this was the one branch of the Royal Army that observed a form of meritocracy. Consequently he learned a great deal about the practical side of soldiering from experienced professionals during a 10-year tour of duty. In addition, he earned his nickname, *Le Beau Soleil*, for his open, sunny disposition.

He left the army in 1791 to marry and become a grocer in Valence. Victor stayed in civilian clothes a mere six months before returning to the army. There, his skills were recognized by a revolutionary army greatly in need of talented leaders. Starting as a grenadier sergeant, he rose to a position of responsibility in time for the Siege of Toulon.

French siege operations received an energizing boost when a young Corsican gunner with the right political connections took charge of the artillery park. During one of his relentless front-line inspections, Bonaparte met Victor and was favorably impressed. Victor in turn recognized an ambitious, natural leader whose talents just might carry the ex-grenadier along.[2] Soon they toured the trenches together, exchanging ideas on how to recapture the port.

The climax of Bonaparte's plan was the assault against a fort the French called *Le Petit Gibraltar*. Having gained renown in earlier attacks, Victor received command of one of the storming columns. So now, under Bonaparte's intense scrutiny, he led his men forward with the élan that would soon be associated with his name: "We received the cannon fire; the scaling ladders were raised, we bounded up them: some were hit by musket fire, by bayonet thrusts; the grenades rained down exploding in our midst; many brave men fell, but they were quickly replaced; the parapet was seized. Victor, although wounded, was among the first to jump down into the redoubt."[3] The attack succeeded and the British were driven from Toulon. In the same decisive assault, Bonaparte received a bayonet thrust in the thigh. Wounded together, they also were promoted for this exploit together, both advancing to the rank of brigadier general. After eight years of service as a private in the Royal Army, Victor rose from sergeant to general in three years in the republican army. It was enough to make him a confirmed republican!

His fate and that of Bonaparte's intertwined again during the latter's Italian Campaign of 1796. By now Bonaparte had risen to army commander while Victor led an infantry brigade. His brigade covered itself in glory during the many hard-fought battles of this memorable campaign. In an army where bravery was commonplace, Victor led one unit with such audacity that the army named it "The Terrible 57th." Bonaparte promoted Victor to full general for these services. But glory had its price. At the head of the 57th he received his second wound.

In 1800 Victor was again in Italy with Bonaparte—now first consul. Commanding a small corps, Victor earned further laurels at the hard-fought Battles of Montebello and, above all, Marengo (see p. 519). But Marengo was a battle whose glory Bonaparte would not share. Only briefly complimented in dispatches, Victor received a saber of honor for his efforts. But the words from the minister of war accompanying this reward attested to his actions: "Victor commanded the army's left at the battle of Marengo, where he conducted himself with great bravery and intelligence."[4]

The Baton in His Knapsack (1801–1814)

In the spring of 1804, all of martial Paris keenly awaited the listing of appointments to the newly created rank of marshal. Fourteen active and four honorary generals received the exalted rank. The newly remarried Claude-Victor Perrin (he had divorced his first wife in 1802 after fathering four children) was not among these. Yet Victor certainly had demonstrated military prowess equaling that of some of the new marshals. Clearly Napoleon had doubts about this man. These doubts had been displayed in 1801, when the First Consul assigned Victor the post of captain-general of Louisiana. Although Victor never actually crossed to America, the fact that he was ordered to this decidedly backwater command indicates Bonaparte felt his services were expendable.

Consequently until 1807 Victor toiled in various positions of lesser responsibility. Generally he served in garrison and administrative posts. Restored to corps command in the spring, he found his greatest opportunity on the battlefield of Friedland.

On June 14, 1807, Napoleon trapped a Russian army with their backs to a deep river. Marshal Ney's decisive attack went awry when a Russian counterattack struck his exposed flank. Into the breach went Victor's corps, directly under the Emperor's watchful eye. He performed masterfully. First he struck the pursuing Russian cavalry in flank, thus closing the gap and giving Ney time to reorganize. Then he massed a 30-gun battery under the gifted artillery general Senarmont. The battery spearheaded the French attack by bold fire and maneuver tactics. Victor's stellar service finally earned him his marshal's baton. He became the nineteenth marshal, the first since the original creation in 1804. It had been a memorable climb for a revolutionary sergeant of volunteers to the exalted ranks of the marshalate. As much as any Frenchman, Victor exemplified the saying that each French soldier carried a baton in his knapsack. He enjoyed the benefits of his new rank for less than a year. Then he was ordered to Spain.

The Spanish war proved a graveyard for many prominent military reputations. High-handed French actions aroused the fierce patriotism of the Spanish peasants who initiated a bloody guerrilla war. Failing to achieve a quick knockout blow, the Emperor personally withdrew from the Peninsula. His marshals were left to clean up the mess.

So Victor spent over three years striving to comply with unrealistic strategic directives from Paris. But like the other marshals, he kept a steady eye on the main chance—career advancement for Claude-Victor Perrin. This advancement faced stiff obstacles that no French peninsular commander, excepting Suchet, overcame. Given the constraints Victor performed better than many.

Shortly after entering Spain, Victor found himself a member of the imperial nobility. Whereas his marshal's baton was fairly earned, elevation to the dukedom of Belluno had less to do with real achievement then with Napoleon's desire to create a new French aristocracy. Indeed, the title itself was somewhat spitefully suggested by Napoleon's sister. It was a punning reference to Victor's nickname, *Le Beau Soleil.** Worse, other ducal titles referred to military victories, thus casting honor upon the recipient. Victor's title has no such significance. .

The Duke of Belluno's operations in the spring and summer of 1809 are a microcosm of French success, defeat, and frustration in the Peninsula. From Paris Napoleon evisaged a joint operation involving Marshal Soult. In practice such coordination proved impossible. The latest news from Soult was over one month old. Unwilling to serve under a senior marshal, Victor claimed the proposed operation was impossible. To support his opinion, Victor exaggerated his own weakness. Such non-cooperation characterized many marshals who felt they could defy orders as long as Napoleon was comfortably away in Paris. Ultimately Victor yielded to higher authority, beginning his advance on March 14, 1809.

His Spanish opponent, General Cuesta, fell back on reinforcements, fighting several tenacious rearguard actions and ambushes in the process. These taught Victor caution. Showing commendable prudence, an attribute ignored by many Napoleonic generals when chasing a seemingly defeated enemy, Victor swept the entire countryside with scouting detachments. He learned that Cuesta had received reinforcements. Anticipating an attack Victor prepared an exceedingly subtle trap at Medellin.

Outnumbered three to two, Victor advanced one-third of his infantry supported on the flanks by all his cavalry. The whole front line presented a concave formation toward the advancing Spanish. Victor's remaining infantry stood in reserve, flanks resting on unfordable rivers. The Spanish attacked all along the four-mile front. Victor planned for his first line to conduct a slow retreat back to the reserves. When the Spanish became disordered, French cavalry were to turn about and crush the enemy flanks. They would be joined by a frontal attack from the infantry. This Cannae-like plan worked almost to perfection and the Spanish army was routed. It had been a tactical masterpiece. However, like most French victories in the Peninsula, Medellin provided little more than glory to the French cause.

* "Beau Soleil," Victor's nickname, implied a cheery (or sunny) disposition; "Belluno," ("beautiful moon") was Pauline Bonaparte's pun. Apparently Victor also had rather short, plump legs, which—in white breeches and stockings—tended to resemble crescent moons. Victor was not amused—he had hoped to become duc de Marengo—but everyone else was vastly amused at his expense.

The remainder of Victor's time in Spain did not enhance his reputation. As part of the forces collected to attack the British at Talavera in the summer of 1809, Victor's men caused one of the two tense moments in Wellesley's victory by almost seizing the dominant battlefield terrain in an extremely bold, unusual night attack. The marshal also urged a French attack to capitalize on a British tactical error the next day, but his advice went unheeded.[5] Next the marshal invaded southern Spain, where he met the British again at Barrosa. Although he exhibited characteristic bravery,[6] his men had the dubious distinction of losing the first French eagle, Napoleon's personal symbol mounted on regimental flag staffs, ever lost to the British in combat. Later Victor was recalled to join in Napoleon's impending invasion of Russia. He had gained several victories and suffered one significant defeat while in Spain. But his reputation was largely intact, which was considerably better than many other marshals could say.

If the "Spanish Ulcer" was a slow disease eating at the bowels of the French Empire, the Russian Campaign of 1812 was a fatal blow delivered to the head. Victor did not participate prominently in most of the campaign. He commanded a reserve formation assigned to the invasion's second wave. As the Emperor began his famous retreat from Moscow, Victor led his men to Smolensk, where he showed his administrative skills by imposing order upon the myriad garrisons that occupied important points along Napoleon's line of retreat. He defended this line and organized depots to receive the retreating army. But as the snows and cold came, Napoleon's army degenerated into a virtual mob surrounding a solid center of formed troops. Then, in late November 1812, this mob ran up against a seemingly impassable barrier, the River Berezina. At this point Victor joined Napoleon. His arrival saved the remnants of the French army.

His force shrunken to a mere 12,000 by disease and combat, Victor faced 30,000 Russians. Over a five-day period, Victor danced a tactical minuet along the frozen, snow-drifted backroads of western Russia. He maneuvered to keep the Russians away from the disorganized French army as Napoleon made plans to bridge the Berezina. And when maneuver could do no more, Victor presented a solid front near the village of Studenka to protect the French rear. For two days Victor fought off Russian attacks as the French retreated over the river to safety. The marshal again demonstrated tactical prowess and courage amid conditions that destroyed the will of many other senior officers. Repeatedly the Russians drove to within artillery range of the fragile French bridges only to be driven back by his tenacious counterattacks. At last, during the second night, Victor led his remnants, still exhibiting good order, across the bridge. His were the last formed units to escape.

The year 1813 brought renewed marching and combat across the plains of central Germany as Napoleon gathered and then lost another huge French army. Victor performed creditable service, particularly at the Battle of Dresden. But the massive French defeat suffered at Leipzig and subsequent retreat to France demoralized many in the French upper command echelon. Victor was one of these. Twenty years of nearly constant combat had taken a toll.

Disappointed by Victor's less than sterling leadership during the 1814 campaign in France, the Emperor delivered his old comrade a stunning rebuke: "The Duke of Belluno's conduct has been dreadful."[7] Relieved of command, Victor suffered extreme humiliation. He pleaded for reinstatement, offering to shoulder a musket and serve as a grenadier private. Touched by this appeal, Napoleon gave him an Imperial Guard command. At the head of this corps at the desperate Battle of Craonne, Victor suffered his last wound in Napoleon's service. It was also the last time Claude-Victor Perrin led troops into combat.

The Twilight Years and the Measure of the Man (1815–1841)

Victor was one of several marshals who sat out the "Campaign of the Hundred Days" when Napoleon briefly returned to power in 1815. Napoleon treated Victor's decision with compassion, issuing an order to remove him from the list of marshals while granting him a retirement pension.[8] Meanwhile, Victor, a former ardent republican, accompanied the Bourbon King Louis XVIII into exile. During the events leading to Waterloo, Victor led an almost monastic life, ever in attendance upon Louis XVIII.[9] Initially ignored by the French royal entourage, his display of new loyalty eventually impressed the king. Upon receipt of news of Waterloo, Victor attended a *Te Deum* victory service with his monarch.

The next phase of Victor's life shows him in the ugliest light. Placed in charge of a committee to investigate veterans' activities, Victor displayed a zeal for rounding up former comrades who had not stood by the king. He was one of two ex-marshals who voted for the death penalty during the trial of Marshal Ney. His persecution of old army men continued even after the committee formally disbanded. Informed in 1822 that an obscure captain did not vote for the royalist candidate, Victor dismissed him from the army and deprived him of his pension.

During the Bourbon reign Victor served in various prestigious capacities. He was a major-general in the Royal Guard, a minister of war, and a darling of the ultra-royalists who admired him for attending the king during the Ghent exile. However, while angling for command of the French invasion of Spain, he ran afoul of a Bourbon favorite. Demoted and falsely blamed for the expedition's logistical troubles, Victor continued to hold high office until the Revolution of 1830. Although offered various important posts by the new government, Victor refused. Instead he retired from official life.

When Napoleon's ashes came home to Les Invalides in 1840, seven former Napoleonic marshals were still alive. Four attended the ceremony. Claude-Victor Perrin chose to stay away. He died in 1841, at age 77.

Victor cannot be included among the top echelon of Napoleonic marshals. Napoleon did not consider him so, and certainly we have no reason to question the Emperor's judgment. But one can place him near the top of the second team. As a military leader, his outstanding characteristics were personal bravery, coolness under fire, defensive tenacity coupled with a will to succeed, and a rare gift for assault tactics. Unlike some of the marshals, he circulated comfortably among his men's campfires, exchanging stories and battlefield gossip. He was an able administrator and yet showed a lack of concern for discipline that was excessive even in light of his peers' carelessness.

As a human being, Victor also presents a puzzling picture. His nickname indicates he must have been a friendly person. But based on his later behavior, particularly after Waterloo, it is hard to find him likeable. Like many high-ranking military men, he possessed a driving ambition and was jealous of his peers. With the exception of Lannes, with whom he developed a sincere mutual affection, he made no friends among the marshalate. Victor particularly detested Soult and Ney. His unwillingness to take orders from any but the Emperor made him a poor subordinate. Indeed this problem proved endemic to the marshalate. They cooperated famously while making their names. As marshals they quarreled bitterly to defend their turf.

Victor deeply grieved his failure to be listed in the original marshalate. Later, when many marshals received battle titles to honor their martial prowess, Victor received a ducal title that reflected no glory. It was his misfortune to distinguish himself most at two of the four battles, Marengo and Friedland, Napoleon refused to share with others. Finally, Victor suffered the disgrace of prominent rebuke in 1814. Even then he continued to serve until knocked out of action by a grave wound.

Claude-Victor Perrin did not provide service in half-measures. As an outspoken republican, he put his life on the line in defense of France. True to the Republic, he opposed Napoleon taking up the imperial purple. But he then provided 10 years of dedicated service to the Empire. However, once abandoning his

Napoleonic loyaltics, he sided with the returning royalty, even though this provided no personal benefits. He gave Louis XVIII the same zealous service he had given Napoleon. When the king fell, he loyally declined further service with Louis's opponents. Victor followed a deeply held code of personal conduct and loyalty. It simply differed from most others.

Napoleon spoke of him only once during his second exile. Referring to the marshal's able conduct at the Berezina, he said, "Victor was better than one might suppose."[*]

The Battle of Marengo (June 14, 1800)

In May 1800 Bonaparte's monumental strategic gamble began as his Reserve Army debouched from the high Alpine passes onto the Italian plains. The first major battle occurred at Montebello, where Victor marched to the sound of the guns to save Lannes's crumbling position. Later, when Lannes became Duke of Montebello, he embraced Victor, attributing his title to his friend's actions. But the victory at Montebello was not enough. Bonaparte needed a decisive victory to cement his new standing as First Consul, the leader of France. He planned for this victory to take place in Italy, the scene of his most memorable triumphs to date. Consequently Bonaparte led his army against the Austrian flank in a surprise advance through Switzerland. From his offices in Paris, the First Consul had predicted this flank maneuver would lead to a decisive battle in the Alessandria area.

On the evening of June 13, this prediction appeared erroneous. General Victor's pickets rested just outside the Austrian bridgehead protecting the entrance to Alessandria. All seemed quiet. Earlier that day portions of Victor's command, acting as the Reserve Army's advance guard, had driven the Austrians from the village of Marengo at the points of their bayonets. Surely, the French high command reasoned, Austrian General Melas would never have ceded Marengo if he meant to fight in front of Alessandria. The high command's lack of vigilance was understandable, albeit entirely mistaken.

Victor's command consisted of two infantry divisions, Gardanne's smallish outfit with 3,600 men stationed in front of the bridgehead, and Chambarlhac's 5,200 men camped in reserve behind Marengo. Supporting them were two brigades of cavalry numbering a paltry 1,000 sabers. Worse, there was a terrible shortage of artillery. The two guns captured on June 13 in

---

[*]Cited by Guy Godlewski, in his article on Victor in *Le Souvenir Napoléonien* No. 328 (Paris: March 1983) p. 14.

Marengo constituted the sole artillery support for two of Victor's four brigades. And now the artillery shortage seemed of consequence, because, contrary to French expectations, the Austrians advanced at dawn on June 14, 1800.

The 28,000-man Hapsburg army had to cross over one of two bridges spanning the Bormida. Both bridge exits converged on a single road, which led to the French positions. Although Melas planned a dawn attack, this constraint meant his army actually made contact with Victor's outposts at 8 A.M. Worse, the narrow front prevented Melas from using his almost three-to-one manpower advantage.

But Victor did not know about the Austrian problems. All he knew was that a large force of white-coated Austrians were driving in his pickets and his commanding general was many miles to the rear, having told his subordinates such an attack would not happen. While probably guilty of a lack of vigilance himself—his most advanced pickets had begun to hear sounds of Austrian movement as early as midnight—Victor recovered quickly, showing admirable battlefield judgment.

First, he told Gardanne's men to absorb the initial shock of the attack by standing fast.[10] This would delay the Austrian advance until Chambarlhac's battalions could deploy behind Marengo. After ordering a dragoon regiment to Gardanne's support, he sent a dispatch to Napoleon notifying the First Consul of the Austrian assault.

Gardanne's two regiments stood in line athwart the Tortona road with the left flank anchored on a bend on the Bormida and the right secured by the stout Pietrabuona farm. Here they endured an intense cannonade as the Austrians deployed for the assault. By 9 A.M. the Austrian formal attack began. The Austrians could deploy only 4,300 men along the restricted half-mile front. Therefore, Gardanne could resist with roughly equal force. Gardanne's men, deployed in line and firing platoon volleys, sent the first Austrian attack reeling backward. Repeated Habsburg efforts utilized newly arriving divisions, but Gardanne's resistance "retarded with a terrible fire the deployment of this column: it finally deployed; with flags flying in the breeze, and musical fanfares as if at a triumphant fete: it threatened to destroy the small French division with its enormous superiority."[11] Victor recognized that the Austrian masses would soon prevail. Around 10 A.M. he ordered Gardanne to withdraw in echelon across Fontanone Creek. Gardanne had gained two hours for the French.

Even now, having lost close to half his men, Gardanne's task remained undone. Victor positioned them to the left of Marengo, behind the creek, where their fire would sweep the flank of the expected Austrian assault against Marengo. This cleverly chosen position presented a substantial barrier to Austrian efforts to expand from their bridgehead. But undaunted, the Habsburgs drove onward, displaying unaccustomed front-line leadership. Nearing the village, the Austrians came up against Fontanone Creek, where a ravine imposed a halt. Gardanne's men capitalized by pouring close-range volleys into the white-coated ranks. For another one and a half hours, the Austrians strove manfully to cross the creek, to no avail.

While Gardanne held the creek line, Victor sent Kellermann's small cavalry brigade to screen his left flank. This precaution paid dividends when Melas changed his direct assault tactics. The Austrian general ordered his cavalry to advance along the willow-covered banks of the Bormida and seek a crossing over the Fontanone to outflank Gardanne's men. At noon, as the Austrians began to cross, Kellermann counterattacked with his cavalry. His charge routed the Austrians. Foiled in his flanking maneuver, Melas returned to his frontal assault against Marengo.

Victor took advantage of the subsequent lull to relieve Gardanne's tired men. He brought up Chambarlhac's three regiments, deploying them with care. Four battalions were stationed in Marengo, with orders to hold at all costs. The remainder of the division lined the creek to the left of the village. In addition, "a valiant auxiliary arrived, Lannes, who ". . . had advanced his troops to render to his brother in arms the same service he had received a few days earlier at Montebello."[12] Lannes stationed his men to the right of Marengo where they confronted an Austrian effort to outflank Victor's line from the north.

A barrage from a 30-gun Austrian battery opened the assault. Stimulated by ample supplies of brandy, fresh Austrian troops, including elite grenadiers, charged against Marengo. Three times the grenadiers penetrated into the village. Three times they were driven out by French bayonet charges.

> Our colonel ran up and down the line, inspiring us with his presence. . . . We could not see one another in the smoke. The guns set the wheatfield on fire, and this caused a general commotion in the ranks. Some cartridge-boxes exploded; we were obliged to fall back and form again as quickly as possible. . . . The situation was restored by the intrepidity of our chiefs, who looked out for everything.[13]

Chambarlhac's division lost close to half its men in the desperate defense of Marengo. Chambarlhac himself, unnerved by the Austrian bombardment, fled for the rear. As his men in

Marengo wavered, French Brigadier Rivaud, in spite of a canister round lodged in his thigh, ran to his drummers and ordered them to sound the charge. This appeal succeeded, as the French drove the grenadiers from Marengo. Confident that Marengo was secure for a time, Victor moved along the creek-line defense, where, acting as a virtual regimental commander in the absence of Chambarlhac, he directed his men's fire and their periodic withdrawals and counterattacks.

It was now 2 P.M. Victor's men, supported since noon by Lannes, had blocked the Austrians for six hours. But events on the French right were about to cause the collapse of the Marengo line. An Austrian force had passed around Lannes's open right flank. This maneuver so stretched the French line that Victor and Lannes realized the next Austrian assault against Marengo could not fail. So they ordered a retreat.

Even this maneuver was performed in great order by Victor's battered men. They formed column and retired in echelon, screened on both flanks by Kellermann's cavalry. For a weary five miles they retreated. The Austrians formed up as if on parade and followed. Melas, feeling the battle was won, retired to have a slight wound dressed and to write victory dispatches to Vienna. While Victor's infantry played no important part in the subsequent dramatic change of fortune, when French reinforcements under Desaix launched a surprise counterattack that decisively routed the Austrian army, they did experience the satisfaction of regaining their original camp-ground outside the Austrian Bridgehead at 10 P.M.

Marengo had been such a close-run affair, and so crucial to the subsequent development of Napoleon's career, that official accounts dwelt on the heroes of the late-afternoon counter-attack. Their feats overshadowed the great importance of Victor's lonely four-hour struggle, when he faced the entire Austrian army.

Victor had displayed characteristic coolness under fire, in the face of a tremendous surprise Austrian assault. Equally important, he accurately gauged his men's ability to hold, as he first let Gardanne's men stifle the Austrian deployment for two critical hours and then relieved them with fresh troops. With these latter he repulsed three major Austrian attacks, until, recognizing they were spent, he directed an orderly retreat while this could still be accomplished. All in all, his tactical finesse well matched his personal courage. Ably seconded by his subordinates, most prominently Kellermann, Gardanne, and Rivaud, Victor himself had provided Napoleon with excellent combat leadership.

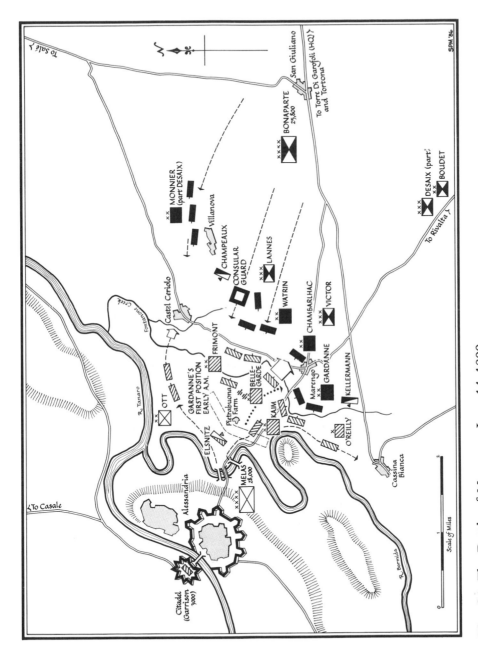

Map 26. The Battle of Marengo, June 14, 1800

TEXTUAL REFERENCES

1. C. V. Perrin, *Extraits des Mémoires inédits de feu* (Paris, 1846), p. 36.
2. *Ibid.,* pp. 27–29.
3. *Ibid.,* p. 64.
4. D. Lacroix, *Les Maréchaux de Napoleon* (Paris, n.d.), p. 307.
5. F. Vigo-Roussillon, *Journal de Campagne* (Paris, 1981), p. 220.
6. C. Oman, *History of the Peninsular War* (London, 1902–30), Vol. 4, p. 327.
7. *New Letters of Napoleon I* (London, 1898), letter of January 19, 1814, to Caulaincourt, p. 327.
8. *Ibid.,* letter of March 26 to Davout, p. 333.
9. J. R. Hull, *The Bourbon Restoration* (London, 1909), p. 336, citing Chateaubriand's observations.
10. Perrin, *op. cit.,* p. 168.
11. *Ibid.*
12. *Ibid.,* p. 171.
13. J. R. Coignet, *The Notebooks of Captain Coignet,* ed. by J. Fortescue (London, 1929), p. 75.

BIBLIOGRAPHICAL NOTE

In Claude-Victor Perrin's *Extraits des Mémoires Inédits de feu* (Paris, 1846) is his detailed campaign account of the Toulon siege and the 1800 campaign of the Reserve Army. Of his *Mémoires de Claude-Victor Perrin* (Paris, 1847), only the first volume, chronicling his life to 1796, has been published. Louis Alexandre Berthier's *Relation de la Bataille de Marengo* (Paris, 1806) is the official, although deliberately misleading, account. It has excellent maps. Albert Jean de Rocca served in Victor's cavalry and provides a lively account of Medellin in *Memoirs of the War of the French in Spain* (London, 1815). Gabriel J. Fabry, in *Campagne de Russe (1812)*, 5 vols. (Paris, 1900–12), provides extensive coverage of Victor's rear area duties and a superb account of the Berezina. In H. Roeder, *The Ordeal of Captain Roeder* (London, 1960), is soldier's view of the retreat from Russia by a German serving in Victor's corps. John R. Hull's *Bourbon Restoration* (London, 1909) describes Victor's prominent role in the Bourbon government.

The Marshals of France; Their Insiginia and Privileges

Uniforms and Insignia of the Napoleonic Marshalate
by Lt. Cdr. Anthony G. Thomas

The oldest sign of a marshal was, and is, the baton. Since Napoleon I's decree, it has been 50 centimeters long. Before 1804 it had varied from a cane to a short truncheon. For most of the previous two centuries, it had approximated the imperial dimension. From at least the sixteenth century, the baton had been *semé de lys*, meaning spangled with *fleurs de lys*.* In 1759 Louis XV had approved a pattern with a royal blue velvet-covered stem, headed gold, with *fleurs de lys* in gold. At one end the gold head carried the name of the marshal, at the other was the inscription *Terror belli, decus pacis*, meaning "Terror of war, honor of peace." Save for the change from *fleurs de lys* to other insignia, the baton has not changed. In Napoleon I's reign, some authorities believe (albeit in error) that the bee at first replaced the *fleur de lys* of the old regime; in fact the surviving batons, illustrations and portraits strongly suggest that eagles were used from the outset, although some privately manufactured replicas (one for Marmont survives) had both bees *and* eagles. At the Restoration, Louis XVIII restored the *fleur de lys*. Louis Philippe in 1830 used stars of five points. Napoleon III brought back the imperial eagle in 1853. Under the Republic Louis Philippe's stars were restored, but were fewer in number than in 1830.

The uniform of a marshal under the First Empire varied, sometimes according to the taste of the wearer, but there was an official pattern. According to this the headgear was a cocked hat with looped and chastened gold lace trimming and ostrich plumes of white at the edge. The cockade was a tricolor with the red at the outermost circle, then white and a blue disk in the center. It was secured to the hat with a strap of black edged in gold. The coat was a single-breasted tailed coat with stand-up collar. The collar and cuffs were ornamented with gold oak leaf embroidery

---

*The royal lilies, emblems of the kings of France.

A Marshal of the Empire in campaign dress.

like that of a general, but larger in size. A plastron of gold oak leaves covered the chest. The oak leaves flowed down the tails of the coat and down the front and back of the sleeves. The buttons bore crossed batons and a trophy of arms. A white silk general's scarf was often worn around the neck, and the waist sash was of gold, parallel stripes interspersed with white. The epaulets were of gold. A double fringe of large thickness encircled the crescent, which carried the crossed batons and four stars, also above the fringe of the sash. White riding breeches and black riding boots completed a magnificent ensemble. There was an equally splended court dress (or *grande tenue*), with wider skirts to the coat (worn without epaulets), white breeches, court buckled shoes, a hat with a panache of ostrich plumes, and a red mantle carrying the plaque of the Legion of Honor. In court dress a straight court sword was carried; in *petite tenue*, as worn on campaign and in action, a curved Mameluke's saber was substituted.

A Marshal of the Empire in full court dress.

About 1809, probably at the initiative of Berthier, red trousers and a képi, copied from the Austrians, began to appear as a form of undress uniform.

In 1816 Louis XVIII made changes. The white cockade replaced the tricolor until 1830. The oak leaf embroidery on the collar and cuffs was, and has remained, on the *képi*, in three rows of thickness in the ratio 10 to 8 to 7. The crossed batons on the epaulets and sash were surrounded by seven stars arranged in a crescent. The seven stars have remained a badge of a marshal ever since. On the short jacket uniforms of later times, they appeared on the cuff in three rows, two to three to two.

In 1872 the tailed coat went, to be replaced by a double-breasted frock coat, embroidery now being confined to collar and cuffs. In 1922 the old uniform was placed in abeyance, from which it returned in 1931 with a single-breasted frock coat. After the Second World War, the sole living marshal at the time, Alphonse Juin, appeared only in khaki service dress with *képi*.

The base colors of the various items of uniform were as follow:

Coat—very dark blue, almost black

Trousers and *képi* top—scarlet, originally of an orange tinge, later (with 40-millimeter-wide gold stripe for full dress tending more toward crimson and black of its same dimension for everyday uniform), crimson tinged scarlet.

Riding breeches—white

Boots—black

Cocked hat—black

French Marshals—From the First Creation to the Present Day

The title borne by the selected soldier was "marshal of France," save during the First Empire (1804–1814), the Hundred Days (March–June 1815), and the Second Empire (1853–1870), when the title of the dignity was "Marshal of the Empire." The number on establishment was officially one until the sixteenth century, when it went up to three, then five, becoming 11 under Henri IV (1593–1610). The number authorized under Louis XIV (1643–1715) was 20, but even this figure was exceeded in the reign of his successor, Louis XV (1715–1774), who in 1762 had 21 marshals. The dignity was abolished by the Convention in 1793, but restored by Napoleon as described in the General Introduction. In 1839 the number was fixed at six in peace and 12 in wartime. In 1875 the dignity was retained but without fixing numbers. A qualification was inserted instead: A recipient of a baton was to have commanded an army victoriously in battle. Under the Republic the dignity has been given several times posthumously.

1047—Gui
1058—Richard
　　　—Ingelard
1068—Dreu
　　　—Oscelin
1080—Floher
1177—Philippe de Tournel
1185—Matthieu de Bourges
　　　—Pierre
　　　—Albéric Clement, Lord of Metz-en-Gatinais; died 1191
1192—Guillaume de Bournel; died 1195
1202—Nevelon d'Arras; died 1204
1204—Henri Clément I, Lord of Metz and Argentan; died 1214
1214—Jean Clément, Lord of Metz and Argentan; died 1262

1226—Guillaume de la Turnelle
1237—Ferry Pasté, Lord of Challeranges; died 1247
1250—Jean Guillaume de Beaumont; died 1257
1257—Gauthier III, Lord of Nemours; died 1262
1262—Henri Clément II, Lord of Metz and Argentan; died 1265
1265—Héric de Beaujeu; died 1270
   —Renaud de Précigny; died 1270
1266—Henri de Courances
1270—Raoul de Sores *dit* Estrées; died 1282
   —Lancelot de St. Maard; died 1278
1272—Geoffroi Ferry de Verneiul; died 1283
   —Florent de Varennes
1282—Guillaume de Bec Crispin; died 1283
1283—Jean II, Squire of Harcourt; died 1302
1285—Raoul de Flament; died 1287
1288—Jean de Varennes; died 1292
1290—Simon de Melun, Squire of Loupe and Marcheville;
   died 1302
1292—Guy de Clermont de Nesle; died 1302
1302—Foucaud de Merle; died 1314
   —Miles de Noyers and Vendeuvre; died 1350
1308—Jehan de Corbeil de Gretz; died 1318
1315—Jean de Beaumont; died 1318
1318—Matthieu de Thrie; died 1344
   —Jean des Barbes, Lord of Chaumont
1322—Bernard Lord of Moreuil; died 1350
1325—Robert Jean Bertran, Baron of Briquebec; died 1348
1344—Charles de Montgomery; died 1381
   —Robert de Waurin, Lord of St. Venant; died 1360
1345—Guy II, Lord of Melloand Offémont; died 1352
1347—Edouard de Beaujeu (1316–1351)
1351—Arnoul de l'Audeneham; died 1370
1352—Rogues, Lord of Hangest and Avesnes Court; died 1352
1352—Jean de Clermont, Lord of Chantilly; died 1356
1356—Jean le Meingre I Boucicault (1310–1367)
1368—Jean de Mauquenchy, Squire of Blainville; died 1391
1369—Louris de Champagne, Count of Sancerre (1342–1402)
1391—Jean le Meingre II Boucicault (1364–1421)
1397—Jean de Rochefort, Squire of Rieux (1342–1417)
1417—Pierre de Rieux and Rochefort (1389–1439)
1418—Claude de Beauvoir, Lord of Chastellux (1385–1453)
   —Jean de Villiers de l'Isle Adam (1384–1437)
   —Jacques, Lord of Montberon; died 1422
1421—Gilbert Motier de La Fayette (1396–1464)
1422—Antoine de Vergy, Count of Dammartin; died 1439
   —Jean de Labaume; died 1435

1424—Amaury de Séverac; died 1427

1426—Jean de Brosse, Baron de Boussac and Sainte Severe (1375–1433)

1429—Gilles de Laval, Lord of Rias and Ingrande (1404–1440)

1439—André de Laval Montmorency (1408–1486)

1441—Philippe de Culant, Lord of Jaloignes; died 1454

1454—Jean Poton, Lord of Xaintrailles (1390–1461)

1461—Joachim Rouhault, Lord of Boismenart; died 1478
  —Jean d'Armagnac, Count of Comminges; died 1473

1464—Wofarrt de Borselles; died 1487

1476—Pierre de Rohan, Lord of Glé and Ham (1450–1514)

1486—Philippe de Crévecoeur, Lord of Esquerdes; died 1494
  —Jean de Baudricourt; died 1499

1499—Jacques de Trivulce, Marquis of Vigevano (1448–1518)

1506—Charles d'Amboise, Lord of Chaumont (1473–1511)

1511—Odet de Foix, Lord of Lautrec (1485–1544)

1514—Robert Stuart, Count of Beaumont (1470–1544)

1515—Jacques de Cahabannes, Lord of La Palisse; died 1525

1516—Gaspard de Coligny, Lord of Chatillon; died 1522

1518—Thomas de Foix; died 1525

1526—Robert III de la Marck, Duke of Bouillon (1491–1537)
  —Theodore de Trivulce (1458–1531)

1538—René, Lord of Montjean; died 1539
  —Claude d'Annebaut, Baron of Retz (1500–1552)
  —Oudart, Lord of Biez; died 1553

1544—Antoine de Lettes, Marquis of Montpezat (1490–1544)
  —Jean Caracciolo, Prince of Melphes (1480–1550)

1547—Jacques d'Albon, Marquis of Saint André; died 1562
  —Robert, Duke of Bouillon, Prince of Sedan (1520–1556)

1550—Charles de Cosse-Brissac, Count of Brissac (1505–1563)

1554—Pierre Strozzi (1500–1558)

1558—Paul de la Barthe, Lord of Thermes (1482–1562)

1559—François, Duke of Montmorency (1530–1579)

1562—François de Scepeaux (1509–1571)

1564—Imbert de la Platière, Lord of Bourdillon (1524–1567)

1567—Artus de Cossé Brissac, Lord of Gonnor, Count of Secondigny; died 1582

1570—Gaspard de Saulx, Lord of Tavannes (1509–1575)

1571—Honorat de Savoie, Marquis of Villars; died 1580

1573—Albert de Gondi, Duke of Retz (1522–1602)

1574—Roger de Saint Lary, Lord of Bellegarde; died 1579
  —Blaise de Montluc (1500–1577)

1576—Louis Prevost de Sansac (1496–1576)

1577—Armand de Gontaut, Baron of Biron (1524–1592)

1579—Jacques de Goyon, Squire of Matignon (1525–1597)
  —Jean VI d'Aumont, Baron of Estrabonne, Count of Cateauroux (1522–1595)

1582—Guillaume, Viscount of Joyeuse; died 1592
1592—Henri de la Tour d'Auvergne, Duke of Bouillon, Prince
 of Sedan (1555–1632)
1594—Charles de Gontaut, Duke of Biron (1562–1602)
 —Claude de la Chatre, Baron of Maisonforte (1536–1614)
 —Charles de Cossé, Duke of Brissac; died 1621
 —Jean de Montluc de Balagny (1550–1607)
1595—Jean de Beaumanoir, Marquis of Lavardin (1551–1614)
 —Henri, Duke of Joyeuese (1567–1608)
 —Urbain de Laval, Marquis of Sablé; died 1629
1597—Alphonse d'Ornano (1548–1610)
 —Guillaume de Hautemer, Count of Fervacques
 (1537–1613)
1613—Concini Concino, Marquis of Ancre; died 1617
1614—Gilles de Courtenvaux, Marquis of Souvre (1540–1626)
 —Antoine, Baron of Roquelaure (1560–1625)
1616—Louis de la Chatre, Baron of Maisonforte; died 1630
 —Piere de Lauzières, Marquis of Themines (1553–1627)
 —Francois de la Grange, Lord of Montigny (1554–1617)
1617—Nicolas de l'Hospital, Duke of Vitry (1581–1644)
1619—Charles de Choiseul, Count of Plessis–Praslin (1563–1626)
 —Jean François de la Guiche, Count of Saint Géran
 (1569–1632)
 —Honoré d'Albert de Luynes, Duke of Chaulnes
 (1581–1649)
1620—François d'Esparbes de Lussan, Viscount of Aubeterre;
 died 1628
1621—Gaspard III de Coligny (1584–1646)
 —Jacques de Caumont, Duke of La Force (1558–1652)
1622—François de Bassompiere (1579–1646)
1625—Henry, Count of Schomberg (1574–1632)
1626—Jean-Baptiste d'Ornano, Count of Montlaur (1581–1626)
 —François Annibal Duke of Estrees (1573–1670)
1627—Timeoeon d'Epinay, Marquis of Saint Luc (1580–1644)
1629—Louis de Marillac (1572–1632)
1630—Henri II, Duke of Montmorency (1595–1632)
 —Jean d'Anduze de St. Bonnet, Marquis of Toiras
 (1585–1636)
1631—Antoine Coeffier, Marquis of Effiat (1581–1632)
1632—Urbain de Maillé, Marquis of Brézé (1597–1650)
1634—Maximilien de Béthune, Duke of Sully (1560–1641)
1637—Charles de Schomberg, Duke of Halluin (1601–1656)
1639—Charles de la Porte, Duke of La Meilleraye (1602–1664)
1641—Antoine III, Duke of Gramont (1604–1678)
1642—Jean Baptiste Budes, Count of Guébriant (1602–1643)
 —Phillippe de la Motte-Houdancourt, Duke of
 Cardonne (1605–1657)

1643—François de l'Hopital, Count of Rosnay (1583–1660)
—Henri de la Tour d'Auvergne, Viscount of Turenne (1611–1675), *MG*
—Jean, Count of Gassion (1609–1647)
1645—César, Duke of Choisseul (1598–1675)
—Josias, Count of Rantzau (1609–1650)
1646—Nicolas de Neufville, Duke of Villeroy (1597–1685)
1651—Antoine, Duke of Aumont (1601–1669)
—Jacques d'Estampes, Marquis of LaFerte Imbaut (1590–1668)
—Henri de Senneterre, Duke of La Ferté (1600–1681)
—Charles de Monchy, Marquis of Hocquincourt (1599–1658)
—Jacques Rouxel, Count of Grancey (1603–1680)
1652—Armand de Caumont, Duke of La Force (1582–1672)
1653—Philippe de Clérembault (1606–1665)
—César d'Albret, Count of Miosoons (1614–1676)
—Louis de Foucault, Count of Daugnon (1616–1659)
1658—Jean de Schulembourg, Count of Montdejeu (1600–1671)
—Abraham de Fabert, Marquis of Esternay (1599–1662)
—Jacques, Marquis of Castelnau (1620–1658)
1668—Bernadin Gigault, Marquis of Bellefonds (1630–1694)
—Francois de Crequy, Marquis of Marines (1620–1687)
—Louis de Crevant, Duke of Humieres (1628–1697)
1675—Godefroy, Count of Estrades (1607–1686)
—Phillipe de Montaut-Benac, Duke of Navailes (1619–1684)
—Jacques-Henri de Durfort, Duke of Duras (1626–1704)
—François d'Aubusson, Duke of La Feuillade (1625–1691)
—Louis Victor Rochechouart, Duke of Montemart and Vivonne (1636–1688)
—François Henri de Montmorency, Duke of Luxembourg (1628–1695)
—Henri Louis d'Aloigny, Marquis of Rochefort (1636–1676)
1676—Guy Aldonce de Durfort Duras, Duke of Lorge (1630–1702)
1681—Jean, Duke of Estrées (1624–1707)
1693—Claude, Count of Choiseul (1632–1711)
—Jean Arnaud, Marquis of Joyeuse Grandpré (1632–1710)
—François de Neufville, Duke of Villeroy (1664–1730)
—Louis François, Duke of Boufflers (1644–1711)
—Anne de Costentin, Count of Tourville (1642–1701)
—Anne Jules, Duke of Noailles (1650–1708)
—Nicolas Catinat, Lord of St. Gratien (1637–1712)
1702—Louis Claude Hector, Duke of Villers (1653–1734), *MG*
1703—Noel Bouton, Marquis of Chamilly (1636–1715)
—Victor Marie, Duke of Estrées (1660–1737)

—François Louis Rousselet, Marquis of Chateaurenault (1637–1716)

—Sebastien le Prestre, Marquis of Vauban (1633–1707)

—Conrad, Marquis of Rosen (1628–1715)

—Nicolas du Blé, Marquis of Uxelles (1652–1730)

—Rene de Froulay, Count of Tessé (1651–1725)

—Camille, Count of Tallart (or Tallard), Duke of Holstun (1652–1728)

—Nicolas Auguste de la Baume de Montrevel (1636–1716)

—Henry, Duke of Harcourt (1654–1718)

—Ferdinand, Count of Marchin (1656–1706)

1706—Jacques de FitzJames, Duke of Berwick (1670–1734)

1708—Charles Auguste de Goyon Matignon, Count of Gacé (1647–1729)

1709—Jacques Bazin, Marquis of Bezons (1645–1733)

—Pierre de Montesquiou, Count of Artagnan (1645–1725)

1724—Victor Maurice, Count of Broglie (1646–1727)

—Antoine Gaston, Duke of Roqelaire (1656–1738)

—Jacques Leonor Rouxel de Grancey, Count of Medavy (1655–1725)

—Léonor Marie du Maine, Count of Bourg (1655–1739)

—Yves, Marquis of Alègre

—Louis d'Aubusson, Duke of La Feuillade (1673–1725)

—Antoine, Duke of Gramont (1671–1725)

1730—Alain Emmanuel, Marquis of Coetlogon (1646–1730)

1734—Armand Charles de Gontaut, Duke of Biron (1663–1756)

—Jacques de Chastenet, Marquis of Purségur (1665–1743)

—Claude François Bidal, Marquis of Asfeld (1665–1743)

—Adrien Maurice, Duke of Noailles (1678–1766)

—Chrétien Louis de Luxembourg-Montmorency, Prince of Tingrey (1675–1746)

—François Marie, Duke of Broglie (1671–1745)

—François de Franquetot, Duke of Coigny (1670–1759)

—Charles Eugene, Duke of Levis Charlus (1669–1734)

1740—Louis de Brancas de Forclquier, Marquis of Cereste (1671–1750)

1741—Louis Auguste d'Albert d'Ailly, Duke of Chaulnes (1676–1744)

—Louis Armand de Brichanteau, Marquis of Nangis (1682–1742)

—Louis de Gand Vilain XIII, Prince of Isenghien (1678–1767)

—Jean Baptiste de Durfort, Duke of Duras (1684–1770)

—Jean Baptiste Demartes, Marquis of Maillebois (1682–1762)

—Charles Louis Auguste Fouquet, Duke of Belle Isle (1684–1762)

—Arminius Maurice, Count of Saxe (1696–1750), *MG*

1745—Jean Baptiste Louis, Marquis of Maulevrier (1677–1754)
1746—Claude Guillaume Testu, Marquis of Balincourt (1680–1770)
—Phillippe Charles, Marquis of La Fare (1687–1752)
—Francois, Duke of Harcourt (1689–1750)
1747—Guy Claude, Count of Montmorencey–Laval (1677–1751)
—Gaspard, Duke of Clermont–Tonnerre (1688–1781)
—Louis Charles, Marquis of La Mothe–Houdancourt (1687–1755)
—Waldemar, Count of Lowendal (1700–1755)
1748—Louis Francois Armand du Plessis, Duke of Richelieu (1696–1788)
1757—Jean Charles, Marquis of Senneterre (1685–1770)
—Jean Hector de Fay, Marquis of La Tour–Maubourg (1684–1764)
—Louis Antoine de Gontaut, Duke of Biron (1701–1788)
—Daniel François de Gelas de Voisin d'Ambres, Viscount of Lautrec (1686–1762)
—Charles François de Montmorencey, Duke of Luxembourg (1702–1764)
—Louis César Le Tellier, Count of Estrées (1695–1771)
—Charles O'Brien de Clare, Count of Thomond (1699–?)
—Gaston Charles Pierre de Lévis, Duke of Mirepoix (1699–1758)
1758—Ladislas Ignace de Bercheny (1689–1778)
—Hubert de Brienne, Count of Conflans (1690–1777)
—Érasme, Marquis of Contades (1704–1795)
—Charles de Rohan, Prince of Soubise (1715–1787)
1759—Victor Francois, Duke of Broglie (1718–1804)
1768—Guy Michel de Durfort de Lorge, Duke of Randan (1704–1773)
—Louis de Brienne, Marquis of Armentières (1711–1774)
—Jean Paul Timoleon de Cosse, Duke of Brissac (1698–1780)
1775—Anne Pierre, Duke of Harcourt (1701–1783)
—Louis, Duke of Ayen and Noailles (1713–1793)
—Antoine Chrétien, Count of Nicolay (1712–1777)
—Charles, Duke of FitzJames (1712–1777)
—Philippe de Noailles, Duke of Mouchy (1715–1794)
—Emmanuel Felicite de Durfort, Duke of Duras (1715–1789)
—Louis Nicolas Felix, Count of Muy (1702–1775)
1778—Claude Louis, Count of Saint Germain (1707–1778)
1783—Augustin Joseph, Marquis of Harcourt, Count of Mailly (1708–1794)

—Joseph Henry d'Esparbes de Lussan, Marquis of
  Aubeterre (1714–1788)
—Charles Just, Marquis of Craon, Prince of Beauvau
  (1720–1793)
—Noel Jourda, Count of Vaux (1705–1788)
—Philippe Henri, Marquis of Ségur (1724–1801)
—Jacques de Stainville, Count of Choiseul (1727–1789)
—Charles Eugene de la Croix, Marquis of Castries
  (1727–1800)
—Emmanuel, Duke of Croy (1718–1787)
—François Gaston, Duke of Levis (1719–1787)
1791—Nicolas Luckner (1722–1794) Count of Luckner
—Jean Baptiste Donatien de Vimeur, Count of
  Rochambeau (1725–1807)

The dignity of marshal was abolished by the Convention in 1793
and restored by Napoleon I in 1804.

1804—Louis Alexandre Berthier, Sovereign Prince of
  Neuchâtel, Duke of Valengin, Prince of Wagram
  (1753–1815)
—Joachim Murat, Grand Duke of Cleves and Berg, King
  of Naples (1767–1815)
—Bon-Adrien Jeannot de Moncey, Duke of Conegliano
  (1754–1842)
—Jean Baptiste, Count Jourdan (1762–1833)
—André Massena, Duke of Rivoli, Prince of Essling
  (1758–1817)
—Charles Augereau, Duke of Castiglione (1757–1816)
—Jean Baptiste Bernadotte, Prince of Ponte-Corvo
  (1763–1844), *KS*
—Nicolas Jean de Dieu Soult, Duke of Dalmatia
  (1769–1851), *MG*
—Guillaume Marie, Count Brune (1763–1815)
—Jean Lannes, Duke of Montebello (1769–1809)
—Edouard Mortier, Duke of Treviso (1768–1835)
—Michel Ney, Duke of Elchingen, Prince of the Moskova
  (1769–1815)
—Louis Nicolas Davout, Prince of Eckmühl, Duke of
  Auerstädt (1770–1823)
—Jean Baptiste Bessières, Duke of Istria (1768–1813)
—Francois Christophe de Kellermann, Duke of Valmy
  (1737–1820)
—Francois Joseph Lefebvre, Duke of Danzig (1755–1820)
—Dominique-Catherine, Marquis of Pérignon (1754–1818)
—Jean Mathieu Philibert, Count Sérurier (1742–1819)

1807—Claude-Victor Perrin, alias Victor, Duke of Belluno
    (1764–1841)
1809—Etienne Jacques, Joseph Alexandre Macdonald, Duke of
    Tarentum (1765–1840)
    —Auguste-Frédéric Louis Viesse de Marmont, Duke of
    Ragusa (1774–1852)
    —Nicolas-Charles Oudinot, Duke of Reggio (1767–1847)
1811—Louis-Gabriel Suchet, Duke of Albufera (1770–1826)
1812—Laurent, Marquis of Gouvion St.-Cyr (1764–1830)
1813—Joseph Anton, Prince Poniatowski (1763–1813)
1815—(restored 1831)—Emmanuel, Marquis of Grouchy
    (1766–1847)
1816—François Henry de Franquetot, Duke of Coigny
    (1737–1821)
    —Pierre de Riel, Marquis of Beurnonville (1752–1821)
    —Henry Jacques Guillaume Clarke, Count of Hunebourg,
    Duke of Feltre (1765–1818)
    —Joseph Hyacinthe du Houx, Marquis of Viomésnil
    (1734–1827)
1823—Jacques Alexandre Law, Marquis of Lauriston
    (1768–1828)*
    —Gabriel Joseph, Count Molitor (1770–1849)*
1827—Louis Aloys, Prince of Hohenlohe–Waldenburg–
    Bartenstein (1765–1829)
1829—Nicolas Joseph, Marquis Maison (1771–1840)*
1830—Louis Victor de Ghaisne, Count of Bourmont
    (1773–1846)*
    —Edmond Maurice, Count Gérard (1773–1852)*
1831—Bertrand, Count Clauzel (1772–1842)*
    —Georges Mouton, Count of Lobau (1770–1838)*
1837—Sylvain Charles, Count Valée (1773–1846)*
1840—Horace, Count Sébastiani (1772–1851)*
1843—Jean Baptiste Drouet, Count of Erlon (1765–1844)*
    —Thomas Bugeaud de la Piconnerie, Duke of Isly
    (1784–1849)*
1847—Honoré Charles, Count Reille (1775–1860)*
    —Guillaume Dode, Viscount of La Brunerie (1775–1851)*
1850—Prince Jérôme Bonaparte (1784–1860),*
    King of Westphalia (1807–1814)
1851—Rémi Joseph Isidore, Count Exelmans (1775–1852)*
    —Jean Isidore, Count Harispe (1768–1855)*
    —Jean Baptiste Philibert, Count Vaillant (1790–1872)
1852—Achille Armand Jacques Le Roy de Saint Arnaud
    (1798–1854)
    —Bernard Pierre Magnan (1791–1865)

      —Esprit Victor Boniface, Marquis of Castellane
         (1788–1862)

1854—Achille, Count Baraguey d'Hilliers (1795–1878)

1855—Amable Pelissier, Duke of Malakoff (1794–1864)

1856—Jacques Louis César, Count Randon (1795–1871)

      —François de Certain-Canrobert (1809–1895)

      —Pierre Joseph François Bosquet (1810–1861)

1859—Marie Edme Patrice Maurice de MacMahon, Duke of
         Magenta (1808–1893), *PR*

      —Auguste Michel Etienne, Count Regnault de St. Jean
         d'Angély (1794–1870)

      —Adolphe, Count Niel (1802–1869)

1861—Philippe Antoine, Count of Ornano (1784–1863)*

1863—Elie Fredéric Forey (1804–1872)

1864—François Achille Bazaine (1811–1888)

1870—Edmond Le Boeuf (1809–1888)

1916—Joseph Jacques Césaire Joffre (1852–1931)

1918—Ferdinand Foch, British Field Marshal, Marshal of
         Poland (1851–1929)

      —Henri Philippe Omer Pétain (1856–1951), *CS*

1921—Joseph Galliéni (1849–1916), *D*

      —Louis Hubert Gonzalves Lyautey (1854–1934)

      —Louis Félix Marie François Franchet d'Esperey
         (1856–1942)

      —Marie Emile Fayolle (1852–1928)

1923—Michel Joseph Maunoury (1847–1923), *D*

1952—Jean de Lattre de Tassigny (1889–1952), *D*

      —Philippe Marie François deLeclerc, Viscount of
         Hautecloque (1902–1947), *D*

      —Alphonse Pierre Juin (1888–1967)

1984—Pierre Joseph Koenig (1898–1970), *D*

Special Note: Charles André Joseph Marie de Gaulle (1890–1970), President of the French Republic from 1959 to 1969, was offered the "highest rank" in 1946, but refused it.

Key to Abbreviations:

MG, Marshal General; (only three ever appointed).

D, Died before promotion—posthumous title.

PR, President of the French Republic (1873–1879).

CS, Chief of the French state (1940–1945); in reality nominally
    in the sight of the Germans only, in the last year.

KS, Crown Prince of Sweden, 1810; King of Sweden and Norway,
    1818–1844.

*Served under Napoleon I, and subsequently became a marshal.

The Post-Napoleonic Marshalate

Since Waterloo, 50 marshals have been created, the most recent in 1984, when Pierre Joseph Koenig, commander of the Forces of the Interior, that is, the Resistance and Maquis fighters in 1944, was posthumously made a marshal 14 years after his death. No less than 27 marshals created after 1815 had served in the armies of the First Empire, 17 of them as general officers, and some lived to serve the Second Empire. Of the marshals made after 1815, two at least, Gérard and Clauzel, had been predicted by Napoleon I as future marshals.

The marshalate has contained many members of foreign descent, and most interesting was MacMahon, descended from an Irish émigré, who was raised to the nobility of France by Louis XV in 1763. The future marshal, a royalist at heart, tried to resign from the French Army at the declaration of the Second Republic in 1848. He stayed to become a marshal and a duke of the Second Empire. In 1861 he represented Napoleon III at the coronation of William I, king of Prussia, at Königsberg, now Kaliningrad. The future victor of the Franco–German war courteously assigned a young page of honor to attend the Marshal Duke of Magenta. His name was Paul von Beneckendorff und von Hindenburg. Like MacMahon he was to receive a baton from an Emperor whom he would himself succeed as President. As president, Marshal MacMahon has been criticized by some commentators for his part in the events of 1877, but Raymond Poincaré, a President himself and a noted constitutional lawyer, considered the criticism unjust.

Field-Marshal von Hindenburg, mentioned above, flowered late in his career. So did Pétain, his French counterpart. In 1912 both were regarded as finished by their respective governments. Yet both not only achieved the highest rank in the army, but also became chief of state. Both also did business with Adolf Hitler. Pétain's career was strangely interwoven with that of Charles de Gaulle. Originally an admirer of Pétain, whose regiment he chose to enter in 1912, de Gaulle became the dedicated opponent of the marshal in the year 1940. Of the refusal of the baton by Charles de Gaulle, there are two interpretations. It may be that de Gaulle felt his services to France from 1940 were political, not military, and that a military honor was wrong. On the other hand, he may have seen himself as above such trinkets as marshals' batons, a figure unique in history, dwelling on a high plane with perhaps Charlemagne and Napoleon I.

The law of 1875 is still in force, and it is therefore unlikely that many marshals will be made in the future as far as can be seen.

Table of Ranks in the French Army, 1790~1815

Non-commissioned Officers and Other Ranks

RANK	NOTES ON FRENCH RANKS	U.S. EQUIVALENT (OR FUNCTION) AND BRITISH ARMY RANKS (WHEN DIFFERENT)
Appointé	Suppressed Nov. 22, 1793	Private first class [senior soldier (Guards) or lance corporal in the British army]
Caporal or *brigadier*	Infantry or cavalry and artillery	Corporal
Caporal or *brigadier fourrier*	Since 1788	Company clerk and supply sergeant (or company quarter-master sergeant in the British army)
Sergent or *maréchal des logis*	Infantry or cavalry	Sergeant (corporal of horse in Houschold cavalry of the British army)
Sergent-major or *maréchal des logis chef*	Infantry or cavalry	Company first sergeant (or staff sergeant in the British army)
Adjudant		Company sergeant major or warrant officer second class
Adjudant-chef		Regimental sergeant major or warrant officer first class

Commissioned Officers

RANK	NOTES ON FRENCH RANKS	US EQUIVALENT (OR FUNCTION) AND BRITISH ARMY RANKS (WHEN DIFFERENT)
Sous-lieutenant		Subaltern, second lieutenant
Lieutenant	From April 1795 this rank was always held by quartermasters	Lieutenant, first lieutenant
Capitaine	From August 1793 all *adjudants-majors* (junior staff officers) held this rank	Captain
Commandant, adjudant major		Major, staff officer second grade
Chef de bataillon or *chef d'escadron*	This rank was replaced by that of *Lieutenant-colonel* from February 1793	Major
Adjudant général chef de bataillon	A staff appointment, not a rank; from February 1793 it became *adjudant général lieutenant-colonel*, but this post was suppressed in 1795	Staff officer first class; lieutenant-colonel
Chef de brigade or *colonel*	Commanded a *demi-brigade* (later *régiment*) of infantry or a regiment of cavalry or artillery	Colonel (or Brigade-Major)
Adjudant général chef de brigade	A staff appointment from 1793; *adjudant commandant* from July 1800	Senior colonel or brigadier-general
Général de brigade	Formerly (until February 1793) *maréchal de camp*	Brigadier-general (or sometimes major-general in the British army of the period)

Général de division	Formerly (until February 1793) *lieutenant-général*	Major-general (or sometimes lieutenant-general in the British army of the period)
Major général	An appointment, not a rank	Army chief-of-staff
Lieutenant du général d'armée	An appointment, not a rank; existed only from 1799 to 1801	Lieutenant-general (or general in the British army), second-in-command, or wing commander
Général d'armée	An appointment, not a rank; became *général en chef* from February 1793	Commander-in-chief or army commander
Maréchal d'Empire	Replaced *Maréchal de France* (suppressed February 1793) after 11-year interval	General of the Army (or Field Marshal in the British army)

The Republican Calendar

Although most dates in the book have been given in conventional form, some are written in accordance with the republican calendar, which was adopted on November 24, 1793, but was backdated to the proclamation of the Republic on September 22, 1792, and remained in use until 1805.

By the republican calendar, the year began on September 22 (1 *Vendémiare*) and ended on September 21 (35 *Fructidor*). From the backdated introduction of the new system, each year was given a number: *"l'An I", "l'An II,"* etc. Thus, *"l'An IV"* ran from September 22, 1796, until September 21, 1797.

The 12 months were divided into four seasons; each month was of 30 days' duration with five supplementary days (six in a leap year) added in *Fructidor* (the twelfth month) to make up the 365 (or 366) total. Each month was further divided into three 10-day "decades."

The months were as follows:

Autumn
Vendémiare—September 22–October 21 ("month of vintage")
Brumaire—October 22–November 20 ("month of mists")
Frimaire—November 21–December 20 ("month of cold")

Winter
Nivôse—December 21–January 19 ("month of snows")
Pluvôise—January 20–February 18 ("month of rains")
Ventôse—February 19–March 20 ("month of wind")

Spring
Germinal—March 21–April 19 ("month of sowing")
Floréal—April 20–May 19 ("month of blossom")
Prairial—May 20–June 18 ("month of lush meadows")

Summer
Messidor—June 19–July 18 ("month of harvest")
Thermidor—July 19–August 17 ("month of heat")
Fructidor—August 18–September 21 ("month of fruits")

APPENDIX D

Note on Military Organizations and Tactics

For readers unaccustomed to military organizations in the Napoleonic period, the following observations may be of use.[*]

A French army, from 1800, was made up of a varying number of army corps (*corps d'armée*). The army corps was the key operational unit. It was an all-arm organization with its own staff (headed by a marshal or senior general), two or more infantry divisions, a light-cavalry division (which might include a "heavy" regiment of cuirassiers), and an artillery detachment under corps command (6 to 12 or occasionally more 12-pdrs and a proportion of howitzers). It also held engineer and bridging detachments, and its own supply and medical service. The size of corps varied enormously, depending upon Napoleon's view of the aptitude of its commander and the requirements of its operational role on a particular campaign. A corps composition was fluid and its organization highly flexible, so changes could be—and frequently were—implemented in mid-campaign to disconcert enemy intelligence. A large corps would be 40,000 or more men; a small one 20,000 men, or even less. A corps was, in effect, a miniature army, and could march and subsist on its own as it was capable of fighting several times its own number until assistance arrived.

An infantry division (approximately 16,000 men in theory though rarely in practice) was commanded by a general and usually comprised two brigades, each of which contained two regiments (called *demi-brigades* in the Revolutionary and Consulate periods up to 1803). A division often controlled a battery of six guns, habitually four 8-pdrs and two 6-inch howitzers. A regiment had three batallions (of up to 1,200 men apiece), together with a medical detachment, a military band, and a small transport section for the munitions and baggage. It sometimes controlled a battery of four 4- (or later 6-) pdrs and two howitzers, particularly

[*] For a fuller description the reader is directed to D.G. Chandler, *The Campaigns of Napoleon* (New York, 1966), pp. 66–90, 133–201 and 332–382 (to include Napoleon's headquarter's organization).

in the later years of the Empire when greater reliance was placed on firepower to offset a drop in the standard of the average infantry formation.

A battalion—the basic tactical unit—was often commanded by a major and comprised a number of companies. In the earlier days of the Empire, there were nine companies in a batallion—including one *voltigeur* (lit. 'leaper') or light company which fought in a skirmishing screen ahead of the rest, and one grenadier company of élite troops. From 1809, however, the batallion was reorganized into a six-company establishment, two of which were still made up of grenadiers and *voltigeurs*. In addition to regiments of line infantry as described above, there were complete units of light infantry or *tirailleurs* comprising (in 1808, for example), one *carabinier* company (the equivalent of the line grenadiers), one *voltigeur* company and four of *chasseurs*.

An army commander also controlled special reserves of artillery (12-pdrs and howitzers) and cavalry (whole divisions of cuirassiers for heavy work, dragoons for many tasks—including fighting dismounted with carbines when occasion demanded—and light cavalry, including hussars, chasseurs and lancers (from 1809)—for scouting and covering roles), as well as the main trains and convoys of the army.

The Imperial Guard was the elite organization of the entire army, and comprised infantry, cavalry, guns and services. The Old, Middle and Young Guards made up the infantry component; the Mamelukes, the *chasseurs-à-cheval* and the Polish and Dutch lancers, together with the Horse Grenadiers and the *Gendarmerie d'Élite* were the cavalry elements; and large numbers of foot artillery, together with horse and "flying" batteries (i.e., all gunners rode their own horses rather than clung to the ammunition limbers) made up the artillery. The Guard's size grew from 2,100 in 1800 (the Consular Guard) to as many as 112,500 by 1814—but for the "great campaigns" it averaged some 12,000 men, and in 1812 all of 56, 169 could claim membership of the Guard for the march on Moscow.

Tactics were complex. The infantry used a combination of column and line—the former for mobility and shock-action based on the threat of the bayonet, the latter for maximum firepower. A French batallion column had a two-company frontage some 50 yards wide by 21 yards (or 12 ranks) deep on the nine company establishment. After 1809, the dimensions were adjusted to give a frontage of 75 yards and a depth of 15 yards. The light infantry company habitually skirmished ahead sniping at enemy-mounted officers, gunners and other tempting targets. Troops were trained to change battle formation rapidly—and formed a square to receive cavalry.

Cavalry used squadron charges with the sword and sabre, or fire-action with carbines and pistols. Their first duty was to defeat the enemy cavalry—then his infantry. Only rarely did they do much damage to a well-composed square, but like sheepdogs they kept the infantry in these formations until horse artillery and infantry could be bought up.

Artillery employed round-shot (cannon-balls) and canister (musket balls in a tin container), using direct or ricochet fire to achieve maximum damage. Howitzers (and mortars, used for attacking enemy defenses) employed exploding shells. It is estimated that the great majority of casualties in battle were caused by artillery fire.

Marshals were responsible for orchestrating the activities of their horse, foot and gun detachments to the maximum effect, including the proper handling of reserves. They delegated the detail of minor tactics at brigade, squadron or battalion level to subordinate commanders. The following passage gives some idea of the sequence of a corps "grand tactical" battle—the level at which most marshals operated (although some, like Massena and Soult, were given command of armies in Napoleon's absence, particularly in Spain and Portugal):

> To draw together the threads . . . let us summarize the tactical sequence of an imaginary Napoleonic battle. As will be seen, the true secret of success in the field lay in the careful coordination of cavalry, infantry and guns into one continuous process of attack, each arm supplementing the activities of the other two. Through interarm cooperation lay the road to victory.

"At the outset, a heavy bombardment would be loosed against the enemy formations, causing fearful losses if they failed to seek shelter, and generally lowering their power of resistance. Under cover of this fire, swarms of *voltigeurs* would advance to within musketry range and add a disconcerting "nuisance" element by sniping at officers and the like. The preliminary phase would be followed by a series of heavy cavalry and infantry attacks. The secret of these was careful timing and coordination. The first cavalry charges were designed to defeat the hostile cavalry and compel the enemy infantry to form squares rather than to achieve an immediate breakthrough. This task was left to the hurrying infantry columns, which under ideal circumstances would have moved up to close range before the horsemen fell back, and before, therefore, the enemy could resume his linear formation. Clearly, a unit drawn up in square or rectangular formation could produce only a greatly reduced output of fire in any one direction, and this diminution of firepower enabled the French columns to get to close grips without suffering phenomenal casualties—providing all went well. If the attack succeeded, the newly deployed French infantry would blaze a gap through the enemy lines; their accompanying batteries of horse artillery would unlimber and go straight into action at point-blank range, and finally the French cavalry, after reforming, would sweep forward again to exploit the breakthrough."[*]

This description is very generalized as every action or battle was unique, and details varied according to circumstances. However, the broad principles outlined above supply a broad indication of a sequence that was often attempted.

[*]See *"The Campaigns of Napoleon"*, *op. cit.*, p. 363–4.

Select General Bibliography

A. General Works on the Overall Military and Other Aspects of the Napoleonic Period

Chandler, D. G. *The Campaigns of Napoleon* (New York, 1966).

————. *Dictionary of the Napoleonic Wars* (New York, 1979).

Connelly, O. *Historical Dictionary of Napoleonic France* (New York, 1985).

Esposito, V. J. and Elting, J. R. *A Military History and Atlas of the Napoleonic Wars* (New York, 1964).

Glover, M. *Warfare in the Age of Bonaparte* (London, 1980).

Herold, C. J. *The Age of Napoleon* (New York, 1963).

Rothenberg, G. E. *The Art of Warfare in the Age of Napoleon* (London, 1977).

B. General Works on the Marshalate

Note: For volumes on individual marshals, see the Bibliographical Note at the end of each chapter.

Brunon, J. *Les Maréchaux de France à travers neuf siècles d'histoire* (Paris, n.d.).

Chardigny, L. *Les Maréchaux de Napoléon* (Paris, 1977).

Currie, L. *The Baton in the Knapsack* (New York, 1935).

Delderfield, R. F. *The March of the Twenty-Six: The Story of Napoleon's Marshals* (London, 1962).

Dunn-Pattison, R. P. *Napoleon's Marshals* (Boston, 1909).

Fraser, E. *The War Drama of the Eagles: Napoleon's Standard-Bearers on the Battlefield in Victory and Defeat from Austerlitz to Waterloo* (London, 1912).

Gavard, C. *Galerie des Maréchaux de France* (Paris, 1839).

Headley, J. T. *Napoleon and His Marshals*, 2 vols. (New York, 1850).

Humble, R. *Napoleon's Peninsular Marshals* (London, 1973).

Johnson, D. *Napoleon's Cavalry and Its Leaders* (London, 1978).

Lachouque, H., and Brown, Anne S. K. *The Anatomy of Glory* (London, 1961).

Lacroix, D. *Les Maréchaux de Napoléon* (Paris, n.d.).

d'Orgeval, Le Barrois. *Le Maréchalat de France des Origines à Nos Jours,* 2 vols. (Paris, 1932).

M. le Duc de Lévis-Minepoix (ed.), *Les Maréchaux de France, Livre d'Or* (Casablanca, 1960).

Macdonell, A. G. *Napoleon and His Marshals* (London, 1934).

Martineau, A. *Tableaux par corps et par batailles des Officiers tués et blessés pendant les guerres de l'Empire, 1805–1815* (Paris, 1899).

Masson, F. *Cavaliers de Napoléon* (Paris, 1896).

Morvan, J. *Le Soldat Imperial, 1800–1814,* 2 vols. (Paris, 1904).

Panckoucke, C. *Portraits des Généraux Francais, 1792–1815,* 2 vols. (Paris, 1818).

Phipps, R. W. *The Armies of the First French Republic and the Rise of the Marshals of Napoleon I,* 5 vols. (Oxford, 1926–39).

Six, G. *Dictionnaire biographique des genéréaux et amiraux français de la Révolution et de l'Empire,* 2 vols. (Paris, 1934).

———. *Les Généreaux de la Révolution et de l'Empire* (Paris, 1947).

Young, P. *Napoleon's Marshals* (London, 1973).

Index A: Names

Abercromby, Sir R., British General: 85

Alexander I, Tsar of Russia: 31, 144, 154, 206, 226, 246, 343, 389, 426

Alvintzi, Josef, Austrian General: 195, 274, 289–90

Augereau, Marshal P.F.C., Duke of Castiglione: lxvii; background, 2; political views of, 4; meets Napoleon, 6; character of, 7, 11, 13; early military experience of, 2–4; marriages of, 3, 4, 12; service in the Pyrenees, 5, 193, 407; transferred to Italy, 6, 8; at Castiglione, 7; in Paris region, 7; role in *coup de Fructidor*, 8; further service, 9, 10; created Marshal, 10; role in 1805, 11; at Jena, 11; in Poland, 11, 12; sick at Jena, 12, 13–15; convalescent, 12; made Duke, lxvii; in Austria, 12; in Spain, 12; replaced by Macdonald, 244; in Reserve, 1812, 12; in Germany, 1813, 12, 245; at Naumburg, 12; role in 1814, 12; denounces Napoleon, 12; disgraced, 13; death of, 13; Napoleon's view of, liv; view of Napoleon, 12; relations with other marshals, 6, 8, 9, 12; mentioned, xlii, 6, 7, 10, 96, 127, 131, 432, 444, 452; picture of, 1

Bagration, Prince Peter, Russian General: 203, 427, 435, 436

Barclay de Tolly, Russian General: 102, 145, 428, 431

Battles: See INDEX B

Barras, Paul, French Director: 81, 84, 272, 339, 443

Beaulieu, Austrian General: 443, 444

Bennigsen, General L, of Hanover: 13, 14, 105, 143, 151, 153, 230, 362

Beresford, Marshal W.C. of England: 423, 473, 474

Bernadotte, Marshal J.P., Prince of Pontecorvo, King of Sweden: 18; origins, 20; early career, xxxiv, 20–3; with Army of the North, 22; character of, 21, 24; transfer to Italy, 23, 24; at Vienna, 24, 25; political views of, xlvii, 25, 26, 27; marries Desiree Clary, 25; Minster of War, 26; commands Army of the West, 26; in Hanover, 27; created a marshal, 27; at Austerlitz, 27–8; in 1806, 28, 111; almost courtmartialed, 28, 111; leads pursuit, 28; contacts Swedes, 28; service in East Prussia, 28; wounded, 28; in 1809, 28, 29; at Wagram, 28, 29, 249; disgraced, 29; with Army of Antwerp, 29; plots, 29; Crown-Prince of Sweden, 30; joins Allies, 31; commands Allied Army of the North, 32, 33; at Gross Beeren, 393; at Dennewitz, 35–7; at Leipzig, 33; occupation of Norway, 34; King of Sweden, 34; death of, 35; Napoleon's view of: liv, 29, 30, 369; view of Napoleon, 26, 369; relations with colleagues, 33, 34, 317, 369, 450; feud with Davout, 28; mentioned, xxxiv, xxxvi, xxxviii, 9, 11, 104, 107, 110, 111, 200, 486; picture of, 19

Berthier, Marshal L.A., Prince of Neuchâtel and of Wagram: 42; origins, 44; early career, 44–5, 181; with Army of Italy, 45; Napoleon's C. of S., 45–52; character of, 50–1, 370; in the Orient, 46; commands Army of the Reserve, 46, 52–6; at Marengo, 46; embassy to Spain, 46–7; passion for Mme. Visconti, 46; marriage of, 48; created a marshal, 47; court positions, 47; awards, 48; C. of S. to the Grand Army, 47, 143; "wounds" Massena, 282; fiasco in 1809, 48; at Wagram, 48; princedom conferred, 48; in Russia, 49, 396; in last campaigns, 49; deserts Napoleon, 49; mysterious circumstances of death, 49, 505; Napoleon's view of, liv, 29, 30, 50, 130, 370; view of Napoleon, 30, 50, 396; relations with colleagues, 51, 205, 367, 369, 467; feuds, 28; mentioned, xxxiii, xxxvi, 84, 102, 109, 110, 273, 287, 305, 315, 342, 388, 470, 495–6; picture of, 43

Bessières, Marshal J.B., Duke of Istria: 60; origins, 62; character of, 69; early career of, 62, 336; in the

Grouchy, Marshal Marquis E. de (*cont.*)
Louis XVIII, 146; rallies to Napoleon,
146; suppresses the Midi, 146;
created a marshal, 146; role
in Hundred Days, 146–9; at Ligny,
147; at Wavre, 148–9; criticisms
of, 149; refuted, 149; conduct after
Waterloo, 149; escapes to USA,
149; amnestied and returns
to France, 149; second marriage of,
150; restored to the marshalate,
150; death, 150; Napoleon's
opinion of, lv, 144, 145; opinion of
Napoleon, 146, 149; relations
with colleagues, 140, 149; as a
cavalryman, 149, 153; mentioned,
xxxviii, 105; picture of, 139
Gudin, General C.E. de la S.: 100, 101,
109, 112, 113, 114
Guard, the Imperial (and predecessors):
63, 68, 110, 152, 198, 201, 211,
223, 225, 316, 317, 341, 373, 431, 432,
465, 500, 517, 574
Guard, the National: 44, 62, 80,
106, 156, 184, 204, 219, 223, 305, 306,
307, 325, 394, 404, 480
Gneisenau, A.W. von, General, of
Prussia: 47

Hoche, General L.L.: 122, 140, 219, 220,
221, 460, 464
Hohenlohe, General Prince, of Prussia:
142, 487
Houchard, General J.N.: 159

Jannissaries, the, of the Sultan: 353
John, Archduke, of Austria: 248
Jomini, General Baron A. H., of
Switzerland: 361, 362, 369, 375
Joseph, King of Spain: (see *Bonaparte,
Joseph.*)
Josephine Beauharnais, Empress:
(see *Bonaparte*, Josephine)
Joubert, General B.C.: 140, 241, 274, 278,
289, 410, 450, 482, 484
Jourdan, Marshal Count J.B.: 156;
origins, 158; character of, 168;
political views of, 158; early career
under Bourbons, 158; and at
the Revolution, 159; rapid
promotion, 160; commands Army of
the North, 160; victor of
Wattignies, 160, 313; commands
the Moselle, 161, 220; victor
of Fleurus, 161–2; defeated at
Wurzburg, 162; resigns, 163; political
appointments in Paris, 163;
commands on the Danube, 163, 222,
385; defeated at Stockach, 163,
276; replaced, 163; dismissed after

Brumaire, 163; created a marshal,
163; reasons for his choice,
163; as Governor of Naples, 163–4;
role in Spain, 164; defeated
at Talavera, 164–5; recalled, 165,
468; Governor of Madrid and
C. of S. to Joseph, 165–8; defeated at
Vitoria, 168–72; recalled to
France, 168; Governor of Les
Invalides, 168; death, 168;
Napoleon's view of, lv, 165, 168;
relations with Joseph, 163–4;
with colleagues, 164; mentioned, xlii,
108, 122, 124, 220, 276, 460,
465; picture of, 157
Junot, General A. Duke of Abrantes: 25,
283, 285, 480, 491

Kalkreuth, Prussian General: 228, 229
Kellermann, Marshal F.C. (the Elder),
Duke of Valmy: 176; origins,
178; political views of, 175, 182;
early service under Bourbons,
178–9; and the Revolution,
179; character of, 179, 182; political
views of, 179, 182; commands
Army of the Centre, 181; victor of
Valmy, 181, 184–7; commands
in the Alps, 182; and in Italy, 183;
arrested, 183; reinstated, 183;
resumes old commands, 183; retires
from active service, 183; political
posts, 183; created a marshal, 183;
reasons for being chosen, 183;
created Duke of Valmy, 184; death,
184; Napoleon's opinion of, lv;
relations with colleagues, 181;
mentioned, xxxiii, xlvi, 45, 223;
picture of, 177
Kilmaine, General C.E.S.J. de: 8
Kléber, General J.B.: 22, 23, 122, 196,
220, 313, 360, 361
Kray, General, of Austria: 276
Kutusov, Field-Marshal Prince M.G., of
Russia: 68, 100, 103, 202, 433–6

Lafayette, General the Marquis de: 159
La Tour Manbourg, General M.V.N.
de F.: 145
Lannes, Marshal J, Duke of Montebello:
190; origins, 192; character
of, 205; politics of, xli; early career,
192; in Spain, 192–3; in Italy,
193–6; at battle of Arcola, 195; in the
Orient, 196–8, 352; divorces
first wife, 198; in campaign of 1800,
198–200; at Montebello, 199,
200, 519; at Marengo, 200, 521–2;
second marriage, 201; embassy
to Portugal, 201–2; created marshal,

Marshalate, the (*cont.*)
war-weariness of, li, liii; and
Fontainebleau mutiny, liii; wounds
shared by: xxx, xxxvii; mentioned,
see Introduction liv–lvii, and
individual chapters *passim*. List of,
from earliest times, 528–37.
The post-Napoleonic Marshalate:
538

Marmont, Marshal, A.F.L.V., Duke of
Ragusa: 254; origins: 256; character
of, 256; political views of, xli;
commissioned, 256; early career of,
256–7; with Bonaparte in Italy,
256–7; as his ADC, 257; in Egypt,
257; returns to France, 257;
at *Brumaire*, 257; in Italy, 1800,
257–8; at Marengo, 258;
appointments, 258; during 1805, 141,
258–9; in Dalmatia, 259; created
Duke of Ragusa, 259; in Austria,
1809, 259; at Znaim, 259; created a
marshal, xxxiv, 259, in Illyria,
260; commander in Spain, 260–2,
287, 288; wounded and defeated at
Salamanca, 262, 265–7, 498,
in Germany, 1813, 262–3; in France,
1814, 263–4, 322; betrays Napoleon,
264, 307; in 1815, 264; struck
from list of marshals, 264; under the
Bourbons, 264; during the
Revolution of 1830, 264; flees
abroad, 264; death, 264; Napoleon's
view of, lv, 258, 260, 264; view
of Napoleon, 256, 257; views
of others on Marmont, 256;
relationships with others, 166, 264;
mentioned: xlii, 25, 108, 110,
145, 147, 480, 525

Massena, Marshal A., Duke of Rivoli,
Prince of Essling: 270; origins,
272; in character of, 163, 287, 291–2,
386; political views of, xli; early life,
272; in Bourbon army, 272;
resigns, 272; and the Revolution,
xxxv, 272; family, 282; rapid
promotion, 272; at Toulon, 272; in
North Italy, 1795, 193, 272,
445, 481; and, under Bonaparte,
1796–7, 273–4; at Rivoli, 274, 289; in
1797–8 in Switzerland, 163,
274–6, 314, 463; battle of First
Zurich, 277; Second Zurich, 278; in
Italy, 1800, 278–81, 464, 484;
surrenders Genoa, 281; retired, 281;
created a marshal, 282; commands
in Poland, 1807, 282; on sick
leave, 282; created Duke of Rivoli,
282; in Austria, 1809, 282–3;
at Aspern-Essling, xxx, 210, 211, 282;

at Wagram, xxx, 208, 249, 283;
invades Portugal, 1810, 283; rows
with collagues, 283, 284; at
Busaco, 285–6; before Torres Vedras
lines, 286–7; retreats, 287; at
Fuentes de Oñoro, 288; recalled, 288;
disgraced, 288; accepts Bourbons,
1815, 289; rejoins Napoleon,
289; rejoins Bourbons, 289;
appointments, 289; retired, 289;
death, 289; Napoleon's opinion of,
lvi, 279, 288, 291; views of Napoleon,
lvii; relations with colleagues:
68, 69, 283, 287, 364; others' opinions
of, 126, 284; mentioned, xl,
xliii, 46, 66, 67, 82, 110, 124, 131, 385,
452, 465, 483; picture of, 271

Melas, General, of Austria: 200,
241, 279, 281, 484, 519, 520, 522
Menard, General J.F.X. de: 275
Menou, General J.F. de B.: 97, 198, 340
Merle, General P.H.V.: 133
Metternich, Prince von, of Austria: 259
Milhaud, General Count E.J.B.: 373
Miloradovitch, General M., of Russia:
326, 366
Molitor, General G.J.J.: 209
Moncey, Marshal B.A.J. de, Duke
of Conegliano: 296; origins,
298; character, 301, 305, 306;
political views of, xli, 299; service in
Bourbon army, 298; dismissed,
298, 302; commissioned, 298; and
the Revolution, 298–9; commands in
West Pyrenees, 299–300; in
La Vendée, 301; denounced, 302;
under Moreau on the Rhine, 302–3;
in Italy, 1800, 303; commander
in Italy, 1801, 303; created a
marshal, 303; further command,
303; created Duke of Conegliano,
304; serves in Spain, 206, 303–5;
recalled, 304; further appointments,
305; in France, 1814, 305; at
Clichy, 305; Napoleon's abdication,
305; and Ney's courtmartial,
305–6; reconciled to Bourbons, 305,
306; commands in Pyrenees,
1823, 306; governor of Les Invalides,
1833, 306; death 306; Napoleon's
opinion of, 304, 306; view of
Napoleon, 305; relations with
colleagues, 305–6; mentioned, xli, 53,
131, 371; picture of, 297
Monnier, General J.C.: 200
Moore, General Sir John, of England:
164, 207, 364, 462
Morand, General Count C.A.L.A.:
100, 101, 109, 112, 113, 114, 208
Moreau, General J.V.: xli, 53, 96, 122,

Index B: Battles, Actions, Sieges and Treaties